New Business Ventures and the Entrepreneur

New Business Ventures and the Entrepreneur

Howard H. Stevenson
Sarofim-Rock Professor of Business Administration
Harvard University Graduate School of Business Administration

Michael J. Roberts
Assistant Professor
Harvard University Graduate School of Business Administration

H. Irving Grousbeck
Lecturer in Business Administration
Stanford University Graduate School of Business

IRWIN

Chicago • Bogotá • Boston • Buenos Aires • Caracas
London • Madrid • Mexico City • Sydney • Toronto

©¹ THE MCGRAW-HILL COMPANIES, INC., 1974, 1985, 1989, and 1994

Senior sponsoring editor: Kurt L. Strand
Editorial assistant: Michele Dooley
Marketing manager: Kurt Messersmith
Project editor: Jean Lou Hess
Production manager: Ann Cassady
Designer: Mercedes Santos
Art manager: Kim Meriwether
Compositor: Carlisle Communications, Inc.
Typeface: 10/12 Times Roman
Printer: R.R. Donnelley & Sons Company

Library of Congress Cataloging-in-Publication Data

Stevenson, Howard H.
    New business ventures and the entrepreneur/Howard H. Stevenson,
Michael J. Roberts, H. Irving Grousbeck. — 4th ed.
        p.   cm.
    Includes indexes.
    ISBN 0–256–11030–1
    1. New business enterprises.   2. New business enterprises—United
States.   I. Roberts, Michael J.   II. Grousbeck, H. Irving.
III. Title.
HD62.5.S75   1993
658.1'1 — dc20   93–24704

Printed in the United States of America
    5 6 7 8 9 0 DOC 0 9 8 7

To
Patrick Rooney
Liles (1937–
1983) teacher
scholar of
entrepreneurship
business leader
athlete
friend

We have several objectives in writing this book. We believe that the topic of entrepreneurship is an exciting and important one. For those students of management who have decided to pursue a career as an entrepreneur, we think this book will provide some of the knowledge and skills required. For those who may be undecided, or perhaps committed to a more "traditional" career, many of the ideas in this book have value for those in more structured business settings. Executives are often called upon to deal with, and even to manage, entrepreneurs. Friends and acquaintances may contemplate starting new ventures and want the advice and/or financial support of acquaintances in management positions.

Most importantly, we believe that all students of management have a great deal to learn from the study of entrepreneurship. The process of identifying and pursuing opportunity, the hallmark of the entrepreneur, has become increasingly important in restoring the competitive position of many U.S. industries in the international marketplace.

Organization and Contents

This book is organized into four parts:

- *Part I:* Evaluating Opportunity and Developing the Business Concept. This first section of the book serves as an overview, and also looks at the first two steps in the process of starting a new venture. Its first three chapters provide a working definition of entrepreneurship, a framework for understanding the entrepreneurial process, and a method for analyzing new venture opportunities. Remaining chapters look at methods of valuing business opportunities as well as the process of preparing a business plan. The cases require evaluating business opportunities and formulating strategies to exploit opportunities.

- *Part II:* Assessing and Acquiring Necessary Resources. This part looks at two of the entrepreneur's critical steps—assessing required resources and acquiring those resources. The chapters focus on understanding the techniques for acquiring both financial and nonfinancial resources. The cases cover a variety of issues, including deal structure, securities law, venture capital, and intellectual property.

- *Part III:* Acquiring an Existing Business. In this part, we look at another avenue to an entrepreneurial career: purchasing an existing business. Chapters describe the search process, as well as some of the tax and legal dimensions of acquisitions. The cases look at several examples of individuals who attempt to purchase an existing business.

- *Part IV:* Managing the Enterprise and Harvesting Value. Here we look at some of the unique challenges of managing an entrepreneurial firm. Included are some approaches to harvesting the economic value that the entrepreneur has created. Chapters examine managing growth and the problem of bankruptcy, as well as the process involved in a public offering. Cases focus on the operating issues faced by the managers of new ventures and the topic of managing growth in a rapidly expanding business.

Together, these sections trace the entrepreneurial process from the initial idea through business operations to harvest.

Throughout the book, we have exhibited some of our own biases. One of which we are aware has to do with the material that has been included as exhibits. Whenever possible, we have included actual documents: business plans, prospectuses, leases, laws, and legal opinions. While some of this material is detailed and highly specific, it is well worth the effort. This is the stuff of which real business is made; better to discover some of the subtleties of the tax code or lease provisions now than when you're sitting down to form a real venture.

Although the detail is included, please do not consider the technical notes, the exhibits, and the appendices as substitutes for detailed current investigation of law, regulation, markets, and practices. This is a rapidly evolving field. Although every effort has been made to be clear, current, and complete, you must consult good attorneys, accountants, and investments advisers before proceeding.

Acknowledgments

Patrick R. Liles taught the New Ventures course at Harvard from 1969 to 1977. In a very real sense, his early work in the field, his first edition of this book, and his vision of the entrepreneur provided a strong foundation on which to build. We dedicate this book to Pat, both in recognition of his accomplishments and our respect for them, and out of our own sense of loss.

In addition to Pat's involvement with the course, many others participated in its teaching and development over the past 40 years. We are indebted to Myles Mace, Frank L. Tucker, Malcom Salter, Thomas Raymond, Philip Thurston, Jim Morgan, Richard Reese, Richard Von Werssowetz, John Van Slyke and Matt Weisman for building the New Ventures course at Harvard and providing a solid foundation for our own work. Recently, Amar Bhide has begun teaching the Entrepreneurial Management course at Harvard. He has made a very real contribution to our work in this area, and he was kind enough to contribute several pieces of his work to this edition. Many other students and scholars of entrepreneurship not at Harvard have contributed helpful comments: Jeffry Timmons, Barry Unger, Steve Brandt, Zenas Block, Karl Vesper, and Neil Churchill.

Thanks are also due:

- Peter Lombard and Ricardo Rodriquez for their help with ICEDELIGHTS.
- Richard Von Werssowetz for his help with Commercial Fixtures, Inc., and Steven B. Belkin.
- Richard E. Floor, of the law firm of Goodwin, Procter & Hoar, Boston, for his help with Viscotech, Inc., and the chapters on Securities Law and Private Financing and Securities Law and Public Offerings.
- Martha Gershun for Eastwind Trading Company, Dragonfly Corporation and the chapter on bankruptcy.
- Jose-Carlos Jarillo Mossi for his help with R&R.
- E.J. Walton for his help with CVD vs. A.S. Markham Corp., National Demographics & Lifestyles (A), and the chapter on the Business Plan.
- E.J. Walton, Lynn Radlauer, Ned Lubell, David Hull, Byron Snider, Robert Stevenson, and Robert Winter for their help with Purchasing a Business: The Search Process.

- Susan Harmeling for her work on the Howard Head and Karen Vincent cases, and for her help with Valerie Morgan.
- David Dodson, of Stanford Business School, for his work on Tom Fisher.
- Laura Pochop for her help with Vintage Directions, Inc.
- Marjorie Tillman for her help with Glenn De-Kraker.
- L. A. Snedeker for her help with Tripledge Products, Inc. and Gordon Biersch Brewing Company.
- Karen Moriarty for her help with Postal Buddy.
- Bill Sahlman for permission to use Parenting Magazine.
- Amar Bhide for permission to use Vinod Khosla and Sun Microsystems (A), Image Presentations, Inc., and the Note on Analyzing New Ventures.

A special thanks to the reviewers for the book. These were:

- Professor Arnold C. Cooper, Purdue University.
- Professor Morton I. Kamien, Northwestern University.
- Professor Henry T. Madden, University of Iowa.
- Professor Robert W. Pricer, University of Wisconsin at Madison.
- Professor William J. Scheela, Bemidji State University.

The case writing and research was sponsored by the Division of Research; we are grateful to the Division as well as to the Associates of the Harvard Business School, who provided much of the funding. Dean John McArthur has been a supporter of many of our efforts in the entrepreneurship area. Without the support of many alumni this activity would not have been possible. Arthur Rock and Fayez Sarofim gave the first chair at Harvard to reestablish a focus on entrepreneurship. Subsequently, the classes of 1954, 1955, 1960 and 1961 have each funded additional chairs. To further the work of the class of 1955, a chair was dedicated in memory of Dimitri d'Arbeloff, the entrepreneurial leader of Millipore. Joel Schiavone of the class of 1961 has also pledged to donate a chair. The depth of alumni interest and support has been most remarkable and rewarding as we have worked to build this area.

The task of compiling this text was an arduous one. We wish to express our appreciation to Cari Feiler, who kindly lent her energy and enthusiasm to the revision of this manuscript. Audrey Barrett was helpful in securing the permissions needed to complete the book.

We are indebted to the entrepreneurs who gave so willingly of their time, energy, and ideas so that we could collect this case material. They provide one of the most critical elements of entrepreneurial success: role models. Robert Reiss, Bob Donadio, Joe Connolly, Lesley Berglund, Jim Pottow, Greg Berglund, Lisa Mangano, Jennifer Runyeon, Chip Fichtner, Sidney Goodman, Steven Belkin, Heather Evans, Robin Wolaner, Jock Bickert, Rob Johnson, Tom Fisher, Dan Gordon and Dean Biersch, Vinod Khosla, Mark Edwards, Vincent Lamb, Glenn DeKraker, and Howard Head are all real people who have shared their experiences with us; others have chosen to remain anonymous. To all we owe thanks for their cooperation. Ultimately, it is through the sharing of their experiences that we can learn.

Finally, each of us would like to make a more personal statement of thanks to our families:

- To my wife Fredi and to Willie, Charley, and Andy, thanks for the patience in helping me to pursue this passion; and to my late parents, Ralph and Dorothy Stevenson, and aunt and uncle, Boyd and Zola Martin, thanks for helping me get a running start into this field.

  H.H.S.

- To my parents, Herb and Joan Roberts, for all their love, support and encouragement.

  M.J.R.

- To my wife Sukey for her love, laughter, adaptability, and constant encouragement, and to my mother Emily for loving lessons of the value of integrity and hard work.

  H.I.G.

C O N T E N T S

PART IV

**MANAGING THE ENTERPRISE AND
HARVESTING VALUE**

I EVALUATING OPPORTUNITY AND DEVELOPING THE BUSINESS CONCEPT

In this first part of the book, we present in Chapter 1 a framework for defining entrepreneurship. Following this, we consider two fundamental issues the entrepreneur must address:

- Is this a good opportunity?
- What business strategy will most fully exploit the opportunity?

What Is An Opportunity?

One of the entrepreneur's most important tasks is to identify opportunities. The capacity to creatively seek out opportunity is the starting point of entrepreneurship for both the individual and the firm.

To qualify as a good opportunity, the situation must meet two conditions:

1. It must represent a future state that is desirable.
2. It must be achievable.

Obviously, this issue cannot be addressed in isolation. It is difficult to understand how attractive an opportunity is until one has developed an idea of what the business strategy will be, what resources will be required to pursue the opportunity, how much those resources will cost, and, finally, how much value will be left for the entrepreneur. Nonetheless, evaluating the opportunity is the starting point for this thought process.

In Chapter 2, ''The Start-Up Process,'' we describe the key steps in starting a business, as well as some of the analytical thinking that drives the decisions that must be made at each juncture.

Chapter 3, ''Analyzing New Ventures,'' presents a framework for evaluating the viability of a potential venture: Can the entrepreneur develop a strategy based on competence, creativity, commitment, or change that will overcome the barriers presented by competition?

Chapter 4, "Valuation Techniques," looks at some of the quantitative techniques for assessing the financial value of a business opportunity. It is important to remember, though, an opportunity may have significant nonfinancial value that these techniques cannot measure. Some opportunities, for example, may not be worth much but may open doors to other opportunities that have considerable value. For some entrepreneurs, the opportunity to work on an interesting idea, with good people, and to be one's own boss compensates for what may be only a mediocre opportunity in a financial sense.

Chapter 5, "The Business Plan," describes the uses of a business plan and how you can write one to meet your needs, as well of those of potential investors.

Developing the Business Concept

Once an opportunity is identified, the entrepreneur must develop a business concept and strategy to exploit the opportunity. Often, this strategy will proximately determine the success or failure of a business, even if the entrepreneur has identified a wonderful opportunity. Federal Express, for instance, decided to serve the same market that Emery Air Freight was serving. But Federal Express chose a much different strategy: a high fixed-cost hub system that was critically dependent on volume. Federal Express's strategy has allowed it to operate at lower costs and thus to surpass Emery in the express delivery market.

To maximize the odds of its success, a new venture should offer products or services that can profitably meet the needs of the markets it attempts to serve. But a new venture has an important advantage over an existing business. It can be created specifically to respond to market needs. Too often existing firms spend enormous resources searching for a market for the products or services produced by their operating assets.

The Cases

R&R and Eastwind Trading—the first two cases—are really "bookends." R&R describes the brief—but successful—history of a business, while Eastwind looks at two women contemplating an entrepreneurial career. Vintage Directions and Tripledge Products describe exciting business opportunities that must be evaluated by the entrepreneurial team before the commitment of additional resources.

Commercial Fixtures deals with assessing and valuing an opportunity. This case points out the difficulty of trying to evaluate an opportunity in a vacuum; clearly, the business is attractive at some price. But what exactly *is* that price? On what does it depend? ICEDELIGHTS provides an overview of the start-up process that raises a host of issues, including opportunity evaluation, resource assessment and acquisition, and valuation and financing. Finally, Postal Buddy considers a revolutionary change in the way the U.S. Postal Service works—will the entrepreneur be able to raise sufficient capital to persevere?

1 A PERSPECTIVE ON ENTREPRENEURSHIP

The term *entrepreneurship* has entered the business vocabulary as the 1980s' equivalent of *professionalism*, the managerial buzzword of the 1970s. Many individuals aspire to be entrepreneurs, enjoying the freedom, independence, and wealth such a career seems to suggest. And larger corporations want to become more "entrepreneurial," their shorthand for the innovative and adaptive qualities they see in their smaller—and often more successful—competitors.

Our purpose in this chapter is to shed some light on the concept of entrepreneurship. We will define entrepreneurship as a management process and will discuss why we believe encouraging entrepreneurial behavior is critical to the long-term vitality of our economy. Finally, we will suggest that the practice of entrepreneurship is as important—if not more important—to established companies as it is to start-ups.

Increasing Interest in Entrepreneurship

It would be difficult to overstate the degree to which there has been an increase in the level of interest in entrepreneurship. A strong indicator of such interest is provided by the unprecedented rise in the rate of new business formation. The number of annual new business incorporations has doubled in the last 10 years, from annual rates of about 300,000 to over 600,000.

These trends are mirrored in the capital markets that fund these start-ups. The decade 1975–1984 saw explosive growth in the amount of capital committed to venture capital firms in the United States. There was a concurrent dramatic increase in the amount of money raised in the public capital markets by young companies.

In addition to interest on the part of individuals who wish to become entrepreneurs and investors who wish to back them, there has been a wave of interest in what some refer to as *intrapreneurship*, or entrepreneurship in the context of the larger corporation. Building on the wealth of books and articles on the subject, some large firms seem to have recognized their shortcomings on certain critical dimensions of performance and have structured themselves in an attempt to be more innovative.

Indeed, we believe that the strengthening of entrepreneurship is a critically important goal of American society. The first 30 years of the postwar period in the United

This note was prepared by Howard H. Stevenson.
Copyright © 1983 by the President and Fellows of Harvard College
Harvard Business School Note 9–384–131

States were characterized by an abundance of opportunity, brought about by expanding markets, high investment in the national infrastructure, and mushrooming debt. In this environment, it was relatively easy to achieve business success, but this is no longer true. Access to international resources is not as easy as it once was; government regulation has brought a recognition of the full costs of doing business, many of which had previously been hidden; competition from overseas has put an end to American dominance in numerous industries; technological change has reduced product life in other industries; and so forth. In short, a successful firm is one that is either capable of rapid response to changes that are beyond its control or is so innovative that it contributes to change in the environment. Entrepreneurship is an approach to management that offers these benefits.

Defining Entrepreneurship

As we have discussed, there has been a striking increase in the level of attention paid to entrepreneurship. However, we've not yet defined what the term means.

As a starting point, it may be helpful to review some of the definitions scholars have historically applied to entrepreneurship. There are several schools of thought regarding entrepreneurship, which may roughly be divided into those that define the term as an economic function and those that identify entrepreneurship with individual traits.

The functional approach focuses on the role of entrepreneurship within the economy. In the 18th century, for instance, Richard Cantillon argued that entrepreneurship entailed bearing the risk of buying at certain prices and selling at uncertain prices. Jean Baptiste Say broadened the definition to include the concept of bringing together the factors of production. Schumpeter's work in 1911 added the concept of innovation to the definition of entrepreneurship. He allowed for many kinds of innovation including process innovation, market innovation, product innovation, factor innovation, and even organizational innovation. His seminal work emphasized the role of the entrepreneur in creating and responding to economic discontinuities.

While some analysts have focused on the economic function of entrepreneurship, still others have turned their attention to research on the personal characteristics of entrepreneurs. Considerable effort has gone into understanding the psychological and sociological sources of entrepreneurship—as Kent refers to it, ''supply-side entrepreneurship.'' These studies have noted some common characteristics among entrepreneurs with respect to need for achievement, perceived locus of control, and risk-taking propensity. In addition, many have commented on the common—but not universal—thread of childhood deprivation and early adolescent experiences as typifying the entrepreneur. These studies—when taken as a whole—are inconclusive and often in conflict.

We believe, however, that neither of these approaches is sound. Consider, for example, the degree to which *entrepreneurship* is synonymous with *bearing risk, innovation,* or even *founding a company.* Each of these terms focuses on *some* aspect of *some* entrepreneurs. But, if one has to be the founder to be an entrepreneur, then neither Thomas Watson of IBM nor Ray Kroc of McDonald's will qualify; yet, few would seriously argue that both these individuals were not entrepreneurs. And, while risk bearing is an important element of entrepreneurial behavior, it is clear that many entrepreneurs bear risk grudgingly and only after they have made valiant attempts to get the capital sources and resource providers to bear the risk. As one extremely successful entrepreneur said, ''My idea of risk and reward is for me to get the reward and others to take risks.'' With respect to the ''supply-side'' school of entrepreneurship, many questions can be raised. At the heart of the matter is whether the psychological and social traits are either necessary or sufficient for the development of entrepreneurship.

Finally, the search for a single psychological profile of the entrepreneur is bound to fail. For each of the traditional definitions of the entrepreneurial type, there are numerous counterexamples that disprove the theory. We simply are not dealing with one kind of individual or behavior pattern, as even a cursory review of well-known entrepreneurs will demonstrate. Nor has the search for a psychological model proven useful in teaching or encouraging entrepreneurship.

Entrepreneurship as a Behavioral Phenomenon

Thus, it does not seem useful to delimit the entrepreneur by defining those economic functions that are ''entrepreneurial'' and those that are not. Nor does it appear particularly helpful to describe the traits that seem to engender entrepreneurship in certain individuals. From our perspective, entrepreneurship is an approach to management that we define as follows: *the pursuit of opportunity without regard to resources currently controlled.*

This summary description of entrepreneurial behavior can be further refined by examining six critical dimensions of business practice. These six dimensions are the following: strategic orientation, the commitment to opportunity, the resource commitment process, the concept of control over resources, the concept of management, and compensation policy.

We shall define these dimensions by examining a range of behavior between two extremes. At one extreme is the ''promoter'' who feels confident of his or her ability to seize opportunity regardless of the resources under current control. At the opposite extreme is the ''trustee'' who emphasizes the efficient utilization of existing resources. While the promoter and trustee define the end points of this spectrum, there is a spectrum of managerial behavior that lies between these end points, and we define (overlapping) portions of this spectrum as entrepreneurial and administrative behavior. Thus, entrepreneurial management is not an extreme example, but rather a range of behavior that consistently falls at the end of the spectrum.

The remainder of this chapter defines these key business dimensions in more detail, discusses how entrepreneurial differs from administrative behavior, and describes the factors that pull individuals and firms toward particular types of behavior.

Strategic Orientation

Strategic orientation is the business dimension that describes the factors that drive the firm's formulation of strategy. A promoter is truly opportunity driven. His or her

FIGURE 1–1

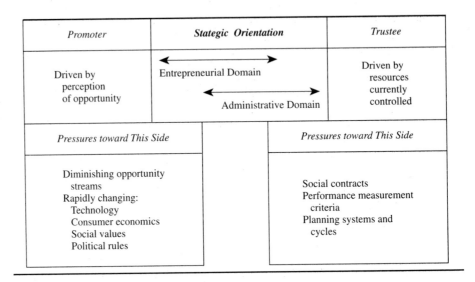

Promoter	***Stategic Orientation***	*Trustee*
Driven by perception of opportunity	Entrepreneurial Domain ← → ← → Administrative Domain	Driven by resources currently controlled
Pressures toward This Side		*Pressures toward This Side*
Diminishing opportunity streams Rapidly changing: Technology Consumer economics Social values Political rules		Social contracts Performance measurement criteria Planning systems and cycles

orientation is to say, "As I define a strategy, I am going to be driven only by my perception of the opportunities that exist in my environment, and I will not be constrained by the resources at hand." A trustee, on the other hand, is resource driven and tends to say, "How do I utilize the resources that I control?"

Within these two poles, the administrator's approach recognizes the need to examine the environment for opportunities but is still constrained by a trusteelike focus on resources: "I will prune my opportunity tree based on the resources I control. I will not try to leap very far beyond my current situation." An entrepreneurial orientation places the emphasis on opportunity: "I will search for opportunity, and my fundamental task is to acquire the resources to pursue that opportunity." These perspectives are represented in **Figure 1–1.**

It is this dimension that has led to one of the traditional definitions of the entrepreneur as opportunistic or — more favorably — creative and innovative. But the entrepreneur is not necessarily concerned with breaking new ground; opportunity can also be found in a new mix of old ideas or in the creative application of traditional approaches. We do observe, however, that firms tend to look for opportunities where their resources are. Even those firms that start as entrepreneurial by recognizing opportunities often become resources driven as more and more resources are acquired by the organization.

The pressures that pull a firm toward the entrepreneurial range of behavior include the following:

- Diminishing opportunity streams: Old opportunity streams have been largely played out. It is no longer possible to succeed merely by adding new options to old products.

- Rapid changes in:
  - Technology: Creates new opportunities at the same time it obsoletes old ones.
  - Consumer economics: Changes both ability and willingness to pay for new products and services.
  - Social values: Defines new styles and standards and standards of living.
  - Political roles: Affects competition through deregulation, product safety, and new standards.

Pressures that pull a firm to become more administrative than entrepreneurial include the following:

- The ''social contract'': The responsibility of managers to use and employ people, plant, technology, and financial resources once they have been acquired.
- Performance criteria: How many executives are fired for not pursuing an opportunity, compared with the number that are punished for not meeting return on investment targets? Capacity utilization and sales growth are the typical measures of business success.
- Planning systems and cycles: Opportunities do not arrive at the start of a planning cycle and last for the duration of a three- or five-year plan.

Commitment to Opportunity

As we move on to the second dimension, it becomes clear that the definition of the entrepreneur as creative or innovative is not sufficient. There are innovative thinkers who never get anything done; it is necessary to move beyond the identification of opportunity to its pursuit.

The promoter is willing to act in a very short time frame and to chase an opportunity quickly. Promoters may be more or less effective, but they are able to engage in commitment in a rather revolutionary fashion. The duration of their commitment, not the ability to act, is all that is in doubt. Commitment for the trustee is time consuming and, once made, of long duration. Trustees move so slowly that it sometimes appears they are stationary; once there, they seem frozen. This spectrum of behavior is shown in **Figure 1–2.**

It is the willingness to get in and out quickly that has led to the entrepreneur's reputation as a gambler. However, the simple act of taking a risk does not lead to success. More critical to the success of the entrepreneurs is knowledge of the territory they operate in. Because of familiarity with their chosen field, they have the ability to recognize patterns as they develop and the confidence to assume that the missing elements of the pattern will take shape as they foresee. This early recognition enables them to get a jump on others in commitment to action.

Pressures that pull a business toward this entrepreneurial end of the spectrum include:

- Action orientation: Enables a firm to make first claim to customers, employees, and financial resources.

FIGURE 1–2

Promoter	Commitment to Opportunity	Trustee
Revolutionary with short duration	← Entrepreneurial Domain → ← Administrative Domain →	Evolutionary of long duration
Pressures toward This Side		*Pressures toward This Side*

Action orientation
 Short decision windows
 Risk management
 Limited decision
     constituencies
		Acknowledgment of
		     multiple constituencies
		 Negotiation of strategy
		 Risk reduction
		 Management of fit

- Short decision windows: Due to the high costs of late entry, including lack of competitive costs and technology.
- Risk management: Involves managing the firm's revenues in such a way that they can be rapidly committed to or withdrawn from new projects. As George Bernard Shaw put it, "Any fool can start a love affair, but it takes a genius to end one successfully."
- Limited decision constituencies: Requires a smaller number of responsibilities and permits greater flexibility.

In contrast, administrative behavior is a function of other pressures:

- Multiple decision constituencies: A great number of responsibilities, necessitating a more complex, lengthier decision process.
- Negotiation of strategy: Compromise in order to reach consensus and resultant evolutionary rather than revolutionary commitment.
- Risk reduction: Study and analysis to reduce risk slows the decision-making process.
- Management of fit: To assure the continuity and participation of existing players, only those projects that "fit" existing corporate resources are acceptable.

Commitment of Resources

Another characteristic we observe in good entrepreneurs is a multistaged commitment of resources with a minimum commitment at each stage or decision point. The promoters, those wonderful people with blue shoes and diamond pinky rings on their left hands, say, "I don't need any resources to commence the pursuit of a given oppor-

FIGURE 1-3

Promoter	*Commitment of Resources*	Trustee
Multistaged with minimal exposure at each stage	Entrepreneurial Domain ⟵⟶ ⟵⟶ Administrative Domain	Single-staged with complete commitment upon decision
Pressures toward This Side		*Pressures toward This Side*
Lack of predictable resource needs Lack of long-term control Social needs for more opportunity per resource unit International pressure for more efficient resource use		Personal risk reduction Incentive compensation Managerial turnover Capital allocation systems Formal planning systems

tunity. I will bootstrap it." The trustee says, "Since my object is to use my resources, once I finally commit I will go in very heavily at the front end."

The issue for the entrepreneur is this: What resources are necessary to pursue a given opportunity? There is a constant tension between the amount of resources committed and the potential return. The entrepreneur attempts to maximize value creation by minimizing the resource set and must, of course, accept more risk in the process. On the other hand, the trustee side deals with this challenge by careful analysis and large-scale commitment of resources after the decision to act. Entrepreneurial management requires that you learn to do a little more with a little less. **Figure 1-3** addresses this concept.

On this dimension we have the traditional stereotype of the entrepreneur as tentative, uncommitted, or temporarily dedicated — an image of unreliability. In times of rapid change, however, this characteristic of stepped, multistaged commitment of resources is a definite advantage in responding to changes in competition, the market, and technology.

The process of committing resources is pushed toward the entrepreneurial domain by several factors:

- Lack of predictable resource needs: Forces the entrepreneurs to commit less up front so that more will be available later on, if required.
- Lack of long-term control: Requires that commitment match exposure. If control over resources can be removed by environmental, political, or technological forces, resource exposure should also be reduced.

- Social needs: Multistaged commitment of resources brings us closer to the "small is beautiful" formulation of E. F. Shumacher by allowing for the appropriate level of resource intensity for the task.
- International demands: Pressures that we use no more than our fair share of the world's resources (e.g., not the 35 percent of the world's energy that the United States was using in the early 1970s).

The pressures within the large corporation, however, are in the other direction—toward resource intensity. This is due to the following:

- Personal risk reduction: Any individual's risk is reduced by having excess resources available.
- Incentive compensation: Excess resources increase short-term returns and minimize the period of cash and profit drains—typically the objects of incentive compensation systems.
- Managerial turnover: Creates pressures for steady cash and profit gains, which encourages short-term, visible success.
- Capital allocation systems: Generally designed for one-time decision making, these techniques assume that a single decision point is appropriate.
- Formal planning systems: Once a project has begun, a request for additional resources returns the managers to the morass of analysis and bureaucratic delays; managers are inclined to avoid this by committing the maximum amount of resources up front.

Control of Resources

When it comes to the control of resources, the promoter mentality says, "All I need from a resource is the ability to use it." These are the people who describe the ideal business as the post office box to which people send money. For them, all additional overhead is a compromise of a basic value. On the other hand, we all know companies that believe they do not adequately control a resource unless they own it or have it on their permanent payroll.

Entrepreneurs learn to use other people's resources well; they learn to decide, over time, what resources they need to bring in-house. They view this as a time-phased sequence of decisions. Good managers also learn that there are certain resources you should never own or employ. For instance, very few good real estate firms employ an architect. They may need the best, but they do not want to employ him or her, because the need for that resource, although critical to the success of the business, is temporary. The same is true of good lawyers. They are useful to have when you need them, but most firms cannot possibly afford to have the necessary depth of specialization of legal professionals constantly at their beck and call. **Figure 1–4** illustrates this dimension.

The stereotype of the entrepreneur as exploitative derives from this dimension: The entrepreneur is adept at using the skills, talents, and ideas of others. Viewed positively, this ability has become increasingly valuable in the changed business environment; it need not be parasitic in the context of a mutually satisfying relationship. Pressures toward this entrepreneurial side come from these:

FIGURE 1–4

Promoter	*Control of Resource*	Trustee
Episodic use or rent of required resources	Entrepreneurial Domain ←——————→ ←——————→ Administrative Domain	Ownership or employment of required resources
Pressures toward This Side		*Pressures toward This Side*
Increased resource specialization Long resource life compared to need Risk of obsolescence Risk inherent in any new venture Inflexibility of permanent commitment to resources		Power, status, and financial rewards Coordination Efficiency measures Inertia and cost of change Industry structures

- Increased resource specialization: An organization may have a need for a specialized resource like a VLSI design engineer, high-tech patent attorney, or state-of-the-art circuit test equipment, but only for a short time. By using, rather than owning, a firm reduces its risk and its fixed costs.
- Risk of obsolescence: Reduced by merely using, rather than owning, an expensive resource.
- Increased flexibility: The cost of exercising the option to quit is reduced by using, not owning, a resource.

Administrative practices are the product of pressures in the other direction, such as the following:

- Power, status, and financial rewards: Determined by the extent of resource ownership and control in many corporations.
- Coordination: The speed of execution is increased because the executive has the right to request certain action without negotiation.
- Efficiency: Enables the firm to capture, at least in the short run, all of the profits associated with an operation.
- Inertia and cost of change: It is commonly believed that it is good management to isolate the technical core of production from external shocks. This requires buffer inventories, control of raw materials, and control of distribution channels. Ownership also creates familiarity and an identifiable chain of command, which becomes stabilized with time.
- Industry structures: Encourage ownership to prevent being preempted by the competition.

FIGURE 1–5

Promoter	Management Structure	Trustee
Flat with multiple informal networks	Entrepreneurial Domain ← → ← → Administrative Domain	Formalized hierarchy
Pressures toward This Side		*Pressures toward This Side*
Coordination of key noncontrolled resources Challenge to legitimacy of owner's control Employees' desire for independence		Need for clearly defined authority and responsibility Organizational culture Reward systems Management theory

Management Structure

The promoter wants knowledge of his or her progress via direct contact with all of the principal actors. The trustee views relationships more formally, with specific rights and responsibilities assigned through the delegation of authority. The decision to use and rent resources and not to own or employ them will require the development of an informal information network. Only in systems where the relationship with resources is based on ownership or employment can resources be organized in a hierarchy. Informal networks arise when the critical success elements cannot be contained within the bounds of the formal organization. **Figure 1–5** illustrates this range of behavior.

Many people have attempted to distinguish between the entrepreneur and the administrator by suggesting that being a good entrepreneur precludes being a good manager. The entrepreneur is stereotyped as egocentric and idiosyncratic and thus unable to manage. However, although the managerial task is substantially different from the entrepreneur, management skill is nonetheless essential. The variation lies in the choice of appropriate tools.

More entrepreneurial management is a function of several pressures:

- Need for coordination of key noncontrolled resources: Results in need to communicate with, motivate, control, and plan for resources *outside* the firm.
- Flexibility: Maximized with a flat and informal organization.
- Challenge to owner's control: Classic questions about the rights of ownership as well as governmental, environmental, health, and safety restrictions undermine the legitimacy of control.

FIGURE 1–6

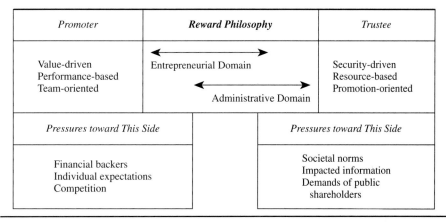

> • Employees' desire for independence: Creates an environment where employees are unwilling to accept hierarchical authority in place of authority based on competence and persuasion.

On the other side of the spectrum, pressures that push the firm toward more administrative behavior include these:

> • Need for clearly defined authority and responsibility: To perform the increasingly complex planning, organizing, coordinating, communicating, and controlling required in a business.
> • Organizational culture: Often demands that events be routinized.
> • Reward systems: Encourage and reward breadth and span of control.

Reward Philosophy

Finally, entrepreneurial firms differ from administratively managed organizations in their philosophy regarding reward and compensation. First, entrepreneurial firms are more explicitly focused on the creation and harvesting of value. In start-up situations, the financial backers of the organization—as well as the founders themselves—have invested cash and want cash out. As a corollary of this value-driven philosophy, entrepreneurial firms tend to base compensation on performance (where performance is closely related to value creation). Entrepreneurial firms are also more comfortable rewarding teams.

As a recent spate of takeovers suggests, more administratively managed firms are less often focused on maximizing and distributing value. They are more often guided in their decision making by the desire to protect their own positions and security. Compensation is often based on individual responsibility (assets or resources under control) and on performance relative to short-term profit targets. Reward in such firms is often heavily oriented toward promotion to increasing responsibility levels. **Figure 1–6** describes this dimension.

FIGURE 1–7 Summary

Pressures toward This Side	Promoter	Key Business Dimension	Trustee	Pressures toward This Side
Diminishing opportunity streams Rapidly changing: Technology Consumer economics Social values	Driven by perception of opportunity	**Strategic Orientation** Entrepreneurial Domain ↕ Administrative Domain	Driven by resources currently contolled	Social contracts Performance measurement criteria Planning systems and cycle
Action orientation Short decisions windows Risk management Limited decision constituencies	Revolutionary with short duration	**Commitment to Opportunity** Entrepreneurial Domain ↕ Administrative Domain	Evolutionary of long duration	Acknowledgement of multiple constituencies Negotiation of strategy Risk reduction Management of fit
Lack of predictable resource needs Lack of long-term control Social need for more opportunity per resource unit Interpersonal pressure for more efficient resource use	Multistaged with minimal exposure at each stage	**Commitment of Resources** Entrepreneurial Domain ↕ Administrative Domain	Single-staged with complete commitment upon decision	Personal risk reduction Incentive compensation Managerial turnover Capital allocation systems Formal planning systems

FIGURE 1-7 *(Continued)*

	Entrepreneurial Domain		Administrative Domain	
Increased resource specialization Long resource life compared to need Risk obsolescence Risk inherent in any new venture Inflexibility of permanent commitment to resources	Episodic use or rent of required resources	**Control of Resources** ↑↕↓ Entrepreneurial Domain ↑↕↓ Administrative Domain	Ownership or employment of required resources	Power, status, and financial rewards Coordination Efficiency measures Inertia and cost of change Industry structures
Coordination of key noncontrolled resources Challenge to legitimacy of owner's control Employees' desire for independence	Flat with multiple informal networks	**Management Structure** ↑↕↓ Entrepreneurial Domain ↑↕↓ Administrative Domain	Formalized hierarchy	Need for clearly defined authority and responsibility Organizational culture Reward systems Management theory
Individual expectations Competition Increased perception of personal wealth creation possibilities	Value-based Team-based Unlimited	**Compensation/Reward Policy** ↑↕↓ Entrepreneurial Domain ↑↕↓ Administrative Domain	Resource-based Driven by short-term data Promotion Limited amount	Societal norms IRS regulations Impacted information Search for simple solutions for complex problems Demands of public shareholders

15

The pressures that pull firms toward the promoter end of the spectrum include the following:

- Individual expectations: Increasingly, individuals expect to be compensated in proportion to their contribution, rather than merely as a function of their performance relative to an arbitrary peer group. In addition, individuals seemingly have higher levels of aspiration for personal wealth.
- Investor demands: Financial backers invest cash and expect cash back, and the sooner the better. Increasingly, shareholders in publicly held firms are starting to press with a similar orientation.
- Competition: Increased competition for talented people creates pressure for firms to reward these individuals in proportion to their contributions.

On the other side, a variety of pressures pull firms toward more trusteelike behavior:

- Societal norms: We still value loyalty to the organization and find it difficult to openly discuss compensation.
- Impacted information: It is often difficult to judge the value of an individual's contributions, particularly within the frame of the annual compensation cycle performance review that most firms use.
- Demands of public shareholders: Many public shareholders are simply uncomfortable with compensation that is absolutely high, even if it is in proportion to contribution.

Summary

These characteristics have been gathered onto one summary chart (see **Figure 1–7**). In developing a behavioral theory of entrepreneurship, it becomes clear that entrepreneurship is defined by more than a set of individual traits and is different from an economic function. It is a cohesive pattern of managerial behavior.

This perspective on entrepreneurship highlights what we see as a false dichotomy: the distinction drawn between entrepreneurship and intrapreneurship. Entrepreneurship is an approach to management that can be applied in start-up situations as well as within more established businesses. As our definition suggests, the accumulation of resources that occurs as a firm grows is a powerful force that makes entrepreneurial behavior more difficult in a larger firm. But the fundamentals of the behavior required remain the same.

Still, our primary focus will be on the start-up. The situational factors that define a start-up situation do much to encourage entrepreneurship. As we look at the start-up process, however, it is worth keeping in mind that many of these lessons can be applied equally well in the large corporate setting.

2 THE START-UP PROCESS

"A Perspective on Entrepreneurship" describes a paradigm for understanding entrepreneurial behavior. The paradigm breaks general management down into a number of key dimensions: strategic orientation, commitment to opportunity, commitment of resources, control of resources, management structure, and reward structure. It describes a range of managerial behavior along each of these dimensions and discusses the type of behavior that can be characterized as entrepreneurial.

This note serves as a conceptual bridge between what entrepreneurial behavior *is* and an in-depth look at the *actual process of* entrepreneurship as it is practiced in the start-up of a business. Entrepreneurship involves the process of pulling together a unique package of resources to pursue an opportunity. Because the entrepreneur never controls *all* of the necessary resources, pursuing the opportunity requires "bridging the resource gap." Such a process requires a series of choices that must be made in a manner both internally consistent and externally appropriate to the environmental context.

This note will describe the elements of the entrepreneurial process as well as the analysis that can help with each step of the process. It is critical to think about these issues *before* actually starting a business. This activity is often called opportunity or "prestart" analysis. It is analogous to gauging the depth of the water before taking the plunge. There should be three dominant goals for this process:

- To understand the dimensions of the opportunity and reach a conclusion regarding its attractiveness or unattractiveness.
- To understand the magnitude—and key elements—of the effort that will be required to exploit the opportunity.
- To identify a course of action—a strategy—for weaving one's way through the obstacles and the risks inherent in any venture.

A typical end product of this phase of analysis is a business plan, although it is entirely possible that the result will be a decision that the idea does *not* present an attractive opportunity.

The stages of prestart analysis flow in a natural order that corresponds to the process of starting a business: evaluating the opportunity, developing the business

This note was prepared by Michael J. Roberts under the direction of Howard H. Stevenson.
Copyright © 1984 by the President and Fellows of Harvard College
Harvard Business School Note 9–384–179

concept, assessing required resources, acquiring necessary resources, managing the venture, and harvesting and distributing value. Yet, to perform a thorough analysis, one must iterate through the full set of elements. For example, one dimension of the opportunity evaluation stage clearly involves an examination of potential financial returns. But it is difficult to project these returns without first developing the business concept, assessing the resources required to execute it, and looking down the road to see what kinds of returns the providers of those resources will require at harvest. Thus, a thorough prestart analysis requires an examination of all these elements of the process before the first concrete step is taken. The remainder of this note will discuss each of the steps in this process in turn.

Evaluating the Opportunity

An attractive, well-defined opportunity is the cornerstone of all successful ventures. The way in which the opportunity is defined will shape the remainder of the venture. There are several key questions that need to be answered in order to adequately evaluate the opportunity.

What Are the Dimensions of the "Window of Opportunity"?

An opportunity has several critical dimensions: its raw size, the time span over which it is projected to exist, and the rate at which it is expected to grow over time.

The raw size of the market is naturally a critical dimension because it has a direct bearing on the potential sales volume of the new venture and, thus, financial returns. All things being equal, of course, bigger is better. But things are not always equal. Large markets may attract large, powerful competitors and, thus, smaller niche markets may be more hospitable.

Growth rate is related to size, and, again, new ventures often thrive in rapid growth environments. By gaining—and holding on to—a piece of a small market and growing with that market, small ventures can become big business.

Every opportunity exists only for some finite amount of time, which varies greatly depending on the nature of the business. For example, in the popular music business, the opportunity for a new hit tune is usually only a few months. By contrast, in real estate, opportunities for even a single property may span several decades. It is important to understand (1) the time period and the economic life over which the opportunity will exist and (2) the appropriate time span for our own analysis of the opportunity. These are not always the same.

The risk and reward potential of an opportunity are also likely to vary over time. Certain parts of the economic life of the opportunity may have greater potential than others, and a careful analysis of the timing and magnitude of opportunities for harvesting can often indicate certain time limits to our analysis and plans. Looking again at real estate, for example, the syndication of tax shelters typically exploits only part of the total economic opportunity and over only a fraction of the total economic life of an income-producing property. Thus, it may be advantageous to pursue the underlying opportunity for only part of its total existence.

One key to exploiting the opportunity is to understand the forces that are creating it. Technological change, government regulation (or its relaxation), and shifts in consumer preferences and market demand can all create opportunity. By spotting patterns early, the entrepreneur can seize the initiative in creating a venture to exploit the opportunity.

The entrepreneur must identify the best period over which to pursue an opportunity and match his or her concept of how value can be created with an analysis of his or her own goals, skills, and time frame.

Is the Profit Potential Adequate to Provide a Satisfactory Return on Investment of Capital, Time, and Opportunity Costs?

An opportunity must earn a sufficient return to justify taking an entrepreneurial risk. *Adequate* is a relative term and depends on the amount of capital invested, the time frame required to earn the return, the risks assumed in the process, and existing alternatives for both capital and time.

Opportunities that demand substantial capital, require long periods of time to mature, and have large risks usually make little sense unless enormous value is being created. In all too many cases, such opportunities may create considerable value, but not for the original entrepreneurs. The numerous rounds of financing reduce the founders' percentage of ownership to such an extent that, ultimately, there is little recompense for the effort and risk.

Adequate also depends on our alternatives and opportunity costs, which vary with individuals, time, and circumstances. What may be attractive and viable for one person may be unrealistic for another, due to the availability of more attractive alternatives. Still, opportunities are likely to have the following financial characteristics:

- Steady and rapid growth in sales during the first five to seven years in some well-defined niche in the market.
- A high percentage of "recurring revenue." That is, once sold, a customer becomes a recurring source of revenue, not simply a one-time sale.
- High potential for operating leverage with increased experience and scale of operations.
- Internally generated funds to finance and sustain growth.
- Growing capacity for debt supported by:

  — Buildup of hard assets that can be used as collateral.
  — Increase in earnings and cash flow to service debt.

- Relatively short time frame during which significant value can be created and sustained—usually from three to five years.
- *Real* harvest options to turn equity into aftertax cash or equivalents.
- Rate of return on investment of 40 percent or more (after taxes).

Does the Opportunity Open up Additional Options for Expansion, Diversification, or Integration?

Good opportunities create additional options in a variety of different ways. Since the future is often unknown, it is critical the entrepreneur *not* be locked into a single, unvarying course. Good opportunities allow for midcourse corrections.

Poorer opportunities foreclose or limit future options. Opportunities that consume resources, eliminate alliances, or narrow technological options are inferior to those that build in flexibility.

Will the Profit Stream Be Durable in the Face of Likely Obstacles?

One thing is certain—circumstances will change over time, particularly if the venture is successful. This success will create all sorts of pressures on performance, including imitative competitors, product substitutions, changing technology, changing customer preferences, personnel turnover, and changing relationships with both suppliers and buyers. It is absolutely essential, therefore, to evaluate whether, having committed to the venture, it may become vulnerable to an erosion of its profit stream. This requires identifying and combatting potentially fatal vulnerabilities and recognizing that some are internal to the venture, such as personnel turnover, while others, such as competitive reactions, are external factors. Internal factors can be managed, and external ones must be carefully monitored.

Does the Product or Service Meet a Real Need?

Successful products meet a real need in terms of functionality, price, distribution, durability, and/or perceived quality. The provision of real value is fundamental to any new venture. Except in pure trading or promotion activities, the creation of value ultimately depends on the ability to offer products and services that satisfy some real need among customers.

A new venture must convince potential customers of the need and the benefits of its products and services in a reasonable period of time and at an affordable marketing and selling cost.

Entrepreneurs often *(a)* fail to understand how or even if their products and services will meet a customer's real needs and *(b)* underestimate how much time and marketing expense will be required to achieve the required level of sales.

Summary

By undertaking an analysis of the opportunity, the entrepreneur should be able to identify critical risks that the venture will face. These can never be eliminated entirely, but it is certainly advantageous to know exactly what they are. Moreover, the judicious application of effort and resources should be of considerable help in managing these risks.

Developing the Business Concept

Having undertaken an analysis of the opportunity, it is appropriate to develop a business concept—or strategy—that fully exploits the opportunity. For instance, assume one felt that there existed an extraordinary opportunity in the retailing of fresh-baked breads. A strategy would still need to be developed to address the maze of choices the entrepreneur would face:

- Franchising versus company-owned stores.
- Mall versus freestanding sites.
- On-premise preparations and baking versus central preparation and frequent delivery.
- Specific geographic region to be targeted versus national rollout.

An investigation of the following issues will help the entrepreneur make some of these strategic choices.

Can Barriers to Entry Be Created?

Barriers to entry help sustain superior returns and can be created based on cost, distribution power, patents, trade secrets, product differentiation, and/or focus. Given a good idea, some real advantage, and success, a venture will, in fact, have only a finite lead time. Competition *will emerge*. Frequently, the first competitors will enter the market with a ''copy and cut price'' strategy for their products and pricing. Thus, we must anticipate competitive threats and devise measures to protect our lead time and our competitive advantage from encroachment over time. An often fatal error for the new firm is the failure to plan for expected competitive reaction and therefore to plan adequately for the renewal that must occur in order to assure that the advantages sought will be durable.

Are the Customers Identifiable, Reachable, and Open to Change?

In order to successfully attract new customers, they must not only be identifiable and reachable, but also must be willing to obsolete any investments they have made to other firms' people, procedures, and/or facilities and equipment.

Often a new venture's success depends on the ability to sell some sort of *change* to the customer: a new process, product, or service. In effect, the customer will be asked to do something different in order to do business with us. Typically, this requires some form of new investment or expenditures by the customer and involves changing the way he or she does business. Becoming integrated into the customer's procedures is often the most effective barrier to entry of competition; it is, however, often the major hurdle that a new product or process must overcome.

It is essential, therefore, that the change being sold be *affordable* to the customer and yield a clearly visible benefit. Assuming customers elect to buy our products and services, we must be able to satisfy and reward them with real benefits at prices and terms the customer can accept and is willing to pay.

It is particularly useful to identify *specific* groups of potential customers within markets and to compare the real benefits received with the products and services offered. Specificity as to the particular customer is an absolute prerequisite to the effective planning of distribution approaches. Those opportunities that postulate the existence of a generalized market are almost always less successful than those based on the knowledge of specific customers and the means by which to reach them.

Will the Suppliers Control Critical Resources and Capture the Innovative Rents or Profits?

As a result of "make or buy" analyses and the desire to be "lean and mean," new companies frequently elect for some period of time not to invest in certain facilities or technology on which their venture will depend. In such cases, the new venture may become dependent on its suppliers, who could be in a position to squeeze extra profits from the venture because they control critical resources.

Will the Buyers Be so Strong as to Demand Uneconomic Concessions?

This area is a potential mine field particularly in established markets. It is often the case when a new or small business attempts to break into a market or sell products or services to large corporations that the buyers enjoy such great advantages in purchasing (e.g., terms of delivery, price, credit, quality standards, etc.) that they wring concessions from the smaller business rendering the transactions uneconomic or excessively risky.

Summary

The process of developing the business concept is critical. The opportunity evaluation develops a perspective on a market need, but the entrepreneur must still develop a business strategy that meets that need in a way that generates a superior return. The forces that drive the development of the business strategy include both external market focus and the economics of various approaches to serving that market.

Assessing Required Resources

An entrepreneur can be viewed as a person who finds ways to bridge the gap between what he or she has in the way of skills and resources and what is actually needed to pursue the opportunity. Those who already have the skills and resources under personal control are closer to "investors" rather than entrepreneurs.

Much entrepreneurial failure occurs because there is too great a mismatch between the resources controlled by the entrepreneur and those required to pursue the opportunity successfully. Every venture depends on having the ability to control a *minimum* set of critical skills, resources, and relationships, and to gain, as necessary, any required approvals. The key questions are: What is the minimum resource set required, and how can the entrepreneur get and maintain control over these resources?

In answering these questions, it is useful to ask several much more specific questions that test our ability to assemble this minimum package.

What Skills, Resources, and Relationships Does the Entrepreneurial Group Already Possess?

The creation of real and lasting value depends on the ability to bring something new to the table. The less one brings, the more fragile and vulnerable the venture will be. The more one brings that can be protected and sustained, the more unique and potentially durable will be the venture.

Rarely does an individual entrepreneur possess or even substantially control all of the skills, resources, and relationships that are required to pursue an opportunity over the longer term. It is important to assess and understand what skills, resources, and relationships are truly controlled by the venture and to understand the resulting advantages and vulnerabilities.

Who Are the Likely Suppliers of the Remainder of the Resources?

The full set of resources required for the venture will include the following:

- Financial.
- Marketing and sales.
- Technological.
- Production.
- Product development.
- Personnel.
- Managerial.
- Systems.

Whatever we lack but need, we must come up with. The key to bridging the gap is to understand from where and how the needed resources can be obtained. Often one of the most difficult parts of the problem is simply *identifying* and understanding alternative sources of supply.

The "resourcefulness" of many entrepreneurs often shows most clearly in this area, particularly in their ability to "make do." The ability to find ingenious ways to get hold of and *use* — not necessarily *own* but *use* — needed resources is a survival skill. In-depth knowledge of an industry and a market is particularly useful in meeting this challenge. The entrepreneur can calibrate quality, honesty, cost, and risk through personal experience and knowledge.

Personal experience also improves credibility and increases the desire of potential suppliers of resources to participate. Suppliers prefer investing their own risk capital of time and product in a known quantity with whom they have personal experience or at least personal ability to calibrate knowledge and planning.

What Skills and Resources Must Be a Part of the Internal Organization?

First, in order to achieve critical economies of scale, a certain critical mass must be obtained. The best companies include and control, as part of their internal organization, those elements and resources that yield distinctive competitive advantages as their experience level and scale of operations increase.

Next, if possible, competitors should be preempted from controlling critical resources. This is a particularly important strategic issue for small companies seeking to compete against larger established players, who may offer similar products or services. Human resources are often the major ones that can be preempted by start-up ventures. To accomplish this, however, careful attention must be paid early on to the venture's legal and economic structure.

Finally, for those resources that require continued coordination through direct authority relationships, internal control will be critical. Some resources can be managed through contractual relationships that are essentially self-enforcing (e.g., suppliers making product to specification). Creation of good alternative possibilities results in achievable price, quality, and delivery standards without direct authority over these items.

In other cases, direct contractual or other authoritative relationships must be established, an example being the creation of a new marketing organization. The feedback needs, the ambiguity of the task, and the requirements for noneconomic action such as missionary selling are often precursors to the need for direct authority-based control. In later stages as the marketing process becomes more routine and systematic, expansion can often be achieved without expanding employment.

For Each Resource or Skill, What Amount Is Required?

The entrepreneur must address the issue of how much of a given resource is optimal, versus the absolute minimum requirement. A bare-bones plan usually has lower costs but higher levels of operating risk. On the other hand, comfort usually means higher cost, but not necessarily lower operating risk.

Somewhere in the middle, there is usually a calculated level of risk that one is willing to assume. Often an entrepreneur believes his or her particular skills, knowledge, or experience allows risk to be managed differently than conventional wisdom might dictate. The entrepreneur therefore is prepared to assume a risk that others believe to be unwise, but in which, in fact, he or she believes there is minimal downside.

The keys are to understand what is needed for the venture, what causes increased risks and to devise an effective strategy to mitigate those risks assumed. The assumption that more resources provide less risk is clearly incorrect. The entrepreneur must know how and why that statement is incorrect.

What Is Really Unique about the Proposed Business Concept?

There are several bases on which to build a long-term competitive advantage, including:

- Cost structure.
- Technology.
- Product features or quality, including augmented product definitions.
- Marketing and sales channels.
- Financial resources.
- Focus.
- People.

It is absolutely essential to have a strategy in mind and a clear understanding of the venture's competitive basis, both in the short run and over time. Unless the entrepreneur controls the resources that generate the truly unique features in the approach, there is high vulnerability. Suppliers, customers, or innovative competitors can exploit this vulnerability to the long-term disadvantage of the venture.

What Quality Trade-offs Can Be Made among the Required Skills and Resources?

It is rarely necessary to have a uniform level of quality in every required resource. An important insight is understanding quality trade-offs. Many fine businesses have been built based on the utilization of used equipment. Management valued quality more highly in the output rather than in the appearance of the manufacturing floor.

What Are the Major Requirements for Regulatory Compliance?

Compliance with governmental and other regulatory constraints is a critical but often overlooked step in the new venture analysis. Key aspects include:

- Licenses.
- Operating procedures.
- Product approvals and testing.
- Insurance and bonding.

It is a telling mark of inexperience and naïveté to pursue the opportunity without ensuring full compliance with the extensive sets of laws, regulations, and standards of business practice. We live in an extremely complex domestic and international environment; it is frequently necessary to obtain formal approval, licenses, or other sanctions in order to simply conduct our activities.

Some of the required sanctions and approvals can be obtained by complying with known laws and/or by compliance with regulations issued by federal, state, and local government agencies. Other sanctions and approvals, such as Underwriters Laboratory approval of the safety of certain kinds of consumer and industrial products, must be obtained from public and private organizations, which have lengthy and frequently expensive application, testing, and approval processes. Still, in other cases, such as in commercial building construction or many government and large private sector contracts, the standard business practice may require formal and legally enforceable bonding of supplier and/or contractor performance by insurance companies, and so forth.

What Critical Checkpoints Will Mark the Lowering of Risks?

Major long-term objectives are most relevant and useful when they can be broken down into achievable intermediate milestones. As a venture develops, it typically becomes more viable. Many entrepreneurs frequently think in terms of "plateaus" and "If only we could. . . ." Preplanning of these checkpoints and plateaus helps us understand how the risk of a venture can or will be reduced over time. These same plateaus act as useful benchmarks in the acquisition of additional resources. They mark times when new players can be induced to play, new types of financing become available, or new suppliers and subcontractors enter the picture based on risk stages having been passed. The entrepreneur who is conscious of passing these checkpoints and bases his or her strategy on passing plateaus can often maintain a higher percentage of ownership.

Are There Adequate Resources to Surmount Potential Variations from the Plan?

Things will go wrong and at the worst possible time. There is an old rule of thumb in business that new ventures can have variances of three and two: three times as much time and twice as much money, or vice versa. In times of financial distress, the "golden rule" takes effect—the party with the gold (i.e., cash) rules. The refinancing of a venture in times of financial distress is most often done on a confiscatory basis. In the venture capital industry, this is called *down and dirty* financing.

The strain and bargaining disadvantage for an entrepreneur created by a major financial crisis provides a rare predatory opportunity for those with cash to exact excessive concessions from those with money already trapped in the deal. Rarely does new money coming into a deal ever agree to take (bail) old money out. The rule is last-in, first-out. To make matters worse, new money frequently demands not only that old money stay in the deal, but also that it retreat in terms of legal priority, control over the affairs of the venture, and any future opportunities to exit.

With this in mind, a plan without contingencies and reserves is no plan at all. The knowledgeable investor, supplier, customer, and employee will want to know what will be done and how it will affect their own expectations and rewards from the venture.

Obviously, however, it is not feasible to have enough resources available up front to surmount every potential contingency. On the other hand, the plan must deal with the *likely ones,* and the entrepreneur must have a back-up vision of the future that will allow survival in the face of potential misfortunes.

Summary

The process of critically assessing required resources is an important step in the venture creation process. One of the most important ways in which the entrepreneur can create value is by doing more with less. On the other hand, both the prudent management of risk and the maintenance of competitive advantage depends on sufficient amounts of the right resources.

Acquiring Necessary Resources

It is always necessary to structure some kind of legal vehicle and organization for conducting the affairs of the venture and for controlling the skills and resources that must be assembled.

Having determined the resources that are critical to the venture, it is time to acquire them. Note that *acquire* does not translate into *own*. One of the most valuable techniques of leverage available to the entrepreneur is to obtain the desired measure of control—without ownership—through such approaches as rents, royalties, and other incentives to encourage the owners of resources to make them available for the entrepreneur's use.

For Each Critical Skill or Resource, What Mechanisms for Control Are Available?

In addition to the classic approach of ownership and direct control, there are several alternatives for controlling resources, including:

- Contractual agreements.
- Long-term noncontractual supply arrangements.
- Ad hoc need fulfillment.

The analysis that determines which control mechanism should be used focuses on understanding the critical factors required for success in the business and evaluating how feasible it is to achieve the required level of performance from each resource under each of the alternative control mechanisms. In general, direct ownership and administrative control of a resource—hiring people, buying plant and equipment—is the most expensive approach and should only be followed for the most critical resources.

What Are the Critical Agenda Items for the Potential Providers of the Required Resources and Skills?

The potential providers have complex and multi-item needs of their own that must be fulfilled in order to persuade them to allow you to use their resources. In addition to financial return, these needs may include:

- Financial reward.
- Professional advancement.

- Operating integration.
- Risk avoidance.
- Social status.
- Political response to outside constituency.

These factors frequently provide the foundation pieces for deals. One of the keys to unlocking someone else's resources on favorable terms is to know what the other person or organization values most. Frequently, there are complex factors at work that have little to do with money.

Can Incentives Be Structured to Meet the Agenda Items Above?

It is difficult to establish and maintain meaningful control over any resource without providing incentives for the owner/possessor of the resource to cooperate with you.

"Thin" relationships and deals can be dangerous and unreliable over time. In cases where incentives are inadequate, it is often wise to enhance them to motivate others to work *actively* on your behalf. This keeps parties in the deal for positive reasons, but typically requires some kind of concession on the entrepreneur's part.

Will the Opportunity Provide Enough Return to Meet the Resource Providers' Needs and to Provide the Entrepreneurial Reward?

New business ventures are always bounded in many ways and can support only so many players. However, there are many different types of "returns" in any venture, including noncash returns such as enhanced technical position, prestige, franchises on market segments, and so forth.

Skilled entrepreneurs know how to allocate all the important financial and other returns among the key players. The problem comes when the returns are just not sufficient to meet the expectations of the key players. These are known as *thin deals*.

Summary

The ability to obtain control over required resources in a creative manner is one of the hallmarks of the successful entrepreneur. By renting, leasing, or borrowing, and with the correct structuring of incentives and the clever use of subcontractors, entrepreneurs can substantially lower the resource requirements and fixed costs of the business. This both lowers risk and raises potential financial returns.

Managing the Venture

Once the critical resources have been assembled, it's time to deploy them and actually start the business. The early days will be quite hectic, as the entrepreneur, assembled management team, and employees begin to learn the business and their jobs. Everything that happens will be happening for the first time, and someone will have to make a decision about how it should be handled. This raises a number of issues, including the following questions.

Does the Management Concept Include Both the Critical Internal and External Elements of the Organization?

Somehow, the entrepreneur must devise and apply a formal or informal system of management to the venture. This management system must include within its scope both what is going to be internal to the venture (e.g., people, production processes, etc.) and what will be kept outside of the venture's organization (e.g., key suppliers or distributors with whom the venture may have contracts and agreements).

Often the entrepreneurial venture is distinguished by the control that it exerts over resources that it does not legally own or employ. The control and influence can only be intelligently and purposefully exercised if there is a managerial relationship with those resources. The relationship is neither hierarchical nor a pure market transaction. It does provide for continuity, clear mechanisms for feedback and evaluation, and yet it must also be mutually beneficial over the long term if it is to endure.

How Will Employees Be Selected and Attracted?

The task of selecting employees for the venture is complicated, given both the resource scarcity of the early days and natural uncertainty over the skills that will be required. Even if the entrepreneur could afford to hire proven managerial talent, it is not clear exactly what skills would be required.

Most entrepreneurs respond to this dilemma by hiring eager, young men and women who can be retained relatively inexpensively and who seem willing to perform a wide variety of tasks. Occasionally, these individuals can be groomed and become good managers. More often, however, it is necessary for the entrepreneur to bring in some seasoned professionals as the firm matures and is financially able to afford their services.

Thus, at the start, it is important for the entrepreneur to have a picture of the managerial resources that will be needed over the course of the venture and to work at developing them. When this approach fails, the entrepreneur must be willing to reach outside the firm for the required skills.

How Will the Evolution of the Entrepreneur's Role Be Managed?

The entrepreneur must be aware that his or her role will evolve considerably as the business grows and matures. As the scope of activity in the firm expands, the entrepreneur will have little choice but to delegate responsibility to a layer of middle managers. This, in turn, will create a new role for the entrepreneur as a "manager of managers," and new skills will be required to execute this role.

Summary

The management of the growing venture is an extremely challenging task, demanding skills that differ dramatically from those required to start the business. The ability to surmount these challenges depends on a recognition that they exist and that difficult changes in behavior and management style will be required.

Harvesting and Distributing Value

If the business is successful, significant value will have been created. The issue then becomes harvesting and distributing that value. Outside investors will be one source of pressure, as they will want to turn their initial cash investment back into cash. The personal desires of the entrepreneur and key employees may also press for some form of harvest. This raises a number of issues, including the following questions.

Is There a Specific Mechanism for Harvesting?

Not all ventures have the same alternatives for harvesting; some cannot be harvested at all and must simply be operated for cash. Often personal service businesses fall into this category. On the other hand, businesses that create assets are often harvestable even without the owner having to quit active business life.

Business ventures that have no realistic prospects for a harvest represent mainly investments that have been made in providing a job for oneself, one's partners, and employees. However, for those business ventures that can be harvested, it is important to understand the range of real options that the venture may have. These include:

- Acquisition by a larger company.
- Public offering of stock via:
  — IPO: typically new shares are issued by the company and sold to raise more financing and establish the market value of the stock.
  — Secondary offering: shares held by principals and early investors are sold to the public or new investors (may be part of IPO).
- Sale of the company:
  — To a third party.
  — To other management and employees.
- Liquidation and distribution of proceeds.

Of these mechanisms, acquisitions, mergers, and public offerings are most frequently used in venture capital situations. However, timing and market conditions are critical to the harvest. Public offerings are often the most elusive harvest form for entrepreneurs. On becoming paper millionaires, many founders find themselves the last to realize the aftertax cash gains from public offerings. Acquisitions and mergers have also often provided only illusionary harvesting mechanisms. The entrepreneur who substitutes his or her own undiversified holdings for undiversified holdings in another firm often loses both control and wealth.

It is critical to understand both the goals and the detailed mechanisms by which a harvesting strategy is to be executed.

Has the Venture Been Structured Financially and Legally so as to Maximize the Aftertax Yield from Harvest?

Here is where the devil is in the details and where foresight is essential. The IRS has been as aggressive as taxpayers have been creative in pursuing aftertax dollars.

Substantial and frequently extensive legal and tax-related preplanning is always required. Some issues have significant lead times extending over several years. For example, achieving capital gains treatment of a partial liquidation and discontinuance of a line of business requires of a corporate vehicle that certain conditions be met for periods prior to and after the liquidation transaction.

What Conditions Will Trigger a Harvest?

Timing is everything. There may indeed be many factors that will determine when it is time to cash in. These could include the following items:

- Need for large amounts of capital to press on to a major stage of growth.
- Peaking of profit potential.
- Changes in tax laws.
- Changes in debt or public equity markets.
- Economic cycles.
- Age, health, and interests of principals and founders.

What Conditions Could Preclude a Harvest?

Depending on the nature of the venture, from time to time certain factors may work against harvesting or prevent it altogether. Among the more important external factors are these:

- Economic and market cycles.
- Tax law changes.
- Competitors.
- Changes in laws and regulations.

The more important internal factors include:

- Major management or operating problems.
- Loss of trade secrets.

How Will Responsibilities to Other Participants Be Fulfilled at Harvest?

All of your creditors, investors, partners, and key employees have or develop expectations about what they will gain from the venture. If you ever intend to do business with them again after the harvest transaction, you will want to ensure that they come away from the experience reasonably happy.

Summary

The harvest is a bittersweet experience for many entrepreneurs. While it represents the culmination of a long effort to build financial value, it can also represent the end of an extremely rewarding managerial experience. Yet, the fear of "giving up the baby" should not be allowed to interfere with sound financial planning. Moreover, many entrepreneurs have a unique ability to build a business, but less of a competitive advantage in the actual management of the company over the long term. They should be willing to recognize where their strengths lie and focus on applying them in the appropriate situations.

Conclusion

Starting a new venture is obviously a complex activity. It entails foresight and planning regarding all of the issues required to manage and to eventually harvest the venture. In addition, it also requires a certain attitude—or point of view—on the general management task. This attitude stems from the unique role and responsibilities of the entrepreneur. Unlike other managers who may have responsibility for a certain aspect or a specific function, the entrepreneur is ultimately accountable for the entire venture. It is this extremely close identity with the business that makes success so very rewarding and failure so difficult. This unique role breeds a certain set of attitudes including:

- An action orientation: The entrepreneur cannot afford to merely elucidate the dimensions of the problem—he or she *must act*.
- An attention to detail: Because the entrepreneur is ultimately accountable for the venture, he or she cannot afford to delegate final responsibility for "details" to others, including trained professionals. The entrepreneur *must* be familiar with legal, financial, and tax details that can impact the business significantly.

Indeed, the whole process of entrepreneurship involves far more than the problem solving often associated with management. The entrepreneur is a finder and exploiter of opportunities. Consequently, successful students of entrepreneurship must develop a similar attitude toward case situations: going beyond analysis of the case problems to an elucidation of the range of alternatives and the selection of a particular plan of action designed to seize the opportunity.

You need not know the answer to everything before you start. You must, however, start with the expectation that it is your responsibility to know the answers and to respond adequately to those steel-hearted outsiders who will ask them of you. And they will ask.

It is an inescapable fact that whatever omissions you make and risks you fail to identify in the prestart phase will be automatically included in the venture. On the other hand, early identification and management of risk factors and the magnitude of the task can be opportunities for substantial profit.

One of the most common and often fatal mistakes for many first-time entrepreneurs is to believe that much of the responsibility for the prestart phase can be delegated (e.g., particularly to professionals and technical experts such as lawyers and accountants), while forgetting that the accountability for the venture's results always rests with the lead entrepreneur and his or her team.

Despite its potential difficulty and complexity, prestart analysis must have a very strong mandate in favor of decisiveness, timeliness, and go–no-go actions. You cannot get bogged down in "analysis paralysis."

If you can look across the scope of issues suggested in this note for your own prestart analysis and respond with well-considered answers, then you have passed through the first gate on the journey of your entrepreneurial venture.

3   ANALYZING NEW VENTURES

Seize the day or look before you leap? Apparently, many entrepreneurs act before they analyze. Of the hundreds of thousands of new businesses that are started every year, only a small number ever turn a true profit, and only the merest handful sustain attractive returns over the long haul. The great majority fold or drag along, providing their owners with incomes comparable to the wages they could earn as employees. And although bad luck plays an important role, many failures are predestined and predictable.

Then, too, we find a great many individuals whose endless research precludes action: By the time they can fully investigate an opportunity, it no longer exists. Entrepreneurs may also lose their enthusiasm, as continued analysis lengthens the list of flaws and calls into question the positives. Corrosive pessimism replaces the previously unrealistic vision of the venture.[1]

This note is intended to help would-be entrepreneurs realistically assess and, I hope, improve their prospects without being paralyzed by analysis. In the sections that follow, I will discuss:

1. A framework for assessing viability. The framework will help entrepreneurs address a basic issue: Can the enterprise survive in a competitive marketplace?

2. Criteria for evaluating attractiveness. Assuming viability, how does the entrepreneur compare the potential rewards with the risks?

3. Judgments and shortcuts. Given limited resources and considerable ambiguity, how does the entrepreneur determine analytical priorities and draw conclusions from conflicting data?

4. Acting on the analyses. What concrete actions should follow the investigation?

Framework for Assessing Viability

Launching a profitable enterprise requires establishing a unique edge. Entrepreneurs often focus on whether customers will buy their goods or services but not on why sales

---

[1] The evidence also raises issues about the value of planning and analysis for entrepreneurs who do take the plunge. A National Federation of Independent Business study of 2,994 start-ups showed that founders who spent a long time in study, reflection, and planning were no more likely to survive their first three years than founders who seized opportunities that came by without much planning. (*Inc.*, July 1992, p. 49.)

This note was prepared by Professor Amar V. Bhide.

Copyright © 1992 by the President and Fellows of Harvard College.

Harvard Business School Note 9–393–053

will lead to profits. Of course, a start-up must attract customers; but, for revenues to exceed expenses, an enterprise must enjoy higher prices or lower costs than its competitors. Therefore, to assess viability, entrepreneurs must analyze the adequacy of their competitive edge and not just their ability to meet customer needs.

The Importance of a Competitive Edge

Competition is the mortal enemy of profits. Economic theory tells us that under conditions of perfect competition, all firms face market prices for their inputs and outputs that leave no room for profit. If for some reason, demand increases, causing prices and margins to rise, new supply enters the market and marginal costs quickly equal marginal revenues. Similarly, if market prices for inputs decline, competitors pass on the benefit to consumers. Firms' owners receive a market return for their capital or a market wage for their time and effort; starting a business creates no "surplus."

Prospects for start-ups in imperfect markets are worse. According to industrial organization theory, structural factors can lead to abnormally high or low returns for competitors in an industry. Barriers to entry may allow a small number of incumbents to set prices well above their costs. Conversely, barriers to exit combined with supplier or customer bargaining power may lead to chronic losses. In either case, the structural factors that interfere with free competition create a hostile environment for new entrants. High industry profits indicate that entrants face disadvantages that prevent them from replicating the profit margins of the incumbents. Chronic industry losses suggest that the start-up has to do much more than match incumbents' prices and costs.

As an intellectual proposition, few would quarrel with the need for start-ups, particularly in imperfect markets, to establish price or cost advantages. In practice, however, many entrepreneurs dilute the much-better-than-your-rivals imperative to an as-good-as standard. Perhaps they have been conditioned to believe that profitability is the natural state for an enterprise and that losses are the consequence of a pathological hubris or ineptitude. Just as we expect every healthy newborn to survive infancy, entrepreneurs assume that their ventures will naturally succeed. But, in fact, competition makes the demise of start-ups normal, to-be-expected events; their profitable survival should be considered extraordinary. Principles of good management—listening to customers, maintaining quality, paying attention to costs, and so on—which may be sufficient to preserve a going business, cannot be counted on to sustain a new venture.

Basic Building Blocks

We can easily list several tangible and intangible assets that constitute a firm's competitive edge. They include low-cost leases in attractive locations, proprietary technology, dominant market share, brand name, and an installed base of captive customers. But we cannot easily describe how an entrepreneur acquires such assets at a price that yields attractive returns. What does an entrepreneur actually do?

The evidence suggests that there is no standard formula. Looking behind the technology, scale, or brands of successful firms we find a variety of stories involving insight, cunning, nerve, perseverance, or happenstance; efforts to find a common script seem futile. For example, some scholars and entrepreneurs regard risk taking as the ultimate source of profit and competitive advantage, whereas others emphasize innovation. The reality is that the extent of risk taking and innovation that we find in successful ventures varies considerably: Some are practically risk-free, others require a major gamble; some winners are based on a revolutionary concept, and others show little originality.

A useful middle ground—between looking for a single factor and concluding that all successful ventures are unique—is to stipulate that entrepreneurs establish an edge through a combination of actions characterized by exceptional commitment, creativity, and competence:

Commitment.   Investing in assets that have limited salvage value. Many tangible and intangible assets that provide a competitive edge require prior expenditures of time or money that are more or less irreversible. For example, a brand name may require an advertising campaign, a low-cost source of raw materials may derive from an investment in exploration, and a proprietary technology may involve years of research and development.

Creativity.   Innovation or insight. Competitive advantage may be gained by some new insight or technology developed by the entrepreneur such as the invention or use of a new product, manufacturing process, distribution channel, marketing strategy, organizational structure, or contracting approach.

Competence.   Doing or getting difficult things done. Entrepreneurs (and managers) vary in their training, enthusiasm, innate skills, contacts, control over resources, and other attributes; accordingly, we often see great differences in the ability to execute tasks such as managing a product development team, closing a sale, raising money, or negotiating with employees. And, if many rivals follow similar strategies—in Drucker's terms, when many know what the right things to do are—then doing things right can lead to significant competitive advantages.

These three Cs, which distinguish successful entrepreneurs from the crowd, often reinforce and complement one another. For example, for an entrepreneur of limited means, committing to an advertising campaign may require an exceptional competence in fund-raising or creativity in structuring deals. Similarly, a breakthrough concept for a new product is, by itself, not always profitable. Concepts can be difficult to sell because others are skeptical or because, once revealed, they lose their value. Therefore, entrepreneurs may have to commit time and money to produce a working prototype before they can expect a gain on their creativity.

The Role of Change

A fourth C—exogenous *change*—can catalyze or magnify an entrepreneur's commitment, creativity, or competence. For example, collapsing real estate or energy markets can help entrepreneurs to invest in valuable properties at bargain prices. The widespread diffusion of microwave ovens created opportunities for innovations in food technology and packaging. The microcomputer revolution allowed entrepreneurs to use their technical or marketing competencies (and exceptional drive) to build profitable and growing businesses.

Change, though, does not always help entrepreneurs. A great retailing concept may be unprofitable if a tight real estate market pushes rents too high. A high-growth market may attract so many entrepreneurs that none can make a profit. As a general rule, well-publicized changes and predictable trends produce fewer opportunities for profit than obscure or confusing disturbances. For example, the obvious aging of the population or the growing demand for day care are less likely to provide profitable opportunities than the uncertainties surrounding a new operating system for microcomputers or the length and depth of the commercial real estate recession. (The truly creative or exceptionally capable entrepreneur can, of course, profit from even well-publicized trends—although the California gold rush made paupers of the thousands who were caught in the frenzy, Levi Strauss was able to make a fortune by supplying rugged jeans to the prospectors.)

Issues to Be Analyzed

The viability of an enterprise depends, we have argued, on whether it can overcome competition: An enterprise will flourish only if its combination of commitment, creativity, and competence, possibly reinforced by external change, outweighs the profit-destroying competitive forces it confronts (**see Figure A**).

Analyzing this balance requires consideration of several issues:

1. What competitive hurdles must the start-up overcome?

A complete analysis (as described in Porter's *Competitive Strategy*) will cover all elements of industry structure affecting profitability; a start-up faces competition not only from rivals offering the same goods but also potentially from substitutes, suppliers, buyers, and other new entrants. In addition to an external industry analysis, entrepreneurs should turn their attention inward to identify their weakness (regarding capital availability, relationships, technology, and so on) vis-a-vis their competitors'. As a rule, most start-ups can expect to face significant "liabilities of newness."

The analyses should be dynamic, with the entrepreneur identifying both existing and potential competitive hurdles. And, ideally, the analyses should provide both qualitative and quantitative indications of the hurdles faced. The entrepreneur should be able to identify, for example, the two or three basic problems faced by a new entrant—the ability of a few suppliers to squeeze industry participants, severe price competition due to overcapacity, the strong preference of customers for proven substitutes, and so on. Entrepreneurs should also be able to quantify the extent of the problems faced: What are the dollars-and-cents cost advantages of the incumbent's scale? What R&D expenditures are likely to be needed to invent around the incumbent's patents and the advertising costs required to gain a point of market share? What period of training (or amount of signing bonuses) does it take to create an adequately skilled work force? If the industry suffers from excessive rivalry, how much higher must our margins have to rise to be profitable?

FIGURE A   **How New Ventures Overcome Barriers to Profitable Market Entry**

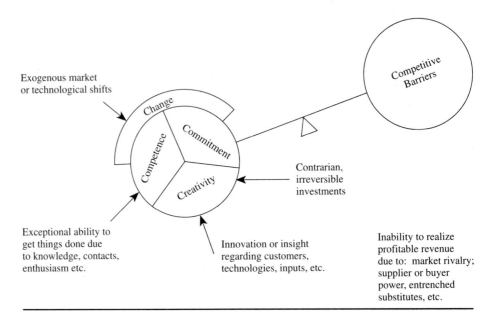

2. What are the quantitative and qualitative dimensions of the competitive edge the start-up seeks to establish?

The purpose of the analysis is to establish, as concretely as possible, the strategic and financial goals for the start-up. A complete analysis will identify minimum price and cost goals needed to earn a fair return on the time and money invested, as well as the corresponding competitive assets—for example, brand name or new production process—that must be acquired for the start-up to attain its price and cost targets. For example, a computer start-up might determine that it can expect a 20 percent price premium for a new machine that is 1.7 times as fast as competing products by using a new parallel-processing architecture the founders expect to develop. All too often, however, entrepreneurs are vague about the dimensions of the competitive advantage they seek. A typical superficial analysis results in the expectation of an unspecified "premium" price for a "better" product.

A full analysis will also include the dimension of time. The development of a new technology may be sufficient to overcome competitive barriers if it is completed by January, but worthless if delayed till December. In a changing market, the when of competitive advantage is as important as the what.

3. What distinctive actions will provide the start-up with its expected edge? That is, how and why is the entrepreneur's commitment, creativity, or competence special?

The analysis provides an important reality check for the entrepreneur's hopes of establishing a valuable brand name, technology, or other competitive edge: Without concrete acts of distinctive commitment, creativity, and competence (or extraordinary luck!) an entrepreneur cannot realistically expect to gain price or cost advantages.

Entrepreneurs should not confuse the absolute level of commitment, creativity, and competence with the amount of commitment, creativity, and competence required to actually differentiate the venture from its competitors. Starting a new disk-drive company, for example, may require significant investment, running into the tens of millions of dollars. But if many other competitors are making (or previously have made) similar investments, then the entrepreneurs' outlays are unlikely to provide a competitive edge; they are merely an entry ticket. Similarly, in launching a new fast-food chain, a high level of operational competence may be necessary though not sufficient to establish a competitive edge if rivals operate at high levels of operational excellence. But conversely, in a business (such as providing transportation services to rock bands) with many fly-by-night or unreliable operators, modest professionalism can provide a meaningful edge.

As previously suggested, external change can create or destroy distinctiveness. A million-dollar investment in an energy exploration venture may represent an unusual commitment in a depressed market, but not in a boom. The ability to install PC networks was a valuable distinguishing competence for entrepreneurs starting computer dealerships in 1985, but cannot be expected to provide a great edge today, as knowledge of LANs has become widely diffused.

4. Is the edge adequate—can the start-up's combination of Cs overcome the competitive hurdles it faces?

The capstone issue of adequacy has two dimensions. One is magnitude—high barriers to entry and significant competitive obstacles require a materially distinctive package of Cs. In a mature market with fierce entrenched competitors, for example, minor innovation is unlikely to provide an adequate basis for profitable entry. The other dimension of adequacy is appropriateness—the entrepreneur's package of distinctiveness must somehow match the specific competitive challenges faced. An exceptional willingness to make large irreversible investments, for example, may be worthless in a rapidly changing industry in which the winners are determined by the speed and quality of their execution.

The analysis of adequacy may be aided by an item-by-item examination of the start-up's income statement. Each item may be associated with a competitive edge—or handicap—and the underlying distinctive competence, creativity, or commitment that is expected to provide the edge. For example, the entrepreneur may look behind projected revenues to assumptions about relative pricing and market share and the specific distinctive actions that justify the assumptions.

Criteria for Evaluating Attractiveness

Assuming that a venture meets the test of viability, the entrepreneur must assess its attractiveness. Is the enterprise likely to provide an attractive return on the entrepreneur's investment of time and money? Discounted expected cash flow (DCF) apparently provides a standard, unbiased measure of attractiveness, but, from an entrepreneur's point of view, its utility is limited. In fact, evaluating a venture's attractiveness requires the consideration of several factors, both quantifiable and unquantifiable.

Limitations of DCF

The economic characteristics of new ventures vary considerably in their expected gross margins, capital intensity, ratio of fixed to variable costs, and so on. The attractiveness of the DCF method lies in its ability to provide a single, well-grounded measure of the economic attractiveness for any kind of venture, eliminating the biases inherent in other measures. Evaluating projects by their expected payback period, for example, will favor ventures that are expected to generate high but short-lived profits over those that promise sustainable profits after a long gestation period. Discounting a venture's expected cash flows (at a discount rate reflecting the expected volatility of these flows) provides for a more reasonable trade-off between longevity and a quick return of capital.

But, although DCF analysis may be a useful starting point, it has serious limitations from an entrepreneur's point of view. First, we may question whether the risks and returns of an entrepreneurial venture can be captured by a single DCF calculation. Knight[2] argued a long time ago that entrepreneurs can expect a profit only to the extent that they bear unmeasurable and unquantifiable risk, which he called uncertainty; if the magnitude and volatility of a venture's cash flows can be reasonably estimated, it cannot be expected to yield a true profit.

Second, a DCF analysis of attractiveness does not reflect the constraints of time and money faced by an entrepreneur. Unlike the idealized diversified investors of finance theory, entrepreneurs cannot back several projects simultaneously. Indeed, they often lack the resources required even for a single venture and cannot always count on others to supply the needed skills or funds at an acceptable price. Such constraints influence significantly a venture's attractiveness. For example, an unexpected need for cash (because, say, one large customer is unable to make timely payment, or raw materials have to be bought to meet an unexpected surge of orders) may shut down a venture or force the entrepreneur to give away an unreasonably large share of the equity to the one investor who is willing to provide the funds. Therefore, whereas a diversified investor might be indifferent between opportunities of equal expected DCFs, an entrepreneur should avoid the one that may unexpectedly need more cash at short notice.

A wealth-constrained, one-venture-at-a-time entrepreneur should also favor projects with:

1. Large Payoffs.   A diversified investor can evaluate projects one at a time, implementing a simple rule of backing all opportunities that have a positive NPV. Entrepreneurs, however, must compare the opportunity of the moment with future oppor-

---

[2] Frank H. Knight, *Risk, Uncertainty, and Profit* (Boston: Houghton Mifflin, 1921).

tunities they may have to forgo and should favor those ventures whose rewards are substantial enough to merit an exclusive, long-term commitment.

2. Low Costs of Exit.   The undiversified entrepreneur's risks are lower with projects that can be shut down without a significant loss of time, money, or reputation. Thus, for example, ventures whose failure is known quickly are better than projects that are not expected to make a profit for a long period and therefore cannot be reasonably abandoned in the interim.

3. Strategic Flexibility.   Launching a venture requires entrepreneurs to make irreversible investments in industry or in market-specific knowledge and contacts. Consequently, entrepreneurs should favor projects in which they can modify a failing strategy or concept and salvage some value from the knowledge and contacts they have invested in.

4. Options for Cashing In.   An entrepreneur locked into an illiquid business cannot easily pursue other more attractive opportunities and faces problems of fatigue and burnout. Therefore, given two businesses with the same expected DCF, entrepreneurs should prefer the one in which their interest can be easily sold. A diversified investor, however, is indifferent to cash flows derived from a share of a business's profits and its sale.

Issues to Be Analyzed

Instead of relying solely on a single DCF computation, therefore, an entrepreneur should also analyze several issues that bear on the magnitude of a venture's payoffs, the exit options available, and so on. Questions that can be usefully analyzed include:

1. What is the size and growth of the potential market?

Large, growing markets are more likely to provide the magnitude of payoff necessary to justify an entrepreneur's dedication to a single project and opportunities for sale of the business. The start-up does not have to wrest share from rivals or secure a monopoly position in order to achieve sizable revenues and profits. Opportunities to develop related businesses and find unexpected growth options are more abundant.

Market growth and size also make for a more forgiving environment. If one customer niche proves unreceptive, the entrepreneur has a greater opportunity to prospect for another, because a large and growing market often contains customers with a variety of needs and buying criteria.

2. How concentrated is the industry?

The expansion opportunities and second chances available to an entrepreneur are usually inversely correlated with industry concentration. Financial services such as leasing and insurance, which are relatively fragmented, are more likely to allow an entrepreneur to change course or develop another niche than a concentrated industry such as packaged goods.

3. How much capital is required?

Delays and failure to meet projections are more likely to cause a cash crisis in a capital-intensive business. High capital requirements also raise the costs of abandoning a venture by increasing the personal wealth and reputation that the entrepreneur must stake in order to attract outside investors.

4. Can the investment be phased?

Some businesses require significant upfront commitment of capital and other resources; the cost of exit from such businesses is higher than when investment can be made in tranches as critical, risk-reducing milestones are achieved.

5. How complex are the operations and technology?

Complex businesses are more likely to suffer from delays and cost overruns, leading to a cash crisis, than businesses with simple operations and technology.

6. Is the competitive edge sustainable?

Businesses with a sustainable competitive advantage, such as a proprietary technology or brand name, can more easily be sold to other firms or to the public markets than businesses that rely on their founders' personal skills and hustle.

7. How long is the payback period?

The entrepreneur's loss of self-esteem, reputation, and, of course, personal wealth due to the closing of a venture are lower if it has already returned the out-of-pocket investment made in it. Therefore, the shorter the so-called payback period, the lower the costs of exit are.

8. What is the margin for error in covering fixed costs?

Failure to meet a fixed obligation—for example, the payroll, rent, or mortgage payment—is usually the proximate cause of a cash crisis. Accordingly, businesses with low fixed costs and high gross margins that can "break even" (i.e., cover fixed costs) at modest sales volumes are more attractive than businesses that need to attain a high percentage of their projected sales to cover fixed costs.

9. What growth rate can internal funds sustain?

High profit margins and low capital intensity allow a business to finance rapid growth through internally generated funds. And the ability to grow without relying on potentially slow or demanding investors not only increases the size of the entrepreneurs' payoff but may also be of strategic value in rapidly expanding industries where it is critical to maintain market share.

Although the particular issues addressed may be different, the analysis of a venture's attractiveness is closely related to that of its viability: For example, an analysis of a venture's distinctive commitment is closely linked to an analysis of its capital intensity and the degree to which investment can be phased. The degree to which a venture depends on the personal competence of its founders influences the sustainability of its competitive advantage. And both sets of analysis use the same set of projected financial statements.

Judgments and Shortcuts

The Importance of Judgment

Assessing a venture's viability and attractiveness requires the entrepreneur to distinguish between critical and marginal issues and to weigh conflicting evidence. Consequently, entrepreneurs cannot rely on a mechanistic flowchart or template; judgment is crucial.

The entrepreneur has to judge which issues need careful analysis and what can be taken for granted. For example, whole tomes have been written about the competitive analysis of industries, and it would take several entrepreneur years to complete the tasks detailed therein. Similarly, there is no end to the level of detail and sophistication that can go into an analysis of a project's break-even point, capital requirements, payback period, or DCF. Without judgment of priorities, entrepreneurs may be tempted to do a little of everything, investigate in great depth issues that may not be critical but for which data are available, or be so intimidated by the task as to avoid all analysis.

The entrepreneur must also identify the critical obstacles and sources of competitive advantage. Generating a long list of problems is of little utility; start-ups *will* generally be capital constrained, will confront customers who are tied by inertia or switching costs to their current suppliers, will incur higher costs due to lower scale or lack of learning, and so on. Unless the purpose of the exercise is merely to smother the idea with objections, the entrepreneur must distinguish between deal-breaking problems and petty irritants. Similarly, it is possible to describe many innovations—from packaging to basic product design—that a venture starting with a clean slate can adopt. The entrepreneur must somehow identify the innovations that will truly sway customers from the nice-to-have frills.

Judgment is then required to weigh the critical pros and cons. Can the capabilities of the established competitors' direct sales force be topped by a creative plan to use distributors? Can customers' loyalty to their current suppliers be overcome with a new ergonomic product design? There is no common unit of measurement to weigh the pros and against the inevitable cons, and equally experienced and astute entrepreneurs can easily disagree.

Evaluating attractiveness requires judgment because ventures that shine by one measure are often questionable on another. For example, establishing sustainable advantages that permit a business to be sold easily usually requires significant investment, long gestation, and considerable operational and technological complexity; the entrepreneur's costs of exit and risks of cost overruns and cash crises are correspondingly high. Conversely, ventures with quick payback and low fixed costs often do not create sustainable advantages. And the entrepreneur cannot use objective formulas to determine how much sustainability is worth giving up for lower initial risk.

Archetypal Comparisons

Some entrepreneurs have great natural judgment, perhaps because of outstanding innate intelligence or instincts. Here we are concerned with how entrepreneurs can draw upon their direct and indirect experiences to draw inferences about the attractiveness and viability of opportunities more consciously.

Drawing on experience presents a dilemma. On the one hand, no two ventures are exactly alike. Useful general rules are rare and some—for example, entrepreneurs have to be risk takers in order to succeed — can be downright misleading. On the other hand, if we treat all ventures as unique and sui generis, the question of learning from experience becomes moot. Therefore, to use experience as an aid to evaluating a venture, the entrepreneur needs to exercise judgment in choosing cases that are meaningfully similar and restraint to prevent carrying the analogy too far. Thus, in launching a PR firm, an entrepreneur may look to the experiences of start-ups in consulting or advertising (rather than, say, in mini-steel mills) while taking into account the differences that might arise due to variations in the nature of PR, consulting, and advertising services.

A good starting point is to rely on the experience of archetypal ventures: Start-ups that cut across many industries and that face similar issues and trade-offs. Knowledge of some common archetypes that we will discuss next can help the entrepreneur set analytical priorities, identify the key requirements for viability, and provide a quick indication of the expected risk-returns.

The Polar Cases

The two archetypes most different from each other may be called the *revolutionary venture* and the *solo contractor*. Revolutionary ventures are rarely undertaken; require significant commitment, creativity, and competence; entail high payoffs and risks; and merit careful preparation and analysis. Solo contracting is commonplace, requires little creativity or commitment, entails modest rewards and risks, and does not call for much advance planning (**see Figure B**).

Revolutionary ventures, as exemplified by Federal Express, Xerox, and Polaroid, offer customers radically new products or services for which there are no close substitutes. Their success requires significantly distinctive acts of creativity, commitment, and competence. Creativity is required to conceive of new product attributes and to develop the technology to develop them; competitive markets rarely fail to provide valuable products or services unless there are serious technological problems involved in providing them. For example, Federal Express founder Fred Smith may not have been the first to think of the need for reliable overnight package delivery, but he did pioneer the hub-and-spoke logistics needed to get the job done.

Creative marketing is also important. The start-up must understand how the revolutionary offering will really be used and the barriers to its adoption, identify and educate segments that are likely to derive the most value, and adopt a pricing strategy without much assistance from market benchmarks.

Significant commitment is required to develop, test, and install new technology. New technology in turn will often prevent the entrepreneur from renting existing

FIGURE B   **Characteristics of Archetypal Ventures**

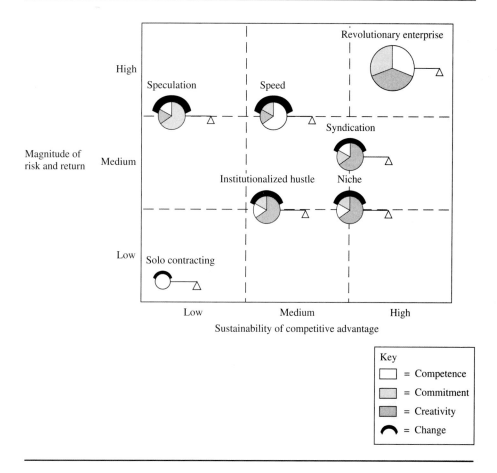

NOTES
1. The size of the circles indicates the magnitude of the distinctive competence, commitment, creativity, or change required to overcome competitive barriers.
2. Risk and returns are indicated for the venture as a whole; the entrepreneur's risks and returns depend on the nature of the deal struck with other stakeholders in the enterprise.
3. The magnitude of the risks depend on the absolute level of commitment required.

production facilities from others and require irreversible investment in fixed capital. Federal Express, for example, had to acquire its own fleet of aircraft. And with potential delays in technology development, slow market acceptance, and high fixed investment, the venture is likely to consume considerable capital in start-up costs.

Entrepreneurs require an unusual breadth of competencies and skills to effect a revolution. They need charisma and the evangelical ability to attract investors, customers, employees, and suppliers to a potentially outlandish vision and to retain their support in the face of inevitable delays and disappointments. To the extent the venture cannot easily subcontract and must develop a variety of its own functional resources, the entrepreneur must have the organizational and leadership skills to recruit, motivate, and integrate employees with diverse skills and temperaments. In addition, the entrepreneur may require considerable technical skills in deal making, strategic planning, managing overhead, and so on. The revolutionary entrepreneur, in other words, would appear to require almost superhuman qualities: Ordinary mortals need not apply.

External change is not, however, a critical ingredient and may actually be disruptive. The revolutionary start-up generally throws a stagnant, mature industry into tumult instead of riding external changes. In fact, great external change and uncertainty may prevent the start-up from acquiring the resources it needs to foment revolution; investors may be hesitant to invest in a radical product and technology until the environment settles down.

Revolutionary ventures offer entrepreneurs an opportunity to win or lose on a grand scale. A successful venture can create enormous financial value by establishing a firm with sustainable, near-monopoly rents that can be taken public at high earnings multiples. Success may also bring public recognition and make the entrepreneur into a near-cult figure. But the risks are also substantial. Revolutions may fail for any number of reasons: the product is flawed, cannot be made or distributed cost-effectively, serves no compelling need, or requires customers to incur unacceptable switching cost. Worse, the failure may not be apparent for several years, locking the entrepreneur into an extended period of frustrating endeavor. Even revolutions that are successful may not be financially rewarding for their founders, especially if they encounter delays en route. Investors may dump the visionary founders or demand a high share of the equity for additional financing.

Given the high risks, revolutionary ventures merit the most careful and complete analysis, and, in the typically stable environment, there is little need to rush the launch. Entrepreneurs should focus particularly on analyzing:

1. The costs and benefits to customers of switching from substitutes.
2. The technological and operational problems to be overcome.
3. First mover advantages and their sustainability. Unless the pioneer is protected by sustainable barriers to entry, the benefits of the hard-fought revolution become a public good rather than the source of entrepreneurial profit.
4. The amount and timing of cash required and the willingness of investors to provide it.

With all the analysis and preparation in the world, however, the founder of a revolutionary venture must anticipate recurring disappointments and a high probability that years of toil may come to naught. Successful revolutions are rare and invariably exhausting. Therefore, the most important analysis is self-analysis; unless there is an extraordinary fit, entrepreneurs should not undertake revolutions.

Solo contracting, as exemplified by an individual offering consulting, accounting, or other services, is, in contrast to the revolutionary venture, commonplace and represents the great majority of start-ups.

The archetype is usually found in service (rather than product) businesses, with fragmented competitors and low barriers to entry. The commitment and creativity required is correspondingly low; entrepreneurs can follow me-too strategies and do not need to invest significant capital. They need some basic technical or professional competence and the ability to attract clients, but excellence in deal making, leadership, or organization building is of little value in a business with few assets and one employee. External change can influence the degree of technical competence required. For example, the availability of good tax preparation software has allowed more individuals to offer tax preparation services by reducing the perceived importance of the preparer's knowledge of tax law.

Profitability usually depends on the perceived superiority of the contractors' skills and its value in the eyes of customers. For example, customers are more likely to pay a larger premium for the services of a stellar strategy consultant than they would for a personal trainer. In general, however, the absolute magnitude of returns is relatively low. Earnings are capped by the hours the entrepreneur personally puts in. The business cannot be sold at much of a premium, and there are no employees whose billings the entrepreneur shares in. But the risks are modest. No great capital investment is required, the market provides quick feedback on viability, and, if the venture fails, the entrepreneur can seek employment in the same or a related field. The serious hazards of physical illness or the obsolescence of skills are not much greater for an independent contractor than for an employee.

Little formal analysis is possible or necessary before launch; independent contractors will generally already have an estimate of their reputation, contacts, and ability to attract clients. Some introspection about lifestyles and work environment may, however, serve as a useful antidote to the glamour of "becoming your own boss." Although they escape the bureaucracy of a firm, they may be at the greater mercy of clients, have to initially undertake less interesting projects, and suffer the loneliness of working without colleagues.

Intermediate Archetypes

Between the exceptional, high-risk high-reward revolutionary venture and the common and sedate independent contracting business, we can identify several other archetypes based on:

• **Trading or speculation** in, for example, real estate, securities or oil and gas properties. As with independent contracting, no firm or organization is required. The entrepreneur buys goods or assets at a low price and sells them at a high price without much added value or processing; the transformation effected is mainly temporal.

The main source of profits lies in the speculator's contrarian commitment of funds to make unfashionable or out-of-favor purchases. Change, which creates confusion and panic among buyers and sellers of the asset, is an essential catalyst. Creativity and competence in arranging financing or in structuring transactions can be helpful, but great innovation or exceptional ability to execute is not required.

The speculators' risks and returns increase with the capital put at risk, the financial leverage obtained, and the price volatility of the asset acquired. Assets with inelastic supply or demand generally exhibit wide price swings. Risks are generally not staged — the entrepreneur is fully exposed when the asset is acquired. Liquidity or exit options often turn on the success of the speculation: if, as expected, prices rise, the speculator can expect many buyers for the asset owned, but if prices decline or stay depressed, market liquidity for the asset will be generally poor. But, like independent contracting, the enterprise is not sustainable; each deal or speculation stands on its own.

Two sets of analysis are crucial. One relates to the market dynamics for the asset being acquired, or, more specifically, why the prices of the asset may be expected to rise. Entrepreneurs should determine whether prices are temporarily low (due to, say, an irrational panic or a temporary surge in supply), in secular decline because of permanent changes in supply or demand, or merely correcting after an irrational prior surge. The other analysis is of the entrepreneurs' ability to hold or carry the asset till it can be sold at a profit, because it is difficult to predict when temporarily depressed prices will return to normal. Carrying capacity depends on the extent of borrowing used to purchase the asset, the conditions under which financing may be revoked, and the income produced by the asset. Rental properties or a producing well that provides ongoing income, for example, can be carried more easily than raw land or drilling rights. For certain kinds of assets — for example, mines and urban rental properties — the entrepreneur should also consider the risks of expropriation and windfall taxation.

• **Institutionalized hustle** as exemplified by the start-up of investment management, investment banking, head-hunting or consulting firms.[3] These ventures are generally found in fragmented service industries with relatively low barriers to entry and may be considered scaled-up versions of individual contracting, from which they often evolve. They require more creativity, competence, and commitment, expose entrepreneurs to greater risks, and offer greater returns.

As with individual contracting, the ability to execute and the perceived quality of the service provided is more critical than a unique technology, installed base, or captive distribution channel. Start-ups can succeed without a unique strategy or major innovation. But, compared with an individual who provides the same service, the entrepreneur requires greater creativity and competence, primarily in the areas of marketing and organization building. Rather than sell their personal capabilities, entrepreneurs must be able to sell the ability of their firms to deliver superior service. Similarly, entrepreneurs must be able to build their firms' reputations rather than their own.

The entrepreneur also requires exceptional competence and some creativity in a variety of organizational and institution-building tasks: recruiting, establishing incentives and control systems, articulating and reinforcing firm values, and so on. Without excellence in organization development, the venture is liable to break apart, as there are few natural economies of scale to hold the firm together. And it is the ability of the organization as a whole — rather than of individual employees — that allows the firm to charge a premium for its services and sustain high levels of capacity utilization.

---

[3] For a detailed discussion, see Amar Bhide, "Hustle as Strategy," *Harvard Business Review,* September–October 1986.

The financial and other commitments required are somewhat greater than for independent contracting. Professional firms usually have to sign long-term leases, invest in furniture and leasehold improvements, invest in recruiting and client development, and pay fixed salaries for employees. The total amounts, however, are modest because little fixed capital is required, and, in any event, though some investment may be necessary, the willingness to make commitments is not an important source of competitive advantage.

The magnitude of the returns to the entrepreneur who can institutionalize hustle are usually much greater than those available to an independent contractor providing the same service. Building a firm gives founders a share of the revenues generated by employees, as well as the satisfaction of building an organization. Success through building does not, however, provide quite the bonanza as through a revolutionary enterprise because the earnings based on hustle are not as highly valued as earnings from a proprietary advantage. Even so, compared with independent contractors, the builders of service firms have more attractive exit options as they can sell their equity to employees, other firms, or—somewhat rarely—to the public.

With the greater commitment required to build a firm, entrepreneurs can face significant personal risks; for example, they may have to provide personal guarantees for leases and bank loans drawn to finance working capital. But the risks are not as great as those faced by the revolutionary entrepreneur. Investment can be staged, with employees and facilities stretched and the expansion of new capacity delayed until it is clear there is demand. And it does not take long for entrepreneurs to discover whether the market can support their venture.

A detailed analysis of competitors and industry structure is rarely of much value. The ability to seize short-lived opportunities and execute them brilliantly is of far more importance than a long-term competitive strategy. Self-assessment, organizational design, and short-term cash forecasts deserve greater attention. Entrepreneurs should ask themselves whether they have the personal qualities, motivation, contacts, and reputation needed to build a firm. Partnership agreements, terms for offering equity to later employees, performance measurement criteria, and bonus plans are important determinants of firm success and are best thought through before launch rather than hastily improvised later on. And, although projections of long-term cash flows are not meaningful, back of the envelope, short-term cash forecasts and analyses of break-evens can keep the entrepreneur out of trouble. Overall though, the analytical preparation required for such ventures is modest.

• **Networking,** or **syndication,** which covers diverse examples such as the Yellow Pages, want-ad publications, 1-900 chat lines, and syndicates organized to bid at Resolution Trust Corporation auctions. The entrepreneur seeks to profit from coordinating the activities and interests of agents who could not otherwise because they are competitors, such as the merchants who advertise in the Yellow Pages, or, because they lack an alternative channel for communicating, the teenagers who patronize the 900 numbers. The role played by the venture can range from putting participating agents in touch with one another, providing the medium for their interaction, or guaranteeing their performance.

New networks are usually the result of an entrepreneur's creativity in identifying the value that can be created by coordinating unrelated agents, developing or using a new technology to achieve the coordination. But, especially in geographically limited networks (such as videotape-enhanced dating agencies), entrepreneurs can profit from copying an idea developed in another location. The extent of irreversible investment required depends on two factors: the minimum number of members required and the value added by the start-up. Establishing a network that requires a large number of participants, to be useful (such as a Yellow Pages) requires large investments in marketing, as compared with, say, forming a syndicate with a dozen investors. Similarly, a networking venture in which the entrepreneur adds significant value (say, by developing and maintaining the channels of communication) is likely to require greater commitment than one in which the venture merely puts the participants in touch with one another.

Basic competencies in marketing and operations are necessary to establish large networks, but are not in themselves the basis of competitive advantage. For small syndicates in which a few participants expose themselves to considerable risk, personal selling abilities are often the single most important factor for determining success. Besides selling the benefits of joining the network, entrepreneurs must be able to convince participants of their honesty and create the perception that the network will be completed soon.

Risk-returns vary widely with the nature of the network. The ideal network provides long-lived utility, does not require a high fixed-cost infrastructure, and increases in value with the number of participants, though it can be useful and profitable even with a small number. Entrepreneurs who first establish such networks can both stage their investment and enjoy large sustainable returns that they can easily cash in. A few ventures (Want-Ads, for instance) approach this ideal, but more often, network opportunities are either high risk and sustainable or low risk and short-lived. The former networks (for instance MCI) require significant upfront investment and high fixed costs to recruit and serve a large number of participants but cannot be easily replicated. The latter entail lower risk because they are smaller but only serve a temporary function (such as RTC syndicates) or can be easily copied and lack economies of scale (such as dating clubs).

The depth and breadth of analytical tasks depends on the type of network as well. In the small low-risk networks, the entrepreneurs learn by doing or, more specifically, by trying to sell. Besides, to the extent the opportunity is short-lived, the urgency of getting started precludes much research. Resources devoted to analysis should not be much greater than with independent contracting. Large networks, however, usually merit the same kind of effort as revolutionary ventures. Entrepreneurs should carefully analyze the costs and benefits to customers, barriers to entry created, long-term cash flow requirements, technical feasibility, and so on, as well as their personal fit with the venture.

• **Speed** as exemplified by several high-tech ventures in disk drives, software for windows, nonstop computing, and workstations. Launching these ventures involves a race to dominate a new market created by a well-publicized external change. The genre is particularly common in high-tech businesses. For example, a new component or building block, such as the 386 chip or the Windows operating system, can set up a race to launch new downstream products, such as personal computers or word processing software. Or a new downstream market, such as laptop computers, creates opportunities to produce new components, such as small disk drives, which many ventures try to develop first.

Success in these ventures depends mainly on superior competence in engineering, production, and marketing. The entrepreneur usually does not require great creativity. Target customers and their needs are common industry knowledge. Choices about components, technologies, and distribution channels are limited, and the advantages and disadvantages of the alternatives are well known. Adopting an unconventional approach—for example, by departing from industry standards—can actually scare off investors and potential customers. Superior commitment rarely provides a competitive advantage; investment requirements, though substantial, merely represent the entry fee for the race.

The winner is determined by the ability to design and produce a quality product on time and on budget and then sell it effectively. Losers usually get left in the dust because they lack a product that works, not because they have pursued a poor strategy. Correspondingly, entrepreneurs need superior skills in recruiting and managing functional experts and adequate competence in fund-raising and deal making.

The risks of such a venture are usually high compared with the potential returns. Substantial resources are consumed before a winner is determined, and investment cannot be easily staged. The winner of the current race may be overtaken when a new upstream component or downstream product sparks a fresh contest. Exit options are subject to the moods and vagaries of the IPO (initial public offering) market: When the venture is hot, the IPO market might not be. Yet the downside for the entrepreneur is often cushioned by the willingness of investors to bear most of the financial risk. And, compared with a revolutionary venture, success or failure is apparent relatively soon, allowing the entrepreneur to remain or move on to other opportunities.

Entrepreneurs evaluating ventures based on speed should pay special attention to analyzing the following questions:

1. Can the entrepreneur acquire and manage the talent and money required to succeed?

2. How many winners can the market accommodate? The race to dominate the operating systems for PCs, a market that is likely to produce only one winner, is riskier to join than the race to develop word processing software, in which two or three products can win.

3. What are the rewards for winning? If the winner is likely to be challenged soon by a new generation of ventures or if returns are likely to be depressed because of buyer power, it may not be worth entering the race.

4. How important is the thrill of the chase and the agony of defeat? Ventures based on speed cannot be easily justified on a financial basis, given the high uncertainties that cannot be resolved by analysis and the risks that cannot be insured. Therefore, the entrepreneur should be able to derive satisfaction from the race itself and have the personal fortitude to deal with failure.

• **Niche marketing,** which includes manufacturers of all-natural foods, no-frills airlines, exotic adventure tours, and art movie houses. The entrepreneur seeks to profit from catering to the specialized preferences of customer segments that are not well served by mainstream competitors.

The successful enterprise usually requires not just marketing creativity, but technological or operational creativity as well. The entrepreneur cannot generally rely merely on the insight that certain customer segments—for example, consumers averse to preservatives or price-sensitive travelers—are being poorly served. More often than not, technological and economic constraints rather than poor understanding of customer needs prevent special segments from being well served. Given the preferences of the mass market, for example, it may be impossible to sell all-natural foods at a price that even aficionados would be willing to pay. High union wages and limited landing slots may preclude no-frills airfares. A breakthrough in production or distribution (a "mini-revolution") may therefore be necessary to serve niche markets.

Exceptional competence or willingness to commit resources is usually not the basis of the niche players' advantage, and, in any case, the total investment that can be justified is limited by the size of the segment served. A packaged good serving a fringe market, for example, cannot afford national advertising and therefore must rely on word of mouth to build brand awareness. Large capital requirements can, in fact, indicate an unviable concept.

External technological or market change often provides attractive opportunities to establish a niche without extraordinary innovation. For example, the personal computer revolution created opportunities in a variety of complementary goods and services such as add-on boards, math co-processors, and software training videos and books. Ventures to exploit these new niches did not have to solve major technological problems. Some could also enjoy (relatively) long-term first-mover advantages because the small markets were not interesting to the big players.

The magnitude of the payoffs from niche ventures are, in the aggregate, lower than from revolutionary enterprises; however, the entrepreneur is more likely to keep a higher share of the value created. Capital requirements are usually lower and the time required to achieve financial self-sufficiency is shorter; therefore, the entrepreneur's equity interest is less likely to be diluted through multiple rounds of financings. Entrepreneurs can realize the value of their businesses through the cash they can throw off, or through sales, depending on their size, to individuals or to competitors serving the broader market.

The niche start-up typically confronts two significant risks: the costs of serving a specialized niche may be higher than the benefits to the customers, and the absolute rewards are too small or distant to attract the necessary resources or justify the entrepreneur's effort. The entrepreneur should therefore carefully analyze the following questions:

1. What are the incremental costs of serving a niche rather than the broad market? Niche ventures often face significantly higher costs due to their lack of scale and the difficulty of marketing to a small diffused segment.

2. How special is the offering from the point of view of the target customers? Established companies may vie for share through marginal tailoring of their products and services; the startup should provide significant price or performance advantages to its target customers.

3. Are the smaller absolute returns from a niche strategy offset by sustained profitability or quick payback? A niche strategy will generally not provide sustained profits without a technological or operational innovation or early entry into an obscure new market. Entrepreneurs who rely on a pure marketing innovation should expect competition to catch up and should therefore at least seek compensation in a quick payback on their investment of time and money.

4. Does the venture require significant investment or talent? The relatively small total returns will usually not allow the entrepreneur to raise much external capital or recruit superstars to the team at attractive terms.

The archetypes I have described are not intended to be mutually exclusive or collectively exhaustive. Nor do I suggest that entrepreneurs should maintain purity of style and avoid hybrids. For example, there is nothing intrinsically flawed about a venture to establish a network that provides a revolutionary service to participants. Archetypes are merely an aid to pruning the analytical task efficiently. If a venture straddles two archetypes, entrepreneurs should construct an analytical approach that combines the relevant features of both or think of another analogy that is more appropriate. What should be avoided is a laundry-list approach, in which all possible issues are halfheartedly analyzed as well as a blind just-do-it attitude.

Conclusion: Acting on the Analyses

Except with obviously unviable ideas that can be easily ruled out through elementary logic, the purpose of analysis is not to find fault with new ventures or find reason for abandoning them. Analysis should be considered as an exercise in what to do next more than what not to do. The problems and risks uncovered should be treated with solutions. For example, suppose analysis leads the entrepreneur to conclude that the commitment of personal funds and time is too great, given the potential returns. Rather than terminate consideration of the venture, the entrepreneur should think creatively about solving the problem. Perhaps the investment in a fixed plant can be reduced by modifying the technology to use more standard equipment that can be rented. Or, under the right terms, a customer might underwrite the risk by providing a large initial order. Or expectations and goals for growth might be scaled down, and a niche market could be tackled first. If no solutions can be found, the problems identified should at least lead entrepreneurs to acquire the knowledge, contacts, or reputation that would improve their chances in the future.

Nor should the entrepreneur think of analysis as a distinct activity that precedes implementation. Businesses cannot be launched like space shuttles, with every detail of the mission planned in advance. Action and analysis in new ventures cannot be easily separated. The attractiveness of a new venture, for example, may depend on the terms obtained from buyers or suppliers—below-market rents can turn a restaurant from a mediocre proposition to a money machine. But an entrepreneur's ability to negotiate below-market rents cannot easily be determined from a general prior analysis; he or she must enter into a serious negotiation with a specific landlord for a specific property. And performing a lot of other analyses without first testing the ability to get a good lease can be a serious waste of time and money.

Entrepreneurs also cannot expect to even approach the zero-defect goal that designers of space shuttles seek. Market research for a new product, for example, cannot provide definitive conclusions about buyer behavior. Slippage can arise between research and reality because the potential customers interviewed are not representative of the market, their enthusiasm for the concept or prototype wanes as they see the actual product, or they may lack the authority to sign purchase orders.

Given the uncertainties of a new venture, the returns from more fact gathering, interviews, or cash flow projections diminish rapidly. In fact, to paraphrase Cardinal Newman, the quest for the perfect start-up plan is often the enemy of the good. Initial analyses only provide plausible hypotheses, which must be tested and modified through action. Analogies and investigation of a few critical questions can identify some of the important obstacles the start-up faces, but the entrepreneur must expect to confront unanticipated problems as well. Similarly, the entrepreneur should be alert to exploit markets that prior research had indicated were unattractive. Entrepreneurs do not implement a detailed blueprint; their strategy and tactics evolve from constant and closely integrated guesswork, analyses, and action.

4   VALUATION TECHNIQUES

One of the entrepreneur's critical tasks is determining value. This is important not only for the individual about to purchase a company, but also for the entrepreneur who is starting a firm and is attempting to estimate the value the business may have in the future. Finally, understanding value is a key step for the entrepreneur about to harvest a venture, either through sale or taking the business public.

Financial theorists have developed many techniques that can be used to evaluate a going concern. Of course, for a large public company, one could simply take the market value of the equity. For a going concern with a long history of audited financials, earnings and cash flow projections are possible. But the valuation of a small, privately held business is difficult and uncertain at best.

This note will briefly outline some of the more widely used valuation approaches, including:

- Asset valuations.
- Earnings valuations.
- Cash flow valuations.

Asset Valuations

One approach to valuation is to look at the underlying worth of the assets of the business. Asset valuation is one measure of the investor's exposure to risk. If within the company there are assets whose market value approximates the price of the company plus its liabilities, the immediate downside risk is low. In some instances, an increase in the value of the assets of a company may represent a major portion of the investor's anticipated return. The various approaches to asset valuation are discussed below.

Book Value

The most obvious asset value that a prospective purchaser can examine is the book value. In a situation with many variables and unknowns, it provides a tangible starting

---

This note was prepared by Michael J. Roberts under the direction of Howard H. Stevenson.

Copyright © 1984 by the President and Fellows of Harvard College

Harvard Business School Note 9–384–185

point. However, it must be remembered that it is only a starting point. The accounting practices of the company as well as other things can have a significant effect on the firm's book value. For example, if the reserve for losses on accounts receivable is too low for the business, it will inflate book value and vice versa. Similarly, treatment of asset accounts such as research and development costs, patents, and organization expense can vary widely. Nevertheless, the book value of a firm provides a point of departure when considering asset valuation.

Adjusted Book Value

An obvious refinement of stated book value is to adjust for large discrepancies between the stated book and actual market value of tangible assets, such as buildings and equipment that have been depreciated far below their market value, or land that has substantially appreciated above its book value that stands at the original cost. An adjustment would probably also reduce the book value of intangible assets to zero unless they, like the tangible assets, also have a market value. The figure resulting from these adjustments should more accurately represent the value of the company's assets.

Liquidation Value

One step beyond adjusted book value is to consider the net cash amount that could be realized if the assets of the company were disposed of in a "quick sale" and all liabilities of the company were paid off or otherwise settled. This value would take into account that many assets, especially inventory and real estate, would not realize as much as they would were the company to continue as a going concern or were the sale made more deliberately. Also, calculation of a liquidation value would make allowances for the various costs of carrying out a liquidation sale.

The liquidation value, it should be noted, is only an indication of what might be realized if the firm were liquidated immediately. Should the company continue its operations and encounter difficulties, most likely a subsequent liquidation would yield significantly less than the liquidation value calculated for the company in its current condition.

The liquidation value of a company is not usually of importance to a buyer who is interested in the maintenance of a going concern. One would assume, however, that the liquidation value would represent some kind of a floor below which the seller would be unwilling to sell because he should be able to liquidate the company himself.

Replacement Value

The current cost of reproducing the tangible assets of a business can at times be significant in that starting a new company may be an alternative means of getting into the business. It sometimes happens that the market value for existing facilities is considerably less than the cost of building a plant and purchasing equivalent equipment from other sources. In most instances, however, this calculation is used more as a reference point than as a seriously considered possibility.

Earnings Valuations

A second common approach to an investor's valuation of a company is to capitalize earnings. This involves multiplying an earnings figure by a capitalization factor or price-earnings ratio. Of course, this raises two questions: (1) Which earnings? and (2) What factor?

Earnings Figure

One can use three basic kinds of earnings:

- *Historical earnings.* The logic behind looking at historical earnings is that they can be used to reflect the company's future performance; there is no logic in evaluating a company on the basis of what it has earned in the past. As will be discussed below, however, historical earnings should be given careful consideration in their use as a guide to the future. They should provide concrete realism to what otherwise would be just a best guess.

    Historical earnings per se can rarely be used directly, and an extrapolation of these figures to obtain a picture of the future must be considered a rough, and frequently a poor, approximation. To gain the benefit from the information in a company's financial history of past operations, it is necessary to study each of the cost and income elements, their interrelationships, and their trends.

    In pursuit of this study, it is essential that random and nonrecurring items be factored out. Expenses should be reviewed to determine that they are normal and do not contain extraordinary expenses or omit some of the unusual expenses of operations. For example, inordinately low maintenance and repair charges over a period of years may mean that extraordinary expenses will be incurred in the future for deferred maintenance. Similarly, nonrecurring "windfall" sales will distort the normal picture.

    In a small, closely held company, particular attention should be given to the salaries of owner-managers and members of their families. If these salaries have been unreasonably high or low in light of the nature and size of the business and the duties performed, adjustment of the earnings is required. An assessment should also be made of the depreciation rates to determine their validity and to estimate the need for any earnings adjustments for the future. The amount of federal and state income taxes paid in the past may influence future earnings because of carryover and carryback provisions in the tax laws.

- *Future earnings under present ownership.* How much and in what ways income and costs are calculated for future operations depends to a large degree on the operating policies and strategies of management. The existing or future owners' approach will be influenced by a host of factors: management ability, economic and noneconomic objectives, and so on. In calculating future earnings for a company, these kinds of things must be considered and weighed.

    A calculation of value based on the future earnings of the company should provide an indication of the current economic value of the company to the current owner. To an investor, including the present owner as an investor, this figure should provide an economic basis for that individual's continued activity and investment in the company. (As we shall discuss later, there is usually more to a potential seller's position than just an economic analysis of his or her own future as an investor.) To an investor who anticipates a change in management with his investment, a calculation of value based on earnings from the current owner's continuing with the company is *not* a meaningful assessment of the value of the company to the investor.

- *Future earnings under new ownership.* These are the earnings figures that are relevant to the investor who is investing in the turnaround of a dying company or in the reinvigoration of a stagnant one. The basis for the figures—the assumptions, relationships between costs and income, and so on—will probably show significant variance from the company's past performance. Plans may be to change substantially the nature of the business. The evaluation and investment decision may also involve large capital investments in addition to the purchase price of the company.

It is the future earnings of the new operation of the business that are helpful in determining the value of the company to the entrepreneur as these are the earnings that will influence the economic return. Most likely these kinds of projections will have large elements of uncertainty, and one may find it helpful to consider the high, low, and most likely outcomes for financial performance.

In addition to deciding on an earnings period on which to focus, there is also the issue of "what earnings?" That is, profit before tax, profit after tax, operating income, or earnings before interest and taxes (EBIT). Most valuations look at earnings after tax (but before extraordinary items). Of course, the most important rule is to be consistent: don't base a multiple on earnings after tax, and then apply that multiple to EBIT. Beyond this, the most important factor to consider is precisely what you are trying to measure in your valuation. A strong argument can be made for using EBIT. This measures the earning power and value of the basic, underlying business, *without the effects of financing*. This is a particularly valuable approach if the entrepreneur is contemplating using a different financial structure for the business in the future.

Price-Earnings Multiple

Next, we have the issue of what multiple to use. Assuming that the investor's primary return is anticipated to result from sale of the stock at some future date, the investor should then ask the question: Given the anticipated pattern of earnings of this company, the nature of the industry, the likely state of the stock market, and so on, what will the public or some acquisitive conglomerate be willing to pay me for my holdings? In terms of some multiple of earnings, what prices are paid for stock with similar records and histories? To estimate with any degree of confidence the future multiple of a small company is indeed a difficult task. In many instances, working with a range of values might be more helpful. This great uncertainty for a potential investor in estimating both a small company's future earnings *and* future market conditions for the stock of that company in part explains why his or her return on investment requirements for a new venture investment are so high.

Again, it is important to remember to be consistent: Always derive the multiple as a function of the same base you wish to apply it to—profit after tax, EBIT, or whatever.

Up until this point, we have been discussing methods of arriving at a value for the business as a whole. While the entrepreneur is naturally concerned with this issue, he or she is also concerned with the valuation of his or her piece of the business.

Residual pricing is a technique that addresses this issue. Essentially, residual pricing involves:

- Determining the future value of a company in year *n* through one of the methods described above.
- Applying a target rate of return to the amount of money raised via the initial sale of equity.
- Using this information to develop a point of view on how much equity the entrepreneur must give up in order to get the equity financing required.
- The ''residual,'' or remaining equity, can be retained by the entrepreneur as his return.

For example, if a company is projected to have earnings of $100,000 in year 5, and if (after some analysis) it seems that the appropriate P/E for the company is 10, then we can assume that the company will be worth $1 million in year 5. Now if we know that the entrepreneur needs to raise $50,000 from a venture capital firm (in equity) to start the business, and if the venture firm requires a 50 percent annual return on that money, then that $50,000 needs to be worth $50,000 $\times$ (1 + 50 percent)^5 = $380,000. So in theory at least, the entrepreneur would have to give 38 percent of the equity to the venture firm in order to raise this money.

Cash Flow Valuations

Traditional approaches to evaluating a company have placed the principal emphasis on *earnings*. Assuming that the company will continue in operation, the earnings method posits that a company is worth what it can be expected to earn.

But this approach is only partially useful for the individual entrepreneur who is trying to decide whether or not to invest in a business. Again, the entrepreneur must distinguish between the value of the business as a whole and the portion of that value that can be appropriated for himself or herself. The entrepreneur must address the need to acquire resources from others and must understand that he or she will have to give up a portion of the value of the business in order to attract these resources. In addition to personal or subjective reasons for buying a business, the entrepreneur's chief criterion for appraisal will be return on investment. Because an entrepreneur's dollar investment is sometimes very small, it may be useful to think of return more as a return on his or her *time,* than a return on his or her dollar investment. To calculate the latter return, the entrepreneur must calculate his or her *individual* prospective cash flow from the business. It is the entrepreneur's return *from* the business, rather than the return inherent in the business itself, which is important. As we shall see, there are several different types of cash flow that can accrue to the entrepreneur.

Operating Cash Flows

Cash or value that flows out of the business during its operations include:

- *Perquisites*. Perquisites are not literally cash at all, but can be considered cash equivalents in terms of their direct benefits. Business-related expenses charged to the company (e.g., company car and country club memberships) are received by the individual and are *not taxed* at either the corporate or personal level. Their disadvantage is that they are limited in absolute dollar terms.

- *Return of capital via debt repayment*. This class of cash flow is a *tax-free* event at both the corporate and personal level. An additional advantage to this type of flow is that it can occur while enabling the entrepreneur still to maintain a continuous equity interest in the company. Its disadvantage is, of course, that it requires him or her to make the original investment.

- *Interest and salary.* Both of these items constitute personal income and are taxed as such at the personal level. However, no tax is imposed at the corporate level.

- *Dividends*. As a means of getting cash from a venture, dividends are the least desirable as the resulting cash flow has undergone the greatest net shrinkage. Dividends incur taxes first at the corporate level (at the 15 percent or 34 percent rate as income accrues to the corporation) and then again at the personal level (at the personal income tax rate as the dividend payment accrues to the individual). At the maximum corporate income tax rate of 34 percent and the maximum personal income tax rate of 28 percent, we can see that this double taxation can reduce $1 of pretax corporate profit to $0.48 aftertax cash flow to the individual.

Terminal Value

Another source of cash is the money the entrepreneur pulls out of the business when the venture is harvested. Again, there are several elements to this aspect of return.

- *Return of capital via sale:* If the owner/manager sells all or part of the business, the amount he or she receives up to the amount of his or her cost basis is a *tax-free* event at both the corporate and personal level. Since a sale of his or her interest is involved, however, it is evident that unlike a return of capital via debt repayment, the owner/manager does not maintain his or her continuous equity interest in the concern. Also, like a cash flow based on debt retirement, an original investment is necessary.

- *Capital gain via sale:* When capital gains are realized in addition to the return of capital on the sale of stock, no tax is imposed at the corporate level; a sale of assets typically generates personal *and* corporate taxes.

Tax Benefits

While not precisely cash flow, tax benefits can enhance cash flow from other sources. For example, if a start-up has operating losses for several years, and if these losses can be passed through to the individual, then they create value by sheltering other income. Because entrepreneurs are often in a low-income phase when starting a business, these tax benefits may be of limited value to them. However, if properly structured, these tax benefits can provide substantial value to investors who can use them. In a situation where the structure and form of the organization (i.e., a corporation), does not permit the losses to flow through to the individual, these losses can be used to offset income of the corporation in prior or future years.

The entrepreneur must also take into account his negative cash flows. Three types of negative cash flows are particularly important:

- Cash portion of the purchase price.
- Deficient salary.
- Additional equity capital.

Frequently, the most critical aspect of the cash portion of the purchase price is that it must be small enough for the entrepreneur to be able to pay in the first place. In this kind of situation, the seller finances the purchase of his company by taking part of the purchase price in the form of a note. The seller then receives cash later on from future earnings of the company or from its assets. Of course, the less cash he or she is required to put up, the more cash the entrepreneur has available for other uses and the greater the opportunity he or she has to produce a high ROI. On the other hand, too much initial debt may hamstring a company from the start, thereby hurting the venture's subsequent financial performance and the entrepreneur's principal source of return—be it the cash withdrawn from the company or the funds received from eventual sale of the company.

The significance to the entrepreneur of a negative cash flow based on a deficient salary is clear—a lower income for personal use than could be obtained elsewhere. In addition, there is the effect that these early negative flows may have on the entrepreneur: Faced with an immediate equity requirement for working capital or fixed assets, the owner/manager may be forced to seek outside investors, thereby diluting his or her future value in the business and also introducing the possibility of divergent goals in the financial and other aspects of the company's operations.

At this point in our analysis, it will appear obvious to some that the next step for the entrepreneur is to find the present value of the cash flow he or she predicts for the venture—in other words, discounting the value of future cash flows to arrive at a value of the venture in terms of cash today. We shall see, however, that in many respects this approach raises more questions than it answers, and therefore its usefulness to the analysis is questionable at best.

The essence of the problem is that present value is basically an investment concept utilizing ROI to determine the allocation of a limited supply of funds among alternatives, whereas the entrepreneur is faced basically with a personal situation where return on both investment and *time* are key. In addition, the entrepreneur may have made a considerable investment in generating the particular option, and it is difficult to weigh this tangible opportunity against unknown options. Because the entrepreneur does not have a portfolio of well-defined opportunities to choose from, he needs to define some standard of comparison. This is typically the salary that could be obtained by working.

In an investment analysis utilizing present value, the discount rate is selected to reflect uncertainty associated with cash flows; the higher the uncertainty, the higher the discount rate and, consequently, the lower the present value of the cash flows. In the corporate context, there is usually a minimal ROI criterion for noncritical investments to keep the ROI greater than the firm's cost of capital.

For the individual entrepreneur, however, the decision to buy or to start a company is fundamentally a subjective one. Return on investment and time for this kind of decision is measured not only in terms of dollars, but also in terms of what he or she will be doing, who his or her associates will be, how much time and energy will have to be expended, and what lifestyle will result. Different kinds of ventures present *different kinds of return* on time. As cash to the entrepreneur is an important enabling factor for *some* of the things the entrepreneur is seeking, it is important that he or she calculate what these cash flows might be and when they can be expected. However, because decisions affecting cash flow also affect the other returns to the entrepreneur and because these other returns may be at least as important as the financial returns, a present value calculation often is not the most important measure.

In thinking about the attractiveness of a particular opportunity, an entrepreneur rarely has easily comparable alternatives. More than likely the decision is either to go ahead with a venture or to stay where he or she is until something else comes along. Perhaps the most useful way to think of this position is to imagine an individual looking down a corridor that will provide a range of opportunities—opportunities to achieve different levels of financial and other rewards with their accompanying risks and sacrifices. Financial theorists, for instance, have recently begun to study investments in terms of their ability to generate a future stream of growth opportunities.

Summary

The previous discussion has outlined a variety of different approaches to the valuation of a firm. It is important to remember that no single approach will ever give the "right" answer. To a large extent, the appropriateness of any method of evaluation depends on the perspective of the evaluator. However, both in this course and in "real life" one must come to some point of view on the worth of a firm, no matter how scant the data. This is very important, even if the value is only a preliminary one, because it permits the individual to delve further into the issues at hand.

Nonetheless, the true purpose of the analysis is not to arrive at "the answer" but to:

- Identify critical assumptions.
- Evaluate the interrelationships among elements of the situation to determine which aspects are crucial.

- Develop *realistic* scenarios, not a best case/worst case analysis.
- Surface and understand potential outcomes and consequences, both good and bad.
- Examine the manner in which the value of the business is being carved up to satisfy the needs of prospective suppliers of resources.

No single valuation captures the true value of any firm. Rather, its value is a function of the individual's perception of opportunity, risk, the nature of financial resources available to the purchaser, the prospective strategy for operation, the time horizon for analysis, alternatives available given the time and money invested, and prospective methods of harvesting. Price and value are not equivalent. If the entrepreneur pays what the business is worth, he has not appropriated any value for himself. The difference is determined by information, market behavior, pressures forcing either purchase or sale, and negotiating skills.

5 THE BUSINESS PLAN

A business plan is a document that articulates the critical aspects, basic assumptions, and financial projections regarding a business venture. It is also the basic document used to interest and attract support—financial and otherwise—for a new business concept. The process of writing a business plan is an invaluable experience, for it will force the entrepreneur to think through his or her business concept in a systematic way.

This chapter will raise and address issues that most entrepreneurs encounter as they prepare their business plans. One of the factors that makes crafting a good plan so difficult is the fact that it has a multitude of purposes. As described, the plan is a blueprint for the company itself and, as such, is intended to help the firm's management. The plan is also typically used to attract potential investors. Finally, the plan may serve as the legal document with which funds are raised. These several uses highlight a constant conflict: To the extent that the plan is a ''marketing document'' for the company, it is likely to be a more optimistic, one-sided presentation than a critical business analysis. For the purposes of legally raising funds, however, the document needs to contain a full disclosure of risks and legal ''boilerplate'' (see Securities Law and Public Offerings). Many a prospectus, for instance, contains the phrase—in big bold letters—''This investment is highly speculative and is suitable only for individuals who can afford a total loss of their investment.'' Thus, it becomes extremely critical to understand exactly what purpose the ''plan'' is serving and what audience such a purpose implies. Even if the document is clearly written to appeal to potential investors, it is important to know exactly what kind of investor. A busy venture capitalist or other professional investor will be more demanding than a private individual, who rarely invests in new enterprises. Similarly, a commercial banker reading the same document would have a different set of questions. Thus, the first rule is to keep in mind *who* the reader is and make sure the document addresses his or her particular concerns.

The bulk of this chapter will focus on preparing a business plan for the professional investor—venture capitalist or otherwise. A plan that meets the needs of this most demanding investor can be scaled down or used for other private individuals, who may well have professional financial advisors review the document anyway. This plan for investors may well include portions of an internal plan that includes far more detailed operating and contingency plans that would be suitable for investors.

This note was prepared by Michael J. Roberts.
Harvard Business School Note 9–389–020

To be clear, however, when we say a business plan, we do *not* mean a legal document for *actually* raising funds, although many entrepreneurs do think of these two documents as identical. First, a prospectus (or "offering memorandum," "investment memorandum," or "offering circular") needs to contain so much legal language and protective boilerplate as to be an ineffective marketing document. Second, we do not recommend proposing a "deal" (exact type and price of the security) in the business plan. Professional investors simply have far more expertise in crafting the security, and pricing is typically a matter of negotiation. Nonetheless, it is important to be clear on how much money you are seeking to raise and how it will be paid back. If money is being sought from less experienced private investors, the situation is more complicated. Not to propose a deal implies negotiating with many separate individuals who may have very different ideas about the type of security they are interested in and how it should be priced.

One approach that can be used to resolve these issues raised by the multiple objectives of the business plan is to follow the distribution of the plan with a more formal offering memorandum. In this way, only those investors who seem genuinely interested are actually solicited. And this second offering memorandum can be used to meet the legal requirements of a fund-raising document.

The Plan

The following sections of this chapter will describe the various sections of a standard business plan. Overall, it is important that the plan be relatively short (40 or so pages is appropriate) and clearly written. Do not assume that the reader will be an expert in the technology or market you are interested in. Finally, think of the plan as an argument, for every point you make—the attractiveness of the market, the price you can charge for the product, its competitive advantages—offers evidence to support your claims.

To achieve this level of end product, it is often helpful to get others to read drafts of the plan. Certainly, members of the management team should prepare their section of the plan and read all of the others. Financial advisors or accountants can also play a valuable role. It is also a good idea to review other entrepreneurs' business plans to get a feel for how others have approached the task. If you can, talk to some of these individuals about their experiences writing the plan and raising funds. Finally, if you can speak with lawyers, accountants, and even some investors (whom you won't be targeting), you're bound to learn from them as well.

It is also a good idea to have a plan read by a legal advisor—presumably the same person who will help you incorporate and draft the other legal documents necessary for financing and starting the business. The securities laws are quite complicated, and you'll need expert advice to assure that you're not running afoul of them. (See Securities Law and Private Offerings.) Counsel will want to assure that you are not making any claims that could later pose problems (i.e., "Investors are guaranteed an attractive financial return"). In addition, there is some standard boilerplate that will help protect you from possible securities laws violations. Copies of the plans should all be individually numbered and a log kept detailing who received them.

The Executive Summary

These few pages are the *most* critical piece of any business plan. Investors will turn immediately to this section in order to get their first impression of the venture. To ensure that this section encompasses all that it should, it should be written last.

The executive summary must clearly but briefly explain:

- The company's status and its management.
- The company's products or services and the benefits they provide to users.
- The market and competition for the product.
- A summary of the company's financial prospects.
- The amount of money needed, and how it will be used.

The Company

This section should describe the company's origins, objectives, and management. The plan should describe how the company will be organized, who will fill these roles, and what their responsibilities will be. Some background on the founders should be given and their more extensive résumés referenced in an appendix. The "story" of how the company came into being should be briefly told so that potential investors get some sense of its history. The section should describe the current status of the company: number of employees, sales and profits (if any), products, facilities, and so forth. Finally, this section should paint a picture of where the company hopes to go and how it envisions getting there—its strategy.

The Product or Service

Having introduced the product in the previous section, the plan should describe it in more detail here. What needs does the product meet, especially compared to competitor's products. If the product exists and is in use, some detailed descriptions of that usage, the results, and some customer testimonials will prove valuable. If the product has yet to be manufactured, a description of how you intend to make it—and what the key milestones in the process are—is also important. If a patent or proprietary technology is employed, it should be explained here (although the proprietary aspects, of course, should not be divulged).

The Market

A common mistake is to deal with the marketing portion of the business plan in a cursory manner. Investors want evidence that the founders of a company have studied the market, understood it, and indeed are driven by their desire to satisfy its needs. To convey this, the plan should address:

- The size, rate of growth, and purchasing characteristics of the target market. Investors will be interested in—and will want to assure that the entrepreneurs are interested in and understand—market segments, the buying process, and how purchase decisions are made.

- The company's perspective on the market. Investors will be curious about the entrepreneur's perspective on the market. Why do you think the company is bringing something new to the market? What trends in the market does the company see, and what changes does the company anticipate in the future?

- The reaction the company expects from the market. What hurdles does the company expect in introducing its product? How will it overcome them? What features and benefits does the company expect will be particularly popular?

Competition

No business plan is complete without a section that describes the competitive firms and products. Again, investors want to be assured that the entrepreneurs understand whom they will be competing against. Information on competitors' products, prices, and marketing approaches should be included.

Sales and Marketing

This section of the plan should explain the manner in which the product will be sold. The plan should describe how target customers will be identified and how awareness will be built through advertising, promotion, or direct mail. The plan should also detail what distribution channel will be utilized, and how the product will be sold—by a direct sales force, reps, direct mail, and so forth. This section should also address how the company will introduce its product to the marketplace. This might include public relations, advertisement, special promotions, or targeted growth.

Operations

In this section, entrepreneurs should explain how the product will be manufactured: the facilities required, the use of subcontractors, and what equipment will be needed to actually produce the product. In general, investors would prefer to see a firm purchase or subcontract much of its manufacturing needs, at least initially. In addition, it is often desirable to lease facilities. The other aspects of operations, including distribution, should also be touched on.

Financials

In this section, investors expect to see realistic financial projections, typically for a five-year time horizon. The following information should be included: an income statement, balance sheet, cash flow forecast, and break-even analysis. While the five-year forecasts should be relatively detailed, it is also important to highlight the key dimensions of the firm's financial performance—sales, earnings, and cash surplus (or deficit)—in some summary form.

It is critical that the financials be driven by *thoroughly documented assumptions*. For instance, don't just develop a sales forecast. Present detailed assumptions about unit volume and price. The same is true for expenses. This not only gives the investor the data he or she needs to evaluate your plan, it also speaks volumes about your careful thinking. The financials should also clearly state the amount of money being sought and to what uses it will be put.

Investors will also be interested in how the venture plans on turning their cash investment back into cash. That is, what is the anticipated exit route for the investor: a public offering, a sale of the company, or a repurchase of shares by the firm? In the financial section, try to give potential investors some idea of how they can cash out.

While it's impossible to know what's going to happen in the future, investors will familiarize themselves with other firms in the industry in order to develop a sense of the appropriateness of the numbers forecasts. Once they are satisfied that the projections are realistic, investors will use these financials to help them value the firm and calculate a potential price for their investment.

Finally, some would-be entrepreneurs make use of public accounting firms to prepare their financials. They feel that the opportunity to present their projections on a prestigious accounting firm's stationery lends credibility to the numbers, and they may well be right. Some entrepreneurs are also anxious to use this approach to gain access to the network of wealthy private investors with which these accounting firms are well connected. While you may consider this approach on its merits, one point is clear. To use an accounting firm in such a manner is no substitute for having these critical financial skills as part of the venture's start-up team. Someone who is part of the team *must* have the ability to develop income statement and cash flow forecasts and budgets.

Appendix

The résumés of all key personnel and their responsibilities should be included in this section. In preparing the résumés, entrepreneurs should make sure that they portray themselves as a well-balanced team. In addition, any sample product literature, letters from customers or suppliers, and so forth can be included in the appendix.

After the Plan Is Written

When the plan is finished, it's time to distribute it to potential investors. It is wise to avoid simply sending the plan to all the venture capitalists you can find. Investors generally avoid plans that come in "over the transom" and far prefer to look at a plan that has been recommended by a financial advisor, lawyer, or company founder that they know and whose judgment they trust.

There are a number of different sources of capital available to entrepreneurs. They run the gamut from friends and family members, with limited or no experience providing capital, to professional investors, who manage a portfolio of investments in young firms. Each of these sources is attractive for different reasons, and it's up to the entrepreneur to understand the advantages and disadvantages of each. Within each category, *who* you raise money from is vitally important. The ability to attract successful, professional investors will lend credibility to your venture idea and will introduce you to a wide range of helpful contacts. Finally, many of these people are successful because they provide excellent guidance, and it will be to your benefit to avail yourself of it.

Because venture capital is such a visible portion of this spectrum of potential sources, it's worth knowing a bit about it. The venture capital industry is a highly fragmented network of individuals and small firms that accounts for $15 to $20 billion of capital. Other potential investors include Small Business Investment Corporations (SBICs) and the venture capital aims of larger corporations. Firms in the venture capital industry can be distinguished along four basic dimensions:

- The size of the investment pool. As with any industry, venture capital firms differ in the amount of money under management. Large firms might manage 10 to 20 times more capital than smaller firms.
- The stage(s) at which they prefer to invest. Venture capitalists tend to specialize in certain phases. Some prefer to invest in the seed and development stage so that they can own a larger part of the venture. Other VCs balk at the risks of this strategy and instead prefer to invest in later stage companies. Venture capitalists typically divide the investment process into four distinct rounds or stages.

  — Seed: This stage is the highest risk stage of investment because the company is usually newly organized and lacks an operational track record. In many situations, the company is little more than an idea.

  — Development: This stage is also characterized by high risk. Companies in this stage are usually building a prototype product and exploratory marketing.

  — Revenue: Investments made in this stage are characterized by less risk than those made in the seed and development stages. This is true because more information is available for venture capitalists to consider. Companies seeking funds in this stage usually have completed a prototype and have begun to market it to their customers.

  — Profitable: Investments made in this stage are characterized by the least amount of risk. Venture capitalists prefer companies in this round because they are usually seeking capital to expand and grow.

- The minimum and maximum amount allocated in each investment. These amounts range anywhere from $150,000 to $5 million or more. Firms syndicate deals among many different companies to meet investment requests, which may be larger than the maximum amount considered.
- Preferred industries for investment. Venture firms may specialize by industry, believing that their ability to select attractive investments and add value is related to their degree of industry knowledge and expertise. Traditionally, high-technology industries such as microcomputers, telecommunications, and

biotechnology have been popular with venture capitalists. More recently, low-tech and service sector businesses have become increasingly popular.

With these differences in mind, it's helpful to understand how venture capitalists tend to evaluate deals. They are quite busy and will rarely spend more than 5 to 10 minutes on an initial review of a plan. During this brief time, they will read the executive summary to get an understanding of the company's status and goals.

Plans that do not meet their criteria are rejected. Plans that seem to present an interesting investment opportunity are reviewed further. During this phase, venture capitalists try to understand and evaluate the key fundamentals of the business. These include:

- The management team. Professional investors are attracted by individuals with proven industry expertise and management ability, and some start-up experience is even better.
- The product/market. Venture capitalists like products that exist (in real life, not just in someone's mind), can be manufactured, and that have some evidence of acceptance into the market.
- The financials. Providers of capital like to see that their investment is likely to turn into value for them, typically within a three- to seven-year time horizon.

For all of these reasons, it is worth devoting some time and energy to a strategy to ''get in the door.'' A 50-pound document and a form letter addressed to ''To Whom It May Concern'' is clearly a bad strategy. An introduction from a lawyer, another venture capitalist, or an entrepreneur whom the firm has backed are all superior options. Learn about the venture firm, its past investments, its strategy, and its people, and try to position your proposal in a way that fits with these elements.

Still, the process of evaluating a business plan is an imprecise art, not a science. Venture capitalists—who specialize in judging the potential of a business—make many investments that fail to live up to their expectations. Thus, many investors will use their ''intuition'' about a market, a business, and the entrepreneur to help make their decision.

Summary

Essentially, the plan serves as a vehicle to get you in the door to talk to investors. They will probe you about the plan and also about your career and management experiences, and those of any other members of the team. A professional investor will present a good many potential problems. After all, the road to starting and managing a new venture is littered with unanticipated problems and difficult challenges. By gauging how you respond to the issues inherent in the fund-raising process, the investor will be able to judge your diligence and business sense as well as the ''fire in your belly''— sure to be as critical a factor in your success as a well-crafted plan.

1–1 R&R

During the summer of 1983, Bob Reiss observed with interest the success in the Canadian market of a new board game called *Trivial Pursuit*.® His years of experience selling games in the United States had taught him a rough rule of thumb: the sales of a game in the United States tended to be approximately 10 times those of sales in Canada. Since Trivial Pursuit had sold 100,000 copies north of the border, Reiss thought that trivia games might soon boom in the United States and that this might represent a profitable opportunity for him.

Reiss's Background

After his graduation from Harvard Business School in 1956, Reiss began working for a company that made stationery products. His main responsibility was to build a personalized pencil division, and he suggested that he be paid a low salary and a high sales commission. He was able to gain an excellent understanding of that market and by 1959 could start on his own as an independent manufacturer's representative in the same industry. His direct contact with stores that sold stationery products revealed that many of them were beginning to sell adult games. He decided to specialize in those products.

In 1973, Reiss sold his representative business to a small American Stock Exchange company in the needlecraft business in exchange for shares. He then set up a game manufacturing division and ran it for that company, building sales to $12 million in three years.

Reiss decided to go into business for himself again in 1979 and left the company. He incorporated under the name of R&R and worked with the help of a secretary from a rented office in New York; Reiss promised himself that he would keep overhead very low, even in good years, and never own or be responsible for a factory. In addition to being a traditional manufacturer's representative, he did some consulting for toy manufacturers, using his extensive knowledge of the market.

The Toy and Game Industry

One of the main characteristics of the toy industry was that products generally had very short life cycles, frequently of no more than two years. Fads extended to whole categories of items: one class of toys would sell well for a couple of years and then fade

This case was prepared by Jose-Carlos Jarillo Mossi under the direction of Howard H. Stevenson.

away. Products that were part of categories tended to ride with the fate of that category, regardless to some extent of their intrinsic merit. Many new products were introduced every year, which made the fight for shelf space aggressive.

Promotional plans for a new product were a key factor in buy or no-buy decisions of the major retailers. At the same time, fewer and fewer retailers were dominating more of the market every year. The largest one, Toys "Я" Us, for example, had 14 percent of the entire market in 1984. The success of a product was often based on less than a dozen retailers.

A few large manufacturers were also becoming dominant in the industry, because they could afford the expensive TV promotional campaigns that retailers demanded of the products they purchased. Billing terms to retailers were extremely generous compared to other industries, thus increasing the need for financial strength. Financing terms ran from a low of 90 days to 9 to 12 months. In general, major retailers were reluctant to buy from new vendors with narrow product lines unless they felt that the volume potential was enormous. On the other hand, the large manufacturers tended to require a long lead time for introducing new products, typically on the order of 18 to 24 months.

The industry was also highly seasonal. Most final sales to the public were made in the four weeks prior to Christmas. Retailers decided what to carry for the Christmas season during the preceding January through March. There was a growing tendency among them, however, not to accept delivery until the goods were needed, in effect using the manufacturer as their warehouse.

The Trivia Game Opportunity

Trivial Pursuit was developed in Canada and introduced there in 1980. Its 1983 sales were exceptionally strong, especially for a product that had been promoted primarily via word of mouth. The game was introduced in the United States at the Toy Fair in February 1983 by Selchow & Righter, makers of Scrabble, under license from Horn & Abbot in Canada. Earlier, the game had been turned down by Parker Bros. and Bradley, the two largest game manufacturers in the United States.

Trivial Pursuit in the United States had a $19 wholesale price, with a retail price varying from $29.95 to $39.95, about 200 percent to 300 percent more expensive than comparable board games. Selchow was not known as a strong marketer and had no TV advertising or public relations budget for the game. The initial reaction at the Toy Fair in February had been poor. Yet by August the game had started moving at retail.

Reiss thought that if the success of Trivial Pursuit in Canada spilled over to the United States, the large game companies would eventually produce and market their own similar products. This would generate popular interest in trivia games in general and constitute a window of opportunity for him. The only trivia game in the market as of September 1983 was Trivial Pursuit. Two small firms had announced their entries and were taking orders for the next season. Bob Reiss decided to design and market his own trivia game.

Developing the Concept

Reiss' first task was to find an interesting theme, one that would appeal to as broad an audience as possible. On one hand, he wanted to capitalize on the new ''trivia'' category that Trivial Pursuit would create; on the other, he wanted to be different, and therefore could not use a topic already covered by that game, such as movies or sports. Further, his game would have its own rules, yet be playable on the Trivial Pursuit board.

As was his custom, Reiss discussed these ideas with some of his closest friends in the manufacturer's representative business. Over the years, he had found them a source of good ideas. One of the reps suggested television as a topic. Reiss saw immediately that this had great potential: not only did it have a broad appeal (the average American family watches over seven hours of TV per day), it offered a great PR opportunity. A strong PR campaign would be needed since Reiss knew clearly that he was not going to be able to even approach the advertising budgets of the large manufacturers, which would probably surpass $1 million just for their own trivia games.

Because licensing was common in the toy industry and was a way to obtain both an easily recognizable name and a partner who could help promote the product, Reiss realized he could add strength and interest to his project if he could team up with the publishers of *TV Guide*. This magazine had the highest diffusion in the United States, approaching 18 million copies sold each week. It reached more homes than any other publication and could be called a household name.

On October 17, 1983, Reiss sent a letter, printed below, to Mr. Eric Larson, publisher of *TV Guide*.

Mr. Eric Larson, Publisher   October 17, 1983
TV Guide
P.O. Box 500
Radnor, PA 19088

Dear Mr. Larson:

I am a consultant in the game industry and former owner of a game company.

Briefly, I would like to talk to you about creating a game and marketing plan for a TV GUIDE TRIVIA GAME.

In 1984, trivia games will be a major classification of the toy industry. I'm enclosing copy of a forthcoming ad that will introduce a game based on the 60 years of *Time* magazine. I am the marketer of this game and have received a tremendous response to the game, both in orders and future publicity.

This project can benefit both of us, and I would like to explore the opportunities.

Sincerely,

Robert S. Reiss

In a follow-up phone conversation, Mr. Bill Deitch, assistant to the publisher of the magazine, asked Reiss for some detailed explanation on the idea. Reiss sent the following proposal:

Mr. Bill Deitch   November 14, 1983
TV GUIDE
P.O. Box 500
Radnor, PA 19088

Dear Mr. Deitch:

In response to our phone conversation, I will attempt to briefly outline a proposal to do a TV Trivia Game by *TV Guide.*

WHY A TV GAME? It is a natural follow-up to the emerging craze of trivia games that is sweeping the country. This category should be one of the "hot" categories in the toy/game industry in 1984. This type of game got its start in Canada three years ago with the introduction of Trivial Pursuit. It continues to be the rage in Canada and was licensed in the United States this year. It is currently the top selling nonelectronic game. It retails from $29.95 to $39.95 and is projected to sell 1 million units. It is not TV promoted. The Time Game, with 8,000 questions covering six general subject areas, only began to ship two weeks ago and had an unprecedented initial trade buy, particularly with no finished sample available for prior inspection.

WILL TV GUIDE BE JUST ANOTHER TRIVIA GAME? No. The next step is to do specialty subjects. Trivial Pursuit has just done a Motion Picture Game with excellent success. Our research tells us that a TV-oriented game would have the broadest national appeal.

THE MARKETS. This type of game has wide appeal in that it is nonsexual and is of interest to adults and children. We feel we can place it in over 10,000 retail outlets ranging from upscale retailers like Bloomingdale's and Macy's to mass merchants like Toys "Я" Us, Sears, Penney, Kmart, Target, etc. There is also a good mail-order market. The market is particularly receptive to good playing, social interactive games at this time. Video games are in a state of decline as their novelty has worn off. (To say nothing about profits.)

WHO WILL DEVELOP THE GAME? Alan Charles, a professional game developer who did the Time Game, is free at this moment to do work on the project. He has satisfied the strict standards Time, Inc. has set for putting its name on a product and mine for play value and product graphics in a highly competitive market.... No easy task.

WHO WILL PRODUCE AND MARKET THE GAME? There are two options for producing the game.
1. Give it to an established game company who would assume all financial risk as well as production and distribution responsibilities. Under this set-up, *TV Guide* would get a royalty on all goods sold.
2. *TV Guide* assumes all financial responsibilities for game. Production and shipping would be handled by a contract manufacturer. Bob Reiss would be responsible for hiring and supervising a national sales force to sell the game. This is not an unusual option, and I do have experience in this. All sales are on a commission basis. This way, *TV Guide* gets the major share of the profits.

   Attached exhibit explores some rough profit numbers for *TV Guide,* via both options.

POSITIONING OF GAME. We see the game as noncompetitive to Trivial Pursuit and Time Magazine Game. It can be developed to retail at $14.95, as opposed to $39.95 for Trivial Pursuit and $29.95 for Time. (Mass merchants generally discount from these list prices.) The TV Game should be able to be played by owners of both games as well as on its own. The name *TV Guide* is important to the credibility of the product. Sales of licensed products have been growing at geometric rates in the last decade. Consumers are more comfortable buying a product with a good name behind it.

PROMOTION OF GAME. Pricing of the product will have an ad allowance built into it. This will allow the retailers to advertise in their own catalog, tabloids and/or newspaper ads. An important part of promotion should be ads in *TV Guide.* Ads can be handled two ways: one, with mail-order coupon and profits accruing to *TV Guide;* the other, with listing of retailers carrying the item. As you have so many regional splits, the listing could be rather extensive. Financially, you would probably opt for the first option on a royalty arrangement and the second if you owned the product.

This product lends itself perfectly to an extensive public relations program. This is an excellent product for radio stations to promote. This should be pursued vigorously.

BENEFITS TO TV GUIDE
• Profits from royalties or manufacturing.
• Extensive publicity through wide distribution on U.S. retail counter, including the prestigious retailers as well as the volume ones. This is the unique type of product that can bridge this gap.
• Good premium for your clients. Can be excellent premium for TV stations. Can be used as a circulation builder. In projecting profits, I have not included premiums. The numbers can be big, but they are difficult to count on.

TIMING. To effectively do business in 1984, all contracts must be done and a prototype developed for the American Toy Fair, which takes place in early February 1984. Shipments need not be made until late spring.

WHO IS BOB REISS? He is a graduate of Columbia College and Harvard Business School who started his own national rep firm in 1959, specializing in adult games when it became a distinct category in 1968. He sold his company in 1973 to an American Stock Exchange company. He remained there for five years and built Reiss Games to a dominant position in the adult-game field. For the last three years, he has been consulting in the game/toy industry and recently acted as broker in the sale of one of his clients, Pente Games, to Parker Bros.

I am enclosing some articles that have a bearing on the subject matter. I think what is needed, as soon as possible, is a face-to-face meeting, where we can discuss in greater detail all aspects of this proposal as well as responsibilities for all parties.

Sincerely,

Robert S. Reiss

RSR/ck

encl.

Rough Profit Potentials to TV Guide

Assumptions
1. Average wholesale cost of $7.15 after all allowances. (This would allow department stores and mail order to sell at $15. Discounters would sell at $9.95 to $11.95.)
2. Cost to manufacture, $3 each.

3. Royalty rate of 10 percent. (Range is 6 percent to 10 percent, depending on licensor support and name. Assuming 10 percent, based on fact you would run No Cost ads in *TV Guide*.)
4. Mail-order retail in *TV Guide* is $14.95, and you would pay $4 for goods. Postage and handling would be a wash with small fee charged to customer.

Option I: Royalty Basis
Projected retail sales: 500,000 units.
*Royalty to *TV Guide* of $357,500.
Mail-order sales: 34,000 units. (.002 pull on 17 million circulation.) Based on full-page ad with coupon. It is extremely difficult to project mail-order sales without testing—too many variables. However, this is a product that is ideal for your audience.
*Profit to *TV Guide* of $372,300.

Option II: You Own Goods
Costs: (rough estimate)

Manufacture	$	3.00
Royalties to inventor		.36
Fulfillment		.30
Sales costs		1.43
Amortization of start-up costs		.10
Total cost	$	5.19
Profit per unit	$	1.96
Profit on 500,000 units	$980,000.00	
(Does not include cost of money.)		

Another phone conversation followed in which *TV Guide* showed a clear interest in pursuing the subject. Reiss answered with a new letter on December 12, 1983, that outlined clearly the steps that had to be followed by both parties should they want to go ahead with the venture. Reiss had to send still another letter with a long list of personal references that *TV Guide* could contact. *TV Guide* finally opted to be a licensor, not a manufacturer. They would give Bob Reiss a contract for him to manufacture the game or farm it out to an established manufacturer, provided he stayed involved with the project. *TV Guide* would receive a royalty that would escalate with volume. Royalties were normally paid quarterly, over shipments; Reiss, however, proposed to pay over money collected, which *TV Guide* accepted. As part of the final deal, *TV Guide* would insert, at no cost, five ads in the magazine worth $85,000 each. These would be "cooperative ads"; that is, the names of the stores selling the game in the area of each edition would also be displayed. Reiss thought that including the names of the stores at no cost to them would be a good sales argument and would help ensure a wide placement of the product.

Developing the TV Guide Trivia Game

The actual game was designed by a professional inventor, whom Reiss knew, in exchange for a royalty of 5 percent—decreasing to 3 percent with volume—per game sold. No upfront monies were paid or royalties guaranteed. Although the inventor delivered the package design in just a few weeks, the questions to be asked were not yet formulated, and Reiss realized he could not do this alone. *TV Guide*'s management insisted that their employees should develop them. Reiss would pay per question for each of the 6,000 questions he needed; employees could moonlight on nights and weekends. Reiss felt it was important to put questions and answers in books rather than cards like Trivial Pursuit. The cost would be considerably lower, and the most serious bottleneck in manufacturing—collating the cards—would be eliminated. Overall, the presentation of the game tried to capitalize on the well-known *TV Guide* name (**Exhibit 1).** The game also lent itself well to this approach, as the question books imitated the appearance of *TV Guide* magazine (**Exhibit 2).**

Initially, Reiss had not wanted to include a board with the game; he wanted people to use Trivial Pursuit's board and had made sure that the rules of the new game would take this into account. However, *TV Guide* wanted a complete game of its own, not just supplementary questions to be played on someone else's game. Another advantage of including a board, Reiss realized, was that a higher price could be charged.

Since *TV Guide* had opted for being merely a licensor, it was Reiss's responsibility to set up all the operations needed to take the game to market in time for the 1984 season, and there were only two months left until the February Toy Fair, where the game had to be introduced.

His first consideration was financial. He estimated that the fixed cost of developing the product would be between $30,000 and $50,000, but some $300,000 would be needed to finance the first production run. Those funds would be needed until the initial payments from sales arrived a few months later.

Reiss seriously considered raising the required money from the strongest among his manufacturer's representatives in the toy business, thinking they would push hard to sell the game to every account. Eventually, he decided against this approach: not only would it not contribute that much to the venture, reps could be motivated to sell in other ways. Perhaps more important, Reiss feared the prospects of perhaps 20 partners who "would be every day on the phone asking how things are going."

Another option that passed through his mind, which he dismissed promptly, was venture capital. He realized that he would have to give up too much and, even worse, that venture capitalists would not understand this kind of deal—one that had very attractive short-term profits but few long-term prospects.

Trivia Incorporated

With the agreement with *TV Guide* in hand, Reiss called Sam Kaplan—a longtime friend who lived in Chicago. Kaplan, 65 years old, had a sizable personal net worth, yet kept working at his small but successful advertising agency (25 employees) "for the fun of it," as he liked to say. Reiss thought that teaming up could be an important help, and Kaplan was indeed enthusiastic about the idea.

Reiss proposed to establish a company, Trivia Inc., that would develop the project. The equity would be split evenly among the two partners. Kaplan, besides lending his line of credit to purchase supplies for the initial run, would use his office to handle day-to-day details. (In fact, Trivia Inc. ended up having only one full-time employee.) Also, because of his vast knowledge of printing and his contacts, Kaplan could secure press time and paper supplies on short notice, and he would supervise the product's manufacturing. This was especially important, since the special paper stock on which the game was printed was then in short supply, and long lead times were generally needed to obtain it. Kaplan would also produce all the ads and the catalog sheets. Reiss would take responsibility for sales and marketing of the product and would pay all reps and coordinate the publicity and the relations with *TV Guide*. An important part of the agreement was that R&R (Reiss's company) would have the exclusive rights to market the game and would receive a commission of 20 percent of the wholesale price from which it would pay the commissions to the reps.

Production, Shipping, and Billing

From the beginning, Reiss's intention was not to be a manufacturer. Through Kaplan's connections, they found not only good suppliers for the question books, the board, and the boxes, but they also even got lower costs than expected. But they still had to tackle the problem of assembly and shipping. Kaplan was a longtime consultant to Swiss Colony, a manufacturer of cheese based in Madison, Wisconsin. This company specialized in mail sales and had developed a strong capability to process mail orders. As a result, Swiss Colony's management had decided several years earlier to offer that fulfillment capability to other companies. They took the orders, shipped the product, and billed to the retailer.

In the deal ultimately reached, Trivia Inc. would have the components sent by the different suppliers to Madison on a "just-in-time" basis, and Swiss Colony would put the boards, dice, and questions in the boxes, package, and ship them. Swiss Colony would charge $.25 per box, including billing for the games, and would send complete daily information on sales to Trivia Inc. Trivia Inc. would pay $2,500 for a customized computer program. With all these measures, Reiss and Kaplan were able to lower their estimated costs by 30 percent and attained the flexibility they wanted. The final cost of manufacturing, assembling, and shipping was about $3.10, not including the royalties paid to the inventor and to *TV Guide*.

A final point was financing the accounts receivable, once the sales started rolling in, and collecting the debts. Reiss was somewhat afraid that the bills of some of the smaller stores carrying the game would be very difficult to collect, since R&R did not have the resources to follow up closely on its collections; moreover, Trivia Inc. needed the leverage of a factor in order to collect from the larger retailers on time. He and Kaplan decided to use Heller Factoring to check credit, guarantee payment, collect the money, and pay Trivia Inc., all for a fee of 1 percent over sales. Trivia Inc. would not need any financing for operations: after 45 days of shipping, Trivia Inc. would always be in a positive cash flow. Thanks to Heller and Swiss Colony, Trivia Inc. had practically no administrative work left to itself.

Selling the Game

Selling was the most important issue for Reiss. He knew that placing the goods in the stores and selling them to the public (selling through) were two distinct, many times unrelated, problems. In any case, however, he thought that the game needed to be priced below Trivial Pursuit to make up for both the lack of a complete national advertising campaign that major manufacturers would launch, and the lack of the kind of brand recognition that Trivial Pursuit was achieving. Accordingly, the wholesale price was set at $12.50, with a retail list price of $25.

Reiss distinguished carefully between two different channels: the mass merchandisers and the department/gift stores. An important part of the overall strategy was to sell quickly to upscale retailers who would establish a full retail markup (50 percent). These were mainly department stores, such as Bloomingdale's or Marshall Field's, and mail order gift catalogs and specialty gift stores. This, it was hoped, would help sell mass merchandisers and give them a price from which to discount. Such a two-tiered approach was not common in the industry. On long-life products, many times only the full-margin retailers got the product the first year. But Reiss felt that this could not be done with his product, because it could well be only a one-year product. Mass merchandisers, however, had to be reached, since they accounted for at least 70 percent of the market. (**Exhibit 3** shows some of the stores Reiss thought had to be reached.)

Two different sets of reps were employed for the two different channels; on average, they received a 7 percent commission on sales. Reiss's personal knowledge of buyers for the major chains proved invaluable. He was able to obtain quick access to the important decision makers at the major chains. They also followed, when possible, the distribution pattern of *TV Guide* magazine. It was soon apparent that the statistics on demographics reached by *TV Guide,* which Reiss made sure all buyers saw **(Exhibit 4),** had a major impact. As Reiss said, "It appeared that every outlet's customers read *TV Guide*." The cooperative ads in the magazine, with the possibility of including the store's name, were also a powerful attraction for different buyers, as Reiss had expected: the name of their stores would be displayed in far more homes than it would with a conventional advertising campaign in national magazines. The stores would not be charged to have their name in the ads, but minimum purchase orders would be requested. Many large customers, such as Kmart and Sears, placed large orders before the product was even finished. (**Exhibit 5** shows a cover letter that was sent to supermarket buyers.)

Promotion

In order to promote the game to the public, Trivia Inc. had a four-part plan, beginning with the five ads in *TV Guide* **(Exhibit 6).** The first ad broke in mid-September 1984 and was strictly for upscale retailers, with $25 as the price of the game. *TV Guide* had eight regional issues, and different stores were listed in each area with a total of about 120, including Bloomingdale's, Marshall Field's, Jordan Marsh, and J. C. Penney. They all had to place minimum orders. The second ad, shown on October 6, was just for Sears. The third, on November 10, was devoted to mass merchandisers and did not include a retail price. The fourth, two weeks later, listed four of the most important toy chains: Toys "Я" Us, Child World, Lionel Leisure, and Kay Bee. The appeal to the public, then, was not just the ad: Reiss knew that showing well-known upscale stores carrying the game initially was the best way to obtain instant credibility for the product. Finally, Kmart, the largest U.S. chain, gave Trivia Inc. an opening order to all its 2,100 stores, even before the game went into production, in exchange for the exclusivity in the fifth ad to be run in *TV Guide* on December 8, 1984. In that ad, Kmart offered a three-day sale at $16.97.

The second part of the plan also tried to give credibility to the game. Trivia Inc. offered the department stores a 5 percent ad allowance (a 5 percent discount from wholesale price) if they put the product in newspaper ads, tabloids, or catalogs. For similar reasons, Reiss wanted to have the game placed in mail order gift catalogs. Their sales in the toy-game business were only moderate, but catalogs gave a lot of product exposure because of their large circulation figures.

The final part of the plan was to obtain free media publicity. The publisher of *TV Guide* magazine wrote a letter to be sent to the producers of such shows as "Good Morning, America," "CBS Morning News," "The Tonight Show," and to 25 top TV personalities, together with a sample of the game. Through *TV Guide* 's PR agency and the joint efforts of *TV Guide* and Trivia Inc., many newspapers, radio, and TV stations were reached. In all, more than 900 press kits were sent to media organizations. As a result, the game was mentioned on many talk shows (TV and radio), and news of it was published in many newspapers **(Exhibit 7).** The cost of this campaign was split between Trivia Inc. and *TV Guide*.

The Results

By October 1983, Selchow, manufacturer of Trivial Pursuit, started falling behind trying to meet the demand. By Christmas, when sales exploded, there was no hope of keeping up—and one of the most serious manufacturing problems was the bottleneck of collating the cards. By the February 1984 Toy Fair, most of the major manufacturers offered trivia games, which was projected to be the hottest category for the year.

R&R sold 580,000 units of the *TV Guide* Game in 1984 at the full wholesale price of $12.50. There were few reorders after mid-October, as the market became saturated with trivia games (over 80 varieties) and Trivial Pursuit flooded the market. By Christmas 1984, all trivia games became heavily discounted; many retailers ran sales on Trivial Pursuit at $14.95, having paid $19.00.

Bad debts for Trivia Inc. were about $30,000 on approximately $7 million billings, with hope of recovering $15,000. Losses from final inventory disposal (it was decided to close out the game) were less than $100,000.

TV Guide was extremely pleased with the royalty collected from the venture. Kaplan, through his 50 percent ownership in Trivia Inc., made over $1 million net. The total cost of designing and launching the product had been $50,000.

Commenting on the whole deal, Reiss said:

I think the critical aspects of success in being a contract manufacturer are to take care of your suppliers and to take care of your sales representatives. We want our suppliers to charge us full markup, so that we are a good customer to them, and we try hard to give them enough lead time to deliver. We pay on time always, no matter what happens. In exchange, we demand perfect work from them. They understand and like this relationship. We need their cooperation, because we are completely dependent on them.

The other aspect is how to deal with your customers, which for us are the manufacturer's representatives and the buyers of major chains. The manufacturer's reps are used to the fact that when sales really do pick up in any product and they can make a lot of money, many manufacturers try to "shave" their commissions, perhaps feeling that the reps are making too much money. I never do that: I am happy if they make millions, and they know it. I also pay on time always. With this, I have developed a loyal and experienced work force and have no fixed or upfront sales cost.

All of these factors allowed us to move quickly. My contacts enabled me to print and manufacture the game for the same cost as a big company. But a Parker Bros. or Milton Bradley would have incurred fixed costs of roughly $250,000 just for design and development and would then have committed to an advertising and promotion budget of at least $1 million.

The Future

According to Reiss, the big question at the end of 1984 was, "Do we add on a new version of the *TV Guide* Game, do a new trivia game, or go onto something new in spite of the great market penetration and success of our game?"

He had been doing some planning for a new game to be called WHOOZIT? and, instead of questions, it would show photographs of famous people that the players would have to recognize. He had a preliminary royalty deal with Bettman Archives, who had the exclusive marketing rights to all the photographs of the news service UPI, in addition to its own extensive archives. But he was unsure about what the best follow-up for the success of 1984 could be.

The market, however, did not seem to be in the best condition. The 1984 Christmas season had ended with large unsold inventories of Trivial Pursuit and other trivia games. Some major companies, like Parker Bros., Lakeside, and Ideal, had closed out their games at low prices, further flooding the market. Many buyers were saying that trivia games, as a category, were over, although they seemed to accept Selchow's estimate of 7 million units of Trivial Pursuit sold in 1985. That figure was well below the 20 million units sold in 1984 but was still an exceptionally high figure compared with other board games. Selchow had also announced a plan to spend $5 million to promote the game in 1985. Some upscale retailers, however, had announced their intention to abandon Trivial Pursuit and other trivia games, mostly because of the heavy discounting.

Reiss thought that one of the reasons why the public seemed to have lost interest in trivia games is that they were hard to play; too often, none of the players knew the answers. In retrospect, he thought that the *TV Guide* Game had had the same problem. But that would be different with WHOOZIT? He was thinking of making easier questions and giving several chances to each player, and he really expected the new game to be enjoyable.

In addition to improving the intrinsic playability of the game, Reiss wanted to have more flexibility selling it. He planned to offer three different price points, one of the versions having only the questions so it could be played on the Trivial Pursuit board. In spite of all these improvements, however, he was not sure whether he should try to replicate the success obtained with the *TV Guide* Game and wondered what his best strategy for a follow up could be.

EXHIBIT 1   **Photo of the Game**

TV GUIDE'S TV GAME, the new board game for two to 20 players, contains more than 6,000 trivia questions and answers pre-pared and authenticated by the editors of TV GUIDE. It provides both a nostalgic trip through the days of Lucy and Uncle Miltie, and a journey through today's video environment...its people, its programs, and the world we all experience TV GUIDE'S TV GAME can be played as a family game (for ages 10 to adult), a party game with up to four teams with five or more players on a team, or without the board using just the questions and answers.

EXHIBIT 2 Book with Trivia Questions

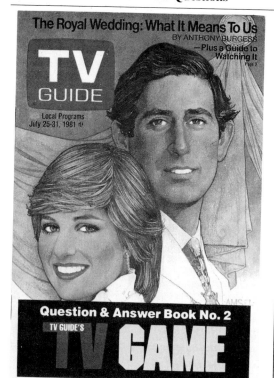

Name the three pitchers who each posted 20 victories for the 1956 Cleveland Indians. **Herb Score, Early Wynn & Bob Lemon**

Gene Stephens of the Red Sox shared the American league RBI title in 1949 and 1950—both times with teammates. Who were they? **Ted Williams (1949) and Walt Dropo (1950)**

On Oct. 19, 1957, this player scored a goal against Chicago's Glenn Hall—making him the first NHL star to score 500 goals in a career. **Maurice ("Rocket") Richard**

In 1921, Babe Ruth set an American league record with 171 runs batted in. Who held the old RBI mark? **Ty Cobb, who drove in 144 runs in 1911**

This Depression-era slugger was the first man to win back-to-back American League MVP honors. **Jimmy Fox (1932-33)**

Who was the last National Leaguer to win the Triple Crown? **Joe Medwick (St. Louis Cardinals, 1937)**

These two Hall of Famers are the only players to win baseball's Triple Crown twice. **Ted Williams (1942, 1947); Rogers Hornsby (1922, 1925)**

Joe DiMaggio's record 56-game hitting streak in 1941 broke a record that had stood since 1897 (44 games). Who held it? **Willie Keeler**

In 1962, he set a National League record by stealing 104 bases. **Maury Wills**

His 145 career knockouts is one boxing record that may never be broken. **Archie Moore**

He reigned over the heavyweight division for a record 11 years, nine months. **Joe Louis (1937-49)**

⓭

SPORTS

He sang "The Gold and Beyond" at the 1984 Winter Olympics. **John Denver**

Johnnie B. Baker Jr. is better known to baseball fans as _____. **Dusty Baker**

What two components make up skiing's Nordic combined event? **Cross-country skiing and jumping**

What is baseball manager Whitey Herzog's real first name? **Dorrel**

What is baseball player Biff Pocoroba's real first name? **Biff**

What is the maximum number of golf clubs a player may carry? **14**

The foil and saber are two of the three types of weapons used in fencing. What is the third? **Épée**

What is the maximum a professional middleweight boxer can weigh? **160 pounds**

What is the inside diameter of a regulation basketball hoop? **18 inches**

How high is the crossbar between a set of football goal posts? **10 feet**

Who was Joe Frazier's opponent in his final pro bout? **Jumbo Cummings**

As a freshman, he quarterbacked the University of Miami to a 31-30 upset of Nebraska and a national championship in early 1984. **Bernie Kosar**

In 1982, this team beat Stanford on a last-second five-lateral kickoff return that included a run through the Stanford marching band. **California**

EXHIBIT 3   Stores to Be Reached

	Number of Outlets
Sears	879
Penney	450
Federated	451
Dayton Hudson	1,149
R. H. Macy	96
Allied Stores	596
Carter Hawley Hale	268
Associated Dry Goods	332
Mercantile	79
Kmart	2,174
Woolworth	N/A
Wal-Mart	751
T.G.&Y.	754
Zayre	848
Bradlees	132
Murphy	386
Rose's	195
Kay Bee	500
Spencer Gifts	450
Hook's Drug	120
Toys " Я " Us	200

Bob Reiss thought that some 5,000 independent stores would be suitable targets, too.

Exhibit 4   Data on *TV Guide's* Audience

February 3, 1984

Mr. Robert Reiss
President
R&R
230 Fifth Avenue
New York, New York 10001

Dear Bob:

I had our Research Department pull together some statistics about *TV Guide* that should be useful in discussing the audience dimensions of our magazine with major department stores and mass merchandisers.

First off, *TV Guide's* circulation averages over 17 million copies each week.

Included in *TV Guide's* average issue audience are:

1. 37,838,000 adult readers age 18 and over.
2. 8,829,000 teenage readers 12–17.
3. 46,667,000 total readers age 12 and over.
4. 19,273,000 readers 18–34.
5. 28,085,000 readers 18–49.
6. 10,312,000 adult readers in homes with one or more children 10–17 years of age.
7. 16,334,000 adult readers in homes with $25,000+ household income.
8. 11,815,000 adult readers with one or more years of college.
9. 4,344,000 adult readers who bought games or toys for children 12–17 in the past year.
10. 3,688,000 adult readers who bought games or toys for adults 18+ in the past year.

Exhibit 5   **Letter to Supermarket Buyers**

TRIVIA
INCORPORATED
Exclusive Marketing Agent
R&R
230 Fifth Avenue, New York, NY 10001
1-212-686-6003 Telex 238131-RR UR

June 29, 1984

Mr. Lamar Williams
General Mdse. Buyer
JITNEY JUNGLE STORES of AMERICA
P.O. Box 3409
453 N. Mill St.
Jackson, MI 39207

Dear Mr. Williams:

Once every decade a product comes along that is just right!

We think we have that product for you. It has two key elements:

1. It is licensed by *TV Guide*. I'm sure we don't have to tell you about the sales strength of *TV Guide* with its 17 million-plus weekly circulation, 46 million readers, etc. If your supermarket is typical, *TV Guide* is one of your best sellers and has earned its exalted position next to the cash registers.

2. The trivia game explosion has taken America by storm and duplicated its Canadian heritage, where trivia games have reigned for four years.

We have put these two elements together and, with *TV Guide*'s help, developed a *TV Guide* Trivia Game with over 6,000 questions and answers. The enclosed catalog sheet gives full description and pricing. All our sales are final. We will advertise the game in five full page color ads in *TV Guide* this fall and will reach your customers.

We feel this game is ideally suited to be sold in your stores. We would be happy to send you a sample and/or answer any questions you may have.

We look forward to the opportunity of working with you.

Sincerely,
Robert S. Reiss

Robert S. Reiss

RSR/ck
encl.

EXHIBIT 6   Ads in *TV Guide* Magazine

EXHIBIT 7   Press Coverage of the Game

TV, too, gets into the trivia act

By BRUCE CHADWICK

SO YOU KNOW who was the only vice president to resign. So what? Okay, you know who threw the ball that Babe Ruth hit into the seats for his 60th home run. Big deal. And you know the name of the drummer in Glen Miller's band. Who cares?

Think you're so smart at trivia? All right, in addition to Matt Dillon, who was the only other character seen during the entire run of "Gunsmoke"? What business did John Walton and his father run in "The Waltons"? In the early days of "All in the Family," what was the name of the company where Archie Bunker worked?

Gotcha, didn't we? Well, to find out all the answers, see below, and also see "TV Guide's TV Game," the latest in the avalanche of trivia games that are flooding stores.

What's different about this one, though, is that it is limited to television.

It's a board game with cards and dice. You land on squares that have questions in seven categories: drama, sports, comedy, news, kids, movies and other TV (questions are divided into three levels of difficulty and many are aimed at today's youngsters and yes, there is a Mr. T question). Whoever gets the most right answers wins. The game is designed for individual or team play.

"Trivia games are hot because people are tired of video games and computer games in which the player is isolated," said Bob Reese, head of Trivia Inc. and the game's founder. "People want to play games with other people and match wits with talking faces, not TV screens. That, plus the yen for nostalgia, is making all trivia games, not just ours, big sellers."

Reese wanted to get into trivia games when Trivial Pursuit became a best seller last fall. He needed something different and turned to television.

Milburn Stone

Mary Tyler Moore

"Everyone watches television, so everyone will be interested in playing and, in fact, everyone will do reasonably well at this game," he said.

Reese turned to TV Guide because the magazine specializes in television coverage and has an extensive research department and library.

Researchers at TV Guide, led by Teresa Hagen, compiled a list of over 6,000 questions from over 20,000 submitted by writers there. Each question/answer had to have two written sources. Those that did not were dropped.

"It was harder than you'd think," said Hagen. "We needed a good balance of questions, easy to very difficult, and wanted a game that everyone, regardless of age, had a decent chance of winning."

The real research problems came in early television history.

"We had a very difficult time finding out firsts—the first comedy show, soap opera, president on TV, baseball game on TV—because early records were destroyed or sketchy."

They uncovered some unusual facts about television. As an example, the "Armed Forces Hour," an early '50's musical variety show, was only a half hour long. Dr. Ed Diethrich, owner of the USFL Arizona Wranglers, once performed open-heart surgery on live TV. Mary Tyler Moore's first major TV show was not "The Dick Van Dyke Show," but "Richard Diamond, Private Detective."

Hagen thinks the game is more than trivia. "We found that in playing it, we'd slide into conversations about what our own lives were like in relation to TV, like who our own heroes were, and our attitudes about things 20 years ago," she said. "We hope the game triggers conversations about life as well as TV."

The other continuing character on "Gunsmoke" was Milburn Stone; the Waltons ran a lumber mill and Archie Bunker worked at Prendergast Tool and Die Co.

Source: *Daily News*, New York: Burrelle's, June 12, 1984.

1–2 EASTWIND TRADING COMPANY (A)

It was a cold day in January 1991 and Gail Pasternak and Martha Gershun sat down at their favorite table in the Prospect Restaurant in Kansas City, Missouri. Over the past several weeks, they had eaten more meals over meetings there than they cared to count. But today was the culmination of all those deliberations and all that number crunching. Today, they would decide whether or not they wanted to proceed with plans to form the Eastwind Trading Company and purchase the 6 million fresh water pearl buttons that would form the basis of the business.

History

Gail and Martha first started talking about their venture in the fall of 1989 when they worked together in the marketing department of a small computer software firm. Gail had come upon a unique collection of 6 million antique, handmade, fresh water pearl buttons in the basement of a local fabric shop (**Exhibit 1**). The fabric store owner and her husband, Susan and George Swanson, had been marketing the buttons to other fabric stores and had made money converting some of the buttons to jewelry. Gail and Martha decided to bid on the business with the intent of making jewelry out of the inventory that did not have predrilled holes. (Many antique buttons used metal shanks to give the seamstress a place to run the thread. These shanks could be cut off, leaving a lustrous, semiprecious stone that could be mounted as earrings, cufflinks, money clips, necklaces, or rings.)

After two months of investigation into the jewelry business, the women decided they wanted to make the Swansons an offer for the business. They did not believe a bank would lend them money to buy such a fledgling firm with uncounted inventory and no real organization. They were reluctant to spend their savings to help buy the business because their own jobs at the software firm were so insecure. If they spent their money to buy the buttons and then lost their jobs, what would they do to live?

With the help of a local financial consultant, Gail and Martha offered the Swansons a deal requiring seller financing. They would work in the business full-time for no salary and over time earn 70 percent of the firm's stock. The women felt this was a

This case was prepared by Martha Gershun under the direction of Howard H. Stevenson.

Copyright © 1993 by the President and Fellows of Harvard College

Harvard Business School Case 9–393–119

good deal for the Swansons. They would own 30 percent of a firm of far greater size than their present operation. And the entrepreneurs would have built a company with no cash investment.

The Swansons did not see it that way. They viewed the deal as unfair to them and of questionable profitability. In February 1990, they sold their buttons to Michael Monroe, a contract construction executive from Branson, Missouri, for $200,000 in cash.

The Present

In November 1990, Gail received a call from Michael Monroe. He wanted to sell the buttons. He said that he had bought the company for his daughter to run. Now, she was getting married and moving to Africa as a missionary. He had put $40,000 into the business since he bought it. Did Gail and Martha want to buy it for $200,000?

The two women weren't sure. A lot had changed since they had offered to buy the company from the Swansons. The software firm where they had worked had sold out to a Canadian company. Martha had a new job that she loved, marketing cellular telephone service. Gail had built a free-lance advertising business and was considering merging with a local advertising firm. Furthermore, they needed steady salaries more than ever. Martha had purchased a four-seater airplane that required steady cash to keep it in the air, and Gail was in the middle of a complex divorce settlement.

The women took a small-business consultant and flew Martha's plane down to Branson to take another look at the buttons. Michael Monroe had increased drastically the value of the business by organizing the inventory and developing a full-color catalog. The consultant advised Gail and Martha that he thought purchasing the buttons was "bankable" even in this anemic lending environment. He offered to set them up with bankers in the Kansas City area who were willing to make loans to new ventures.

The women decided to buy the business. They would sell it to bankers as a pure button business, ignoring the more profitable, but riskier concept of selling the buttons as jewelry. They agreed that Gail would work in the business half-time, drawing a reasonable salary and keeping half of her free-lance clients as supplemental income. Martha would continue her job, but would devote evenings and weekends to the business. They also decided to seek $300,000 in financing: $200,000 to buy the business and $100,000 in working capital.

Gail and Martha spent the next two weeks talking to bankers. (Exhibit 1 shows their business plan for the banks, and **Exhibit 2** contains some pro forma projections.) In addition to their plan, they brought each banker a catalog from the business and several of the beautiful pearl buttons. Over and over they heard the same objections. If the business got into financial trouble, the banks were not prepared to try and sell off the buttons. Basically, the banks were not willing to bet on such an unconventional deal.

Finally, Stadium Bank offered to submit the loan to the Small Business Administration (SBA). If the SBA would guarantee the loan, then Stadium would lend the money. After another anxious two weeks, the SBA word came through—it would guarantee a loan of $225,000 to the Eastwind Trading Company at 1 3/4 percent over prime, adjusted quarterly, for 5 1/2 years. The first six months would be interest-only payments. After that, payments would be $4,997/month. The time needed to pay off the loan would depend on fluctuations in the interest rate. There were only two major stipulations. Gail and Martha had to come up with $75,000 in equity before the loan would be granted. And they would each have to guarantee the loan personally.

Martha had stock, which her grandmother had given her over the years, now worth about $40,000. If she sold that, her tax liability could be as much as $5,000 at the end of the year. Additionally, each of the women had $5,000 in cash to invest in the business. They had other assets, too. Gail owned a grand piano and a BMW; Martha owned the airplane. While there were loans against these items, they certainly had value if the loans were paid off, possibly as much as $10,000 in total.

Gail and Martha decided that they needed outside financing. They recast the numbers they had shown the bank, pulling management salaries way down and adding payments to the outside board members; they also recast the financials using more optimistic projections **(see Exhibit 3).** They calculated that 1 percent of their business was worth $4,767 using a 35 percent discount rate and conservative numbers, and $9,142 using a 35 percent discount rate and more optimistic projections.

Over the next several weeks, Gail and Martha talked to many investors. Few wanted to invest funds; all wanted to give them advice. Finally, they put together several options. Each investor had different reasons for being interested in the deal, and each one wanted different concessions before putting in money. Now, as Gail and Martha sat down at the Prospect yet again, they reviewed their list of potential investors to determine how to structure their business.

1. John Walsh, a wealthy local entrepreneur, was interested in investing $25,000 for 8 percent of the firm. He wanted reassurances that the business would be an ongoing concern, with Gail and Martha agreeing to exploit the distribution channels they would open up for the buttons with other follow-up products. He was concerned that the women had not been thorough enough in their evaluation of the implementation problems involved in shipping so many buttons, but he promised to keep his hands out of the firm and let Gail and Martha run their own show. He wanted cash kept in the firm and thus preferred a straight corporate structure. Additionally, he wanted some mechanism to ensure that in the event of a liquidation, his paid-in capital would be returned before Gail and Martha made any profit.

2. Roger Johnson, one of Martha's close friends, offered to invest $15,000 for 4.8 percent of the firm's equity. He was willing to buy as much as 8 percent of the firm if Martha would loan him the additional $10,000 until he could get the cash—probably about 3 months. Roger had some interest in sitting on the firm's board of directors, but primarily agreed to let the women run the firm the way they wanted. He was interested in a contractual limit to their salaries and wanted cash dividends as soon as possible. Thus, he wanted the corporation to elect the tax advantages of an ''S'' corporation.

3. Dr. Dick Powell and Tom English, a local psychologist and a wealthy insurance executive, were interested in investing together. They offered Eastwind $65,000 for 25 percent of the firm as follows: $5,000 in equity financing,

$45,000 loan to the business (subordinated to the SBA loan), and a $15,000 personal loan to Gail and Martha, repayable in the second year at 10 percent interest. Dick, in particular, showed a real fascination with the buttons and had lots of ideas about how they could be sold. He wanted to be actively involved in marketing the business and had lots of ideas for new product lines. The duo wanted the business to retain earnings for expansion and thus preferred a straight corporate structure.

4. Martha's sister Eleanor offered to pay $10,000 for 3.2 percent of the firm. She lived in New York and didn't really care about voting or how the business was run. Quite wealthy in her own right, she thought this investment would be a lark and might pan out well.

Martha turned to Gail and said:

Now that we have received approval on the SBA guarantee, we have really got to make our decisions about the start-up equity. It's fun so far, but business school just didn't prepare me for the amount of hassle we had to take from prospective investors. The worst ones are the ones who don't understand that what they are asking for isn't even good for them; the smart, but greedy ones, I can handle! We've got to figure out how to handle our minority investors. Because we are looking for relatively little cash, most of what I know about venture capital isn't so relevant.

Now, Gail and Martha had to make the tough decisions. Should they proceed with the business? How much outside money did they need? Who did they want as their minority shareholders? How much of their company should they give away? What price was their equity worth? How should the Eastwind Trading Company ownership and management be structured?

On a more personal level, Gail and Martha wondered: How much of their own money were they willing to risk? How poor were they willing to be? How did they feel about one of them putting in more money than the other?

Exhibit 1   Eastwind Trading Company Business Plan

Financing Request

We are seeking $300,000 in debt financing to purchase the Swanson Pearl Button Company, the world's only wholesale supplier of handmade fresh water pearl buttons. The loan will be secured by the finished goods inventory valued at between $1 million and $4 million. The loan will be paid out of business operations, over a seven-year period, with interest-only payments during the first year.

The total capitalization of $300,000 will be divided as follows:
—$200,000 to purchase the business, including all inventory, accounts receivable, customer lists, and related supplies.
—$100,000 working capital, used to reestablish marketing distribution through sales representatives.

The Swanson Pearls: What They Are, Where They Came From

The Swanson Pearl Buttons are the only remaining collection of handmade fresh water pearl buttons in the world. These 6 million buttons represent the final inventories of the factories that manufactured pearl buttons at the turn of the century in Muscatine, Iowa, the "Pearl Button Capital of the World." The factories closed when cheaply manufactured plastic buttons far underpriced pearl buttons in the 1920s. Today, with a resurgence of interest in high-quality materials, pearl buttons are in increasing demand for high-quality garments.

Pearl buttons can no longer be manufactured in large quantities and wide varieties of colors. Not only has pollution seriously deteriorated oyster beds, but the labor intensive process by which they were manufactured is no longer cost-effective. The Japanese are currently manufacturing small quantities of "processed" pearl buttons of a very inferior quality with poor market acceptance.

Thus, the Swanson Pearls are unique and valuable. Their naturalness and quantity virtually identify them as a natural resource. Their history gives them value as antiques. Their finite quantity increases their value every year.

The pearls carry the Swanson name because they were discovered by George and Susan Swanson. Mrs. Swanson, a dressmaker for Kansas City socialites, had pursued a lengthy search for pearl buttons for her expensive custom clothing. When she exhausted all current manufacturer possibilities, she focused on finding pearl buttons that had possibly been left over from the early 1900s.

After an exhaustive and unproductive search, the Swansons accidentally happened upon this last collection of pearls, still in their original boxes, in an old fishery in Muscatine, Iowa, where they had been forgotten since their owner died in the 1950s.

The Swanson Pearl Button Company History

George and Susan Swanson, 1987–1990

The Swansons moved the buttons to Kansas City, placed them in a storeroom, separated 200 styles, and began to market them to fabric stores through a color flyer. Most of the buttons remained unseparated and in boxes. In the three years that they owned the buttons, the Swansons sold approximately 600,000 at an average of 65 cents apiece, or $390,000. The South provided most of the revenue through one effective sales representative. There was spotty distribution throughout the Mid- and Northwest.

The Swansons decided to sell the company when George Swanson developed health problems and could no longer manage the company.

Michael Monroe, 1990

In February 1990, the Swansons sold the buttons to Michael Monroe of Branson, Missouri, for $200,000 cash. Mr. Monroe bought the company for his daughter to run. This fall, she decided

EXHIBIT 1   *(continued)*

to move out of the country. During the time that he owned the buttons, Mr. Monroe invested $40,000 in mailing supplies and marketing. He developed internal control systems and sale processes and inventoried all of the buttons, increasing the available button styles to over 800. He developed a catalog, which he sent to 1,200 fabric stores.

Despite the fact that the company is now well organized, there is no selling effort beyond the initial catalog mailing. Even at this slow selling pace, the company has averaged $2,000 per month since February. The company is essentially sitting still, only filling orders for standing customers. In late November, Mr. Monroe announced that the buttons were up for sale again.

No books or financial records were provided to Mr. Monroe when he purchased the buttons from George and Susan Swanson. At present, the only financial records are Mr. Monroe's lists of orders received and filled. The business currently has no outstanding debts or accounts payable. As the firm was purchased in February 1990, no income tax forms have yet been filed.

Our Plan

Current Status

Distribution is through catalog sales only and is confined to 100 accounts. Most accounts are in the Mid- and Northwest. There are virtually no buttons sold east of the Mississippi and very few sold on the West Coast. They currently wholesale for an average of 65 cents apiece. Average order size is $25 per account per month.

Market Research

Our market research tells us that:
- There are over 14,000 fabric stores in the United States (Standard Rate and Data Service).
- Button pricing is very flexible, because of the unique nature of the buttons and the fact that they add little to the end cost of a garment. Current accounts felt that prices could be much higher.

Strategies for Increasing Revenue

Our plan is to:
- Raise the price of the buttons 30 percent to an average price of 85 cents each.
- Hire sales representatives at 20 percent commission to effectively cover the entire country.
- Provide retailers with selling incentives and merchandising assistance.
- Approach clothing manufacturers and designers for large sales of buttons for use on designer clothing.
- Implement a direct mail campaign to reach the remaining 12,000+ fabric stores.

Backgrounds of Key Personnel

Gail Pasternak

Gail Pasternak will bring to the business extensive experience in business management and all facets of marketing.

From 1982 to 1989, Ms. Pasternak was president and creative director of Pasternak, Kizer and Associates, a Kansas City advertising agency. During that time, she designed and implemented extensive marketing, public relations, and advertising programs for a wide variety of clients, including Data Phase, Continental Healthcare Systems, KLSI Radio, Cramer, Inc., Mid-America Health Network (HealthNet), and many others. She was responsible for many successful programs for her clients and received numerous creative awards for her work. During that time, she also managed the business, which employed from 4 to 10 people.

Ms. Pasternak also served as Director of Marketing Services for Data Phase Corporation. In that role, she was responsible for the development and implementation of marketing plans for the company's three computer products.

EXHIBIT 1   *(concluded)*

Since February, Ms. Pasternak has been working as a consultant and free-lance writer for the advertising community. She is currently involved in such accounts as National Photo, Ralston Purina (protein division), Mid-America Health Network (HealthNet), Johnson County Bank, and International Soccer.

Ms. Pasternak holds a BA in Journalism, 1977, from Beaver College, Glenside, PA, and a BFA in Graphic Design, 1983, from the Kansas City Art Institute.

Martha Gershun

Martha Gershun will bring to the business extensive marketing, financial, and general management experience. She has worked for the data communications subsidiary of United Telecom, managing the corporate planning process and setting direction for new product introduction. She was responsible for the development of United Telecom's entry into the provision of data services for multitenant buildings.

Ms. Gershun also worked for Data Phase in Kansas City, as Product Manager for a new series of microcomputer software. In this capacity, she was responsible for the management of the product's development, documentation, marketing, and sales effort.

Ms. Gershun is presently employed with United TeleSpectrum, the subsidiary of United Telecom that provides cellular mobile and paging service to 27 markets nationwide. As Manager of Market Development, she is responsible for the company's cellular business, handling all advertising and public relations, sales material, billing implementation, market research, and new product development.

Additionally, Ms. Gershun has worked for the Boston Consulting Group, Boston, MA, doing strategic planning and acquisition studies, and for Amherst Associates, Chicago, IL, doing financial planning for the health-care industry. She holds a BA *cum laude* from Harvard College, 1983, and an MBA from the Harvard Business School, 1988. She also holds a post-graduate diploma in economics from the University of Stirling, Scotland.

EXHIBIT 2   Financials

Pro Forma Income Statement
February 1991 to January 1992

	February	March	April	May	June	July	August	September	October	November	December	January	FY 1991
Revenue													
Buttons:													
Shops/mail[a]	3,100	3,100	3,100	3,875	3,875	3,875	4,844	4,844	4,844	4,844	4,844	4,844	49,989
Shops/reps	—	—	—	5,000	6,500	8,000	9,500	11,000	11,000	11,000	11,000	11,000	84,000
Clothing mfg.	—	—	—	—	—	—	5,000	5,000	10,000	10,000	20,000	20,000	70,000
Total number	3,100	3,100	3,100	8,875	10,375	11,875	19,344	20,844	25,844	25,844	35,844	35,844	203,989
Sales	$ 2,015	$ 2,015	$ 2,635	$ 7,544	$ 8,819	$10,094	$16,442	$17,717	$21,967	$21,967	$30,467	$30,467	$172,149
Expenses													
Commissions	—	—	—	850	1,105	1,360	1,615	1,870	1,870	1,870	1,870	1,870	14,280
Rent[b]	500	500	500	500	500	500	500	500	500	500	500	500	6,000
Utilities	100	100	100	100	100	100	100	100	100	100	100	100	1,200
Moving expense	1,000	—	—	—	—	—	—	—	—	—	—	—	1,000
Stationery and miscellaneous	2,000	—	—	—	—	—	2,000	—	—	—	—	—	4,000
Supplies[c]	500	100	100	100	100	100	100	100	100	100	100	100	1,600
Computer	—	2,000	—	—	—	—	—	—	—	—	—	—	2,000
Advertising[d]	10,000	5,000	5,000	5,000	2,000	2,000	2,000	3,000	1,000	1,000	1,000	1,000	38,000
Travel[e]	—	2,000	2,000	2,000	1,000	1,000	1,000	1,000	1,000	1,000	1,000	1,000	14,000
Staff[f]	640	640	640	640	640	640	640	640	640	640	640	640	7,680
Insurance[g]	300	300	300	300	300	300	300	300	300	300	300	300	3,600
Management[h]	2,500	2,500	2,500	2,500	2,500	2,500	2,500	2,500	2,500	2,500	2,500	2,500	30,000
Professional fees[i]	1,700	200	200	200	200	4,450	200	200	200	200	200	3,200	11,150
Earnings before income tax	($17,225)	($11,325)	($8,705)	($4,646)	$ 374	($2,856)	$ 5,487	$ 7,507	$13,757	$13,757	$22,257	$19,257	$ 37,639

[a] Current sales = 3,100 buttons with average price of .65 each. We will increase average price in April by 30 percent to .85.

[b] 1,100 square feet commercial space.

[c] Business presently owns office furniture and mailing supplies.

[d] Direct mail to remaining 12,000 fabric stores.

[e] To recruit reps and manufacturing accounts and attend trade shows.

[f] Person to fill orders at $8/hr. × 20 hrs./wk.

[g] Buttons for $1 million and life insurance on both principals for $1 million.

[h] Gail full time at $30,000 until FY 1992, then at $60,000 (includes benefits); Martha full-time starting FY 1993.

[i] Legal, consulting, accounting, bookkeeping.

Exhibit 2 (continued)

Pro Forma Cash Flow Statement
February 1991 to January 1992

	February	March	April	May	June	July	August	September	October	November	December	January
Sources												
Sales	—	$ 2,015	$ 2,015	$ 2,635	$ 7,544	$ 8,819	$10,094	$16,442	$17,717	$21,967	$21,967	$ 30,467
Loan proceeds	$300,000	—	—	—	—	—	—	—	—	—	—	—
Cash from principals	10,000	—	—	—	—	—	—	—	—	—	—	—
Uses												
Purchase price	200,000											
Commissions	—	—	—	—	850	1,105	1,360	1,615	1,870	1,870	1,870	1,870
Rent	1,000	500	500	500	500	500	500	500	500	500	500	500
Utilities	100	100	100	100	100	100	100	100	100	100	100	100
Moving expense	1,000	—	—	—	—	—	—	—	—	—	—	—
Stationery, miscellaneous	—	2,000	—	—	—	—	—	2,000	—	—	—	—
Supplies	—	500	100	100	100	100	100	100	100	100	100	100
Computer	—	—	2,000	—	—	—	—	—	—	—	—	—
Advertising	—	10,000	5,000	5,000	5,000	2,000	2,000	2,000	3,000	1,000	1,000	1,000
Travel	500	1,500	2,000	2,000	1,500	1,000	1,000	1,000	1,000	1,000	1,000	1,000
Staff	320	640	640	640	640	640	640	640	640	640	640	640
Insurance	3,600	—	—	—	—	—	—	—	—	—	—	—
Management	1,250	2,500	2,500	2,500	2,500	2,500	2,500	2,500	2,500	2,500	2,500	2,500
Professional fees	—	1,700	200	200	200	200	4,450	200	200	200	200	200
SBA charge	3,000	—	—	—	—	—	—	—	—	—	—	—
Cash position before debt service	$ 99,230	($17,425)	($11,025)	($8,405)	($3,846)	674	($2,556)	$ 5,787	$ 7,807	$14,057	$14,057	$ 22,557
Cumulative cash position before debt service	$ 99,230	$ 81,805	$ 70,780	$62,375	$58,529	$59,203	$56,647	$62,434	$70,241	$84,298	$98,355	$120,912

Exhibit 2   *(concluded)*

Pro Forma Income Statement
FY 1992–1995

	FY 1992	*FY 1993*	*FY 1994*	*FY 1995*
Revenue				
Buttons:				
Shops/mail	66,847	76,874	88,405	101,666
Shops/reps	144,000	172,800	207,360	248,832
Small manufacturing	300,000	400,000	500,000	600,000
Total number	510,847	649,674	796,400	950,498
Sales $	$434,212	$552,223	$676,400	$807,923
Expenses				
Commissions	$ 28,800	$ 34,560	$ 41,472	$ 49,766
Rent	6,000	6,000	6,000	6,000
Utilities	1,800	1,800	1,800	1,800
Moving expense	—	—	—	—
Stationery and				
miscellaneous	2,000	3,000	4,000	4,000
Supplies	6,000	9,000	12,000	17,000
Computer	10,000	—	—	—
Advertising	48,000	72,000	72,000	72,000
Travel	24,000	36,000	36,000	36,000
Staff	15,360	15,360	30,720	20,720
Insurance	3,600	3,600	3,600	3,600
Management	90,000	180,000	210,000	210,000
Professional fees	7,600	8,740	10,051	11,559
Earnings before				
income tax	$191,052	$182,163	$248,757	$365,478
Total buttons sold = 3,110,773				

Exhibit 3 Financial Projections

Eastwind Scenario One

	1991	1992	1993	1994	1995	1996	1997	1998	Total
Revenue									
Number of buttons:									
Shops/mail	49,989	66,847	76,874	88,405	101,666	101,666	101,666	101,666	688,779
Shops/reps	84,000	144,000	172,800	207,360	248,832	248,832	248,832	248,832	1,603,488
Clothing mfg.	70,000	300,000	400,000	500,000	600,000	600,000	600,000	600,000	3,670,000
Total number of buttons	203,989	510,847	649,674	796,400	950,498	950,498	950,498	950,498	5,962,267
Total sales[a]	$172,149	$434,212	$552,223	$676,400	$807,923	$807,923	$807,923	$807,923	$5,066,676
Expenses									
Commissions	$ 14,280	$ 28,800	$ 34,560	$ 41,472	$ 49,766	$ 49,766	$ 49,766	$ 49,766	$ 318,176
Rent	6,000	6,000	6,000	6,000	6,000	6,000	6,000	6,000	48,000
Utilities	1,200	1,800	1,800	1,800	1,800	1,800	1,800	1,800	13,800
Moving expenses	1,000	0	0	0	0	0	0	0	1,000
Stationery and miscellaneous	4,000	2,000	3,000	4,000	4,000	4,000	4,000	4,000	29,000
Supplies	1,600	6,000	9,000	12,000	17,000	17,000	17,000	17,000	96,600
Computer	2,000	10,000	0	0	0	0	0	0	12,000
Advertising	38,000	48,000	72,000	72,000	72,000	72,000	72,000	72,000	518,000
Travel	14,000	24,000	36,000	36,000	36,000	36,000	36,000	36,000	254,000
Staff	7,680	15,360	15,360	30,720	30,720	30,720	30,720	30,720	192,000
Insurance	3,600	3,600	3,600	3,600	3,600	3,600	3,600	3,600	28,800
Professional fees	11,150	7,600	8,740	10,051	11,559	11,559	11,559	11,559	83,777
Management	30,000	90,000	120,000	120,000	120,000	120,000	120,000	120,000	840,000
Board payments	4,000	4,000	4,000	4,000	4,000	4,000	4,000	4,000	32,000
Total expense	$138,510	$247,160	$314,060	$341,643	$356,445	$356,445	$356,445	$356,445	$2,467,153
Earnings before income tax	$ 33,639	$187,052	$238,163	$334,757	$451,478	$451,478	$451,478	$451,478	$2,599,523
Debt service	$ 42,000	$ 60,000	$ 60,000	$ 60,000	$ 60,000	$ 0	$ 0	$ 0	$ 282,000
Net income (before tax)	($ 8,361)	$127,052	$178,163	$274,757	$391,478	$451,478	$451,478	$451,478	$2,317,523

NPV at 25% $695,443
NPV at 30% $572,310
NPV at 35% $476,709

1% of the business is worth $4,767 today. $50,000 = 10.5% of the business.

[a]Assumes no inflation.

EXHIBIT 3 (concluded)

Eastwind Scenario Two

	1991	1992	1993	1994	1995	Total
Revenue						
Number of buttons:						
Shops/mail	49,989	66,847	153,748	176,810	203,332	650,726
Shops/rep	84,000	144,000	345,600	414,720	497,664	1,485,984
Clothing mfg.	70,000	300,000	800,000	1,000,000	1,200,000	3,370,000
Total number of buttons	203,989	510,847	1,299,348	1,591,530	1,900,996	5,506,710
Total sales[a]	$172,149	$434,212	$1,104,446	$1,352,800	$1,615,846	$4,679,453
Expenses						
Commissions	$ 14,280	$ 28,800	$ 34,560	$ 41,472	$ 49,766	$ 168,878
Rent	6,000	6,000	6,000	6,000	6,000	30,000
Utilities	1,200	1,800	1,800	1,800	1,800	8,400
Moving expenses	1,000	0	0	0	0	1,000
Stationery and miscellaneous	4,000	2,000	3,000	4,000	4,000	17,000
Supplies	1,600	6,000	9,000	12,000	17,000	45,600
Computer	2,000	10,000	0	0	0	12,000
Advertising	38,000	48,000	72,000	72,000	72,000	302,000
Travel	14,000	24,000	36,000	36,000	36,000	146,000
Staff	7,680	15,360	15,360	30,720	30,720	99,840
Insurance	3,600	3,600	3,600	3,600	3,600	18,000
Professional fees	11,150	7,600	8,740	10,051	11,559	49,100
Management	30,000	90,000	120,000	120,000	120,000	480,000
Board payments	4,000	4,000	4,000	4,000	4,000	20,000
Total expense	$138,510	$247,160	$ 314,060	$ 341,643	$ 356,445	$1,397,818
Earnings before income tax	$ 33,639	$187,052	$ 790,386	$1,011,157	$1,259,401	$3,281,635
Debt service	$ 42,000	$ 60,000	$ 60,000	$ 60,000	$ 60,000	$ 282,000
Net income (before tax)	($ 8,361)	$127,052	$ 730,386	$ 951,157	$1,199,401	$2,999,635
NPV at 25% $1,231,196						
NPV at 30% $1,057,254						
NPV at 35% $ 914,225						

1% of the business is worth $9,142 today. $50,000 = 5.5% of the business.

[a]Assumes no inflation.

1–3 VINTAGE DIRECTIONS, INC.

The four founders, Lesley Berglund, Jim Pottow, Greg Berglund, and Lisa Mangano, had just returned from their Christmas vacations and were trying to hammer out a time when they would all be available for an investor pitch. After a few attempts, Jim interrupted the negotiations. "Well, guys, I wasn't quite ready to tell you this, but I won't be here to make the meeting. I'm moving back to Toronto."

Lesley, Jim's partner for the spring 1991 field study that had led them all into the fine wine distribution business, had suspected that he might be making that kind of announcement. After handling the bulk of the financial and operational responsibilities for Vintage Directions, Inc., (VDI) for six months, Jim could no longer ignore his family's pressure to leave California and join their Canadian convenience store business.

The team had planned ahead, with a vesting stock program, for the possible departure of any of the founders. But Jim's announcement generated mixed emotions. On the one hand, VDI might have a better chance of surviving with the reduction in overhead. Yet Jim's departure would mean an important transition for the team and a serious reassessment of how many managing founders the business could sustain, and equity investors it could attract, in light of its unexpectedly modest initial growth.

Background

In December 1990, George Schofield, the president of a Napa Valley wine company, commissioned a study at Harvard Business School that second-year students Lesley Berglund and Jim Pottow agreed to conduct. The purpose of the study was to examine the various marketing possibilities for his inventory of 1981–1987 Cabernet Sauvignon from 11 different Napa and Sonoma Valley wineries. Schofield's company, Unique Wines, Inc., (UWI) had been engaged in the purchase and aging of premium California Cabernet Sauvignon since 1983, through annual investor contract offerings. By 1991, UWI had 13,400 cases of wine covering seven consecutive vintages (1981–1987), with a market retail value of $3 million. According to Lesley:

> George is an extremely respected man in the Napa Valley, and he has been a friend of the family for years. He used to be the CFO of Mondavi, and he has been acting CFO at several small wineries, as well as for my father's Caterpillar tractor dealership.

This case was prepared by Research Associate Laura Pochop under the supervision of Professor Howard Stevenson.

Harvard Business School Case 9–393–043

He knew that I had a sales and marketing background, and his strengths are really more in financial forecasting, so he asked me if I would be interested in looking into what he might *do* with all those Cabernets.

I have harbored a not-so-secret dream of becoming involved in the wine industry for what seems like forever. I think I wrote my college application essays about it! But I had never really identified a good opportunity. I didn't want to move home to Napa and just work for one winery after business school—I thought that would be too limiting.

When George approached me about the field study, I had already accepted an offer with the international consulting firm where I had worked the previous summer. Unlike most of my friends, I didn't need to spend my second year recruiting, so I was open to the chance to pursue my interest and learn a great deal more about the wine industry.

Jim was someone who I had met in my first year. He was very interested in wine, in an enthusiast sense, even though he didn't grow up in the industry. We weren't really that close, but we had several occasions to discuss wine and I thought he might be interested in the field study.

During the course of their study, conducted under the supervision of the agribusiness and entrepreneurship departments at HBS, Lesley and Jim first investigated the recent dynamics in the U.S. wine industry and found reason for both caution and optimism. Though both total and per capita wine consumption had been declining steadily since 1987 **(see Exhibit 1),** the "superpremium" ($7.00–13.99 per bottle) and "ultrapremium" ($14 per bottle and up) wine segments had been growing **(see Exhibit 2).** They then turned to an analysis of the channel dynamics to estimate the returns Unique Wines, Inc., might be able to realize through different sale options **(see Exhibit 3).** In light of the channel economics and the returns that they imagined George's investors would demand, Lesley and Jim decided to investigate direct mail (DM) as the most efficient and effective distribution channel for UWI's wines. Lesley spent her spring break immersing herself in the sparse available literature on direct mail:

I guess I became really kind of a nerd; I went to Jamaica over break and took about 12 books on direct mail to the beach with me every day. But I was really becoming intrigued with the concept. Jim and I had tried to investigate HBS sources of information on direct marketing but had come up with nothing. I talked with a whole bunch of professors, but at that time there was really no direct-mail "guru" at HBS. I had taken Entrepreneurial Management in the fall. Our exam was the Ruth Owades case—that case, dealing with a direct-mail startup, was the sum total of my direct-mail knowledge!

At that point, I was trying to make some personal decisions about how deeply I wanted to get involved with the project. I had already spent my consulting company signing bonus on my last semester's tuition. But I was really falling in love with the idea, and the chance to help George out. We thought that fine wine consumers turned out to be the perfect fit with the direct-mail channel: they were easy to identify and reach through their connections to various wine publications, interest groups, and winery visits.

And the more I learned about direct marketing, the more I realized that it incorporated everything I loved about sales and marketing—the chance to be creative and try to think of new ways to present ideas—but surmounted the things I found really frustrating—the lack of feedback on whether or not a campaign really works. With a direct-mail campaign, it almost seems like a science; you send out a certain number of pieces, calculate your return rates, and figure out if your strategy was successful. You don't have to guess the way I had to at Clorox—did we sell more bleach this month because of a new marketing strategy or was it because my sales force was particularly aggressive?

Lesley and Jim completed a business plan that centered around marketing the UWI wines through the DM channel. The business plan won an Uhlmann Award for excellence in an agribusiness field study. Throughout the field study, Lesley had been sharing her ideas and progress with her brother Greg, who was working in Boston at a computer company called Aegis Associates. Greg was then enmeshed in partnership negotiations at Aegis. He described his situation:

> Aegis was a very entrepreneurial company that sold PCs, mainly to architects and engineers. When I got there, right after I graduated from college, it had dwindled from a four-person operation to a one-person shop. I was in sales and I was doing very well. Around the time that Lesley began telling me about her field study, I had been negotiating with the CEO for a 50 percent equity position, which it looked like I was going to be able to get for virtually nothing.
>
> At the same time, I was involved in a very serious romantic relationship with a woman that Lesley had introduced me to the year before named Lisa Mangano. She had been a year ahead of Lesley at HBS and had taken a job in Chicago in the spring before we met. So we spent that year seeing each other long distance. At first one of us would fly out one weekend a month, then every other weekend, and then just about every weekend. That whole time we were trying to figure out what to do about being in the same city, but we were both very strong-willed people and had come to a stalemate. We couldn't decide whether I should leave my excellent job in Boston to go to Chicago, or she should leave her excellent job in Chicago to be with me in Boston.

Lisa also heard from Lesley about the progress of her field study:

> I was working for Leo Burnett in Chicago, but I had seen Lesley fairly often when I was out visiting Greg. I remember the first time she told us about it—we were on this Christmas Caribbean cruise and we joked that maybe some day the three of us would be running a giant direct-mail wine company. At the time it seemed ironic how well the idea seemed to fit the three of us. My parents ran a small direct-mail printing business in New York, and I had been on the creative end of advertising before and after business school. Greg and Lesley had grown up on their family's vineyard in the Napa Valley, and Greg had been working on some data-base management projects at Aegis. And, of course, Greg and I were looking for a solution that would get us to the same city.

After turning in the field study, Lesley began to seriously investigate the possibilities of pursuing a wine-related venture with George Schofield after graduation. Over Easter weekend, Lisa flew out to huddle with Greg and Lesley about the potential of forming a management team. Lisa remembers the meeting as an intense but valuable immersion into the realities of working within such a small team:

> Lesley had this friend who owned a farm out in Lincoln, Massachusetts, so the three of us went out there and locked ourselves in for the Easter weekend. We talked through a lot of issues—our personal strengths and weaknesses, the risks and opportunities of the business, how the team dynamics might play out. We thought it was a real strength that we had such distinct areas of expertise, but there were some definite concerns. We weren't sure that the venture would be able to grow fast enough to support all of us, especially since I had piled

up such heavy personal debt from business school. Or if the market had the potential to ever support us all. We also knew we had different expectations and different ''pain thresholds'' in terms of personal cash flow.

Between the three of us, we knew we had a great deal of the skills necessary to make it really work. The weakest link, we knew, was on the financial side. But Lesley had seen during the field study that Jim was very sophisticated in terms of computer modeling and financial control systems and had a definite curiosity about the venture. He had been doing some recruiting, but hadn't come up with anything ideal. His family was working under the assumption that he would go back to Toronto and use his B-school education at the business that they owned. So if he decided to do the venture he felt that he always had something to fall back on if things didn't immediately take off.

But eventually we decided to do it. At that point, it was still a feeling of ''let's give it a shot for six months.'' We were all basically curious about how it would turn out—was there an opportunity out there, could we get financing, did we know enough to really do this?

Vintage Directions, Inc.

In July 1991, Vintage Directions incorporated with the goal of building three integrated business segments focused on developing the direct-mail/direct-marketing channels for the premium wine industry. The three segments were designed to meet specific wine industry and premium wine consumer needs:

Library Cabernets—To sell a rare supply of ultrapremium, properly aged California Cabernet Sauvignon through a direct-mail offer, under the collection brand name *Ambrosia*. The focus centered on offering mixed cases of 10-year-old Cabernets from the UWI collection.

Additional Wines and Related Products—To expand Ambrosia into a full catalog of premium, hard-to-find wines, wine accessories, gourmet foods, and related gifts. Ambrosia was designed to offer selection, convenience, and value to premium wine buyers.

Marketing and Management (M&M) Services—To leverage Vintage Directions' own direct-marketing infrastructure by offering related services to individual wineries and gourmet food companies. Strategically critical to VDI's success, the income from M&M Services was projected to cover overhead while the base business of Ambrosia was built up over time. M&M Services was also intended to allow the VDI management team to go down multiple learning curves by managing DM campaigns for other companies.

According to Lesley, the three other partners definitely wanted to focus on the first two segments of the business:

Nobody but me was too excited about taking time away from Ambrosia to do M&M, and I had mixed feelings about the trade-offs involved. I would rather cover overhead with cash flow from M&M Services than take on more debt, and I can see the benefits that we can get through expanding our DM knowledge base. But the others, and particularly Jim, feel that we came out here to build a direct-mail wine empire, and nothing should distract us from that goal.

The United States Wine Market.   The domestic retail market for premium wines reached $2.9 billion in 1991, up by a compound annual growth rate of 5.5 percent in dollars since 1984. In 1991, this market consisted of $1.4 billion in "popular premium" wines ($3.00–$6.99 per bottle), $1.02 billion in "superpremium" wines ($7.00–$13.99 per bottle), and $460 million in "ultrapremium" wines ($14.00 per bottle and up). Continued growth in dollar sales of higher-priced super- and ultrapremium wines have more than offset a steady decrease in per capita consumption since 1987. As a result, demand for lower-priced jug wines and low-end imports have decreased dramatically. The resulting phenomenon is dubbed by the wine industry as a trend toward "drinking less but drinking better."

The high-end wine segment in which Ambrosia specializes is popular with both consumers and wineries, showing sustained growth and offering participating wineries larger profit margins in what is an overall shrinking market. This market segment is dominated by small independent producers, with 70 percent of case sales driven by wineries that produced fewer than 100,000 cases per year. No "typical" winery exists in this fragmented industry segment. These wineries range from boutiques, which make and sell only a few thousand cases of high-end wine, to Robert Mondavi Winery, one of the largest premium wine producers in the world with production in the hundreds of thousands of cases per year.

The 1980s saw a change in the distribution channel structure of the wine industry. While the traditional three-tier structure still exists, there has been significant consolidation in the number and power of wine wholesalers (the middle link in the chain from manufacturer to broker and/or wholesaler/distributor to retailer). As the number of wholesalers decreased, the number of brands being carried by each wholesaler has increased, thereby decreasing wholesaler attention to any one brand. The increased power of wine wholesalers was being felt most strongly by smaller wineries, who had little leverage over distributors even before the consolidation. It was these wineries in particular that could be helped most by DM, and on which VDI focused.

Drinking Less, But Drinking Better.   VDI research confirmed that while total U.S. wine consumption continued its decline, the super- and ultrapremium wine segment's growth was strong. In addition, industry experts attested to the fact that the taste/quality of premium California Cabernet Sauvignon begins to peak at 10 years of age, but unfortunately most of these wines are sold after only three years and thus consumed "before their time."

VDI's primary research, through consumer surveys, focus groups, and in-depth interviews with wine industry personnel, revealed that fine wine drinkers wanted to buy, and were willing to pay a premium price for, properly aged California Cabernet Sauvignon, but often had difficulty finding them on retail shelves. In addition to age and availability, research showed that these consumers had a strong demand for selection and variety and had increased knowledge of wines and would be responsive to a DM offer that addressed these needs.

Direct Marketing.   In the late 1980s, several factors were thought to be revolutionizing the direct-mail world. From the consumers' point of view, DM met their changing demographic needs for convenience. The increase in dual-income households had decreased the time available for shopping and led to a surge in "armchair" shopping via mail-order catalogs or direct-response offers. Traditional negative consumer reaction to DM had dissipated with more sophisticated offerings from direct marketers. Past concerns that the product "won't fit/work/be any good/be what I expected" were handled through confidence-building money-back guarantees and excellent customer service. Long delivery lead times were replaced by prompt, even overnight, fulfillment. Ordering and payment became easier with the increased use of 1-800 numbers and credit cards. The success of upscale direct marketers, such as L. L. Bean and The Sharper Image, proved that not only cheap, low-quality goods were offered through the DM channel. Instead consumers were increasingly able to find high-end items that offered an emotional "image"-based appeal, yet also offered a value in terms of price, availability, and/or selection.

From the manufacturer's point of view, one primary benefit of DM was greater channel control. Through DM, manufacturers were able to target their consumers precisely. They could tell a complete "story" without relying on the ability and incentives of intermediary channel members. Other key benefits for the manufacturer included the ability to control marketing costs and increase profits through DM. Every aspect of a DM campaign was designed to generate a response that is measurable, testable, and data-base driven, thus converting the abstract aspect of marketing into a universal language of numbers.

VDI believed that its selection of products, beginning with the hard-to-find properly aged California Cabernet Sauvignon, would meet both of these needs. Information technology breakthroughs in data-base management and desktop publishing continued to increase the effectiveness and profitability of this channel option and promised to allow Vintage Directions to develop efficiencies of scale by managing multiple winery mailing lists.

The Premium Wine Consumer.   VDI found that although 42 percent of the U.S. population drinks wine, almost half (49 percent) of the total U.S. wine volume was consumed by only 3 percent of the population. In 1989, this translated into 5 million adults drinking five bottles per week. Therefore, VDI concluded that the wine consumer market niche was a perfect fit for direct marketing: large volumes of wine were consumed by a small, but identifiable and reachable segment.

Fit with Mail-Order Consumer Profile.   Further industry research performed by VDI indicated that the consumer segment most likely to buy via direct marketing strongly overlapped the premium wine drinker profile **(see Exhibit 4).** Specifically, they were of the same age group (35–45 years), tended to have advanced educations (college or graduate school) and high income levels ($60,000 plus per year).

Direct Mail for Premium Wine Consumers.   VDI consumer surveys and focus group results showed that the proposed concept of selling premium California Cabernet Sauvignon through a direct-marketing channel had strong potential with both wine enthusiasts/experts and those who wish to become enthusiasts/experts. Fifty-five percent of the respondents to a VDI survey, all frequent consumers of California Cabernet

Sauvignon or French Bordeaux, indicated that they would consider purchasing wine through a mail-order/direct-response offer. A clear desire for mixed cases of hard-to-find, properly aged premium wines, for which these consumers are willing to pay a premium price, also emerged from the primary research. VDI intended to enhance its direct-marketing offer by meeting those identifiable needs.

Secondary Markets.   VDI also intended to pursue the new restaurant (made up of high-end restaurants that had not had time or capital to build an extensive wine cellar yet still wanted to offer an impressive wine list) and corporate gift markets, both of which remained untapped by the DM channel.

Geographic Scope.   VDI focused its offer on premium wine enthusiasts in California and its five "reciprocal" states (where it was legal to sell wine via DM). In 1991, the reciprocal states included: New Mexico, Colorado, Oregon, Missouri, and Wisconsin. Two additional states, Illinois and Washington, were expected to be added in 1992. These eight states consumed a total of 191 million gallons of wine annually, or 35 percent of total U.S. wine consumption. A grass-roots approach was to be pursued in each state that would include local PR efforts through area food and wine experts, and through wine-interest/enthusiast groups. The super- and ultrapremium wine market size in these eight states was estimated at over $533 million in annual sales.

Competition.   At the time VDI incorporated, there were only a handful of companies offering wine by direct mail, most of which handled either small, boutique wines or special labels for bulk wine. Some of these were "wine-of-the-month" clubs, which usually offered two bottles per month of selected wines of varying quality.

Some wineries also pursued DM themselves, but at varying levels of seriousness and effectiveness. Only 19 of the 700 plus California wineries had been acknowledged by their peers as industry experts in DM.

VDI viewed new DM competitors emerging as a reflection of the industry belief that there was both room and need for more direct marketing of wine. The entries also demonstrated that barriers were relatively low. VDI sought to raise the entry and mobility barriers to new and existing competitors by building brand equity in the Ambrosia name and its associated DM products.

Team/Operations.   The complimentary backgrounds of the VDI team covered all functional areas of the operation (**see Exhibit 5** for team résumés).

Lesley Berglund's professional experience was in consumer products sales management and merchandising as well as strategic management consulting. For five years before HBS, she managed large-scale consumer products sales projects and teams. She completed a number of distribution channel strategy consulting projects. As a third generation Napa Valley native, Lesley had extensive contacts in the California wine industry. Her focus at VDI was on product management for the Ambrosia catalog (product procurement, positioning, and pricing as well as supplier relations). She split the remainder of her time between raising capital and developing new business leads for M&M Services projects.

Greg Berglund's professional experience in MIS included substantial background in systems design, integration, and installation of microprocessor-based hardware platforms for small to medium-sized businesses. His software application expertise contributed directly to VDI's need for sophisticated data-base management of its mailing lists. All operational issues associated with the data base were managed by Greg. He also was prepared to use his computer expertise to recommend and obtain hardware and software, install systems, and train staff for VDI's M&M Services clients.

Lisa Mangano's professional experience included account management and production for several advertising agencies and an NBC-TV affiliate. She offered a breadth of knowledge of both the process and production of direct-marketing campaigns through her background in both advertising and her family's New York-based direct-mail printing business. Lisa's creative and copy writing talents led the design and production of the Ambrosia catalog as well as DM campaigns for VDI's M&M Services clients. In addition, Lisa looked forward to managing Ambrosia's advertising and public relations campaigns.

Jim Pottow's experience as an analyst with an international consulting firm included evaluating start-ups and providing strategic and financial consulting to small businesses. His work in his family's Canadian retailing business exposed him to consumer product sales and customer relations. Jim's focus at VDI had been financial management and order processing. In addition to designing and maintaining the financial model on which the business plan was based, his duties included bookkeeping, inventory management, accounts payable, order input, and tracking.

All team members evenly split the duties of manning the phones to take customers' orders as well as the manual labor process of packing and shipping orders. VDI had no additional employees.

Financing.   The initial capitalization for the corporation was a nominal amount split evenly among Greg, Lesley, Lisa, and Jim. The founders also agreed to forgo salary for the first six months of operation. A special $25,000 debt issue was also arranged for George Schofield that was convertible to 1,000 shares of the company in lieu of principal repayment. George indicated that he would convert his debt into equity once the remaining financing was secured.

Nearly immediately after incorporating, the management team began going after start-up financing, focusing primarily on family and friends. They decided to attempt to raise initial capital of $200,000 through straight debt, under the following terms:

- $200,000 in straight debt to be raised in blocks of $5,000, with a minimum investment of $15,000.
- Fixed annual interest rate at the maximum allowed by California State Usury Law (then estimated at 11.5 percent).
- Interest payments deferred for 18 months.
- Interest payments made quarterly after the first 18 months.
- Repayment of the principal, 25 percent at the end of year 3, 75 percent at the end of year 4.
- Principal personally guaranteed by the founders, based on future earnings.

VDI also offered these investors access to Ambrosia wine at a 20 percent discount over the life of the loan.

Making presentations on the debt offer forced Lesley to confront her commitment to the consulting firm:

> I had already negotiated with them for a start date in January, because I originally wanted a six-month break. They knew that I would be spending the time working on a wine project in Napa Valley, but after that they were expecting me in their San Francisco office.
>
> But when you are trying to attract investors for a service business like VDI, you aren't selling assets, you're selling yourselves. We had to be able to say that they would be investing in the team—Lesley, Greg, Lisa, and Jim—and we were stable and committed to making VDI succeed. So unless I resigned from my future employer, I would need to talk out both sides of my mouth, and I knew I couldn't do that. I went to the consulting firm in July and told them I wouldn't be coming back. We worked out a schedule to repay my signing bonus and they were very understanding and supportive of me; they encouraged me to reapply if the wine project didn't work out.

The initial debt offering brought in $45,000 from three investor groups that each invested in $15,000 units.

Direct-Mail Performance.   The first test of VDI's concept came in September 1991, when it spent $9,000 for outside creative work, printing, and postage to send out a test mailer focused on mixed cases of ultrapremium 10-year-old Cabernet Sauvignon under the Ambrosia brand name. This first mailing was a 12,000-piece newsletter and generated $12,000 in revenue with a 0.29 percent response rate (number of orders generated/number of pieces mailed) and an average order size of $366. This first attempt tested 12 different lists; VDI determined from the response that 5 of the original lists performed well enough to justify repeat mailings.

Next VDI expanded Ambrosia into a full catalog offering 50 wines, sparkling wines, ports, wine-related gifts, and gourmet food baskets, which represented products from several top vintners. In November, a 16-page catalog was mailed to 45,000 names from the 50 different lists, including the 5 that had tested highest in the September mailing. This catalog cost $33,000 for outside creative work, printing, and postage. This time, the response was $35,000 in revenue with a .31 percent response rate and an average order of $255. In this mailing, the library Cabernet collection still accounted for 61 percent of total revenue, but there was interest demonstrated in a broader product mix, including white wines, younger vintages, and a broad range of prices. VDI considered breadth important since the top 10 items (20 percent of total items offered) only accounted for 50 percent of sales. The net unit sales mix from the first mailing was 50 percent red wine, 30 percent white wine, and 20 percent non-wine products despite the fact that 80 percent of all products offered were red wine. Of the 50 different lists tested in the November mailing, 11 were deemed successful enough for further mailings. (See **Exhibit 6** for statistical data including analysis of per piece ''in-the-mail'' costs, response rates, and average order size.)

As of January 1992, the Ambrosia house list of buyers included over 150 customers who had spent an average of $310 per order (as compared to a DM industry average order size of $60). The reorder rate between the first and second mailer was high, at 43 percent. The reorder rate within the second mailing alone was also high at 10 percent. One-thousand eighty dollars spent on test ads in *The Wine Spectator* and *Wine & Spirits* magazines generated 93 potential customers who called VDI to request a catalog. Of these prequalified leads (referred to as "two-step" customers), 4 percent actually ordered.

Strategic Considerations.   With the second "test" mailing complete, VDI decided to focus only on the mailing lists that had proven to be successful. These successful list categories were dominated by proven direct-mail buyers of wine (lists of their best customers provided for free by the wineries) and/or wine accessories (rental names from various catalogs). They planned to concentrate on improving response rates by cutting back the number of pieces mailed to 20,000 for the Spring 1992 catalog and concentrating just on these proven list segments.

New initiatives that the team was considering were:

- A wine industry cooperative consumer data-base management project that would allow winery participants (and Ambrosia) to rent proven direct-mail wine buyer names from each other. This project would also generate substantial management fees for VDI.
- A program tested in the winter 1991 mailing that included an introductory cover letter from the vintner who lent VDI its mailing list when catalogs were mailed to new winery lists.
- An aggressive advertising and PR program to generate more qualified two-step names, followed up with an outbound telemarketing program.

As the team members examined the financial results to date **(see Exhibit 7),** they saw a need to switch from the original debt financing offer to an equity offer. The original debt instrument had provided $45,000. With George Schofield's $25,000 convertible note, total capitalization stood at $70,000. Management had also made an interim loan of $10,000 to the company to get through the November mailing. This drained the balance of their personal savings accounts and made the need to start drawing salaries in January critical. Furthermore, VDI had realized after the first test mailer that capital needs would exceed the original $200,000 estimate. (See **Exhibit 8** for proposed capitalization recap.) They had tentatively agreed on an equity offer under the following terms:

> VDI investors would purchase 5,000 shares of common stock (equaling 33.3 percent equity in the company) for $30 per share totaling $150,000 subject to provisions regarding anti-dilution, protective provisions, redemption rights, right of first refusal, key man insurance, and co-sale. In addition, the team was considering providing for a seat on the board of directors for investors obtaining 1,000 shares of stock or more.

Personal Considerations.   The downtime after the completion of the second mailing left the team with some time to consider the personal aspects of being young entrepreneurs. Greg's previous success at an entrepreneurial company had convinced him that he was cut out for the often frantic pace, but he was concerned that he might be creating a life that lacked balance.

In every sense of the expression, I think you can say that I have put all of my eggs in one basket. I have my career, my family, and my personal life all tied up in the same tiny office. Lisa and I talk about it all of the time—is the success of our business dependent on the success of our relationship, and vice versa? I also feel pangs every day about what I gave up in Boston; even though I left on relatively good terms I probably couldn't go back. Lesley knows that she could always go back to consulting, and Lisa's old manager at Leo Burnett often calls her to let her know there's always a place for her. But I feel a little bit trapped, although I could always throw in the towel and go to business school.

Lisa was much less worried about the problems that might come from mixing her professional and personal life, but more concerned about the material sacrifices that came along with VDI:

A lot of people think that Greg and I are insane to do this, but I have a really different outlook because of my parents. They ran this small company while I was growing up and it only made their relationship stronger—they actually *like* being together 24 hours a day.

The thing that is weighing on me now is the constant panic I feel about money. I'm not starving or anything, but this really isn't the way I thought I would be living as a 28-year-old business school graduate. I'm willing to work hard, but I'm not sure I see the reward at the end of the line.

Lesley felt that her transition had probably been the least traumatic, but was beginning to notice the strain her career choice was making on her:

It was probably less frightening for Greg and me to come out here than for Jim or Lisa, since we grew up in the area and knew a lot of people. The isolation factor of country living has only recently become an issue, but it is a serious one. We have been much too busy to worry about a social life, but it has finally dawned on me that I haven't really done anything besides work in a long, long time.

I am living with my grandmother to save money, but I don't think that can go on forever. Lisa and Greg are living together and they kind of have their social life taken care of, so maybe they feel less isolated.

It's funny; our original idea was that this is direct mail, we could be located anywhere. Maybe eventually we could move down to San Francisco or somewhere in the Bay Area, but right now we still have too much to do with the wineries. Since I have the most contact with the wineries I would have to commute the one and one-half hours north from San Francisco nearly every day.

Jim Pottow's Decision.   The decision of Jim to leave the company just six months into its launch affected the remaining team members in different ways, but all three agreed that it did not spell disaster for VDI. Greg saw Jim's decision as almost noble:

I know that Jim has done a lot for us, and feel very positively about him as a person. But I can still see his leaving as a positive step for us. In many ways, I feel like he's leaving to help us, to do what he can to make sure we survive. It was becoming obvious that we are just plain overstaffed and we definitely have too much horsepower. Four is a lot of mouths to feed.

I also think that Jim might be feeling like much of the work he had to do is done, whereas the things that call on the strengths of Lisa and me, and to a lesser extent Lesley, are just now really beginning. Jim has set up some powerful systems for us when and if we do experience the growth that we're all hoping for. But I don't think he's willing to wait around until that happens.

Lisa's reaction to Jim's announcement was colored by her own financial concerns:

My very first thought was, "Now, what do *I* do?" At this point, I've completely blown through my savings, and we still haven't been able to agree on a partner draw structure so that we can begin to take some form of salary out of the company. I'm truly desperate—I have a loan repayment schedule that doesn't really lend itself to being a struggling entrepreneur. I have even made an arrangement to take on a temporary bar management position so I can bring in some cash. For three nights a week in January, I am going to be the night manager at a friend's bar near here.

There are also things that have been very tough on both Jim and I about being out here. Lesley is living with her grandmother, and Greg and I are living at their mother's house. Their father is giving us free office space, and everywhere you go around here its Berglund, Berglund, Berglund. It's very hard for me to take, and I think it is that much harder for Jim.

Lesley was surprised at how little discussion and controversy the move generated:

It's strange. He just said it, and we all kind of took it in. None of us will try to stop him, in part because we have talked about this and planned for a graceful "divorce" and in part because we know it might be the best thing for all of us. But it does raise a whole lot of questions in regard to ownership, and how are we going to be able to raise the capital we need. We're really underfinanced right now, but we've also got to concentrate on transfer of knowledge issues and splitting up the work that Jim was doing between the three of us who will be left.

Jim leaving is also going to make it more difficult for us to make a decision to switch over from debt to equity, which we've been discussing. He wants to walk away with his 10 percent of the company, and it makes me at least extremely reluctant to go out there and give away another 30 or 40 percent. We also have to resolve the salary issue, because Lisa isn't the only one who has gone through all of her savings. The fundamental thing I think we should get straight now is just what we all expect and are willing to put up with, and if it looks like we will be able to make that happen or not. Essentially we have to figure it all out: do we have a business here or not?

EXHIBIT 1   The Wine Market (1981–1990)

Year	Gallons (Millions)	Change Previous Year (%)
1990	508.1	−(2.8)
1989	522.9	−(5.2)
1988	552.2	−(4.2)
1987	576.7	−(1.9)
1986	586.6	1.1
1985	580.3	4.7
1984	554.4	5.0
1983	528.1	2.7
1982	514.0	1.6
1981	505.7	5.4

SOURCE: Beverage Marketing Corporation; Wine Institute

Wine per Capita Consumption

Year	U.S. Resident Population (000)	Per Capita Consumption (Gallons)	
		Amount	Change (%)
1990	249,891	2.04	−(3.3)
1989	247,737	2.11	−(6.2)
1988	245,901	2.25	−(5.1)
1987	243,510	2.37	−(2.5)
1986	241,078	2.43	0.0
1985	238,740	2.43	3.4
1984	236,158	2.35	3.9
1983	233,981	2.26	1.8
1982	231,534	2.22	0.9
1981	229,307	2.20	4.3

SOURCE: Beverage Marketing Corporation; Wine Institute; U.S. Bureau of Census

Exhibit 2   U.S. Wine Industry Product Breakdowns

Wine sales can be divided into 5 separate categories. Part A shows how the popularity of each has shifted over time along with the maturing of the American palate away from sweeter/fortified wines to premium table wines, particularly in the last few years.

(A) Percent of Wine Sales

	1980	*1987*	*1989*
Table wines	75.0%	58.3%	64.7%
Wine coolers	na	21.0%	18.0%
Champagne/sparkling wines	6.2%	7.3%	7.3%
Dessert/fortified wines	16.8%	12.3%	8.9%
Vermouths	1.8%	1.1%	1.1%

Source: The Wine Institute

Table wines are further divided into generics and varietals. Since any varietal over $3 per bottle is called a "premium wine," further distinctions have been made in Part B.

(B) Market Segments (1991)

	Price Range	*Dollar Sales (billion)*
Popular premium	$ 3.00–$6.99/Bottle	$1.4
Superpremium	$ 7.00–$13.99/Bottle	$1.02
Ultrapremium	$14.00 and up/Bottle	$ .460
Total		$2.9

Source: The Gomberg-Fredrickson Report, March 3, 1992.

VDI competes in both the super- and ultrapremium segments of the wine industry. No further breakdown is available above $14 per bottle price range, where Vintage Directions, Inc., markets most of its high-end wine.

Exhibit 3   Wine Industry Channel Economics

By taking the same bottle of wine sold at a $10 retail price to the consumer through various channel options, we can understand the economic impact of alternate distribution channel strategies available to Unique Wines, Inc. These rough examples are listed in order of increasing profitability to UWI. Distribution and inventory costs are ignored.

(A) Direct Sales to Retailers/Restaurants

Initially the most expensive option, but sales reps' effectiveness can improve efficiencies as volume increases. High control of the sales process is maintained.

Retailer price to consumer	$10.00
UWI price to retailer	$ 6.65
Less: Sales' rep salary	$ 2.00 (assume $30,000 salary driving 15,000 case sales)
Net cash to UWI	$ 4.65/bottle

(B) Distributor Channel to Retailers/Restaurants

Less expensive than direct sales, but very little, if any, channel control.

Retailer price to consumer	$10.00
Distributor price to retailer	$ 6.65
UWI price to distributor	$ 5.00
Net cash to UWI	$ 5.00/bottle

(C) Broker Channel

More profitable than distributor channel, but this does not demonstrate increased distribution charges. Also very little channel control.

Retailer price to consumer	$10.00
UWI price to retailer	$ 6.65
Less: 15% broker commission	$ .67
Net cash to UWI	$ 5.98/bottle

(D) Direct Mail

Bypasses the three-tiered channel system. Once DM program scale is hit, increases UWI profitability vs. other alternatives. Also provides complete control of the sales process.

UWI price to consumer	$10.00
Less: 25% DM variable costs	$ 2.50
Net cash to UWI	$ 7.50/bottle

Exhibit 4   Wine Consumer Profile

Roper Survey:

In June 1990, a Roper Survey interviewed a nationally representative sample of 1,500 adults. Their findings on wine consumer demographics included:

51% of wine drinkers are men (58% of ''frequent'' wine drinkers)
47% are Republican (vs. 38% Democrats)
44% are White

Consumption increases as income levels increase. Average wine drinking household income = $40,000 vs. ''frequent'' drinkers = $67,000 and nondrinkers = $30,900. Peak age for wine consumption is 30 to 44 years old, and as these baby boomers continue to age a further shift from beer to wine is expected. Attitudes and habits of these consumers include:

80% believe its OK to drink wine (vs. 20% who favor renewed prohibition)
75% support warning labels on all packaging and advertising
75% of all wine is consumed at home, over dinner

The total sample ranked wine #7 as a ''healthy beverage,'' ahead of beer and spirits. Wine drinkers are ''believers,'' for they rank wine #3, equal with milk and tap water.

Les Amis du Vin:

The demographic profile for *Les Amis du Vin's* 80,000 readers validates the findings from the Roper Survey and gives further insight into the premium wine consumer's habits. Their reader profile is as follows:

38% are between 35 and 49 years old
56% are men
64% have completed graduate work or degree
61% have incomes greater than $50,000 (30% have incomes greater than $80,000)
81% are married
38% have a 2-person household (childless yuppies)
88% own their own home

Primary Research:

The following recaps a survey conducted by the company in March 1991. Over 2,500 surveys were sent out to Harvard Business School students, faculty, staff, and administration, and to consultants and staff at the MAC Group, resulting in a 4% response rate. Nondrinkers of fine red wine were discouraged from responding. In April 1991, this research was followed up with two focus groups. Highlights from this research include:

• A strong response to a mixed case/direct-marketing offer of 10-year-old Cabernet Sauvignon across heavy drinkers (67%), moderate drinkers (89%), and even light drinkers (75%) of fine red wine.
• Evidence that such a DM offer would meet consumers desire for aged wines, mixed cases, and information about the wines.
• Most heavy and moderate drinkers of fine red wine read *The Wine Spectator, Gourmet, Food & Wine, Wine Enthusiast,* and *The Wine Advocate.*

GREGORY ROSS BERGLUND

Business Experience

1989–present   AEGIS ASSOCIATES, INC.   CAMBRIDGE, MA
Marketing Representative—for a start-up 7-person value added reseller
- Focused on the systems integration of personal computers; Novell networking, computer aided design, and systems implementation consulting
- Assisted in firm sales growth from $.3 to $1.5 million in 18 months.
- Significant events/roles include:
  Offered partnership—50% equity in the firm, 9/90—age 23
  Management role—initiated, wrote, and implemented a firmwide mission statement, operating principle, and operating policy; established core process oriented business systems
  Technical manager & resource—managed two full-time technicians: sold, planned, assembled, installed, managed, tuned, trained, and supported Novell networks & CAD systems

summer 1988   BERGLUND, INC.   NAPA, CA
Accounts Receivable Collector—for a Caterpillar Inc. dealership
- Collected delinquent debts from recent sale of assets
- $1.7 million (90%) collected in 90 days—300% of objective

Education

1985–1989   WESLEYAN UNIVERSITY   MIDDLETOWN, CT
- BA in Economics, June 1989

fall 1987   THE NATIONAL OUTDOOR LEADERSHIP SCHOOL   LANDER, WY
- Studied Sociology, Geology, Ecology, & Wilderness Management

1981–1985   THE THACHER SCHOOL   OJAI, CA
- Small college preparatory school
- Commendations: Physics and Music
- Senior prefect, "A" camper (top 6%), horse owner

Other Achievements

WESLEYAN UNIVERSITY OARSMAN: 1986 First Freshman Boat: 1987 First Varsity Boat. Success driven by top physical conditioning and working with and through others. 1st place New England Intercollegiate Rowing Championships (1987); Silver Medalist at Dad Vail National Regatta (1987).

FANATIC OUTDOORSMAN: At the National Outdoor Leadership School (NOLS) developed leadership, cooperative, and survival skills in stress-filled conditions while rock climbing, caving, high altitude backpacking, winter camping, and high desert surviving.

Personal

Born in Napa Valley, California.

LESLEY P. BERGLUND

Education

9/89–6/91 HARVARD GRADUATE SCHOOL OF BUSINESS ADMINISTRATION   Boston, MA
M.B.A. Candidate, June 1991. General Management curriculum. Tutor for first-year Marketing and Management Communications courses. HBS Show Board Member '91, Design Director '90. Vice President, Small Business & New Enterprise Club.

8/80–6/84 WESLEYAN UNIVERSITY   Middletown, CT
B.A. in Economics, June 1984. International curriculum concentration.

Fall 1982 Instituto Internacional   Madrid, Spain
Studied comparative economics, politics, and culture in Spanish.

Summer 1982 Richmond College   London, England
Studied multinational business organizations.

Experience

Summer 1990 to present THE MAC GROUP, Management Consulting   Cambridge, MA

Summer Associate
- *Distribution Channel Strategy.* Headed an in-depth analysis of the existing distribution channel activities, flows, and economics for the U.S. personal computer industry.
- Continuing as an independent consultant for MAC to identify channel system voids, overlaps, and constraints, and to develop an optimal needs-based channel strategy for PC manufacturing client.

9/85–7/89 THE CLOROX COMPANY, Special Markets Sales Division

5/89–7/89 Sales Merchandising, Special Assignment   Oakland, CA
- Developed and introduced "*Ad Power*," a revolutionary sales tool now used by both field sales and the trade.

7/87–4/89 Northeast Area Sales Manager   Boston, MA
- Set company record by reaching ASM level after 22 months vs. normal 6-year track.
- Achieved broad-scale sales successes: $30 million in annual sales throughout 14 states. Exceeded annual volume and merchandising objectives by 25%. Doubled national accounts' volume.
- Hired, trained, and managed 4 Clorox Account Managers
- Initiated and designed "*MVP*," a $1.5 million volume-based co-op allowance program. Sold program to senior management. Coordinated implementation across functions including sales, marketing, finance, information, and legal services.

2/86–6/87 New England District Manager   Boston, Ma

9/85–1/86 Philadelphia Territory Manager   Philadelphia, PA

8/84–8/85 PROCTER & GAMBLE DISTRIBUTING COMPANY, Beverage Division
Sales Representative   Philadelphia, PA

summer 1983 CODORNIU, S.A., Sparkling Wine Manufacturer   Barcelona, Spain
Translator, Export, Public Relations and Marketing Departments

Capabilities

Recognized Problem-Solver: Effected client and internal corporate organizational changes through analytical and creative recommendations.

Effective Communicator: Developed persuasive sales and public speaking skills. Formulated incisive written and graphic presentations.

Motivational Manager: Applied interpersonal skills to produce outstanding results through diverse personnel and clientele.

Personal

Proficient in Spanish and basic French. Avocations include the wine industry, agribusiness, and real estate. Avid reader and varsity tennis player.
Born in Napa Valley, California 7/17/62.

LISA MANGANO

Education

1988–1990   HARVARD GRADUATE SCHOOL OF BUSINESS ADMINISTRATION   BOSTON, MA
Master in Business Administration degree, June 1990. General Management curriculum. Tutor for first-year Management Communications course. Marketing Club Career Fair host/coordinator. Active member Arts & Media Club, Entrepreneurship Club. Elected section representative to Southeastern Club. Winner of *Harbus News* Scholarship for media related employment (Summer 1989).

1982–1986   UNIVERSITY OF RICHMOND   RICHMOND, VA
Bachelor of Arts, *summa cum laude,* in Sociology and Speech Communications. Cumulative GPA 4.00; graduated first in class of 545. Scholastic honors include Phi Beta Kappa, Mortar Board (Scholarship, Leadership, and Community Service), Omicron Delta Kappa (Leadership), and Alpha Kappa Delta. Rhodes Scholarship Nominee. Other activities include election as secretary of Student Athletic Board, secretary of Westhampton College Judicial Board, and award of Undergraduate Research Grant in Sociology.

Business Experience

9/90–Present   LEO BURNETT COMPANY, INC.   CHICAGO, IL
Client Service Associate. Managing new product account for Kraft General Foods. Responsible for tracking and reporting business results, and for working with client and agency to develop and implement marketing and business plans.

Summer 1989   WESH-TV BROADCASTING COMPANY   ORLANDO, FL
News Intern. Assisted in news-gathering, writing, and producing three daily evening news broadcasts. Worked closely with anchors, reports, producers, and technicians on all aspects of the management and operation of the NBC affiliate station.

1987–1988   LOWELL/HARRISON, INC.   ROCKVILLE CENTRE, NY
Media Director/Account Executive. Developed and presented extensive media plans and analyses to clients on an annual and on-going basis. Managed client relations with major health-care and consumer accounts for this small, quickly growing agency. Worked in all facets of the field, from writing ad and public relations copy to creating, presenting, and producing multimedia campaigns. Personally responsible for origination, selection, and implementation of new computer system.

1986–1987   DREXEL BURNHAM LAMBERT INC.   NEW YORK, NY
Financial Analyst, Corporate Finance. Prepared in-depth industry and company analyses for proposed financings. Participated in drafting and filing documents and prospectuses; organized marketing of offerings.

Other Experience

Extensive public speaking experience. Internships held with two major advertising agencies and the UR departments of Athletic Marketing and Sports Information. Conducted search for new university president as only undergraduate member of UR Presidential Selection Committee. Currently serve as key career consultant for the University of Richmond.

Personal

Involved in family printing business. Enjoy snow-skiing and all water sports. Avid reader on a broad range of topics.

JAMES G. POTTOW

Education

1989–1991   HARVARD GRADUATE SCHOOL OF BUSINESS ADMINISTRATION   BOSTON, MA
Candidate for Master in Business Administration degree, June 1991. Course concentration in General Management and Entrepreneurship. Selected by faculty to tutor first-year students. Elected treasurer of boat club and president of Rugby Club. Regular contributor to *Harbus* newspaper.

1983–1987   QUEEN'S UNIVERSITY   KINGSTON, ONT
Awarded Honors Bachelor of Commerce degree, June 1987. Majors in Marketing and Finance. Awarded D. I. McCleod Academic Scholarship. Selected to represent Queen's at National Business Conference. Co-editor of faculty newspaper. President, University Wine Society. Member of Queen's Rowing Team.

1985–1986   CAMBRIDGE UNIVERSITY   CAMBRIDGE, U.K.
Initiated a Junior Year Abroad program for Queen's students at Girton College. Structured an advanced year of study in Economics. Honors on all exams. Member of College May Boat and College First Rugby Team.

Experience

Summer 1990   RISC SERVICES, S.A.   PARIS, FRANCE
Project Manager: Developed business plan for a $100 million gold jewellery retail chain for potential corporate investors/partners. Responsible for directing input from design, marketing, real estate, operations and information technology teams, as well as preparing summary document/presentation including financial projections and analysis.

1987–1989   BAIN AND COMPANY, INC.   LONDON, U.K.
Associate Consultant: Designed and implemented competitive strategy for large multinational companies across several different industries as a member of small client teams.
- Designed national brand and distribution strategy for major drinks manufacturer, resulting in the $3 million repurchase of key distribution rights.
- Worked directly with senior partner in evaluating $3 billion acquisition proposal, having previously screened several medium-sized acquisitions.
- Assessed market attractiveness of "add-on" services for industrial packaging manufacturer. Interviewed customers, competitors, and suppliers.
- Conducted market penetration study for large U.K. retailing chain.

Summer 1987   GENERAL FOODS CANADA   TORONTO, ONT
Marketing Analyst: Researched and formulated product development and marketing strategy for the convenience store industry. Structured own workplan, ran successful test market of new product, and presented conclusions directly to senior management.

Summer 1984   THE BECKER MILK COMPANY, LTD   TORONTO, ONT
Convenience Store Manager: Managed store with $500,000 annual sales and $60,000 inventory. Reversed declining sales trend and showed substantial performance improvement by concentrating on better merchandising, customer relations, suggestive selling and staff motivation.

Personal

Canadian and British citizenship. Interests include film, music, wine, skiing, writing.

EXHIBIT 6A   The Ambrosia Catalog

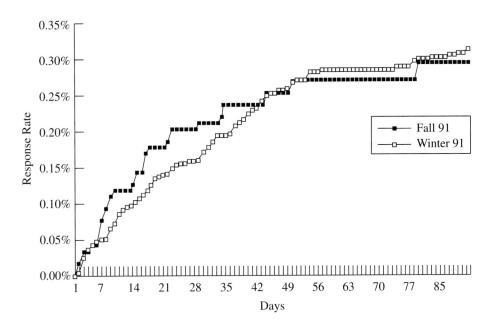

EXHIBIT 6B   The Ambrosia Catalog

	1991 Test Mailer				1991 Winter Catalog				Projected 1992 Spring Catalog			
	Total Cost	Cost per	Unit	Split	Total Cost	Cost per	Unit	Split	Total Cost	Cost per	Unit	Split
Printing	$2,229	$0.19		25%	$13,243	$0.29		41%	$8,800	$0.44		37%
Creative	1,060	$0.09		12%	4,069	$0.09		12%	10,000	$0.50		42%
Postage	3,584	$0.30		40%	12,388	$0.28		38%	3,300	$0.17		14%
Mailing list	2,081	$0.17		23%	2,991	$0.07		9%	1,900	$0.10		8%
Total in the mail	$8,954	$0.75		100%	$32,691	$0.73		100%	$24,000	$1.20		100%
Total pieces mailed	12,000				45,000				20,000			
Total orders	35				138				121			
Response rate	0.29%				0.31%				0.61%			
Total cases sold	32	0.91	/order		126	0.91	/order		169	1.4	/order	
Total revenue	$12,810	$366	/order		$35,244	$255	/order		$45,000	$372	/order	
Gross margin	31%				43%				34%			
Net income	$3,971	$113	/order		$15,155	$110	/order		$15,300	$126	/order	
Less: Fulfillment	(1,272)	(36)	/order		(3,825)	(28)	/order		(3,388)	(28)	/order	
Less: In the mail	(8,954)	(256)	/order		(32,691)	(237)	/order		(24,000)	(198)	/order	
Net profit/loss	($6,255)	($179)	/order		($21,361)	$(155)	/order		($12,088)	($100)	/order	

Exhibit 6C   The Ambrosia Catalog

List Performance	1991 Test Mailer				1991 Winter Catalog			
List Source	*# Mailed*	*% Total*	*Response Rate*	*Profit/Name*	*# Mailed*	*% Total*	*Response Rate*	*Profit/Name*
Winery lists	5,431	45%	0.20%	($0.49)	10,967	24%	0.40%	($ 0.51)
DM wine accessories	2,000	17%	0.20%	($0.52)	11,128	25%	0.20%	($ 0.62)
Wine clubs	0				7,370	16%	0.10%	($ 0.52)
DM food & gift	0				4,542	10%	0.20%	($ 0.66)
Publications	2,000	17%	0.20%	($0.64)	6,380	14%	0.00%	($ 0.74)
B&B guests	1,662	14%	0.10%	($0.62)	1,100	2%	0.00%	($ 0.65)
Two step	0				93	0%	3.70%	$ 0.05
Other/referral	907	8%	1.70%	$1.10	3,385	8%	1.50%	$ 0.06
House list	0				35	0%	43.00%	$48.00
Total	12,000	100%	0.29%	($0.52)	45,000	100%	0.31%	($ 0.47)

EXHIBIT 7A   Vintage Directions, Inc., Income Statement

	Actual 1991 6 Months		1992 Total		1993 Total		Forecast 1994 Total		1995 Total		1996 Total	
Revenue												
Ambrosia sales revenue	$ 48,000	97%	185,054	72%	1,673,459	88%	3,552,836	93%	5,655,858	94%	7,856,431	95%
Ambrosia co-op ad dollars (nonwine)	0	0%	0	0%	8,000	0%	16,000	0%	20,000	0%	24,000	0%
List rental income	0	0%	0	0%	12,555	1%	23,366	1%	69,026	1%	91,233	1%
M&M Services income	1,308	3%	73,693	28%	200,000	11%	220,000	6%	242,000	4%	266,200	3%
Total revenue	$ 49,308	100%	$ 258,747	100%	$1,894,014	100%	$3,812,202	100%	$5,986,884	100%	$8,237,865	100%
COGS/COPS:												
Ambrosia product costs	31,251	63%	109,182	42%	970,606	51%	1,954,060	51%	2,997,605	50%	3,928,216	48%
Total Ambrosia fulfillment	4,489	9%	17,138	7%	117,142	6%	248,699	7%	395,910	7%	549,950	7%
Total COPS—M&M Services	0	0%	37,061	14%	100,000	5%	132,000	3%	145,200	2%	159,720	2%
Total COGS/COPS	35,740	72%	163,381	63%	1,187,748	63%	2,334,758	61%	3,538,715	59%	4,637,886	56%
Gross profit	13,568	28%	95,366	37%	706,266	37%	1,477,444	39%	2,448,169	41%	3,599,979	44%
Operating expenses												
Selling expenses												
Catalog fixed	5,129	10%	19,246	7%	40,000	2%	40,000	1%	40,000	1%	40,000	0%
Catalog variable	37,572	76%	76,749	30%	200,000	11%	282,000	7%	282,000	5%	282,000	3%
List building	1,947	4%	28,404	11%	72,000	4%	72,000	2%	72,000	1%	72,000	1%
Total sales and marketing	44,648	91%	124,399	48%	312,000	16%	394,000	10%	394,000	7%	394,000	5%
General and administrative												
Rent	0	0%	13,920	5%	18,120	1%	22,820	1%	23,975	0%	25,189	0%
Salaries & wages	0	0%	94,384	36%	286,722	15%	451,018	12%	619,787	10%	839,468	10%
Other	11,131	23%	22,559	9%	75,761	4%	76,244	2%	119,738	2%	164,757	2%
Total general & administrative	11,131	23%	130,863	51%	380,603	20%	550,082	14%	763,500	13%	1,029,414	12%
Total operating expenses	55,779	113%	255,261	99%	692,603	37%	944,082	25%	1,157,500	19%	1,423,414	17%
Total operating income	−42,211	86%	−159,896	62%	13,663	1%	533,361	14%	1,290,669	22%	2,176,565	26%
Depreciation	4,371	9%	2,555	1%	3,842	0%	4,642	0%	5,042	0%	5,442	0%
Amortization	1,980	4%	2,180	1%	2,380	0%	2,380	0%	2,380	0%	600	0%
Interest income	29	0%	2,137	1%	8,842	0%	27,603	1%	67,111	1%	123,756	1%
Interest expense	2,525	5%	4,944	2%	4,725	0%	3,544	0%	0	0%	0	0%
Income before taxes	−51,058	−104%	−167,438	−65%	11,558	1%	550,398	14%	1,350,358	23%	2,294,279	28%
Income taxes	800	2%	800	0%	800	0%	165,119	4%	405,107	7%	917,712	11%
Net income	$ −51,858	−105%	$ −168,260	−65%	$ 10,758	1%	$ 385,279	10%	$ 945,250	16%	$1,376,568	17%

EXHIBIT 7B   Vintage Directions, Inc., Balance Sheet

	Actual 1991 6 months	Forecast 1992 Total	1993 Total	1994 Total	1995 Total	1996 Total
Current assets						
Cash	$ 3,560	− 23,704	$ 70,704	$ 517,264	$1,503,329	$2,946,231
Accounts receivable	0	0	14,569	29,325	46,053	63,368
Inventory	10,267	6,597	10,638	21,959	34,012	46,001
Prepaid & other	0	500	0	0	0	0
Total current assets	$ 13,827	$ − 16,607	$ 95,912	$ 568,547	$1,583,393	$3,055,601
Noncurrent assets						
Deposits	1,200	2,400	2,400	2,400	2,400	2,400
Loans to Officers	9,000	9,000	0	0	0	0
Total Fixed Assets	4,371	15,210	19,210	23,210	25,210	27,210
Accumulated Depreciation	− 4,371	− 6,926	− 10,768	− 15,410	− 20,452	− 25,894
Total Fixed Assets, Net	0	8,284	8,442	7,800	4,758	1,316
Organization Expenses	9,902	11,902	11,902	11,902	11,902	11,902
Accumulated Amortization	− 1,980	− 4,161	− 6,541	− 8,922	− 11,302	− 11,902
Intangible Assets Net	7,922	7,741	5,361	2,980	600	0
Total noncurrent assets	$ 18,122	$ 27,425	$ 16,202	$ 13,180	$ 7,758	$ 3,716
Total assets	$ 31,949	$ 10,818	$ 112,114	$ 581,727	$1,591,151	$3,059,316
Current liabilities						
Accounts Payable	$ 4,242	$ 678	$ 98,979	$ 194,563	$ 294,893	$ 386,490
Accruals	0	0	0	0	0	0
Bank Line of Credit	0	0	0	0	0	0
Loans from Officers	6,000	0	0	0	0	0
Total current liabilities	$ 10,242	$ 678	$ 98,979	$ 194,563	$ 294,893	386,490
Noncurrent liabilities						
Loans from Officers	1,025	1,025	0	0	0	0
Interest Payable	2,450	9,144	2,406	2,406	0	0
Subordinated Debt @ 10.5%	45,000	45,000	45,000	33,750	0	0
Subordinated Conv. Debt @ 10.5%	25,000	0	0	0	0	0
Total noncurrent liabilities	$ 73,475	$ 55,169	$ 47,406	36,156	0	0
Shareholder equity						
Common Stock/Paid in Capital	90	175,090	175,090	175,090	175,090	175,090
Retained Earnings (Deficit)	− 51,858	− 220,119	− 209,361	175,918	1,121,168	2,497,736
Total shareholder equity	$ − 51,768	$ − 45,029	$ − 34,271	$ 351,008	$1,296,258	$2,672,826
Total liabilities & equity	$ 31,949	$ 10,818	$ 112,114	$ 581,727	$1,591,151	$3,059,316

Exhibit 7C   Vintage Directions, Inc., Cash Flow

	Actual 1991 6 Months	Forecast				
		1992 Total	1993 Total	1994 Total	1995 Total	1996 Total
Net Income (Loss)	$ −51,858	$ −168,260	$ 10,758	$ 385,279	$ 945,250	$1,376,568
+ Depreciation	4,371	2,555	3,842	4,642	5,042	5,442
+ Amortization	1,980	2,180	2,380	2,380	2,380	600
Gross Cash Flow	$ −45,507	$ −163,525	$ 16,980	$ 392,301	$ 952,673	$1,382,610
Change in Working Capital						
Decrease/(increase) accounts receivable	0	0	−14,569	−14,755	−16,728	−17,315
Decrease/(increase) inventory	−10,267	3,670	−4,041	−11,320	−12,053	−11,990
Decrease/(increase) prepaid and other	0	−500	500	0	0	0
Increase/(decrease) accounts payable	4,242	−3,564	98,301	95,584	100,330	91,598
Increase/(decrease) accruals	0	0	0	0	0	0
Net change in working capital	$ −6,025	$ −394	$ 80,191	$ 69,509	71,548	$ 62,292
Cash from (for) operations	−51,532	−163,919	97,171	461,810	1,024,221	1,444,902
Investing activities						
Decrease/(increase) LT deposits	−1,200	−1,200	0	0	0	0
Decrease/(increase) capital expenditures	−4,371	−10,839	−4,000	−4,000	−2,000	−2,000
Decrease/(increase) intangible assets	−9,902	−2,000	0	0	0	0
Total investing activities	$ −15,473	$ −14,039	$ −4,000	$ −4,000	$ −2,000	$ −2,000
Financing activities						
Increase/(decrease) bank line of credit	0	0	0	0	0	0
Decrease/(increase) loans to officers	−9,000	0	9,000	0	0	0
Increase/(decrease) loans from officers	7,025	−6,000	−1,025	0	0	0
Increase/(decrease) interest payable	2,450	6,694	−6,738	0	−2,406	0
Increase/(decrease) sub. debt	45,000	0	0	−11,250	−33,750	0
Increase/(decrease) sub. convertible debt	25,000	−25,000	0	0	0	0
Increase/(decrease) common stock	90	175,000	0	0	0	0
Total financing activities	$ 70,565	$ 150,694	$ 1,238	$ −11,250	$ −36,156	0
Net change in cash	3,560	−27,264	94,408	446,560	986,065	1,442,902
Beginning cash balance	0	3,560	−23,704	70,704	517,264	1,503,329
Ending cash balance	$ 3,560	$ −23,704	$ 70,704	$ 517,264	$1,503,329	$2,946,231

EXHIBIT 7D Vintage Directions, Inc., Income Statement

	1/92 Actual	2/92 Actual	3/92 Actual	4/92 Actual	5/92 Actual	6/92 Actual	7/92 Budget	8/92 Budget	9/92 Budget	10/92 Budget	11/92 Budget	12/92 Budget	Total 1992 Budget	
Revenue														
Ambrosia sales revenue	0	3,842	2,593	2,488	18,720	16,924	8,049	8,049	8,049	38,780	38,780	38,780	185,054	72%
Ambrosia co-op ad dollars (nonwine)	0	0	0	0	0	0	0	0	0	0	0	0	0	0%
List rental income	0	0	0	0	0	0	0	0	0	0	0	0	0	0%
M&M Services income	1,275	1,958	8,068	946	6,468	14,978	5,000	7,000	7,000	7,000	7,000	7,000	73,693	28%
Total revenue	$ 1,275	$ 5,800	$ 10,661	$ 3,434	$ 25,188	$ 31,902	$ 13,049	$ 15,049	$ 15,049	$ 45,780	$ 45,780	$ 45,780	$ 258,747	100%
COGS/COPS:														
Ambrosia product costs	0	2,267	1,530	1,468	11,045	9,985	4,749	4,749	4,749	22,880	22,880	22,880	109,182	42%
Total Ambrosia fulfillment	609	220	287	163	938	2,277	724	724	724	3,490	3,490	3,490	17,138	7%
Total COPS—M&M Services	0	996	6,392	117	1,190	6,516	4,350	3,500	3,500	3,500	3,500	3,500	37,061	14%
Total COGS/COPS	$ 609	$ 3,483	$ 8,209	$ 1,748	$ 13,173	$ 18,778	$ 9,823	$ 8,973	$ 8,973	$ 29,870	$ 29,870	$ 29,870	$ 163,381	63%
Gross profit	$ 666	$ 2,317	$ 2,452	$ 1,686	$ 12,015	$ 13,123	$ 3,226	$ 6,076	$ 6,076	$ 15,910	$ 15,910	$ 15,910	$ 95,366	37%
Operating Expenses														
Selling Expenses														
Catalog fixed	0	750	6,259	512	2,325	0	0	0	9,400	0	0	0	19,246	7%
Catalog variable	827	395	518	4,417	1,502	7,960	1,300	1,500	58,830	500	500	500	76,749	30%
List building	750	540	3,383	1,111	1,080	540	1,080	3,000	7,920	3,000	3,000	3,000	28,404	11%
Total sales and marketing	$ 1,577	$ 1,685	$ 10,160	$ 6,040	$ 4,907	$ 8,500	$ 2,380	$ 4,500	$ 74,150	$ 3,500	$ 3,500	$ 3,500	$ 124,399	48%
General and administrative														
Rent	1,000	1,000	1,000	1,000	1,240	1,240	1,240	1,240	1,240	1,240	1,240	1,240	13,920	5%
Salaries and wages	4,600	4,336	4,683	8,222	5,183	18,561	6,994	7,066	8,541	11,066	7,566	7,566	94,384	36%
Other	1,662	867	2,209	1,814	2,484	2,917	2,345	1,545	1,545	1,781	1,545	1,845	22,559	9%
Total general and administrative	$ 7,262	$ 6,203	$ 7,892	$ 11,036	$ 8,907	$ 22,718	$ 10,579	$ 9,851	$ 11,326	$ 14,087	$ 10,351	$ 10,651	$ 130,863	51%
Total operating expenses	$ 8,839	$ 7,888	$ 18,052	$ 17,076	$ 13,814	$ 31,217	$ 12,959	$ 14,351	$ 85,476	$ 17,587	$ 13,851	$ 14,151	$ 255,261	99%
Total operating income	$ -8,173	$ -5,571	$ -15,600	$ -15,390	$ -1,799	$ 18,094	$ -9,733	$ -8,275	$ -79,400	$ -1,677	$ 2,059	$ 1,759	$ -159,896	-62%
Depreciation	149	149	149	232	232	232	232	232	232	232	232	254	2,555	1%
Amortization	165	165	165	165	165	165	198	198	198	198	198	198	2,180	1%
Interest income	113	131	141	138	116	125	108	58	471	237	234	243	2,115	1%
Interest expense	613	394	394	394	394	394	394	394	394	394	394	394	4,944	2%
Income before taxes	-8,988	-6,148	-16,167	-16,042	-2,473	-18,759	-10,449	-9,041	-79,753	-2,264	1,469	1,156	-167,460	-65%
Income taxes	0	0	0	800	0	0	0	0	0	0	0	0	800	0%
Net income	$ -8,988	$ -6,148	$ -16,167	$ -16,842	$ -2,473	$ -18,759	$ -10,449	$ -9,041	$ -79,753	$ -2,264	$ 1,469	$ 1,156	$ -168,260	-65%

EXHIBIT 7E Vintage Directions, Inc., Balance Sheet

	1/92 Actual	2/92 Actual	3/92 Actual	4/92 Actual	5/92 Actual	6/92 Actual	7/92 Budget	8/92 Budget	9/92 Budget	10/92 Budget	11/92 Budget	12/92 Budget
Current assets												
Cash	$ 134,246	$ 128,025	$ 112,474	$ 91,944	$ 89,980	$ 77,831	$ 60,773	$ 52,275	$ −26,256	$ −27,977	$ −25,966	$ −23,704
Accounts receivable	0	0	0	0	0	4,752	0	0	0	0	0	0
Inventory	10,267	10,267	10,077	10,077	10,077	9,127	9,127	9,127	8,447	8,447	8,447	6,597
Prepaid & other	0	500	500	500	500	500	500	500	500	500	500	500
Total current assets	$ 144,513	$ 138,792	$ 123,052	$ 102,522	$ 100,558	$ 92,211	$ 70,401	$ 61,902	$ −17,309	$ −19,030	$ −17,018	$ −16,607
Noncurrent assets												
Deposits	1,200	1,200	1,200	2,400	2,400	2,400	2,400	2,400	2,400	2,400	2,400	2,400
Loans to officers	9,000	9,000	9,000	9,000	9,000	9,000	9,000	9,000	9,000	9,000	9,000	9,000
Total fixed assets	8,968	8,968	8,968	13,901	13,901	13,901	13,901	13,901	13,901	13,901	13,901	15,210
Accumulated depreciation	−4,520	−4,670	−4,819	−5,051	−5,283	−5,514	−5,746	−5,978	−6,210	−6,441	−6,673	−6,926
Total fixed assets, net	4,448	4,298	4,149	8,850	8,618	8,387	8,155	7,923	7,692	7,460	7,228	8,284
Organization expenses	9,902	9,902	9,902	9,902	9,902	9,902	11,902	11,902	11,902	11,902	11,902	11,902
Accumulated amortization	−2,145	−2,310	−2,476	−2,641	−2,806	−2,971	−3,169	−3,367	−3,566	−3,764	−3,962	−4,161
Intangible assets net	7,757	7,592	7,427	7,261	7,096	6,931	8,733	8,535	8,336	8,138	7,940	7,741
Total noncurrent assets	$ 22,404	$ 22,090	$ 21,775	$ 27,511	$ 27,115	$ 26,718	$ 28,288	$ 27,858	$ 27,428	$ 26,998	$ 26,568	$ 27,425
Total assets	$ 166,917	$ 160,882	$ 144,827	$ 130,033	$ 127,672	$ 118,929	$ 98,689	$ 89,760	$ 10,119	$ 7,968	$ 9,549	$ 10,818
Current liabilities												
Accounts payable	$ 4,242	$ 3,742	$ 3,242	$ 4,678	$ 4,178	$ 3,678	$ 3,178	$ 2,678	$ 2,178	$ 1,678	$ 1,178	$ 678
Accruals	0	0	0	0	0	9,903	0	0	0	0	0	0
Bank line of credit	0	0	0	0	0	0	0	0	0	0	0	0
Loans from officers	0	0	0	0	0	0	0	0	0	0	0	0
Total current liabilities	$ 4,242	$ 3,742	$ 3,242	$ 4,678	$ 4,178	$ 13,581	$ 3,178	$ 2,678	$ 2,178	$ 1,678	$ 1,178	$ 678
Noncurrent liabilities												
Loans from officers	1,025	1,025	1,025	1,025	1,025	1,025	1,025	1,025	1,025	1,025	1,025	1,025
Interest payable	2,406	3,019	3,631	4,244	4,856	5,469	6,081	6,694	7,306	7,919	8,531	9,144
Subordinated debt @ 10.5%	45,000	45,000	45,000	45,000	45,000	45,000	45,000	45,000	45,000	45,000	45,000	45,000
Subordinated conv. debt @ 10.5%	25,000	0	0	0	0	0	0	0	0	0	0	0
Total noncurrent liabilities	$ 73,431	$ 49,044	$ 49,656	$ 50,269	$ 50,881	$ 51,494	$ 52,106	$ 52,719	$ 53,331	$ 53,944	$ 54,556	$ 55,169
Shareholder equity												
Common stock/paid in capital	150,090	175,090	175,090	175,090	175,090	175,090	175,090	175,090	175,090	175,090	175,090	175,090
Retained earnings (deficit)	−60,846	−66,994	−83,161	−100,003	−102,477	−121,236	−131,685	−140,727	−220,480	−222,744	−221,275	−220,119
Total shareholder equity	$ 89,244	$ 108,096	$ 91,929	$ 75,087	$ 72,613	$ 53,854	$ 43,405	$ 34,363	$ −45,390	$ −47,654	$ −46,185	$ −45,029
Total liabilities and equity	$ 166,917	$ 160,882	$ 144,827	$ 130,033	$ 127,672	$ 118,929	$ 98,689	$ 89,760	$ 10,119	$ 7,968	$ 9,549	$ 10,818

Exhibit 7F Vintage Directions, Inc., Cash Flow

	1/92 Actual	2/92 Actual	3/92 Actual	4/92 Actual	5/92 Actual	6/92 Actual	7/92 Budget	8/92 Budget	9/92 Budget	10/92 Budget	11/92 Budget	12/92 Budget	Total 1992 Budget
Net income (loss)	$ −8,988	$ −6,148	$ −16,167	$ −16,842	$ −2,473	$ −18,759	$ −10,449	$ −9,041	$ −79,753	$ −2,264	$ 1,469	$ 1,156	$ 168,260
+ Depreciation	149	149	149	232	232	232	232	232	232	232	232	254	2,555
+ Amortization	165	165	165	165	165	198	198	198	198	198	198	198	2,180
Gross cash flow	$ −8,673	$ −5,834	$ −15,853	$ −16,446	$ −2,077	$ −18,363	$ −10,019	$ −8,611	$ −79,323	$ −1,834	$ −1,899	$ −1,608	$ 163,525
Change in working capital													
Decrease/(increase) accounts rec.	0	0	0	0	0	−4,752	4,752	0	0	0	0	0	0
Decrease/(increase) inventory	0	0	190	0	0	950	0	0	680	0	0	1,850	3,670
Decrease/(increase) prepaid and other	0	−500	0	0	0	0	0	0	0	0	0	0	−500
Increase/(decrease) accounts payable	0	−500	−500	1,436	−500	−500	−500	−500	−500	−500	−500	−500	−3,564
Increase/(decrease) accruals	0	0	0	0	0	9,903	−9,903	0	0	0	0	0	0
Net change in working capital	0 $	−1,000 $	−310 $	1,436 $	−500 $	5,601 $	−5,651 $	−500 $	180 $	−500 $	−500 $	1,350 $	−394
Cash from (for) operations	$ −8,673	$ −6,834	$ −16,163	$ −15,010	$ −2,577	$ −12,761	$ −15,671	$ −9,111	$ −79,143	$ −2,334	$ −1,399	$ 2,958	$ 163,919
Investing activities													
Decrease/(increase) LT deposits	0	0	0	−1,200	0	0	0	0	0	0	0	0	−1,200
Decrease/(increase) capital expenditures	−4,597	0	0	−4,933	0	0	0	0	0	0	0	−1,309	−10,839
Decrease/(increase) intangible assets	0	0	0	0	0	0	−2,000	0	0	0	0	0	−2,000
Total investing activities	$ −4,597	0	0 $	$ −6,133	0	0 $	−2,000	0	0	0	0	0 $	−1,309 $ −14,039
Financing activities													
Increase/(decrease) bank line of credit	0	0	0	0	0	0	0	0	0	0	0	0	0
Decrease/(increase) loans to officers	0	0	0	0	0	0	0	0	0	0	0	0	0
Increase/(decrease) loans from officers	−6,000	0	0	0	0	0	0	0	0	0	0	0	−6,000
Increase/(decrease) interest payable	−44	613	613	613	613	613	613	613	613	613	613	613	6,694
Increase/(decrease) sub. debt	0	0	0	0	0	0	0	0	0	0	0	0	0
Increase/(decrease) sub. convertible debt	0	−25,000	0	0	0	0	0	0	0	0	0	0	−25,000
Increase/(decrease) common stock	150,000	25,000	0	0	0	0	0	0	0	0	0	0	175,000
Total financing activities	$143,956 $	613 $	613 $	613 $	613 $	613 $	613 $	613 $	613 $	613 $	613 $	613 $	150,694
Net Change in Cash	130,686	−6,221	−15,550	−20,530	−1,964	−12,149	−17,058	−8,499	−78,531	−1,721	2,012	2,261	−27,264
Beginning Cash Balance	3,560	134,246	128,025	112,474	91,944	89,980	77,831	60,773	52,275	−26,256	−27,977	−25,966	3,560
Ending Cash Balance	$134,246 $	128,025 $	112,474 $	91,944 $	89,980 $	77,831 $	60,773 $	52,275 $	−26,256 $	−27,977 $	−25,966 $	−23,704 $	−23,704

EXHIBIT 7G Vintage Directions, Inc., Assumptions

	Actual 1991 6 Months	Percent of Revenue	1992 Total	Percent of Revenue	1993 Total	Percent of Revenue	Forecast 1994 Total	Percent of Revenue	1995 Total	Percent of Revenue	1996 Total	Percent of Revenue
Ambrosia Catalog												
Catalog/year	2		2		4		4		4		4	
Average catalog size	28,000		55,000		100,000		150,000		150,000		150,000	
Total catalogs mailed	56,000		110,000		400,000		600,000		600,000		600,000	
Catalog annual growth	N/A		96%		264%		50%		0%		0%	
Total response rate	0.30%		0.49%		1.20%		1.64%		2.55%		3.45%	
Total orders	155		543		4,781		9,869		15,286		20,675	
Average order size	$310		$340		$350		$360		$370		$380	
Ambrosia sales revenue	$48,000	97%	$185,000	72%	$1,673,459	88%	$3,552,836	93%	$5,655,858	94%	$7,856,431	95%
Annual sales growth			285%		805%		112%		59%		39%	
Co-op ad dollars/catalog	$0	0%	$500	0%	$2,000	0%	$4,000	0%	$5,000	0%	$6,000	0%
Annual co-op ad dollars	$0		$1,000		$8,000		$16,000		$20,000		$24,000	
Total Ambrosia customers	35		261		3,167		8,495		15,369		23,037	
Total Ambrosia prospects	93		1,631		7,296		10,977		13,392		14,977	
Rental income/name	$0.10		$0.10		$0.10		$0.10		$0.10		$0.10	
Number of times rented/year	0		0		12		12		24		24	
Mailing list rental revenue	$0	0%	$0	0%	$12,555	1%	$23,366	1%	$69,026	1%	$91,233	1%
Product costs as percent of Ambrosia sales	65%		59%		58%		55%		53%		50%	
Fulfillment cost as percent of Ambrosia sales	9%		9%		7%		7%		7%		7%	
M&M Services												
M&M Services income	$1,308	3%	$73,693	28%	$200,000	11%	$220,000	6%	$242,000	4%	$266,200	3%
M&M annual income growth	0%		5534%		171%		10%		10%		10%	
COPS as percent of M&M income			50%		50%		60%		60%		60%	
Selling expenses												
Fixed catalog costs	$5,129	10%	$19,246	7%	$40,000	2%	$40,000	1%	$40,000	1%	$40,000	0%
Total variable catalog costs	$37,572	76%	$76,749	30%	$200,000	11%	$282,000	7%	$282,000	5%	$282,000	3%
Per piece variable catalog costs	$0.67		$0.70		$0.50		$0.47		$0.47		$0.47	
List building (advertising & PR)	$1,947	4%	$28,404	11%	$72,000	4%	$72,000	2%	$72,000	1%	$72,000	1%
List building percent of Ambrosia sales	4%		15%		4%		2%		1%		1%	
Overhead costs												
Office/warehouse space (Sq. Feet)	2,000		1,600		1,900		3,300		3,300		4,300	
Total office/warehouse rent	$0	0%	$14,708	6%	$21,720	1%	$42,210	1%	$44,321	1%	$61,817	1%
Head count	4		4		7		12		15		19	
Total salaries with benefits	$0	0%	$100,953	39%	$286,722	15%	$451,018	12%	$619,787	10%	$839,468	10%
Other overhead		23%		9%		4%		2%		2%		2%

129

Exhibit 7H Ambrosia Assumptions Details

	Actual 1991 Third Quarter	Actual 1991 Fourth Quarter	Est. 1992 Jan.–June	Est. 1992 July–Dec.	Actual 1991 Total	Est. 1992 Total	Est. 1993 Total	Est. 1994 Total	Est. 1995 Total	Ext. 1996 Total
Response Rates										
Winery lists	0.20%	0.35%	0.31%	0.35%	0.30%	0.34%	0.40%	0.50%	0.50%	0.50%
Rental lists	0.15%	0.10%	0.30%	0.20%	0.11%	0.21%	0.30%	0.20%	0.30%	0.30%
Other/referral	1.70%	1.50%	1.50%	1.50%	1.54%	1.50%	1.50%	1.50%	1.50%	1.50%
Two-step list		3.70%	2.60%	3.00%	3.70%	2.87%	4.00%	4.00%	4.00%	4.00%
Customer base		43.00%	10.00%	10.00%	43.00%	10.00%	10.00%	10.00%	10.00%	10%
House list telesales		0.00%	0.00%	4.00%		2.71%	6.00%	6.00%	6.00%	6.00%
Total response rates	0.29%	0.31%	0.61%	0.47%	0.30%	0.49%	1.20%	1.64%	2.55%	3.45%
Pieces mailed										
Winery lists	5,431	10,967	10,256	20,000	16,398	30,256	100,000	200,000	200,000	200,000
Rental lists	5,662	30,520	6,500	63,109	36,182	69,609	251,137	315,816	278,969	241,789
Other/referral	907	3,385	2,339	5,000	4,292	7,339	20,000	20,000	20,000	20,000
Two-step list	0	93	750	1,631	93	2,381	21,503	38,869	50,263	57,738
Customer base	0	35	155	261	35	416	7,360	25,315	50,768	80,473
House list telesales	0	0	0	0	0	0	0	0	0	0
Total pieces mailed	12,000	45,000	20,000	90,000	57,000	110,000	400,000	600,000	600,000	600,000
Orders by list										
Winery lists	11	38	32	70	49	102	400	1,000	1,000	1,000
Rental lists	8	31	20	126	39	146	753	632	837	725
Other/referral	15	51	35	75	66	110	300	300	300	300
Two-step list	0	3	20	49	3	68	860	1,555	2,011	2,310
Customer base	0	15	16	26	15	42	736	2,532	5,077	8,047
House list telesales	0	0	0	76	0	76	1,732	3,851	6,062	8,293
Total orders	34	138	123	422	172	544	4,781	9,870	15,287	20,675
Average order size:										
Cases	0.9	0.9	1.4	1.2	0.9	1.2	1.2	1.2	1.2	1.2
Dollars	$368	$255	$373	$330	$310	$340	$350	$360	$370	$380
Total cases sold	31	124	170	506	156	676	5,738	11,843	18,343	24,810
Total catalogs sent	12,000	45,000	20,000	90,000	57,000	110,000	400,000	600,000	600,000	600,000
Average catalog size					28,500	55,000	100,000	150,000	150,000	150,000
List building costs (Ad/PR)	$0	$1,947	$7,404	$18,000	$1,947	$25,404	$72,000	$72,000	$72,000	$72,000
List building costs/name	$0	$21	$12	$20	$21	$17	$10	$10	$10	$10
Two-step names generated	0	93	600	900	93	1,500	7,200	7,200	7,200	7,200
Telesales commissions	$0	$0	$0	$1,997	$0	$1,997	$48,490	$110,911	$179,431	$252,097
TS commissions as a percent of revenue	0%	0%	0%	8%	0%	8%	8%	8%	8%	8%
House List										
Two-step names	0	93	750	1,631	93	1,631	7,296	10,977	13,392	14,977
Customer base	0	35	155	261	35	261	3,167	8,495	15,369	23,037
Total house list	0	128	905	1,892	128	1,892	10,463	19,472	28,761	38,014
Total Ambrosia revenue	$12,810	$35,244	$45,274	$139,219	$48,054	$184,493	$1,673,459	$3,552,836	$5,655,858	$7,856,431

EXHIBIT 8   VDI Proposed Capitalization

Capital Sources	Paid In	Date	Number of Shares	Equity
Founders equity*				
Greg Berglund	$25	7/01/91	2,510	16.7%
Lesley Berglund	$25	7/01/91	2,510	16.7%
Lisa Mangano	$25	7/01/91	2,510	16.7%
Jim Pottow	$15	7/01/91	1,470	9.8%
External equity				
Proposed Investors	$150,000	1/31/92	5,000	33.3%
Convertible debt†				
George Schofield	$25,000	7/15/91	1,000	6.7%
Private debt				
External Sources	$45,000	9/01/91	n/a	n/a
Management Infusion	$10,000	11/1/92	n/a	n/a
Total capital	$230,000		15,000	100%

*Reflects Jim Pottow's value of vested equity shares in VDI after six months of full-time work, with unvested shares redistributed equally to the remaining three founders.

†Convertible debt of $25,000 will swap into equity as soon as 5,000 shares in external equity shares are issued or reserved.

1–4 TRIPLEDGE PRODUCTS, INC.

By early 1989, Tripledge Products was apparently on the verge of enormous growth. Accordingly, the company needed capital to build inventory and finance the projected ramp-up. In total, the management was seeking a $500,000 investment: a $150,000 term loan secured by all assets except inventory and receivables, a $75,000 term loan secured by existing inventory, a $100,000 revolving credit line secured by new inventory purchases and receivables, and $175,000 in convertible, redeemable preferred stock.

The current management of Tripledge, Jennifer Runyeon (president) and Chip Fichtner (chairman), had purchased the assets of Tripledge Wiper Corp. in October of 1988. Tripledge Wiper Corp. had been in Chapter 11 at the time the two partners spotted an ad in *The Wall Street Journal* seeking an investor. The company sold a unique, patented, three-bladed wiper through automotive aftermarket retail stores, the traditional distribution channel. However, the expense of competing in this market proved overwhelming, and despite a profitable shift to offshore manufacturing, the company ultimately was unable to pay off an unsecured note, which was called by its largest shareholder and lender in November of 1987. The company promptly declared bankruptcy.

Despite this dire financial situation, Runyeon and Fichtner traveled to the company's headquarters to begin due diligence on Tripledge Wiper in the summer of 1988. They soon came to believe that they had stumbled on a product with great untapped potential. However, the best price that the two could negotiate was $2 million for 50 percent of the company as a going concern, which not only seemed very high, but was too much to raise from prospective investors. After unsuccessfully attempting to lower the price, they returned to Texas.

Runyeon and Fichtner had been friends since attending high school together in Greenwich, Connecticut. Upon their graduation in 1978, the two proceeded together to Southern Methodist University in Texas. Fichtner soon dropped out to join Merrill Lynch as a commodities broker. He was so successful that he ultimately departed at age 20 to join Bear, Stearns & Company in Dallas as the youngest vice president in the firm's history. During summers and after graduation, Runyeon began working for him, first as an assistant and then as a broker. Continuing their alliance, the two founded their own investment banking firm, Randall and Powell, in January of 1988, while still

This case was prepared by L.A. Snedeker under the supervision of H. Irving Grousbeck.

Development of this case was funded by Mr. and Mrs. Glenn M. De Kraker.

Stanford Business School Case S–SB–131

working in their traditional jobs in commodities trading. The enterprise was still thriving when the Tripledge opportunity arose.

After returning to Texas, the two received a call from the Tripledge owners in August of 1988. Now desperate, they sought to liquidate the assets of the company. Runyeon, Brackett, and Fichtner ultimately bought those assets for $150,000 with a loan supplied by a friend's father, himself a stockbroker, plus a small continuing royalty on each wiper blade sold. After the purchase, the previous president of Tripledge Wipers remained in his position for a short time; Runyeon stayed in New Jersey to learn from him about the company and the industry. When it became obvious that his plans for the venture did not match those of Runyeon and Fichtner, they asked him to leave, which he did amicably. Thereupon, Runyeon packed up the company in a U-Haul and moved its headquarters to Dallas.

Given their limited financial resources, the owners of Tripledge Wiper (now renamed Tripledge Products, Inc.) were not able to invest much capital in marketing. Thus, they decided to avoid entrenched retail competition, which was essentially dominated (90 percent of the OEM market and 78 percent of the automotive aftermarket) by two companies: Anco and Trico, both founded in the 1920s. Indeed, the automotive aftermarket was a low-margin, commodity business with little service offered to the consumer. Until the entrance of Tripledge, that is.

Because of the high-quality, patented design of their wiper (which actually did work better than ordinary wipers), Runyeon and Fichtner believed they could sell directly to the consumer, rather than to the retail level. The duo investigated a concept in direct-response marketing known as "syndication." Syndicators were third-party entrepreneurs who sold advertising time on TV (those infamous 1-800 number commercials), print ads in magazines, and credit card billing inserts on the basis of nothing in advance and a percentage of sales. Thus, the up-front investment in advertising would be zero. Moreover, in the case of billing inserts, Tripledge would receive the bonus of an implicit endorsement by the credit card company. Daring to raise the suggested retail price of the wipers from $12.95 to $19.95, the company forged ahead with this strategy in limited tests.

The tests, conducted in early 1989, proved extremely successful. In particular, cash flow was attractive, since more than 60 percent of the TV test orders were charged on credit cards. The company thus received its payments within 5 days; through traditional retail channels, the store would pay Tripledge 45 to 90 days after receipt of the product. Given the results of these tests, Runyeon and Fichtner believed the future of their company was promising. Accordingly, they began planning for the associated ramp-up, in expectation of sharply increased orders as they rolled out the syndicated advertising campaign. It was with these expectations that they sought $500,000 in loans and equity.

(What follows are excerpts from the actual document written by the management of Tripledge seeking financing for their anticipated growth.)

Executive Summary

The automobile windshield wiper market in the United States is enormous. There are more windshield wipers than telephones in the United States. Approximately

87,500,000 replacement wipers were sold in the United States in 1988, generating retail sales of over $400 million. Because conventional wipers are made from natural rubber, they deteriorate rapidly and must be replaced every 6–18 months.

Tripledge Products, Inc., produces the world's only synthetic automobile windshield wiper using a proprietary compound developed by Tripledge with Du Pont labs. Tripledge Wipers were patented in the U.S. in 1984. Since then six foreign patents have been issued. Tripledge Wipers are in service throughout the world and have a large, untapped export sales market.

The Tripledge wiper is unique in design, patented, and lasts a lifetime. The product has a proven sales history with hundreds of thousands sold and a successful direct-response marketing approach, with significant profit margins.

In order to refinance acquisition debt, finance additional inventory purchases, and provide additional direct-marketing support, Tripledge Products, Inc., (TPI) and its exclusive marketing affiliate, Dauntless Marketing Inc. (DMI), are seeking $500,000 in new capital in a combination of secured debt and preferred stock with a royalty. Based on achieving slightly over a 2.0 percent share of the U.S. windshield wiper replacement market in 1989, the combined companies (DMI/TPI) could earn over $5.0 million pre-tax, pre-interest, and dividends.

By providing the requested infusion of capital, an investor can achieve not only unusually high current income (in excess of 55 percent cash on cash, in the first year alone) but can also expect aggressive long-term growth. In addition, the investment can be secured by a *first lien on all assets* and an attachment to the combined companies' cash flow stream.

Capital Request Summary

Debt

$150,000   Term loan secured by all assets of Tripledge Products, Inc., with the exception of inventory and receivables; 3 years.

$ 75,000   Term loan secured by existing inventory; 1 year.

$100,000   Revolving credit line secured by new inventory purchases and receivables; 2 years.

Capital Stock

$175,000   Convertible, redeemable, adjustable rate preferred with the "dividend" being a royalty equal to $.25 per pair of wipers sold; 5 years.

$500,000   Total investment

Yield

Based on current interest rates and pro forma income, the above debt and equity package could yield a cash on cash return of $279,508, or 55% in the first 12 months.

History of the Company

In October 1988, Tripledge Products, Inc. (TPI), a Delaware corporation, was formed for the purpose of purchasing all assets of Tripledge Wiper Corp. (TWC), a Delaware corporation in Chapter 11 of the U.S. Bankruptcy Code. TWC had developed and successfully marketed an extrudable multiedged windshield wiper that is unique both in design and in material formulation.

The material formulation is a breakthrough in elastomeric chemistry. It is the first wiper to be made of Du Pont Nordel®, a long-lasting EPDM synthetic rubber. The exact formula was developed for Tripledge Wiper Corporation through proprietary research performed in cooperation with Du Pont's Chestnut Run Elastomer Laboratory. In determining the perfect balance of ingredients, hundreds of variations were initially tested and further refinements took several years to complete.

The patented multiedged shape was developed after two years of experimentation and testing. In each direction, three edges work together to produce a superior wipe quality.

The company was issued U.S. patent #4,473,919 on October 2, 1984. Foreign patents have been issued in Great Britain, Canada, France, and Italy, and Japan is pending.

The company has developed valuable die and process technology that make possible the mass production of the product by the extrusion process. This results in lower costs than conventional wipers, which are compression-molded.

Consumer benefits include superior wipe quality, a long-lasting product, and the elimination of wiper noise.

TWC filed bankruptcy in November 1987 due to the largest shareholder and lender calling an unsecured note. The company had not been operating profitably due to its inability to assemble wipers in the United States cost effectively. Once the assembly was shifted offshore, the company became profitable, although not sufficiently profitable to retire a large unsecured note.

U.S. Windshield Wiper Market

In 1981, the Federal Trade Commission made a comprehensive study of the U.S. wiper market and the domestic producers. The study was in connection with a proposed antitrust action against Champion Spark Plug's acquisition of Anco Industries. Anco was the second-largest producer of windshield wipers in the United States and the largest supplier to the replacement aftermarket. Anco had a 34.3 percent market share in 1980.

The Federal Trade Commission report is the only accurate base upon which the current market size can be evaluated. According to this report, in 1978 there were 70,973,394 aftermarket wipers sold in the United States.

The U.S. domestic manufacturer new car production in 1986 was 7.8 million units. Assuming the U.S. producers sell 70 percent of the new cars sold in the United States, there were over 11 million new cars sold in the United States in 1986.

In 1988, U.S. registered autos approximated 150 million with each car having at least two wipers (many have 3), the total wipers in use in the United States is *at least* 300 million.

For our projections, we have used publicly available sales figures and the 1978 base as reported by the Justice Department to estimate 1988 aftermarket only sales of 87,500,000 units.

Although the market has historically grown about 15 percent in dollar volume over each of the last five years, our pro formas assume 1988 constant unit volume for 1989 and 1990 over 1988.

Foreign Wiper Market

During 1988, TWC's Japanese distributor purchased over $250,000 of Tripledge Wipers. The product retails for $49.95 in Japan and has been extensively advertised on TV. Other high-potential markets include Europe, Canada, and South America. The Japanese distributor has indicated it will continue ordering approximately 10,000 pairs per month.

The Product

Tripledge Wipers versus All Others.   Three features make Tripledge wipers better:

1. The trade secret formula
2. The patented Tripledge shape
3. The product's extrudability

The Trade Secret Formula.   All conventional wipers sold today are made of natural rubber compounds, which are known to deteriorate rapidly. When tires, hoses, and fan belts were made of natural rubber they cracked, rotted, and dried out regularly.

Tripledge wipers are made of Du Pont Nordel®, a special blend of EPDM (Ethylene Propylene Diene Monomer)—a synthetic rubber family known for its long-lasting chemical characteristics. EPDM is already used in long-lasting radial tires and many automotive components.

The proprietary Tripledge formula was specially blended to clean your windshield cleaner than other wipers and last for the life of your car. It is also an extrudable compound specially formulated to cure evenly in state-of-the-art industrial microwave curing units.

In order to obtain a superior formula, the founders of the company requested applied research from the E.I. du Pont de Nemours & Co., Inc., in Wilmington, Delaware, on a proprietary basis. Its research chemist, Dr. Henry J. Leibu, personally supervised the Tripledge project at Du Pont.

The Tripledge formulation was compounded by Dr. Leibu in cooperation with Du Pont's Chestnut Run Elastomer Laboratory. This is the laboratory where Neoprene and other synthetic rubber formulations were discovered, and it's been one of the preeminent elastomeric chemistry labs since the science was born.

Dr. Leibu joined Tripledge in 1982, upon retiring from a 32-year career as a research chemist for Du Pont specializing in elastomers. He holds many patents for work in the field of elastomeric chemistry and worked extensively with Du Pont on automotive EPDM compounds. From 1972–76, he served as Du Pont's international liaison with the Michelin Company in France on the tire project. Dr. Leibu remains a consultant to Du Pont as well as Tripledge.

The trade secret formula is a valuable company asset and no other wiper company has been able to successfully compound a wiper using a synthetic rubber formula.

The Patented Shape.   Tripledge lifetime wipers work better than conventional wipers because they have five edges. In each direction, three specially designed edges work together to produce the cleanest windshield possible. The first edge clears off the bulk of the water or snow without actually touching the glass, the sharply pointed second edge cleans the windshield of bugs, road oil, and grime, and the final edge squeegees the glass perfectly clean.

Only Tripledge lifetime wipers take off road oil, dirt, and bugs, in addition to rain. Functionally, Tripledge lifetime wipers are the best wipers available. They are already used by police, firemen, ambulance and taxi drivers and literally hundreds of thousands of satisfied consumers across the country.

Tripledge lifetime wipers never lose their flexibility, which causes conventional wipers to crack and tear. They don't become porous and, therefore, won't stick to your windshield in ice and snow or in the heat of midsummer. Tripledge lifetime wipers are impervious to ozone and sunlight aging and are guaranteed for the life of your car. No other wiper company can offer such a guarantee.

The hollow barrel shape of the Tripledge lifetime wiper has a special purpose. Automotive wipers sit idle more often than they are used. "Compression-set" during rest deforms the squeegee and causes conventional wipers to chatter. The hollow barrel of the Tripledge Lifetime Wiper, however, causes the "compression-set" to be absorbed by the patented barrel design, allowing the Tripledge lifetime wiper to conform to the curvature of your car's windshield. This eliminates chatter and unpleasant noises produced by conventional wipers.

The Manufacturing Advantage.   Conventional wipers are pressed into shape by the compression molding process. First, rubber is colandered into sheets about one-quarter inch thick. Then, they are placed into molds that resemble large waffle irons. These molds press the rubber into mats of 50 wipers. When the excess is trimmed off, the "mat" is about the size of a household door mat. Cycle time is high and mold maintenance is expensive. The mats are then slit into 50 individual wipers of the proper length. Many molds and molding machines are needed to meet the needs of a mass market. Molding is labor intensive compared to extrusion, and equipment and tooling costs are considerably greater for a high-output molding operation than for extrusion.

Tripledge lifetime wipers are extruded at a high rate of speed and cut at the end of the extrusion line to the precise length necessary by a mechanical cutter. Two people can handle the entire extrusion process; one feeding the specially pre-mixed compound into the machine at one end, and the other boxing the cut pieces on the other. They can make 12,000 Tripledge lifetime wiper squeegees in an eight-hour shift with a single die, twice that much with a two-cavity die, and quadruple the output with a four-cavity die.

Conventional wipers are very difficult to extrude because their shape does not lend itself to extrusion, and the edges come out wavy. The radial shape of the Tripledge lifetime wiper, however, is the perfect shape to extrude.

The Product Line.   The Tripledge Lifetime Wiper includes the patented Tripledge squeegee mounted in a high-quality galvanized steel superstructure. The entire superstructure is electro-painted black. Plastic bushings separate all metal-to-metal connections. The louvered design reflects the ''Euro-styling'' original equipment found on the finest German-made cars. This style is now popular universally on upscale production cars.

In order to properly fit the broad spectrum of American and import cars and trucks, the company produces 17 different part numbers (SKUs). The line includes five different blade-to-arm connections in lengths ranging from 11 inches to 22 inches.

Together with the patent, the trade secret formula, and the secret die technology, the risk of knockoffs is greatly diminished.

The Competition

The U.S. windshield wiper market is substantially concentrated. Until the early 70s, two companies completely dominated the market on all levels. In 1986, it is estimated that these two companies—Anco and Trico—still dominate 90 percent of the OEM market and 78 percent of the aftermarket.

Anco, 1075 Grant Street, Gary, Indiana 45440. Anco is a wholly owned subsidiary of the Champion Spark Plug Company. It was founded in the early 20s by Mr. John W. Anderson, a pioneer in windshield wiper development. Until his death in the late 60s, Mr. Anderson controlled 94.4 percent of the company. After his death, his holdings passed to the John W. Anderson Foundation, which sold the stock to the Champion Spark Plug Company in 1987 for about $40 million. Subsequently, it acquired the remaining 5.6 percent from private owners.

Upon acquiring Anco, Champion merged the two sales forces and began mass marketing programs to expand aftermarket sales away from strictly traditional distributors. Historically, Anco has maintained the dominant aftermarket position, while Trico has maintained the dominant OEM position.

Trico Products Corp., 817 Washington St., Buffalo, New York 14203. Trico was the first wiper company and developed all the early wiper systems for automobiles. Currently, Trico remains the market leader in the design of OEM wiper systems and has historically strong ties with all OEM suppliers around the world.

During the late 20s, when General Motors was being formed and was short of capital, Trico accepted a large amount of GM stock for GM's debt. This direct ownership has put Trico in an unusually strong position as a GM supplier and gave it the power to dictate wiper system details to GM.

During its prime, Trico was terrifically profitable and built up assets in the securities of Ford Motor Company, Exxon Corporation, and GM. Under the leadership of the company's founder, the manufacturing operations were concentrated in Buffalo, New York, with licensing agreements in foreign countries.

After the founder's death, the company was run by the son of the founder. During the 1970s, Trico became overburdened with an expensive sales force and inefficient production facilities. For several years, the company lost money on wiper sales but remained strong financially due to its previous investments in blue-chip securities. During the 1980s, a professional manager was hired as president to turn the company around.

Tridon, Inc., 2190 S. Service Road, Oakville, Ontario, Canada. Tridon was originally a metal stamping operation and one of the largest suppliers of metal hose clamps to the auto industry. In the late 60s, Tridon teamed up with the Gates Rubber Company, makers of automotive hoses, to produce a wiper. The Tridon/Gates product was poorly marketed and failed in the market, but Tridon continued making wipers and developed several innovations in the field.

Tridon tested new compound formulations and developed the first plastic superstructure to be given OEM approval. Currently, Tridon wipers are original equipment on many Ford Motor Company Products.

Pylon Mfg. Co., 201 Hillsboro Plaza, Deerfield Beach, Florida 33441. This company was started by Andy Granatelli's STP Corp., but was spun off to its president, Rodney K. Longman, in a leveraged buyout in the 60s. Mr. Longman developed the company into a tough competitor by making packaging innovations, copying the Anco appearance, and refining production methods continually.

Recently, Masco Industries purchased Pylon Mfg. Co. from Mr. Longman and retained his services for five additional years. The terms of this sale are not known.

Parker-Hannifin Corp., 1000 Pennsylvania Ave., Brooklyn, New York 11207. This huge conglomerate has a position in the auto parts industry through its Roberk subsidiary, which manufactures auto antennas, mirrors, and wipers. It has been successful by developing an extremely low-priced wiper product and capturing large retail chains (such as Kmart) with a "universal fitting" short line.

Roberk is able to maintain its price competition by being the primary manufacturer of each of its component parts.

Robert Bosch Corp., 2800 S. 25th Ave., Broadview, Illinois 60153. This is the U.S. sales division of a large West German auto parts manufacturer. In Germany, the company makes a variety of parts for OEM use as well as sales in the aftermarket.

The company manufactures spark plugs, starter motors, automotive wiring, driving and fog lights, and wipers. In the United States, its position in the wiper aftermarket is very small, and many accounts we contacted complained of the company's inability to ship complete orders on a timely basis.

Bosch wiper blades are original equipment on many European cars including Mercedes-Benz, Porsche, Audi, *The Bosch superstructure and the Tripledge superstructure are identical in design, color, and material.*

History of the Wiper Market

When automobiles were first introduced, they were buggies with a motor drive. Early autos had no windshields and, therefore, needed no wipers. Henry Ford began using wipers only on later versions of the Model T and from then on.

When wipers first appeared, they swung in a semicircle from the top and were hand-operated by the driver. This type of wiper was introduced on some cars as early as 1917, but they didn't become common until the early 20s. Passenger side wipers weren't felt to be necessary and weren't added until the mid-20s. Until the late 40s, all wipers were rubber squeegees pressed into a rigid metal holder. No articulation was necessary as windshields were flat.

During this period, from 1921 until 1950, the wiper market was characterized by consumers who were loyal to the brand of wipers that came on the car as original equipment. The OEM suppliers were the only legitimate aftermarket suppliers. For this reason, it was important to compete fiercely at the OEM level (then just "The Big Three") in order to gain the replacement business.

Anco and Trico completely dominated the industry during this period, and many reliable sources will admit that price fixing and personal kickbacks were commonplace. Profits were kept low at the OEM level and artificially high in the "traditional after-market" where position was protected.

The relationship between Trico and General Motors during this period also bears noting. Trico owned a large amount of GM stock and was able to place a great deal of pressure on GM as to the wiper system's blade-to-arm connection and design elements. When synthetic rubber was first used on autos in the 30s, Trico was able to reject its use for wipers and stick to natural rubber, which was quick to deteriorate and produced profitable aftermarket sales. Anco enjoyed a secondary position and made no attempt to rock the boat.

During this period, from 1950 until 1967, car production was at an all-time high and the replacement market was prosperous, protected, and profitable.

Just as blocking patents expired in the late 60s, another trend was gaining force that opened the door for competition to Anco and Trico—discount department stores. These large-volume retailers were buying in volume and selling below the prices offered by "traditional" stores. Sears and Kmart, the two leading discount department stores, developed tremendous buying power and their market dominance is legendary.

Due to the high sales volume they created, auto parts and accessories were an important part of the discount department store's inventory. Today, Kmart is the largest seller of wipers, with annual estimated sales of over 6 million units. The "name brands" were preferred, but when they weren't available, the powerful buyers (not customers) found other sources. In the case of wipers, as in many other areas, the name brand manufacturers were faced with the decision to support their protected market or enter the new "mass market." Because their established relationships with their best accounts were on the line, many manufacturers refused to sell to mass merchandisers.

With Sears and Kmart looking for a wiper line and Anco and Trico not prepared to respond, other companies entered the market. Roberk, Tridon, and Pylon were all started within a few years of each other in the 60s. They were formed with the intention of gaining major accounts where OEM connections were not important but where *price* was the competing factor.

Buyers at these major chains were not seeking improved or innovative products; they specialized in offering traditional products at greatly reduced prices. Therefore, none of the new market entrants was interested in an improved wiper. In fact, at the slim profit margins they were charging, the new manufacturers as well as the chain buyers liked the replacement factor and there was no perceived need for a lifetime wiper.

Meanwhile, in almost every other field, OEM suppliers were fiercely competing to produce better products, and synthetic rubbers and plastics were made in a wide variety of formulas to meet the differing requirements of the belts, hoses, tubes, and tires that the auto industry needed. Yet the wiper industry slept and carried out very little product development on the squeegee portion of the wiper and has made almost no improvements in it in 70 years.

During this era, Americans bought only American-made cars and blade-to-arm connections were not changed regularly from model to model. Then, in the 60s and early 70s, the public started buying imported cars from Europe and later Japan, which had different wiper systems.

Since the percentage of imported cars was relatively low, the mass merchandisers were not interested in expanding their shelf space to fit a few oddball cars. Wiper manufacturers started supplying plastic adaptors to fit these new connections. This gave rise to a popular trend in the wiper market, "the 7-SKU Universal Line." For the past 20 years, buyers have embraced this marketing concept and have been ignoring the recent effect the Japanese have been making in the automobile business.

Management—Tripledge Products

Jennifer P. Runyeon, President.   Ms. Runyeon is also the president of Randall and Powell, Inc., an investment banking firm, and Contemporary Financial Futures Corp., a commodity brokerage firm.

Prior to her association with Contemporary Financial, she worked as a commodity broker with J. C. Bradford & Co. in Nashville. Ms. Runyeon has a bachelor's of business administration degree from Southern Methodist University in Dallas.

Elliott M. Brackett, Vice President.   Mr. Brackett was formerly a stockbroker with Rotan Mosle and Southwest Securities in their Dallas offices. Mr. Brackett has a bachelor's of business administration degree from Southern Methodist University. Mr. Brackett is also associated with Randall and Powell.

Management—Dauntless Marketing, Inc.

J. Jovan Philyaw, President.   Mr. Philyaw has been involved in direct-response marketing for seven years: first, as a creator of special promotions for Gordon's Jewelers and later as a consultant for several major TV-marketed products. Mr. Philyaw is the exclusive marketing consultant for the blockbuster best-selling book *Fit for*

Life (over 5 million copies sold) and is a part owner of all marketing rights to *Fit for Life* follow-on products.

C. C. Fichtner.   Mr. Fichtner is also associated with Randall and Powell as the managing director of corporate finance. In 1981–82, he was vice president in charge of managed commodity accounts with Bear, Stearns & Co. (youngest VP at age 20 in Bear, Stearns history). Previously he was the largest managed account broker world-wide with Merrill Lynch & Co.

Since 1982, he has been president and CEO of the parent of various start-up companies, including a savings and loan holding company (sold in 1985) and an NASD registered brokerage firm with five offices that was sold to a NYSE member firm in 1986.

Consultants.   Dr. Henry J. Leibu, director: research & development, compounded the original formula for the Tripledge lifetime wiper while working as a research chemist for E. I. Du Pont de Nemours & Co., Inc. Currently, Dr. Leibu has retired from the Du Pont company and works part-time for Tripledge as a consultant. His work in monitoring the quality on a batch-by-batch basis and his refinements over the past five years have been invaluable to the company.

From 1949 until 1982, Dr. Leibu worked entirely in the Du Pont company in fields relating to elastomers research and rubber technology. He is author of a number of published technical articles and holds many patents in the field, including some for filled EPDM automotive molding compounds and vulcanization of EPDM compounds.

Dr. Leibu was born in Switzerland and educated at the Swiss Federal Institute of Technology in Zurich. He holds a doctor of science in process technology from that institution. In addition, he studied chemistry at Oxford University.

From his graduation in 1945 until 1949, Dr. Leibu held a teaching and research associate position in the Swiss Federal Institute of Technology, in charge of the high-pressure synthesis laboratory.

From 1972 to 1976, Dr. Leibu worked on the development of EPDM tire polymers and tire retreading systems of Nordel®. He was Du Pont's international liaison with the Michelin Company on the tire program during this period.

From 1976 until his retirement from the Du Pont company in 1982, Dr. Leibu worked on research for new EPDM and Hypalon® polymers and developed special EPDM compounds for tire sidewalls with enhanced ozone resistance. He had direct responsibility for injection molding of elastomers, single ply roofing materials, Nordel® pond liners, and the corresponding developments of adhesives systems.

Dr. Leibu's broad technical knowledge in elastomers, thermoplastics, and plastics combined with his 30 years' experience in process technology is responsible for the technology behind the Tripledge lifetime wiper and will be a valuable asset in developing future products for the company.

Marketing History

Typically, the automotive aftermarket parts business is a low-margin "commodity" business that requires several layers of sales intermediaries between the manufacturer and the consumer—manufacturer to distributor to jobber to auto parts store or service station to consumer. Fortunately, the Tripledge wiper is unique in that it has no direct competition due to its patented design, lifetime warranty, and superior performance. With proper marketing, it can be sold directly to the consumer at very attractive noncommodity type product prices and profit margins.

When TPI purchased the assets of Tripledge Wiper Corp. (TWC) in October 1988, the company was selling 70 percent of its product through ads in men's "handyman" magazines such as *Popular Mechanics* and 30 percent through the traditional automotive parts channels. The suggested retail price was $14.95 per pair, which was the price advertised in magazines, plus $2.50 shipping and handling. TWC was selling to distributors as low as $2.49 per wiper.

One customer, a catalog company similar to Sharper Image, Sporting Edge/B.N. Genius, had begun selling the product through its catalogs at $16.95 per pair plus $5.00 shipping and handling. After the purchase of assets, TPI raised the minimum wholesale price to $6.98 per pair with a suggested retail of $19.95 per pair. Subsequently, the wholesale price has been raised to $7.98 per pair. By the end of December, Tripledge wipers has become the number five all-time best seller for Sporting Edge/B.N. Genius. Thanks to aggressive insertions of the catalog in almost every domestic airline magazine during November, Sporting Edge/B.N. Genius sold over 10,000 pairs during November and December. Obviously, the product had universal appeal beyond the men's handyman magazines.

In November 1988, TPI contracted with Dauntless Marketing, Inc.,[1] to handle Tripledge wipers in all direct-response markets including TV, radio, direct mail, credit card syndications, and non-handyman print media. DMI, in return, guaranteed minimum 1989 sales of 250,000 pairs.

Direct-Response Marketing

DMI produced a one-minute and two-minute TV commercial that was tested in three different TV markets between December 15, 1988, and January 15, 1989.

The measure of a product's sales potential on television is the cost per order, or CPO.

CPO = Spot cost in dollars ÷ Number of pairs sold.

In each test, the Tripledge wipers achieved uniquely low CPOs, getting as low as $3.25 per order on national cable spots on Christian Broadcast Network. In local cable tests on Gannett's Channel 56 in Boston, the product achieved a $6.60 CPO, *without* offering COD orders, which can account for a 25 to 40 percent increase in sales. Using the *highest CPO* from the test of less than $8.00, the gross profit per pair sold was a promising $6.41 per pair.

---

[1]Dauntless Marketing Inc. was the name of the entire company from October 1988 through summer 1989. At that time, the team decided it needed a more descriptive name and changed the company name to Lifetime Automotive.

Sale price	$19.95
+ Shipping & handling	3.50
Gross TV sale	$23.45
Less	
Product cost	$ 3.75
800# cost	1.85
Credit card fee	.98
UPS/postage	1.80
Label	.05
Tape, stuffing	.06
Shipping labor	.33
Box	.22
	$ 9.04
Advertising cost per order	$ 8.00
	$17.04
Net profit	$ 6.41

The cash flow is very attractive in direct-response marketing as over 60 percent of the TV test orders were charged to Mastercard, Visa, or American Express. (Calculations above assumed 100 percent, therefore 40 percent of the orders are $.98 more profitable.)

The company receives good funds on MC/Visa/Amex orders within five days of the airing of the spot, and usually within three days. On orders paid by check, the orders are held two weeks for the check to clear. COD orders are paid by the freight carrier within 14 days. In any case, the company has no bad debts and is assured of payment *prior to* shipment—a significant departure from the typical automotive product buyer (i.e., Kmart, who will pay within 45 to 90 days *after* receipt of the product).

In short, the TV tests showed that putting a *maximum* of $8.00 per order into advertising would produce not only the return of the $8.00, but also a gross profit of $6.41 per pair with a total time frame of less than seven days average. *Tripledge wipers were a smash hit on TV.*

Future Marketing Strategy

Direct Response—TV Syndicators.   Using the test results from TV, DMI approached a number of the TV time syndicators. Media Arts Inc., owners of the direct-response ad time on USA Network, Nashville Network, and several other cable channels, has begun testing the product. Media Arts pays $9.00 per pair of Tripledge wipers (cash with orders) and passes on the shipping and handling charge of $3.50 to TPI. TPI pays nothing for the advertising and has no risk or additional cost. Several other similar arrangements are being negotiated.

Gross Profit Analysis

Revenue	$12.50 per pair
Product cost	3.75
UPS/postage	1.80
Tape/stuffing	.06
Shipping labor	.33
Box	.22
	$ 6.16
Gross profit	$ 6.34 per pair

Direct-Response TV—Per Order.   Some 300 local broadcast, local cable, and national cable television channels will advertise a successfully proven product like Tripledge wipers on a "per order" or PO basis. PO TV advertising limits the cost of TV marketing to a fixed cost per order. Using Direct Response Marketing, Inc., of California, DMI has negotiated a fixed cost per order of $8.00 with a number of channels including Turner Broadcasting.

In PO TV time buys, the advertiser can "buy" orders at a fixed price. The TV station runs the commercial until the purchased amount of orders is acquired. The advertiser pays nothing for TV time except for the fixed PO price, in this case $8.00. On February 1, 1989, DMI escrowed $50,000 to buy 6,666 orders from various stations. The orders are all guaranteed within 30 days of execution. The escrowed funds are not released to the station until the orders are delivered. If the first amount escrowed is successful, Tripledge wipers can be sold nationwide on a *risk-free* basis at a fixed advertising cost.

Gross Profit Analysis—Per Order

Sale price	$19.95
+ Shipping & handling	3.50
Gross TV sale	$23.45
Less	
Product cost	$ 3.75
800# cost	1.85
Credit card fee	.98
UPS/postage	1.80
Label	.05
Tape, stuffing	.06
Shipping labor	.33
Box	.22
	$ 9.04
Advertising cost Per Order	$ 8.00
	$17.04
Net profit	$ 6.41

Direct-Response TV—Risk Buys.   Based on the success of the December–January tests, HDM Worldwide Direct, an affiliate of Young and Rubicam, has agreed to extend DMI/TPI $50,000 per week in credit to buy TV time on various broadcast and cable channels. HDM Worldwide Direct will be paid the standard agency commission of 15 percent from the TV stations. Using national cable test results of CPOs less than $4.00, the gross profit analysis shows a net of $10.79 per pair. A profit worth the risk of buying our own time rather than exclusively using the no risk PO and syndicator markets. Using the existing $50,000 per week budget and a conservative $5.00 CPO, almost 500,000 orders can be generated over the next 12 months from risk buys alone, using no cash outlay on the part of the company.

Direct Response—Credit Card Syndicators.   Every month, in hundreds of millions of credit card billing statement envelopes and separate mailers, billions of dollars of merchandise are sold to American consumers. Only the products that in tests produce superior response rates make it into the national credit card mailings. Products are generally not sold by the company sending the bill, but by credit card syndicators such as *World Book Encyclopedia,* who own the ''space'' in the bill envelope.

In February and March 1989, ads and order coupons for Tripledge wipers can be found in credit card bills mailed by J.C. Penney, Texaco, and Citgo. A response rate of .004 (four tenths of 1 percent) is considered successful and will gain the product national rollout. Although only 30 percent of the way through the normal 45-day response measurement time, Tripledge has already been slated for national rollout in Texaco and Citgo.

Over the next three months, World Book will put Tripledge in full runs in Texaco (2,600,000), Citgo (700,000), and based on the J.C. Penney mailing, which just went out, Sears (22,000,000) in May. This accomplishment is significant in the fact that major oil companies and auto parts retailers are endorsing a mail-order product in direct competition with their own dealers and stores. If these are successful, most of the major credit card mailings will carry an ad for Tripledge wipers in late spring, including J.C. Penney— 12,000,000; Shell Oil— 4,500,000; Mobil Oil— 2,800,000; Amoco— 2,700,000; Montgomery Ward— 6,000,000; Exxon— 2,600,000; Unocal— 1,400,000; Sun— 1,200,000; and possibly even the major bank cards such as Mastercard, Visa, Discover, and American Express.

Direct-Response Marketing—Print Syndication

Tripledge Wiper Corp. survived on direct-response print advertising from 1984 through October 1988. Even using poorly laid out ads, short hours manning the 800 number, and a limited budget, the product was sold to well over 100,000 Americans. One *free* mention in Du Pont's company employee magazine generated over 10,000 orders in three months. Tripledge wipers are proven producers in print advertising.

DMI approached several of the national print media syndicators who own the direct-response space in dozens of national magazines. One, National Syndications, Inc., has asked for the exclusive rights to national print for Tripledge wipers, pending the first test. During late February or early March 1989, Tripledge wipers will be featured in a two-thirds-page ad in *Parade Magazine. Parade Magazine* reaches 33 million households each Sunday and a two-thirds-page ad costs over $200,000. The first test will be limited to 2 million households. If a .005 (one half of 1 percent) response rate is achieved (10,000 orders), NSI will roll the product out nationally. Based on Tripledge's previous print response rates, we expect over 1 percent. On a national ad in *Parade,* a 1 percent response rate would produce 330,000 orders.

U.S.A. Weekend, Gannett's clone of *Parade* that reaches 28 million households, has also asked to test ads for Tripledge wipers.

Print syndication is similar to TV in that the syndicator takes all the risk in return for buying the product at a favorable rate. In the case of NSI and Parade outlined above, NSI will pay TPI/DMI $8.50–$9.50 per pair based on volume and pass on the $3.50 shipping and handling to TPI/DMI for fulfillment.

Direct Response—Print—Risk Buys.   TPI/DMI will continue to buy print ads directly as they have done successfully for four years. Concentration will be placed on those magazines that have historically produced the best results, including *Popular Mechanics, Popular Science,* various AAA Motorclub magazines, and airline magazines. The print media risk buys will be continued as long as the CPO remains below $8.00. HDM Worldwide Direct is handling these placements on credit.

Direct Marketing—Catalogs

As the fifth best selling product in the four-year history of The Sporting Edge/B.N. Genius catalog, Tripledge wipers are proven sellers to catalog buyers. Sporting Edge/B.N. Genius sold an average of 250 pairs per day during November–December 1988, with over 10 percent shipped Federal Express at the buyer's expense.

Other catalogs will be carrying the Tripledge wipers during 1989, including Brookstone, Amway, J.C. Whitney, Herrington, Beverly Hills Motoring Accessories, Vista U.S.A. (the Exxon Motorclub catalog), Attitudes, and Sharper Image. Sharper Image will include Tripledge wipers in its June catalog mailing of 2.5 million catalogs, an exposure roughly three times that of B.N. Genius/Sporting Edge. Tripledge wipers will also be carried in the 100 plus Sharper Image catalog stores. The stores will have a display of wipers and continuous-loop video extolling the virtues of Tripledge wipers. Customers will place orders in the store and receive the product by mail. Sharper Image will pay TPI/DMI $9.50 per pair plus $4.50 for fulfillment.

Catalog companies typically buy the product in bulk and provide their own fulfillment, although Sporting Edge/B.N. Genius currently pays TPI $4.50 per pair for fulfillment.

Financing Request

Term Loan

Amount	$150,000
Collateral	First lien on all assets including patents, customer lists, trademarks, furniture, fixtures, equipment, computers, tooling, dies, etc; excepting inventory and receivables
Rate	Prime plus 3 floating adjusted quarterly, payable quarterly
Term	Two years
Amortization	5 year with quarterly principal payments, balloon at end of year two
Use of proceeds	Pay off existing secured debt
Documentation	Promissory note, security agreement, UCC-1 filing in Texas, Oklahoma, and New Jersey

Term Loan

Amount	$75,000
Collateral	First lien on all existing inventory
Rate	Prime plus 3 floating, payable quarterly
Term	1 year
Amortization	Proceeds from sales of existing inventory at $4.00 per unit with minimum of 25% of principal amount per quarter
Use of proceeds	Pay off existing secured debt
Documentation	Promissory note, security agreement, UCC-1 filing in Texas, Oklahoma, and New Jersey

Term Loan

Revolving Credit Line

Amount	$100,000
Collateral	First lien on all purchased inventory and receivables
Rate	Prime plus 3 floating with interest payable quarterly
Term	2 years
Amortization	2 1/2% principal reduction quarterly
Use of proceeds	Purchase new inventory
Documentation	Promissory note, security agreement, UCC-1 filing in Texas, Oklahoma, and New Jersey

Preferred Stock, Series A

Amount	$175,000
Number of shares	1,750
Purchase price	$100.00 per share
Par value	$1.00
Liquidation preference	$100.00 per share
Convertible	Into 20% of the then outstanding common and options, fully diluted
Redemption	$58,333 per year at the end of the third, fourth, and fifth year if not converted
Dividend	Cash, payable semiannually at $.25 per pair of wipers sold in the preceding six months with a minimum of $10.00 per share annually; can be structured preferably as royalty
Other covenants	Under the proposed terms of the concurrent financing described in this memorandum, no common stock dividends shall be paid until all secured debt is retired, which would also apply to any holder of the above upon conversion.

TRIPLEDGE PRODUCTS, INC.
Balance Sheet
(As Of December 31, 1988)

Assets

Current assets

Cash in bank—Dallas	253.57	
Cash in bank—Bridgeport	9,014.66	
Petty cash	250.00	
Total cash		$ 9,518.23
Trade accounts receivable	83,084.98	
Inventory	94,243.08	
Prepaid expenses	8,769.00	
Current vendor and utility deposits	6,317.00	
Total other current assets		192,414.06
Total current assets		$201,932.29

Depreciable assets

Furniture and fixtures	15,311.22	
Office equipment	30,776.99	
Machinery and equipment	15,000.00	
Extrusion dies	4,365.00	
Less: Accumulated depreciation	(3,338.00)	
Net depreciable assets		$ 62,115.21

Deferred assets

Organizational costs	17,200.00	
Tripledge name and logo	58,500.00	
Patents	112,000.00	
Less: Accumulated depreciation	(6,356.50)	
Net deferred assets		$181,343.50

Other assets

Market research and other projects	16,368.22	
Customer list and data base	3,600.00	
Total other assets		$ 19,968.22
Total assets		$465,359.22

Liabilities and owners' equity

Current liabilities

Trade accounts payable	43,272.03	
Taxes payable	2,006.95	
Current notes payable	260,653.00	
Current royalties payable	841.12	
Total current liabilities		306,773.10
L/T Royalties (estimated)		166,500.00
Total liabilities		$473,273.10

Shareholder equity

Common stock issued and outstanding	1,000.00	
Current year to date net income	(8,913.88)	
Total shareholder equity		(7,913.88)
Total liability/owner equity		$465,359.22

149

TRIPLEDGE PRODUCTS, INC.
Income Statement
(For December 1, 1988, through December 31, 1988)

	Current Period	Percent	Year-to-Date*	Percent
Income				
Aftermarket wholesale—wipers	$ 78,108.91	88.06	$154,073.58	85.70
DMI P.I. Sales—wipers wholesale	1,139.98	1.29	1,139.98	0.63
Mail order/phone order—retail	9,455.72	10.66	24,568.28	13.66
Less: Returns and allowances	(1,614.34)	(1.82)	(4,167.11)	(2.32)
Total income	$ 87,090.27	98.18	$175,614.73	97.68
Direct costs				
Cost of goods sold	41,367.87	46.64	83,416.98	46.40
Shop/warehouse labor	3,828.70	4.31	8,412.67	4.68
Freight and shipping supplies	15,109.86	17.04	24,113.85	13.42
Equipment depreciation	371.00	0.42	1,593.36	0.89
Total cost of production and shipping	$ 60,677.43	68.40	$117,536.86	65.38
Sales commissions	543.19	0.61	793.46	0.44
Credit card processing discount	378.23	0.43	805.74	0.45
Order processing payroll	5,248.66	5.91	15,522.25	8.63
Total selling costs	6,170.08	6.96	17,121.45	9.52
Total direct costs	$ 66,847.51	75.36	$134,658.31	74.90
Gross profit	$ 20,242.76	22.82	$ 40,956.42	22.78
Operating expenses				
Administrative payroll	4,197.19	4.73	21,163.76	11.77
Group health insurance and other cost	2,652.18	2.99	3,824.32	2.13
Consultants	4,106.08	4.63	4,889.08	2.72
Legal counsel	515.85	0.58	1,450.85	0.81
Computer technician	0.00	0.00	757.24	0.42
Total personnel: payroll and contract	$ 11,471.30	12.93	$ 32,085.25	17.85
Advertising and promotion	8,139.99	9.17	22,095.41	12.29
Travel and entertainment	1,379.61	1.55	15,361.75	8.54
Total indirect marketing expense	$ 9,519.60	10.73	$ 37,457.16	20.83
Rent and utilities	4,025.83	4.55	7,502.72	4.18
Telephone	3,891.24	4.38	8,185.58	4.56
Office supplies	505.02	0.57	1,021.31	0.57
Postage and delivery	708.75	0.80	1,892.00	1.05
Outside reproductions	0.00	0.00	100.74	0.06
Computer lease and maintenance	373.22	0.42	746.44	0.42
Computer supplies	164.65	0.19	369.10	0.21
Computer software	0.00	0.00	84.00	0.05
Fax machine lease and repair	111.49	0.13	192.98	0.11
Postage meter lease and repairs	171.72	0.19	515.16	0.29
Miscellaneous	79.87	0.09	833.04	0.45
Depreciation and amortization	2,722.00	3.07	8,153.00	4.54
Total office and general expense	$ 12,753.79	14.38	$ 29,596.07	16.46
Total operating expenses	$ 33,744.69	38.04	$ 99,138.48	55.14
Total income (loss) from operations	$(13,501.93)	(15.22)	$(58,182.06)	(32.36)

(continued)

TRIPLEDGE PRODUCTS, INC.
Income Statement—Continued
(For December 1, 1988, through December 31, 1988)

	Current Period	Percent	Year-to-Date*	Percent
Extraordinary item—other income				
Realize discount on inventory purchases	0.00	0.00	54,606.90	30.37
Other expense				
Interest expense—general	2,114.41	2.38	5,338.72	2.97
Net income before taxes	$(15,616.34)	(17.60)	$(8,913.88)	(4.96)
Net income (loss) after taxes	$(15,616.34)	(17.60)	$(8,913.88)	(4.96)

*Includes mid-October through December.

Tripledge Products, Inc., Notes to Financial Statements (December 31, 1988)

1. **Organization and operations**

   Tripledge Products, Inc., (the "Company") is a Delaware Corporation. It was organized September 9, 1988. The principal office of the Company is located in Dallas, Texas, with fulfillment centers in Bridgeport, New Jersey, and Hugo, Oklahoma.

2. **Significant accounting policies**

   The Company maintains the books on the accrual basis of accounting. Income is recorded when earned and expenses are recorded when incurred.

   Depreciation is provided on the straight-line basis. Assets are recorded at cost and depreciation is provided over the assets' useful life. Intangible assets are amortized over the life of their expected benefit to the Company: patents—13 years; name and logo—5 years; deferred organizational costs—5 years.

3. **Extraordinary item**

   A one-time adjustment for accounting purposes was entered in October 1988. Salable goods inventory was verified prior to closing the Asset Purchase Agreement on October 4, 1988. The purchase price allocation, in the closing documents, valued that inventory at exactly 50% of the standard cost of those goods. This purchase of inventory was then treated as is generally accepted for trade discounts on purchases. The inventory was adjusted to standard cost and the discount taken as extraordinary income.

4. **Income taxes**

   The Company is a tax paying entity for federal income tax purposes and is organized and files tax returns as a subchapter C corporation. No provision for taxes was made for 1988 due to net operating loss.

5. **Long-term royalties**

   According to provisions of the Asset Purchase Agreement dated October 4, 1988, the Company agrees to make deferred payments as follows: from the closing date through December 31, 1990, the Company shall pay to Tripledge Wiper Corporation an amount equal to two percent (2%) of the Company's gross revenue derived from the sale of patented products, and from January 1, 1991, through December 31, 1993, the Company shall pay to Tripledge Wiper Corporation an amount equal to one and one-half percent (1.5) of the Company's gross revenue derived from the sale of patented products. Such amounts shall be payable annually on March 1 of each calendar year for the preceding calendar year, commencing on March 1, 1989, and ending on March 1, 1994.

6. **Stockholder equity**

   The Company is authorized and has issued 100,000 shares of common stock. Par value of the stock is 1 cent (.01).

TRIPLEDGE PRODUCTS, INC.
Pro Forma Income Statement
Year One

	Note (#)	March 89	April	May	June	July	Aug.	Sept.	Oct.	Nov.	Dec.	Jan. 90	Feb.	Annual Totals	Percent of Category
Gross net sales	1	216,472	432,944	649,415	865,887	865,887	865,887	865,887	865,887	865,887	865,887	865,887	865,887	9,091,814	1.000
Units sold	2	22,787	45,573	68,360	91,146	91,146	91,146	91,146	91,146	91,146	91,146	91,146	91,146	957,033	0.282
COGS	3	85,449	170,899	256,348	227,865	227,865	227,865	227,865	227,865	227,865	227,865	227,865	227,865	2,563,481	0.844
Net sales		$131,022	$262,045	$393,067	$638,022	$638,022	$638,022	$638,022	$638,022	$638,022	$638,022	$638,022	$638,022	$6,528,332	0.844
Other income															
Fulfillment center	Sched 1	13,532	36,774	58,067	81,309	79,487	79,487	79,487	79,487	79,487	79,487	79,487	79,487	825,578	0.107
List rental	4	886	1,251	1,798	2,527	3,256	3,985	4,714	5,444	6,173	6,902	7,631	8,360	52,927	0.007
Misc. item upsl	Sched 2	7,770	15,540	23,311	31,081	31,081	31,081	31,081	31,081	31,081	31,081	31,081	81,081	326,348	0.042
Total net income		$153,211	$315,610	$476,242	$752,939	$751,846	$752,575	$753,304	$754,033	$754,762	$755,492	$756,221	$756,950	$7,733,185	
Operating expenses															
G&A TPI COR	Sched 3	54,220	54,220	76,320	76,320	96,780	96,780	96,780	96,780	96,780	96,780	96,780	96,780	1,035,320	0.551
G&A DMI COR	Sched 4	20,420	20,420	24,320	24,320	52,700	52,700	52,700	52,700	52,700	52,700	52,700	52,700	511,080	0.272
Intangible amortization	Sched 5	1,926	1,926	1,926	1,926	1,926	1,926	1,926	1,926	1,926	1,926	1,926	1,926	23,115	0.012
Curr res	5	4,272	8,545	12,817	11,393	11,393	11,393	11,393	11,393	11,393	11,393	11,393	11,393	128,174	0.068
Warr res	6	4,329	8,659	12,988	17,318	17,318	17,318	17,318	17,318	17,318	17,318	17,318	17,318	181,836	0.097
Total operating expenses		$85,168	$93,770	$128,372	$131,277	$180,117	$180,117	$180,117	$180,117	$180,117	$180,117	$180,117	$180,117	$1,879,526	
Earnings before interest, taxes, royalties		68,043	221,840	347,870	621,661	571,729	572,458	573,187	573,916	574,645	575,374	576,104	576,833	5,853,660	
YTD Earnings before interest, taxes, royalties		68,043	289,883	637,753	1,259,415	1,831,143	2,403,601	2,976,788	3,550,704	4,125,349	4,700,723	5,276,827	5,853,660		
Non operating expenses															
Interest expenses	7	3,792	3,792	3,792	3,792	3,792	3,792	2,917	2,917	2,917	2,917	2,917	2,917	40,250	0.087
Royalties/TWC	8	4,329	8,659	12,988	17,318	17,318	17,318	17,318	17,318	17,318	17,318	17,318	17,318	181,836	0.394
Royalties/Series A	9	5,697	11,393	17,090	22,787	22,787	22,787	22,787	22,787	22,787	22,787	22,787	22,787	239,258	0.519
Cum Series A	10	5,697	17,090	34,180	56,966	79,753	102,539	125,326	148,112	170,899	193,685	216,472	239,258		
Total non operating expenses		$13,818	$23,844	$33,870	$43,896	$43,896	$43,896	$43,021	$43,021	$43,021	$43,021	$43,021	$43,021	$461,345	
Net profit pretax		54,225	197,997	314,000	577,765	527,833	528,562	530,166	530,895	531,624	532,353	533,083	533,812	5,392,315	
YTD Profit pretax		54,225	252,222	566,222	1,143,988	1,671,820	2,200,382	2,730,548	3,261,443	3,793,067	4,325,421	4,858,503	5,392,315		
Tax /@ .35	11	18,979	69,299	109,900	202,218	184,741	184,997	185,558	185,813	186,069	186,324	186,579	186,834	1,887,310	
Earnings after taxes, interest, royalties		35,246	128,698	204,100	375,548	343,091	343,565	344,608	345,082	345,556	346,030	346,504	346,978	3,505,005	
YTD earnings after tax		35,246	163,944	368,044	743,592	1,086,683	1,430,248	1,774,856	2,119,938	2,465,494	2,811,523	3,158,027	3,505,005		

Schedule #1
TPI Fulfillment center

	Note (#)	March 89	April	May	June	July	Aug.	Sep.	Oct.	Nov.	Dec.	Jan. 90	Feb.	Annual Totals
Gross revenue	#1	$79,753	$159,506	$239,258	$319,011	$319,011	$319,011	$319,011	$319,011	$319,011	$319,011	$319,011	$319,011	$3,349,616
Units shipped	#2	22,787	45,573	68,360	91,146	91,146	91,146	91,146	91,146	91,146	91,146	91,146	91,146	957,033
Fixed overhead	Sched #1A	9,710	9,710	11,660	11,660	13,482	13,482	13,482	13,482	13,482	13,482	13,482	13,482	150,596
Variable expenses														
UPS/USPS @1.80		41,016	82,031	123,047	164,063	164,063	164,063	164,063	164,063	164,063	164,063	164,063	164,063	1,722,659
Boxes @.22		5,013	10,026	15,039	20,052	20,052	20,052	20,052	20,052	20,052	20,052	20,052	20,052	210,547
Labels @.03		684	1,367	2,051	2,734	2,734	2,734	2,734	2,734	2,734	2,734	2,734	2,734	28,711
Shipping supplies @.06		1,367	2,734	4,102	5,469	5,469	5,469	5,469	5,469	5,469	5,469	5,469	5,469	57,422
Printed material @.04		911	1,823	2,734	3,646	3,646	3,646	3,646	3,646	3,646	3,646	3,646	3,646	38,281
Labor @.33	#3	7,520	15,039	22,559	30,078	30,078	30,078	30,078	30,078	30,078	30,078	30,078	30,078	315,821
Total variable expenses		$56,511	$113,021	$169,532	$226,042	$226,042	$226,042	$226,042	$226,042	$226,042	$226,042	$226,042	$226,042	$2,373,442
Variable expense per order		2.48	2.48	2.48	2.48	2.48	2.48	2.48	2.48	2.48	2.48	2.48	2.48	
Total expenses		$66,221	$122,731	$181,192	$237,702	$239,524	$239,524	$239,524	$239,524	$239,524	$239,524	$239,524	$239,524	$2,524,038
Total cost per order		2.91	2.69	2.65	2.61	2.63	2.63	2.63	2.63	2.63	2.63	2.63	2.63	
Center net income		$13,532	$36,774	$58,067	$81,309	$79,487	$79,487	$79,487	$79,487	$79,487	$79,487	$79,487	$79,487	$825,578
YTD		13,532	50,307	108,373	189,682	269,169	348,656	428,143	507,630	587,117	666,604	746,091	825,578	
Average cost per order		2.66												
Average net profit per order		0.84												

1. Gross net sales: Sales at average of $9.50 per pair net of order acquisition cost such as advertising.

2. Units sold: Total *pairs* sold, wipers only.

3. Cost of goods sold: Units sold X Cost per pair. Assume $3.75 per pair March–May (extra cost for air shipping) and $2.50 per pair thereafter.

4. List rental income: Calculated on beginning base of 88,000 names at $.008 per month *plus* monthly names as added at the same rate.

5. Currency reserve: Calculated at 5% of product cost, total content to cover possible dollar devaluations against the new Taiwanese dollar and the Korean won.

6. Warranty reserve: Calculated at 2% of gross net sales.

7. Interest expense: Assumes current prime rate of 11%, debt is that contemplated in this offering.

8. Royalties/TWC: 2% of gross net sales paid annually to Tripledge Wiper Corp. as part of original asset purchase agreement.

9. Royalties/Series A: $.25 per pair of wipers sold payable semiannually to holders of the proposed Series A preferred stock.

10. CUM Series A will be paid out semiannually.

11. Tax: At 35% assumes increase in current federal income tax and no state income tax.

153

ATTACHMENT TO BUSINESS PLAN

motor/age

TRIPLEDGE® Wiper Corp.
3165 Tucker Road
Bensalem, PA. 19020

Bud Groner, S.A.E.
257 Georgetowne Blvd.
Daytona Beach, FL 32019

November 25, 1987

(904) 788-7260

ATTENTION: Mr. Rick Bell, Pres.

Dear Sir:

Thank you for the opportunity to test and evaluate your product, "Tripledge Wiper Blades." After a year of testing these new and of different design of other types of blades, I am pleased to report that these blades have been more than "equal" to other types I have tested and/or evaluated. I find these to be of superior material, especially in the heat of the Florida sun, and combined with the salt spray and moisture in this climate, I have found that they exceed my expectations.

These Tripledge® Blades also wipe well, without smear, after a full year of Florida climate and sun. I have used these in excess of highway speeds, (up to 100 mph) and find these blades to perform as well as any other blade I have used and tested.

After several months of highway use, I do clean these blades, (as I do any blade) with household ammonia, to remove the road grime and highway oil and tar accumulation that builds up from day to day highway driving, and this keeps the blades working as well as the first day I tried them.

It is my personal opinion that the Tripledge® Wiper Blade is of excellent quality, and should give years of satisfactory service to the consumer.

It is refreshing to see a manufacturer with a refreshing idea!
Sincerely yours,

Bud Groner, H-P EDITOR
Chilton's MOTOR/AGE MAGAZINE

ATTACHMENT TO BUSINESS PLAN

ATTACHMENT TO BUSINESS PLAN

Quality American-Made "Pressure Checkers" Inform You When Tires Need More Air

A tire that's lost just a few pounds of pressure can *significantly lower* your car's mileage and road-hugging ability. Pressure Checkers let you see at a glance when a tire needs more air.

Precision-made, they work on virtually any tire, replacing the valve cap. An orange indicator, enclosed in a clear plastic dome, raises up when pressure drops between 2 and 5 psi. Tested and approved by TUV, the demanding West Germany regulatory authority.
#611400 Pressure Checkers,
Set Of 4 $9.95 *(1 lb.)*

Rechargeable Cobra Lamp Sheds Light Three Different Ways

With its sculptured, European design, the Cobra Lamp is one of the most elegant...and thoughtfully engineered...lighting devices we've ever seen.

It gives you a choice of *three* lighting configurations. For broad, evenly dispersed light, switch on the energy-conserving fluorescent bulb. Or use the spotlight to cast an intense, focused beam. For roadside emergencies, set the Cobra on end to warn traffic in both directions *for up to 12 hours* with its 360° red and yellow flasher.

The Cobra quickly pays for itself in battery savings. Its built-in, rechargeable cells reach full power in 15 hours. During a bad storm, plug the lamp into an outlet. If the power goes off, it *automatically* turns on, guiding your way to it. Rugged, moisture-resistant ABS case measures 14 1/2Hx4Wx4"D. Includes UL-listed AC recharger and DC adaptor.

Keep a Cobra at home, in your car, boat, RV, or cabin. It's a rugged, economical, beautifully designed lamp built to last a *lifetime*.
#611495 Cobra 3-Way Lamp
$39.95 *(3 lbs.)*

Rechargeable Cobra Lamp, designed in Great Britain, provides 4 to 6 hours of fluorescent light, Up to 3 hours of spotlight, or up to 12 hours of flashing light...from a single charge.

Sav-A-Tow Gets Your Car Moving In Minutes...Every Time!

When no amount of rocking back and forth helps, your car can be free in a minute! Simply slide Sav-A-Tow against a tire, and the "alligator" teeth on the bottom grab the slippery road, while the tire grips the 76 raised studs on top. Made of tough polyethylene to support up to 3000 lbs. at 0° F. It's impossible to be spun out. Works on snow or ice, in sand or potholes.
#641622 Sav-A-Tow, Each $19.95 *(3 lbs.)*; *Save $4.00!* 2 for $35.90 *(6 lbs.)*

Patented *Triple-Edge* Wipers Keep Your Windshield Clear!

The unique, *patented* design of these superb wiper blades keeps your windshield clear and streak-free!

Triple-Edge Blades have *three* wiping edges instead of one. The first removes most of the water; the second cleans away bugs and dirt; and the third *squeegees* the glass clean.

Backed by our 1-year performance warranty, Triple-Edge Wiper Blades are made of DuPont® Nordel, the same material used on 50,000 mile radial tires. It *never* breaks down. Black metal frames.
#611524 Triple-Edge Wiper Blades, Pair $19.94 *(1 lb.)*
#611526 Rear Triple-Edge Blade $9.95 *(1 lb.)*

Specify year, make and model of your car.

Improve driving safety with Triple-Edge wiper blades. They're the *last set* you'll ever buy.

Order Toll-Free most items in this catalog by 1:00 p.m. (your time) weekdays, and you'll receive your order by 10:30 a.m. the next day (in most delivery areas)!

1–5 COMMERCIAL FIXTURES INC.

It would take only a few quick strokes of his pen to fill out the bid form and but an instant to seal the envelope. Gordon Whitlock caught himself in momentary wonder that this simple form would have such a dramatic effect on the next few years of his life. Tomorrow, February 23, 1992, at 12 o'clock noon, the envelopes from Gordon and his partner, Albert Evans, would be opened to determine which of them would buy out the other and own Commercial Fixtures Inc., the company built by their fathers. After working together for over 25 years, the two partners had decided that this was the best way to resolve differences of opinion that had arisen over how to manage the company.

Company Description

Commercial Fixtures Inc. (CFI) manufactured custom-engineered fluorescent lighting fixtures used for commercial and institutional applications. Sales in 1991 were $4 million with profits of $115,000.

Most sales were standard items within the nine major lines of products designed and offered by the company. Ten percent of sales were completely custom designed or custom built fixtures, and 15 percent of orders were for slightly modified versions of a standard product. In 1991, CFI shipped 66,000 fixtures. Although individual orders ranged from one unit to over 2,000 units, the average order size had been fairly consistently 15–20 fixtures. Modified and custom designed fixtures averaged about 25 per order. Gordon Whitlock, CFI president, described their market position:

> Our product marketing strategy is to try to solve lighting problems for architects and engineers. We design products that are architecturally styled for specific types of building constructions. If an architect has an unusual lighting problem, we design a special fixture to fit his needs. Or if he designs a lighting fixture, we build it to his specifications. We try to find products that satisfy particular lighting needs that are not filled by the giant fixture manufacturers. We look for niches in the marketplace.
>
> Having the right product to fit the architect's particular needs is the most important thing to our customer. Second is the relationship that the architect, the consulting engineer, or the lighting designer has with the people who are representing us. The construction business is such that the architect, engineer, contractor, distributor, and manufacturer all have to work as a team together on a specific project to ensure its successful completion. The architect

This case was prepared by Richard O. von Werssowetz and H. Irving Grousbeck under the direction of Philip H. Thurston.
Harvard Business School Case 9–393–115

makes a lot of mistakes in every building he designs, unless he just designs the same one over and over. Consequently, there's a lot of trading that goes on during the construction of a building, and everybody's got to give and take a little to get the job done. Then the owner usually gets a satisfactory job, and the contractors and manufacturers make a fair profit. It requires a cooperative effort.

Most of our bids for orders are probably compared with bids from half a dozen other firms across the country. Since a higher percentage of our orders are for premium-priced products, we are not as price sensitive as producers of more commonplace lighting fixtures. It is difficult for a small firm to compete in that market. As many as 30 companies might bid on one standard fixture job.

CFI owned its own modern manufacturing facility located outside Denver, Colorado. Production consisted of stamping, cutting, and forming sheet metal, painting, and assembly of the fixture with the electrical components that were purchased from outside suppliers. The company employed a total of 104 workers, with 34 in sales, engineering, and administration and another 70 in production and assembly.

The company sold nationwide through regional distributors to contractors and architects for new buildings and renovations. Prior to 1989, CFI sold primarily to a regional market. At that time, marketing activities were broadened geographically. This was the primary reason that sales had been increasing over the last few years even during a weak construction market. (See **Exhibit 1** for historical sales, earnings, unit sales, and employment.)

Background

Commercial Fixtures Inc. was formed in Golden, Colorado, in 1936 by Jonathan Whitlock and Julius Lacy. Each owned one half of the company. Whitlock was responsible for finance and engineering and Lacy for sales and design. They subcontracted all manufacturing for the lighting systems they sold.

After several years, differences in personal work habits led Whitlock to buy out Lacy's interest. Jonathan Whitlock then brought in Paul Evans as his new partner. Evans had been one of his sheet metal subcontractors. Paul Evans became president and Whitlock, treasurer. Ownership was split so that Whitlock retained a few shares more than half because of his experience with Lacy.

In 1940, CFI began manufacturing and moved its operations to a multifloor 50,000-square-feet plant also located in Golden. The company grew and was quite profitable during the war years and during the following boom in construction of the early 1950s. Whitlock and Evans were quite satisfied with the earnings they had amassed during this period and were content to let the company remain at a steady level of about $1 million in sales and about $15,000 in profit after taxes.

Jonathan Whitlock's son, Gordon, joined CFI as a salesman in 1969 after graduating from MIT and then Colorado Business School. Paul Evans' son Albert, who was a graduate of Trinity College, also became a CFI salesman in 1970 when he was discharged from the service. The two sons were acquaintances from occasional gatherings as they were growing up, but had not been close friends.

In 1972, Jonathan Whitlock had a heart attack and withdrew from the management of the business. Although he remained an interested observer and sometime advisor to his son, Jonathan was inactive in company affairs after this time. Paul Evans assumed complete management overview of the company.

Gordon Whitlock moved inside to learn about other parts of the company in 1973. His first work assignments were in manufacturing and sales service. Albert Evans joined his father in the manufacturing area a year later. Gordon became sales manager, Albert became manufacturing manager, and at Paul Evans' suggestion, another person was added as financial manager. These three formed a middle management triumvirate that worked well together, but major decisions were still reserved for Paul Evans, who spent less and less time in the office.

As the new group began revitalizing the company, a number of employees who had not been productive and were not responding to change were retired early or asked to leave. When the man who had been Paul Evans' chief aide could not work with the three younger managers, they ultimately decided he had to be discharged. Paul Evans became so angry that he rarely entered the plant again.

For several years, the three managers guided the company as a team. However, there were some spirited discussions over the basic strategic view of the company. As sales manager, Gordon Whitlock pressed for responding to special customer needs. This, he felt, would be their strongest market niche. Albert Evans argued for smooth production flows and less disruption. He felt they could compete well in the "semi-standard" market.

In 1975, the fathers moved to restructure the company's ownership to reflect the de facto changes in management. The fathers converted their ownership to nonvoting Class A stock. Each transferred 44 percent of his nonvoting stock to his son. Jonathan Whitlock decided to relinquish his voting control at this time in an effort to help things work as the new generation took over. Accordingly, Gordon and Albert were each issued 50 percent of the Class B voting shares.

That same year, Gordon Whitlock began to work with an individual in forming a company in the computer field that rented extra space from CFI. CFI provided management and administrative support, helping the new company with bidding and keeping track of contracts. Although Albert Evans was not active in this company, Gordon split his partial ownership in this new company with Albert because they were partners and because Gordon was spending time away from CFI with the computer company.

With the heavy demands of the start-up over the next three years, this new effort began to weaken the relationship between Gordon and Albert. At the same time, Albert and the financial manager began to have strong disagreements. These seemed to arise primarily from forays in cost analysis, which led the financial manager to question some of Albert's decisions. There were also differences of opinion over relations with the work force and consistency of policy. Albert preferred to control the manufacturing operation in his own way. Gordon felt Albert could be more consistent, less arbitrary, and more supportive of the work force. When the computer company was sold in 1981, the financial manager joined it as treasurer and resigned from CFI.

Growing Conflict

The departure of the financial manager led to a worsening of the relationship between Gordon and Albert. Gordon had been made company president in 1976. Gordon recalled the decision:

> Paul Evans had resigned as president and the three of us were sitting around talking about who should be president. Albert Evans finally said, "I think you should be it." And I said, "OK."

Yet even with this change, the three managers had really operated together as a team for major decisions. Now, Gordon was upset that they had lost an excellent financial manager, someone critical to the operation (due, in his opinion, partially to the disagreements with Albert). There was also no longer a third opinion to help resolve conflicts. The financial manager was replaced with an old classmate of Albert's, and the new manager became one of several middle level managers who had been hired as the company grew.

The pressures of growth created more strains between Gordon and Albert. Sales had reached $1 million and had begun to tax CFI's manufacturing capacity. Gordon felt that some of the problems could be alleviated if Albert would change methods that had been acceptable during slacker periods but hindered intense production efforts. Albert had different views. Both agreed to look for additional space.

The transition to a new factory outside Denver, Colorado, in 1983 eased the stresses between the partners. A major corporation had purchased an indirect competitor to obtain its product lines and sold CFI the 135,000-square-feet plant. CFI also entered into an agreement to manufacture some of the other company's light fixtures as a subcontractor. The plant was in poor condition and Albert Evans took over the project of renovating it and continuing production of the other company's lines. Gordon Whitlock remained in Golden running the CFI operation alone until it became possible to consolidate the entire operation in Denver. Gordon described this interlude:

> The next year was a sort of cooling off period. Albert was immersed in his operation, and I was geared into the continuing operation. Albert had always enjoyed projects of this sort and was quite satisfied with this arrangement.
>
> Then in 1985 we hired a plant manager to run the Denver plant, and Albert came back to work in Golden. By that time, of course, a lot of things had changed. All of Golden had been reporting to me. I had somewhat reshaped the operation, and the people had gotten used to my management style, which was different than Albert's.
>
> Albert's reaction was to work with the design and engineering people, but he really wasn't involved very much with the daily manufacturing any more. He developed a lot of outside interests, business and recreation, that took up much of his time.
>
> I was very happy with that arrangement because it lessened the conflict. But when he did come back, the disagreements were worse. I guess I resented his attempts to change things when he only spent a small amount of time in the company.
>
> Then in 1986 we made the decision to sell the Golden plant and put the whole company in Denver. We were both involved in that. Most of our key people went with us. Albert and I were very active in pulling together the two groups, in integrating the operation.

That began a fairly good time. I was spending my time with the sales manager trying to change the company from a regional company to a national one and was helping to find new representatives all over the country. Evans spent his time in the engineering, design, and manufacturing areas. There was plenty of extra capacity in the new plant, so things went quite smoothly. In particular, Albert did an excellent job in upgrading the quality standards of the production force we acquired with the plant. This was critical for our line of products and our quality reputation.

This move really absorbed us for almost two years. It just took us a long time to get people working together, to produce at the quality level and rate we wanted. We had purchased the plant for an excellent price with a lot of new equipment and had started deleting marginal product lines as we expanded nationally. The company became much more profitable.

As the company expanded, a group of six people formed the operating team. Albert Evans concentrated on applications engineering for custom fixtures and new product design. In addition, there were a sales manager, financial manager, engineering manager, the plant manufacturing manager, and Gordon. Disagreements began again. Gordon recounted the problems:

Our operating group would meet on a weekly or biweekly basis, whatever was necessary. Then we would have monthly executive committee meetings for broader planning issues. These became a disaster. Albert had reached the point where he didn't like much of anything that was going on in the company and was becoming very critical. I disagreed with him as did the other managers on most occasions. Tempers often flared and Albert became more and more isolated.

He and I also began to disagree over which topics we should discuss with the group. I felt that some areas were best discussed between the two of us, particularly matters concerning personnel, and that other matters should be held for stockholders meetings. The committee meetings were becoming real battles.

In 1990, Paul Evans died. Although he had remained chairman of the board, he had been generally inactive since 1974. Jonathan and Gordon Whitlock and Albert Evans became the only directors.

Search for a Solution

Gordon Whitlock was discouraged by the continuing conflicts with his partner and had sought advice on how to remedy the situation from friends and associates as early as 1982. In 1990, Gordon was beginning to believe that he and Albert had just grown too far apart to continue together. However, Gordon had to find a mutually agreeable way to accomplish a separation. One partner could buy the other out, but they would have to agree on this and find an acceptable method. Albert seemed to have no interest in such an arrangement.

During 1990, the differences between the partners grew. The vacillations in leadership were disruptive to the operation and made other employees very uncomfortable.

By early 1991, the situation was growing unbearable. Gordon recalled the executive committee's annual planning meeting in January:

It was a total disaster. There were loud arguments and violent disagreements. It was so bad that no one wanted ever to participate in another meeting. We were all miserable.

What was so difficult was that each of us truly thought he was right. On various occasions other people in the company would support each of our positions. These were normally honest differences of opinion, but politics also started to enter in.

When Gordon returned from a summer vacation in August, he was greeted by a string of complaints from several of CFI's sales agents and also from some managers. Gordon decided that the problems had to be resolved. Gordon sought an intermediary:

I knew that Albert and I weren't communicating and that I had to find a mediator Albert trusted. I had discussed this before with Peter Dowling, our attorney. Peter was a boyhood friend who had grown up with Albert. I felt he had very high integrity and was very smart. Albert trusted him totally, and Peter was probably one of Albert's major advisors about things.

When I first talked to Dowling in March, he basically said, "Well, you have problems in a marriage, and you make it work. Go make it work, Gordon." He wasn't going to listen much.

Then in early September I went back to say that it wasn't going to work any more. I asked him for his help. Peter said that Albert had also seen him to complain about the problems, so Peter knew that the situation had become intolerable.

Dowling prepared a memorandum describing the various options of changing management and/or ownership that were available to partners who were having disagreements. Gordon decided to encourage one of Dowling's options that called for each partner to name a price for the business. Previously, some of Gordon's own advisors had suggested this same outlet.

Both directly and through Dowling, Gordon pressed Albert to agree to such an arrangement. Although Albert, too, was unhappy with their conflicts, he was hesitant to accede.

Gordon felt that there were several principal reasons for Albert's reluctance. One was the fact that Albert's only work experience was with CFI. This was limited primarily to managing manufacturing operations he had known for years. Second, Gordon thought Albert was very uncertain as to how to value the company since he had little formal training in financial analysis and had not been directly involved in the financial operations. Gordon felt that this made Albert's task of setting a bid price more difficult than his own. Finally, there was the emotional tie to the company and the avoidance of such a momentous decision.

As discussions began to result in the formulation of a buy-sell agreement, Albert's reluctance waxed and waned. Just before Christmas, Evans called Whitlock, who was sick at home, and said he had decided to fire the financial manager and become the treasurer of the company. He could look at the figures for a year or so and then make a better decision. Gordon felt the financial manager was essential and could not be discharged. He thought this was really more of an attempt to buy time.

After two more months of give and take in developing a formula and bid conditions, Whitlock and Evans finally signed a mutual buyout agreement on February 17, 1992. It called for sealed bids in a specific format with the partner offering the higher price buying out the other (**Exhibit 2**). The bids would be submitted in one week. Gordon credited Peter Dowling with convincing Albert to sign:

> I think Peter got him to sign it by sheer force of personality. By saying this situation is just not right, it's screwing up the company, you're not happy. You won't be happy until it's solved. This is a reasonable way to solve it, and you damn well ought to take the chance. Because later, if you pass this up, it's just going to get worse.

Valuing the Company

Before preparing his bid, Gordon reviewed the thinking he had done since first considering the idea of buying or selling the company. He began with the company's current position. With the serious discussions going on about the buyout agreement, preparation of the financial statements for 1991 had been accelerated, and they were already completed. (These are shown together with the results for 1990 and 1989 as **Exhibit 3.**)

Gordon had also begun developing the bank support he might need to fund a buyout. The company's banker indicated that he would loan Gordon funds secured by his other personal assets if Gordon was the buyer, but that since he had not worked with Albert, the bank would decline to finance an acquisition with Albert as the buyer. In addition, the bank would continue the company's existing line of credit, which was secured by CFI's cash and accounts receivable. The maximum that could be borrowed with this line was an amount equal to 100 percent of cash plus 75 percent of receivables. Both types of borrowing would be at 1 percent over the prime rate (then about 9 percent).

Gordon had worked with the banker to begin financial projections he could use in establishing his bid. These projections set out pro forma operating results *before* taking the bid conditions into consideration. By structuring the financial projections in this manner, the results of *operating* assumptions could be separated from *bid* structures. Various combinations of bid conditions could be easily tested based on this set of business operating results. Long-term debts that would be assumed with the business were included within the operating projections. Other bank financing requirements would be influenced by the bid terms and were left separate. The banker completed one sample projection using the minimum $500,000 bid and token $10,000 per year non-complete payments (**Exhibit 4**).

To be conservative, Gordon had made the sales projections about 10 percent lower each year than he really thought they would achieve. Because fixed costs would not rise appreciably with modest increases in sales, any improvements in sales volume would be particularly advantageous to profits. The asset and liability assumptions were based on company experience, but there could be fluctuations in items such as lengths of receivables and inventory turns. He felt he should consider how these various changes would impact his financing requirements and his price assessment.

Gordon also had sought out common valuation techniques. By looking through business periodicals and talking to friends, he found these methods were not necessarily precise. Private manufacturing companies were then most often valued at between 5 and 10 times aftertax earnings. Book net asset value also helped establish business worth, but was often adjusted to reflect differences between the market values of assets and the depreciated values shown on balance sheets. For CFI, this was true because they had obtained their new plant at an excellent price. Gordon felt it alone was probably worth $200,000 more than stated book.

To Gordon, the variations in worth suggested by these different methods not only reflected the uncertainty of financial valuation techniques, but also showed that a business had different values to different people. His bid would have to incorporate other more personal and subjective elements.

One important consideration was what amount of personal resources he could and should put at risk. Both he and Albert were financially very conservative. Neither of them had ever had any personal long-term debt—even for a house. Gordon could gather a maximum of $650,000 of assets outside of CFI that could be pledged to secure borrowing. His bank had already confirmed that he could borrow against those assets. However, for him to put his entire worth at risk, he would want to be very comfortable that the price was a reasonable one. Gordon described his feelings:

> You get very protective about what you have outside the company. The problem you always have with a small company is that most of your worth is tied up in it, and you may have very little to fall back on if something goes sour. We both have never been big leverage buyers or anything like that.

Besides the element of increased financial risk, there were several other considerations that tempered Gordon's willingness to pay a very high price. Since they had moved to the plant in Denver, the one-hour commute to work had been a bit burdensome. It would be nice not to have that drive. Gordon also felt he had good experience in the complete general management of a business, and his engineering undergraduate degree and MBA gave him a certain flexibility in the job market. This was important, because for both financial and personal reasons, he felt he would still have to work should he lose the bid.

On the other hand, some factors encouraged Gordon to be aggressive. His father cautioned him to be reasonable, but Gordon knew his father would be very disappointed if Gordon lost the company. And Gordon himself had strong emotional ties to CFI. Gordon also developed a point of view that in some ways he was buying the entire company rather than half:

> I'm sitting here with a company that I have no control over because of our disagreements. If I buy the other half share, I'm buying the whole company—I'm buying peace of mind, I could do what I want, I wouldn't have to argue. So I'd buy a "whole peace of mind" if I bought the other half of the company.

Gordon felt that differences in personal values had been the major reasons two friends had suggested two very different bids. Both had been business school friends and had been very successful entrepreneurs. However, one suggested a bid value for the other half of the company of $850,000 and the other suggested $1,100,000. Gordon commented:

Philip, who suggested the lower bid, was much more similar to me in lifestyle. He was involved with his family and a number of other activities. Mark, who suggested the higher bid, was unmarried and intensely involved in his company. The company was his life. However, all of the many friends I consulted cautioned me that I would be better off financially if I bought the company and urged me not to "get cute" and undervalue it.

Finally, Gordon considered his competitive position versus Albert. Although Albert had not accumulated the personal resources that Gordon had, he did have a relative with a private company that Gordon knew had an accumulated earnings problem and had the ability to match Gordon's resources. This relative would also be giving Albert financial advice in setting a value for the company. Albert also probably had fewer job prospects if he sold out. His undergraduate study was in liberal arts and his entire experience was within CFI. Gordon also thought Albert might have some doubts about his ability to manage the company on his own.

The Bid

The bid structure was a very simple one. The minimum bid was $500,000 in cash. Additional amounts could be added either to the cash portion and/or to a five-year noncompetition agreement. The bids would be evaluated on a present-value basis using an 8 percent discount rate. That rate was selected as equivalent to cash invested at the current return of AAA-rated bonds. Both Gordon Whitlock and Albert Evans were satisfied that was fair. The minimum cash payment had been established to protect the interests of the seller and to reduce possible future uncertainty and unpleasantness if the company's position should change substantially. The noncompetition payments would be obligations of CFI but also would be personally guaranteed by the buyer.

Now it was time to decide on a price and then try to get some sleep. Gordon put the form down and walked around the room. He sat down once again, uncapped his pen, and began to enter his bid.

EXHIBIT 1 Historical Performance

Year	Net Sales	Profit after Tax	Number of Fixtures Shipped	Total Employees	Hourly Employees
1991	$4,412,191	$115,209	66,000	104	70
1990	$3,573,579	$101,013	58,000	94	58
1989	$2,973,780	$106,528	52,000	82	52
1988	$2,935,721	$ 63,416	54,000	82	50

EXHIBIT 2   **Buy/Sell Agreement**

AGREEMENT made on this 17th day of February 1992, between Albert W. Evans of Denver, Colorado (hereinafter called *Evans*) and Gordon M. Whitlock of Denver, Colorado (hereinafter called *Whitlock*).

WHEREAS, Evans and Whitlock each own shares of the voting and nonvoting capital stock of Commercial Fixtures Inc. (CFI) and desire to arrange for the purchase by one (or the purchase by CFI) of all shares of capital stock of CFI owned by the other;

NOW, THEREFORE, in consideration of the foregoing and of the mutual agreements contained herein, Evans and Whitlock agree as follows:

1. Evans and Whitlock will each submit to David Austin, the named senior partner of CFI's accounting firm, by noon on February 23, 1992 (the "Bid Date"), a proposal to purchase (or to have CFI purchase some or all of) the other's shares of capital stock of CFI (such proposal to be on the Bid Form attached hereto as Attachment A):

   a. Such proposal shall include all of the stock owned by the other and shall specify the number of shares to be purchased by him, and by CFI and the purchase price, which price shall be not less than $500,000 in the aggregate and shall be paid in full at the Closing hereinafter specified, except as the parties shall otherwise agree.

   b. Such proposal shall specify the amount of the equal annual payments to be made by CFI over the five-year period from 1992 through 1996 in consideration of a noncompetition agreement for such period covering the United States to be executed by the seller in the form attached hereto as Attachment B [not included], such annual payments made in equal installments at the end of each calendar quarter commencing March 31, 1992.

2. If either Evans or Whitlock fails to submit such a proposal by the Bid Date (except for causes beyond his reasonable control in which event a new Bid Date will be established by Austin), the party so failing shall sell his capital stock to CFI upon the terms specified in the other's proposal. If neither party submits such a proposal by the Bid Date this agreement shall terminate.

3. With respect to each proposal, Austin shall add the amount of the purchase price submitted under Section 1(a) and the amount of the annual payment to be made under Section 1(b) above (discounted to present value as at January 1, 1992, as to all payments to be made on or after January 1, 1992, at the rate of 8 percent per annum), and thereby determine which of the submitted proposals is the highest price (the determination to be made as set forth in the Bid Form Computation attached hereto as Attachment C). The party submitting the highest proposal shall be the buyer (which term shall include CFI to the extent such proposal provides that it shall purchase shares). If both offers are determined by Austin to be equal, the buyer shall be determined by an auction as follows:

   a. The parties with such others as they choose to bring shall meet at Austin's offices at a time and a date specified by Austin.

   b. Commencing with Evans (unless he declines to raise his bid in which case commencing with Whitlock) the parties shall submit successive bids of not less than $5,000 in excess of the last bid submitted by the other party.

   c. A party shall have 15 minutes after the bid of the other party in which to submit his own bid, and if he fails to submit a bid at least $5,000 higher than other party's last bid, then the last highest bid will be the buyer, except that if neither party raises his original bid then Austin shall determine the buyer by a flip of the coin.

   d. If a party fails to attend such meeting, the other party shall be the buyer, unless such failure was for causes beyond the reasonable control of the party in which case Austin shall set a time and date for another meeting.

All determinations of Austin under this and the preceding Section, which shall include the question of whether causes beyond the reasonable control of a party prevented the party from acting, shall be final and binding on the parties. Compliance with this agreement shall be determined by Austin, and his determination thereof shall also be final and binding on the parties.

4. If Whitlock is the seller, Evans shall cause CFI at the Closing either (*a*) to redeem for $75,107.50 all shares of capital stock of CFI owned of record or beneficially by Jonathan Whitlock upon tender of certificates for the same endorsed to CFI or (*b*) to continue to pay a $10,000 annual pension to Jonathan Whitlock and to pay the premiums on the $75,000 life insurance policy held by CFI on Jonathan Whitlock's life and to place such insurance policy in a separate trust which trust shall be the beneficiary under such policy, all in such a manner as to place such policy and proceeds beyond the reach of CFI's creditors, and promptly upon receipt the proceeds of such policy shall be paid by the trust to Jonathan Whitlock's estate in consideration of the endorsement to CFI or the certificate for the shares of capital stock to CFI held by the estate. The bills of Peter Dowling to CFI, including those for arrangements leading to this agreement, shall be the responsibility of CFI regardless of which party is the buyer.

5. Austin shall notify the parties in writing promptly upon any determination that a party has failed to satisfy Section 2 hereof and promptly upon any determination made under Section 3 above. The closing date on which the buyer shall make his payment under Section 1(a) and the seller shall endorse his shares of capital stock to CFI to the buyer, shall be April 15, 1992, or such earlier date as the buyer shall designate. If the buyer shall fail to make the Section 1(a) payment at the Closing, the other party will become the seller upon the lower terms of the original seller's proposal, and Austin shall reschedule the

---

EXHIBIT 2   *(concluded)*

Closing on a date within 90 days. If at the new Closing the new buyer fails to make the Section payment, this agreement shall terminate. Payment of amounts owed by CFI under Section 1(b) above (and under Section 4 if Whitlock is the seller) shall be personally guaranteed by Evans or Whitlock, as the case may be, and overdue payments of such amounts shall bear interest at the rate of 15 percent from the date due. There shall be credited against payment to be made under Section 1(b) with respect to 1992 commencing March 31, 1992, the amount of salary received by the seller for 1992. At the Closing the seller shall execute an agreement not to compete with CFI for five years in the United States. The seller's employment, salary, Blue Cross/Blue Shield, group insurance, all other payments and benefits, except those provided herein, shall terminate at the Closing. The seller may retain the CFI automobile now used by him, and ownership thereof will be transferred to the seller by CFI.

WITNESS our hands and seals on the date first set forth above.

_____
Albert W. Evans

_____
Gordon M. Whitlock

Attachment A—Bid Form

PURCHASE PRICE (SECTION 1-a) $_____

NONCOMPETITION AGREEMENT (SECTION 1-b) $_____

AMOUNT PER YEAR $_____

TOTAL AMOUNT (5 YEARS) (TO BE PAID IN EQUAL
   QUARTERLY PAYMENTS) $_____

_____   _____
Date   Signature

Attachment C—Bid Computation Form

			Evans	Whitlock
Purchase price (1a):			$_____	$_____
Noncompetition agreement (1b):				
	Evans	Whitlock		
Yearly amount for five years:	$_____	$_____		
Discounted value (DV):				
Adjusted purchase price:			$_____	$_____

The discounted value shall be the present value of the yearly amount paid quarterly for 20 quarters discounted at an interest rate of 2 percent per quarter.

This shall be computed as follows:

$$DV = \frac{\text{Yearly amount}}{4} \times 16.3514 = \text{Yearly amount} \times 4.08786.$$

EXHIBIT 3   **Financial Statements**

COMMERCIAL FIXTURES INC.
Balance Sheets
Years Ended December 31

Assets	1991	1990	1989
Current assets:			
Cash	$ 51,248	$ 3,778	$ 70,520
Accounts receivable			
Customers	600,361	430,750	318,356
Refundable income taxes	23,001	—	—
Other	—	2,276	5,289
	623,362	433,026	323,645
Less allowance for doubtful receivables	3,500	3,500	3,500
	619,862	429,526	320,145
Inventories			
Raw materials	291,790	259,550	277,072
Work in process.	534,438	483,357	316,113
	826,228	742,907	593,185
Prepaid insurance and other	14,028	20,134	26,070
Total current assets	1,511,366	1,196,345	1,009,920
Property, plant, and equipment:			
Buildings and improvements	341,426	325,686	295,130
Machinery and equipment.	210,493	173,073	135,419
Motor vehicles.	32,578	32,578	29,421
Office equipment.	42,866	43,905	36,949
	627,363	575,242	496,919
Less accumulated depreciation	273,284	233,444	185,215
	354,079	341,798	311,704
Land.	11,101	11,101	11,101
Total property, plant, and equipment	365,180	352,899	322,805
Other assets:			
Cash surrender value of life insurance policies (less loans of			
$19,748 in 1991, $19,590 in 1990 and $19,432 in 1989) . . .	81,978	77,215	72,569
Total assets.	$1,958,524	$1,626,459	$1,405,294

EXHIBIT 3   *(continued)*

Liabilities	1991	1990	1989
Current liabilities:			
Current maturities of long-term debt	$ 12,184	$ 10,558	$ 9,000
Note payable—bank*	325,000	200,000	—
Note payable—officer	—	30,000	39,000
Accounts payable:			
Trade	389,582	295,208	313,203
Employees' withholdings	4,875	3,197	3,070
Amount due for purchase of treasury stock	—	—	75,000
Accrued liabilities:			
Salaries and wages	93,713	57,534	48,413
Commissions	41,474	26,010	12,878
Sundry	14,528	11,357	4,796
Income taxes	—	18,036	19,800
	149,715	112,937	85,887
Total current liabilities	881,356	651,900	525,160
Long-term debt	176,522	189,122	195,710
Stockholders' equity:			
Contributed capital			
6% Cumulative preferred stock—authorized 10,000 shares			
of $10 par value; issued 2,000 shares	20,000	20,000	20,000
Common stock			
Class A (nonvoting)			
Authorized 15,000 shares of $10 par value; issued			
8,305 shares	83,050	83,050	83,050
Class B (voting)			
Authorized 5,000 shares of $10 par value; issued and			
outstanding 20 shares	200	200	200
	103,250	103,250	103,250
Retained earnings	892,396	777,187	676,174
	995,646	880,437	779,424
Less shares reacquired and held in treasury—at cost			
2,000 shares 6%			
cumulative preferred stock	20,000	20,000	20,000
2,308 shares Class A common stock	75,000	75,000	75,000
	95,000	95,000	95,000
Total stockholders' equity	900,646	785,437	684,424
Total liabilities	$1,958,524	$1,626,459	$1,405,294

*Converted to long-term debt in balance sheet projections in Exhibit 4.

Exhibit 3   *(continued)*

Statement of Earnings

Year Ended December 31

	1991	1990	1989
Net sales	$4,412,191	$3,573,579	$2,973,780
Cost of goods sold			
Inventories at beginning of year.........................	742,907	593,185	416,512
Purchases...	1,599,426	1,275,665	1,109,781
Freight in...	19,520	26,595	20,966
Direct labor	430,154	360,568	328,487
Manufacturing expenses	977,299	802,172	673,643
	3,769,236	3,058,185	2,549,389
Inventories at end of year..............................	826,228	742,907	593,185
	2,943,008	2,315,278	1,956,204
Gross profit	1,469,183	1,258,301	1,017,576
Product development expenses............................	131,746	128,809	102,299
Selling and administrative expenses.......................	1,112,542	915,140	740,801
	1,244,288	1,043,949	843,100
Operating income	224,895	214,352	174,476
Other deductions or (income)			
Interest expense......................................	56,259	37,790	32,416
Payments to retired employee...........................	10,000	10,000	20,000
Miscellaneous	(923)	(1,551)	(6,193)
	65,336	46,239	46,223
Earnings before income taxes............................	159,559	168,113	128,253
Provision for income taxes..............................	44,350	67,100	49,000
Earnings before extraordinary income	115,209	101,013	79,253
Extraordinary income—life insurance proceeds in excess of cash			
surrender value......................................	—	—	27,275
Net earnings...	$ 115,209	$ 101,013	$ 106,528
Earnings per share of common stock	$19.15	$16.79	$13,10

EXHIBIT 3   *(concluded)*

Statement of Changes in Financial Position

	Year Ended December 31		
	1991	*1990*	*1989*
Working capital provided from operations:			
Earnings before extraordinary income	$115,209	$101,013	$ 79,253
(Add item not requiring outlay of working capital)			
Depreciation.	55,978	50,658	44,267
Working capital provided from operations.	171,187	151,671	123,520
Extraordinary income from life insurance proceeds	—	—	27,275
Capitalized equipment lease obligation	—	5,295	—
Proceeds from cash surrender value of life insurance policies. . . .	—	—	51,877
Total working capital provided.	171,187	156,966	202,672
Working capital applied:			
Additions to property, plant, and equipment.	68,259	80,752	47,107
Increase in cash surrender value of life insurance policies—			
net of loans	4,763	4,646	5,954
Reduction of long-term debt.	12,600	11,883	8,996
Purchase of 2,308 shares of nonvoting Class A stock	—	—	75,000
Total working capital applied	85,622	97,281	137,057
Increase in working capital.	$ 85,565	$ 59,685	$ 65,615
Net change in working capital consists of:			
Increase (decrease) in current assets:			
Cash.	$ 47,470	$(66,742)	$ 64,854
Accounts receivable—net	190,336	109,381	(3,548)
Inventories.	83,321	149,722	176,673
Prepaid expenses	(6,106)	(5,936)	(4,980)
	315,021	186,425	232,999
Increase (decrease) in current liabilities:			
Current portion of long-term debt	$ 1,626	$ 1,558	$ 500
Notes payable to bank.	125,000	200,000	—
Note payable officer	(30,000)	(9,000)	—
Accounts payable	96,052	(17,868)	107,153
Amount due for purchase of treasury stock.	—	(75,000)	75,000
Contribution to profit-sharing trust.	—	—	(20,000)
Accrued liabilities	54,814	28,814	(7,619)
Income taxes	(18,036)	(1,764)	12,350
	229,456	126,740	167,384
Increase in working capital.	$ 85,565	$ 59,685	$ 65,615
Working capital at beginning of year.	544,445	484,760	419,145
Working capital at end of year.	$630,010	$544,445	$484,760

EXHIBIT 4   Pro Forma Financial Statements

Income Statement for Projections

Historical Percentages			Projected Percentages				(Thousands of Dollars)		
1989	*1990*	*1991*	*1992*	*1993*	*1994*		*1992*	*1993*	*1994*
100.0	100.0	100.0	100.0	100.0	100.0	Net sales	4,800	5,100	5,400
65.78	64.79	66.70	67.0	67.0	67.0	Cost of goods sold	3,216	3,417	3,618
34.22	35.21	33.30	33.0	33.0	33.0	Gross income	1,584	1,683	1,782
28.61*	29.28	28.25	28.0	28.0	28.0	Operating general and admin.†	1,344	1,428	1,512
5.61†	5.93	5.05	5.0	5.0	5.0	Profit before taxes and purchase financing . . .	240	255	270
						Noncompete payments	10	10	10
						Interest for "other bank debt"‡	74	70	63
						Profit before taxes	156	175	197
38.2§	39.9	27.8	39.0	39.0	39.0	Taxes	61	68	77
						Net earnings	95	107	120

*Historical and projected percentages include interest for long-term debt *only* as well as a $25,000 cost reduction for the reduced salary requirements of a replacement for Evans.

†Profit after adjustments to operating G&A.

‡Interest for "other bank debt" is assumed to be 10 percent times "other bank debt" outstanding at the end of the prior year.

§Effective tax rate.

Projected Beginning Equity Position

Total equity, December 31, 1991:	$900,646
Less cash payment of purchase price:	500,000
Beginning equity, January 1, 1992:	400,646

EXHIBIT 4   *(continued)*

Balance Sheet Accounts for Projections

	Historical			Projected				(Thousands of Dollars)			
	1989	*1990*	*1991*	*1992*	*1993*	*1994*		*At Closing 1991*	*1992*	*1993*	*1994*
							Assets:				
							Cash	50	50	50	50
(Days)	39.3	43.9	51.3	52.0	52.0	52.0	Accounts receivable.	620	684	727	769
(Turns)	3.3	3.1	3.6	3.8	4.0	4.1	Inventories	826	846	854	882
							Prepaids	14	15	15	15
							Total current assets	1,510	1,595	1,646	1,716
							Net fixed assets	365	370	370	370
							(Assume policies cash in)	0	0	0	0
							Total assets.	1,875	1,965	2,016	2,086
							Liabilities and Equity:				
(Days)	59.0	47.0	48.9	50.0	50.0	50.0	Operating accounts payable.	394	441	468	496
							Accrued expenses and taxes	150*	150	150	150
($000)	205	200	189				*Total existing long-term debt.*	189	176	163	148
							Liabilities from ongoing operations . . .	733	767	781	794
							Other bank debt	741	702	632	569
							Total liabilities	1,474	1,469	1,413	1,363
							Equity at beginning of year†	401	401	496	603
							Net earnings for year.	NA	95	107	120
							Total equity	401	496	603	723
							Total liabilities and equity	1,875	1,965	2,016	2,086

*In a purchase by an *outside* buyer, this is often zero at closing. These liabilities are paid off rather than transferred, and new accruals are gradually rebuilt in the normal course of business.

†See calculations of beginning equity elsewhere in exhibit.

EXHIBIT 4   *(concluded)*

Sources and Uses of Funds
(thousands of dollars)

	1992	*1993*	*1994*
Sources:			
Net earnings...	95	107	120
Plus depreciation......................................	56	56	56
Funds provided by operations...........................	151	163	176
Increase in accounts payable	47	27	28
Increase in accrual expenses and taxes	0	0	0
Increase in other bank debt.............................	—	—	—
Total sources	198	190	204
Uses:			
Increase in accounts receivables........................	64	43	42
Increase in inventories	20	8	28
Increase in prepaids..................................	1	0	0
Increase in fixed assets*..............................	61	56	56
Decrease in long-term debt............................	13	13	15
Decrease in other bank debt...........................	39	70	63
Total uses...	198	190	204

NOTE: Total sources must equal total uses.

*Reinvestment in plant and equipment is assumed to equal depreciation after the first year.

1–6 ICEDELIGHTS

On March 10, 1983, Paul Rogers, Mark Daniels, and Eric Garfield walked out of their final negotiating session with ICEDELIGHTS. The three were negotiating for the Florida franchise rights to ICEDELIGHTS, a European-style cafe/ice cream shop selling a variety of beverages and frozen desserts.

The session had gone fairly well, and they felt as though they had gotten most of the concessions that they wanted. Yet, mixed with this air of excitement was a sense of trepidation. There was a great deal of work that remained to be done on the deal, not the least of which was the securing of additional financing. In addition, other issues remained: Did the Florida market offer good potential for an ice cream business? Did the deal make good business sense? Was it right for them personally at this point in their careers? Did they have the skills and resources to make the business work, assuming that the deal came off? Did the same factors that made them good friends make them good business partners?

Background

Paul Rogers, Mark Daniels, and Eric Garfield were three second-year students at the New York School of Business (NYSB) who had all been classmates in their first year. (See résumés, **Exhibit 1**.) The idea of starting, or buying, their business arose during the week just prior to the start of second-year classes. The three had rented a house on Cape Cod for a week. Fresh from their summer jobs, they naturally shared their views of what their summer experiences had been like, and what impact these experiences would have on their career choices.

- Paul, 26, had spent two-and-a-half years with State Street Bank in Boston. He had worked for the summer as an associate with the New York investment bank of Warburg Paribas Becker and had enjoyed the experience. Paul, however, was excited by the challenge and rewards of creating and managing an enterprise of his own at an early stage in his career.
- Mark, 25, had spent two years with McKinsey & Co. and had also turned to investment banking for the summer. While he had enjoyed this experience, Mark felt a genuine desire for the independence and satisfaction of owning and managing his own business. He was unsure how additional work in either consulting or investment banking would bring him closer to this goal.

This case was prepared by Michael J. Roberts under the direction of Howard H. Stevenson.
Copyright © 1983 by the President and Fellows of Harvard College
Harvard Business School Case 9–384–076

- Eric, 30, had spent five years with Celanese in the international finance area. After pursuing positions with investment banks and consulting firms, Eric accepted a position with McKinsey's Atlanta office. Although he enjoyed the experience a great deal, Eric also felt drawn toward owning his own business. The independence, financial rewards, and opportunity to manage and truly create an organization seemed unequaled in any other career.

During that week on Cape Cod they spent a great deal of time on the beach and in the local bars discussing their experiences and speculating on what lay ahead. They talked about what they were looking for in a career: each of them wanted a job he would truly enjoy, independence, and great financial rewards. In addition, there was something incredibly appealing about building and managing an organization—really creating a business—being an entrepreneur. Moreover, it was clear that none of the "traditional" opportunities offered this. The idea of "having our own business" took hold.

Each of them had, at different times, thought that running his own business might be fun. During that week, they realized that this opportunity was the only option that would truly satisfy their objectives. Slowly, the focus of their thoughts turned to "How do we get there?"

Their discussions surfaced two fundamentally different approaches:

- The first approach, the "conservative" one, had two possibilities:

  — They could pick an industry, really try to learn a business, develop their management skills, and keep an eye out for opportunities; they were bound to learn a great deal, and they would be making their mistakes on someone else's money. In four or five years, they were bound to spot an opportunity and could then obtain the financing. Everyone says, "the money's there if you have a good idea."

  — Or, they could get into the deal flow; go to work for a venture capital firm or the M&A area of an investment bank. They would learn how to evaluate deals and make contacts with people that could provide financing. Then they would buy something for themselves and run it!

- The second approach was, "Why wait?" They argued that they had the skills and abilities to run a business, not a high-tech or sophisticated manufacturing firm, but surely there were some businesses that they had the collective talent to manage—all they had to do was find one. Further, in four or five years, it would be much harder to do. One would be used to the financial security and lifestyle of corporate life; it wouldn't be easy to go back to $25,000 or $30,000 and 80-hour weeks. Finally, with a spouse, family, car payments, a mortgage, and a summer home or ski house on the way, the risks associated with failure would be far greater down the road.

As school began, they decided that it was certainly worth trying to find a business.

The Search

The three began talking with professors at the business school, lawyers, and business contacts. They asked for advice and mentioned that they were in the market to buy a company. It soon became clear that they needed some concrete specifications regarding the businesses they were interested in, both as a guide to potential sources of information and to show a minimum level of commitment to the project. A brief specifications sheet was pulled together (**Exhibit 2**), which described the businesses they would be interested in and included their résumés.

The process proceeded through October and November with little in the way of results. People were generally helpful and encouraging, but it was very tough to get specific leads.

In late November, Paul's father, Mr. Rogers, mentioned that some friends of the family had recently purchased the ICEDELIGHTS franchise for Oregon and California; he had heard that Florida might be available. The three were excited about the possibility even though retailing had not been one of the industries targeted in their specifications sheet. The skills required to run a food franchise seemed within their range of abilities. It sounded like a fun business, and the potential financial rewards seemed to be great.

ICEDELIGHTS

ICEDELIGHTS was a Boston-based chain of food outlets selling a variety of beverages, pastries, and frozen desserts. There were currently nine stores in the New England area (primarily Boston), with several more scheduled to be opened during 1983. ICEDELIGHTS had sold its first franchise rights (Oregon and California) in June 1982, and the first of these stores was scheduled to open in the summer of 1983.

The four of them met with ICEDELIGHTS on December 10. Bob Andrews, the chairman, revealed that they had received dozens of franchise requests for Florida. He mentioned seven individuals in particular, each with extensive experience in either the fast-food industry or Florida real estate and who clearly had the financial resources required. Yet he felt that, at this time, ICEDELIGHTS was stretched to its capacity. They had grown slowly and carefully and were committed to maintaining a quality operation. Managing their existing locations and their own expansion, as well as providing a high level of assistance to the California franchise, would consume their available resources for the near future.

ICEDELIGHTS' conservative approach was due in large part to problems the company had had in its early years. Bob Andrews purchased ICEDELIGHTS when it had two locations. Early expansion resulted in financial problems when the company did not have the necessary organization and control systems in place.

Following this meeting, they met with the president of ICEDELIGHTS—Herb Gross. As the chief operating officer, he provided the group with a more detailed description of the ICEDELIGHTS operation. He, too, stressed ICEDELIGHTS' commitment to slow, *quality* growth. He felt, however, that there was some possibility that a deal could be worked out. Paul, Mark, and Eric expressed their enthusiasm for the business and their desire to really get involved in the day-to-day, hands-on operations of ICEDELIGHTS. They left impressed with the quality of ICEDELIGHTS' management and its potential for growth.

During this conversation, Paul, Mark, and Eric gained a better understanding of how ICEDELIGHTS worked. The heart of the concept revolved around several factors: first, ICEDELIGHTS sold an Italian "gelati" type ice cream, which was extremely rich and "homemade" looking and tasting. Yet, through a great deal of effort, ICEDELIGHTS had been able to perfect the process of freezing this "homemade" ice cream. This enabled ICEDELIGHTS to manufacture each of the products centrally, freeze them, and then sell on the premises of each store location. Most shops with a high-quality ice cream made the product on the premises. Moreover, ICEDE-LIGHTS had built and developed a very impressive organization. Its ongoing standardization of production, training, accounting, and control systems, store management, and store design and construction convinced Paul, Mark, and Eric that they would receive a great deal of support as a franchise. Finally, by marketing the concept as a café, this chain was able to derive sales throughout the day from coffee, pastry, and light snacks as well as ice cream in the afternoon and evening.

At this point, Paul, Mark, and Eric felt that a real opportunity was finally within their grasp. They realized that a great deal of work lay ahead if they were to have any chance of pulling the deal off. The opportunity to do a field study in the New Ventures area seemed to be an excellent vehicle to both accomplish this effort and get some advice from a knowledgeable advisor. They put together a proposal **(Exhibit 3)**, which was accepted.

The group met briefly with ICEDELIGHTS again in early January. Bob Andrews and Herb Gross indicated that they were interested in pursuing the Florida franchise further. They were very impressed with Paul's, Mark's, and Eric's abilities and willingness to get involved in the day-to-day operations of the franchise. The other groups had all been interested in purchasing the franchise as an investment. They viewed the desire to be involved in the operations as crucial to maintaining the quality of the operation. A dinner was scheduled for January 11 to discuss how to proceed.

The Deal

On January 11, Paul, Mark, Eric, and Mr. Rogers met Bob and Herb at a restaurant in Boston. ICEDELIGHTS' officers indicated that they did want to go ahead with the Florida franchise, but because they were so stretched, they did not want to be legally bound to proceed. Nonetheless, they recognized that, because of their job search situation, Paul, Mark, and Eric did need some security that the deal would come off. So ICEDELIGHTS proposed the following terms:

The franchisees (Paul, Mark, Eric, and Mr. Rogers) would:

- Pay $200,000 up front.

  — $100,000 development fees for the state of Florida.
  — $100,000 in five prepaid franchise fees of $20,000 each. This was prepayment for the first five stores.

- Pay $20,000 per store opened (after the first five, which were prepaid as above).
- Pay a 5 percent royalty on sales.

In exchange, ICEDELIGHTS would allow them to use the ICEDELIGHTS name, sell them products for roughly 32 percent of suggested retail price, train them, train one manager per store opened, and provide them with assistance in finding real estate, selecting locations, and constructing stores. In effect, ICEDELIGHTS would provide them with the first few locations as "turnkey" operations.

Because ICEDELIGHTS did not wish to be legally obligated to proceed if it felt that its operation was still stretched to capacity, these terms would be subject to an option.

The parties would sign an option which specified the terms of the franchise agreement (as above):

- The franchisees (Paul, Mark, Eric, and Mr. Rogers) would make a deposit of $75,000. If ICEDELIGHTS did not agree to proceed within nine months, the group would get back its $75,000 plus interest.
- If ICEDELIGHTS did agree to proceed, the franchisees would pay the remainder of the up-front fee ($125,000) and proceed.
- If the franchisees did not agree to pay the remaining fee and proceed, they would forfeit the $75,000 deposit.

ICEDELIGHTS' officers stressed that they were personally committed to going ahead with the Florida franchise as soon as California was running smoothly. They said that it was in everyone's best interest that they not be obligated to proceed if they did not feel that they could provide the franchisees with the level of support required. They further felt that by locking in the terms of the franchise, they were bringing something to the deal.

Another dinner was scheduled for January 25, two weeks hence, when Paul, Mark, Eric, and Mr. Rogers would deliver their decision to ICEDELIGHTS.

Paul, Mark, and Eric had two weeks to make a decision. The main issue now seemed to be financing. As the former president of a Boston-area bank, Mr. Rogers had a great many friends and associates who were potential sources of financing. Mr. Rogers began approaching them in hopes of finding one or two individuals to back the entire deal.

In the meantime, Paul, Mark, and Eric tried to pull together some financial data that would allow them to generate pro forma financials and estimate both the financing required and the attractiveness of the operation.

First, they compared the terms of the ICEDELIGHTS franchise with those of other leading franchises (**Exhibit 4**). On one hand, ICEDELIGHTS seemed expensive for a new and unproven franchise. Yet it appeared to offer excellent profit potential, and they were obtaining the rights to the entire state of Florida.

They did try to get some idea of the market potential that Florida offered and pulled together the data shown in **Exhibit 5.**

Next, they looked at the store-level income statement (**Exhibit 6**). The operation appeared to be incredibly profitable, particularly in light of the investment required. At $160,000 investment per store, they estimated that they would require $750,000 in financing, as follows:

Up-front fee	$200,000
First three stores	480,000
Working capital	70,000
	$750,000

Next, they had to think about how to structure the deal and how much equity to keep: Could they keep enough to make it financially rewarding to them and attractive enough for investors? Would the operation require continued infusions of cash for growth?

They knew that the more debt they could put in the capital structure the better, due to the deductibility of interest payments and the nondeductibility of dividends. They also knew that there were certain IRS regulations that limited the amount of debt they could have. They looked up the applicable section of the Tax Code, Sec. 385, and its explanation (see **Exhibit 7**). Further, debt and fixed interest payments would both restrict their growth and increase the riskiness of the venture.

After running some preliminary pro formas (**Exhibit 8**), they decided on a first cut at the deal capital structure. It seemed as though they could give 25 percent of their company away and still give investors an attractive return.

Mr. Rogers' contacts had said they were enthusiastic about the concept, but in the two-week period, they were unable to get any firm commitments. Mr. Rogers himself, however, had agreed to invest $75,000 in the venture.

On further reflection, Paul, Mark, and Eric decided that the deal was attractive to them even if they had to give up a good deal more than the 25 percent that they had projected. The enthusiasm that Mr. Rogers' contacts had expressed convinced them they would be able to raise the money. They decided to proceed.

On January 25, they met with ICEDELIGHTS and indicated that the terms were acceptable and that they wanted to go ahead with the deal. They agreed that their lawyers would be in touch to draw up the papers.

Financing

The following weekend, Paul, Mark, and Eric raced to produce a prospectus. They spent all day Saturday writing the document and hosted a previously planned dinner party Saturday evening for eight friends. At 1 A.M. Sunday morning, after a great dinner, a lot of wine, and a cut-throat game of charades, one guest suggested that they charge over to his office to type the document. A normally staid law firm was transformed as 11 typists pounded out the prospectus until 4:30 in the morning. The document, excerpted in **Exhibit 9**, presented the concept for the business and the proposed financing and capital structure.

During the next three weeks, they spoke to friends and associates of Mr. Rogers, presenting their business plan. At the end of three weeks, they had informal ''commitments'' for 15 units, or $405,000. With Mr. Rogers's $75,000, they had $480,000, and were only $270,000 shy.

During this time, it became clear that they would have to give up more than the original 25 percent they had planned. Not surprisingly perhaps, potential investors were somewhat put off by the 75/25 split in the deal. Paul, Mark, and Eric decided that as long as they were giving up more of the company they could raise a bit more money, and they revised the deal as shown in **Exhibit 10.**

In the process of determining the original deal, the three thought that investors would primarily be concerned with their overall return—ROI, IRR, NPV, or whatever. But, in fact, their requirements were more complex:

- Short-term repayment of original investment, with significant control during this phase.
- Long-term capital gain with reduction in investor control once original investment repaid.

There were also significant differences in the level of sophistication of potential investors. Some liked the concept, and that was sufficient. For others, a detailed analysis of investors' versus founders' risk and reward was required.

In addition, there were several other issues that remained to be settled, including:

- Form of organization. They had made a preliminary decision to use a straight corporation, but it was possible that a Sub-S or Limited Partnership made more sense.
- Legal counsel. They had decided to use Ernest Brooke, an acquaintance of Mr. Rogers who had indicated an interest in investing. Yet a few weeks had gone by, and he now seemed more hesitant. Further, he did not have any particular expertise in securities or corporate law and had not been particularly helpful.
- The market. Was Florida really a good spot for this business? Throughout, they had attempted to obtain market information on Florida without spending the time and expense on a lengthy trip. The data they had obtained seemed inconclusive.

Throughout this period, the second-year recruiting season was in full swing. Because they were emotionally committed to the ICEDELIGHTS deal, and because it was consuming so much of their time, none of the three was actively pursuing other opportunities. Each of them had the opportunity to return to the firm where they had worked for the summer, as well as one or two other possibilities.

The Decision

It was now February 22, and they had gotten a preliminary set of documents to review. The time when they would actually have to sign papers and put down their $75,000 seemed to be drawing near. A meeting was set for March 10 to put the finishing touches on the agreement.

At this point, Mark began having some strong doubts about the advisability of proceeding. He expressed them this way:

> I started getting these funny feelings in the pit of my stomach. I guess it was fear. It seemed to me that we had all gotten very caught up in the enthusiasm of the project and had not been as hard-nosed about the business decisions as we should have been.
>
> First, we had not even been to Florida. Eric lived there and was home at Christmas, but we never thoroughly investigated the market. We didn't know if there was competition there, and if there *were* other ice cream shops/cafés, how were they doing? Who knew if the Florida market would be attracted to the rich and different style of ice cream we offered? Finally, this was a "mall-based" retail economy. Who knew how we would do in malls?
>
> Second, I began to question the nature of our agreement and relationship with ICEDELIGHTS. It seemed to me that we were absolutely, critically dependent on them for real estate and product. We didn't have the credibility, contacts, or track record to get the prime

real estate that we needed. We were dependent on Bob Andrews for that. Similarly, one of our real competitive advantages was the cost and quality of our product. They were under no legal obligation to supply us, and we had no right to build our own production facility. What happened if they decided to expand their own operation and couldn't supply us? This gelati is not like hamburger buns—you can't just pick it up anywhere. I thought that our agreements should recognize this dependency and that ICEDELIGHTS should take 25 percent of our company instead of the $200,000 up front. This would give them a real financial incentive to act in our best interests.

Finally, there was my relationship with Paul and Eric. There had been some tension lately. It was obvious that I was more conservative, more risk-averse than they. I was worried about how this might affect our working relationship. I was uncomfortable with the notion that I could be outvoted on a decision and committed to a course of action that I wasn't comfortable with.

At this same time, Mr. Rogers was in Florida and reported that there were a small number of ice cream shops/cafés serving gelati. Further, one of these shops was not doing too well. Obviously, there were a great many of the typical ice cream shops, including Häagen-Dazs, Baskin-Robbins, and several local chains. Still, he felt that there were ample locations to provide for a fast growing business. They also learned that there were two other operations with a similar focus on gelati—Gelateria Italia and Gelato Classico—which were centered in California, but had recently started to franchise.

In preparation for their March 10 meeting, they decided that they would:

1. Go to Florida over spring break to thoroughly investigate the market.
2. Press ICEDELIGHTS to provide further assurances that it would be able to deliver the real estate support and product that they needed.

The issue relative to their attorney was still dragging on. Mark had mentioned his concerns about Ernest Brooke to a friend, John Stors, who was an attorney with a prominent local law firm. John had offered to check with other lawyers in his firm to see if anyone had ever dealt with Brooke. Sure enough, a half-dozen or so lawyers in the office knew Brooke and had dealt with him on tax, real estate, divorce, and estate issues. One mentioned that he had won a case in court over Brooke, a case that Brooke should not have lost. And most damaging of all was the revelation that Brooke was known to be a very close, personal friend of Bob Andrews, ICEDELIGHTS chairman.

Based on this, they decided to use Evan Post and risk alienating Brooke, who seemed willing to invest $30,000 maximum. Post had a reputation as an excellent counsel for small start-ups, as well as good contacts with potential investors. They spoke with Brooke who was quite accommodating and who agreed that the lure of potential investors was attractive, and a legitimate reason for including Evan Post.

Finally, they had exhausted all of Mr. Rogers' contacts and were still about $400,000 short (some investors' ''commitments'' had evaporated over the past month). They had a meeting with a newly formed venture capital partnership just prior to their March 10 meeting. The venture capital firm indicated that it was extremely interested, but it would require more ownership in the company for its investment. This firm was a particularly attractive partner because its principals had extensive experience running a Kentucky Fried Chicken franchise.

At the March 10 meeting, ICEDELIGHTS responded to their concerns. First, they agreed that the franchisees would not have to pay the remaining $125,000 until ICEDE-LIGHTS had furnished them with one suitable location and the lease had been signed. Further, ICEDELIGHTS agreed that the franchisees would have the right to build a production facility if ICEDELIGHTS became unable to supply them with product.

The closing date for the deal was set for March 25; in two weeks they would have to put up their $75,000 and sign the franchise and option agreements.

During this time, they had to decide whether to proceed or not. Three major questions remained:

- Was there real potential for this business in the Florida market?
- Did the option and franchise agreement make good business sense?
- Did the returns justify the risks?

If they did decide to proceed, they had to resolve the remaining financial issues:

- How much of the company could they give up and still have the deal be attractive to them? They had revised the deal as shown in Exhibit 10, but knew that they might have to give up even more of the company.
- Should they go ahead and commit $75,000 under the option agreement before they had the full $825,000 of financing secured, hoping to obtain the remainder before the option was exercised?
- Should they go with less than $825,000 and plan a second offering after the first store was up and running?

Finally, they each had their own personal feelings about the deal.

Mark: ICEDELIGHTS' concessions did reassure me to a certain extent, but I still have some very uncomfortable feelings.

First, the prospects for the business in Florida are still unclear to me; we haven't been to Florida yet, but I have the sense that we will find *some* attractive locations. But in order to meet our projections and investors' expectations, we have to grow extraordinarily quickly.

Second, even if the business does well, we are still critically dependent on ICEDE-LIGHTS. I think that real estate and product are our two key factors for success, and we really can't control them—they are in ICEDELIGHTS' hands. And if they don't perform, our only remedy is to sue. It really scares me to think that we will have the responsibility for $825,000 of other people's money, but can't control the two most important elements of the business.

Finally, I do question whether we have the skills to really make this work. I think that we have been pretty naive so far, and very much caught up in the excitement of actually doing a deal. Fortunately, it hasn't cost any money, and we've learned a lot.

Paul: The concessions that we won from ICEDELIGHTS reassured me of their continuing commitment to the Florida franchise. We would have preferred giving ICEDELIGHTS a small equity stake in the company, but they were not interested in this proposition.

Like Mark, I am concerned about the market; I do want more than just a "gut feel" that the market is there. This issue is particularly pressing because the closing date of March 25 will come before we have a chance to get to Florida over spring break. We need some concrete research before that. Money is also still a problem. We have "informal commitments" for about $300,000 of the $825,000 needed; experience has taught us that these are often more "informal" than they are commitments. A venture capital firm has expressed very strong interest in a $400,000 to $500,000 investment, but we've grown skeptical of verbal commitments and are still looking for other investors.

Both Eric and I have picked up on Mark's concerns and feel that we are dealing with them. I've started to get the impression, though, that Mark is veiling a lot of his more personal concerns about the venture in terms of business risk.

As far as I'm concerned, we've been lucky so far—things have gone very smoothly. Now it is time to start running fast, tying up all the loose ends. I'm exhilarated by the prospect of this, and the thought that we are really right on the verge of finally having our own company.

Eric: I feel that we really have a great opportunity here. I'm really excited by the idea of creating and managing our own organization. It is a fairly simple business, and ICEDELIGHTS has done a great deal to build and standardize the organization. With their systems and support, I am very confident that we can be successful.

I spent Christmas break in Florida, and I believe that the market prospects are very good. The population base is an Eastern, upscale, sophisticated one. The economies of the business are such that we can be profitable even with a small volume. Finally, all of our investors believe that Florida is an attractive market.

I think that ICEDELIGHTS' concessions assured us of the product supply and real estate support that we needed. After we get a few stores up and running, we will have developed a name for ourselves and won't need their real estate assistance anyway.

I understand Mark's concerns, but there are always going to be risks. In this case, they are manageable, and the return justifies them. There is little to be gained by waiting to start our own business; in a few years the risks will seem even greater. Now we have very little to lose.

I really don't feel that any additional assurances will satisfy Mark's doubts. In fact, I think that Mark would be uncomfortable with *any* deal. His lack of commitment is a real problem at this point and needs to be cleared up before it becomes a personal and business problem for all of us.

Eᴄʜɪʙɪᴛ 1   **Résumés**

PAUL ROGERS

Education

1981–1983
NEW YORK SCHOOL OF BUSINESS ADMINISTRATION   NEW YORK, NY
Candidate for the degree of Master in Business Administration in June 1983.

1974–1978
HARVARD COLLEGE   CAMBRIDGE, MA
Bachelor of Arts degree in June 1978. Majored in modern European history. Vice president of the Delphic Club;
presently serves as graduate treasurer.

Work Experience

Summer 1982
WARBURG PARIBAS BECKER   NEW YORK, NY
Corporate Finance. Summer associate. Worked on the initial public offering of a manufacturer of computer
memory devices. Assisted in the preparation of the prospectus, due diligence investigations, and marketing of this
successful offering. In addition, performed preliminary debt rating analysis and lease-versus-buy analysis for
prospective clients.

Summer 1981
NEWBURY, ROSEN & CO., INC.   BOSTON, MA
Corporate Finance. Wrote the prospectus for a $600,000 private placement for a start-up venture in the electronic
test equipment rental industry. Performed industry, competitive, and market analyses.

STATE STREET BANK AND TRUST COMPANY, INC.   BOSTON, MA
1981
Corporate Finance Department. Senior analyst. Worked with three-person team in structuring private place-
ments and assembling prospectuses. Co-authored prospectus for $10 million private placement to regional re-
tailing chain. Participated in presentations of services to a large high-technology firm.

1980–1981
Corporate Services Department. Senior analyst. Assisted vice president of department in establishing a Eurodol-
lar loan syndication portfolio, in which State Street acted as lead manager and agent. Marketed this service to
prospective clients. Made both individual and joint presentations to foreign banks interested in joining syndicates. Managed negotiations among the client, legal counsel, and the banking syndicate for a $10 million revolv-
ing loan syndication to a major toy manufacturer. Helped bring to a closing two additional term loan syndications
totaling $14 million.

1978–1980
Commercial Credit Training Program. Trainee. Completed the training program in 18 instead of the stipulated 24
months.

1975–1978
HASTY PUDDING THEATRICALS   CAMBRIDGE, MA
Producer of this broadway-like musical comedy show. Selected script, hired professional director, set designer,
music arranger, and costume designer, and coordinated an 80-person company. Budget for 1978: $110,000.
Improved financial controls and initiated a fund drive.

Personal Background

Raised in Boston. Have lived and traveled extensively abroad. Flexible on relocation. Fluent in French.

References

Personal references available upon request.   November 1982

Exhibit 1   *(continued)*

MARK DANIELS

Education

1981–1983
NEW YORK SCHOOL OF BUSINESS ADMINISTRATION   NEW YORK, NEW YORK
Candidate for the degree of Master in Business Administration in June 1983. General management curriculum. Awarded First-Year Honors. Representative to Admissions and Financial Aid Advisory Committee.

1975–1979
HARVARD COLLEGE   CAMBRIDGE, MASSACHUSETTS
Awarded Bachelor of Arts, *cum laude,* in Economics, June 1979. Wrote Senior Honors Thesis on strategic implications of cost and market structure in the publishing industry. Served as Editor-in-Chief, Harvard Yearbook Publications; Treasurer, D.U. Club; Class Representative, 1979 Class Committee; Executive Committee member, Harvard Fund. Elected Trustee of Yearbook.

Business Experience

Summer 1982
MORGAN STANLEY & CO.   NEW YORK, NEW YORK
Worked as a summer associate in corporate finance and mergers and acquisitions areas. Assisted in the development and implementation of a strategy for divesting a client's shipping subsidiary. Assisted in the defense of an oil services client engaged in a hostile takeover.

1979–1981
McKINSEY & COMPANY   NEW YORK, NEW YORK
                                                             TOKYO, JAPAN
Functioned as a consultant to top management of McKinsey's clients in the telecommunications, computer, and office products industries. Assessed the competitive cost position of a major international manufacturer of telecommunications products. Managed internal research project on Japanese competition in high-technology industries. Transferred to McKinsey's Tokyo office to develop a strategy for a British client seeking to enter the Japanese office products market. Wrote and presented report to Board of Directors in London.

Current Activities

Currently teaching two courses at New York College, serving as business tutor at Kirk House (an undergraduate residence), and working as an admissions counselor at the New York Business School. Specific responsibilities include:
Tutor, New York College Economics Department, teaching Managerial Economics and Decision Theory.
Teaching Assistant, New York College General Education Department, teaching Business in American Life.
Nonresident Business Tutor, Kirk House, advising undergraduates on careers and graduate education.
Counselor, New York Business School Admissions Office, interviewing prospective students.

Personal Background

Enjoy sailing, racquet sports, travel, and photography.

References

Personal references available upon request.

                                                             September 1982

EXHIBIT 1   *(concluded)*

ERIC GARFIELD

Education

1981–1983
NEW YORK SCHOOL OF BUSINESS ADMINISTRATION   NEW YORK, NEW YORK
Candidate for the degree of Master in Business Administration in June 1983. Pursuing a general management curriculum with emphasis on finance. Awarded COGME Fellowship.

1970–1974
UNIVERSITY OF FLORIDA   GAINESVILLE, FLORIDA
Earned a Bachelor of Science degree in Accounting with additional concentration in Economics. Awarded membership in Beta Alpha Psi and Phi Eta Sigma, two honorary scholastic fraternities.

Business Experience

Summer 1982
McKINSEY & COMPANY, INC.   ATLANTA, GEORGIA
Associate. Analyzed financial performance and product-line profitability, as part of a strategy study, for a major pharmaceutical company. Recommended a new pricing and production strategy. Prepared and presented report to client.

CELANESE CORPORATION   NEW YORK, NEW YORK
1979–1981
International Finance Manager. Supervised the preparation and analysis of strategic plans and operating budgets. Prepared financial analysis for potential foreign acquisitions and divestitures. Collaborated in cost reduction project resulting in annual savings of $5 million.

1978–1979
Financial Analyst. Prepared financial analysis for capital expenditure projects and for actual monthly results versus budget.

1976–1978
International Auditor. Supervised audit team in performing operational audits. Developed audit programs for foreign installations.

1975–1976
MINNESOTA MINING AND MANUFACTURING (3M)   CARACAS, VENEZUELA
Senior Cost Analyst. Prepared product analysis required by the Venezuelan government for the introduction of new products. Analysis included marketing, production, and financial data.

1974–1975
PRICE WATERHOUSE & CO.   MIAMI, FLORIDA
Staff Auditor. Performed financial audits of manufacturing and service organizations.

Personal Background

Fluent in English and Spanish. Enjoy participative sports, reading historical novels, and international travel.

References

Personal references available upon request.

                                                                            September 1982

Exhibit 2 **Specifications Sheet**

Dear:

We are currently second-year students at the New York School of Business and are interested in acquiring a company. We have the skills and abilities necessary to successfully manage a going concern and to create value for our backers and ourselves.

As explained in the attached specification sheet, we seek to acquire a medium-size firm. We feel our skills are applicable to a broad range of industries—from general industrial to consumer goods.

As the accompanying résumés indicate, the three of us have varied and complementary skills. We have backgrounds in planning, finance, control, operations, and general management. We believe that our abilities, combined with hard work and intense commitment, will enable us to succeed in such a venture.

We would greatly appreciate the opportunity to discuss our ideas with you and would be grateful for any suggestions you might have.

Sincerely,

SPECIFICATIONS

GENERAL:	Established manufacturing firms engaged in the production of Industrial and/or Consumer Goods.
SALES VOLUME:	$5,000,000–$10,000,000.
LOCATION:	Preferably, but not exclusively, Northeast.
PRODUCT:	Basic product with established market.
EXAMPLES:	Include, but are not limited to the following:

Industrial equipment
Food packaging and processing
Control systems and equipment
Electronic equipment
Plastic molding
Construction equipment
Oil field machinery
Sporting and athletic goods
Precision instruments

EXHIBIT 3   Field Study Proposal

Outline of Proposed Field Study

STEP I. Understand Existing Operations in New England, including: products, manufacturing, distribution, retail location strategy, advertising/merchandising strategy, cost structure, customer profile, management structure and systems, and personnel requirements.

STEP II. Evaluate Implications for Franchise, including: potential profitability and growth, competition, cost impact, tailoring of concept, relations with franchisor, key risks, and financial requirements.

STEP III. Evaluate and Structure Deal, including: management structure and responsibilities, form of organization, and legal/tax aspects.

STEP IV. Prepare Business Plan, including: introduction, company description, risk factors, products, market, competition, marketing program, management, manufacturing, facilities, capital required and use of proceeds, and financial data and financial forecasts.

EXHIBIT 4   Food Franchises — Terms

	Franchise Fee per Location ($100)	*Royalty (percent of sales)*
ICEDELIGHTS	20	5
Gelateria Italia	15	0
Gelato Classico	30	0
Baskin-Robbins	0	0
Carvel	20	Varies
Swensen's	20	5.5
Häagen-Dazs	20	$0.60/gallon
Long John Silver Seafood	10	4
H. Salt Fish & Chips	10	Varies
Kentucky Fried Chicken	10	4
Church's Fried Chicken	15	4
McDonald's	12.5	11.5
Wendy's	15	4
Burger King	40	3.5
Burger Chef	10	4
Taco Bell	45	5
Domino's Pizza	10	5.5
Pizza Inn	15	4
Shakey's Pizza	15	4.5
Orange Julius	18	6

EXHIBIT 5   Population Growth and Income Levels in Florida

City	1980 Population (000)	1970–1980 Growth (percent)	1979 Median Family Income
Boston*	563	(12.0%)	$14,318
Jacksonville	540	7.1	17,646
Miami	456	3.6	13,384
Tampa	271	7.2	15,412
St. Petersburg	238	10.2	15,476
Ft. Lauderdale	153	10.1	19,275
Hialeah	145	42.2	17,070
Orlando	128	29.3	16,312
Hollywood	121	14.2	19,890
Clearwater	85	63.5	18,528
Gainsville	81	26.6	18,528
Largo	58	141.7	16,252
Pompano	52	36.6	20,447
Boca Raton	49	75.0	26,910
Sarasota	49	20.0	16,661

*For reference only.

EXHIBIT 6   Financials

Pro Forma Income Statement: Store Level

Sales		$550,000
Fixed costs:		
Rent (1,000 to 12,000 square feet)	$ 25,000	
Management salaries	30,000	
Variable costs:		
Cost of product	192,500	
Payroll	52,500	
Royalty to parent (5%)	27,500	
Shipping	16,500	
Advertising	5,500	
Other	11,000	
Rent override*	13,500	
Total costs		374,000
Pretax store contribution		$176,000

Capital Requirements per Store

Construction, leasehold improvements	$ 60,000
Equipment costs	85,000
Fees and miscellaneous expenses, capitalized	15,000
Total	$160,000

*A "percent-of-sales" bonus to the landlord after a base sales level is reached.

Exhibit 7   Section 385 of Tax Code and Accompanying Explanation

---

Law

Treatment of Certain Interests in Corporations as Stock or Indebtedness.

(a) *Authority to Prescribe Regulations.* The Secretary is authorized to prescribe such regulations as may be necessary or appropriate to determine whether an interest in a corporation is to be treated for purposes of this title as stock or indebtedness.
(b) *Factors.* The regulations prescribed under this section shall set forth factors which are to be taken into account in determining with respect to a particular factual situation whether a debtor-creditor relationship exists or a corporation-shareholder relationship exists. The factors set forth in the regulations may include among other factors:

(1) Whether there is a written unconditional promise to pay on demand or on a specified date a sum certain in money in return for an adequate consideration in money or money's worth and to pay a fixed rate of interest.

(2) Whether there is subordination to, or preference over, any indebtedness of the corporation.

(3) The ratio of debt to equity of the corporation.

(4) Whether there is convertibility into the stock of the corporation.

(5) The relationship between holdings of stock in the corporation and holdings of interest in question.

Explanation

The distinction between debt and equity is an important one, because of the different tax treatment accorded to each. Interest paid on debt is deductible, while dividends distributed on stock are not. Similarly, the repayment of principal is tax free.
    In brief, in order to be classified as debt, a security must meet certain tests.

Essentially, the two key factors are:

• Proportionality: If debt is *not* held in proportion to equity, then the security will usually be treated as debt. If, however, the debt securities *are* held in proportion to equity, then the debt may be classified as equity if "debt is excessive."

• Excessive debt: Debt is typically *not* excessive if both of the following apply:

• The outside debt/equity ratio is less than 10:1. The outside ratio includes *all* creditors.

• The inside debt/equity ratio is less than 3:1. The inside ratio excludes debts to independent creditors.

However, even if debt is excessive by these tests, it still may not be excessive if the corporation pays a reasonable rate of interest on the debt, and the financial structure would be acceptable to a bank or similar lender.

Source: Reproduced with permission of the publisher from P-H *Federal Taxes*. Copyright 1983 by Prentice Hall, Inc., Englewood Cliffs, N.J. 07632.

EXHIBIT 8   Preliminary Pro Forma Cash Flow Statement (*in thousands of dollars*)

	Year 1	Year 2	Year 3	Year 4	Year 5	Year 6	Year 7	Year 8	Year 9	Year 10
Number stores, total	2	6	10	15	20	20	20	20	20	20
New stores	2	4	4	5	5	—	—	—	—	—
Existing stores	0	2	6	10	15	20	20	20	20	20
Sales	800	2,600	4,600	7,000	9,500	10,000	10,000	10,000	10,000	10,000
Operating income	130	470	390	1,375	1,900	2,100	2,100	2,100	2,100	2,100
Store opening expenses	100	200	200	250	250	—	—	—	—	—
Franchise fees	40	80	80	95	75	—	—	—	—	—
Corporation overhead	115	205	425	575	725	800	800	800	800	800
Income	(125)	(15)	185	455	850	1,300	1,300	1,300	1,300	1,300
Tax	(60)	(7)	35	200	380	580	580	580	580	580
AT income	(65)	(8)	150	255	470	720	720	720	720	720
− Store investment	250	500	500	625	625	—	—	—	—	—
− Corporation investment	10	20	50	50	50	—	—	—	—	—
+ Depreciation	40	120	200	300	400	400	400	400	400	400
+ Franchise fees (prepaid)	40	80	80	—	—	—	—	—	—	—
Case + or −	(180)	(320)	(270)	(375)	(175)	400	400	400	400	400
Total cash + or −	(305)	(335)	(120)	(120)	295	1,120	1,120	1,120	1,120	1,120
Cumulative cash + or −	(305)	(640)	(760)	(880)	(585)	535	1,655	2,775	3,895	5,015

EXHIBIT 9   **Excerpts from Prospectus**

THE OFFERING

Terms of the Offering

The Company is offering 25 Investment Units. Each Unit consists of 100 shares of its Class A Common Stock (zero par value), offered for $2,000 and $25,000 of the Company's Debentures.

	Per Unit	Total
Equity	$ 2,000	$ 50,000
Debentures	25,000	625,000
Total	$27,000	$675,000

All subscriptions shall be for at least one full unit. The Company currently plans to call for each subscription according to the following schedule:

Approximate Timing	Amount per Unit	Description
Immediately	$ 2,000	Equity
July 1–September 1, 1983	$15,000	Debentures
January 1–March 1, 1984	$10,000	Debentures

The Company reserves the right to accelerate or delay the timing of these contributions as its business requires, and will give investors thirty (30) days written notice of such requirements. Investors who are unable to meet subsequent contribution requirements will forfeit their contributions to date unless a suitable substitute can be found by the investor.

THE SECURITIES OFFERED HEREBY ARE NOT REGISTERED UNDER THE SECURITIES ACT OF 1933 AS AMENDED AND MAY NOT BE SOLD, TRANSFERRED, HYPOTHECATED OR OTHERWISE DISPOSED OF BY AN INVESTOR UNLESS SO REGISTERED OR, IN THE OPINION OF COUNSEL FOR THE COMPANY, REGISTRATION IS NOT REQUIRED UNDER SAID ACT.

Capitalization

The capitalization of the Company as of the conclusion of the Offering, assuming all units are sold, will be as follows:

Debt	$675,000
Equity	$ 75,000

This capital consists of the $675,000 raised from the Offering *plus* $75,000 contributed by the Founders.

The Founders will purchase 7,500 shares of the Company's Class B Common Stock for $25,000 and will also contribute $50,000 in debt.

EXHIBIT 9   *(continued)*

The resulting capitalization is detailed below:

Debt			
Investors	$625,000		
Founders	50,000		
		$675,000	
Equity			
Investors	$ 50,000		
Founders	25,000		
		$ 75,000	
Total capital		$750,000	

Description of Shares and Debentures

The investment units each consist of 100 shares of the Company's Class A Common Stock (zero par value) representing 1 percent of the total outstanding Common Shares of the Company. In total, the Class A stockholders will have representation on the Board of Directors equal to 50 percent of the total number of directors. When the Debentures have been repaid in full, the Class A board representation will be reduced to a pro rata share.

The Founders' Class B stock will be restricted as to dividends until the Debentures have been repaid in full.

The Debentures will be issued with a face value of $5,000 each and will pay interest at 15 percent per annum, cumulative with the first payment deferred until the end of Year 2. Interest payments will be made annually. The Debentures will have a maturity of five (5) years and will be callable.

Use of Proceeds

The amount to be received by the Company from the sale of the Investment Units offered herein is $675,000. The Company intends to use these funds, in addition to the $75,000 contributed by the Founders, for the following purposes:

Development rights for the state of Florida	$100,000
Prepaid franchise rights for the first five stores	$100,000
Capital for three ICEDELIGHTS stores	$480,000
Working capital	$ 70,000
	$750,000

Dividends

The Company plans to pay no dividends for a period of five (5) years, and until such time as the Debentures have been paid in full. Following this five-year period, the Company does have the intention of distributing dividends to its investors. No assurance can be made, however, that the Company will, in fact, be able to pay such dividends. Such payment is a matter to be determined from time to time by the Board of Directors and, of necessity, will be based upon the then existing earnings and cash position of the Company, as well as other related matters.

EXHIBIT 9   *(continued)*

Reports to Stockholders

The Company will furnish its shareholders audited financial statements on an annual basis as well as unaudited quarterly reports of operations and financial condition.

Financial Projections

Following a period of identifying suitable real estate, negotiating loans, and equipping locations, the Company anticipates commencing retail operations no later than early 1984. Ten-year financial projections (attached) are based on the following assumptions.

Store Openings

The Company anticipates opening stores according to the following schedule:*

	Year									
	1	2	3	4	5	6	7	8	9	10
Number of stores opened	3	4	5	5	5	2	2	2	1	1
Cumulative number of stores in operation	3	7	12	17	22	24	26	28	29	30

Sales Level and Growth

Based on its knowledge of sales volumes in existing ICEDELIGHTS locations, and its knowledge of the Florida market, the Company estimates $550,000 in base-level sales. This base level for new stores inflates at the rate of 5 percent per year. Store-level sales grow as follows:

Year	Total Rate of Growth	Real Growth	Inflation
1	15%	10%	5%
2–10	13%	8%	5%

Capital Requirements

Based on its knowledge of existing ICEDELIGHTS locations, the Company estimates a cost per store of $160,000. This breaks down as follows:

Construction costs	$60,000	
Equipment costs	85,000	
Fees and miscellaneous expenses	15,000	
Total capital costs..................................		$160,000

---

*The decline in the rate of openings after Year 5 reflects the Company's desire to show 10-year financial projections and does not serve to indicate the Company's estimate of the total potential of the Florida market.

EXHIBIT 9   *(continued)*

The capital costs are depreciated or expensed as follows:
a. Construction costs over 10 years, the assumed life of a lease.
b. Equipment costs over five years.
c. Architectural fees and other expenses are expensed in the year incurred.

Store Expenses

The Company estimates store level operating expenses as follows (as a percentage of sales):

Cost of product (including packaging)	35%
Payroll	15
Rent (1,000 to 1,200 square feet required)	7
Royalty	5
Shipping	3
Advertising	1
Other (telephone, cleaning, etc.)	2
Total expenses	68%

Amortization

The $100,000 development rights are amortized over the 20-year life of the agreement.

THE ATTACHED PROJECTIONS REPRESENT OUR ASSESSMENT OF THE POTENTIAL FOR THE FLORIDA MARKET. THESE ESTIMATES ARE BASED ON DISCUSSIONS WITH MANAGEMENT AND OUR OWN INVESTIGATION OF THE EXISTING OPERATION. WE BELIEVE THAT THESE FIGURES ARE REPRESENTATIVE OF CURRENT OPERATIONS AND DO FAIRLY REFLECT THE LEVEL OF OPERATIONS ANTICIPATED IN FLORIDA. NONETHELESS, THEY ARE ONLY PROJECTIONS, AND MUST BE VIEWED AS SUCH.

EXHIBIT 9 (continued)

Projected Income Statement

(in thousands of dollars)

	Year									
	1	2	3	4	5	6	7	8	9	10
Net sales	$ 962	$3,340	$6,617	$10,815	$15,719	$20,392	$24,580	$29,386	$34,482	$39,839
Store level expenses:										
Variables	654	2,271	4,500	7,354	10,689	13,867	16,714	19,982	23,448	27,091
Fixed	53	174	330	521	730	900	1,025	1,160	1,784	1,398
Depreciation	69	165	295	430	575	585	574	545	480	415
Operating income	186	730	1,492	2,510	3,725	5,040	6,267	7,699	8,770	10,935
Start-up expenses	103	140	180	173	162	67	69	71	36	37
Corporate overhead	105	215	415	580	680	810	906	1,017	1,110	1,203
Amortization	5	5	5	5	5	5	5	5	5	5
Earnings before interest and taxes	(27)	370	892	1,752	2,878	4,158	5,287	6,606	7,619	9,690
Interest expense:										
Investor	0	216	101	101	75	0	0	0	0	0
Bank		15	15	15	0	0	0	0	0	0
Profit before taxes	(27)	139	776	1,636	2,803	4,158	5,287	6,606	7,619	9,690
Taxes	0	52	357	753	1,289	1,913	2,432	3,039	3,505	4,457
Net income	(27)	87	419	883	1,514	2,245	2,855	3,567	4,114	5,233

EXHIBIT 9 *(continued)*

Projected Balance Sheet
(in thousands of dollars)

	Year									
	1	2	3	4	5	6	7	8	9	10
Assets										
Cash	$320	$105	$ 24	$ 225	$ 936	$3,400	$6,445	$10,153	$14,537	$19,964
Prepaid fee	40	0	0	0	0	0	0	0	0	0
Development agreement	95	90	85	80	75	70	65	60	55	50
Net fixed assets	268	715	1,220	1,632	1,940	1,726	1,541	1,405	1,140	951
Total assets	$723	$910	$1,329	$1,937	$2,951	$5,196	$8,051	$11,618	$15,732	$20,965
Liabilities										
Bank debt	0	100	100	0	0	0	0	0	0	0
Investor debt	675	675	675	500	0	0	0	0	0	0
Total liabilities	675	775	775	500	0	0	0	0	0	0
Equity										
Paid-in capital	75	75	75	75	75	75	75	75	75	75
Retained earnings	(27)	60	479	1,362	2,876	5,121	7,976	11,543	15,657	20,890
Total equity	48	135	554	1,437	2,951	5,196	8,051	11,618	15,732	20,965
Total liabilities & equity	$723	$910	$1,329	$1,937	$2,951	$5,196	$8,051	$11,618	$15,732	$20,965

Exhibit 9 (continued)

Projected Cash Flow
(in thousands of dollars)

	Year									
	1	2	3	4	5	6	7	8	9	10
Net income	($ 27)	$ 87	$419	$ 883	$1,514	$2,245	$2,855	$ 3,567	$ 4,114	$ 5,233
Depreciation	69	165	295	430	575	585	575	545	480	415
Amortization	5	5	5	5	5	5	5	5	5	5
Prepaid expense	60	40	0	0	0	0	0	0	0	0
Cash from operations	107	297	719	1,318	2,094	2,835	3,434	4,117	4,599	5,653
Capital expenditures:										
Development agreement	100	—	—	—	—	—	—	—	—	—
Prepaid fees	100	—	—	—	—	—	—	—	—	—
Store construction and equipment	337	612	800	842	883	371	389	409	215	226
Cash generated: surplus/(deficit)	(430)	(315)	(81)	476	1,211	2,464	3,045	3,708	4,384	5,427
Financing:										
Equity	75	0	0	0	0	0	0	0	0	0
Debentures	675	0	0	(175)	(500)	0	0	0	0	0
Bank debt	0	100	0	(100)	0	0	0	0	0	0
Net cash flow	320	(215)	(81)	201	711	2,464	3,045	3,708	4,384	5,427
Beginning cash	0	320	105	24	225	936	3,400	6,445	10,153	14,537
Ending cash	$ 320	$ 105	$ 24	$ 225	$ 936	$3,400	$6,445	$10,153	$14,537	$19,964

EXHIBIT 9 *(concluded)*

Cash Flow and Internal Rate of Return to One Unit Shareholder
(in thousands of dollars)

	Year										
	0	1	2	3	4	5	6	7	8	9	10
Investment	$27	—	—	—	—	—	—	—	—	—	—
Interest	—	—	$ 8	$ 4	$ 4	$ 3	—	—	—	—	—
Return of principal	—	—	—	—	$ 4	$21	—	—	—	—	—
Share of cash flow (1%)	—	—	—	—	—	—	$25	$30	$37	$44	$ 54
Share of estimated market value at 10 times earnings*	—	—	—	—	—	—	—	—	—	—	$523
Net cash flow to investor	($27)	—	$ 8	$ 4	$ 8	$24	$25	$30	$37	$44	$577

Annualized internal rate of return = 49%

*For illustrative purposes only.

EXHIBIT 10   **Summary of Changes to the Offering**

The Offering

The Company is offering 25 investment units. Each unit consists of 150 shares of its Class A Common Stock (no par value), offered for $5,000 and $25,000 of the Company's 10% debentures.

	Per Unit	Total
Equity	$ 5,000	$125,000
Debentures	25,000	625,000
Total	$30,000	$750,000

All subscriptions shall be for at least one full unit. The Company currently plans to call for each subscription according to the following schedule:

Approximate Timing	Amount per Unit	Description
Immediately	$ 2,500	Equity
July 1–September 1, 1983	17,500	Equity and 3 debentures
January 1–March 1, 1984	10,000	2 debentures

The Company reserves the right to accelerate or delay the timing of these contributions as its business requires, and will give investors thirty (30) days written notice of such requirements. Investors who are unable to meet subsequent contribution requirements will forfeit their contributions to date, unless a suitable substitute can be found by the investor.

The securities offered herein are not registered under the Securities Act of 1933 as amended and may not be sold, transferred, hypothecated or otherwise disposed of by an investor unless so registered or, in the opinion of counsel for the Company, registration is not required under said Act.

Capitalization

The capitalization of the Company, as of the conclusion of the offering, assuming all units are sold, will be as follows:

Debt	$675,000
Equity	$150,000
Total	$825,000

The capital consists of $750,000 raised by the offering plus $75,000 contributed by the founders.

The founders will purchase 6,250 shares of the Company's Class B Common Stock for $25,000 and will also contribute $50,000 in debt.

EXHIBIT 10 (concluded)

Revised Cash Flow and Internal Rate of Return to One Unit Shareholder

(in thousands of dollars)

					Year						
	0	1	2	3	4	5	6	7	8	9	10
Investment	$30	—	—	—	—	—	—	—	—	—	—
Interest		—	$5	$3	$3	$3	—	—	—	—	—
Return of principal		—	—	—	$5	$20	—	—	—	—	—
Share of cash flow (1½%)		—	—	—	—	—	$37	$46	$56	$66	$82
Share of estimated market Value at 10 times earnings*		—	—	—	—	—	—	—	—	—	$785
Net cash flow to investor	($30)	—	$5	$3	$8	$23	$37	$46	$56	$66	$867
Annualized internal rate of return = 52%											

*For illustrative purposes only.

1–7 POSTAL BUDDY

Sidney Goodman read his business plan one last time and sighed. It was March 1990, and Goodman's efforts to raise $2.0 million for his fledgling company, Postal Buddy Corporation (Postal Buddy), had so far been unsuccessful. As he sat in his San Diego office, Goodman knew that he had to make some changes. The capital that he was trying to raise was critical to the funding of Postal Buddy's first major market test. Without the capital to finance a market test of the Postal Buddy concept, two years of hard work and product development would come to a grinding halt.

Postal Buddy Corporation manufactured a freestanding electronic kiosk that enabled immediate, on-line change of address to be sent directly to the United States Postal Service (USPS or Postal Service). Goodman planned to locate Postal Buddy machines in department stores, grocery stores, even college campuses in addition to post offices throughout the country. Initial response from major mailers and the Postal Service had been overwhelmingly positive. The customers, typically people who were moving, like the easy-to-use kiosks, as well as the other products and services that were sold through the kiosk. Product acceptance, Goodman felt, was not going to be Postal Buddy's major hurdle.

Goodman had spent the last year and a half working with the Postal Service on the refinement and deployment of Postal Buddy. Through a series of long and complex negotiations, Goodman had managed to acquire the full cooperation of the postmaster general as well as the right to use the USPS eagle and logo and even funding from the USPS. In addition, Goodman had four patents pending, covering not only the Postal Buddy system and certain components, but the broader concept of a self-service printing kiosk as well. Goodman had received a letter from the U.S. Patent Office just yesterday allowing the major claims of the broadest and most important patent.

In spite of these successes, Goodman was unable to raise any financing from the venture capitalists with whom he had been meeting for the past four months. For one thing, Postal Buddy did not yet have a test market contract with the Postal Service. In addition, while investors liked the concept, no one was willing to back an unproven idea and, in investors' minds, an unproven management team. The nationwide implementation of Postal Buddy, Goodman admitted, would be a daunting task. Goodman believed, however, that the market test would prove the validity of his idea. Once he

This case was prepared by Karen E. Moriarty under the supervision of H. Irving Grousbeck. Postal Buddy® is a registered trademark of Postal Buddy Corporation. Development of this case was funded by the Robert Denzil Alexander Fund.

had accomplished the test, Goodman was confident that Postal Buddy would get the USPS contract. At that point, he could concentrate on assembling a strong management team.

The Postal Buddy Concept

The Postal Buddy concept is that of an on-line, interactive system in a freestanding kiosk that enables people who are moving to electronically change their address with the Postal Service. The change-of-address terminals would be located in postal lobbies, supermarkets, drugstores, college campuses, military bases, and major office buildings. Postal Buddy's goal would be to own and operate a nationwide network of Postal Buddy terminals that would handle a major share of the address changes in the United States. (See **Exhibit 1** for photograph of a Postal Buddy kiosk.)

Through the use of a customized keyboard and software package, Postal Buddy would also prompt the customer to select publications, credit card issuers, government agencies, and a variety of other organizations to be notified automatically of the address change. While these services would be free to the customer, the major mailers and organizations subscribing to Postal Buddy would receive current address lists updated daily. In addition to the subscription fee, they would be charged on a per name basis.

Postal Buddy's customers would not be limited, however, to people who are moving. Customers would be able to purchase products and services vended from the kiosk. Initially, these products would include return address labels, business cards, and change of address postcards preprinted with the customer's old and new addresses. The products would be printed in seconds by a laser printer contained within the kiosk. Consumers would also be able to purchase magazine subscriptions and stamps or put their names on catalog lists. (See **Exhibit 2** for a detailed description of Postal Buddy's products and services.)

Communication and payment would be key aspects of the system. Standard microprocessors would provide the central computer system or host. Each Postal Buddy would contain a standard personal computer. The Postal Buddy network would also use address standardization software and a pre-existing radio network for communication between the kiosks and the host system. Payment for products would be accepted in coins, bills ($1, $5, $10, or $20) or by credit card. To handle these transactions, the company had designed a unique interface board allowing on-line communication between a standard coin and bill acceptor and the PC in the kiosk. Credit card payment would be handled by a clearinghouse for the various credit card issuers.

Verification and security would be provided by the use of measures such as visible photographing of each transaction, the requiring of Social Security numbers and signature verification. In addition, postcards would be sent to the customer's old address to verify the validity of the address change.

Postal Buddy History

In early 1985, Sid Goodman had begun looking for a new venture. After 14 years of running Management Reports Incorporated (MRI), a Cleveland-based computer time-sharing company that he founded to service the real estate property management industry, Goodman was ready for a change. Goodman, who had a degree in accounting and was a CPA, had become increasingly interested in the innovative use of high-speed laser printing systems through his work at MRI. One day in 1983, while tinkering with a Xerox 9700 laser printer, he accidentally stumbled on a technique for duplex, or two-sided, printing of labels, a feat that had until then been impossible because of an inability to feed the heavyweight, wax-coated backing paper through the copier. Goodman applied for and received a patent on the two-fold format of the labels. With MRI generating a healthy $12 million in annual revenues, Goodman decided to sell the company in late 1985 and move to San Diego in order to pursue commercially viable opportunities for his invention.

Goodman spent most of 1986 experimenting with ideas for creative, marketable uses of the label-printing technology. Deciding that the sale of labels might be an opportunity worth pursuing, Goodman and his son Martin created The Welcome Labels Corporation in early 1987. Focusing on the multifamily residential market, the company's strategy was to market the labels, printed with the names and addresses of a new resident, to local apartment management firms. The labels, which were sent to the resident as part of a welcoming package, were printed with promotions for the apartment property on the backing paper. Welcome Labels marketed the idea as an excellent public relations program for the management companies.

As Welcome Labels grew throughout 1987 and early 1988, Goodman noticed an interesting phenomenon: 18 months after the start of the company, it was generating $10,000 a month in reorders at an average $8.50 an order, an amount that was several times what Goodman had expected. It was particularly interesting since customers could buy competitors' labels at $1 per 1,000 labels, while the Welcome labels were priced at $2 for a sheet of 45. When he began questioning the customers about their purchases, Goodman discovered that they loved a number of the labels' features. In particular, customers liked: (1) the format of the labels: the convenient two-fold, perforated sheets and the self-adhesive feature; (2) the heavyweight paper and other quality aspects of the printing; and (3) the ability to have the labels in only five days rather than wait six to eight weeks for the competition's labels. Goodman realized that he had stumbled onto a very successful consumer product.

Despite consumer acceptance of the labels, Goodman recognized that the current distribution channel was never going to provide significant market penetration. The market as then defined was too narrow, both geographically and demographically. Goodman began searching for a new way to broaden the market, experimenting with direct mail, point-of-purchase displays in drugstores, and department store sales. After spending what he termed "a small fortune" on these efforts, Goodman still had no viable alternative means for reaching new markets.

At that point, anxious to find new customers, Goodman revived his concept of the label-vending machine. Figuring that he had nothing to lose by giving it a try, Goodman came up with a sketch and commissioned a cabinetmaker in early 1988 to construct the cabinet. The concept was simple: the cabinet would hold a printer from which the customer could print his or her own labels. In April, Goodman convinced a local drugstore to install the cabinet, which he called the "Label Machine." In its first month, the Label Machine attracted four to five customers per day. Moreover, people were using the machine despite the novelty of the concept and the lack of advertising. Goodman was particularly impressed because of the huge inconvenience involved: since the machine did not take money, customers had to find the store clerk who, in turn, had to issue a special sales receipt for the labels before they could be purchased. In the face of this indisputable market acceptance, Sid Goodman became convinced that he had a winner.

Getting Started

Goodman began thinking about ways to develop and implement the vending machine concept. By midsummer of 1988, Goodman had settled on a plan to own and operate a network of label-vending machines installed in drugstores and other retail locations throughout the country. Knowing that he could not fund a business of such scope alone, Goodman began putting together a business plan. He decided to find a large corporate partner, preferably one in a related business such as stationery or office products. Goodman felt that he could be very flexible; he was even willing to work out a royalty arrangement if a prospective partner required more direct control and ownership of the business.

Dozens of phone calls and meetings later, Goodman was still without a corporate partner and the financial backing for his new venture. No one was willing to give the idea or Sid Goodman a chance. Among the companies he contacted, however, was Dennison Manufacturing, a large manufacturer of stationery, inks, and other office products. Like Goodman's other contacts, the manager of new products was reluctant to even look at the product, let alone sign the nondisclosure agreement that Goodman required. According to Goodman:

> The manager was convinced that any good idea concerning labels was probably already in his files. However, I finally managed to strike a deal with him. I offered to send him the labels and the business plan with an *unsigned* nondisclosure agreement. If he thought that it really was a good idea, then he could send the signed nondisclosure agreement back to me.

Goodman's gamble paid off. The manager like the idea and, by August of 1988, asked Goodman to fly out to the company's Waltham, Massachusetts, headquarters and meet with senior management. At the first meetings, top management was somewhat skeptical of consumers' willingness to pay a comparatively high price for Goodman's labels. However, Dennison was intrigued enough to request a further demonstration, at its own expense, of the vending machine. The outcome of the demonstration was exactly what Goodman had hoped: Dennison's management loved both the machine and the labels. The company agreed verbally to finance the rollout of a label machine network as a separate business unit of Dennison. Management asked Goodman to submit a proposal naming his price for an exclusive license of the product together with a consulting arrangement for its implementation.

Unfortunately for Goodman, Dennison was also undergoing a dramatic reorganization at the time. As he began to get further into the negotiating process, Goodman found himself dealing with new managers who, preoccupied with the reorganization, were not focusing on the details of his proposed deal. Over the next three months, the process slowed to a crawl, as Goodman sought to find a corporate "champion" within Dennison to move the project forward.

Goodman flew back to Dennison headquarters several times, attempting to overcome the bureaucratic stumbling blocks that had derailed his venture. On one such trip, he stopped in Washington on the chance that he could arrange a meeting with USPS officials. After having no success with the Address Information Systems group, his initial contact, Goodman was eventually referred to Tom Berry, executive advisor to the Special Projects and Innovation group. Berry was a retired AT&T executive who had been the executive assistant to the previous postmaster general. His unusual background gave him the unique perspective of both an experienced businessman and an insider in the USPS bureaucracy. Fortuitously for Goodman, Berry had recently taken on the challenge of finding a solution to the Postal Service's enormous change-of-address problem.

The Change-of-Address Problem

Every year, the Postal Service handles 2.25 billion pieces of "undeliverable as addressed" mail from 39 million residential and business address changes. The mail is processed through 209 computerized forwarding units (CFUs) maintained by the Postal Service solely for this purpose. As a result, the expense of the forwarding service to the USPS is a staggering $1.3 billion annually. For example, the Postal Service spends $35 million each year on the purchase of the yellow forwarding labels alone. Costs to major mailers like the publishing industry are similarly large. They incur up-front expenses associated with address change processing and the further burdens of delayed payments and loss of customers through interrupted service.

The current system has two major flaws. First, the address change system utilizes manual cards. The customer must go to the post office, pick up, and then fill out the confusing change of address form. He or she must then fill out change of address cards by hand to notify each mailer. Because it is such a time-consuming process to notify each correspondent, many people choose simply to rely on the Postal Service forwarding service instead.

The second problem is the "effective moving date" processing of the address change. The USPS files each change of address card manually until the actual moving date. Upon the moving date, the card is handed to the mail carrier, who notes that all future mail is to be forwarded to the CFU serving that region. Once mail arrives at the CFU, the Postal Service applies the yellow forwarding address label and then reroutes the mail back into the regular delivery system.

For a fee, notification of address changes can currently be sent at the mailer's request. The new address is also uploaded into the national change of address (NCOA) data base in Memphis to which major mailers can send their mailing lists to be corrected. However, the delay and rerouting results in a number of inefficiencies and costs. Because the system does not allow for advance notification of an address change, mail is often sent out before a new address is received. In addition to the costs of rerouting, customers often do not receive forwarded mail lost in the system, or they experience delays of as much as two months. Considerable effort and money is also wasted by mailers on processing duplicate address changes. Lastly, the process nearly triples the USPS handling process for each piece of forwarded mail.

Initial Involvement with the USPS

As he talked with Goodman in December 1988, Tom Berry's initial reaction to Goodman's label machine was one of extreme interest. Goodman had naively told Berry that his machine could collect address changes from people buying labels; after all, the company just had to ask the customer if the address was new and then enter it into the computer. Berry recognized that Goodman's label machine would provide an immediate, tangible benefit that would motivate the customer to use the machine. If the machine could somehow be designed to incorporate an address change system as well, Goodman suggested, then the Postal Service and mailers would gain enormous benefits from the nationwide network of machines.

Berry, who had just received $25,000 from a consortium of major mailers, was about to undertake a broad focus group study of whether customers would use a terminal in the Post Office to change their address. Unfortunately, he had no prototype to use in the study. He asked if Goodman would be interested in providing a demonstration model for the focus group.

Goodman was ecstatic about the opportunity. Agreeing enthusiastically to provide the terminal at his own expense, he rushed to develop mock-up address change software for the meeting that was only weeks away in January. At his own inspiration, Goodman added features like the vending of the preprinted postcards and business cards. In the process, he redesigned the graphics on the cabinet, got approval to use the USPS logo, and created a new name, Postal Buddy. At the same time, he began the application process for another, broader patent, this time on the concept of a self-service print shop.

Goodman was eager to inform Dennison of the proposed new direction for the project and the exciting opportunity that it represented. Upon hearing the news, the president of one of the newly organized Dennison divisions contacted Goodman. Sid recalled the conversation:

> He told me that Postal Buddy was becoming much larger than they (Dennison) had originally thought. He believed that for it to be successful, the business would need a lot of attention and time. Unfortunately, there was no one at the division level willing to champion the project. The division would still provide funding if I wanted to proceed, but the president thought it would take a long time before Dennison could figure out who would manage the effort.

Goodman took the implicit recommendation and terminated his negotiations with Dennison. Once again without a source of funding, he nonetheless forged ahead with his preparations. The focus group study was about to begin.

Developing a Relationship with the Post Office

By the end of the focus group study, all parties involved — the Postal Service, the mailers, and the customers — were enthusiastic about the Postal Buddy concept. The study's findings indicated that consumers valued four critical aspects of the system: (1) the simplification of the address change process; (2) the ability to notify mailers automatically and at no cost; (3) the perceived control over the unsettling and often stressful moving process; and (4) the ability to receive instantly printed products. In all of the participants' minds, the results of the study were clear: Postal Buddy was a success.

Based on the extraordinary strength of the consumer reaction, Goodman was convinced that the machine had to be used and the labels seen for anyone to really appreciate the allure of the product. He set up the prototype in Berry's office so that the concept could be easily demonstrated to other major mailers. One day not long after the completion of the study, Ron Vandegrift, the national accounts manager, decided to bring the postmaster general by to see the machine. The postmaster general, Anthony Frank, was on his way to a meeting to discuss future developments at the USPS. Vandegrift thought he might find Postal Buddy interesting.

Goodman had been told in advance that he would have only three minutes of the postmaster's time. Instead, Frank was so impressed that he stayed for a 40-minute conversation with Goodman. The postmaster general was unequivocally supportive and enthusiastic about the machine. According to Goodman, Frank's comments about the concept were direct and unqualified:

> This is one of the best ideas I've ever seen. I want it (the project) to work. I want to do whatever we have to to get it tested.

In spite of Frank's declaration of support, Goodman soon became embroiled in the tortuous workings and political struggles of the USPS, the largest civilian bureaucracy in the world. Over the next several months in early 1989, several significant groups emerged in opposition to the Postal Buddy project. Certain of the most important internal groups resented the external development of a major ground-breaking technology in an area that they considered to be rightfully within their domain. In particular, Procurement, a group that in the not too distant past had been the focus of a major scandal, was overly sensitive to the issue of sole-sourcing a project of this magnitude with Postal Buddy.

Resolving the concerns of the different factions and getting the project to move forward was a seemingly impossible task. Goodman did everything he could to accelerate the process, from meeting and negotiating with each of the internal groups at the USPS to threatening the recalcitrant Procurement group with a lawsuit over violation of the nondisclosure agreement if it put the contract out to bid. Still, the process dragged on, with the dissenting groups attempting to stall the project in the hope that the inertia would eventually kill it completely.

At the same time, however, Goodman began marshalling his support at the Postal Service. Frank and Berry both began steadily spreading word of the Postal Buddy concept in the publishing and other major mailing industries. Vandegrift also began working with the major mailers interested in becoming Postal Buddy subscribers. Word of mouth from the consortium participants had spread throughout the industry and, aided by Vandegrift's efforts, the interest in the industry began to increase. With the approval of Berry and Vandegrift, Postal Buddy began collecting $500 as a subscription fee from over 100 of the largest major mailers who wanted to participate in the market test. If the uncooperative groups continued to stall the project, the Postal Service would be in the dubious position of allowing Postal Buddy to receive revenues for a product that had no USPS contract.

Midway through 1989, recognizing the advantage of the attention being generated within the industry, Goodman began pushing the Postal Service toward an agreement with Postal Buddy. His initial goal was to secure a contract and funding for a test market of the product. Goodman knew that a successful test market would be critical to calming fears at the Postal Service about the viability of the product and Postal Buddy's ability to implement the system. In addition, Goodman knew that later-stage financing would depend on the success of the market test.

Goodman also wanted several concessions from the USPS concerning the product. Goodman required the right to print postage on the change-of-address postcards vended through Postal Buddy. Unlike typical postcards, which are preprinted with postage and purchased on a consignment basis, the right to ''manufacture'' postage would allow Postal Buddy to free up an otherwise significant investment in inventory. It would also let Postal Buddy take advantage of the ''float,'' the free use of cash generated from the sale of postage until the payment was due to the Postal Service. Goodman also negotiated for the right to use the USPS eagle and logo on all Postal Buddy machines. Lastly, he wanted the right to claim full authorization of Postal Buddy from the Postal Service, i.e. ''Authorized USPS Change-of-Address System.''

For its part, in addition to concerns about implementation and sole-sourcing, the Postal Service was worried about its control over the Postal Buddy system. The printing of postage was dismissed out of hand, as no company in the history of the Postal Service had ever been granted the right to privately manufacture postage on demand. In addition, Procurement was intent upon owning the rights to any technology that would be intrinsic to the success of such a major program. As a precondition for granting a contract, Procurement began threatening to require rights under the ''rights in technical data'' clause of a government funding contract. Under this clause, the government can claim nonexclusive rights to any technology developed using government funding, even if the technology is patented. If successful, the maneuver would allow the Postal Service to use Goodman's patent royalty-free. Procurement even asserted the right to use eminent domain to claim the patents, which are considered real property and thus subject to seizure by the government, if Goodman didn't cooperate.

As the negotiation process continued, tempers flared between the various parties. However, Goodman's combination of persuasiveness and hardball tactics finally paid off. In September 1989, Postal Buddy and the USPS formalized an agreement. Postal Buddy would be allowed to use the logo and authorization claim. It was also granted the first license to print postage on demand. The Postal Service agreed to invest $500,000 in the project: $200,000 to provide partial funding for the creation of the change-of-address software and $300,000 to help finance the test market project. The test market contract would not be awarded until the fully operational machine had been delivered.

In return, Postal Buddy agreed to create a fully operational Postal Buddy machine at its own expense. By funding the development of the machine himself, Goodman ensured that he could avoid the rights in technical data clause of a government-funded contract. Postal Buddy also ceded ownership of the change-of-address portion of the test market software to the Postal Service, thereby satisfying Procurement's desire for ownership of *something*. The software, however, did not include any of the payment-accepting or printing mechanisms. Therefore, as a stand-alone product, it was essentially useless. Lastly, in an effort to protect the company even further, Postal Buddy required, and was granted, a nonexclusive, irrevocable, royalty-free license to use the USPS-owned test software, thereby protecting its rights to all future products.

In October, Goodman filed three additional patents. They covered the change-of-address system, the customized Postal Buddy keyboard, and the printing of the labels, postcards, and business cards. Postal Buddy was now ready for the next stage.

Planning the Market Test

Despite the fact that he had barely enough funding in hand to develop the first machine, Goodman launched into planning the market test. With the help of the Postal Service and the major mailers, Goodman selected northern Virginia outside of Washington, D.C., an area of 750,000 residential addresses and a 50 percent annual moving rate, for the test location. Goodman proposed that, beginning in January of 1990, Postal Buddy would install 30 units, 15 in post offices and 15 in supermarkets, drugstores, military bases, a college campus, and a major office building. Goodman felt that a six-month test would give the company enough time to adequately judge the efficiency of the system, consumer acceptance of the product, and the best locations for Postal Buddy installation.

After the completion of the market test, Goodman hoped to have enough quantitative data to make a decision about a national rollout. He calculated that such a rollout would entail a minimum of one machine in at least 10,000 major post offices, as well as a significant number of the 50,000 major supermarkets, drugstores, college campuses, military bases, and office buildings in the country. Assuming the market test confirmed the positive results of the earlier study, the ability of Postal Buddy to achieve the national rollout rested on two critical issues: securing financing for the company and getting a long-term Postal Service contract.

Financing

By October of 1989, Goodman's immediate task was to attack the problem of financing. In the past year and a half, the company had generated cumulative net operating losses of $1.1 million. The company's major outside sources of funding to date had been David Hirsch, a managing director of a major investment banking firm who invested in excess of $500,000 in the company, and several of Goodman's friends. (See **Exhibit 3** for the financing history of the company.) In addition, the sale of Welcome Labels in late 1989 generated cash that Goodman was able to use for Postal Buddy. He had also invested $750,000 in the development of the technology prior to the founding of Welcome Labels, had taken no salary for two years, and had advanced significant personal borrowings to the company. As a result, Goodman had run out of resources. Both he and Hirsch were unable to put new cash into the company.

Goodman began rewriting the business plan in preparation for his capital-raising efforts in the venture capital and corporate communities. In December 1989, he began approaching various institutional investors for financing. In Goodman's estimation, Postal Buddy would need $2 million of capital, in addition to the Postal Service's $300,000 contribution, to implement the market test and repay some of the founder debt. As a result, he settled on a private placement offering of 25 percent of the company's common stock in return for the $2 million. (See **Exhibit 4** for a summary of terms.)

Goodman had other financial worries as well. Once the market test was completed, Postal Buddy would need a second round of $5 million in late 1990 to create the capital base necessary to finance the first 4,000 sites in the national rollout. Significantly, Goodman projected that the off-the-shelf nature of the majority of the system's components would allow the company to pursue asset-based financing and thus be completely self-financing after the second round of funding. With the asset loan capacity at 60 percent of the $8,000 full-production cost of the kiosk, Goodman realized that he would have access to an extremely important source of capital. If Postal Buddy were to opt for the conservative deployment assumed in the financial projections, the company would be able to establish a 10,000-machine network without any additional outside capital after the first year. More aggressive plans called for the installation of a 30,000-machine base. (See **Exhibit 5** for Postal Buddy financial projections.) Nonetheless, Goodman realized that he would still have to come up with the first two rounds of financing in order to progress beyond the concept stage of his company.

By March 1990, Goodman's efforts were still unsuccessful. The corporations that he approached were typically not interested in a partnership with a start-up company in an entirely new industry. Others felt that Postal Buddy was not a "strategic" fit with their own interests.

Most venture capitalists, on the other hand, thought that Postal Buddy was an intriguing opportunity with enormous potential. According to Sid, many of them admitted that "Postal Buddy was the stuff that venture capital should be made of." However, as he met with one venture capitalist after another, Goodman was turned down with a variety of polite excuses. For many, the magnitude of the task of deploying a 30,000-machine network that would require constant servicing, reliable networking, and communications coordination was simply too daunting. For others, management concerns rose to the forefront. One venture capitalist in particular was remarkably straightforward in his advice: find a chief operating officer to run the company. As a result, Goodman had thus far come up empty-handed in his search for capital.

A Postal Service Contract

The venture capitalists were equally concerned about the other element critical to Postal Buddy's success: a longer-term contract with the Postal Service. To date, Goodman had been unable to get the Postal Service to commit to a contract for the national rollout. Procurement was still agitating within the organization to put the contract out for bids. In addition, Goodman thought it premature to push for the national contract at this time. Until Postal Buddy delivered the operational machine to the USPS, secured the test market contract, and raised the necessary capital, Goodman did not want to assume any additional commitments. However, given that many of the venture capital firms would not invest in the company without the USPS commitment, Postal Buddy was caught in a no-win situation.

With the financial situation becoming grave, Goodman went back to the Postal Service and pushed hard for progress on the longer-term commitment. While the Postal Service was unwilling to guarantee Postal Buddy a sole-source contract, Goodman finally secured a concession. Because of the patents pending as well as the proprietary nature of the current development work, the Postal Service agreed to "probably" require that any future suppliers of the change-of-address machine license the technology from Postal Buddy.

Current Situation

It was now March of 1990 and Goodman was facing several major decisions. Work was just about complete on the first fully operational Postal Buddy kiosk. Of paramount importance now was the financial situation. The company had been forced to borrow money from shareholders; meanwhile, Goodman's total personal credit card balances were approaching $125,000. However, several encouraging events had occurred recently. With the help of Tanner & Co., a small boutique investment banking firm that had taken an interest in Postal Buddy, Goodman had refined the financial projections one more time. Harold Tanner, previously of Salomon Brothers and a personal friend of Goodman's co-investor, was now tentatively interested in investing $300,000 in the company. In addition, Goodman had just received a letter from the Patent Office reassuring him of the likely granting of the key print-shop patent.

Goodman was very concerned about securing the rest of the necessary capital. Should he relinquish some operating control in the hopes of satisfying potential venture capital investors? He knew from previous conversations with several prestigious venture capitalists that at least one firm would be willing to invest the entire $2 million if a chief operating officer approved by the firm were installed. Goodman wondered whether relinquishing some operating control was worth the security of having venture capital financing.

Or, Goodman wondered, could he raise the money from an untapped source such as private individuals? Goodman already had Harold Tanner interested in investing. Through the network of contacts that he had generated in his fund-raising efforts, Goodman thought that this avenue might be feasible. However, if he pursued this option, the company might run out of money before he could secure the financing. Besides, he had already approached many of the wealthiest individuals among his contacts, with no success.

Goodman also thought about franchising the company if he was unable to raise adequate capital in the first two rounds. He believed that Postal Buddy franchises could achieve successful implementation of the concept and significant market penetration. He was somewhat uncertain, however, as to the Postal Service's reaction to a franchise arrangement.

Goodman had other nagging concerns. Most obvious was the contract with the Postal Service. Goodman wondered how he should approach the upcoming negotiations. Should he be satisfied with a licensing arrangement and allow another company to deal with the hassles of implementing such a huge project? Goodman was not really worried about losing the contract even if the Postal Service wanted to put it out to bid. Not only could another company not come up with a working prototype in such a short time frame, but Goodman also knew that the Postal Service would insist that the contract involve the installation, operation, and ownership of the system by the bidding entity. Goodman didn't believe that anyone would want to commit the $40 to $50 million that it would take to install the 4,000-machine base projected for the first three years. He also realized, however, that he might be wrong.

Goodman was also concerned about hiring a management team to implement the Postal Buddy network. First, Goodman knew that he would have to bring in experienced management to help him run a company that was projected to generate $150 to $500 million in annual revenues after six years. He wondered which positions he should try to fill first. On the one hand, he wasn't really ready to turn over significant operating responsibilities to a newly recruited executive. Rather, he felt that he possessed the capability to manage the company for at least another year until the initial stages of the national rollout. Having been through the exhausting process of shepherding a new idea through the Postal Service bureaucracy, Goodman knew that his hard-won experience would be critical to the market test and to the early stages of the rollout. On the other hand, however, Goodman eventually preferred to work on the creative, research side of the business and leave the management of the organization to someone else. Perhaps now was a better time to hire a COO and, at the same time, resolve the financial issues as well.

Goodman sat back and contemplated the decisions he had to make. He had a lot of work to do to finally get Postal Buddy off the ground.

EXHIBIT 1   **Postal Buddy Kiosk**

Exhibit 2   **Description of Postal Buddy Products**

Address Change Services

Name change:	Changes name for recently married, divorced or widowed customers.
Address change:	Most common use. Changes residential address for a current or future move of a family or individual.
Work address:	Notifies mailers and business associates of a work address change. Cannot currently be done through USPS.

Moving Related Products

Address labels:	Dispenses sheets of 45 pressure-sensitive labels at the cost of $2.39 for the first sheet and $1.49 for additional sheets.
Business cards:	Dispenses 10 microperforated business cards on medium-weight card stock. The cards are available in two different styles, at a cost of $2.50 for the first sheet and $1.50 for each additional sheet.
COA postcards:	Preprints change of address postcards with the customer's old and new address. Each costs $.33, including postage. The postcards will offer significant time savings from the time required to fill out the cards by hand.

Major Mailer Notification

Will notify:
Associations
Book, record, travel, and frequent flyer clubs
Catalogs
Credit cards
Department stores
Insurance companies
Magazines
Journals and national newspapers.

Cost to the customer is free. Cost to the "subscribing" business is $500 plus $.30 per address change. They will receive updated changes on-line via a PC, floppy disk, or magnetic tape.

Government Agency Notification

Will notify:

Department of Veteran Affairs	Military Reserve Units
Federal Election Commission	Office of Personnel Management
Health Care Finance Administration—Medicare/Medicaid	Railroad Retirement Administration
	Social Security Administration
Internal Revenue Service	Voter Registration—Local Election Officials

Subscription/Catalog Services

Subscriptions:	Customers can view magazines that can be screened according to categories. For example, a customer can select [age 19–24, female, tennis] and choose from publications in that category. Can be for self or as a gift. Payment accepted in cash or by credit card.
Subscription extension:	Extend and pay for existing subscriptions.
Catalog requests:	Customers can choose to receive catalogs from a variety of categories. The cost to the customer will be $1.00 to $2.00 per catalog to be applied to the first purchase.

Additional Products and Services

Vacation hold:	Puts customers' mail on temporary hold.
Temporary PO box:	Arranges a temporary PO box for a customer if he or she does not know the permanent address.
Stamps:	Vends stamps in $5 books. Stamps are received on consignment from the Postal Service and are sold at face value.
Congressional updates:	Provides congressional offices with a list of new residents.

EXHIBIT 3   Summary of Financing[a]

	Initial Capitalization December 1988			Private Placement I[f] Proposed Quarter 1, 1990			Private Placement II Proposed Quarter 4, 1990		
	%	*Shares*	*$*	*%*	*Shares*	*$*	*%*	*Shares*	*$*
Sidney Goodman[b]									
Common equity	53.61%	6,000	$ 1,000	34.85%	6,969		29.62%	6,969	
Loan to company			$ 420,000						
David Hirsch[c]									
Common equity	33.88%	3,792	$ 200,000	22.02%	4,405		18.72%	4,405	
Loan to company			$ 340,000						
Others[d]									
Common equity	12.51%	1,400	$ 166,000	8.13%	1,626		6.91%	1,626	
	100.00%	11,192	$1,127,000						
Future management				10.00%	2,000		8.50%	2,000	
Common equity									
Investor group I									
Common equity[e]				25.00%	5,000	$2,000,000	21.25%	5,000	
				100.00%	20,000	$2,000,000			
Investor group II									
Common equity							15.00%	3,530	$5,000,000
							100.00%	23,530	$5,000,000

[a]Includes actual and proposed financings. Does not include $300,000 from the USPS, which is not considered to be an investment in the company.

[b]Includes Martin Goodman's shares. Loan at 9%, half of which is to be repaid after Round 1. The remainder is to be repaid in the first year.

[c]Loan at 9%. Half is to be repaid upon close of Round 1. The remainder is repaid in the first year.

[d]Friends of Sidney Goodman. Certain investments were made prior to December of 1988.

[e]Total shares outstanding were to be rounded up to 20,000 for ease of computation. Additional shares issued to earlier shareholders were to be determined by pro rata allocation.

[f]Use of financing proceeds:

Total cash from financing:	$2,000,000
Less: Fees and expenses	$ 140,000
Net cash from financing	$1,860,000
Repayment of Goodman debt	$ 210,000
Repayment of Hirsh debt	$ 170,000
Total debt repayment	$ 380,000
Net cash available to company	$1,480,000

Exhibit 4   Common Stock Private Placement Summary of Terms

Size of offering	$1,500,000–$2,000,000	
Equity ownership	$2,000,000 for 25%; venture valuation of $8,000,000.	
	$1,500,000 for 20%; venture valuation of $7,500,000.	
	10% ownership is to be reserved for new management	
	participation; 65% will be owned by existing shareholders.	
Voting	Ownership and voting are equivalent.	
Source of funds	Units	20
	Price per units	$ 100,000
	Total sources of funds	$2,000,000
Use of funds	Working capital (cash)	$1,480,000
	Repayment of founder debt	380,000
	Fees and expenses	140,000
	Total uses of funds	$2,000,000
Founder debt	Founder debt that is not to be repaid at the time of the offering will be repaid during the first year of operations.	
Salary payable	Sid Goodman has not been paid a salary for two years. At the time of the second offering (this is the first), Sid is to receive a $200,000 bonus.	
Pre-emptive rights	All shareholders shall have the pro rata right to participate in all future offerings.	
Dilution provisions	For a period of two years, investors in this offering will be protected against dilution from the sale of equity at a lower price. Investors before this offering will not be similarly protected.	
Sale provisions	For a period of two years, investors in this offering will be protected against the sale of the entire company at a price less than the venture valuation. If such a sale is made, investors will receive their principal back before any founders receive any proceeds.	

Board of directors	Management	Investors
	Sidney Goodman	David Hirsch
	Martin Goodman or	Investor group representative
	COO	Investor group representative

EXHIBIT 5   Six-Year Financial Projections

	Year 1	Year 2	Year 3	Year 4	Year 5	Year 6
Income Statement (dollars in 000s)						
Revenue	$ 927	$16,371	$54,502	$95,998	$132,567	169,138
Cost of goods sold:						
Materials	124	3,253	7,182	12,566	17,354	22,141
Transaction costs	48	749	2,408	4,220	5,828	7,436
Modem rental	23	398	1,260	2,206	3,046	3,886
Servicing	136	2,309	8,002	15,273	23,019	32,090
Maintenance	49	755	2,400	4,200	5,800	7,400
Rent	158	2,784	9,264	16,320	22,536	28,754
Setup	62	558	980	800	800	800
Advertising	106	818	2,724	4,800	6,629	8,457
Depreciation	118	1,530	4,820	8,420	11,620	14,702
Total cost of goods sold	$ 824	$13,154	$39,040	$68,805	$ 96,632	$125,666
General and administrative[a]	1,032	1,623	2,114	2,805	3,392	4,040
Research and development	25	100	100	100	100	100
Operating income	(954)	1,494	13,248	24,288	32,443	39,332
Other income:						
Postage float[b]	1	19	60	104	144	184
USPS contract	150	0	0	0	0	0
Earnings before interest and taxes	(803)	1,513	13,308	24,392	32,587	39,516
Interest income	79	130	8	15	102	1,201
Other income (expense)[c]	(16)	(16)	(16)	(16)	(16)	(16)
Interest expense[d]						
Asset-based loan	0	(57)	(783)	(1,150)	(252)	(1,150)
Founder debt	(36)	0	0	0	0	0
Pretax income	(760)	1,586	12,533	23,257	32,437	39,567
Income tax expense	0	358	4,756	8,832	12,320	15,468
Net income	(760)	1,228	7,777	14,425	20,117	24,099
Installed base (year end)	155	1,550	4,000	6,000	8,000	10,000
Cost per machine[e]	$8,000	$ 8,000	$ 8,000	$ 8,000	$ 8,000	$ 8,000
Machine days per year	340	340	340	340	340	340
Movers/machine/day	2.5	2.5	2.5	2.5	2.5	2.5
Mover revenue/machine/day[f]	$12.75	$16.00	$16.00	$16.00	$16.00	$16.00
Customers/machine/day	7.5	7.5	7.5	7.5	7.5	7.5
Total other revenue/machine/day[g]	$30.93	$34.60	$37.35	$37.38	$37.38	$37.38

[a]Includes the San Diego and Virginia offices.

[b]Period of float for sale of stamps assumed to be 45 days.

[c]Amortization of transaction expenses over 10 years.

[d]Interest rate on asset loans assumed at 11%. Interest on founder debt is 9%.

[e]Cost of first 30 machines for the test market is $10,000 per machine.

[f]Revenues from the major mailer notification and sale of change of address postcards.

[g]Revenues from the sale of address labels, business cards, and magazine subscriptions.

EXHIBIT 5   *(concluded)*

	At Closing	Year 1	Year 2	Year 3	Year 4	Year 5	Year 6
Balance Sheet **(dollars in 000s)**							
Current assets							
Cash[a]	$1,480	$ 4,670	$ 68	$ 183	$ 274	$ 9,256	$32,407
Accounts receivable	20	20	225	602	904	1,205	1,506
Note receivable	40	0	0	0	0	0	0
USPS contract receivable	40	0	0	0	0	0	0
Inventory	5	38	389	1,000	1,500	2,000	2,500
Prepaid expenses	3	9	103	274	411	549	686
Total current assets	$1,588	$ 4,737	$ 785	$ 2,059	$ 3,089	$13,010	$37,099
Net property, plant, and equipment	37	1,220	10,850	25,631	33,211	37,592	38,890
Transaction expenses	143	129	114	100	86	71	57
Total assets	$1,768	$ 6,086	$11,749	$27,790	$36,386	$50,673	$76,046
Current liabilities							
Accounts payable	120	9	103	274	411	549	686
Total current liabilities	120	9	103	274	411	549	686
Asset-based loan	0	433	3,793	11,904	5,953	0	0
Founder debt[b]	380	0	0	0	0	0	0
Total debt	380	433	3,793	11,904	5,953	0	0
Shareholder's equity							
Common equity: first offering	2,000	2,000	2,000	2,000	2,000	2,000	2,000
Common equity: second offering	0	5,000	5,000	5,000	5,000	5,000	5,000
Retained earnings	(732)	(1,356)	853	8,612	23,022	43,124	68,360
Total shareholders' equity	$1,268	$ 5,644	$ 7,853	$15,612	$30,022	$50,124	$75,360
Total liabilities and shareholders' equity	$1,768	$ 6,086	$11,749	$27,790	$36,386	$50,673	$76,046

[a]Assumes $0 cash balance prior to Round 1 financing. $300,000 cash from USPS assumed expended previously on product development.
[b]$760,000 balance prior to close of Round 1 less the repayment of $380,000 with financing proceeds.

II Assessing and Acquiring Necessary Resources

This section addresses two of the most important issues faced by entrepreneurs as they start a new venture:

- What resources are needed?
- How are they to be acquired?

Assessing Required Resources

In order to translate the business concept into a reality, the entrepreneur needs first to assess the resources that the venture will require. Entrepreneurs are often required to do more with less. By definition, they are attempting to achieve goals that will require considerably more resources than they currently control.

One of the key skills lies in distinguishing between those resources that are absolutely essential and those that would be nice to have but are not crucial.

Another technique is to distinguish between resources that must be ''owned'' and those that may be rented, contracted for, or even borrowed. Perhaps professional advice can be obtained based on friendship or the promise of future business. Doing more with less requires buying only what is needed and using the rest without actually owning it.

Acquiring Necessary Resources

Having identified the required resources, it then becomes the entrepreneur's task to acquire them. This acquisition should be guided by a number of policies:

- First, the entrepreneur must commit quickly, and sometimes fully, in order to get to the next stage. This, perhaps, is why entrepreneurs are perceived as risk takers.

- Still, the entrepreneur must be flexible in these commitments, shifting resources once the desired end has been achieved.
- Finally, the individual must approach the acquisition process with the intention of giving up as little as possible in order to attract the needed resources. The rest of the value created thus accrues to the entrepreneur.

Chapter 6, "Attracting Stakeholders," considers the task of acquiring resources in the broadest possible light.

Financial Resources

Clearly, financial resources—dollars—are the most frequently needed. Chapter 7, "Alternative Sources of Financing," describes the spectrum of alternatives for obtaining financing. Chapter 8 looks at the technique of structuring a deal in order to obtain the required financial resources. Chapter 9 discusses the securities laws that affect the raising of funds and also describes the business plans and prospectuses that are typically used.

Nonfinancial Resources

The entrepreneur must also secure the nonfinancial resources that the venture needs—a building, plant or office space, technology, management, and other employees. Chapter 10, "Intellectual Property," describes the legal issues that surround ideas: patents, trademarks, trade secrets, confidentiality, and so forth. The entrepreneur must be aware of the serious repercussions that can result either from unfairly using someone else's idea or from failing to protect his or her own idea.

The Cases

The Steven B. Belkin case describes an entrepreneur's attempt to raise funds to finance a start-up venture. In addition to the issues surrounding financing, there are other questions as well: Is the venture a good opportunity? Has the entrepreneur adequately detailed the business concept and the resources needed to exploit the opportunity? What kind of investors should be targeted?

Clarion Optical Co. describes an interesting opportunity for a company's managers to purchase their current employer's business. The case exposes the student to some of the quantitative techniques that lie behind the structuring of a deal.

Viscotech concerns a young company that may have violated the securities laws in its search for funds. The student is asked to address this issue and to recommend a plan for proceeding in light of the potential violation.

Heather Evans considers a situation where a young MBA student is ready to start her clothing business. Can she craft a deal that will make her investors happy while maintaining sufficient equity for herself?

Parenting Magazine focuses on a start-up in the volatile world of publishing. Should Robin work with an existing media company, or should she strike off on her own?

National Demographics & Lifestyles is a venture capital financed company in the business of selling names to the direct-mail industry from its data base. Will its venture backers continue to finance the company, given its inability to ''make its numbers''?

CVD v. A. S. Markham describes a recent legal case in which employees of a large defense contractor left that firm to begin a competitive business. Did they take trade secrets with them or violate their employment agreements?

Finally, Chris Miller considers an ethical issue that arises in the course of a fund-raising effort. Should the entrepreneurs disclose a piece of news to a potential investor?

6 ATTRACTING STAKEHOLDERS

Acquiring resources—or to put it more broadly, attracting stakeholders—is a basic entrepreneurial task. While every enterprise needs employees, customers, suppliers, and financiers who are willing to risk their time and money, attracting these "stakeholders" to an entrepreneurial venture is a particularly difficult challenge. This note first describes the importance of the challenge and then the set of tasks the entrepreneur must work on in order to overcome it: Designing the enterprise to minimize the stakeholder investment needed, selecting the right stakeholders, and then convincing them to participate in the enterprise. We will use the example of a hypothetical entrepreneur (like Steve Jobs) who wishes to launch a revolutionary computer, but the principles we describe are generally applicable to any entrepreneurial venture.

The Challenge of Attracting Stakeholders

Many participants are at risk in any enterprise by virtue of the irreversible investment they make in it. The most obvious are the financial stakeholders—the venture capital firms, institutional and individual investors, bondholders, banks, or factors who provide our entrepreneur with the funds needed for R&D, machinery, new product promotion, and growth in inventory and receivables. Much of this investment is irreversible—if the enterprise fails, liquidation of its tangible and intangible assets will rarely make the financial stakeholders whole, especially when their opportunity costs are properly taken into account.[1]

Employees, customers, and suppliers have an equally important, if less obvious, stake in the success of the enterprise they participate in as well. The individual who leaves IBM to head up marketing for our hypothetical entrepreneur's new computer project may be as much at risk as the venture capitalists who fund it. If the enterprise fails, the marketing manager is unlikely to be made whole for the time and effort she invested; IBM will not have her back in her old position and she may have to eat into her savings while looking for a new job.

Failure of the enterprise may similarly wipe out suppliers' and customers' investments. Suppliers may not recover the costs of designing and producing special

---

[1]This is true, the record shows, even for the lenders whose investment is supposedly secured by assets.
Professors Amar Bhide and Howard Stevenson prepared this note.
Harvard Business School Note 9–389–139

components for the new computer or collect on their receivables. Similarly, customers may find they have invested time and money on hardware that cannot be easily serviced and upgraded.

Moreover, attracting the stakeholders needed to launch a new computer is much more of a challenge for an individual entrepreneur than it is for a large corporation like IBM. Since IBM's managers effectively control the corporation, they can mandate the investment of shareholder funds for a new product. In addition, since IBM has a well-established, profitable franchise in mainframe computers as well as a long-standing reputation for fair dealing, employers, suppliers, and customers have the confidence that they will not be left in the lurch if the new product fails.[2]

The individual entrepreneur who cannot inspire such confidence may therefore face employees, suppliers, customers, and financiers whose perception of their downside risk causes them to demand conditions of exchange that cannot be met if the enterprise is to be viable. In the extreme, they may not participate at all. Suppliers may refuse to dedicate a production run without a cash advance that a fledgling enterprise cannot provide; demands by venture capitalists and key employees for ownership stakes may exceed the total equity pie; and worst of all, conservative purchasing agents may not touch an innovative computer even if it does offer outstanding price/performance.

Minimizing Stakeholder Exposure

The extent to which stakeholders are at risk in a venture depends upon the irreversibility of their investment. While entrepreneurs cannot make the investment required by their ventures fully reversible, they can hold the required "sunkenness" to a minimum and thus overcome stakeholders' reluctance to participate.

Reusable, Off-the-Shelf Inputs

Financiers', suppliers', and employees' risks may be reduced by using components, capital equipment, and other factors of production that can be easily put to alternative uses and, preferably, are available off the shelf. Then, financiers, suppliers, and employees do not have to commit substantial resources, and what resources they do commit can be easily recovered if the enterprise fails.

Using standard fungible inputs affects several strategic choices; for our computer start-up these might include:

- Hardware design that relies on off-the-shelf processors and subsystems.
- A product that is differentiated along easily comprehensible performance dimensions or on price. Then salespeople (or distributors) do not have to acquire special skills or knowledge in order to sell it.

---

[2]They may take heart from the example of the PC Jr. computer, which IBM kept alive for longer than might have been economically justified in order to protect the interests of the stakeholders. None of the employees who worked on the product were let go, as jobs were found for them elsewhere in the IBM organization.

- Software based on an industry standard operating system such as UNIX or MS-DOS.
- An assembly line restricted to elementary capital goods such as a conveyor belt and screwdrivers. Where required, general-purpose machine tools, ovens, and CAD-CAM tools can be used instead of special designs.
- A Silicon Valley, Route 128, or Research Triangle site so that key employees do not have to make an investment to relocate and can find alternative employment more easily.
- Modest volume or market share goals so that suppliers do not have to dedicate special production runs or build new capacity.
- A marketing plan that seeks product awareness through a few influential opinion makers in the industry rather than through advertising or missionary selling.

Even seemingly trivial decisions may matter. For example, using an industry standard accounting or word processing package reduces the training required for accounting and typing staff, enhances their market-ability in the eyes of other employers, and thus reduces their risk in joining a new venture.

Customer Investment

Many of the product design decisions that help reduce other stakeholders' investment in an enterprise will often reduce customers' risks as well. For example, the use of industry standard components in a computer reduces the buyer's risk of being stuck without spare parts should the vendor go out of business. The adoption of an industry standard operating system likewise eliminates the investment a customer might otherwise have to make in adapting existing applications software to a new supplier's hardware. At the simplest level, products that can be easily purchased due to some simple cost or performance advantages do not require the customer to sink much time and money in the purchase decision and in employee education.

Other product decisions may be taken that directly reduce a customer's investment in learning, search, and adaptation. For example, a new computer may be designed to slot easily into customers' existing hardware networks. In the software arena, "open system architecture," which allows the customer (or any other qualified firm) to easily modify or upgrade the product without the assistance of the original vendor may be adopted to reduce the customer's "stake" in the start-up.

Trade-offs

Unfortunately, there is no free lunch. Securing the participation of stakeholders by reducing the "sunkenness" of their investment may reduce the profitability and long-run sustainability of the enterprise. For example, in the case of the computer start-up:

- Industry standard, off-the-shelf components may lead to higher variable costs and rapid knockoffs by competitors.
- Flexible capital equipment designed to have high salvage value may be more expensive.

- A Silicon Valley, Route 128, or Research Triangle location may entail high real estate and labor costs.
- A plug-compatible, me-too product with low switching costs for the customer may be vulnerable to competitors offering marginally better prices or features.

The entrepreneur may thus be squeezed between being unable to get the enterprise off the ground at all because the risks to stakeholders are too high or launching a marginally profitable, short-lived venture.

One key to resolving this dilemma lies in undertaking irreversible investment only where the greatest leverage is expected in terms of profitability or sustainability or where a stakeholder is most prepared to make the investment for idiosyncratic reasons. For example, a computer start-up may seek irreversible stakeholder investment in the one element, such as a proprietary microprocessor, unique architecture, a low-cost, out-of-the-way location, or new distribution channel, where stakeholder investment seems most readily available and/or where the investment will provide the greatest sustainable advantage. This same company will forcefully adhere to industry standards in all other areas. Asking the question: "Is this uniqueness really the key to a major competitive edge?" is often a good starting place.

Another resolution to the viability/sustainability dilemma can lie in phased investment. The enterprise may be launched with very low irreversible investment, gradually building to higher levels as stakeholder confidence is gained. Apple is a case in point. In its early years, its products were based on an industry standard operating system (CP/M), were promoted virtually without any advertising, and were manufactured in plants whose capital equipment consisted largely of conveyor belts and screwdrivers. As the company gained the confidence of stakeholders, however, its new products used a proprietary operating system, were assembled in highly automated state-of-the-art plants, and were launched with multimillion-dollar advertising budgets.

Selecting Stakeholders

Since irreversible investment required by an enterprise cannot be entirely eliminated, another entrepreneurial task is to select stakeholders who are the most willing to and capable of bearing the risk. All other things being equal, the most desirable stakeholders fit one or more of the following characteristics: they are diversified, experienced in the type of risks they are expected to bear, have excess capacity, and are risk seekers. Let us consider these in turn.

Diversification

Diversified stakeholders are more capable of bearing the risk of investing in an enterprise than these undiversified stakeholders. Thus, for a computer start-up:

- The venture capitalist with a large diversified portfolio of investments can be expected to be more capable of providing risk capital than an individual with no other start-up investments.

- The distributor who handles the products of a number of vendors will probably be less concerned about dedicating 10 percent of the time of 10 salespersons to the new machine than any one salesperson considering full-time employment with the start-up.[3]
- The buyer for a firm with an installed base of computers from a variety of manufacturers will likely be more comfortable trying out a new vendor than the buyer at a customer who has standardized on just one.

Experience and Specialization

The risk that a particular individual or firm sees in investing in an enterprise can depend as much upon the investor's past experience and knowledge as upon the objective dangers. Therefore, an entrepreneur should, when possible, seek the participation of stakeholders who are experienced in bearing the risks required of them. Our computer start-up may, for example, seek to establish relationships with:

- Customers who have bought (and preferably successfully used) computers from start-ups in the past rather than customers who have never strayed from ''name'' vendors.
- Law and accounting firms that specialize in new ventures and recognize that an up-front investment in helping a start-up can pay off handily in the long term.
- Employees who have worked for a start-up that failed before and know that being laid off is a setback, not the end of the world. People who have been employed, for example, at IBM for their entire working lives may grossly overestimate the risks of not being able to find a new job.
- Lenders who have dealt with the industry and products often have a feeling of comfort about the downside and experience with the upside, which makes them more adventurous.

Experienced and specialized participants may not only be easier to sign on, but they can also help secure the participation of other stakeholders. Participants in a venture need reassurance about the competence and reliability of each other—the customer who orders a new computer has to be confident that the vendor's service staff is capable, and the key software engineer needs reassurance that the venture capitalists backing the project are solid. Targeting an experienced ''team'' of stakeholders can thus go a long way toward building this necessary mutual confidence.

''Bell cows''—individuals or organizations that have established reputations as leaders and as savvy precursors of the future—are especially valuable. If our entrepreneur can get Arthur Rock, the doyen of high-tech venture capitalists, or Steve Wozniak, designer of the first Apple, to sign on, a number of other investors, employees, suppliers, and customers will participate, too. If Rock or Wozniak are players, then the venture must be real!

---

[3]In general, we may note that employees in a single business start-up will not be able to diversify their risks to the same extent as ''outside'' subcontractors serving many businesses.

Bell cows open doors and they often induce timely commitment for the entrepreneur. They are often the most important form of ''reality check.'' Bell cows stand at the nexus of important networks. Entrepreneurs have two problems: finding them and convincing them.

Finding bell cows requires industry knowledge. The fledgling entrepreneur has to have it or access it. Having industry knowledge is a function of time, effort, and having knowledge to exchange. It helps to know who is doing what. It helps to read the industry trade papers, and it helps to have made friends.

Accessing industry knowledge beyond your own depends on building your team. Both insiders and service providers such as lawyers, accountants, advertising and P/R firms, and consultants are critical. Even more critical is the entrepreneur's reputation for reciprocity and follow-through.

Excess Capacity

The risks of participation are lower for stakeholders with excess capacity who are not required to make any ''new'' investment or incur significant opportunity costs and may even be under pressure to utilize existing resources. Therefore, our illustrative computer start-up may target:

- Customers with a well-staffed, technology evaluation department for whom the time required to assess a new product is ''free'' and who may also be under organizational pressure to make new product recommendations, rather than customers with a small, overworked purchasing department.
- Venture capitalists (or banks) with a large, unused ''quota'' of technology investments (or loans). Often newly raised venture funds or ones that have developed a bad reputation as being ''slow off the mark'' are likely targets.
- Writers of technical manuals and product literature who are not kept fully occupied by their employers or who may work part time for personal reasons.
- The young professionals in an accounting firm who are under pressure to ''build a client base'' in order to make partner.
- Distributors with a ''hole'' in their product line but good customer coverage.
- Board stuffers and other suppliers with unused capacity—especially note those who have recently undergone aggressive capacity expansion programs.

Obviously the stakeholders' unused capacity must be greater than the enterprise's needs for this criterion of selection to be useful; hence as mentioned in a previous section, staged growth and volume goals are a great help in attracting stakeholders. Capitalizing on ''excess'' capacity also requires the entrepreneur to carefully understand the cost structure and organizational dynamics of the target stakeholder.

Risk Seeking

Rather than target those stakeholders whose participation in an enterprise involves the least risk to them, the entrepreneur may instead cultivate risk seekers—individuals or firms who because of their temperament or circumstance take on projects that have a negative expected value. For example, the entrepreneur in our computer start-up might seek:

- "Leading edge" customers for whom the publicity and thrill of being the first user of a new technology far outweighs the economic downside.
- Cultist programmers who derive satisfaction from working for a "Mission Impossible"-type enterprise.
- Very wealthy individuals for whom an investment in the venture is like the casual purchase of a lottery ticket or a contribution made to support the local theater company.

There are, however, risks in seeking the participation of risk seekers. First, they may be fickle—the wealthy individual who invests with our entrepreneur on a lark may not be as prepared to invest in future rounds as a professional, level-headed venture capitalist. Second, the participation of risk seekers may scare away other more conservative players. The reputation of your stakeholders has potential for both a halo effect and a negative aura.

Convincing Stakeholders

Assume that our entrepreneur has formulated a plan that minimizes risk for stakeholders and has identified the most appropriate participants for the computer venture. The most formidable task—a challenging mix of analysis and action—remains. The project must be sold; expressions of interest and encouragement from the participants must be converted into firm commitments. This requires the entrepreneur to possess the necessary attitudes and reputation, go through a process of "ham and egging," and master basic closing techniques.

Entrepreneurial Attributes

A prerequisite for gaining stakeholder commitment is the entrepreneur's enthusiasm and belief in the project. The immediate payoff for stakeholders in an entrepreneurial project is almost always low—their decision to participate is based on expectations of substantial long-term reward. The entrepreneur cannot create this expectation without a strong inner conviction that the project can and will succeed.

Another requirement for the entrepreneur is a reputation for reliability. A track record for success is helpful—a Steve Jobs will have a tremendous edge in launching a new venture—but is not absolutely necessary. What participants will look for is evidence that in the past the entrepreneur has:

- Honored implicit as well as explicit promises and has fairly shared rewards with stakeholders.
- Has not abandoned ventures in midstream when things have gone badly.

Ham and Egging

Besides these attributes and reputation (which an entrepreneur either has or hasn't), there are a number of skills and techniques that can be adopted to secure commitment, one of the most important of which is "ham and egging."

The need for ham and egging arises from the desire of each participant to see the others commit first. Customers are reluctant to spend the time to evaluate, much less place an order for a new computer until the entrepreneur can actually deliver a product; employees are hesitant to sign on until the financing is in place; and investors are unwilling to step forward unless customers have shown a willingness to buy.

The ultimate ham and egging solution is for the entrepreneur to simultaneously convince each participant that everyone else is on board, or almost on board. Not all entrepreneurs have the ability to pull this off or can even feel comfortable trying to. The alternative is to ask for a small increment of commitment from a participant, parlay that commitment into another increment of commitment from the next participant, and repeat the cycle for as many times as is necessary.

Our computer entrepreneur may for example:

- Get customers to spend a little time talking about the general attributes they would like to see in a new machine.
- Use these customer reactions to raise money to build a prototype.
- Persuade an engineer to work part time on the prototype for payment in cash and equity.
- Go back to the customer with the prototype asking for more detailed feedback.

This sequential ham and egging process works particularly well if one or more of the participants is a "bell cow."

Basic Sales Closing Skills

Ham and egging is a process that is somewhat unique to launching new ventures. In addition, the entrepreneur needs to employ techniques that are basic to closing any kind of sale such as developing a schedule, knowing in depth what you are asking for, anticipating objections, managing advisors, and handling the problems after the close.

Developing a Schedule.   Entrepreneurship is like driving fast on an icy road — it requires anticipation. Early in the selling process a schedule must be agreed upon so that the program can be checked and commitment tested. Intermediate points help you to know whether the stakeholder is stringing you along or is really going to participate. One of the greatest dangers in securing the commitment of stakeholders comes when one on whom you depend drops out. It destroys the ham and egging, it damages credibility, and leaves a critical resource gap. A schedule known to all induces social pressure and lets the entrepreneur maintain the appearance of control, since if others don't meet the schedule, the entrepreneur can initiate quickly a search for a replacement.

Knowing What You Need.   It is always nice to have "more." Successful entrepreneurs know what degree of commitment is required at any given moment and ask only for that degree. Knowing the bottom line for both time and commitment is a great aid to effective negotiation.

Anticipating Objections.   Stakeholders have both real and imaginary concerns. Getting to closing on a commitment requires addressing both. Real objections need be met with both acknowledgment and contingency plans. A prospective employee wants to know that you are aware of the real risks that she is taking. Acknowledging that risk and discussing the window of foresight that will be available before problems become serious and even honestly discussing the ''fume date'' is often all the reassurance a prospective employee needs. A customer can be reassured about the risk of committing to your product by understanding how service could be handled even if your firm were gone.

Imaginary objections need be dealt with, too. Often, however, the important thing is to find out why the issue is being raised so that underlying uncertainty can be addressed with realistic answers and well thought through contingency plans.

Handling Advisors.   Lawyers, accountants, and staff have different motives than principals. They often get no credit when things go right, but bear the brunt of blame when things go wrong. Agreed schedules, anticipation of objections, and a sense of being a valued team member are often critical to getting the job done. Your advisors and the stakeholders' advisors often are the roadblocks on the road to commitment. As an entrepreneur, you have to manage them closely and create an expectation and incentives for getting the deal done. Often this means getting them to see the closing of an agreement as the beginning and not the end of the relationship.

Following Up.   Many deals have been broken after a commitment is secured. In spite of the hectic pace of the entrepreneurial life, one of the most critical skills is maintaining the commitment. New objections arise as customers see the problems in implementation. New alternatives arise for employees when their old employer sees their departure and recognizes the potential loss. The details of covenants, warranties, and representations become points of contention, then points of honor, then irreconcilable differences in the process of negotiation. The entrepreneurial task remains one of keeping the sale in place. That can only be done by constant attention and follow-up.

Summary

Securing stakeholders is the critical process for an entrepreneur who seeks to pursue opportunity beyond the resources that he or she currently controls. It requires understanding who will provide the needed resources, what resources will be needed, when they will be needed, and how the provider will benefit from his or her participation. The process is iteratively analytical and action oriented. It requires preparation and skill. It is, however, the key to leveraging an idea into opportunity and opportunity into a real business operation.

7 ALTERNATIVE SOURCES OF FINANCING

One of the most common issues confronted by the entrepreneur revolves around securing financing for the venture. Questions of how and when to raise money and from whom are frequent topics of concern. This chapter will describe some common sources of capital and the conditions under which money is typically lent or invested. Chapter 8, ''Deal Structure,'' discusses the specific terms and pricing of capital.

An Overview

As in most transactions, the owners of capital expect to get something in return for providing financing for the venture. In evaluating potential opportunities, the providers of funds will typically use some form of a risk/return model. That is, they will demand a higher return when they perceive a higher risk.

The entrepreneur's objective, of course, is to secure financing at the lowest possible cost. The art of successful financing, therefore, lies in obtaining funds in a manner that those providers of funds view as relatively less risky.

The entrepreneur can do several things to structure the financing so it will be perceived as ''less risky'':

- Pledge personal or corporate assets against a loan.
- Promise to pay the money back in a short period of time when the investors can judge the health of the business, rather than over the long term when its financial strength is less certain.
- Give investors some measure of control over the business, through either loan covenants or participation in management (i.e., a seat on the board).

Note that these are only a few of the possible mechanisms.

The liabilities side of the balance sheet itself provides a good overview of the potential sources of financing. Because this side of the balance sheet is arranged in order of increasing risk, it follows that the lowest cost forms of financing will usually be available from the higher balance sheet items.

This note was prepared by Michael J. Roberts under the direction of Howard H. Stevenson.

Copyright © 1984 by the President and Fellows of Harvard College

Harvard Business School Note 9–384–187

Start-Up Financing

Start-up financing provides the entrepreneur with a host of unique challenges. The highest risk capital (and therefore potentially highest return capital) is at the bottom of the balance sheet as equity. When a business is in the start-up phase, it is at its riskiest point. Therefore, equity capital is usually an appropriate source of financing during this period. That is not to say that debt capital is unattractive. It may even be available when secured by assets of the business, such as a building or equipment. However, some equity is usually required to get a business "off the ground." There is virtually no getting around the fact that the first investment in the business will be equity capital. This is required to demonstrate commitment on the part of the entrepreneur. Investors perceive, and rightly so, that the individual entrepreneur will be more committed to the venture if she or he has a substantial portion of personal assets invested in the venture. It is this fact that has led some to claim that: "You're better off trying to start a business with $5,000 than with $100,000 in personal resources. If you are relatively poor, you can demonstrate your commitment for a smaller sum." This statement presumes that you will be seeking capital from some *outside* source. If you were going to fund the venture all by yourself, you would naturally prefer to have $100,000 instead of $5,000.

There is another, more practical reason why this start-up phase will usually be financed with the entrepreneur's own funds. In order to raise money, you typically need more than an idea. The entrepreneur will have to invest some money in the idea, perhaps to build a prototype or do a market study, in order to convince potential providers of capital that the idea has potential.

This is not to say that these funds must be equity capital in the purest sense. That is, the money need only be equity from the point of view of potential investors in the business. The entrepreneur can obtain these "equity funds" by mortgaging personal assets like a house or car, borrowing from friends or relatives, even from a personal bank loan or credit card advances. The important fact is that when the money goes into the business, it does so as equity, not as debt to be repaid to the entrepreneur.

Some specialized firms provide "seed capital." Most venture capital firms require that a business move beyond the idea stage before they will consider financing it. Yet some businesses require a good deal of work (and money) to get from the concept phase to the point where they can obtain venture capital financing. Seed funds can provide this kind of capital.

Outside Equity Capital

Typically, the entrepreneur will exhaust his or her own funds before the business is a viable operation. At this point, it is usually still too early to obtain all of the required financing in the form of debt. The entrepreneur must approach outside sources for equity capital.

Private Investors

One popular source of equity capital is private investors, also known as *wealthy individuals*. These investors may range from family and friends with a few extra dollars to extremely wealthy individuals who manage their own money. Doctors frequently come to mind and do, in fact, represent a significant source of private equity capital. Wealthy individuals may be advised by their accountants, lawyers, or other professionals, and the entrepreneur must deal with these people as well.

In order to approach wealthy individuals, you will usually need at least a business plan. A formal offering memorandum has the advantage of providing more legal protection for the entrepreneur in the form of disclaimers and legal language. However, it suffers from appearing overly negative, being more costly to prepare (it usually requires legal counsel), and also being limited by the SEC laws in terms of its distribution. That is, some of the SEC rules permit only 35 "offerees." Some legal advisors believe that you can show the business plan to more individuals and then formally "offer" to only those individuals who have a real interest in investing.

One of the best ways to find wealthy investors is through a network of friends, acquaintances, and advisors. For instance, if you have used a local lawyer and accountant to help you prepare a business plan or offering document, these advisors may know of wealthy individuals who invest in ventures like yours.

At this point, it is worth reiterating the importance of following the securities laws and obtaining the advice of counsel. Because many of these wealthy individuals are "unsophisticated," they can (and often do, if the venture is unsuccessful) claim that they were misled by you, the conniving entrepreneur. A carefully drawn offering document is the key to legal protection in this instance.

Wealthy investors may be well suited to participation in equity financings that are too small for a venture capital firm to consider (e.g., under $500,000). Wealthy investors are also typically thought of as being a less expensive source of equity than venture capital firms. This may be true. It is also true that:

- Wealthy individuals do not often possess the expertise or time to advise the entrepreneur on the operations of the business.
- Wealthy investors are far less likely to come up with additional funds if required.
- These investors are more likely to be a source of "problems" or frustration, particularly if there is a large number of them. Phoning frequently or complaining when things are not going according to plan, they can create headaches for even the most well-intentioned of entrepreneurs.

Venture Capital

Venture capital refers to a pool of equity capital that is professionally managed. Wealthy individuals invest in this fund as limited partners, and the general partners manage the pool in exchange for a fee and a percentage of the gain on investments.

In order to compensate for the riskiness of their investments, give their own investors a handsome return, and make a profit for themselves, venture firms seek a high rate of return on their investments. Target returns of 50 percent or 60 percent are not uncommon hurdles for firms to apply to prospective venture capital investments.

In exchange for this high return, venture firms will often provide advice to their portfolio companies. These people have been through many times what the entrepreneur is usually experiencing for the first time. They can often provide useful counsel on the problems a company may experience in the start-up phase.

Venture firms can differ along several dimensions. Some prefer investing in certain kinds of companies. "High-tech" is popular with most, although perceptions of what precisely this is will vary widely. Some firms have a reputation for being very involved with the day-to-day operations of the business; others exhibit a more hands-off policy.

In approaching venture capitalists, the entrepreneur needs a business plan to capture the firm's interest. Here the document serves a far different purpose than it would in the case of wealthy individuals. A venture capital firm will expend a good deal of effort investigating potential investments. Not only is this sound business practice on their part, but they also have legal obligations to their own investors.

Therefore, a business plan targeted to venture firms should be short, concise, and attempt to stimulate further interest, rather than present the business in exhaustive detail.

Most venture capitalists also report that it is only the naive entrepreneur who will propose the actual terms of the investment in the initial document. While the plan should certainly spell out how much financing the entrepreneur is seeking, to detail the terms (e.g., "for 28 percent of the stock . . .") is viewed as premature for an initial presentation.

One topic, which is frequently of concern to entrepreneurs, is confidentiality. On the one hand, it seems wise to tell potential investors about your good ideas to get them interested in the company; on the other, what if someone else takes them? In general, venture capitalists are a professional group and will not disclose confidential information. It is more difficult, however, to make this statement about private sources of capital, like wealthy individuals.

Whatever the target investor audience, it is generally *not* a good idea to put truly proprietary material in a business plan. These plans are frequently copied and could certainly be left accidentally on a plane or in an office. A business plan might, for example, describe the functions a new product would perform, but should probably not include circuit designs, engineering, drawings, etc.

Venture firms may not invest via a pure equity security. Some may invest a package of debt and equity, convertible debt, or convertible preferred. Each of these has its advantages:

- A debt/equity package provides for the venture firm to get some of its funds back via interest, which is deductible to the company, and results in a tax savings. The investor can also recover tax-free cash based on repayment of loan principal.
- Convertible debt or preferred gives the venture firm a liquidation preference. If the venture should fail, the venture capitalist will have a priority claim on the assets of the business. Often too, the terms can force eventual repayment even if the firm never achieves "public" status.

Venture firms will usually "syndicate" a large investment. That is, they will attempt to interest other firms in taking a piece of the investment. This permits the firm to invest in a larger number of companies and thus spread its risk. This is particularly important on subsequent "rounds" or stages of financing. Other venture firms will want to see that the original firm(s) will continue their investment in the company. If the existing, more knowledgeable investors aren't interested in the company, why should a new venture firm be interested?

Public Equity Markets

Of course, the largest source of equity capital remains the public equity markets: the New York, American, and over-the-counter stock exchanges. Typically, however, a firm must have a history of successful operation before it can raise money in this way. In "hot" markets, some smaller, start-up companies have been able to raise public equity. The process is lengthy, detailed, and expensive. See Chapter 15, "Securities Law and Public Offerings" for a discussion of the public equity markets.

Whether the investment is made by wealthy individuals or a venture capital firm, terms will have to be negotiated. In exchange for their investment, the investor will receive a "security," which represents the terms of his or her investment in the company. In the case of a public offering, the investment bank negotiates the terms on behalf of its clients. Venture capital firms and investment banks, of course, tend to be more sophisticated than the average wealthy investor.

Debt Capital

The other large category of capital is debt. Debt is presumed to be lower risk capital because it is repaid according to a set schedule of principal and interest.

In order to have a reasonable expectation of being paid according to this schedule, creditors lend against:

- Assets: Firms can obtain asset-based financing for most hard assets that have a market value. A building, equipment, or soluble inventory are all assets that a company could borrow against.
- Cash flow: Lenders will allow firms to borrow against their expected ability to generate the cash to repay the loan. Creditors attempt to check this ability through such measures as interest coverage (EBIT ÷ Interest payments) or debt/equity ratio. Obviously, a healthy business with little debt and high cash flow will have an easier time borrowing money than a new venture.

Cash Flow Financing

Cash flow or unsecured financing is of several types and can come from different sources.

- Short-term debt: Short-term unsecured financing is frequently available to cover seasonal working capital needs for periods of less than one year, usually 30 to 40 days.

- Line-of-credit financing: A company can arrange for a line of credit, to be drawn upon as needed. Interest is paid on the outstanding principal, and a "commitment fee" is paid up front. Generally, a line of credit must be "paid-down" to an agreed-upon level at some point during the year.
- Long-term debt: Generally available to solid "creditworthy" companies, long-term debt may be available for up to 10 years. Long-term debt is usually repaid according to a fixed schedule of interest and principal.

Cash flow financing is most commonly available from commercial banks but can also be obtained from savings and loan institutions, finance companies, and other institutional lenders (e.g., insurance companies, pension funds). Because cash flow financing is generally riskier than asset-based financing, banks will frequently attempt to reduce their risk through the use of covenants. These covenants place certain restrictions on a business if it wishes to maintain its credit with the bank. Typical loan covenants concern:

- Limits on the company's debt/equity ratio.
- Minimum standards on interest coverage.
- Lower limits on working capital.
- Minimum cash balance.
- Restrictions on the company's ability to issue senior debt.

These, and other covenants, attempt to protect the lender from actions that would increase the likelihood of the lender not getting its money back.

Asset-Based Financing

Most assets in a business can be financed. Because cash flow financing usually requires an earnings history, far more new ventures are able to obtain asset-based financing. In an asset-based financing, the company pledges or gives the financier a first lien on the asset. In the event of a default on the financing payments, the lender can repossess the asset. The following types of financing are generally available:

- Accounts receivable: Up to 90 percent of the accounts receivable from creditworthy customers can usually be financed. The bank will conduct a thorough investigation to determine which accounts are eligible for this kind of financing. In some industries, such as the government business, accounts receivable are often "factored." A factor buys approved receivables for a discount from their face value, but collects from the accounts.
- Inventory: Inventory is often financed if it consists of merchandise that could be easily sold. Typically, 50 percent or so of finished goods inventory can be financed.
- Equipment: Equipment can usually be financed for a period of 3 to 10 years. One half to 80 percent of the value of the equipment can be financed, depending on the salability or "liquidity" of the assets. Leasing is also a form of equipment

financing where the company never takes ownership of the equipment, but rents it.

- Real estate: Mortgage financing is usually readily available to finance a company's plant or buildings; 75 to 85 percent of the value of the building is a typical figure.
- Personally secured loans: A business can obtain virtually any amount of financing if one of its principals (or someone else) is willing to pledge a sufficient amount of assets to guarantee the loan.
- Letter-of-credit financing: A letter of credit is a bank guarantee that a company can obtain to enable it to purchase goods. A letter of credit functions almost like a credit card, allowing businesses to make commitments and purchases in other parts of the world where the company does not have relationships with local banks.
- Government-secured loans: Certain government agencies will guarantee loans to allow businesses to obtain financing when they could not obtain it on their own. The Small Business Administration, the Farmers Home Administration, and other government agencies will guarantee bank loans.

Asset-based financing is available from commercial banks and other financial institutions. Insurance companies, pension funds, and commercial finance companies provide mortgages and other forms of asset-backed financing. Entrepreneurs themselves can also provide debt capital to a business once it has passed out of the risky start-up period.

Internally Generated Financing

A final category of financing is internally generated. This term describes:

- Credit from suppliers: Paying bills in a less timely fashion is one way to increase working capital. Sometimes, suppliers will charge you interest for this practice. In other instances, the costs may be more severe if a key supplier resource decides to stop serving you.
- Accounts receivable: Collecting bills more quickly will also generate financing.
- Reducing working capital: A business can generate internal financing by reducing other working capital items: inventory, cash, and so forth.
- Sale of assets: Perhaps a more drastic move, selling assets will also generate capital.

Each of these techniques represents an approach to generating funds internally, without the help of a financial partner. Although the purely financial costs are low, the entrepreneur must be wary of attempting to run the business ''too lean.''

Summary

We've attempted to describe the spectrum of financial sources that an entrepreneur can tap both during the start-up phase and as a going concern. Figure 7–1 is an attempt to

FIGURE 7–1 Alternative Sources of Financing

Source	Cost							Control		
		Fixed Rate		Floating Rate						
	Zero	Short-term	Long-term	Short-term	Long-term	Percent of Profits	Equity	Covenants	Voting Rights	Guarantee of Debt
Self			X				X		X	X
Family and friends		X	X	X	X		X		X	X
Suppliers and trade credit	X	X				X				X
Commercial banks		X		X				X		X
Other commercial lenders		X	X		X			X		X
Asset-based lenders/lessors			X			X	X	X		
Specialized finance companies		X	X			X	X	X		
Institutions and insurance companies			X		X	X		X		
Pension funds			X			X	X	X		
Venture capital		X	X				X	X	X	X
Private equity placements							X	X	X	
Public equity offerings						X	X		X	
Government agencies (SBIC)			X		X	X				X
Other government programs			X					X		X

summarize these sources. Along the horizontal axis, we've tried to note whether the provider of capital tries to manage the risk/reward ratio by (1) increasing reward by raising the cost of funds or (2) decreasing risk by asserting some measure of control over the business. This is not an exhaustive list, but an overview of the most popular sources. In every case, there is a high premium on understanding both your own needs and the specific needs of the financier.

8 DEAL STRUCTURE

A critical aspect of the entrepreneur's attempt to obtain resources is the development of an actual "deal" with the owner of the resources. Typically, the entrepreneur needs a variety of resources, including dollars, people, and outside expertise. As in any situation, the individual who desires to own, or use, these resources must give up something. Because the entrepreneur typically has so little to start with, she or he will usually give up a claim on some future value in exchange for the ability to use these resources now.

Entrepreneurs can obtain funds in the form of trade credit, short- and long-term debt, and equity or risk capital. This chapter will focus on the structure and terms of the deal that may be used to obtain the required financial resources from investors. The note will center on financial resources because raising capital is a common problem that virtually all entrepreneurs face.

What Is a Deal?

In general, a *deal* represents the terms of a transaction between two (or more) groups or individuals. Entrepreneurs want money to use in a (hopefully) productive venture, and individuals and institutions wish to earn a return on the cash that they have at risk.

The entrepreneur's key task is to make the whole equal to more than the sum of the parts. That is, to carve up the economic benefits of the venture into pieces that meet the needs of particular financial backers. The entrepreneur can maximize his or her own return by selling these pieces at the highest possible price, that is, to individuals who demand the lowest return. And the individuals who demand the lowest return will typically be those that perceive the lowest risk.

The Deal

In order to craft a deal that maximizes his or her own economic return, the entrepreneur must:

This note was prepared by Michael J. Roberts under the direction of Howard H. Stevenson.
Harvard Business School Note 9–384–186

- Understand the fundamental economic nature of the business.
- Understand financiers' needs and perceptions of risk and reward.
- Understand his or her own needs and requirements.

Understanding the Business

The first thing the entrepreneur must do is assess the fundamental economic nature of the business itself. Most business plans project a set of economics that determine:

- The amount of the funds required.

  — The absolute amount.
  — The timing of these requirements.

- The riskiness of the venture.

  — The absolute level of risk.
  — The factors that determine risk.

- The timing and potential magnitude of returns.

It is important to remember that the venture itself does not necessarily have an inherent set of economics. The entrepreneur determines the fundamental economics when she or he makes critical decisions about the business. Still, there may be certain economic characteristics that are a function of the industry and environment and that the entrepreneur will generally be guided by.

For instance, a venture such as a genetics engineering firm has characteristics that differ greatly from those of a real estate deal. The genetics firm may require large investments over the first several years, followed by years with zero cash flow, followed by a huge potential return many years out. The real estate project, on the other hand, may require a one-time investment, generate immediate cash flow, and provide a means of exit only several years down the road.

One technique for understanding a venture's economic nature is to analyze the potential source of return. Let's take this example—a paint business with the following projected cash flows:

	Year					
	0	*1*	*2*	*3*	*4*	*5*
Cash flow [$000 omitted]	(1,000)	400	400	400	400	5,600

Now, we can break this cash flow down into its components:

- Investment: money required to fund the venture.
- Tax consequences: not precisely a cash flow, but nonetheless a cash benefit that may accrue if an investment has operating losses in the early years.

- Free cash flow: cash that the business throws off as a result of its operations before financing and distributions to providers of capital.
- Terminal value: the aftertax cash that the business returns as a result of its sale. Here, this is assumed to occur at the end of Year 5.

Let's assume that these flows are as follows:

	Year					
Cash Flows ($000)	*0*	*1*	*2*	*3*	*4*	*5*
Original investment	(1,000)					
Tax consequences	—	300	300	0	(100)	(200)
Free cash flows	—	100	100	400	500	800
Terminal value (after tax)	—	—	—	—	—	5,000
Total	(1,000)	400	400	400	400	5,600

Now, we can calculate the IRR of the total investment: 64.5 percent.

Next, we calculate the present value of each of the individual elements of the return *at that IRR,* and then the percent that each element contributes to the total return. Of course, the present value of the total return will be equal to the original investment.

Element	*Present Value* *@64.5% ($000)*	*Element's* *Percent of Total*
Tax consequences	263	26.3
Free cash flows	322	32.2
+ Terminal value	415	41.5
Total	$1,000	100.0%

This analysis illuminates the potential sources of return inherent in the business, as projected.

The task of the entrepreneur is now to carve up the cash flows and returns and sell them to the individuals/institutions that are willing to accept the lowest return. This will leave the biggest piece of the economic pie for the entrepreneur. To do so requires an understanding of the financiers' needs and perceptions.

Understanding Financiers

Providers of capital clearly desire a "good" return on their money, but their needs and priorities are far more complex. Figure 7–1 in Chapter 7 depicts some of the differences that exist among different financial sources. They vary along a number of dimensions, including:

- Magnitude of return desired.
- Magnitude and nature of risk that is acceptable.
- Perception of risk and reward.
- Magnitude of investment.
- Timing of return.
- Form of return.
- Degree of control.
- Mechanisms for control.

The priorities attached to the various elements may differ widely. For instance, institutions such as insurance companies and pension funds have legal standards, which determine the type of investment that they can undertake. For others, the time horizon for their return may be influenced by organizational or legal constraints.

Certain investors may want a high rate of return and be willing to wait a long period and bear a large amount of risk to get it. Still other investors may consider any type of investment, as long as there exists some mechanism for them to exert their own control over the venture. To the extent that the entrepreneur is able to break down the basic value of the business into components, which vary along each of these dimensions, and then find investors who want this specific package, the entrepreneurs will be able to structure a better transaction; a deal that creates more value for himself or herself.

If we return to our example of the paint business, which requires a $1 million investment, we can see how the entrepreneur can take advantage of these differences in investor characteristics.

- The tax benefits, for example, are well suited for sale to a risk-averse wealthy individual in a high marginal tax bracket. Because the benefits accrue as a result of operating losses, if the business does poorly, the tax benefits may be even greater. But let's assume that the wealthy individual believes that these forecasts are realistic and requires a 25 percent return. If we discount the tax benefits at this 25 percent required return, we arrive at a present value of $325,500. Therefore, this individual should be willing to invest $325,500 in order to purchase this portion of the cash flows. There must be economic substance to the transaction other than tax benefits. Care must be taken so that the investor can show prospect for economic gain. For this analysis, this tax-based requirement is ignored.
- The operating cash flows would, in total, be perceived as fairly risky. However, some portion of them should be viewed as a "safe bet" by a bank. Let's assume that the entrepreneur could convince a banker that no less than $60,000 would be available in any given year for interest expenses. Further, if the banker were willing to accept 12 percent interest and take all of the principal repayment at the end of Year 5 (when the business is sold), then she or he should be willing to provide $60,000 ÷ .12 = $500,000 in the form of a loan.

    Now the entrepreneur has raised $825,500 and needs only $174,500 to get into business.

- The terminal value and the riskier portion of the operating cash flows remain to be sold. Let's assume that a venture investor would be willing to provide funds at a 50 percent rate of return.

First, we need to see precisely what cash flows remain:

	Year				
	1	*2*	*3*	*4*	*5*
Total	400	400	400	400	5,600
− Wealthy investor	300	300	0	(100)	(200)
− Bank	60	60	60	60	560
= Remaining	40	40	340	440	5,240

The remaining cash flows in Years 1 through 5 have a present value, at the venture firm's 50 percent discount rate, of $922,140. If we need $174,500, we need to give up $174,500 ÷ $922,140 = 18.9 percent of these flows in order to entice the venture investor to provide risk capital. These flows might well be sold to the tax-oriented investor in order to meet the requirements for economic substance. This leaves the entrepreneur with a significant portion of the above "remaining" flows. One can see how these differences in needs and perceived risk allow the entrepreneur to create value for himself or herself.

Understanding the Entrepreneur's Own Needs

The example we have just worked through was based on the assumption that the entrepreneur wants to obtain funds at the lowest possible cost. While this is generally true, there are often other factors that should affect the analysis.

The entrepreneur's needs and priorities do vary across a number of aspects including the time horizon for involvement in the venture, the nature of that involvement, degree of business risk, and so on. All of these variables will affect the entrepreneur's choice of a venture to pursue. However, once the entrepreneur has decided to embark on a particular business, his or her needs and priorities with respect to the *financing* of the venture will vary with respect to:

- Degree of control desired.
- Mechanisms of control desired.
- Amount of financing required.
- Magnitude of financial return desired.
- Degree of risk that is acceptable.

For instance, in the above example, the entrepreneur could have decided to obtain an additional $100,000 or $200,000 as a cushion to make the venture less risky. This would certainly have lowered the economic return, but might have made the entrepreneur more comfortable with the venture.

Similarly, the bank, which offered funds at 12 percent, or the venture investor might have imposed a series of very restrictive covenants. Rather than accept this loss of control, the entrepreneur might rather have given up more of the economic potential.

In addition, the entrepreneur may need more than just money. There are times when some investors' money is better than others. This occurs in situations where once an individual is tied into a venture financially, she or he has an incentive to help the entrepreneur in nonfinancial ways. For instance, an entrepreneur starting a business that depends on securing good retail locations would prefer to obtain financing from an individual with good real estate contacts than from someone without those contacts. Venture capital firms are frequently cited for providing advice and support in addition to financing.

Summary

Once the fundamental economics of a deal have been worked out, the entrepreneur must still structure the deal. This requires the use of a certain legal form of organization and a certain set of securities.

The vehicles through which the entrepreneur can raise capital include the general partnership, the limited partnership, the S corporation, and the corporation. While these forms of organization differ with respect to their tax consequences, they also differ substantially regarding the precision with which cash flows may be carved up and returned to various investors. In a limited partnership, for instance, virtually *any* distribution of profits and cash flow is feasible so long as it is spelled out clearly and in advance in the limited partnership agreement. (Losses, however, are usually distributed in proportion to capital provided.) In an S corporation, on the other hand, where only one class of stock is permitted, investors can get a return in the form of tax losses that can be passed through, but founder's stock is equivalent to investors' stock, and it is difficult to draw any distinctions in the returns that accrue to the two groups.

Securities can involve debt, warrants, straight or preferred equity, and a host of other legal arrangements. The structuring of securities requires the assistance of good legal counsel with expertise in securities and corporate law, as well as intimate knowledge of the tax code.

In the previous chapter, we looked at alternative sources of financing. Here, we've attempted to describe how the entrepreneur can structure a deal with these potential sources of capital. A well-structured deal will provide the financier with his or her desired return and still create substantial value for the entrepreneur.

9 Securities Law and Private Financing

Many business financing transactions are regulated by state and federal securities laws. The Securities and Exchange Commission (SEC) administers federal securities laws, and state securities laws (Blue Sky laws) are enforced by the respective states.

Securities laws apply to private business transactions as well as to public offerings in the stock markets. This piece will focus on private financing; see Chapter 15, "Securities Law and Public Offerings" for information on the public financing markets. Like tax laws, securities laws are complex and not always grounded in logic. The consequences of violation (even technical violation) can be vastly disproportionate to the harm inflicted and can include severe personal liabilities for management (including innocent management). In addition, a violation can preclude present and future business financings. Treatment and cure of violations, when possible, can be time consuming and expensive. To complicate matters, securities regulation has changed dramatically over the past dozen years first in response to the speculative abuses of the late 60s and, more recently, in an attempt to modify regulations that would facilitate capital formation.

Statements contained in this piece are of necessity general in nature and become outdated with the passage of time, and therefore they should not be relied on in formulating definitive business plans, but used rather as an indication of the nature and extent of securities regulation that may be applicable in various circumstances. In this regard, it should be borne in mind that in addition to the federal securities laws, there are securities laws in each of the 50 states—many of which vary substantially from state to state.

What Is a Security?

The securities laws are applicable only if a *security* is involved in the transaction. The statutory definition of security includes common and preferred stock, notes, bonds, debentures, voting-trust certificates, certificates of deposit, warrants, options subscription rights, and undivided oil or gas interests. In fact, the definition is broad enough to encompass just about any financing transaction, whether or not a certificate evidencing the investor's participation is issued, so long as the investor's participation in the

This note was prepared by Michael J. Roberts and Richard E. Floor under the direction of Howard H. Stevenson.

business is passive or nearly so. Generally, a security is involved whenever one person supplies money or some item of value with the expectation that it will be used to generate profits or other monetary return for the investor primarily from the efforts of others. Thus, a limited partnership interest is a security. So is a cow, if purchased together with a maintenance contract whereby someone else will raise, feed, and sell the cow without the participation of the investor. Similarly, an orange grove is a security if coupled with an agreement to maintain, harvest, and sell the orange crop; a condominium unit is a security if coupled with an agreement to rent the unit to others when not occupied by the owner; and parcels of oil property may be securities if sold with the understanding that the promoter will drill a test well on adjoining land. A franchise may or may not be a security, depending on the extent of the participation of the investor. Generally, a transaction involves a security if there is an expectation of a ''profit'' or monetary return.

Despite the broadness of the above generalizations, there are some financing transactions that are deemed not to involve securities merely because they traditionally have not been considered to involve them. Thus, a note given in connection with a long-term bank loan is generally not considered a security although it falls squarely within the statutory definition. On the other hand, bank transactions only modestly removed from normal commercial practice may be deemed to involve securities. Active participation in the solicitation of a pledge of a third party's securities in connection with an outstanding loan to another party, for instance, would fit within the definition and thus be subject to the securities laws.

Business Financing Disclosures

The financing of a business frequently involves the investment of money or some other item of value by a person who is not a part of management or otherwise familiar with all of the material aspects of the business. In order for an outside investor to make an informed investment decision, she or he must be made aware of the material factors that bear upon the present condition and future prospects of the business and of the pertinent details regarding participation in the business and its profits. The securities laws thus impose an obligation upon a business and its management to disclose such information to a potential investor together with the factors that adversely affect the business or which may reasonably be foreseen to do so in the future. In addition to financings by a company, these laws impose similar disclosure requirements whenever a member of management or a principal equity owner sells his personal security holdings to an outsider.

In financings involving outsiders, it is common practice (whether required or not) for management to prepare a prospectus, offering circular, or memorandum describing the nature, condition, and prospects of the business and the nature and extent of the investor's participation in it (see Chapter 5). In this manner, the pertinent disclosures are set forth in a permanent written record so that there can be no argument as to whether or not the disclosures have been made or what they were. Such a document traditionally discloses the terms of the offering, the use of the proceeds, the capitalization of the business (before and after the financing), contingent liabilities (if any), the operations of the business, its sources of supply, marketing techniques, competitors and market position, its personnel, government regulation and litigation, its management and management's remuneration, transactions between the company and management, the principal equity owners of the business, and balance sheets and earnings statements of the business.

Historically, the SEC has discouraged the disclosure of forward-looking information such as projected earnings or dividends per share, and in fact has implied that disclosure of such information might be inherently misleading. In recent years, however, the commission changed its view and issued a series of rulings, which have now been codified into Rule 175, authorizing the disclosure of projections concerning revenues, income, earnings, dividends, and company objectives, under certain circumstances. In disclosing such information to prospective investors, management must act reasonably and in good faith, disclose any underlying assumptions, and correct information that becomes false or misleading over time.

Despite the fact that disclosure documents are often prepared and reviewed by attorneys and accountants, the law imposes the primary obligation for complete and accurate disclosure upon the company, its management, and principal equity owners.

It thus is essential that each member of management (including outside directors) and each principal equity owner be satisfied that the information in the disclosure document is accurate and complete based on his own personal knowledge of the company and its records. The financial statements, for instance, are generally deemed to be the company's disclosures rather than the accountant's, and the company itself remains principally responsible for their accuracy, even when an audit has been performed. In fact, the company has no "due diligence" defense at all in a federally registered offering and is absolutely liable if any material misstatements or omissions occur anywhere in the prospectus.

A disclosure document that satisfies these disclosure standards often appears negative in its presentation. Such a document need not be unduly so in order to provide the necessary protection, and, in any event, what appears "negative" to management may not necessarily appear negative to the financial community, which is accustomed to reading disclosure documents of this type.

In order to alleviate this negative effect, some entrepreneurs will first prepare a "business plan," which is *not* an offering/disclosure document. The purpose of this document will be to stimulate investor interest. Having screened investors, the entrepreneur will then circulate a more formal offering/disclosure document. This technique is often effective, but still imposes a duty on the entrepreneur not to make any misleading claims in the business plan. In a public offering, such an approach (called *gun-jumping*) would clearly be illegal. See Figure 9–1 for an outline of a business plan and prospectus.

Private Offerings

Private offerings are distinct from public offerings in a number of ways. Public offerings typically involve larger sums of money and may be sold through brokers. Public

---

FIGURE 9-1   Business Plan and Prospectus Outline

Business Plan
1. Introduction (or executive summary)
   Short description of:
   • Business objectives
   • Product
   • Technology and development program
   • Market and customers
   • Management team
   • Financing requirements
2. Company description
   • History and states
   • Background and industry
   • Company's objectives
   • Company's strategies
3. Risk factors
4. Products
   • Product description and comparisons
   • Innovative features (patent coverage)
   • Applications
   • Technology
   • Product development
   • Product introduction schedule and major milestones
5. Market
   • Market summary and industry overview
   • Market analysis and forecasts
   • Industry trends
   • Initial product(s)
6. Competition
7. Marketing program
   • Objectives
   • Marketing strategy
   • Sales and distribution channels
   • Customers
   • Staffing

8. Management
   • Founders
   • Stock ownership
   • Organization and personnel
   • Future key employees and staffing
   • Incentives (employee stock purchase plan)
9. Manufacturing
10. Service and field engineering
11. Future products (product evolution)
    • Engineering development program
    • Future R&D
12. Facilities
13. Capital requirements
14. Financial data and financial forecasts
    • Assumptions used
    • 3-year plan
    • 5-year plan
15. Appendixes
    • Detailed management profiles
    • References
    • Product descriptions, sketches, photos
    • Recent literature on product, market, etc.
Prospectus
When used as a legal prospectus, or offering memorandum, the following additions or changes should be made:
• Affix federal and state securities legends.
• Affix disclosures.
• Add a detailed use of Proceeds section.
• Add a section that describes the securities offered, in detail.
• Expand on the Risk Factors section to include dilution, nontransferability, and other risk factors that relate specifically to the securities being offered.
Remember—Obtain the counsel of a competent securities attorney.

NOTE: Use and dissemination should be restricted; document should be treated as confidential.

offerings require that the company go through an expensive and lengthy ''registration'' process to register the securities with the SEC. This process is discussed more fully in Chapter 15, ''Securities Law and Public Offerings.''

Federal securities laws and many state securities laws have long reflected the view that some potential investors are sufficiently sophisticated in business investment matters to be as able to investigate a business and assemble relevant data as are management and regulatory authorities. More recently, Congress has recognized that small businesses wishing to attract capital may be unduly hampered by burdensome filing requirements. In either circumstance, preparation of an orderly and systematic discussion of the business in a formal prospectus and the review of this presentation by government agents is deemed unnecessary because the offerees are competent to assess the venture independently, or because the issuer seeks to raise very limited amounts of capital. Thus, registration is unnecessary, and the company and its management and principal equity owners may rely upon one of the so-called private offering exemptions. Local state securities laws in every state where a *purchaser* is residing should always be reviewed. (It may also be prudent to similarly review state securities laws where any offeree resides, since the offer itself may be a violation even if no sale is made.)

Historically, the principal criteria of the availability of the private offering exemption have been the business acumen or "sophistication" of the offerees, access to material information concerning the company, and the number of offerees *(not purchasers)*. All of these items were highly subjective, and the absence of guidelines often resulted in liability for issuers who mistakenly believed they came within the exemption. Beginning in the 1970s, however, for purposes of federal regulation, the SEC attempted to create more order by releasing a series of rules that provide "safe harbors" within the general ocean of uncertainty embodied in these three traditional criteria. Regulation D represents the commission's most recent attempt to foster coherence and certainty.

Regulation D: The Various Rules

Six administrative rules, three of which set forth general definitions and three of which provide safe harbors for certain private offerings, comprise Regulation D. The operative rules— 504, 505, and 506 —broaden the scope of the private offering exemption. Collectively, they are designed to simplify the existing rules and regulations, to eliminate unnecessary restrictions on small issuers' ability to raise capital, and to create regulatory uniformity at the federal and state levels. Each of the rules requires that a notice be filed with the SEC on Form D.

Rule 504.   The first exemption, Rule 504, is especially useful to issuers seeking to raise relatively small amounts of capital from numerous investors. It permits an issuer to sell up to $1 million of its securities during any 12-month period. Rule 504 does not limit the number or sophistication of the investors or prescribe any specific form of disclosure. The effect of the rule, then, is to delegate substantial responsibility regulating small issuers to the state agencies. Because Rule 504 is designed to assist small businesses, however, it is unavailable to investment companies or to companies that do not have an existing business ("blank check" companies), which must use the separate (and more restrictive) Rule 504A. Companies required to file periodic reports under the Securities Exchange Act are also denied the use of Rule 504.

Rule 506.   In contrast to Rule 504, Rule 506 permits an issuer to sell an unlimited amount of its securities, but only to certain investors. In this regard, the rule represents a continuation of the SEC's effort to codify some of the practices developed by lawyers and courts in applying the general private placement standards of sophistication, information, and numbers and permits issuers to raise potentially substantial amounts of capital without registration. Rule 506 is available for transactions that do not involve more than 35 purchasers. Sales to accredited investors (defined below), relatives of investors, or entities controlled by investors are excluded from this total. The issuer must determine that each nonexempt investor meets the sophistication test, either individually or through a knowledgeable "purchaser representative," but no longer need inquire as to the investor's ability to bear the financial risk of his or her investment. In determining sophistication, the issuer can insist that each purchaser or group of purchasers be represented by a person who would clearly meet any test of sophistication. Subject to certain exceptions, the representative cannot be an affiliate, director, officer, employee, or 10 percent beneficial owner of the company (although he can be paid by the company as long as this is disclosed) and must be accepted by the purchaser in writing as his representative.

Perhaps the most significant aspect of Rule 506 is the "accredited investor" concept. Such investors are presumed to be sophisticated and thus do not count against the 35 investor limitation. They include institutional investors such as banks, savings and loan associations, broker-dealers, insurance companies, investment companies, certain ERISA employee benefit plans, private business development companies, corporations, certain trusts, partnerships and tax-exempt organizations, the issuer's directors, executive officers, and general partners. In addition, individuals whose net worth exceeds $1 million at the time of the purchase, or individuals with incomes in excess of $200,000 (or joint income with spouse in excess of $300,000) in each of the last two years, are considered accredited investors.

When an issuer sells securities under Rule 506 to accredited investors only, it is not compelled to make disclosures of any sort. If the sale involves both accredited and non-accredited investors, by contrast, the disclosure requirements are more complex. Nonreporting companies must disclose (a) the non-financial statement information required by a registration statement available to the company and (b) the financial statement information required by (i) for offerings of up to $2 million, Item 310 of Regulation S-B, except that only the most recent balance sheet must be audited, (ii) for offerings of up to $7.5 million, Form SB-2 (including two-year audited financials), or (iii) for offerings of more than $7.5 million, a form of registration statement available to the company. If obtaining audited financial statements requires "undue effort and expense" for an issuer other than a limited partnership (to which separate provisions apply), then only a balance sheet as of 120 days prior to the offering need be audited. Reporting companies, on the other hand, must furnish (*a*) their most recent Rule 14a-3 annual report, definitive proxy statement, and Form 10-K if requested, *or* the information contained in their most recent Form S-1, Form 10, Form S-11, Form SB-1, Form SB-2, or Form 10-K, and (*b*) any other reports or documents required to be filed under the Securities Exchange Act subsequent to distribution or filing of special reports or registration statements together with information concerning the offering and material changes, regardless of the size of the offering. All companies selling securities to accredited and nonaccredited investors must also furnish nonaccredited investors a written description of any written information accredited purchasers receive and must give all purchasers an opportunity to ask questions and receive answers and to obtain any additional information which the issuer possesses or can acquire without unreasonable effort or expense prior to the sale. Finally, no issuer utilizing Rule 506 may engage in general solicitation or advertising.

Rule 505.   Rule 505 adds some flexibility to Rule 506 for certain issuers. It permits the sale of up to $5 million of unregistered securities over any 12-month period to any 35 investors in addition to an unlimited number of accredited investors. The primary advantage of Rule 505, therefore, is the elimination of the sophistication test for unaccredited investors entirely and with it the elimination of the need for a purchaser representative.

Investment companies and issuers disqualified under Regulation A are ineligible to use Rule 505. Like Rule 506, Rule 505 prohibits general advertising or solicitation through public media of any kind and imposes disclosure requirements identical to the Rule 506 requirements discussed above.

Section 4(6).   Section 4(6) of the Securities Act, enacted as part of the Small Business Investment Incentive Act of 1980 and not technically a part of Regulation D, permits companies to issue up to $5 million of their securities in any single offering without registration and restricts the class of purchasers in any such transaction to accredited investors. Issuers are not required to disclose any specific information and may not engage in any form of solicitation in connection with offers or sales. Given these requirements, any issuer who can meet the requirements of Section 4(6) can also qualify under Rules 505 or 506.

Regulation D: Other Information

In addition to these specific exemptions, Regulation D includes a number of broadly applicable provisions designed to streamline and simplify private offerings. For example, when calculating dollar limitations, issuers must integrate the proceeds from all offers and sales made more than six months before or after a Regulation D offering. The regulation also provides that any securities issued pursuant to one of its exempting provisions (other than securities issued under Rule 504) may not be resold without registration. In this regard, the company must exercise reasonable care to prevent further distribution and should accordingly place restrictive legends on its certificates, enter "stop-transfer" orders, advise purchasers of the restrictions on resale, and secure representations that the securities are purchased for the individual's own account and not with any intention to redistribute. The issuer in a Regulation D or Section 4(6) private offering must file five copies of Form D with the commission not later than 15 days after the first sale.

The burden of proving the availability of an exemption is on the person asserting it. In order for the risk of nonavailability of the exemption to be reduced to an acceptable level, the issuer must complete positive and compelling documentary proof that each of the requirements for exemption has been met. This is particularly important if none of the safe-harbor rules applies. The sophistication of offerees should be thoroughly investigated *before* they are approached, and a memorandum setting forth their background and the reasons for their sophistication placed in the log. In making the initial presentation, use of a private placement memorandum should be made, each such memorandum being numbered and containing a legend that is not to be reproduced or disclosed to outsiders. The number of the memorandum and the date on which it is submitted to the offeree should be set forth in the log. If the offeree becomes an investor, the date on which he or his representative reviews the books and the records of the company, the books and records so reviewed, and the date on which he or his representative engaged in face-to-face negotiation should be recorded in the log. At the end of the offering, a memo should be placed in the log stating that no persons other than those set forth in the log were contacted or offered any of the securities, such memo reciting that *offer* is understood to mean nothing more than creating a situation that can be construed as seeking a commitment (even informal) to acquire a security to be issued by a described company at a given price. The log should be placed in the company's permanent files as evidence of the availability of the private offering exemption as to the financing.

Finally, and perhaps most important, an issuer must remember that all offerings, even if exempt from federal registration, remain subject to the antifraud and civil liability provisions of the federal securities laws and to the general requirements of state Blue Sky laws. Particular note should be taken of the fact that the safe-harbor exemptions provided under Regulation D are generally not available under state Blue Sky laws and that registration may be necessary in a given state for an offering that fully complies with Rules 504, 505, or 506.

Resale of Restricted Securities

Securities issued under one of the private offering exemptions (other than securities issued under rule 504) or held by a member of management or a principal equity owner of the company (no matter how acquired, and whether registered or not) are subject to restrictions on resale that severely limit their liquidity unless the securities are subsequently registered under the Securities Act of 1933. For this reason, it is common practice for venture capital firms, private placement investors, management, and such owners to obtain an agreement from the company to register the securities upon demand or to include them "piggyback" in any other SEC registration that the company might undertake.

If the securities are not registered or covered by Regulation A when they are resold, as a practical matter the resales must be made under SEC Rule 144, or one of the private offering exemptions (not including the Regulation D exemptions for this purpose). Absent such an exemption, the resales will constitute unregistered offerings and subject the issuer and seller to potential liability. In addition, if the securities are transferred without consideration—by gift or upon death, for example—the restrictions generally bind the recipient.

Restrictions upon subsequent resale must be disclosed to potential investors in a private placement or the financing will be deemed by the SEC to violate the antifraud provisions of federal securities laws. This disclosure is often recited as part of the "investment letter" signed by the investor.

Consequences of Violation

As a practical matter, in the past a vast majority of securities laws violations have not been investigated or litigated. However, the possibility of nonenforcement provides little comfort to potential defendants when commercial transactions of any size are involved. Moreover, transactions of today are potential lawsuits five years from now, when investors may be more aware of their rights under the securities laws and more inclined to enforce them.

The consequences of violation of the securities laws in connection with a company's prior financings are rarely serious so long as its operations continue to be successful and this success is reflected in the price of its securities. If public estimates of a company's success have been too conservative, however, an investor who has sold his securities too cheaply may complain. Investors and regulators tend to scrutinize company disclosures in minute detail when a business turns sour, with the hopes of discovering some technical or other securities law violation to use in unwinding a financing, or holding management responsible.

The most serious consequence of violation of the securities laws is potential civil liability that may be incurred by those persons deemed to have violated such laws or to have aided and abetted violations. When a corporation or other business entity is involved, management (i.e., officers and directors, general partners, etc.) and the company's principal equity owners may be held liable as controlling persons. In this regard, the corporate entity, which serves as an effective shield from liability in other situations, affords no protection from securities laws violations. The magnitude of the liabilities that may thus be incurred can be enormous. If a violation involves improper disclosure, the applicable statute of limitations does not begin until the person harmed discovers or reasonably should discover the improper disclosure. Furthermore, agreements to indemnify management and owners from liability for securities laws violations are of little use. Insurance from these liabilities is expensive and often difficult to obtain.

Suit under the securities laws by damaged investors or others is relatively easy to bring. Such suit may be brought in federal court in any jurisdiction in which any defendant is found or lives or transacts business, and service of process may be made anywhere in the world. A single plaintiff may bring a class action on behalf of all persons similarly situated, and courts award attorneys' fees liberally to successful or settling plaintiffs' attorneys as an inducement to bring such suits as private guardians of the public.

A company that makes an offer to an ineligible offeree in a nonregistered offering in which the private or intrastate offering exemption is relied on is thus subject to a contingent liability to all investors in the offering for the aggregate amount of their investment. Under past practice, this contingent liability was deemed by the SEC staff to be cured by a subsequent registered or Regulation A offer to the investors to repurchase the shares sold in violation of the registration provisions. Subsequent financings without either the offer to repurchase or a disclosure of the contingent liability violate the antifraud provisions of the securities laws. Under recent SEC staff interpretations, even a registered offer to repurchase may not remove the contingent liability, and the contingent liability must be disclosed in subsequent financings until the three-year statute of limitations has run, or else an antifraud violation will occur.

Uncorrected securities laws violations can preclude subsequent Regulation A or registered financings. The SEC may take administrative, civil, or criminal action, which can result in fine, imprisonment, court order requiring restoration of illegal gains, order suspending or barring activities with or as a broker-dealer, or other sanctions reflecting the nature and seriousness of the violation.

Summary

Like many areas of the law, securities regulation is complex territory, fraught with countless opportunities for the entrepreneur to stumble. In the case of securities laws, an error can be particularly costly, making it difficult for the individual or the company to raise funds. For this reason, competent legal counsel is vitally important.

10   INTELLECTUAL PROPERTY

In recent years, the world's major industrial economies have become considerably more knowledge based. That is, high value-added, knowledge-intensive industries (such as electronics and service businesses) have grown at the expense of resource-based and commodity businesses. The rationale for this trend is clear: The major economic powers have focused their efforts on developing knowledge-intensive industries as a way to increase the income and standard of living of their populace, while decreasing their economy's dependence on diminishing natural resources.

As the U.S. economy has become more knowledge intensive, legal minds have grappled with the issue of intellectual property. Who owns an idea? How can valuable knowledge and information be protected?

This chapter will address the various categories of protection afforded by the law, describe the nature of what can be protected, and discuss how that protection is achieved.

Intellectual Property

The area of intellectual property has challenged the legal system for hundreds of years and continues to do so. Common law has historically protected the property rights of individuals and corporations. But the area of intellectual property has presented new challenges to the legal system. If someone stole your wedding band, it would be fairly easy to prove—that individual would have the ring, and you would be without it.

Yet, how can you tell when someone has taken an idea or a concept? Intellectual property issues are particularly relevant in situations where an individual is working on some state-of-the-art process for his or her employer. During the course of developing the design, the employee has some "inspiration" that is outside the scope of the project's original bounds. Does this idea belong to the employer or the employee? Does it matter whether the inspiration occurred on the company's premises or while the employee was at home in the shower? Could the employee continue to work for the employer, but set up an independent business to exploit the idea?

This note was prepared by Michael J. Roberts under the direction of Howard H. Stevenson.
Copyright © 1984 by the President and Fellows of Harvard College
Harvard Business School Note 9–384–188

A special patent law and patent court system were developed to deal specifically with these questions. Recently, however, intellectual property issues have arisen outside the bounds of traditional patent and trade secret law. The legal system is currently in the midst of grappling with these perplexing issues.

Intellectual Property and the Law

Historically, it has been a specific goal of U.S. public policy to create the incentives required for the progress of technology. One of the means to this end has been through the system of patents and copyrights. These classes of intellectual property have arisen out of the statutes of the United States government, which are, quite literally, the laws of the United States as passed by Congress.

They include subjects such as:

• Title 11: Bankruptcy
• Title 23: Highways
• Title 39: Postal Service
• Title 50: War and National Defense

Each of the titles lays down the law relating to the subject at hand, as well as the administrative systems the U.S. government will put in place to support each of the areas.

Specifically relating to intellectual property are two titles:

• Title 17: Copyrights
• Title 35: Patents

Patents and copyrights receive protection directly under this statutory framework, but the law in these areas is not governed exclusively by the language of the U.S. Code itself. Through their application and interpretation of the statutes in individual cases, judges define (and indeed create) relevant legal standards. Such ''common law,'' or judge-made law, adapts the patent and copyright laws to modern circumstances (short of congressional amendments of the statutes themselves).

Out of common law principles have grown other areas of law that address intellectual property issues. These areas include trademarks, trade secrets, and confidential business information. Each of these topics will be explored in detail.

Patents

Patents are issued by the U.S. Patent and Trademark Office. There are three specific types of patents:

• Utility patents: for new articles, processes, machines, etc.
• Design patents: for new and original ornamental designs for articles of manufacture.
• Plant patents: for new varieties of plant life.

It is important to understand the concept of a patent. A patent *does not* grant an individual exclusive rights to an invention. The inventor *already* has that exclusive right by dint of having invented the device in the first place; he or she can merely keep the invention a secret and enjoy its exclusive use.

Rather, the government grants the inventor the ''negative right'' to exclude others from making or using the invention. This right is granted in exchange for placing the information in the public domain.[1]

For instance, let's assume that the electronic calculator was a patentable invention, and that Mr. B was issued a patent on the device. Now, let us further assume that the idea of a checkbook holder with an electronic calculator was also patented, and that Mr. C was issued a patent on this invention. Mr. C would have the right to prevent others, including Mr. B, from manufacturing this device. However, Mr. C *could not* produce his article without the consent of Mr. B. In the event that patent infringement does occur, the patent holder can sue in civil court for damages. Should the patent holder become aware of potential infringement before the actual infringement occurs, he or she can sue for an injunction to prevent the infringement from actually occurring.

As mentioned, these kinds of legal battles occur in the civil courts. The purpose of the patent court system is to mediate patent claims. For example, when a patent claim is published in the *Patent Gazette,* others could come forward and challenge the patentability of the invention in the patent court system. One basis of challenge is for another inventor to claim that he or she was actually the first inventor. For this reason, it is recommended that inventors keep a daily record of their progress in a notebook. These notes should record the inventor's progress and be signed and witnessed on a daily basis. In the event of a challenge, such a record will prove invaluable.

The three types of patents each cover different kinds of intellectual property and are governed by different regulations.

Utility Patents.   A utility patent is issued to protect new, useful processes, devices, or inventions. First, what constitutes a patentable invention? The invention must meet several requirements:

- It must fall within one of the statutory categories of subject matter. There are four broad classes of subject matter: machines, manufacture, composition of matter, and processes.
- Only the actual, original inventor may apply for patent protection. In the case of corporations, for instance, the patent, when issued, is always granted to the individual and then *assigned* to the corporation.
- The invention must be new. That is, it will be considered novel if it is:

  — Not known or used by others in the United States.

  — Not patented or described by others in a printed publication in this or a foreign country.

---

[1]David A. Burge, *Patent and Trademark Tactics and Practice* (New York: John Wiley & Sons, 1980), p. 25.

— Not patented in this country.

— Not made in this country by another who had not abandoned, suppressed, or concealed it.

- The invention must be useful, even if only in some minimal way.
- The invention must be nonobvious. If the invention has been obvious to anyone skilled in the art, then it is not patentable.[2]

Finally, even if an invention meets all of these requirements, a patent can be denied if the application was not filed in a timely fashion. Specifically, if you used, sold, described in print, or attempted to secure a foreign patent application *more than one year prior* to your U.S. application, the patent will be denied.

Utility patents are issued for a term of 17 years.

The process of obtaining a patent is quite laborious. Patent attorneys, who specialize in the area, will draft the patent application, which includes specific claims for the patentability of the invention. After several iterations of discussions with the patent office, some or all of the claims may be approved. This process frequently takes two years or longer.

Following acceptance of the patent by the Patent Office, a general description of the invention is published in the *Patent Gazette*. Interested parties may request a copy of the full patent from the Patent Office for a very nominal fee.

During the time between application for a patent and its issue, the invention has "patent pending" status. In some ways, this offers more protection than the actual patent. The invention will not be revealed by the government during this time, and others may be afraid to copy the invention for fear of infringing on the forthcoming patent.

Design Patents. A design patent protects the nonfunctional features of useful objects. In order to obtain a design patent, the following requirements must be met:

- Ornamentality: The design must be aesthetically appealing and must not be dictated solely by functional or utilitarian considerations.
- Novelty: The design must be new. The same criteria used for a utility patent will be applied here.
- Nonobvious: The design must not be obvious to anyone skilled in the art. This is a difficult standard to apply to a design and is quite subjective.
- Embodied in an article of manufacture: The design must be an inseparable part of a manufactured article.[3]

Design patents are issued for 3½, 7, or 14 years, depending on the election of the applicant at the time of the application.

---

[2]Illinois Institute for Continuing Legal Education, *Intellectual Property Law for the General Business Counselor* (Chicago: Illinois Bar Center, 1973), pp. 1–16 through 1–24.

[3]Burge, *Patent and Trademark,* pp. 137–38.

Plant Patents.   A plant patent is obtainable on any new variety of plant that that individual is able to reproduce asexually. The new plant must be nonobvious. A plant patent is issued for a term of 17 years.

Copyrights

Copyright protection is afforded to artists and authors, giving them the sole right to print, copy, sell, and distribute the work. Books, musical and dramatic compositions, maps, paintings, sculptures, motion pictures, and sound recordings can all be copyrighted.

To obtain copyright protection, the work must simply bear a copyright notice, which includes the symbol © or the word *copyright,* the date of first publication, and the name of the owner of the copyright.

Copyrighted works are protected for a term of 50 years beyond the death of the author.

Trademarks

A trademark is any name, symbol, or configuration that an individual or organization uses to distinguish its products from others.

Trademark law is *not* derived from statutes of the Constitution, but is an outgrowth of the common law dealing with unfair competition.

Unfair competition is deemed to exist when the activities of a competitor result in confusion in the mind of the buying public.

Trademarks are typically brand names that apply to products, and service marks are names that apply to services.

There are several regulations that govern the proper use and protection of trademarks.[4] The scope of protection under the law is a function of the nature of the mark itself. Principal categories are:

- Coined marks: A newly coined, previously unknown mark is afforded the broadest protection (e.g., Xerox as a brand of copier, Charmin as a brand of toilet tissue).
- Arbitrary marks: A name already in use and applied to a certain product by a firm, but without suggesting any of the product's attributes (e.g., Apple Computer, Milky Way candy bars).
- Suggestive marks: A name in use, but suggesting some desirable attribute of the product (e.g., Sweet-n-Low as a low-calorie sweetener, White-Out correction fluid).
- Descriptive marks: A name that describes the purpose or function of the product. Descriptive marks cannot be registered until, over time, they have proven to be distinctive terms (e.g., *sticky* would probably not be approved as a trademarked brand name for glue).

---

[4]Burge, *Patent and Trademark,* p. 114.

- Unprotectable terms: Generic names, which refer to the general class of product. Escalator, for instance, once a trade name, is now a generic term for moving staircases. One could not introduce a new brand of orange juice and call it *O.J.*

In order to maintain a trademark, an owner must continue to use it and protect it. In this vein, some consumer product companies routinely produce and sell a few hundred items of several brand names that they have trademarked and wish to protect, but are not in normal production. Similarly, Coca-Cola has a crew of agents who routinely order "a coke" in establishments that do not serve Coca-Cola. If they are served a soda, they prosecute. In this way, they can maintain that they have attempted to keep their brand name from becoming a generic term. Aspirin, Cellophane, Zipper, and Escalator are all names that have lost their trademark status.

Until a trademark is registered with the Patents and Trademark Office, it is desirable to use the™ symbol after the name of a product,^{SM} for services. After registration, the legend ® should be used.

Trade Secrets

A trade secret is typically defined as any formula, device, process, or information that gives a business an advantage over its competitors. To be classified as a trade secret, the information must not be generally known in the trade.

One cannot, by definition, patent a trade secret because the patent laws require that the invention be fully disclosed.

One advantage of a trade secret is that the protection will not expire after the 17-year term of the patent. Coke, for instance, maintains its recipe as a trade secret rather than patent it. Yet, should the information become public knowledge, its advantage could disappear quickly, and the inventor would have no claim on the process because it had not been patented.

Finally, should a firm decide to maintain a patentable advantage as a trade secret, and should another firm independently discover and patent that invention, this "second" inventor will have the right to collect royalties or force the "first" inventor to cease patent infringement. For this reason, many corporations routinely "defensively patent" and publish inventions so that others cannot.

In order for a company to maintain trade secret status for advantageous information, the company must keep the information secret and take precautions to keep it secret. These precautions include:

- Having certain policies relating to secret information.
- Making employees sign confidentiality and noncompete agreements.
- Marking documents *confidential* or *secret*.

Confidential Business Information

The courts have also seen fit to protect a class of information less "secret" than a trade secret, but that is nonetheless confidential. The key here is that the information is disclosed in confidence, with the clear understanding that the information is confidential. Even if the information is in the public domain, if the recipient derives some value from the confidential disclosure he or she can be held liable for claims of unjust enrichment. There are several cases, for instance, where an inventor disclosed an idea to a second party; the second party searched out the idea in *existing* U.S. patents, found the idea was already the subject of a patent, and bought that patent from the holder. The courts held that the second party had to give the patent to the inventor because of the confidential nature of their relationship.[5]

Employee's Rights

Much of the law has evolved in an attempt to protect the rights of the enterprise. This has always been balanced, however, by the employee's right to earn a livelihood in the *best* potential source of livelihood. For instance, as an atomic engineer, the courts would protect my right to make a living as an atomic engineer, not merely earn a wage as a waiter or a bartender.

When a relationship between an employee and employer is severed, it is often the content of the written documents that will govern who has rights to what. Employment contracts, confidentiality, nondisclosure, and noncompete agreements all come into play. For this reason, prospective employees are well advised to read these documents carefully and negotiate, rather than merely sign all of the papers that are typically associated with the first day on the job.

An employee can bargain away some of his or her rights in this area by signing inventions agreements, noncompete contracts, or employment agreements. However, the courts will not let an employee bargain away his or her fundamental right to earn a living from the best potential source.

If an employee signed an agreement that the courts found to be overly restrictive, the entire agreement would be thrown out. It is this fact that gives rise to the lawyer's advice that "It is better to sign an unreasonable employment agreement than a reasonable one."

There are three dimensions to the reasonableness test that the courts apply to employment agreements:

- Time horizon.
- Geographic scope.
- Nature of employment.

For instance, an employment contract that required an employee not to compete for six months, in the state of New York, as a designer of petroleum process facilities might be viewed as reasonable, while an agreement that specified a time horizon of one year and a geographic area of the United States would probably be viewed as unreasonable.

---

[5]Illinois Institute for Continuing Legal Education, *Intellectual Property Law,* pp. 6–9, 10.

Summary

It is clear that the body of legal knowledge in the intellectual property area is evolving rapidly. Yet the processes that the law prescribes remain vitally important; in this area in particular, dotting the ''i's'' and crossing the ''t's'' is key. Whether it be keeping notebooks and records, filing patent claims, or reading the fine print on an employment contract, it is hard to overemphasize the importance of understanding the details.

In order to gain sufficient command of the relevant body of law, specialized legal counsel is called for. In an area that is changing so rapidly, one cannot rely on prior practices and ''industry standard policies'' for protection.

References

American Bar Association. *Sorting out the Ownership Rights in Intellectual Property: A Guide to Practical Counseling and Legal Representation.* Chicago: American Bar Association, 1980.

Burge, David A. *Patent and Trademark Tactics and Practice.* New York: John Wiley & Sons, 1980.

Gallafent, R. J.; N. A. Eastway; and V. A. F. Dauppe. *Intellectual Property Law and Taxation.* Kensington, Calif.: Oyez, 1981.

Illinois Institute for Continuing Legal Education. *Intellectual Property Law for the General Business Counselor.* Chicago: Illinois Bar Center, 1983.

Johnston, Donald F. *Copyright Handbook.* New York: R. R. Bowker Company, 1978.

Lietman, Alan. *Howell's Copyright Law.* BNA Incorporated, 1962.

White, Herbert S. *The Copyright Dilemma.* Chicago: American Library Association, 1977.

2–1 STEVEN B. BELKIN

Wake up, Steven! It must be some mistake, but American Express is calling and says it's important. It's something about your credit rating.

His wife's voice roused Steven Belkin from a fitful sleep. A cascade of problems swept through his mind as Joan handed him the telephone:

This must be about my $15,000 overdue credit card bill. Joan hasn't realized I'm in quite so deep . . . she's going to be a bit shaken by this. I can see I'd better reassure her when I get off the phone . . . but to tell the truth, if I don't find investors soon, I'm really in trouble.

It was 11:30 the night of December 5, 1973. Steven Belkin had charged many of his expenses while trying to set up a new group travel business. Finding investors was proving much more difficult than he had anticipated, and he had had to let his bill slip for a couple of months. Steven was going to have to find a new financing strategy fast to keep The Travel Group from being a one-way ticket to disaster.

Background

Steven Belkin, age 26, had lived in Grand Rapids, Michigan, as a youth. There he had his earliest business experiences. When he was 12, his grandfather had given him some salvaged automatic letter openers. Steven decided to set up a raffle with $1 tickets and the letter openers as the prize. He enjoyed selling the tickets and felt wonderful telling the purchasers who had won. Another time he sold light bulbs door to door. Taking the idea from a school fund-raising project, he made it a summer job for his own profit. Steven's parents were of modest means, and financial pressures were a source of family discord. Steven resolved that his own excellence and success would provide family happiness.

Several people advised Steven that the way to success was to couple engineering with business school. After graduating from high school where he had been captain of his basketball and tennis teams, Steven received an industrial engineering degree from Cornell. He concentrated on obtaining good grades at Cornell and also was active in student government and other school activities to improve his chances for admittance to graduate school. After graduation in 1969, Steven entered the MBA program at Harvard. Steven recalled an interview he had set up:

This case was prepared by Richard O. von Werssowetz under the direction of Howard H. Stevenson.

Copyright © 1982 by the President and Fellows of Harvard College

Harvard Business School Case 9–383–042

I tried to figure out how best to improve my odds to get in. I came down and had an interview and talked to different people. I don't know if it helped — they say it doesn't, but I don't know. I always took the attitude to absolutely give everything you have. Then if you don't make it, at least you have given all you've got.

Steven saw life as a series of plateaus. At Cornell, grades had been important to reach the next level. Having reached business school, Steven now wanted to concentrate on learning about different kinds of business and on getting to know his classmates. Steven recalled:

I felt I needed to get there faster than the usual course. It wasn't OK for me to get there in the regular process, riding someone else's wave. I needed to get ready to jump on my own wave. In order to do that, to speed up the process, I needed to have more experience and contacts than my years. You get that extra knowledge from the experiences of others. And the families and friends of your classmates are a wealth of contacts.

Steven and another student obtained the résumé concession at Harvard Business School, which not only helped with expenses but also gave him a chance to meet all members of his class.

Innovative Management.   During the summer between the first and second years of the MBA program, Steven decided he wanted to do consulting for small businesses. He asked friends and professors for leads, with little success. However, he did find that four graduating students were starting a new consulting company in that area that they would name Innovative Management (IM). Actually, one student had some possible business sources and had found a financial backer who would provide $50,000 for working capital. That student had asked the others to join for a salary and 5 percent portions of equity. Steven joined in the same fashion and the group quickly got underway. Steven described their start-up:

We would go to bankers and individual venture capitalists who had made loans or investments in companies that weren't doing as well as they had hoped. We offered to go in and analyze the situation and either suggest that they write off the situation or propose a plan to improve the company. Then we would actually go in and implement our suggestions.

The bankers and private investors we approached often didn't have the time or the ability to do this type of analysis. So they would go to the head of a company in trouble and point out that things weren't going very well, then suggest that the company employ us for the study as a condition of providing more funds. The companies would pay our fees, which usually were $4,000 to $5,000.

Initially, we would approach a new source of projects and offer to do the first job at no cost. After we showed what we could do, they would usually give us additional assignments.

Our customers were companies with annual sales from $2 million to $10 million. Most were fairly new entities. Usually we could provide a needed control system, a marketing strategy — an entire business plan. Although the owners usually were under considerable pressure to let us in, they often were very stimulated by what we did. They knew they had problems and they didn't have the luxury of our education. After we gave our report to the financial backer, we also gave it to the company. Often we could provide our recommendation in only three or four days.

By the end of the summer, we were so successful that we began hiring additional business school graduates. I continued to manage several others during my second year of school.

In addition to running the résumé service and continuing his consulting business, Steven did a survey of interest in small business among students in the top 10 business schools as his second-year project.

My purpose was to show that there was a strong interest among these students in new ventures and starting your own company even though most schools were not teaching that. The survey confirmed this, and I used the data to write some articles that we used to publicize our consulting firm. For example, we had stories in the *Boston Globe* and the SBANE [Small Business Association of New England] paper.

People are always fascinated about people who do surveys and who have statistics. It makes you an instant expert to have a survey! It bought us new contacts and more credibility.

Looking back, Steven commented that he had done too much during the second year:

I was incredibly busy. I cut a lot of classes. But the income was tempting, and I was just ready to get the second year over with. But you are always going to have work, yet you only have the second year of business school once. I missed an awful lot. I didn't realize then that the cases contained so much practical experience—I felt they were "text booky." I just didn't absorb that they really reflected day-to-day problems.

During the last half of the second year, Steven explored the job market, interviewing primarily with consulting firms. Although none of the firms caught his fancy, Steven thought the process was worthwhile:

It was a terrific educational experience to be able to talk to these high-caliber people in the different companies where they were trying to sell you and tell you all about their companies. But I guess I was a bit spoiled after already having my teeth in it, giving suggestions to people and seeing them implement them the next week. The big companies seemed a little academic—nothing, really, compared to what I was doing.

Steven remained with Innovative Management when he graduated in June 1971. A year later, however, the company was sold and Steven decided to leave. Steven explained:

We grew from 5 people to 22 in that first two years. Then one of the individual venture capitalists who had given us some work wanted to buy the company. The other four founders wanted to sell, but I thought that we would lose our objectivity as an affiliated consultant. I wasn't very happy about it, so I left the firm.

Group Touring Associates.   Having decided to leave Innovative Management, Steven Belkin reviewed his situation. Financially, he had limited resources. Steven had been earning almost twice the $12,000 typical starting salary of his class. Joan, whom he had married just after graduation, worked as a teacher for a smaller salary. Steven had received $15,000 for his interest in the consulting company but also still owed several school loans that were not yet due for payment. Their net worth was about $10,000. Steven had no special ideas for starting a different business and was not attracted to seeking a job with a larger company. It appeared to him that he should continue small business consulting on his own.

The sale of IM took place at the end of the summer of 1972. Before Steven embarked on an independent course, however, he was approached by Frank Rodgers, the original investor in Innovative Management. Rodgers had been squeezed out of that investment when the company was sold. Rodgers said he would like Steven to work for him helping other companies in which Rodgers had investments, and Steven agreed.

Steven found he had a special attraction for a group travel company that was one of Rodgers' first assignments. This company, Group Touring Associates (GTA), developed tours that were sold to various groups by mail using their membership lists. GTA had been started by Robert Goode in 1966 with the backing of Rodgers and a few other private investors. Rodgers had invested $200,000 to date; the others, another $200,000.

Sales had grown to $1.8 million over the past year, but GTA had yet to make a profit. Losses had been increasing from $50,000 four years ago to over $250,000 last year. Robert Goode had convinced his investors to continue their backing by pointing to the rising sales. He contended that the front-end marketing costs of mailings and of setting up the trips would cause him to show losses as he grew. On the other hand, the unearned customer deposits made prior to the trips provided much of the cash needed for the growing operation. Rodgers agreed that some losses might have been necessary as the company got its start, but now was alarmed by the continuing deficits. Rodgers felt that the deposit cash flow was disguising more fundamental problems and wanted Steven to help the situation.

After a brief analysis of the business, Steven felt GTA had excellent potential and that it could be built profitably with better management. He accepted an offer to join the company and became GTA's executive vice president:

> Looking back at my other consulting clients, there wasn't one business that I wanted to do. I had done one project for another tour operator, but they marketed through travel agents and student groups. The combination of group travel with direct mail made this very fascinating to me—this was the business for me. OK, I needed solid experience in this one. This was a good opportunity, and I could earn a piece of the action.

A year later, Steven could point with pride to sales that had grown 50 percent and to a profit of over $150,000. Steven credited the turnaround to basic planning and well-managed execution:

> There was little organization when I came: no business plan, budgets, or anything like that. What I did was to clearly define our product and focus our operational and selling efforts. All within a budget and a plan. Before, the salespeople would try to find what trips various groups might be thinking about and come back and try to put one together. I introduced the strategy of defining the trips with the greatest general demand, then putting the trips together, and having the salespeople fill them up.
>
> This strategy let us buy better, put together better promotional material, and better control our costs. I was very sensitive to the fact that we were in the direct-mail business

rather than just the group travel business. We had to provide better value for the travel dollar and promote it well by mail.

At the end of his first year as executive vice president, Steven reopened discussion about his future role in GTA with Robert Goode. He had initially accepted a salary of $22,000 with the understanding that they would renegotiate his position after Steven had proven himself. Now Steven felt he should receive a $30,000 salary and also be given 10 percent of the company. Robert would not agree. Steven recalled:

> Robert and I went back and forth quite a bit. GTA was finally making money, and I felt I deserved part ownership. Robert wouldn't go over $25,000 in salary and wanted to wait another year for the equity.
>
> As we reached an impasse, Frank Rodgers arranged several more meetings between us. However, now that the company was profitable, Goode no longer needed more equity, and Rodgers didn't have enough power to force Goode to agree to my demands. I think Robert also felt that he had run the company for six years and, now that I had gotten GTA over the hurdle, he wanted to be the boss again.
>
> I tried very hard to reach an agreement; I wanted to stay. I felt that if I could be earning the $30,000 and have 10 percent of a profitable, growing company, I would be on my way to being successful. I was really running the show; I felt I was going to make money; I was fulfilling my entrepreneurial goals.

Considering an Independent Course

As Robert Goode's position hardened, Steven began to consider leaving GTA to start his own group travel packager. Looking at the industry structure made him feel this segment was a good opportunity. Potential air travelers could arrange pleasure trips directly on their own, choose ground packages offered by "tour wholesalers" such as American Express, or select complete air/ground packages such as those organized by GTA using chartered airlines. Traits of these choices are shown in **Table 1.**

Although the group air charter industry had only developed over the last 10 years after the introduction of jet air service, this mode of touring had already become a popular travel alternative. Steven felt the key attractions were lower cost, professional tour management, and the comfort and peace of mind of the sponsoring organizations' endorsements.

The lower costs were the direct result of the use of chartered aircraft—the group tour organizer guaranteed to pay for all seats and took the risk of filling the flight. Many travelers were willing to accept the fixed schedules of charters to take advantage of the lower prices. The offer of complete tour packages with professional tour guides was convenient, especially for travelers unfamiliar with the desired destination. Also, each traveler was a member of a group that sponsored the tour and could feel that his or her own representative would make sure the tour was a good trip and that the group would receive everything for which they had paid. This was particularly important in 1973 because there had been some recent publicity about tours that had been stranded or given inferior accommodations or service.

TABLE 1   **Comparison of Pleasure Travel Options**

	Direct Selection by Traveler	Use of "Tour Wholesaler"	Charter Tours
Air travel	Via scheduled airline	Via scheduled airline	Chartered airplane
Land arrangements	Individual plans and arranges directly with provider or through retail travel agents	Provided by tour wholesaler	Provided by group travel wholesaler
Flexibility	Complete	Travel timing flexible	Fixed departure and return schedules
		Only selected destinations and accommodations	Only selected destinations and accommodations
Usual cost	Highest price	Sold as service; cost often same as direct	30 percent to 40 percent lower
Sold by	Individual carriers, hotels, etc.; retail travel agents	Retail travel agents	Group-sponsored direct mail, some retail travel agents
Other limitations			Must be member of "affinity group"

Steven saw these advantages as clear distinctions between group charter companies and tour wholesalers that used scheduled air carriers. The tour wholesalers also marketed primarily through retail travel agents whereas charter tours were normally sold using direct mail.

Looking at competition, Steven knew there were 10 major group tour operators in the United States. GTA ranked about seventh in that list. Where GTA provided tours for about 8,000 people per year, the largest U.S. operators moved about 50,000 customers yearly. As he viewed the market, he felt there was certainly room for one more:

> In the United States, there were regulations that you had to belong to an organization to go on a group trip. These had been eliminated about six years ago in Europe. With that, some of the group tour operators did more business than some of the scheduled carriers. The largest European companies running group charters were moving over a million people per year each. These regulations were relaxing in the United States, so I felt there would be great opportunities.

Steven received encouragement from Alan Lewis, GTA's most productive salesman. During Steven's negotiations with Robert Goode, Steven had described his growing frustration to Lewis. When Steven mentioned that he would be happy for Alan to join him if he left, Alan suggested that Steven should go out on his own whether or not Goode agreed to his demands. Alan would like to join him and was anxious to get an ownership position himself.

Steven's discussions with Goode made no further progress, so Steven resigned and left in early September 1973. Alan Lewis also resigned, and the two of them began to develop The Travel Group, their own group travel business.

The Travel Group

Steven's idea for The Travel Group (TTG) was to duplicate the strategy that had been successful for Group Touring Associates. They would start with limited tour offerings to the most popular destinations, then expand as their reputation grew. They would use five sales representatives to call on groups across the United States to develop sponsors for direct-mail promotions. They would carefully control their customer service and tour operations to minimize costs and gain customer satisfaction.

The tours they would offer were complex logistical tasks with large financial commitments. Running a tour meant chartering an entire plane, which would accommodate up to 200 passengers. The company would also have to commit to blocks of hotel rooms and meals and provide ground transportation and other assorted support services. Once the package was planned, promotional material had to be written, printed, and distributed. Then inquiries had to be answered and reservations made.

To run the company, Steven would be president and major shareholder. He would be responsible for raising the capital they would need, for negotiating the trip arrangements, and for setting up the internal operations. Alan Lewis would be executive vice president. He would hire and manage the sales force, cover key clients personally, and work with sponsoring groups to fill the tours. Steven described their deal:

> I had planned to give five key salespeople 5 percent of the company each. Alan convinced me to give him the entire 25 percent, and he would give away whatever was necessary to hire the others. Thus, we became partners, but I would have a minimum of 51 percent ownership, Alan up to 25 percent, and the remainder would be for me or the investors. He ended up keeping all 25 percent after hiring four other excellent salespeople. Equity for our financial backers would come out of my share.

Steven and Alan immediately swung into action. Steven concentrated first on creating a business plan, while Alan began his search for salespeople and selling efforts for an initial tour he and Steven had outlined. By October 1, 1973, the business plan was finished, and Steven prepared to raise $250,000:

> Developing the plan was fairly straightforward. We knew the basic charter travel destinations and seasons. We planned to run one airplane a week in season during the first year, two planes a week the second, and build each year. It was important to run "back to back" tours as much as possible so that the chartered plane could take one tour and return with the prior week's group. I added cost projections and made cash flow assumptions to give an overall financial plan.
>
> The plan showed an accumulated deficit of $155,000 for the five months before our first tour. Then I expected profits and tour deposits to provide cash for growth. I felt I should raise $250,000 for a safe cushion to fund that deficit with room for unexpected costs, delays, or errors.

The business plan for The Travel Group is shown in **Exhibit 1.** Steven intended this document to be a simple, easy to follow business plan rather than a formal investment memorandum. He explained his reasoning:

Most people make business plans so complicated that people understand nothing and get scared by them. If you repeat things two or three times, then they say, "Oh, yes. I understand that." They think they understand what they are investing in. If you keep giving them more and more inputs and ideas, they just can't absorb it.

When people finish reading my verbal description, they understand what I have said. That does not mean they understand the business. But they have understood what I said, so therefore they think they understand the business.

Financing Strategy.   Steven and Alan had direct experience in the operational tasks confronting them. Finding the needed financing was less familiar. However, several of Steven's earlier IM consulting assignments had involved raising money for smaller companies. Steven described IM's role:

> Some situations we investigated needed more equity along with the strategic and management changes we might suggest. If asked to implement our plan, we would agree to raise the money along with providing an executive vice president to bolster management and increase the company's credibility to investors. In return, we would receive part of the equity.
>
> We tried to keep this from being threatening to the president. Rather, we worked to convince the president that we'd be adding some new skills and helping to make the company valuable. Not like we were after the president's job.
>
> We'd approach individual venture capitalists for investments of $25,000 to $50,000 each. Our total needs were usually $100,000 to $200,000. The Rodgers family was very well connected, and we had developed other contacts in the course of our projects.
>
> Pricing was rather arbitrary. The company probably didn't have earnings, and we were selling the future. There was no scientific approach. We tried to show that the investors would double their money in a three-year period, then double it again to a value four times their original investment by the end of year five.
>
> Structurally, these investments sometimes ended up as a combination of debt and equity. This might be a loan with stock warrants. If all went well, they'd get most of their money back in a year or so and keep an equity ride with the warrants. The investors were very interested in not losing—not making mistakes, and less worried about how to get their equity out. That was less well structured—something down the road.

With this limited fund-raising experience, Steven developed a financing strategy. First, he assessed the situation from an investor's point of view. TTG had a large upside. Few start-ups could show the rapid sales growth Steven had projected. There were good margins that gave an excellent profit potential and unusually attractive cash flows. The management team had strong credentials. Steven's education was a plus, and both he and Alan had been successful running a similar company. They would also be using an experienced sales force. The group travel market in the United States had much less penetration than in Europe and should grow rapidly. Finally, there was little sophisticated competition in this industry, so their management skills would give them an extra advantage.

To demonstrate long-term potential, Steven could also show evidence that a group tour operator could be attractive as a public stock offering. One large U.S. tour operator had gone public in 1967 at a price of $10 per share. Within two years, the price had risen as high as $93 per share. The shares were currently trading for about

$8, but this was primarily the result of that company's poor results in diversifying into restaurants, cruise ships, and hotels.

Steven decided that this set of characteristics made TTG a good deal for institutional venture capital groups. He would attempt to raise the $250,000 in five units of $50,000. He hoped that two or three investors would subscribe to the entire total. Steven felt this was a better alternative than going to wealthy individual investors for smaller units:

> I thought the larger shots would be easier. I had the right background and credentials and a good business plan. I was sophisticated enough to present it to institutional investors. I felt this was a good package to offer, that they would buy me and would buy the business plan.

As insurance, Steven would also present the plan to a few individual investors, but his main thrust would be the institutional groups.

For leads, Steven turned to the "hit" list he had been developing since he had been in business school:

> I kept a notebook of people I met who might be good contacts. I'd put in notes on meetings and phone calls, addresses, correspondence. Some were filed in various institutional categories—others were just alphabetical.
>
> I put the people I would approach in priority by relationships. I wasn't going to ask people directly to invest. Rather, I would ask for their help: "What should I do to raise money?" I didn't want to put them on the defensive—once you ask them if they'd invest they have to protect themselves. This way, they could talk to me totally straight and really give me advice. If they *were* interested, then they would say they'd like to look at my plan further. Either way, they'd often recommend someone else to see.

Prospects, 5: Investors, 0.   Steven had contacts with five well-known institutional venture capital companies. He approached each, describing his idea and asking advice. Out of these five, two were interested enough to ask to consider his plan. After being initially encouraged by this interest, Steven soon began to feel that none of these firms was likely to invest. He described the problem areas he encountered:

> First, I was confronted with the developing fuel crisis. There were headlines in the newspapers saying airlines were canceling charter flights. Only needed scheduled flights would be flying. There I was telling people I was starting a new charter company just as TWA was grounding all of its charters!
>
> I had to explain that I could buy space on regular flights if necessary, but that the *charter airlines* would continue to run. The charter airlines were separate airlines encouraged by the government so that additional aircraft would be available in a national emergency. They only flew charters and were not canceling their flights. I also argued that if flights were rationed, my old relationships with the airlines and the professionalism we would be bringing in would give us preference in charter assignments.
>
> I felt I was making some of the venture capital companies comfortable about the fuel problem, but I also found them reluctant to invest because there were no hard assets to "lend" against. They'd say, "There's nothing there! You aren't buying any machinery; all the money's going for working capital. There's no product line, no proprietary technology."

I believe they were thinking that if it didn't work, with hard assets they could still minimize their losses somehow and get something out of it. I got the feeling they were just more liberal bankers, which was different from my earlier concept of venture capitalists.

Approaching Wealthy Individuals.   Scheduling appointments and follow-up visits with the venture capital companies took most of October with some discussions continuing into November. At the same time, Steven also was calling on wealthy acquaintances in a more casual way:

I'd say, "You know I'm raising money on Wall Street, but this might be something you'd be interested in. I'd like to get your input. Do you have any suggestions?" I'd mostly ask for advice and references to other venture capitalists or investment bankers.

As it became evident that the venture capital companies were not showing great enthusiasm, Steven more seriously pursued wealthy individuals:

I primarily approached other successful business executives who either still ran their own businesses or had sold their businesses in the last few years. I thought that a $50,000 investment would be easy for them. It was a lot tougher than I thought.

By November, I was letting everyone know I was trying to start this company. I was using every contact I could to get referrals to wealthy investors.

Out of all of his contacts, Steven developed two serious leads. One investor who was also a friend indicated he might provide $20,000. The other wanted Steven to come back when he had raised most of the remainder of the offering. Steven had expected wealthy individuals to be excited by the opportunity he saw in TTG. Now he found that wealthy individuals were going to be more difficult to attract as investors than he had anticipated.

Offer of a Bank Loan.   Steven's discussions with the wealthy individual who knew him did lead to an unexpected offer of debt financing. Steven explained:

I didn't think any part of my deal was bankable at all. I clearly felt that all equity money would be required. Yet the one wealthy individual who was my friend said he did think the idea had merit and that he would introduce me to his bank. He gave me a very strong personal endorsement and to my surprise, his banker said he would match every dollar of equity I raised with one dollar of debt!

Once this bank opened my eyes, I approached several downtown banks to see what they would do. They wouldn't have any part of a loan—there were no assets to lend against.

The bank willing to give me a credit line was located outside of the main metropolitan area. They were more aggressive to compete, but they also saw TTG as a good cash flow generator and needed the deposits.

The loan offer opened welcome new possibilities to Steven. Now if he could raise as little as $125,00 in equity, the total of $250,000 would be available to him. However, the use of the debt line would greatly increase his own exposure because the bank would be lending against his personal guarantee. He was not anxious to do this himself, and the idea was frightening to Joan:

> I was signing a $125,000 note, but my net worth was less than $10,000. Sure. I decided it didn't make any difference—if things went bad, I couldn't pay it anyway, so why worry about it? I would be more concerned about signing a $25,000 note because I conceivably could pay that.
>
> But they also required Joan to sign it, and this was very, very stressful for her. It was overwhelming and very upsetting. We talked about it, and I said it was the same way for me too. But if it's $125,000 or it's a million, it doesn't make any difference right now.

The note Steven and Joan Belkin signed was a contingent line of credit at 2 percent over the prime lending rate. The credit line would equal the amount of TTG's equity up to a maximum of $125,000. Steven could draw on the line at his discretion. However, both he and Joan were very anxious not to use this credit so that they would not actually incur the personal liability of their guarantee.

Growing Pressures.   Signing the credit line agreement and the slow progress in raising the needed equity were not the only sources of the pressures Steven felt building. There was also the hectic pace of beginning TTG operations.

If TTG was to run its first tour during the late winter season, the package must be put together and ready for sale by the beginning of January. To do this, Steven and Alan had been continually working to develop their first trip and get their sales effort underway since October. By October 15, they had hired a secretary who had worked with them at GTA and set up operations in Steven's apartment. By the end of October, they had added another secretary and the first additional salesman. Steven described what it was like:

> We just assumed we would get the money and that we had to make it work. So we had to get the sales.
>
> Joan was teaching, so she went off to work at seven o'clock and came home about 3:30. She had been very, very helpful in putting together the business plan, but she's a very organized person and had her own work to do. When all the people were in the apartment, that started getting to her. Not only would there be no privacy and no quiet to plan her classes and grade her papers, but sometimes we'd raid the refrigerator for lunch, and she'd find that what she had planned for supper had disappeared. We would often work past seven o'clock talking to the West Coast. She could go into a bedroom by herself, but in that small two bedroom apartment, it was more of a prison than a refuge.
>
> On November 15, we rented a 10-foot by 20-foot office that had been the rental office in my apartment building so things were a bit better, but we still used my apartment. We were sharing desks and had no place to have meetings with potential backers or sales contacts. I always met people at the airport, said I was just leaving on a flight, then waited until they had gone before going back to our office.

Steve Belkin and Alan Lewis were funding the office expenses and salaries for the other employees from their own pockets. So far they had invested almost $10,000 in cash. In addition, each of them was charging every possible expense on their personal American Express credit cards. Since both of them were traveling around the United States and Europe to talk to group sales prospects, interview sales representative candidates, and set up the first tour, they had accumulated outstanding charges of about $15,000 each. They had both been heavy users of their credit cards before, which gave them high credit limits. They had made no payments since September and were starting to get overdue reminder letters, which emphasized they were about to lose their hard-earned credit.

As business paused for the Thanksgiving holiday, Steven wasn't quite sure how much he should be thankful. There was little progress finding equity investors, and Steven's bills and responsibilities grew.

He felt he had to provide others emotional support just when he was the least sure of what he might have done to his own position:

> I was having to play Mr. Completely-in-Control: "Everything is great. We're going to get our money." The only one who was really starting to worry was Alan. He was the only one I really talked to. He hadn't had much exposure to raising money. I was starting to let him know I was getting nervous, and he didn't know how to read that. "What does it mean when Steve's nervous?"
>
> I'd also gone far enough that everyone knew I was doing this. It's not like I could have a quiet failure. I'd gone to close friends and family for contacts—the ones I'd worked so hard to impress. I'd always been Mr. Successful: "Here's Steve. He went to Harvard, was captain of his tennis team and basketball team, and always got good grades. He had his own consulting firm." Now Mr. Successful was starting his own company, and Mr. Successful was in trouble.

What Now?

By the first week of December, Steven knew he had only a few weeks left before TTG would start to unravel. Finding money was the key:

> I felt I really had to switch gears here. I had to scrape it together. Initially I wanted to do it the business school way. Now, I had to become a street fighter. I might have to go out and beg, and it would be very difficult for me to go to people and say, "I need your help."
>
> I only had a little time. Should I put more emphasis on the venture capital route and really try to close one of those? Should I continue with the wealthy investors? Or should I go to friends and relatives and try to piece it together in fives and tens? Because I had so little time left, I really felt the main options I should consider were to find one venture capitalist for $250,000 or to go to friends for small amounts.

In deciding on his last-ditch strategy, Steven also contemplated whether he should change his offering to be more attractive. Pricing had never been explicitly discussed with the institutional venture firms. When talking to wealthy individuals, Steven was offering to sell 250,000 shares at $1 per share. He and Alan would be issued 750,000. What ways of repricing or restructuring the deal would help him to raise his equity fast?

"This is not exactly how I thought it would be," Steven thought to himself as he struggled to find a creative solution that December evening. "This is a good opportunity. Why haven't I been successful raising the money yet? I wonder if it was a mistake to resign so quickly? Well, here I am. Maybe I'll think of something tomorrow." It seemed that he had just drifted away, when the phone rang.

EXHIBIT 1   **TTG Business Plan—October 1, 1973**

[The entire narrative of the business plan is reproduced below. Title pages have been removed and the layout has been condensed. Only selected financial exhibits are included.]

1. THE INTRODUCTION

The Travel Group is being formed to meet the tremendous need for low cost group travel. People now have more leisure time than ever before, and they are becoming aware that group vacations are available at prices almost everyone can afford. A week in Europe or the Caribbean for $199 per person is an affordable price for most people.

The group travel industry is less than 10 years old. The market penetration for this new industry has barely begun. There are unlimited groups available. Alumni organizations, professional associations, religious groups, fraternal organizations, employee associations, unions, corporations, women's clubs, etc. The Travel Group will be concentrating on "prime groups." These are organizations that are known to be extremely responsive to group travel (e.g., Shriners, medical associations, bar associations, teacher associations).

The Travel Group will provide "deluxe" group tours. The attitude of management is to send "prime groups" during "prime season." Hotel accommodations will be at deluxe hotels (e.g., Hilton, Sheraton, Hyatt), and air transportation will be via scheduled carriers (e.g., United, Braniff, American) when possible.

The Travel Group will be classified as a "back-to-back wholesaler" in the travel industry. The corporation will market its group tours to travel agents throughout the United States. This should comprise less than 10 percent of the sales during the first two years, but eventually should produce 25 percent of the sales volume.

The primary source of sales for The Travel Group will be through direct sales. The corporation will have its own sales force, and each salesman will be assigned a different territory.

During the first year of operations, The Travel Group projects the movement of only 6,861 passengers. The four salesmen that management will offer positions currently move more than 18,000 passengers per year. Thus, the first year projection of less than 7,000 passengers is quite conservative. Management has also allowed six months before the departure of the first flight. This will provide the sales force with more than sufficient time to sell the first back-to-back charters to Hawaii.

Sales of $2,766,397 are projected during this first year and a profit of $169,223.

The second year of operations, 1975, should produce sales of $8,059.589 with a profit before tax of $832,636. In five years, 1978, The Travel Group should achieve a sales volume of $18,241,542 and a before tax profit of $2,150,121.

There is a tremendous positive cash flow in the group charter business. This allows for rapid expansion without additional financing. The potential of The Travel Group is open-ended, but management will expand cautiously.

II. THE INDUSTRY

The back-to-back group charter business is in the early stages of growth. The industry is less than 10 years old. The management in the industry is quite unsophisticated. Financial and management controls are lacking. The market penetration of group charters has barely begun. Few companies have creative and organized marketing programs.

The main regulatory organization in the industry is the Civil Aeronautics Board (CAB). The trend in the past two years has been for more and more "low cost group travel." The CAB is oriented toward making travel available at a cost affordable for the mass public. This is very favorable for firms like The Travel Group, and, thus, governmental regulation should be beneficial to the company.

The United States is several years behind Europe in low cost vacations. In 1972 group vacation charters provided more revenue to the European airlines than the regularly scheduled flights.

In the United States, the same growth pattern is developing. In the past four years, charters on the North Atlantic have grown at the rate of 58 percent per year. In 1972 charter flights accounted for 30 percent of all passengers flown on the North Atlantic.

Exhibit 1   *(continued)*

It is easy to understand this tremendous growth in the group charter business by simply looking at the money saved by a typical vacationer.

Assume an individual would like to travel to Hawaii for one week. He departs on a weekend, flies coach class, and all accommodations are deluxe:

	Regular Rate	*Group Charter Rate*	*Savings*
Airfare	$510	$225	$ 285
Hotel	140	84	56
Dinners	56	40	16
Transfers	20	10	10
Tour operator's fee	0	113	− 113
Total cost	$726	$472	+ $ 254
	****	****	****

Thus, an individual can save 35 percent, or $254, during a one-week visit to Hawaii.

III. THE COMPANY

The Travel Group will be selling deluxe back-to-back group charters. *Back-to-back* means that, for a set period of time, groups will be sent *every* week to a particular destination. The aircraft, which takes one group to the destination, will pick up the group that is ending their vacation. This allows substantial savings on airfare. There is also tremendous buying power at the hotels because rooms are utilized every week.

These cost advantages will allow The Travel Group to sell vacations to destinations all over the world at savings of 35 percent or more (see Industry section).

The Travel Group will have salesmen assigned to different territories in certain sections of the country. These salesmen will call on prime traveling groups. They will be selling deluxe packages, principally during prime season. The "sell" is usually easy because the organization has nothing to lose and much to gain. The Travel Group will pay for the mailing of a brochure describing the vacation to all the members of the organization. For each reservation the group produces, the organization will be given about $15. Thus, if a group fills a 150-seat airplane, the organization will receive $2,250 (150 × $15) and will have provided vacations for its members at substantial savings.

Groups that will be approached by the sales force include Shriners, Masons, medical associations, bar associations, Elks, Moose, alumni associations, teacher associations, unions, employee groups, and Knights of Columbus. There is an unlimited number of groups. Management will develop a mailing list of all the prime groups in the country to provide additional direction for the sales force.

The cash flow in the business is very favorable. Deposits from passengers are often received more than 90 days in advance. Final payments from passengers are due 45 days before departure. Payments to the airlines occur 30 days before departure, and hotel bills are not paid until 30 days after departure. Thus, the majority of receipts are in-house 45 days in advance of departure while disbursements occur 15 to 90 days after the initial receipts are in.

IV. THE COMPETITION

The group travel industry is in its early stages of growth. The industry is less than 10 years old, and there is only a limited number of group tour operators. Sophisticated and experienced management is scarce in the industry. The few back-to-back group travel companies that do exist have had substantial sales growth in the past three years. In the last 18 months, there have been several new companies started that have been running back-to-back charters. One of these companies had sales of close to $8 million during its first year and before tax profits of over $500,000.

EXHIBIT 1   *(continued)*

Competition in the industry has not developed to the point of pricing of the same packages. Sales growth is achieved by contacting the proper groups and then appropriately following up these leads.

Back-to-back operators always concentrate on a few destinations. With the vast number of destinations, there is limited competition among tour operators in providing packages to the same place. For instance, one of the new tour operators is just specializing in running trips to Greece, while another has programs just to the Orient.

Currently the East Coast is the only section of the country that has become familiar, to some extent, with group charters. Amazingly, 60 percent of all charter flights are out of New York. The South, Midwest, and Central States have barely been touched.

Less than five back-to-back tour operators have a national sales force. The Travel Group's national sales force will be comprised of experienced travel salesmen who are currently working in different territories throughout the United States for other tour operators.

V. THE MANAGEMENT

There are two key departments in the group charter business. One is sales, and the other is operations. By providing a well-organized business plan and by making equity available, The Travel Group has attracted some of the most qualified people in the industry.

Mr. Steven B. Belkin will be president. He will be responsible for directing the operations of the company. Mr. Belkin is thoroughly familiar with the day-to-day operations as well as the overall business planning of a back-to-back tour operator.

He is a graduate of Cornell University and Harvard Business School. He was one of five founders of Innovative Management, a small business consulting firm in the Boston area. Some of his consulting projects included the development and implementation of a marketing program for a ski charter travel firm, running a chain of sporting goods stores with sales of over $6 million, and serving as president of a film school and production company. When Mr. Belkin left and sold his interest in this consulting firm, it had grown to 22 full-time consultants.

For more than a year, Mr. Belkin has been devoting full time to a travel group charter firm, which was in severe financial difficulties. With the development and implementation of a new business plan, creation of a national sales force, and tighter management and financial controls, this firm has now been turned around. The year before Mr. Belkin's involvement, the firm had sales of approximately $1 million with a loss of over $250,000. This year the company has already reported a respectable profit for the first six months and has more than doubled the previous year's sales.

The sales force that is available is comprised of some of the best salesmen in the industry. Each man has thorough familiarity and personal contacts with the prime groups in the different sections of the country.

The sales team will have a minimum of six months before the first back-to-back charter will start. This should provide more than sufficient time to sell the program. During the first year of operations, the sales force needs to move only 6,861 passengers. This year the four salesmen being considered moved more than 18,000 passengers. Thus, the first-year programs should be sold fairly easily, and this will allow the sales team to start concentrating on the second-year programs well in advance.

VI. THE FINANCIALS

[Some exhibits omitted.]

A. TRIP COST ANALYSIS
    Exhibit I Hawaii
    Exhibit II San Juan
    Exhibit III Ad hoc
    Exhibit IV Acapulco
    Exhibit V Spain

EXHIBIT 1   *(continued)*

A great deal of time and effort has been devoted to the preparation of the following financial exhibits. Management will use them for budgeting as well as for projections.

The Trip Cost Analysis section clearly outlines the revenues and expenses associated with each trip on both a per passenger and per airplane basis. The airfare, hotel, meals, transfers, mailing, giveaways, and load factor are all expenses that have been determined by historical statistics and actual experience.

The Profit and Loss Statements for the first two years have been prepared on a month-to-month basis. Management has determined the number of planes and passengers that can be accommodated each month to a particular destination. During the first year of operation, no passengers are projected to be moved until June. There is a good possibility that ad hoc programs will be sold before this time, so sales and profit could be greater than projected.

The Cash Flows have been prepared for the first two years on a month-to-month basis. The cash flow assumptions are very important, and management feels the assumptions made are conservative.

The five-year, pro forma profit and loss statement illustrates the potential of this new and growing business. The Travel Group hopes to have sales of over $18 million within five years and profits before tax of over $2 million.

EXHIBIT 1
COST ANALYSIS PER PASSENGER
HAWAII

Selling price	$429	+10% =	$	471.90
Direct costs: Air	$225			
Hotel	84			
Meals	40			
Transfers	10		−359.00	
Gross profit before acquisition costs			$	112.90
Acquisition costs:				
Mailing cost 10¢ brochure				
+ Nonprofit mailer				
(.50% return rate)	$ 20.00			
Giveaways ($20/reservation)	20.00			
Load factor (90%)	20.00		−60.00	
Gross profit			$	52.90
			*********	

****

EXHIBIT 1 *(continued)*

Hawaii Trip Analysis per Plane

Total sales	= $471.90 × 135 passengers	= $63,706
Cost of sales	= $419.00 × 135 passengers	= $56,565
Total profit	= $ 52.90 × 135 passengers	= $ 7,141

Options: $10 net/passenger = $1,350/plane
(Options include additional profit on such items as bus tours, which are arranged through the charter operator.)

EXHIBIT VI
THE TRAVEL GROUP, INC.
PRO FORMA PROFIT AND LOSS STATEMENT (1974 AND 1975)

	1974	1975
SALES	$2,766,397	$8,059,589
Cost of sales	2,345,594	6,870,953
Gross profit	$ 420,803	$1,188,636
General and administrative	251,580	356,000
Profit (before tax)	$ 169,223	$ 832,636
	*********	*********
Earnings per share	$. 17	$ .83
Value/share (10 multiple)	$1.70	$8.33
Number of planes	44	128
Number of passengers	6,861	22,183

EXHIBIT 1 *(continued)*

EXHIBIT VII
THE TRAVEL GROUP, INC.
PLANE AND PASSENGER PROJECTIONS
FIRST YEAR OF OPERATION (1974)

	January	February	March	April	May	June	July	August	September	October	November	December	Total
HAWAII													
Passengers						750	600	750	600	600	750	600	4,650
Planes						5	4	5	4	4	5	4	31
SAN JUAN													
Passengers											895	716	1,611
Planes											5	4	9
AD HOC													
Passengers						150	150	150	150			600	600
Planes						1	1	1	1			4	4
TOTAL PASSENGERS	0	0	0	0	0	900	750	900	750	600	1,645	1,316	6,861
TOTAL PLANES	0	0	0	0	0	6	5	6	5	4	10	8	44

EXHIBIT 1 (*continued*)

EXHIBIT VIII
THE TRAVEL GROUP, INC.
PRO FORMA PROFIT AND LOSS STATEMENT
FIRST YEAR OF OPERATION (1974)

	January	February	March	April	May	June	July	August	September	October	November	December	Total
SALES													
Hawaii (150-seat plane)	(31 planes)	(4,650 passengers)				318,530	254,824	318,530	254,824	254,824	318,530	254,824	2,766,397
Hawaii options (net)						7,500	6,000	7,500	6,000	6,000	7,500	6,000	
San Juan (179-seat plane)	(9 planes)	(1,611 passengers)									263,120	210,496	
San Juan options (net)											4,475	3,580	
Ad hoc programs	(4 planes)	(600 passengers)				65,835	65,835	65,835	65,835				
TOTAL SALES	44 planes	6,861 passengers				391,865	326,659	391,865	326,659	260,824	593,625	474,900	2,766,397
COST OF SALES													
Hawaii						276,070	220,856	276,070	220,856	220,856	276,070	220,856	
San Juan											219,200	175,360	
Ad hoc programs						59,850	59,850	59,850	59,850				
TOTAL COST OF SALES						335,920	280,706	335,920	280,706	220,856	495,270	396,216	2,345,594
General and administrative costs	15,000	15,000	18,000	18,000	22,716	22,716	22,716	22,716	22,716	24,000	24,000	24,000	251,580
Net profit (before tax)													$ 169,223
													**********

EXHIBIT 1   *(continued)*

EXHIBIT XII
CASH FLOW ASSUMPTIONS

A. Receipts
1. Deposits and final payments are only received 15 days before the date of the trip (very conservative since final payments are due 45 days before departure, and deposits are often received 90 days in advance).
2. Net Operational Tour Receipts are received the week of the trip.

B. Disbursements
1. Airlines are paid 30 days in advance.
2. Hotels are paid 30 days after the trip (requires letter of credit and cash deposits).
3. Meals and transfers are paid 30 days after the trip.
4. Acquisition costs are paid 30 days in advance.
5. Ad hoc program payments require $10,000 deposit 30 days before departure and the balance paid the week before departure.
6. General and administrative expenses are assumed to be paid/disbursements during the month they are expensed. (Conservative since telephone and travel and entertainment expenses are usually not disbursed until a minimum of 30 days after being expensed. These two expense categories are approximately 20% of G + A expenses.)

Exhibit 1 *(continued)*

EXHIBIT XIII
THE TRAVEL GROUP, INC.
CASH FLOW PROJECTIONS
FIRST YEAR OF OPERATION (1974)

	January	February	March	April	May	June	July	August	September	October	November	December
RECEIPTS												
Hawaii					159,265	286,677	286,677	286,677	254,824	286,677	286,677	254,824
Hawaii options (net)						7,500	6,000	7,500	6,000	6,000	7,500	6,000
San Juan										131,560	236,808	210,496
San Juan options (net)											4,475	3,580
Ad hoc programs					32,918	65,835	65,835	65,835	32,918			118,504
TOTAL RECEIPTS	—	—	—	—	192,183	360,012	358,512	360,012	293,742	424,237	535,460	593,404
DISBURSEMENTS												
Hawaii					192,375	153,900	282,825	226,260	244,350	264,735	226,260	244,350
San Juan										100,000	80,000	199,200
Ad hoc					10,000	59,850	59,850	59,850	49,850			92,880
General + administrative	70,608	15,000	18,000	18,000	22,716	22,716	22,716	22,716	22,716	24,000	24,000	24,000
TOTAL DISBURSEMENTS	70,608	15,000	18,000	18,000	225,091	236,466	365,391	308,825	316,916	388,735	330,260	560,430
MONTHLY CASH SURPLUS (DEFICIT)	(70,608)	(15,000)	(18,000)	(18,000)	(32,908)	123,546	(6,879)	51,186	(23,174)	35,502	205,200	32,974
BEGINNING CASH BALANCE	—	(70,608)	(85,608)	(103,608)	(121,608)	(154,516)	(30,970)	(37,849)	13,337	(9,837)	25,665	230,865
ENDING CASH BALANCE	(70,608)	(85,608)	(103,608)	(121,608)	(154,516)	(30,970)	(37,849)	13,337	(9,837)	25,665	230,865	263,839

EXHIBIT 1   (continued)

EXHIBIT XIV
THE TRAVEL GROUP, INC.
CASH FLOW PROJECTIONS
SECOND YEAR OF OPERATION (1975)

	January	February	March	April	May	June	July	August	September	October	November	December
RECEIPTS												
Hawaii	254,824	286,677	286,677	254,824	254,824	286,677	286,677	286,677	286,677	286,677	286,677	382,236
Hawaii options (net)	6,000	6,000	7,500	6,000	6,000	6,000	7,500	6,000	7,500	6,000	7,500	6,000
San Juan	210,496	236,808	236,808	157,872	52,624					105,248	210,496	315,744
San Juan options (net)	3,580	3,580	4,475	3,580	1,790						3,580	3,580
Acapulco	237,008	266,634	266,634	177,756	59,252					118,504	237,008	355,512
Acapulco options (net)	5,400	5,400	6,750	5,400	2,700						5,400	5,400
Spain					148,006	333,014	333,014	333,014	333,014	148,006		
Spain options (net)						4,500	5,625	4,500	5,625	4,500		
TOTAL RECEIPTS	717,308	805,099	808,844	605,432	525,196	630,191	632,816	630,191	632,816	668,935	750,661	1,068,472
DISBURSEMENTS												
Hawaii	226,260	264,735	226,260	244,350	226,260	264,735	226,260	282,825	226,260	282,825	226,260	398,250
San Juan	175,360	195,360	175,360	159,200	95,360	47,680				80,000	80,000	255,360
Acapulco	92,880	234,900	211,680	194,940	118,800	59,400				92,880	92,880	304,560
Spain					174,600	218,250	252,900	316,125	252,900	97,875	78,300	
General and administrative	28,000	28,000	28,000	28,000	28,000	30,000	30,000	30,000	30,000	32,000	32,000	32,000
TOTAL DISBURSEMENTS	522,500	722,995	641,300	626,490	643,020	620,065	509,160	628,950	509,160	585,580	509,440	990,170
MONTHLY CASH SURPLUS/(DEFICIT)	194,808	82,104	167,544	(21,058)	(117,824)	10,126	123,656	1,241	123,656	83,355	241,221	78,302
BEGINNING CASH BALANCE	263,839	458,647	540,751	708,295	687,237	569,413	579,539	703,195	704,436	828,092	911,447	1,152,668
ENDING CASH BALANCE	458,647	540,751	708,295	687,237	569,413	579,539	703,195	704,436	828,092	911,447	1,152,668	1,230,970

EXHIBIT 1   *(concluded)*

EXHIBIT XV

THE TRAVEL GROUP, INC.

PRO FORMA PROFIT AND LOSS (1974–1978)

	1974	1975	1976	1977	1978
SALES	$2,766,397	$8,059,589	$12,029,894	$15,124,878	$18,241,542
Cost of sales	$2,345,594	$6,870,953	$10,305,490	$12,910,496	$15,481,421
Gross profit	420,803	1,188,636	1,724,404	2,214,382	2,760,121
General and administrative	251,580	356,000	480,000	540,000	610,000
Profit (before tax)	$ 169,223	$ 832,636	$ 1,244,404	$ 1,674,382	$ 2,150,121
Earnings per share	$.17	$.83	$1.24	$1.67	$2.15
Value/share (10 price/earnings)	$1.70	$8.33	$12.44	$16.74	$21.50
Number of planes	44	128	192	240	288
Number of passengers	6,861	22,183	33,275	41,595	49,915

2–2 CLARION OPTICAL CO.

It was early September of 1992, and Jerry Stone and Iris Randal were having dinner and discussing their plans to purchase Clarion Optical Co., their current employer. They had decided to attempt to purchase Clarion almost two months ago. Since then, they had spent most of their time talking with potential financial backers and had learned a great deal about potential financing sources.

Now, they needed to make a decision about how to finance and structure the purchase of Clarion. They needed to resolve:

- How to structure the deal for the purchase of Clarion.
- What form(s) of legal organization to use.
- Whom to approach for financing, how much money to raise, and on what terms.

Background

Clarion Optical was located outside of Atlanta, Georgia, and had been founded by Cyrus Atkins in 1946. Clarion began as a manufacturer of high-quality glass for optical uses and as a grinder and polisher of lenses for optical instruments. In the late 1970s, Clarion's chief engineer, Jerry Stone, had pushed Atkins, and Clarion, into the custom contact lens business (i.e., lenses for individuals who could not wear standard off-the-shelf products). This business had proved to be so profitable that Clarion had reached the point where it was once again a single-product company, having phased out of the optical instrument market. (See **Exhibit 1** for most recent financial statements.)

Since Cyrus's gradual retirement from the business began in the mid-1980s, Stone had been president and had taken over more and more responsibility for the firm's operations.

In early 1992, Clarion's new chief engineer, and one of Stone's early pupils in the lab, Iris Randal, had come to Jerry with an idea for a new product line—implantable lenses for the human eye. The incidence of cataracts was on the rise and new surgical techniques had made the replacement of the human eye lens a commonplace procedure.

Iris had developed a new substance from which to make the lens, which was far less costly and created a better lens than existing technology. Jerry and Iris began developing a business plan to explore and capitalize on the opportunity.

This case was prepared by Michael J. Roberts under the direction of Howard H. Stevenson.

Copyright © 1993 by the President and Fellows of Harvard College

Harvard Business School Case 9–393–116

The Sale of Clarion

Two months before, Cyrus Atkins had told Jerry that he had decided that it was time to sell Clarion. Cyrus, a widower, was nearing 80 and had two older children who were successful and well-established professionals. Cyrus had amply provided for them in his large estate, of which his 100 percent ownership of Clarion represented only a part. His interest in Clarion was his last major illiquid holding, and Cyrus was convinced that he should sell the company and tidy up his estate.

Jerry expressed an immediate interest in purchasing the company, and Atkins was pleased at the prospect of Clarion remaining ''in the family.'' He told Jerry that he would give him ample time to try to put together a financing package. Atkins said that he was willing to sell Clarion for 10 times its 1991 earnings of $200,000, or $2 million.

Jerry was convinced that the new implantable lens technology had great potential and was the key to Clarion's future success. He also had a great deal of respect for Iris's engineering and management abilities and decided that she should be part of the management team that attempted the buyout.

Jerry was convinced that the other key staff would remain on. After all, they would not be getting a new boss—he had been managing Clarion for many years.

Jerry discussed the idea with Iris, and she was thrilled with the prospect of owning a piece of Clarion. She also had a great deal of confidence in the new lens technology and was excited to learn that Jerry planned to make this a keystone of his plan for the business. They raced to put together the money.

Valuing the Assets

On the advice of a friend in the banking industry, Jerry and Iris took Clarion's balance sheet and attempted to determine the fair market value of Clarion's assets. A valuation was performed, and they were pleasantly surprised that this value exceeded book value and Atkins's asking price. (See **Exhibit 2.**)

- Land and Building: A 20-year-old, fully depreciated structure, the $200,000 figure on the books represented only the cost of the land. The building was in excellent shape and was owned and used exclusively by Clarion. The structure housed all manufacturing, shipping, and management. There was ample space for any contemplated expansion of the business. Jerry and Iris researched the market and determined that the fair market value of the structure was as follows:

  — Land $250,000
  — Building $750,000

- Equipment: Clarion's equipment was fairly new, but rapid depreciation had decreased its book value to $100,000. Jerry and Iris were convinced that it was worth $500,000.

- Inventory: Because of the custom nature of its work, Clarion kept large stocks of high-quality optical glass on hand. Much of this had been purchased a year or two ago on particularly favorable terms. Now, this $200,000 of book value inventory was worth $500,000.

- Accounts Receivable: Most of Clarion's customers were well-established optical shops who paid their bills on time. The $300,000 book value of accounts receivable was an accurate reflection of their true worth.
- Cash: The cash, of course, was worth $200,000, and Jerry and Iris were convinced that $100,000 would give them sufficient working capital.

Having convinced themselves that Clarion's assets were indeed worth $2.5 million, Jerry and Iris set about investigating potential financing sources.

Financing the Purchase

Jerry and Iris's business plan indicated that they would need an additional $1 million over the purchase price to fund the research and development effort required to get them into the lens business. This raised their ''magic number'' to at least $3.0 million. They then began investigating potential sources of this money.

- New England Pension Trust: Jerry and Iris contacted this tax-free pension fund, an extremely conservative financier. The trust indicated that it would be willing to lend up to 80 percent of the value of the land and building—a mortgage at 12 percent.
- Michael Grund: An extremely wealthy acquaintance of Jerry's, Michael had agreed to consider an investment of up to $250,000 if it showed an aftertax IRR of at least 30 percent. Michael was in the 50 percent tax bracket with respect to personal income, and 40 percent with respect to capital gains.
- Georgia Bank and Trust Co.: A local bank, Georgia B&T had agreed to lend up to 80 percent of the book value of accounts receivable, and 40 percent of the book value of inventory, at 15 percent.
- Rebel Ventures: This local venture capital firm was excited by the venture and had agreed to give Jerry and Iris up to $3.5 million on any investment that showed a 60 percent pretax IRR. It would, however, require the management team to put up $40,000 of its own funds.
- Bank of Atlanta: The bank had agreed to lend either the company or Jerry and Iris personally up to $300,000 at 17 percent with Jerry and Iris's personal guarantees as security. While they each had little (about $20,000 each) in liquid assets, each had a tangible net worth of close to $250,000 due to their own and their spouses' investments in their separate homes.
- General Insurance Corporate Credit: The credit area of this large insurance company had agreed to purchase the existing equipment from Clarion for $300,000 and lease it back to Clarion for five years at $100,000 per year.

With this information in hand, they went to speak with two friends to ask for advice on how to structure the deal:

- Bill Lawrence, an old friend in the real estate business.
- Henry Adams, the trustee at the local bank.

Lawrence's Suggested Structure.   Bill Lawrence suggested financing the deal in the following way:

- Have Grund buy the building and land in a separate transaction for $1 million, and then have Clarion rent it back from Grund (transaction described in **Exhibit 3**). He could:

    — Take an 80 percent mortgage from the bank @ 12 percent.
    — Keep the tax losses and cash flow for his investment of $200,000.
    — Clarion would agree to buy the building and land back at some price at the end of Year 7, in order to give Grund his required 30 percent return.

- Buy the rest of the company for $1 million and finance as follows:

— Excess cash	$100,000
— Borrow on accounts receivable	300,000
— Borrow on inventory	80,00
— Sale/leaseback of equipment	300,000
— Note/personal guarantee	220,000

This would permit Jerry and Iris to retain 100 percent of the equity. It did have its drawbacks though:

- Risk: It seemed as though there would be very little, if any, margin for error in their projections.
- R&D schedule: Without a major influx of venture capital, Jerry and Iris thought it would take three years to generate sufficient cash flow to perform the $1 million worth of R&D required. This would:

    — Delay Clarion's entry into the market.
    — Reduce its share when it did enter.
    — Make the market smaller in the early years because Clarion would not be out developing the market.
    (See **Exhibit 4** for relative market scenarios.)

- Cost: Finally, when they did enter the market, they would not have sufficient funds flow to purchase equipment. This would require them to subcontract production and fulfillment (this firm would also finance working capital needs), which would raise COGS to 30 percent (10 points higher than the 20 percent COGS if they manufactured in-house).
- Salaries: Jerry, who was making $60K/year, and Iris, making $40K/year, would each take a salary cut to $20,000 per year until the business started generating cash.

Adams's Suggested Structure.   Adams suggested that they finance the entire purchase with venture capital funds. This would obviously reduce their share of the equity, but would reduce the risk as well. This financing structure would have important implications:

- Investment: They would invest in the plant and equipment necessary to produce the lens, which would:

  — Reduce the COGS to 20 percent of sales.
  — Increase depreciation charges.

- Fixed charges would drop:

  — No rent.
  — No lease payments.
  — No interest payments.

- Personal stake: They would each invest $20,000 of their own funds in the initial purchase of the company.

The Decision

Jerry and Iris knew that these proposals represented the two extreme ends of the financing spectrum, but they thought that running out the numbers would help them get a feel for what the important issues and trade-offs were.

They finished dessert and coffee and went back to the office to lay out all of their assumptions (see Exhibit 4) and crunch through the numbers.

EXHIBIT 1   **Clarion Financials**

Historical Financial Statements
Year Ended December 31, 1991
(in thousands of dollars)

Income Statement

Sales............................	$1,010
Cost of goods sold	300
Selling, general and administrative	100
Executive salaries	200
Operating income	$ 410
Depreciation......................	10
Net income	400
Taxes	200
Profit after tax	$ 200

Balance Sheet

Cash............................	$ 200		
Accounts receivable	300		
Inventory	200		
Equipment	100		
Land and building.................	200	Owner's equity	$1,000
Total assets......................	$1,000	Total equity	$1,000

EXHIBIT 2   **1991 Balance Sheet Comparison (in thousands of dollars)**

	Book Value	Appraised Value
Cash..	$ 200	$ 200
Accounts receivable	300	300
Inventory	200	500
Equipment	100	500
Land and building	200	1,000
Total assets.................................	$1,000	$2,500

EXHIBIT 3   Real Estate Transaction

Assumptions
- Mortgage: 25 years
  $800,000
  12%
  Constant payment of $102,000 per annum
- Amortization schedule: ($000)

Year	1	2	3	4	5	6	7
• Interest payment	96.0	95.3	94.5	93.6	92.6	91.4	90.2
• Principal payment	6.0	6.7	7.5	8.4	9.4	10.6	11.8

- Principal value of mortgage outstanding at end of Year 7 equals $740,000.

Real Estate Cash Flows

(in thousands of dollars)

Year	1	2	3	4	5	6	7
Rent	$ 165.0	$ 173.0	$182.0	$191.0	$200.0	$211.0	$221.0
Maintenance.	40.0	41.0	42.0	44.0	45.0	46.0	48.0
Taxes	25.0	25.0	25.0	25.0	25.0	25.0	25.0
Net operating income . . .	100.0	107.0	114.0	122.0	130.0	140.0	148.0
Finance payment	102.0	102.0	102.0	102.0	102.0	102.0	102.0
Pretax cash flow	(2.0)	5.0	12.0	20.0	28.0	38.0	46.0
+ Amortization	6.0	6.7	7.5	8.4	9.4	10.6	11.8
− Depreciation	150.0	120.0	96.0	76.8	61.4	49.0	39.2
= Taxable income	(146.0)	(108.3)	(76.5)	(48.4)	(23.0)	0.5	18.5
+ Tax benefit/(cost)	73.0	54.1	38.2	24.2	11.5	(.2)	(9.2)
= Aftertax cash flow . . .	71.0	59.1	50.2	44.2	39.5	37.8	36.8

NOTE: Finance payment is a level stream that includes both interest and principal. Amortization (principal repayment) must therefore be added back to pretax cash flow to arrive at a taxable income figure. Taxes are figured at 50% personal rate.

Cash Flows on Sale of Building and Land
Sale transaaction at assumed prices of $1,000,000 and $1,100,000

Calculation of tax due:

Sale	$1,000,000	$1,100,000
− Net book value	407,600	407,600
Gain on sale	$ 592,400	$ 692,400
Tax (40% rate)	236,960	276,960

Calculation of net cash proceeds:

Sale proceeds	$1,000,000	$1,100,000
− Tax liability	236,960	276,960
− Mortgage balance	740,000	740,000
Net cash proceeds	$ 23,040	$ 83,040

EXHIBIT 4   **Scenario Cash Flows**

Assumptions
1. *Sales* (see Schedule A, attached)
   - All Debt: They thought that under this scenario, it would take three years to fund the $1 million of R&D required out of cash flow. In this case, Clarion could not enter the implantable lens market until Year 4, at which point it could only attain 40 percent market share; and the market would be smaller, because it would not have been out developing it.
   - All Equity: Clarion could finish the R&D in one year and enter the market in Year 2. It could obtain a larger market share and grow the entire market.
   - Both: In either case, sales of the existing contact lens product line would stagnate at whatever level they were at when implantable lens sales began.
2. *COGS*
   - All Debt: Cost of implantable lens equal to 30 percent sales, due to subcontracting.
   - All Equity: Cost of implantable lens equal to 20 percent of sales.
   - Both: Cost of existing contact lens product equal to 30 percent sales.
3. *SG&A ($000)*

Year:	1	2	3	4	5	6	7
• All Debt	108	120	129	500	600	700	800
• All Equity	107	500	600	700	800	900	1000

4. *Executive Salaries ($000)*

Year:	1	2	3	4	5	6	7
• All Debt	40	40	40	200	300	400	500
• All Equity	100	100	100	200	300	400	500

5. *R&D*
   $1 million required to complete R&D on implantable lens.
   - All Debt: Funded out of cash as available; Jerry and Iris assumed that this could be completed in three years.
   - All Equity: Funded in Year 1 out of venture capital.
6. *Depreciation*
   - All Debt: Equal to zero in all years: No plant, equipment, building to depreciate.
   - All Equity: Depreciation on existing building and equipment equal to $150,000 each year for seven years. Depreciation on new equipment purchased is calculated on a straight-line basis over a five-year life, beginning in the year of actual purchase (i.e., if $1 million worth of equipment purchased in Year 1, then $200,000 taken in Years 1 through 5). (See *Investment*, line 13, for investment required.)

SCHEDULE A
Sales Revenue Scenarios (in millions of dollars)

	All Debt					All Equity				
		Implantable Lens Sales					Implantable Lens Sales			
Year	Contact Lens Sales	Market Size	Clarion Share	Resultant Sales	Total	Contact Lens Sales	Market Size	Clarion Share	Resultant Sales	Total
1	1.10	1.0	0	0	1.10	1.1	1.0	0	0	1.1
2	1.28	2.5	0	0	1.28	1.1	5.0	60%	3	4.1
3	1.60	5.0	0	0	1.60	1.1	10.0	60%	6	7.1
4	1.60	10.0	40%	4	5.60	1.1	20.0	60%	12	13.1
5	1.60	20.0	40%	8	9.60	1.1	40.0	60%	24	25.1
6	1.60	40.0	40%	16	17.60	1.1	60.0	60%	36	37.1
7	1.60	65.0	40%	26	27.60	1.1	80.0	60%	48	49.1

EXHIBIT 4   *(concluded)*

7. *Interest*
   - All Debt:
   - $300,000 borrowed against accounts receivable is outstanding over the entire seven years, at 15 percent per annum. No principal repayments made.
   - $80,000 borrowed against inventory is outstanding over the entire seven years, at 15 percent per annum. No principal repayments made.
   - $220,000 note, personally guaranteed is outstanding over five years, principal and interest paid according to following schedule.

Year:	1	2	3	4	5
Interest	38	32	26	19	10
Principal	31	37	43	50	59

   - All Equity: No interest charges.
8. *Lease Payments*
   - All Debt: Lease payments on machinery are $100,000 per annum for five years, at which time ownership reverts to Clarion.
   - All Equity: No lease payments.
9. *Rent*
   - All Debt: As shown in Exhibit 3.
   - All Equity: No rent payments.
10. *Maintenance and Real Estate Taxes*
    - All Debt: No maintenance expenses or taxes.
    - All Equity: As shown in Exhibit 3.
11. *Taxes:* 50 percent of income. Assume that losses are offset against following year's income (i.e., if Clarion has losses of $200,000 in Year 1 and pretax profit of $1 million in Year 2, income tax in Year 2 is calculated on a pretax base of $800,000).
12. *Depreciation:* (See line 6)
13. *Investment*
    - All Debt: Purchase of building in Year 7 at price required to give 30 percent return.
    - All Equity: Annual investment required in ($000)

Year:	1	2	3	4	5	6	7
Working Capital	63	600	600	1,200	2,400	2,400	2,400
Equipment	1,000	1,000	2,000	4,000	8,000	12,000	15,000

14. *Principal Repayment*
    - All Debt: On $220,000 personally guaranteed note only; see above under *Interest.*
    - All Equity: None.
15. *Terminal Value:* Assume that the company is sold at the end of Year 7 for 10 × Year 7 aftertax earnings under both scenarios.
16. *Other:* In addition, they realized that they needed to make other assumptions in order to judge the two scenarios.
    - Assume Jerry and Iris's personal investment in business as follows:
      - All Debt: Investment of 0 in Year 0 plus $60,000 in "lost salary" in each of Years 1 through 3.
      - All Equity: Investment of $40,000 in Year 0.
    - Calculate cash flows to Jerry and Iris *jointly* (i.e., do not make any assumptions about how equity, investment, or cash flows are divided between the two parties).
    - Assume that in the equity scenario, only return occurs via sale of equity at end of Year 7 —no dividends paid or other distributions made.
    - Assume that in the debt scenario, free cash flow is taken out at end of each year, including the end of Year 7.
    - Calculate flows and returns to Jerry, Iris, and Rebel Ventures on a *prepersonal tax* basis (i.e., include taxes at the corporate level in your calculations, but *do not* include any personal taxes on dividends or distributions out of Clarion). Also, do not include Jerry and Iris's salaries as part of the cash outflows in calculating returns.
    - Include the price of the building repurchase in Year 7 as an investment in that year in the debt scenario.
    - In the all-debt scenario, assume that all available cash is spent on R&D until the $1 million project is complete; you must "plug" the figure for R&D for each year (i.e., free cash flow should equal zero in years where R&D project is ongoing).
    - Assume Rebel Ventures will invest whatever cash is required to keep Clarion cash positive up to its stated $3.5 million limit.

2–3 VISCOTECH, INC.

Kenneth Jones, president of Viscotech, walked through the lobby of the Park Tower Building and headed toward a small restaurant near Chicago's business district. He needed some time away from the office, time to ponder the difficult situation in which he found himself. It was March 1989, and only seven months ago, Jones had left his position with a large pharmaceutical firm to become Viscotech's president. Stock, options, and a hefty salary increase had made the future seem bright. Now, all that seemed to be slipping away.

Jones had just come from a meeting with an attorney, Paul Benjamin, who had informed Jones that Viscotech might have committed violations of U.S. securities laws. Jones had to evaluate this information in light of the entire chain of events that had led up to that morning's meeting with Benjamin. As he considered his predicament, he realized that he needed to evaluate both Viscotech's and his own exposure to a potential SEC violation.

Viscotech

Viscotech was incorporated in 1982 by Dr. Samuel Evans, a surgeon and professor at the Midwestern Medical School; Louis Brown, a research scientist at the Chicago Institute of Technology; Dr. Harold Stein, a nutritional specialist at the Midwestern Medical School; and Melvin O'Connor, an accountant and attorney in the Chicago area.

The company was founded in order to design, develop, and market a device that could measure the viscosity of saliva. It had long been known that this type of analysis of saliva could help physicians assess nutritional inadequacies in patients.

Between 1982 and 1987, the company had spent almost $500,000 pursuing its research agenda. These funds had been obtained from the company's founders in the form of debt and equity.

By late 1987, Viscotech had succeeded in obtaining several patents that covered the core technology used in the device. Viscotech had focused its efforts on developing its first product, the Doctor's Office Device. This device would be simple, easy to use, and would allow doctors to perform a comprehensive nutritional analysis in their offices. In addition, the technology had broader applications in the feeding and breeding of cattle and swine.

This case was prepared by Professor Michael J. Roberts, Richard E. Floor of Goodwin, Procter & Hoar, Boston, and Professor Howard H. Stevenson. Professor Michael J. Roberts updated this case.
Copyright © 1993 by the President and Fellows of Harvard College
Harvard Business School Case 9–393–117.

The announcement of the device had received a great deal of favorable attention in the medical press. By the end of 1987, Viscotech had developed a working prototype of the device, which was ready for more extensive clinical testing and subsequent submission to the Food and Drug Administration for approval.

1988 — The Need for Capital

In early 1988, it became clear to Viscotech's principals that the company would require another infusion of cash in order to:

- Complete testing and receive FDA approval.
- Develop engineering and manufacturing specifications.
- Research new applications for the technology.

In April of 1988, a group of physicians who were friends of Viscotech's founders indicated that they were interested in investing in the venture. At about the same time, O'Connor had been in touch with the venture capital community seeking funds for Viscotech. At a meeting in late April, the four founders decided to pursue the raising of capital from other acquaintances in the medical community because the venture firms were offering too meager a price for an equity investment.

At this point, O'Connor agreed to proceed with the raising of funds in this manner. In order to protect the founders, he thought it prudent to raise money with a very carefully drawn offering circular. However, because his schedule was quite full with other business commitments, O'Connor knew that he would be unable to prepare such a document for several months.

The Medical Investment Fund Trust

Because of these constraints and the fact that Viscotech needed money quickly, O'Connor suggested that funds be raised through another vehicle — the Medical Investment Fund Trust (MIFT). MIFT could then invest the money in Viscotech, and then Viscotech could spend these funds. Later that year, an offering circular would be presented, and each investor given the option to withdraw and receive his or her funds back. If investors chose to subscribe, they would agree to exchange their investment in MIFT for Viscotech shares.

O'Connor was confident that the trust offered a means of raising money on an interim basis, while avoiding the final commitment until the offering circular was issued. As such, the structure was similar to an arrangement O'Connor and Viscotech had used several years earlier to raise funds.

It was decided that investors who advanced funds through MIFT would receive a certificate representing shares in MIFT. MIFT, in turn, would be granted an option on shares of Viscotech. They would attempt to raise $2,000,000 in 250 units of $8,000 each. Each unit would represent a claim on 0.1 percent of Viscotech stock.

In June 1988, O'Connor drew up the trust instrument and a brief description of MIFT for potential investors (see **Exhibit 1**). This package contained information on Viscotech that had previously been made public. Prior to distributing the MIFT package, the company raised $100,000 from six relatives and friends of the principals to meet its needs during the interim.

Beginning in June, and continuing throughout the summer, acquaintances of Viscotech's principals advanced funds to MIFT. The funds were routinely forwarded to O'Connor's office and disbursed by him.

As part of the financing effort, Viscotech conducted a series of informational seminars for friends and acquaintances of the principals. These discussions centered around the technology, the history of the company, and potential markets for the company's devices. No formal offers were made at these seminars, nor were there any discussions of price. Many of the individuals who were present, however, did subsequently invest.

In August, O'Connor began to realize that his schedule was not going to be free for quite some time. Therefore, he contacted a friend of his, Leonard Atkins, an experienced attorney with the Chicago firm of Dewey & White. O'Connor informed Atkins of the MIFT arrangement and told Atkins that he wanted him to draw up an offering circular to close the MIFT financing. Atkins suggested that Viscotech undertake a private offering, but O'Connor said that he would prefer to have the SEC review any materials. Accordingly, they decided to attempt to raise funds through a Regulation A offering. This plan was approved at the annual shareholders' meeting in mid-August, and Atkins was given instructions to proceed.

Kenneth Jones

Later that August, Viscotech hired Ken Jones as its president. The original principals were able to spend only a portion of their time on Viscotech because of their medical and research responsibilities. In addition, as the product got closer to market, the principals felt the need for an individual with business experience.

Jones had graduated from the U.S. Naval Academy, and subsequent to his sea duty had attended the Midwest Business School. He had worked for a major international pharmaceutical firm as a product manager for four years before joining Viscotech. Jones was given 1,620 shares of Viscotech, options on further shares, and a salary of $65,000 per year.

Jones did not become heavily involved in the financing efforts because most of the potential investors were acquaintances of the founders. He did understand the MIFT arrangement, however, and understood from O'Connor that Atkins had cleared this vehicle for raising funds. Jones did attend and speak at several of the informational seminars, and he was briefed by Atkins on what to say. Specifically, Atkins told him to be wary of making statements that could be interpreted as "promises about Viscotech's future performance."

During the fall, Jones met with Atkins and O'Connor several times regarding the Regulation A offering. Jones edited several drafts of the offering circular. During this process, Atkins was supplied with Viscotech's financial statements prepared by O'Connor, which showed the liability for stock subscriptions through MIFT and detailed the expenditures of funds received. At one point, Jones asked Atkins how MIFT would be treated, and Atkins responded by saying, "We don't need to talk about MIFT."

By early December of 1988, $976,000 had been raised by MIFT from 34 investors. By February, the Regulation A offering circular was in draft form. Atkins had prepared the material for submission to the SEC. The principals decided to send the material off in early March.

The SEC Issue

The last weekend in February, Ken casually mentioned the financing plans to a friend at a neighborhood party. This friend, an attorney with the prestigious local firm of Cole & Eggers, thought that something sounded a bit odd. He suggested that Ken see one of his colleagues, Paul Benjamin, an expert on securities law. Ken made arrangements to see Benjamin during the first week of March and sent him a draft of the circular.

Jones explained the events of the past months to Benjamin, and they reviewed a copy of the circular. The attorney felt that the use of MIFT as a vehicle to insulate Viscotech was not effective, and that both Jones and Viscotech were exposed to SEC charges arising out of the manner in which MIFT had raised its funds. He recommended that Jones "come clean" and go to the SEC. Benjamin felt that this would show Jones's good faith and limit his own personal exposure to SEC charges. In addition, he advocated "freezing" all existing funds in MIFT as a further show of good faith. Viscotech could then raise its funds with a Rule 505 offering that required notifying the SEC but did not require SEC approval. Benjamin drafted a version of this offering, which appears as **Exhibit 2**, and which gives investors the option of withdrawing their investment. Benjamin also stated that the company would have to hire an individual to prepare the required two years of audited financial statements since O'Connor had had a financial interest in Viscotech while his firm was involved in the company's accounting.

What to Do

Jones's head was spinning when he left Benjamin's office. He wanted to do what was legal and ethically right. Yet, he also knew how desperately Viscotech needed funds to gear up for manufacturing and marketing of the Doctor's Office Device. Going to the SEC seemed to minimize his personal risk, but could implicate the rest of the company's principals and would surely harm the company's chances of raising money. Viscotech could go ahead with the Rule 505 offering, which merely required notifying the SEC. Benjamin said that there was a low probability that the SEC would request further documentation or the actual offering circular. However, in the event that the SEC did request the offering circular, Benjamin advised that it be very conservatively drafted, like the version excerpted in Exhibit 2. Ken felt, however, that this draft was *so* conservative that many investors would be likely to take recission (i.e., request the return of their investment) if they received this document.

Ken didn't know what to do. Any course that would successfully raise the funds Viscotech needed seemed to involve a good deal of risk.

Eᴄʜɪʙɪᴛ 1   **MIFT Offering Circular**

Confidential Investment Memorandum

Medical Investment Fund Trust

The Medical Investment Fund Trust (MIFT) has been formed as a vehicle to raise funds for Viscotech, Inc. Each $8,000 investment in MIFT will represent a claim on 200 (roughly 0.1 percent) of Viscotech's shares. MIFT seeks to raise $2,000,000 in this manner.

In the near future, Viscotech, Inc., will distribute an offering memorandum to those individuals who have invested in MIFT. At that time, any investor who desires to do so shall have the right to sell his/her MIFT shares back to the company for the amount of the original investment.

The Business˙

Viscotech was formed in 1982 by Dr. Samuel Evans, Midwestern Medical School; Louis Brown, Chicago Institute of Technology; Dr. Harold Stein, Midwestern Medical School; and Melvin O'Connor, Esq., O'Connor & O'Connor. The company has spent $500,000 of its founders' funds perfecting a technology that can assess nutritional inadequacies in patients through an analysis of saliva.

Patents

The company has filed and been granted 15 patents, which cover the core aspects of Viscotech's technology. In addition, the company has filed for 63 additional patents, which have yet to be ruled on. These patent applications have been made in 20 countries.

Products

Viscotech plans to produce the following devices:

- Doctor's Office Device: A complex instrument capable of analyzing deficiencies in a patient with respect to vitamins, minerals, blood sugar, amino acids, hormones, and trace elements.
- Home Device: A simpler instrument that will enable individuals to easily assess their own vitamin, mineral, and blood sugar levels.
- Farm Animal Device: A simple instrument that will allow breeders of cattle and swine to determine the optimal feed content for their animals.

With the tremendous increase in individuals' concern with their own nutritional well-being, the company is confident that these instruments will be extraordinarily successful. Imagine being able to take a simple test, using saliva, to determine the adequacy of vitamin and mineral intake, and to make dietary adjustments accordingly.

Markets

The markets for these products offer tremendous potential. In addition to lucrative U.S. markets, incredible potential exists in Third World markets where malnutrition is a problem. Individuals will now be able to test undernourished people to determine the precise therapeutic treatment. The government of India has indicated a strong interest in making a grant of $250,000 to Viscotech for the purpose of developing such an instrument for its use. The company currently plans to introduce the following devices:

The Doctor's Office Device: There is no other product available that performs these tests with the ease, accuracy, speed, and inexpensive price of the Viscotech instrument.

- Projected Potential Market: The potential market is projected to be doctors dealing regularly with patients with nutritional problems:

EXHIBIT 1   *(continued)*

	Nutritionists	*G.Ps*	*Total*
United States	14,000 of 24,000	6,000 of 56,000	20,000 of 80,000
Europe	10,000 of 20,000	5,000 of 70,000	15,000 of 90,000
Rest of world	4,000(est.)	1,000(est.)	5,000
Total potential market			40,000

- Average Instrument Usage
  - —6 tests per patient per month, or 75 tests per year.
  - —4 ongoing patients per doctor.
  - —75 × 4 = 300 tests per doctor per year.

- Sales Price
Instruments	$3,000.00 each
Disposables	$ 2.40 per test

Market introduction is projected for the third quarter of 1990 in both the United States and Europe. First-year projected sales of 250 instruments represents a less than 1 percent penetration of the potential market, with second-year sales of 400 instruments reaching a cumulative penetration of 1.9 percent.

Viscotech plans to initially distribute the doctor's instrument through regional dealers and manufacturers' reps in the major metropolitan areas where the primary market is concentrated. Given the large number of potential customers and the need to demonstrate the instrument to each of these potential customers, economics dictate that Viscotech make use of existing sales and distribution channels into these targeted doctors' offices. Viscotech will have a small, highly qualified in-house sales team to manage this distributor network. Viscotech will also handle all product services directly.

The Home Device: This device will allow individuals to safely and easily sample their own saliva to determine the levels of key nutritional variables: vitamins, minerals, and blood sugar levels.

Viscotech has developed working prototypes of the saliva collection device and the measuring device that comprise the Home Device System. Both components are significantly different from those used with the Doctor's Office Device.

At present the company is having a prototype mold constructed for the saliva collection device with a capability to produce 3,000–5,000 parts. Availability is scheduled for mid-September, after which we will begin the first in-use testing of the Home Device.

We estimate that design finalization will take 1–2 years and market introduction 2–3 years.

- Projected Potential Market: the potential market is projected to be men and women in the 15–45 age group that are currently using vitamins, dietary supplements, or have a nutritional problem. This represents an immediate worldwide market of about 100 million individuals:

United States	25 million
Europe	34 million
Japan	12 million
Rest of world	30 million
	101 million

- Average Instrument Usage: Minimum average of 5 tests per month or 70 tests per year.

EXHIBIT 1   *(continued)*

- Sales Price
  Instrument $45.00
  Disposables $ .90
- Estimated Manufacturing Cost
  Instrument $10.00
  Disposables $ .20
- Total Potential Dollar Market
  Annual disposable sales   7 billion tests   @ $ 0.90 = $6.3 billion
  One time instruments sales   100 million   @ $45.00 = $4.5 billion
- Sales Projections: Market introduction in the United States is projected for the second quarter of 1992. Projecting sales in such an enormous market is at best difficult. If a 1 percent share of the potential market were achieved during the first five years, end-user purchases of disposables would be $60 million annually, and instrument sales would average $9 million annually. The company feels that it is possible to achieve a 20 percent share of the potential market during the next 5–10 years.
- Marketing and Distribution: An arrangement with a very large multinational consumer marketing company appears to provide the most logical and reasonable path to the marketplace. Such a company could provide both the dollar investment and expertise required to successfully develop sales of the Home Device. Additionally it could provide indemnity for Viscotech against any product liability claims.

Discussions with International Pharmaceutical have taken place over the last six months and have developed to an advanced point. International has the broadest line of any company in the field and is part of a premier, highly successful company in the health care industry. International has made two offers in writing (June 8 and July 12), and Viscotech has made one counterproposal in writing (July 31).

The Farm Animal Device: The instrument system proposed for use by doctors in managing patients is, conceptually, equally applicable for increasing the productivity of food animals such as swine, dairy cattle, and beef cattle.

The objective is to develop an effective instrument system and verify its feasibility for improving the rate of weight addition in swine and cattle. This development process entails empirically modifying the doctor's instrument system to accommodate the saliva of swine and cattle.

Swine and cattle were chosen because they appeared to offer the greatest immediate commercial opportunity.

- Both are maintained and bred primarily in large confined herds, which facilitates management and recordkeeping.
- Both represent large potential markets in terms of numbers of annual breedings.
- Swine represent the largest per capita consumed meat in the world.

Dairy Cattle: Projected Potential Market: The potential market is projected to be only farms with over 50 milk cows, where the payback on an instrument system would be very high.

- Projected Potential Market: Farms with over 50 milk cows.
  United States—50,000 farms out of total 588,000 farms with milk cows
           These farms have 4.8 million of the total 12.5 million milk cows in the United States. Our potential market in the United States is, therefore, 8.5 percent of total farms that have 38.5 percent of total milk cows.
  Europe—estimated 40,000 farms have 5 million of the over 50 million milk cows in Europe.
  Rest of world—conservative estimate 10,000 farms.
  Total market potential— 100,000 farms.

EXHIBIT 1   *(continued)*

- Average Instrument Usage
  - 11 tests per cow per year.
  - 144 cows per farm, which assumes 50 percent of sales will be to farms with 50–100 cows and 50 percent to farms with over 100 cows. This assumption results in penetration of market potential being greater for disposables than instruments.
  - 11 × 144 = 1,584 tests per farm per year.

- Sales Price

Instrument	$2,500 each
Disposables	$2 per test

Viscotech is currently funding a research program with dairy cattle at the University of the Midwest.

Market introduction is projected for the third quarter of 1985. First-year sales of 210 instruments represent a less than .5 percent penetration of the potential U.S. market. Second-year sales of 525 instruments brings the cumulative penetration to .7 percent of the total world market.

Distributor arrangements for sale to the dairy industry have not yet been set up.

Swine: Projected Potential Market: The potential market is projected to be only larger operations that average 250 sows. The animals are in a confined controlled environment, and the economic payback of an instrument system would be very high.

- Projected Potential Market

  United States—8,000 operations averaging 250 sows in confinement, which account for 40 percent of total 5 million sows in the United States.

  Europe—estimated 4,000 operations accounting for 25 percent of 4 million sows.

  Rest of world—estimated 2,000 operations accounting for 10 percent of 5 million sows.

- Average Instrument Usage
  1. 19 tests per sow.
  2. 250 sows per farm.
  3. 19 × 250 = 4,750 tests per farm per year.

Note: This averages 13 tests per day, meaning larger operations of 400–600 sows would definitely need two or three instruments for scheduling purposes. Instrument sales are projected conservatively at one per operation, but with replacement sales beginning after five years of heavy usage.

- Sales Price

Instrument	$2,500 each
Disposables	$1.25 per test

Note: Economics of sow breeding require lower cost per test to provide attractive payback. Competitively, lower disposables' price can be justified based on much higher volume of testing per farm as compared to dairy cattle. Gross margin will be reduced significantly, but still remain attractively above 40 percent.

Viscotech has recently signed a joint R&D/Distribution agreement with National Swine Breeders, Inc. This company is the largest producer of hybrid breeding stock in the United States.

Market introduction is projected for the second quarter of 1990. First-year sales of 100 units represents a 1.25 percent penetration of the potential U.S. market. Second-year sales of 200 instruments brings the cumulative penetration to 2.1 percent of the potential world market.

EXHIBIT 1   *(concluded)*

Projected Income Statements ($000)

	1991	1992	1993
Sales	$2,726	$7,629	$23,400
Commissions (33%)	908	2,391	7,722
Cost of goods sold	661	1,974	5,850
Gross profit	1,157	3,264	9,828
Research and development	352	438	512
Sales and marketing	283	441	742
General and administrative	511	630	803
Interest	77	65	0
Depreciation	12	19	28
Profit before tax	(78)	1,668	7,743
Tax	—	—*	3,716
Profit after tax	(78)	1,668	4,027

*Due to prior losses and tax credits.

EXHIBIT 2   Viscotech Investment Memorandum

<u>Confidential Investment Memorandum and Recission Offer</u>

50,000 SHARES OF COMMON STOCK

This Confidential Investment Memorandum has been prepared in connection with the offering by Viscotech, Inc. (the "Company") of up to 50,000 shares of its Common Stock, $.10 par value, at $40 per share. The minimum subscription is 100 shares ($4,000).

This memorandum presents background information, has been prepared for the confidential use of private investors, and is not to be reproduced in whole or part. This offering is not made pursuant to any registration statement of Notification under Regulation A filed with the Securities and Exchange Commission, and the securities offered hereby are offered for investment only to qualifying recipients of this offering. The Company claims an exemption from the registration requirements of the Securities Act of 1933, as amended under Section 4(2) of that Act and Rule 505 thereunder.

Nothing set forth herein is intended to represent or in any manner imply that the stock offered hereby has been approved, recommended, or guaranteed by the Government of the United States or of any state, or by any of the agencies of either.

THE SECURITIES OFFERED HEREBY ARE HIGHLY SPECULATIVE AND INVOLVE A HIGH DEGREE OF RISK. PURCHASE OF THESE SECURITIES SHOULD BE CONSIDERED ONLY BY THOSE PERSONS WHO CAN AFFORD TO SUSTAIN A TOTAL LOSS OF THEIR INVESTMENT. SEE "RISK FACTORS."

THIS OFFERING INVOLVES IMMEDIATE SUBSTANTIAL DILUTION FROM THE OFFERING PRICE. FOR FURTHER INFORMATION CONCERNING THIS AND OTHER SPECIAL RISK FACTORS, SEE "RISK FACTORS" AND "DILUTION."

The offering price has been determined arbitrarily, and bears no relationship to the book value per share. Since all such shares must be acquired for investment only, no market for the shares offered hereby will arise, and no sales of such stock will be permitted in the future except pursuant to an effective registration statement or an exemption from registration under the Securities Act of 1933, as amended. Hence, the Company can offer no assurance that the stock will be salable at any time when the subscriber desires, or that the stock will be able to be resold at any time at or near the offering price.

The offering of the common stock is not underwritten. The Company plans to sell shares of common stock by personal solicitation or otherwise, through efforts of its distributors and officers. Such persons will receive no compensation other than reimbursement of out of pocket expenses incurred by them in connection with the sale. Such officers may be deemed "underwriters" as that term is defined in the Securities Act of 1933, as amended.

Unless 50 percent of the shares offered hereby are sold within 90 days from the date hereof, all subscribers' funds will be returned to them without interest or deduction.

EXHIBIT 2   *(continued)*

TABLE OF CONTENTS

Risk Factors

Viscotech, Inc. (the "Company") was incorporated under the laws of the State of Illinois on December 17, 1982, to do research on, and to develop, instruments and devices to measure precisely and accurately the amount of, and the variations in, elasticity and viscosity (known as viscoelasticity) of saliva in humans and other mammals. It has not yet marketed any such instruments or devices.

Prospective investors should be informed of the following risk factors involved in this offering:

(A) Insolvency:
1. To date, the Company has been engaged only in research and development, has generated no sales, and is, consequently, currently insolvent.
2. A substantial portion of this offering has already been raised and the funds have been used to pay current obligations. (See "Use of Proceeds.")
3. Even if the offering is fully subscribed, unless operations soon become profitable, or the Company raises additional funds elsewhere, investors will stand to lose their entire investment.
(B) Dilution:
In the event all the shares offered hereby are sold, those persons who purchase these shares will incur an immediate substantial dilution in the book value of $33.73 per share from the offering price of $40 per share while the book value of the presently outstanding shares will increase from a negative $3.91 per share to $6.37 per share solely by reason of the proceeds raised through the offering.

(C) No Operating History:
The Company has no operating history, and there is no assurance that it will operate profitably.

(D) No Present Product Market:
The Company has no contracts or commitments from potential users of its products and can give no assurance that the products will be marketed successfully.

(E) Limited Personnel:
The Company has only three full-time employees, a Chief Executive Officer, and two Engineers. The development of the devices it intends to market has been, and will continue to be, of an indeterminate time, dependent upon part-time efforts of its founders, and of outside consultants.

(F) Food and Drug Administration Approval:
The Food and Drug Administration has not approved the Company's complete instrument system for sale, and no assurance can be given that it, or any other governmental agency with jurisdiction, will do so.

(G) Use of Proceeds for Research and Development in Other Areas:
A significant amount of the Company's funds will be used for further research and development in the fields of animal husbandry, consumer products, industrial products, and possibly other areas, and no assurance can be given that this research and development will be successful.

(H) Need for Additional Funding:
The Company believes that it will be necessary to secure funding in addition to that offered pursuant hereto in order to enable the Company to achieve its objectives. The Company will seek to raise such additional funds through any one or more of loans, grants, or additional equity. Should the Company seek to raise additional equity, it may be required to do so at a price per share less than that being offered pursuant hereto, in which case investors will suffer a dilution in the value of their shares. The Company can give no assurance that such additional funding will be available to it on any basis.

(I) Competition:
Many companies with resources far greater than those available to the Company are involved in the field of nutrition and may be able to compete with the Company.

(J) Dividends:
The Company has never paid dividends, and does not expect to do so in the foreseeable future.

(K) No Cumulative Voting:
The common stock of this Company does not have cumulative voting rights. Hence, the holders of more than 50 percent of the shares voting for the election of directors may elect all the directors if they so choose. Since the present management holds more than 50 percent of the shares to be outstanding, it will be in a position to reelect itself as directors.

Business
It has long been known that the viscoelasticity of saliva decreases in the event of nutritional deficiency. To date, however, to the knowledge of the Company, there is no instrument or method capable of accurately measuring this decrease at a reasonable cost and evaluating the extent and cause of nutritional inadequacy. Such measurements can be of significant aid to doctors in diagnosing the problems of overweight, obese, or anorexic individuals and to breeders of such animals as cattle and swine. The instruments that the Company has developed are, it believes, capable of making such measurements on minute quantities of saliva, which consists of a variety of nonhomogeneous materials, without homogenizing them or otherwise destroying their integrity. The instruments developed by the Company do not rely on hormonal, chemical, or other ingested material, nor on any

EXHIBIT 2   *(continued)*

implanted devices. Rather, a sample of saliva is extracted and placed on a grid in the instrument, which is capable of determining the exact amount of viscoelasticity present in the sample.

Food and Drug Administration approval is a necessary prerequisite to the marketing of the Company's products for human medical use in the United States. Approval has been granted for the Company's saliva aspirator. Application for approval of the Company's Doctor's Device (the first major product that the Company intends to market) will be submitted subsequent to the completion of clinical trials presently in progress. There can be no assurance that approval will be forthcoming. A delay in the grant of such approval, or the attachment thereto of conditions, or the denial thereof, might have a serious, adverse effect on the Company.

Although the Company has developed prototype machines and other products for use by doctors, clinics, and other medical personnel, such machines have not been distributed, and so their effectiveness in the field remains unproven. The Company has distributed a limited number of its products to users who are not associated with the Company, in order to secure from them reports as to results and other comments. The Company cannot guarantee that such reports or comments will be favorable.

In addition, the Company is planning to contract for the production of several hundred Doctor's Devices to be available for sale to doctors, clinics, and hospitals for delivery commencing in 1989. Although the Company has had negotiations with manufacturers, no commitments or contracts have been made. In consequence, no assurance can be given that the machines can be produced within the projected time and at a favorable price, or that if produced, a sufficient number can be sold to offset the investment.

The Company is presently attempting to develop a device at a commercially reasonable price that would enable a person to sample his own saliva and determine his own nutritional levels. There can be no assurance that its efforts will be successful within a reasonable time and at reasonable cost, or that in any event, Food and Drug Administration approval will be granted, or that such a device would have the degree of consumer acceptance necessary for economic viability.

The Company also has research projects planned to measure bronchial secretions, synovial fluid, spinal fluid, serum, and meconium, any or all of which may be of importance in other branches of medicine. In addition, the Company is supporting research at a university agricultural school to experiment in the application of the Company's concepts in the field of swine production.

All of these activities will take considerable time to complete. No assurance can be given that any will be completed successfully, or within the resources of the company, or that if successfully completed, commercially salable products can be developed and marketed.

Patents

The Company has filed and been granted patents on certain applications of its basic concepts and has filed further patent applications which are presently pending. Patent applications corresponding to certain of the Company's U.S. patents have been filed in twenty or more countries. A schedule setting forth the patent status is included as Appendix A. The Company can offer no assurance that any pending patent application will be granted, that the grant of any patent ensures that the product covered thereby can be marketed successfully, that any patent is valid and enforceable, or that any of its patents cannot be circumvented or attacked by others. Nor can it assure that any of its present or future products will not infringe on patents of others.

Use of Proceeds

The net proceeds of this offering, assuming the sale of the 50,000 shares offered hereby, will be approximately $1,800,000 after deducting estimated expenses of $200,000. The Company will apply the net proceeds to satisfy its liability on Stock Subscriptions which as of the date hereof totals $976,000 (see Note 8 of Financial Statements), such liability having been created by the receipt by the Company of subscriptions to this offering prior to the issuance of this Confidential Investment Memorandum. The funds creating this liability have been used since June 1988, as follows:

EXHIBIT 2   *(continued)*

- $300,000 to reduce bank indebtedness.*
- $250,000 to pay current indebtedness to creditors.
- $30,000 to process patent applications.
- $396,000 for working capital, including the salary of the Company's President, other employees, research and development, and other expenses of the Company.

The balance of the proceeds from the offering ($1,124,000) will be used to pay the estimated expenses of the offering (approximately $200,000), and the balance ($924,000) added to working capital.

Since there is no underwriting for the shares being offered, there is no assurance that all of the shares will be sold. As of the date of this offering, the Company has received subscriptions for the purchase of substantially all shares offered hereby, and has accepted funds for the purchase of 24,400 of the shares offered hereby. Such subscriptions cannot be accepted except pursuant hereto. Unless subscriptions pursuant hereto are received within 90 days from the effective date of this Memorandum for at least 30,000 shares offered hereby, all subscribers' money will be returned to them without interest or deductions. In any event, any subscriber who has sent money to the Company for the purchase of the securities offered hereby prior to the receipt of this Confidential Investment Memorandum, who so requests or who fails to complete and return the subscription form attached hereto within such 90-day period will be refunded his or her subscription money in full without interest or deduction.

Certain Transactions
     Indebtedness to Affiliates
     As of February 28, 1989, the Company was indebted to certain of its officers and other related parties as follows:

Creditor	Amount Due	Date Due	Consideration
Louis J. Brown	$ 7,500	Sept. 1, 1990	Services rendered.
Harold J. Stein	$25,000	Sept. 1, 1990	Services and expenses.
Fredericks Communication	$63,562	$2,000/month commencing Oct. 1, 1989	Expenses; employees' services.
O'Connor & O'Connor	$23,000	Sept. 1, 1990	Expenses; employees' services.
Melvin I. O'Connor	$16,782	Sept. 1, 1990	Cash advanced.

All amounts due bear interest ranging from 8 percent to 12 percent per year.

Mr. Brown and Dr. Stein are consultants to the Company. The debt to Mr. Brown represents accrued consulting fees; and that to Dr. Stein represents approximately $11,000 in accrued consulting fees and approximately $14,000 advanced by him as salary to a nurse engaged to assist him in his research for the Company.

Fredericks Communication, and its subsidiaries, furnished services in fabricating parts, materials, and devices used by the Company, and also conceived, developed, and produced slide shows, display equipment, and audiovisual shows used by the Company at exhibits and medical meetings. The indebtedness to Fredericks consists of services of employees and out of pocket expenses.

---

*The remaining balance of $65,000 indebtedness to the bank is to be paid, by agreement, $5,000 per month, commencing April, 1989. The Company's original indebtedness of $365,000 to the bank was personally guaranteed by certain of the Company's directors. The proceeds of the loan were used in part to repay Company indebtedness to its directors.

Exhibit 2   *(continued)*

The indebtedness to the Company's accountants is produced by services of employees and out of pocket expenses in recordkeeping, statement and tax return preparation, and clerical services.

Melvin I. O'Connor advanced funds at various times. The liability to him represents interest on various loans ($4,282) and the remaining balance on these cash loans to the company ($12,500).

The Company intends to continue its arrangements with Mr. Brown for consulting services at a cost to the Company of $1,500 per month, plus out of pocket expenses. In addition, the Company intends to use, as required, the services of Dr. Stein and the staff accounting services of the Company's accountants at the generally applicable rates of each for such services. If the Company deems it advisable it may utilize the services or facilities of other affiliates for compensation to be negotiated in each instance. The Company has negotiated an informal arrangement with Fredericks Communication Co., Inc., whereunder the latter has constructed an office and engineering laboratory in a building owned by Fredericks Communication Co., Inc., and has leased it to the Company on a tenant- at-will basis. Such arrangement has not been formalized by any written agreement.

Fredericks Communication Co., Inc.

Fredericks Communication Co., Inc. ("Fredericks"), originally known as Fredericks Recording Co., Inc., was contracted by the Company in 1986 to supply the Company with disposable grids, then contemplated to be plastic squares with uniform ridges. Thereafter, the Company and a subsidiary of Fredericks known as Fredericks Research & Development, Inc., entered into a joint venture to procure, manufacture, or have manufactured for it the grids required by the Company on an exclusive basis. On November 17, 1988, the Company acquired by merger Fredericks Research & Development, Inc., for 10,980 shares of the Company's stock (after giving effect to the August 1988 stock split). At that time Fredericks Research & Development, Inc.'s share of expenses (excluding fixed costs, overhead, and executive salaries) for research and development on Company products was $46,466.34.

The Company has used Fredericks to procure substantially all of the molds, dies, boxes, aspirators, machinery, extruders, and other equipment required by the Company. Fredericks also provided research and development for the grids and other items in connection with the Company's business, and rendered assistance to the Company in conceiving, designing, and producing film strips, slides, and other display material used by the Company in its presentations at trade and other shows. Fredericks principals, Messrs. Smith, Green, and Marvin, in September 1987, purchased 3,960 shares of the Company's stock, after giving effect to the August 1988 stock split, for $120,000 ($30.30 per share). Messrs. Smith, Green, and Marvin loaned the Company $50,000 cash, which was repaid in July 1983, and Mr. Green, along with other Company principals, endorsed a Company Note for $165,000 to a bank in July 1988. Mr. Smith has been at various times Clerk, Assistant Clerk, and Director of the Company, and both he and Mr. Green are currently Directors.

Fredericks has charged the Company for these various services, for its actual costs of materials, services of its staff and special personnel other than executive personnel. The Company intends to continue its arrangements with Fredericks respecting procurement and the providing of other services, and to reimburse Fredericks in connection with these activities for Fredericks's expenses and services of its personnel other than executive personnel.

Capital Structure and Description of Common Stock

The capitalization of the Company as of the date of this Offering Circular, and as adjusted to give effect to the sale of the shares offered hereby, is as follows:

EXHIBIT 2   *(continued)*

	Prior to Offering	Following Offering if All Shares Sold
Notes payable—bank	$365,000	$ 65,000
Notes payable—shareholders	135,844	135,844
Accounts payable	47,506	47,506
Stock subscriptions	976,000	-0-
Capital stock	14,412	19,412
Additional paid-in capital	462,028	2,257,028

The Company's Common Stock, of $.10 par value, is its only authorized class of capital stock. At all meetings of stockholders, holders of Common Stock are entitled to one vote for each share held. The holders of Common Stock have no preemptive or subscription rights. All the outstanding shares of Common Stock are fully paid and nonassessable and are entitled to dividends if and when declared by the Board of Directors.

The Common Stock of the Company does not have cumulative voting rights. Hence, the holders of more than 50 percent of the shares voting for the election of directors may elect all the directors if they so choose. Since the present management holds more than 50 percent of the shares to be outstanding, it will be in a position to reelect itself as directors.

Dividends

Holders of shares of the Company's Common Stock are entitled to receive dividends as may be declared by the Board of Directors out of funds legally available therefore and to share pro rata in any distribution to shareholders. The Company does not contemplate the payment of any dividends in the foreseeable future.

New Financing

The Company believes that it will be necessary to secure funding in addition to that offered pursuant hereto in order to enable the Company to achieve its objectives. By letter dated March 8, 1988, the Indian U.S. International Industrial Research & Development Foundation, a foundation sponsored and funded by the governments of the United States and India, advised the Company that its Board had approved a first-year grant of up to $250,000 to be expended on research and development of the Company's products, subject to various conditions and the negotiation of a formal contract. The Company believes that conditions to this grant will include (a) establishment of a joint program with an Indian company for research, development, preproduction, and premarketing of the Company's products, (b) expenditures by the Company and its Indian partners on the program during the first year of the grant of amounts equivalent to those received from the grant during the same time. The Company cannot give assurances that a final contract for the grant will be executed, or that if it is, the Company will be able to satisfy the conditions thereof.

Remuneration

Mr. Jones was engaged as Chief Executive Officer on September 1, 1988, at a salary of $65,000 per year. Mr. Brown is paid consulting fees of $1,500 per month. None of the other officers or directors are compensated. In November 1986, O'Connor & O'Connor, of which Mr. O'Connor is a partner, were issued 900 shares of stock (after giving effect to the 12 for 1 split) in satisfaction of $7,500 of liability to them for cash advances and staff services rendered. The shares were distributed to the partners of O'Connor & O'Connor, other than Mr. O'Connor, who disclaims any benefit therefrom or control thereover. Mr. Jones has devoted full time to his duties as president of the Company since September 1, 1988, and is currently in the process of moving his residence to Illinois.

Exhibit 2   *(continued)*

Applicable Regulations

As indicated above, the products contemplated by the Company for use by doctors and by individuals require approval of the Food and Drug Administration (FDA). There is no assurance that the Company will be able to comply with the FDA regulations or that the necessary approval of the Company's operations and all the products can be achieved. To date it has only received such approval for its aspirators. The Company is in the process of compiling clinical data with respect to the balance of its products, to be supplied to the FDA as required. The Company believes that these contemplated products, however, may be utilized in animal husbandry without FDA approval and, if manufactured abroad, may be utilized outside the United States without FDA approval, although they may require approval by appropriate regulatory agencies in each country. The Company also believes that no government regulations are applicable to any of the contemplated uses in industry, inasmuch as no hazardous procedures are associated with the utilization of the Company's proposed products.

Litigation

The Company is not involved in any litigation and knows of no threatened or contingent liabilities.

The Company, at the request of any subscriber or Advisor (as defined in the Subscription Agreement), will make available for inspection copies of these documents, will provide answers to questions concerning the terms and conditions of this Offering, and will provide such additional information that is necessary to verify the accuracy of the information contained herein or that may otherwise pertain to the Company or to this investment, to the extent the Company has such information or can acquire it without unreasonable effort or expense.

Exhibit 2 *(continued)*

Financial Statements

Consolidated Balance Sheet
(Unaudited)

	February 28,		June 30,				
ASSETS	1989	1988	1987	1986	1985	1984	1983
Current assets:							
Cash	$ 21,110	$ 1,104	$ 6,437	$ 4,745	$ 1,207	$ 10,331	$ 12,514
Inventories (Notes 1 and 2)	150,023	18,359	—	—	—	—	—
Subscriptions receivable (Note 3)	131,000	—	73,413	—	—	—	3,000
Prepaid items	1,000	—	—	—	—	—	—
Total current assets	303,133	19,463	79,850	4,745	1,207	10,331	15,514
Fixed assets (Notes 1 and 4)	31,274	26,775	2,074	—	—	—	—
Other assets:							
Patents and patent applications	325,753	183,753	115,467	59,595	33,942	17,637	—
Unamortized organization and other expenses	831	673	279	171	287	403	519
	326,584	184,426	115,746	59,766	34,229	18,040	519
Total assets	$ 660,991	$ 230,664	$ 197,670	64,511	$ 35,436	$ 28,371	$ 16,033
LIABILITIES AND SHAREHOLDERS' EQUITY/(DEFICIT)							
Current liabilities:							
Medway advances (Note 5)	$ —	$ —	$ —	$ —	$ 43,850	$ 33,850	$ —
Current maturities of note payable —bank (Note 6)	50,000	—	—	—	—	—	—
Current maturities of amounts due to shareholders (Note 7)	10,000	269,000	2,500	9,000	—	16,000	16,000
Accounts payable and accruals	47,506	196,487	44,075	22,833	6,912	184	1,702
Total current liabilities	107,506	465,487	46,575	31,833	50,762	50,034	17,702
Long-term debt:							
Note payable—bank (Note 6)	15,000	—	—	—	—	—	—
Amounts due to shareholders (Note 7)	125,844	—	—	—	—	—	—
	140,844	—	—	—	—	—	—
Amounts received on stock subscriptions (Note 8)	976,000	20,000	—	—	—	—	—
Shareholders' equity/(deficit) (Note 9):							
Common stock, par value $.10 Authorized 300,000 shares Issued 144,120 shares	14,412	476,440	461,440	103,940	37,940	9,940	9,940
Additional paid-in capital	462,028	—	—	—	—	—	—
Accumulated deficit	(1,039,799)	(731,263)	(310,345)	(71,262)	(53,266)	(31,603)	(11,609)
	(563,359)	(254,823)	151,095	32,678	(15,326)	(21,663)	(1,669)
Total liabilities and shareholders equity/(deficit)	$ 660,991	$ 230,664	$ 197,670	$ 64,511	$ 35,436	$ 28,371	$ 16,033

The accompanying notes are an integral part of the consolidated financial statements.

EXHIBIT 2 *(continued)*

Consolidated Statement of Operations and Accumulated Deficit
(Unaudited)

	Feb. 28,	June 30,					
	1989	1988	1987	1986	1985	1984	1983
Sales	$ —	$ —	$ —	$ —	$ —	$ —	$ —
Expenses:							
Rent	1,888	—	—	—	—	—	—
Office and clerical expenses	11,385	10,853	17,975	6,575	27	130	—
Meetings expenses	7,741	3,266	5,305	2,959	1,340	681	118
Advertising, shows, public relations	9,482	46,355	26,524	5,499	—	—	—
Telephone	3,130	2,021	946	—	—	—	—
Taxes	2,276	1,520	948	160	114	184	114
Miscellaneous	1,086	106	142	116	116	116	58
Interest	12,385	8,750	—	—	—	—	—
Depreciation	819	—	—	—	—	—	—
Payroll and payroll expenses	33,909	—	—	—	—	—	—
Research and development (Note 11)	224,435	348,047	187,243	2,687	20,066	18,883	11,319
	308,536	420,918	239,083	17,996	21,663	19,994	11,609
Net loss	(308,536)	(420,918)	(239,083)	(17,996)	(21,663)	(19,994)	(11,609)
Accumulated deficit, beginning	(731,263)	(310,345)	(71,262)	(53,266)	(31,603)	(11,609)	—
Accumulated deficit, ending	($1,039,799)	($ 731,263)	($ 310,345)	($ 71,262)	($ 53,266)	($ 31,603)	($ 11,609)

The accompanying notes are an integral part of the consolidated financial statements.

Exhibit 2 *(continued)*

Consolidated Statement of Changes in Financial Position
(Unaudited)

	8 Mos. Ended Feb. 28, 1989	Years Ended June 30,					
		1988	1987	1986	1985	1984	1983
Resources provided:							
From operations:							
Net loss	($ 308,536)	($ 420,918)	($ 239,083)	($ 17,996)	($ 21,663)	($ 19,994)	($ 11,609)
Add items not affecting working capital:							
Depreciation and amortization	904	325	251	116	116	116	58
Working capital applied to operations	(307,632)	(420,593)	(238,832)	(17,880)	(21,547)	(19,878)	(11,551)
Amounts received on stock subscriptions	956,000	20,000	—	—	—	—	—
Proceeds of bank note	15,000	—	—	—	—	—	—
Amounts due shareholders	125,844	—	—	—	—	—	—
Capital investment	—	15,000	357,500	66,000	28,000	—	9,940
	789,212	(385,593)	118,668	48,120	6,453	(19,878)	(1,611)
Resources applied:							
Purchase of fixed assets	5,403	25,026	2,325	—	—	—	—
Other assets	158	394	108	—	—	—	577
Patents and patent applications	142,000	68,286	55,872	25,653	16,305	17,637	577
	147,561	93,706	58,305	25,653	16,305	17,637	577
Increase/(decrease) in working capital	$ 641,651	($ 479,299)	$ 60,363	$ 22,467	($ 9,852)	($ 37,515)	($ 2,188)
Changes in the components of working capital:							
Increase/(decrease) in current assets:							
Cash	$ 20,006	($ 5,333)	$ 1,692	$ 3,538	($ 9,124)	($ 2,183)	$ 12,514
Inventories	131,664	18,359					
Subscriptions receivable	131,000	(73,413)	73,413			(3,000)	3,000
Prepaid items	1,000						
	283,670	(60,387)	75,105	3,538	(9,124)	(5,183)	15,514
Increase/(decrease) in current liabilities:							
Medway advances	—	—		(43,850)	10,000	33,850	—
Current maturities of notes payable—bank	50,000						
Current maturities of amounts due to shareholders	(259,000)	266,500	(6,500)	9,000	(16,000)	—	16,000
Accounts payable and accruals	(148,981)	152,412	21,242	15,921	6,728	(1,518)	1,702
	(357,981)	418,912	14,742	(18,929)	728	32,332	17,702
Increase/(decrease) in working capital	$ 641,651	($ 479,299)	$ 60,363	$ 22,467	($ 9,852)	($ 37,515)	($ 2,188)

The accompanying notes are an integral part of the consolidated financial statements.

EXHIBIT 2   *(continued)*

NOTES TO CONSOLIDATED FINANCIAL STATEMENTS
February 28, 1989
(Unaudited)

Note 1 —Summary of Significant Accounting Policies
    Principles of Consolidation
    The consolidated financial statements include the accounts of Viscotech, Inc., and its wholly owned inactive subsidiaries, Nutrico, Inc., and Animal Technology, Inc. All intercompany balances and transactions have been eliminated in consolidation.

    The Company was organized December 29, 1982; and the subsidiaries were organized in December 1985: Nutrico, Inc., for the exploitation of the Company's concepts related to industrial viscometry and Animal Technology, Inc., for the exploitation of the Company's concepts related to animal nutrition.

Inventories
    Inventories are valued at the lower of cost (first-in, first-out basis) or market.

Fixed Assets
    Fixed assets are carried at cost and depreciated on the straight-line method over estimated useful lives as follows:

Display equipment	Five (5) years
Molds and dies	Seven (7) years
Machinery	Ten (10) years
Office equipment	Ten (10) years

Note 2 —Inventories
    Inventories consisted of the following:

	February 28, 1989	June 30, 1988
Machines completed awaiting modification	$116,500	$16,500
Machine parts	15,000	—
Aspirators—finished	8,138	500
Grids	3,961	—
Packing materials	5,799	1,121
Instruction booklets, tapes, calibrating fluids, etc.	625	238
	$150,023	$18,359

Note 3 —Stock Subscriptions
    The Company has offered its shares through the Medical Investment Fund Trust. The Company has not yet received payment for all shares subscribed.

Exhibit 2   *(continued)*

Note 4 — Fixed Assets

Fixed assets consisted of the following:

	February 28,	June 30,	
	1989	1988	1987
Display equipment	$ 2,183	$ 2,183	$2,183
Molds and dies	23,730	22,163	—
Machinery	5,367	2,758	—
Office furniture	1,141	—	—
	32,421	27,104	2,183
Less accumulated depreciation	1,147	329	109
	$31,274	$26,775	$2,074

Note 5 — Medway Advances

In fiscal years 1984 and 1985, the Company received nonrefundable advances from Medway, Inc., to finance research and patent applications. Medway, Inc., was given an exclusive marketing arrangement during this period. Medway's contract for exclusive marketing expired in December 1985.

Note 6 — Note Payable — Bank

In July 1988, the Corporation borrowed $365,000 from a bank, unsecured but guaranteed by several shareholders. Of the proceeds, $255,000 was used to repay the shareholders who had loaned that amount to the Corporation. The note, which bears interest at the bank's prime rate plus 2 percent, originally matured in January 1989. At that time, $300,000 was paid. The remaining balance is to be paid in monthly installments of $5,000, commencing in April 1989.

Note 7 — Due to Shareholders

In February 1984, several shareholders-creditors accepted term notes for amounts due them as follows:

Shareholder-Creditor	Amount	Interest	Payable	Nature of Debt
Louis Brown	$ 7,500	8%	Sept. 1, 1990	Services rendered
Harold J. Stein	25,000	Prime	Sept. 1, 1990	Research services, out of pocket expenses
Fredericks Communications	63,562	Prime	$2,000/month commencing Oct. 1, 1990	Out of pocket expenses, services of employees
O'Connor & O'Connor	23,000	8%	Sept. 1, 1990	Out of pocket expenses, services of employees
Melvin I. O'Connor	16,782	8%	Sept. 1, 1990	Cash advances
	$135,844			

Exhibit 2   (continued)

Louis Brown and Harold J. Stein had been employed as consultants at $1,500 per month each. In addition, Dr. Stein advanced the salary and expenses of a nurse employed by the Company in his office.

Fredericks Communications and its subsidiaries furnished services in fabricating parts, materials, and devices used by the Company, and also conceived, developed, and produced slide shows, display equipment, and audiovisual shows used by the Company at exhibits and medical meetings. The indebtedness to Fredericks consists of services of employees and out of pocket expenses.

The indebtedness to O'Connor & O'Connor is produced by services of employees and out of pocket expenses in recordkeeping, statement and tax return preparation, and clerical services.

Melvin I. O'Connor advanced funds at various times. The liability to him represents interest on various loans ($4,282) and the remaining balance on these cash loans to the Company ($12,500).

Note 8 — Amount Received on Stock Subscriptions

Funds have been received from subscribers to the stock of the Corporation. Issuance of the stock has been delayed pending approval of a registration under Regulation A of the Securities and Exchange Commission. The registration involves 50,000 shares of $.10 par value stock, to be issued at $40 per share. At June 30, 1988, 500 shares had been subscribed and paid for, and at February 28, 1989, a total of 24,650 shares had been subscribed.

Note 9 — Common Stock

On August 31, 1989, the Corporation voted to change its authorized capital stock from 12,500 shares of no par value to 300,000 shares of $.10 par value and to exchange 12 shares of the newly authorized stock for each share of old stock then outstanding. This exchange of shares has been given effect in the accompanying financial statements by transferring from common stock to additional paid-in capital the amounts in excess of par as of February 28, 1989.

Note 10 — Merger

On August 31, 1988, the shareholders voted to issue 915 shares of old no par stock (equivalent to 10,980 shares of new $.10 par stock) to Fredericks Research & Development Corporation in exchange for all the outstanding stock of that corporation and to merge Fredericks Research & Development Corporation into the Company. The assets acquired from Fredericks Research & Development Corporation were certain technical procedures in production and the right to limited participation with the Company in certain production profits. No value was recorded for the assets acquired from Fredericks; accordingly, common stock was credited and additional paid-in capital charged for the par value of the shares issued.

Note 11 — Operations

The Corporation has used most of its resources since its inception in research and development of its concepts for measuring the viscoelasticity of oral mucus in humans and animals and developing instruments for commercial medical application. Expenditures to date are as follows:

Fiscal year June 30, 1983	$ 11,319	
June 30, 1984	18,833	
June 30, 1985	20,066	
June 30, 1986	2,687	($43,850 defrayed by others — Note 5)
June 30, 1987	187,243	
June 30, 1988	348,047	
July 1, 1988 to February 28, 1989	224,435	
	$812,630	

EXHIBIT 2   *(continued)*

Note 12 — Taxes on Income
    The Company's net operating losses are available to offset future taxable income. Losses through 1985 may be carried forward five (5) years and subsequent losses, seven (7) years.
    For tax purposes, the Company has capitalized research and development costs, as discussed in Note 11, which costs will be written off over sixty (60) months from commencement of significant sales.

APPENDIX: ACCREDITED INVESTOR QUESTIONNAIRE

THE INFORMATION IN THIS INVESTOR QUESTIONNAIRE IS BEING SOLICITED SOLELY TO DETERMINE THE STATUS OF THE UNDERSIGNED AS AN ACCREDITED INVESTOR AND THE SUITABILITY OF THE INVESTMENT IN THE _____ STOCK FOR THE UNDERSIGNED. THIS INFORMATION WILL BE KEPT STRICTLY CONFIDENTIAL AND WILL NOT BE USED FOR ANY OTHER PURPOSE.

Investor Questionnaire

    In connection with the potential purchase by the undersigned investor (the "Investor") of shares of the _____ (the "Shares") of _____ Inc. (the "Company") contemplated by a certain Confidential Private Placement Memorandum regarding the Company dated _____, 19_____ (the "Memorandum"), the Investor hereby represents, warrants and covenants to the Company as follows:

    1. Investor Status. The Shares will only be offered for sale to persons and entities who either (i) qualify as "accredited investors" as defined in Rule 501 of Regulation D promulgated under the Securities Act of 1933, as amended, the "Act") [or (ii) are presently holders of the Company's outstanding _____ stock with participation rights entitling them to invest in the Shares.] Answer the following questions yes or no to establish your status as an "accredited investor."

  (a) The Investor, or the Investor and his or her spouse jointly, have a net worth in excess of U.S. $1,000,000. _____

  (b) The Investor's income for each of the past two years has been in excess of U.S. $200,000 (or joint income with the Investor's spouse has been in excess of U.S. $300,000) and the Investor has a reasonable expectation (alone or with his or her spouse, as the case may be) of reaching the same level of income this year. _____

  (c) The Investor is a bank as defined in Section 3(a)(2) of the Act or a savings and loan institution or other institution as defined in Section 3(a)(5)(A) of the Act whether acting in its individual or fiduciary capacity; a broker or dealer registered pursuant to Section 15 of the Securities Exchange Act of 1934; an insurance company as defined in Section 2(13) of the Act; an investment company registered under the Investment Company Act of 1940 or a business development company as defined in Section 2(a)(48) of that Act; a Small Business Investment Company licensed by the U.S. Small Business Administration under Section 301(c) or (d) of the Small Business Investment Act of 1958; a plan established and maintained by a state, its political subdivisions, or any agency or instrumentality of a state or its political subdivisions, for the benefit of its employees, if such plan has total assets in excess of $5,000,000; an employee benefit plan within the meaning of the Employee Retirement Income Security Act of 1974, if the investment decision is made by a plan fiduciary, as defined in Section 3(21) of such Act, which is either a bank, savings and loan association, insurance company, or registered investment adviser, or if the employee benefit plan has total assets in excess of $5,000,000, or, if a self-directed plan, with investment decisions made solely by persons that are accredited investors. _____

EXHIBIT 2   *(continued)*

(d) The Investor is a private business development company as defined in Section 202(a)(22) of the Investment Advisers Act of 1940. _____

(e) The Investor is an organization described in Section 501(c)(3) of the Internal Revenue Code, a corporation, a Massachusetts or similar business trust, or a partnership, not formed for the specific purpose of acquiring the Shares, with total assets in excess of $5,000,000. _____

(f) The Investor is a director or an executive officer of the Company. _____

(g) The Investor is a trust with total assets in excess of $5,000,000, not formed for the specific purpose of acquiring the Shares, whose purchase is directed by a sophisticated person as described in Rule 506(b)(2)(ii) of Regulation D. _____

(h) The Investor is an entity in which all of the equity owners are accredited investors. _____

2. <u>Investor Suitability.</u>   In addition to the requirement of Investor Status, Shares will only be offered for sale to qualified investors with respect to whom the Company has determined that their proposed investment in the Shares is suitable. All potential investors must answer the following questions yes or no to establish their suitability as an investor.

(a) The Investor has adequate means of providing for his or her current needs and personal contingencies, has no need for liquidity in connection with this investment and can afford the loss of his or her entire investment in the Shares. _____

(b) The Investor's overall commitment to investments which are not readily marketable is not disproportionate to the net worth of the Investor, and the Investor's investment in the Shares will not cause such overall commitment to become excessive. _____

(c) The Investor has evaluated the risks of investing in the Shares, has recognized that the Investor could sustain a total loss of the investment, and has determined that the Shares are a suitable investment for the Investor. _____

(d) Name of current business, business address and telephone number:

_____

Type of current business: _____
If applicable, position held in current business, responsibilities involved in position and number of years employed in position:_____

(e) Please provide either (i) the name of your accountant, attorney, broker or other person familiar with your finances who may be contacted to verify the financial information contained in Section 1 of this Investor Questionnaire or (ii) complete the financial information requested on Exhibit A attached hereto:

Name: _____ Relationship: _____

(f) Do any significant contingent liabilities exist for which you may be obligated?
Yes _____ No _____ If yes, please indicate type and amount: _____

(g) Are you involved in any significant litigation which, if determined adversely, would have a material adverse effect on your financial condition? Yes _____ No _____ If yes, please provide details. _____

(h) Please indicate the number and total dollar amount of investments you have made within the last three years in illiquid securities issued by start-up companies, such as the Shares.

Number _____   **Total Dollar Amount** _____

EXHIBIT 2   *(concluded)*

3. General.

(a) The Investor acknowledges that the Company will rely on the Investor's representations contained herein as a basis for the exemption from registration.

(b) The Investor received the Memorandum and first learned of this investment in the jurisdiction of his or her business or residential address set forth on the signature page hereto, and intends that the securities laws of only that jurisdiction shall govern this transaction.

(c) The Investor, if a resident of a foreign jurisdiction, has considered the effect of the securities laws of such jurisdiction on his or her potential purchase of the Shares and such laws do not in any way prohibit, otherwise conflict with, or impose any substantive or procedural limitations on, such potential purchase.

(d) The Investor, either alone or with his or her purchaser representative, has such knowledge and experience in financial and business matters as to be capable of evaluating the merits and risks of the prospective investment in the Shares.

EXHIBIT A

Please provide the following information as of the most recent practicable date, indicating such date below:

Month _____ Day _____ Year _____

ASSETS

Liquid Assets	
(cash, money market funds, publicly-traded stocks and bonds)	$_____
Illiquid Securities	
(non-publicly traded securities, such as the Shares)	$_____
Other Assets	
(real estate, personal property and other assets)	$_____
Total Assets	$_____

LIABILITIES

Current Liabilities	
(liabilities coming due within one year)	$_____
Long-Term Liabilities	
(liabilities coming due in more than one year)	$_____
Total Liabilities	$_____

NET WORTH

Total Assets—Total Liabilities	$_____

2–4 HEATHER EVANS

It was May 10, 1983, and Heather Evans's graduation from Harvard Business School was less than a month away. Although she had just taken the last of her final exams that morning, Heather's thoughts could not have been further from school as she boarded the Eastern Shuttle and headed back to New York. The trip was a familiar one, for Heather had been commuting between school and Manhattan in an attempt to get her dress company off the ground.

Many of the elements of the business were falling into place, but the securing of $250,000 in financing remained elusive. Her business plan had been in the hands of potential investors for over a month now, and her financing group was simply not coming together. Her contact at Arden & Co., a New York investment firm and hoped-for lead investor, was not even returning her phone calls. A number of small, private investors had been stringing along for some weeks, but whenever Heather tried to go that next step and negotiate specific financing terms with any one of them, the rest of the group seemed to move further away. Heather expressed her frustration:

> I was really counting on Arden & Co. to be my lead investor; this would lend both credibility to the deal and give me *one* party to negotiate terms with. Then I could go to these private investors, point to the deal I'd struck with Arden and say, "These are the terms—make a decision."
>
> Now, if I give each of these investors what they want, I'll end up giving the company away. But I do need the money, and fast. In order to get out a holiday (winter) line, I need to start placing orders for fabric in the next month. All this, in addition to the rent and salaries I'm committed to.
>
> I don't know whether I should stick with the private investors I have and somehow try to hammer out a deal; or really work on getting a venture firm as a lead investor—maybe there is still a chance of bringing Arden & Co. around. Maybe I should try to get less money, or move back my timetable and wait for spring to introduce a line.

Heather Evans

Heather Evans graduated from Harvard College in 1979, having earned her bachelor's degree in philosophy in three years. A Phi Beta Kappa graduate, Heather had been a working model throughout her college career, appearing in such publications as *Mademoiselle, Seventeen,* and *GQ.* (See **Exhibit 1**.)

Heather applied to the Harvard Business School during her senior year and was accepted with a two-year deferred admit to the class entering in 1981. She accepted a

This case was prepared by Michael J. Roberts under the direction of Howard H. Stevenson.
Copyright © 1983 by the President and Fellows of Harvard College
Harvard Business School Case 9–384–079

position with Morgan Stanley as a financial analyst. Heather explained the origin of her interest in a business career:

> My father is an attorney with a Wall Street firm, and many of my parents' friends were "deal-makers" who had gone to the Business School. I thought that I would like that kind of work and the lifestyle that went along with it. In addition, my career as a model gave me a taste of running my own business—the independence, the travel, the people—and I loved it. I knew, though, that I would need a good solid background to gain the skills and credibility necessary for success.
>
> I thought that working for an investment bank like Morgan Stanley would give me the technical and financial training that I would need during my career.

Heather left Morgan Stanley and began her two years at HBS with her basic orientation unchanged:

> I was still focused primarily on a deal-making, venture-capital type of career. I had always been interested in the fashion business and thought that I might, at some point, financially back a designer. I decided to work on Seventh Avenue for the summer and got a job as the assistant to Jackie Hayman, president of a woman's clothing company.

Heather saw the business and financial side of the business as well as the design and marketing aspects:

> I was convinced and confident that I could run a business like this. That summer was actually the first time I believed that business school education had much value at all. I was able to understand the business very well, and my education and experience allowed me to grasp the fundamental issues quickly.

Heather returned to HBS in September, committed to starting her own venture in the garment industry.

The Evolution of Heather Evans Incorporated

Heather began by defining the concept of the company and its product line. Based on her experience in investment banking and at business school, Heather was convinced that the current mode of business dress for women—primarily suits—was, in fact, ill-suited to the demands and desires of businesswomen. Heather conceived a line of dresses in natural and wear-worthy fabrics that would better meet these women's needs (see business plan for full description).

In September, she began working with Robert Vin, an assistant designer in New York, in an attempt to transfer her concepts to finished design sketches and patterns. By November, it was clear to Heather that this arrangement was not going to work out; she decided that she would be both the chief designer and operating manager of her firm. Although it was an extremely untraditional approach to a start-up in the garment business, Heather reasoned that it would make more sense for her:

> First, I didn't get along that well with Robert on a personal level. More important, though, I found myself doubting both his design sense and my own ability to judge someone else's design sense. Fundamentally, I had more trust in myself and my abilities as a designer.

Thus was Heather Evans Incorporated born.

Heather spent November and December flying between Boston and New York and developing, in further detail, her concept of the business. By December, Heather had put together a plan of action, which she submitted for approval as a field study (see **Exhibit 2**). After her first-semester exams ended, Heather moved to New York. She scheduled all of her classes on Monday and Tuesday and planned to spend the rest of her time in New York getting the key elements of her business in place.

Staff.   Heather decided that the first person she needed was an assistant designer. "I wanted someone who had the technical training and experience in design that I lacked. I needed someone who knew more about design than I did, but who didn't mind working for me as an assistant."

Heather interviewed several individuals and in early February offered the position to Belinda Hughes, who had served as an assistant designer with two major firms. Heather began paying Belinda (out of her own pocket) to do free-lance work based on detailed discussions with Heather about the content of the line, with the promise that full-time employment would begin in April or May.

Heather also began looking for a pattern-maker: someone who could transform a sample dress into specifications and a design for production.

Heather asked several industry acquaintances, and a vice president at Marjori (a major fashion manufacturer) recommended Barbara Tarpe. Heather called Barbara and the two hit it off. During their meeting, Barbara indicated that she would like an equity position in the company. Heather thought that Barbara could make a significant contribution and that her request was reasonable. Heather genuinely liked Barbara and thought that she would make a good partner.

One week later, before proceeding further, Heather decided to call another friend in the industry who might know Barbara.

> Martin is an old friend, and I trust his judgment; he told me that Barbara was a terrible liar and had no real talent. I looked back at my original notes after our meeting: "Very good rapport with Barbara. She seems *HONEST*. Feel she can run entire inside of business." I didn't hire Barbara and was shocked at how wrong I could be about someone. I had always felt comfortable trusting my own judgment.

Office and Showroom Space.   Heather spent countless afternoons scouring New York's garment district (around Seventh Avenue from 42nd to 34th Streets) for potential showroom, office, and working space. Showroom space is very important, because store buyers visit here during the buying season to make their decisions.

> I decided that I needed about 1,500 square feet of space for an office, sample and pattern-making space, and a showroom. For $7 or $8 per square foot, I could get space in buildings which were somewhat off the main center of the district and which housed other relatively "unknown" designers. For $20–$25 per foot, I could be in a building that was more centrally located and that housed better-known firms.

By late February, Heather had decided to lease 1,500 square feet of space in a building at $10 per foot, for $1,500 per month.

Although the building was in a less desirable location and would get less traffic from buyers than more expensive buildings, Heather reasoned that she should attempt to conserve as much cash as possible. Heather sent a deposit on this space and would begin paying rent May 1.

A month later, an acquaintance in the garment business called and offered Heather space in 550 Seventh Avenue—the most prestigious building in the garment center, housing such designers as Ralph Lauren, Oscar de la Renta, and many other famous names. Heather would have her own office space and would share the showroom space with another designer (who sold a line of clothing that would not compete directly with Heather's). Heather accepted his offer on the spot, even though she would have to start paying rent as of March 15, and the rent was $2,000, substantially more than the other building, and there was less space.

Financing. In the fall, Heather had begun talking informally with potential investors—friends at school and former colleagues in the investment banking and garment industry. She was hesitant, however, to do more than this until she had a business plan and a proposed deal.

Then in February, a friend and recent Business School graduate called to suggest that the two get together for a drink.

> Anne Snelling and I had both worked for Morgan Stanley and then gone on to the Business School. She had graduated one year earlier than I and gone to work for Arden & Co. (a private investment bank). I assumed that our meeting would be social, but Anne was soon putting on the hard-sell for Arden, convincing me that they should do the whole deal. I was quite surprised and pleased. Arden had an excellent reputation, and their financing would be a "stamp of approval" on the deal.

Heather and Anne met once or twice during January and February, and Anne asked Heather to accompany her to Vail for a week of skiing over spring break the first week in March. Heather reasoned that it would be a wise move to go.

> I didn't really feel comfortable taking off for a week—I had an incredible amount to do. Yet I was anxious for Arden's participation, so off to Vail I went. I was unsure whether Anne intended our week to be business or pleasure, but I brought along all of my papers and was prepared to negotiate a deal.
>
> Once we got there, Anne said she wanted to talk about the deal, but was constantly on the phone pursuing other business. I came back to New York feeling pretty discouraged; we had never had a chance to really discuss my business.

Heather called Anne that next week and voiced her concern: time was running out, and Heather still had no clear idea where Arden or Anne stood on the issue.

> Anne suggested that we get together for dinner that evening and tie things up—I was relieved. But when I walked into the restaurant, Anne was sitting there with her sister, Susan, and Susan's fiance. She apologized — they had just flown into the city, and Anne had asked them to join us. I was livid.

At this point, Heather realized that the financing was not going to come as easily as she had hoped, and she began pushing some of her other potential investors to get a sense of their interest. She raced to finish the business plan (see **Exhibit 3**) and sent this out to Arden & Co. and 15 individual investors during the first week in April.

Down to the Wire

During the month of April, the pace of Heather's efforts accelerated and the business began eating up more cash. Belinda's part-time salary was now running about $1,000 per month; rent was running $2,000 per month. Finally, Heather had begun shopping the fabric market and would soon have to order and pay for $3,000 worth of sample fabric.

Heather had already invested about $10,000 of her own funds in the business, and her remaining resources were dwindling quickly. Because of the timing of the cycles in the garment industry (see **Exhibit 4**) Heather would have a great many more expenses before any cash came back into the business; most significantly, she would have to pay for the fabric for the entire holiday line—about $40,000 worth.

Yet Heather was having a difficult time bringing the investor group together. Anne Snelling was not returning her phone calls, and the private investors were interested, but had made no firm commitments. Heather's major problem was trying to negotiate with all of these potential investors individually; without a lead investor, there was no one party to negotiate the terms of a deal with.

The process of raising funds was hampered by Heather's extremely busy schedule. Besides talking to retailers, working on designs, and getting settled in her new office space, Heather was still going to school during this time, and exams were coming up. Heather commented on the strain:

> The spring semester was a rough one; trying to get my company started really took its toll. I had always considered myself a responsible student. I prepared about a half-dozen cases the entire semester and only made it to half my classes. I felt bad about it, but I knew I had to do it to get my business going.

Financing Options

Heather had several options available, but knew that she did not have sufficient time to pursue them all.

Arden & Co.   Heather held out some hope that Arden was still interested in the deal. Perhaps if she really pushed for a commitment, Arden would come through.

Venture Capital Firms.   Heather had spoken with one or two firms that had indicated some interest. She knew that starting fresh with people who were unfamiliar with the company, as well as dealing with the bureaucratic decision-making process, would take a great deal of time. In addition, Heather suspected that they might drive a harder bargain than private investors, but at this point she welcomed the opportunity to negotiate with anyone just to get an idea of what valuation to put on the company.

Helen Neil Fashions, Inc.   Heather had approached another small venture capital firm that had Helen Neil Fashions, Inc., in its portfolio of companies. Helen Neil herself was a proven designer, and the company had established a base of relationships with manufacturers and retailers. The company, however, lacked any real operating management. This venture firm had indicated an interest in financing Heather if she would ally herself with Helen Neil and essentially embark on a joint venture. This idea had not yet been broached with Helen Neil, however, and Heather knew that any deal was dependent on the approval of Helen and her company's management.

Private Investors.   Heather had a pool of 20 or so private individuals who seemed interested in investing in the company. The problem here was the amount of time it took to negotiate with each of these people individually, and their diverse desires for the terms of the investment. Heather was unsure how to structure the deal to satisfy the divergent interests of these individuals whom she was fairly sure would invest under any reasonable set of terms. She had spoken to a small sample of these investors (see **Exhibit 5**) to get their point of view, but was hesitant to speak to any more investors before she could present them with a deal.

Heather's Requirements

Heather had given some thought to the different aspects of the deal and had decided that the following terms were important to her:

- Control of the company: Heather felt that she should be able to control over 50 percent of the equity, as well as have a majority of the voting control of the company.
- License of the name *Heather Evans:* Heather felt that she had already expended considerable effort in building up her own name, and that if she left the company, she should have the right to use it.
- Ability to remain private: Heather did not want to be in a position where her investors could force her to become a public company. Liz Claiborne, a successful women's clothing company, had recently gone public, and potential investors were naturally excited by the returns inherent in a public offering. (See **Exhibit 6** for excerpts from the Liz Claiborne prospectus.) Heather knew that she had to offer her investors some means of exit and getting a return on their investment.

With exams finally over, Heather could concentrate her full energies on pulling together her financial backing and getting the business off the ground.

EXHIBIT 1   Heather Evans Modeling One of Her Designs

EXHIBIT 2   **Field Study Plan**

The purpose of this project is to develop a business plan and a strategy for approaching investors for a women's designer clothing manufacturing company, which I will form upon graduation from HBS. This company will offer high price, high quality dress and jacket combinations to executive women, ages 27 to 45.

The business plan will include:

I. A marketing plan, including an analysis of the relevant market, how I will position my product (in terms of price and image), and a retailing and promotion strategy.
II. A description of the organization, including people and physical plant.
III. Pro forma financial statements, based on sales projections from I, and operating costs from II.
IV. A financing proposal.

The attached time schedule outlines the process of putting together this plan. You will note that I have allotted substantial time to drafting and redrafting the plan, relative to research. This is because I have already spent a lot of time gathering information and find that I now need to organize that information in order to see what is missing. I will, however, spend the first half of January meeting with department store buyers to refine my retailing strategy, which I recognize is weak.

The final product for my Independent Research Report (IRR) will be the business plan actually presented to investors and a broader strategic document describing how the plan fits into my investor strategy.

Field Study Project Schedule Week of:

December 13, 1982	• Settle issue of advisor for IRR.
	• Gather examples of business plans.
December 20	• Complete survey of existing market research and financial information on comparable companies. (Sources: Fairchild Publications' library; 10-Ks ordered from companies.)
December 27	• Vacation.
January 3, 1983	• Prepare preliminary outline of plan.
	• Review outline with advisor.
	• Set up meetings with buyers from Filene's, Nieman's, Macy's, Bergdorf, Saks, Bloomingdales, Nordstrom, and others.
January 10 and 17	• Prepare first draft of plan Parts I and II.
	• Meet with buyers.
January 24 and 31	• Talk with various industry contacts to fill information "holes," especially regarding Part II of plan (e.g., salary levels for various employees, equipment needs and costs, and optimal showroom and design studio locations).
February 7	• Prepare second draft of plan, including detailed pro formas (Part III).
	• Begin interviewing candidates for design assistant, sales/PR director, and business manager positions. (These individuals should be named in the plan.)
February 14	• Review second draft with advisor.
	• Present plan to CPA for review.
	• Prepare list of potential investors and consider order of approach.
	• Select law firm.

EXHIBIT 2   *(concluded)*

February 21 and 28	• Select and recruit key employees. • Revise plan, Parts I–III. • Present revised plan to lawyer. • Explore financial structure alternatives with lawyer, advisor, and others.
March 7	• Draft Part IV of plan. • Determine preferred investor group profile and strategy for approaching investors. • Select factor and discuss terms, to the extent appropriate at that point.
March 14, 21, 28	• Vacation.
April 4 and 11	• Meet informally with key investors. • Finalize plan.
April 18	• Distribute plan to potential investors.

EXHIBIT 3   **Heather Evans Incorporated Business Plan, April 7, 1983** *(Confidential)*

TABLE OF CONTENTS

HEATHER EVANS INCORPORATED BUSINESS PLAN
I. SUMMARY

COMPANY	HEATHER EVANS INCORPORATED, incorporated in New York on March 9, 1983, and located in New York City.
BUSINESS	The Company will design, contract for the manufacture of, and market a line of clothing for professional women.
MANAGEMENT	*Heather H. Evans, President and Designer* Ms. Evans will graduate from Harvard Business School in June 1983. She has worked as assistant to the president of Catherine Hipp, a designer clothing firm; as a financial analyst at Morgan Stanley, an investment bank; and as a photographic model, with Ford Models.
	Belinda Hughes, Assistant Designer Most recently, Ms. Hughes was head designer at Creations by Aria. For two years before that, after her graduation from Parsons School of Design, she worked as Mr. Kasper's assistant at Kasper for J.L. Sports.
CONCEPT	The Company will offer a "designer" line to fit the lifestyle of professional women. Based on her experience in investment banking and at business school, Ms. Evans has conceived a style of clothing, based primarily on dresses, which better fits the lifestyle and demands of businesswomen than the suits and other looks currently offered to them by existing clothing manufacturers.

EXHIBIT 3   *(continued)*

STATUS

The Company has already begun designing its holiday line, obtained show-room and studio space in a prestigious designer building, reserved production capacity in a high-quality factory, and arranged for credit with an apparel industry factor.

In order to present its first line for the Holiday 1983 season, the Company must be assured financing prior to May 1983. The Company is seeking $250,000, to cover start-up expenses, to fund development of its first line, and to provide initial working capital. Thereafter, the Company anticipates that it will generate sufficient cash from operations, which, together with normal industry factoring, will fund growth internally.

Legal Counsel: Kaye, Scholer, Fierman, Hays & Handler
Accountants: Rashba & Pokart
Bank: Citibank

II. CONCEPT

HEATHER EVANS INCORPORATED aims to become a substantial apparel company. Its success formula is a combination of powerful elements:

- a new look,
- for an unmet and quickly growing market,
- promoted and sold by a unique individual, Heather H. Evans,
- within a professionally managed and controlled organization.

Ms. Evans recognized the need for a *new look* for professional women when she shopped for clothes to wear to her job at an investment bank. She found few clothes that fit the functional demands of her work, while having some "style." Since then, she has spoken with hundreds of professional women who voice the same complaint. They work in an environment that strictly defines what is considered appropriate; "Seventh Avenue" does not understand these women.

The HEATHER EVANS "look" will be based on dresses, worn with untailored or softly tailored jackets, with:

- A clean and elegant silhouette.
- Distinctiveness through cut and line, without frills, excessive detail, or sexual suggestiveness.
- Undistracting colors, in solids or subtle patterns (e.g., Glen plaid or pinstripe).
- Comfortable fit.
- Travel-worthy fabrics in all-natural fibers, such as silk-wool blends.
- Quality construction.

Dresses and jackets will be priced and sold separately, along with coordinated skirts and tops, as a *complete* line:

- To permit the customer to coordinate an entire workplace wardrobe from the line.
- To position the line in "sportswear" departments of department stores, which are more updated and better displayed than "dress" departments.
- To avoid resistance to the high price tag of a combined outfit, from a customer who usually buys sportswear pieces.

Each collection will include 30 to 70 pieces, depending on the season, which is comparable to other complete designer sportswear lines. The Company will sell five collections: for the holiday, early spring, spring, transition, and fall seasons. These are the regular "sportswear" market periods.

Unlike most designer collections, which include many kinds of clothes for different activities and different times of day, the HEATHER EVANS collection will include only clothes appropriate for the conservative workplace. This focus is critical in establishing the confidence of upper-strata

---

EXHIBIT 3   *(continued)*

---

professional women in the "look" for officewear. Later, the Company can introduce other lines (e.g., leisurewear) under the HEATHER EVANS name, in order to benefit from its reputation and customer franchise.

HEATHER EVANS clothes will be sold through better department and specialty stores. The line will be marketed as "designer" clothing, but will be priced at the upper end of the "bridge" category, which is the next lower price category. The bridge category was born and grew dramatically with such lines as Liz Claiborne and Evan Picone, which targeted the flood of women into the workplace over the past decade; HEATHER EVANS will capitalize on the second stage of this demographic trend, as women become accepted in large numbers in better-paid, professional and managerial roles. Positioning the line at the top of the bridge category:

- Will place the line in stores next to other lines currently bought by the target customer (e.g., Tahari, Harve Bernard, Nipon Collectibles).
- Responds to growing price resistance among customers, *but*
- Permits the Company to create a quality garment.
- Develops the HEATHER EVANS label for future licensing potential.

Heather H. Evans:

Ms. Evans is uniquely qualified to develop and sell a new style of clothing for conservative businesswomen. As a former investment banker and a graduate of Harvard Business School,

- She has lived the lifestyle of these women, and knows their needs.
- She understands the limits of appropriateness within a formal office environment, which Seventh Avenue designers, who have tried to capture this customer, clearly do not.
- She can gain the confidence of the target customer through identification of her own background with their own lives.

Moreover, as a former model, Ms. Evans has experience at projecting herself through the media and can attract publicity as a designer/personality. She will actively seek to publicize the Company in business media, as well as fashion media, to reach the target customer. She is currently working on stories about the Company with writers from *Vogue* and *Savvy*. (Ms. Evans's résumé is included as Appendix A.)

III. MARKET

HEATHER EVANS will initially position its products as designer clothing for the "formal" professional woman to wear to the office. Later, the Company can serve a virtually unlimited number of markets based on its reputation for quality and taste, as established through its original line of clothing.

PROFESSIONAL WOMEN'S CLOTHING

Target Market:

HEATHER EVANS will target the upper end of a subsegment of the working women's clothing market, identified as "formal professional" women in a 1980 market study by Celanese.

These women are an extremely attractive market because they are:

- a large, fast-growing group,
- with high disposable incomes,
- who are concentrated in metropolitan areas,
- where they buy at a select group of better department and specialty stores,
- with relative insensitivity to price,
- attention to quality,
- apparel brand loyalty,
- and *still-developing tastes and preferences in professional clothing.*

EXHIBIT 3   (continued)

Celanese found the formal professional segment to be a well-defined purchasing group: it "includes accountants, lawyers, sales managers, executives, and administrators who work in highly structured and formal environments. They can be characterized by a strict dress code and overriding concern with presenting a professional image. Members of this group wish to convey occupational status at work and in nonwork activities and can be considered investment dressers."

- 4.3 million women fall within this group.
- They spend $5 billion per year on clothes.
- They represent the fastest growing segment of the working women's clothing market, with real growth forecast at 8–10 percent per year.

HEATHER EVANS will target the upper end of this group, whose concerns about quality and appropriateness are highest, commensurate with their level of income and responsibility.

The following statistics suggest that the upper end of the market is growing even faster than the formal professional market as a whole:

- In 1980, 793,000 women made over $25,000 per year.
- 147,000 women made over *$50,000* per year, up *22 percent* from the previous year.

Thus, HEATHER EVANS will target the new ranks of established executive and professional women. Whereas Liz Claiborne and others capitalized on the initial entry of women into the work force in the 70s, HEATHER EVANS will capitalize on their acceptance in positions of responsibility in the 80s.

Style Trends:

Formal professional women are a ripe market for a well-conceived new clothing label because their tastes and habits in officewear are evolving, but they have few options among existing clothes.

Women in the upper end of the market, HEATHER EVANS's target, are still wearing mostly classic or modified tailored suits, with a blouse and neck ornament. The lower end shows movement toward softer looks and, particularly, dresses. Ms. Evans believes that this trend toward more varied looks will also be seen in the upper end of the market. However, the existing untailored bridge lines, dress lines, and designer sportswear lines are inappropriately styled for that segment.

Manufacturers have recently seen the demand for suits flatten, as interest in dresses has renewed. Responding to this trend, Liz Claiborne and Albert Nipon both opened dress divisions aimed at executive women, priced in the "better" range. The president of Liz Claiborne Dresses voiced the expectations of many in the industry when she told *Women's Wear Daily* that, unlike the 70s when working women wore mostly tailored sportswear for fear of standing out, "in the 80s I think they're going to be a lot more adventuresome in what they wear." As evidence, the dress division of Liz Claiborne hit around $10 million in wholesale sales in less than a year, approximately 10 percent of the entire company's sales.

These examples illustrate the receptivity of the working women's market to new styles and designers. However, the offerings of these companies and others are inappropriate for the more conservative elements. HEATHER EVANS intends to fill this gap.

Competition:

The "designer" fashion market is a relatively easy one to enter, because

- *Competition is fragmented.* For example, although there are no comprehensive trade statistics available, it is worth noting that Liz Claiborne, which is one of the two largest companies in the market, can claim less than 3 percent of the market, with $155 million in latest 12 months sales.

- *Channels welcome new products.* Department store buyers are responsible for identifying and promoting new, promising lines, so that customers perceive the buyer's store as a fashion leader. In particular, major department store chains are seeking new lines in the bridge price range, in which HEATHER EVANS will position its products. They foresee this price category becoming increasingly important.

Retailers are encountering consumer price resistance, which suggests that the designer-priced sportswear market has matured: the continual "trading-up" by customers in the 70s has ended. In response, manufacturers are generally lowering prices, both within existing lines and by introducing new lines in lower price categories. Many designer companies will target the bridge market, where customers are value-conscious, but have disposable income. The Company anticipates that the opportunities created by renewed interest in this area will favor the Company's strategy and outweigh the threat of other new entrants and competition.

DESIGNER PRODUCTS MARKET

Once it has established a franchise in the expensive businesswear market, HEATHER EVANS can expand into any of several immediately related markets:

- Accessories (e.g., belts, shoes, scarves) in a similar price category to coordinate with the original clothing line.
- Leisure clothing in the same price range for the same customer as the original line.
- Lower-priced office-wear for a different, wider customer group (i.e., the rest of the 4.3 million formal professional women).

Finally, numerous tertiary markets exist for a well-managed designer name. For example, Bill Blass has licensed his name for chocolates, while Ralph Lauren has licensed his for a full line of home furnishings.

In the past, these designers have developed their names in the couture or designer sportswear levels; however, the extraordinary success of Norma Kamali, whose clothes retail for $30 to $100, demonstrates that a "designer" name can be made in any price range.

Thus, the Company can serve a virtually unlimited number of markets based on its reputation for taste and quality, as established through its original line of clothing. In Calvin Klein's case, his name is used on products with combined retail sales of $1 billion.

Licensing:

Designers profit enormously from licensing agreements, through which they attach their names to products in return for a 5—10 percent royalty. These products are manufactured and marketed—and often designed—by the licensee. For example,

- Pierre Cardin reaps over $50 million a year in royalties on $1 billion of wholesale sales on 540 licenses, with minimal related expenses.
- The top 10 designers collect over $200 million in royalties between them each year.

Long-Run View:

The designer label has replaced the better department store label as the arbiter of taste and quality for the American consumer. After some designers (most notably Cardin) licensed their names indiscriminately in the name-craze of the mid-70s, consumers became more evaluative about the value of a given designer's name, but they continue to purchase according to that name.

This shift has been disastrous for department stores, which have lost their business to discounters, which carry the same designer names for less with comparable service, and to specialty stores, which offer superior service at comparable prices. Although this shake-up in the retail industry will have repercussions for designers, it is unlikely to reverse a now well-entrenched phenomenon.

Exhibit 3   *(continued)*

IV. MANAGEMENT AND OPERATIONS

ORGANIZATION AND PEOPLE
Design:

The design group is the core of the Company: it creates five new product lines each year, on which the eventual success of the Company will depend. It is important to recognize that sales of the line will depend as much on existing specifications of fit, construction, fabrics, and coordination of pieces within the line as on the design sketches themselves; these are all parts of the design function.

The design process for each line takes approximately nine months, so that several lines are being worked on in various stages at any time. For each line, the design function is to—

- Plan the line; determine the number of styles, colors, and fabric groups, on the basis of overall line balance, ranges of buyer climates and tastes, and other marketing factors.
- Define the theme and tone of the line.
- Choose and order specific fabrics and other supplies, after surveying the market for these products.
- Create and select sketches.
- Cut, drape, and sew samples. Perfect fit of samples.
- Select final samples for the collection.
- Prepare patterns for production and communicate with normal industry contract manufacturers.

Ms. Evans will spend 40 percent of her time on design and production functions. She will oversee the entire process, with emphasis on *planning* and defining the theme of each line, and *selecting* fabrics, sketches, and final samples.

Ms. Hughes and Ms. Evans will work as a team on all design-related tasks. Ms. Hughes has significant expertise in the creative and technical aspects of fashion design. She is experienced in creating specific styles from a general concept for a line. Her vocabulary of stylistic detail, production feasibility, and textile characteristics complement Ms. Evans's market-driven design direction. (Ms. Hughes's background is described in Appendix B.)

Ms. Hughes has already been retained by Ms. Evans on a free-lance basis and is designing a Holiday line. It is expected that Ms. Hughes will join the company on a full-time basis shortly after funding is received.

The Company plans to hire a design assistant in June. The design assistant will make sample patterns, cut the samples, and oversee the sample makers. She will work with an outside pattern maker on production patterns and with the factory to assure that the final product meets the specifications of the sample garments.

The Company plans to hire one sample maker in June and another in September 1983.

Production:

The production function manages the process from the sample through the shipment of the final garment to the stores. The concerns of the production staff are quality, timely delivery, and cost. During the first two years, Ms. Evans and the design assistant will oversee production as part of their design responsibilities.

Following normal industry practice, the Company will subcontract all manufacturing, including the grading and marketing of its patterns, cutting of its piece goods, and sewing of its garments, to independent suppliers. Initially, all its suppliers will be located in New York City and other locations in the northeastern United States. There is capacity available in suitable shops in this area, where management can carefully monitor the quality and timing of production. As production volume increases, the Company may consider manufacturing in Hong Kong, Taiwan, or elsewhere, where manufacturing costs for quality workmanship may be lower.

Malcolm Wong, a contractor located at 226 West 37th Street, has agreed to reserve time to produce production patterns and sew the Company's entire first collection. Mr. Wong's factory is a high-quality, nonunion shop, with 20 operators. Ms. Evans may use other contractors for all or part of the line, if these contractors offer a more favorable price.

The Company has arranged for its shipping to be done through Fernando Sanchez, as part of its rental arrangement with that firm (see Facilities and Equipment). Fernando Sanchez will provide space, shipping personnel, and shipping supplies. After July 1984, the Company expects to add one shipping employee of its own.

Sales and Promotion:

Sales are made during "market weeks," which last approximately three weeks for each of the five seasons, spread through the year. Store buyers write orders based on the sample line, which they view in the Company's showroom or in one of several regional marketplaces. The Company plans to join the New York Fashion Council, Inc., and has tentatively arranged through this group to reserve space in the key regional market shows.

Ms. Evans will spend 40 percent of her time in sales and promotion.

Initially, Ms. Evans will handle all department store sales and some specialty store sales, in the showroom and in "trunk shows" to the Dallas and L.A. markets. Ms. Evans's personal attention is important in this stage to communicate the philosophy of the line, to use her Harvard Business School contacts in department store managements, and to save money.

The Company plans to retain an established, independent representative to sell the line to specialty stores in the Northeast (except New York City). Ms. Evans is currently negotiating with a well-known representative for several designer lines, with whom she has worked previously. The representative will show the line to his customers in the Company's showroom.

Once critical customer relationships have become established and sales volume warrants, Ms. Evans will hire full-time, experienced showroom personnel and, possibly, retain additional independent sales representatives. Ms. Evans will then direct her efforts to more promotional activities and to managing the sales personnel.

Ms. Evans will also carry out an active campaign of nonsales promotion. She will communicate with customer fashion directors, concerning use of samples in cooperative advertising and scheduling personal in-store appearances, and with newspaper and magazine editors to encourage editorial coverage. She will also oversee production of promotional materials to announce the opening of each collection.

Control:

Financial and production control will occupy 20 percent of Ms. Evans's time. These functions are critical to, but often neglected in, apparel manufacturing companies. In particular, fabric purchasing and production decisions must be made so as to maximize sales, yet minimize inventory at the end of the season when it becomes obsolete. Ms. Evans's experience in financial analysis and her business school training are valuable assets in the control function.

The Company plans to hire a part-time bookkeeper during its first months of operation. In July 1984 or thereafter, the Company will retain a full-time office manager.

FACILITIES AND EQUIPMENT

The Company has arranged for showroom and design studio space in the 550 Seventh Avenue building. This is one of the most prestigious buildings in the garment district, with such other tenants as Bill Blass, Halston, Ralph Lauren, and Oscar de la Renta.

HEATHER EVANS's showroom will be within the showroom of Fernando Sanchez, a new and successful high-priced, designer line. Ms. Evans feels that the exposure of the HEATHER EVANS line alongside the Sanchez line and within the 550 Seventh Avenue building will be very beneficial for the

Exhibit 3   *(continued)*

Company. The Company's line does not compete with the Sanchez line and will often be bought by different buyers from a given store.

The Company's design studio and office space will be adjacent to the Fernando Sanchez show-room, with its own entrance. The Company will be provided with shipping space at another location, 226 West 37 Street, as part of its arrangement with Fernando Sanchez. These facilities should be adequate for the first two years of operation.

V. FINANCIALS

The Company anticipates raising $250,000 in equity capital. This level of capitalization is adequate, together with normal industry factoring, to develop and to grow a substantial apparel company, without additional equity financing. This is a business plan and is not intended, of itself, to be an offering of stock or debt.

Industry Financial Characteristics:

High fashion apparel manufacturing offers high returns on capital within a short time frame to those companies whose clothing becomes "*fashion.*"

- Margins run 40 to 60 percent.
- Operating costs after cost of goods sold and sales commissions (approximately 10 percent of sales) are relatively fixed. Basically, the cost of designing a line is the same at $1 million in sales as at $20 million.
- Investment in working capital is low: with 60-day terms from fabric suppliers and receivables factoring, cash received from shipment of finished goods can be applied to the cost of those same goods.
- Investment in fixed assets is limited to equipping and remodeling showroom, studio, and shipping space. All manufacturing is subcontracted.
- After an initial introductory period of one to two years, acceptance of a line may proceed extremely rapidly, with annual sales growth rates of 100 to 500 percent not unusual.

Whether a line does become "fashion" and to what extent depends on a number of variables that cannot be tested or foreseen until the clothing is presented to the fashion press and the consumers. These variables include the appeal of the specific styles and fit of the line, general fashion trends and specific competitive styles offered at the time the line is presented, and media interest in the line. Thus, investors are rewarded for putting at risk the cost of developing, producing, and marketing a line of clothing during an initial introductory period.

Sales Projections:

The Company has prepared sales projections for the first two years of operation, as presented in Exhibit I. These projections are based on typical order sizes for new lines in the Company's price range and reasonable rates of trial by stores, taking into account supplier credit limits.

For reasons mentioned above, having to do with the nature of fashion, the Company cannot meaningfully forecast sales growth beyond the introductory period.

Financial Statements:

Projected financial statements for the company's first and second years of operation are included as Exhibits II and III, respectively. These forecast net income of $167,173 on sales of $1,712,500 in the second year.

A detailed list of assumptions for the forecasted financial statements is included as Exhibit IV. These estimates were developed by Ms. Evans, based on the experience of comparable companies, and discussed in detail with Rashba & Pokart, certified public accountants, who have extensive experience with apparel industry clients.

EXHIBIT 3 (continued)

HEATHER EVANS INCORPORATED

EXHIBIT I

Sales Projections

	Season	Market Period	Shipping Period	Specialty Store			Department Store			
				Number of Orders	Avg. Order Size ($000)	Sales Volume ($000)	Number of Orders	Avg. Order Size ($000)	Sales Volume ($000)	Total ($000)
Year 1	Holiday	August	October–November	38	$2	$75	9	$8	$75	$150
	Early spring	September	December–January	50	1	50	12	4	50	100
	Spring	October	February–April	50	3	150	12	12	150	300
	Transition	February	May–June	58	1	57.5	14	4	57.5	165
	Total									$715
Year 2	Fall	March	July–September	62	3.5	217.5	15	14	217.5	435
	Holiday	August	October–November	60	2	120	15	8	120	240
	Early spring	September	December–January	75	1	75	19	4	75	150
	Spring	October	February–April	94	4	375	23	16	375	750
	Transition	February	May–June	80	1	80	20	4	80	160
	Total									$1,735

Exhibit 3 (continued)

HEATHER EVANS INCORPORATED

EXHIBIT II

Projected Statement of Income
Year Ended May 31, 1984

	TOTAL	JUNE	JULY	AUG.	SEPT.	OCT.	NOV.	DEC.	JAN.	FEB.	MAR.	APRIL	MAY
TOTAL SALES	607,500	0	0	0	0	75,000	75,000	50,000	50,000	100,000	100,000	100,000	57,500
LESS: DISCOUNTS	48,600	0	0	0	0	6,000	6,000	4,000	4,000	8,000	8,000	8,000	4,600
NET SALES	558,900	0	0	0	0	69,000	69,000	46,000	46,000	92,000	92,000	92,000	52,900
COST OF GOODS SOLD													
INVENTORY—BEGINNING	0				24,375	61,875	53,750	41,250	57,500	82,500	82,500	68,688	48,750
PIECE GOODS & TRIMMINGS	257,438	0	0	24,375	24,375	16,250	16,250	32,500	32,500	32,500	18,688	20,000	40,000
CONTRACTING COSTS	116,313	0	0	0	13,125	13,125	8,750	8,750	17,500	17,500	17,500	10,063	10,000
TOTAL	373,750	0	0	24,375	61,875	91,250	78,750	82,500	107,500	132,500	118,688	98,750	98,750
LESS: INVENTORY—ENDING	70,000	0	0	24,375	61,875	53,750	41,250	57,500	82,500	82,500	68,688	48,750	70,000
COST OF GOODS SOLD	303,750	0	0	0	0	37,500	37,500	25,000	25,000	50,000	50,000	50,000	28,750
GROSS PROFIT	255,150	0	0	0	0	31,500	31,500	21,000	21,000	42,000	42,000	42,000	24,150
OPERATING EXPENSES:													
PRODUCTION	149,100	11,300	11,300	11,300	12,800	12,800	12,800	12,800	12,800	12,800	12,800	12,800	12,800
SELLING AND SHIPPING	53,513	1,000	1,000	1,700	1,000	8,825	5,125	3,750	3,750	6,500	10,200	6,500	4,163
GENERAL AND ADMINISTRATIVE	120,369	9,727	9,727	9,727	10,132	10,132	10,132	10,132	10,132	10,132	10,132	10,132	10,132
FACTOR'S CHARGES	24,300	0	0	0	0	3,000	3,000	2,000	2,000	4,000	4,000	4,000	2,300
TOTAL OPERATING EXPENSES	347,282	22,027	22,027	22,727	23,932	34,757	31,057	28,682	28,682	33,432	37,132	33,432	29,395
NET INCOME (–LOSS)	–92,132	–22,027	–22,027	–22,727	–23,932	–3,257	443	–7,682	–7,682	8,568	4,868	8,568	–5,245

SEE ACCOMPANYING SUMMARY OF SIGNIFICANT PROJECTION ASSUMPTIONS AND SUMMARY OF SIGNIFICANT ACCOUNTING POLICIES.

PRELIMINARY DRAFT
For discussion purposes only; all exhibits are tentative and subject to change.

341

Exhibit 3 (continued)

HEATHER EVANS INCORPORATED

EXHIBIT II

Projected Schedule of Operating Expenses
Year Ended May 31, 1984

	TOTAL	JUNE	JULY	AUG.	SEPT.	OCT.	NOV.	DEC.	JAN.	FEB.	MAR.	APRIL	MAY
PRODUCTION EXPENSES:													
DESIGNER'S SALARY	30,000	2,500	2,500	2,500	2,500	2,500	2,500	2,500	2,500	2,500	2,500	2,500	2,500
ASSISTANT DESIGNER AND SAMPLEHAND'S SALARIES	55,500	3,500	3,500	3,500	5,000	5,000	5,000	5,000	5,000	5,000	5,000	5,000	5,000
PATTERN MAKER SALARY	39,600	3,300	3,300	3,300	3,300	3,300	3,300	3,300	3,300	3,300	3,300	3,300	3,300
DESIGN ROOM SUPPLIES	24,000	2,000	2,000	2,000	2,000	2,000	2,000	2,000	2,000	2,000	2,000	2,000	2,000
TOTAL	149,100	11,300	11,300	11,300	12,800	12,800	12,800	12,800	12,800	12,800	12,800	12,800	12,800
SELLING AND SHIPPING:													
SALESMEN'S COMMISSIONS	30,375	0	0	0	0	3,750	3,750	2,500	2,500	5,000	5,000	5,000	2,875
TRAVEL AND ENTERTAINMENT	20,100	1,000	1,000	1,700	1,000	4,700	1,000	1,000	1,000	1,000	4,700	1,000	1,000
FREIGHT OUT	3,038	0	0	0	0	375	375	250	250	500	500	500	288
TOTAL	53,513	1,000	1,000	1,700	1,000	8,825	5,125	3,750	3,750	6,500	10,200	6,500	4,163
GENERAL AND ADMINISTRATIVE:													
RENT	24,000	2,000	2,000	2,000	2,000	2,000	2,000	2,000	2,000	2,000	2,000	2,000	2,000
OFFICE SALARY	9,600	800	800	800	800	800	800	800	800	800	800	800	800
TELEPHONE	8,400	700	700	700	700	700	700	700	700	700	700	700	700
STATIONERY AND OFFICE	12,000	1,000	1,000	1,000	1,000	1,000	1,000	1,000	1,000	1,000	1,000	1,000	1,000
LEGAL AND AUDIT	12,000	1,000	1,000	1,000	1,000	1,000	1,000	1,000	1,000	1,000	1,000	1,000	1,000
DUES AND SUBSCRIPTIONS	3,600	300	300	300	300	300	300	300	300	300	300	300	300
DEPRECIATION AND AMORTIZATION	2,700	225	225	225	225	225	225	225	225	225	225	225	225
INSURANCE	7,200	600	600	600	600	600	600	600	600	600	600	600	600
BUSINESS AND PAYROLL TAXES	13,470	1,010	1,010	1,010	1,160	1,160	1,160	1,160	1,160	1,160	1,160	1,160	1,160
UTILITIES	4,500	375	375	375	375	375	375	375	375	375	375	375	375
EMPLOYEE BENEFITS	22,899	1,717	1,717	1,717	1,972	1,972	1,972	1,972	1,972	1,972	1,972	1,972	1,972
TOTAL	120,369	9,727	9,727	9,727	10,132	10,132	10,132	10,132	10,132	10,132	10,132	10,132	10,132

SEE ACCOMPANYING SUMMARY OF SIGNIFICANT PROJECTION ASSUMPTIONS AND SUMMARY OF SIGNIFICANT ACCOUNTING POLICIES.

PRELIMINARY DRAFT
For discussion purposes only; all exhibits are tentative and subject to change.

Exhibit 3 *(continued)*

HEATHER EVANS INCORPORATED

EXHIBIT II

Forecasted Balance Sheets
June 1983 through May 1984

ASSETS	JUNE	JULY	AUG.	SEPT.	OCT.	NOV.	DEC.	JAN.	FEB.	MAR.	APRIL	MAY
CURRENT ASSETS:												
CASH AND DUE FROM FACTOR	203,398	181,596	159,094	122,262	119,230	124,273	116,816	100,609	109,402	114,495	130,726	125,769
MERCHANDISE INVENTORIES	0	0	24,375	61,875	53,750	41,250	57,500	82,500	82,500	68,688	48,750	70,000
TOTAL CURRENT ASSETS	203,398	181,596	183,469	184,137	172,980	165,523	174,316	183,109	191,902	183,183	179,476	195,769
FIXED ASSETS—NET	17,775	17,550	17,325	17,100	16,875	16,650	16,425	16,200	15,975	15,750	15,525	15,300
OTHER ASSETS	6,800	6,800	6,800	6,800	6,800	6,800	6,800	6,800	6,800	6,800	6,800	6,800
TOTAL ASSETS	227,973	205,946	207,594	208,037	196,655	188,973	197,541	206,109	214,677	205,733	201,801	217,869
STOCKHOLDERS' EQUITY												
CURRENT LIABILITIES:												
ACCOUNTS PAYABLE	0	0	24,375	48,750	40,625	32,500	48,750	65,000	65,000	51,188	38,688	60,000
STOCKHOLDERS' EQUITY	227,973	205,946	183,219	159,287	156,030	156,473	148,791	141,109	149,677	154,545	163,113	157,869
TOTAL LIABILITIES AND STOCKHOLDERS' EQUITY	227,973	205,946	207,594	208,037	196,655	188,973	197,541	206,109	214,677	205,733	201,801	217,869

SEE ACCOMPANYING SUMMARY OF SIGNIFICANT PROJECTION ASSUMPTIONS AND SUMMARY OF SIGNIFICANT ACCOUNTING POLICIES.

PRELIMINARY DRAFT

For discussion purposes only; all exhibits are tentative and subject to change.

EXHIBIT 3 (continued)

HEATHER EVANS INCORPORATED

EXHIBIT II

Projected Statements of Cash Flow
Year Ended May 31, 1984

	TOTAL	JUNE	JULY	AUG.	SEPT.	OCT.	NOV.	DEC.	JAN.	FEB.	MAR.	APRIL	MAY
CASH AND DUE FROM FACTOR—BEGINNING	0	0	203,398	181,596	159,094	122,262	119,230	124,273	116,816	100,609	109,402	114,495	130,726
RECEIPTS:													
INITIAL CAPITALIZATION	250,000	250,000											
NET SALES	558,900	0	0	0	0	69,000	69,000	43,000	46,000	92,000	92,000	92,000	52,900
TOTAL	808,900	250,000	203,398	181,596	159,094	191,262	188,230	170,273	162,816	192,609	201,402	206,495	183,626
CASH DISBURSEMENTS:													
ACCOUNTS PAYABLE—PIECE GOODS & TRIMMINGS	197,438	0	0	0	0	24,375	24,375	16,250	16,250	32,500	32,500	32,500	18,688
CONTRACTORS PAYABLE	116,313	0	0	0	13,125	13,125	8,750	8,750	17,500	17,500	17,500	10,063	10,000
OPERATING EXPENSES—NET	344,582	21,802	21,802	22,502	23,707	34,532	30,832	28,457	28,457	33,207	36,907	33,207	29,170
SECURITY DEPOSITS	6,800	6,800											
PURCHASE OF FIXED ASSETS	18,000	18,000											
TOTAL	683,132	46,602	21,802	22,502	36,832	72,032	63,957	53,457	62,207	83,207	86,907	75,770	57,857
CASH AND DUE FROM FACTOR—ENDING	125,769	203,398	181,596	159,904	122,262	119,230	124,273	116,816	100,609	109,402	114,495	130,726	125,769

SEE ACCOMPANYING SUMMARY OF SIGNIFICANT PROJECTION ASSUMPTIONS AND SUMMARY OF SIGNIFICANT ACCOUNTING POLICIES.

PRELIMINARY DRAFT
For discussion purposes only; all exhibits are tentative and subject to change.

EXHIBIT 3   *(continued)*

HEATHER EVANS INCORPORATED

EXHIBIT III

Projected Statement of Income
Year Ended May 31, 1985

	TOTAL	JUNE	JULY	AUG.	SEPT.	OCT.	NOV.	DEC.	JAN.	FEB.	MAR.	APRIL	MAY
TOTAL SALES	1,171,250	57,500	145,000	145,000	145,000	120,000	120,000	75,000	75,000	250,000	250,000	250,000	80,000
LESS: DISCOUNTS	137,000	4,600	11,600	11,600	11,600	9,600	9,600	6,000	6,000	20,000	20,000	20,000	6,400
NET SALES	1,575,500	52,900	133,400	133,400	133,400	110,400	110,400	69,000	69,000	230,000	230,000	230,000	73,600
COST OF GOODS SOLD:													
INVENTORY—BEGINNING	70,000	70,000	113,750	113,750	105,625	93,125	78,500	56,000	112,875	200,375	200,375	145,125	81,250
PIECE GOODS & TRIMMINGS	585,000	47,125	47,125	39,000	39,000	24,375	24,375	81,250	81,250	81,250	26,000	47,125	47,125
CONTRACTING COSTS	299,625	25,375	25,375	25,375	21,000	21,000	13,125	13,125	43,750	43,750	43,750	14,000	10,000
TOTAL	954,625	142,500	186,250	178,125	165,625	138,500	116,000	150,375	237,875	325,375	270,125	206,250	138,375
LESS: INVENTORY—ENDING	98,375	113,750	113,750	105,625	93,125	78,500	56,000	112,875	200,375	200,375	145,125	81,250	98,375
COST OF GOODS SOLD	856,250	28,750	72,500	72,500	72,500	60,000	60,000	37,500	37,500	125,000	125,000	125,000	40,000
GROSS PROFIT	719,250	24,150	60,900	60,900	60,900	50,400	50,400	31,500	31,500	105,000	105,000	105,000	33,600
OPERATING EXPENSES:													
PRODUCTION	153,600	12,800	12,800	12,800	12,800	12,800	12,800	12,800	12,800	12,800	12,800	12,800	12,800
SELLING AND SHIPPING	114,288	4,163	8,975	9,675	8,975	11,300	7,600	5,125	5,125	14,750	18,450	14,750	5,400
GENERAL AND ADMINISTRATIVE	149,524	10,132	12,672	12,672	12,672	12,672	12,672	12,672	12,672	12,672	12,672	12,672	12,672
FACTOR'S CHARGES	63,020	2,116	5,336	5,336	5,336	4,416	4,416	2,760	2,760	9,200	9,200	9,200	2,944
TOTAL OPERATING EXPENSES	480,432	29,211	39,783	40,483	39,783	41,188	37,488	33,357	33,357	49,422	53,122	49,422	33,816
INCOME BEFORE PROVISION FOR INCOME TAXES	238,819	–5,061	21,117	20,417	21,117	9,212	12,912	–1,857	–1,857	55,578	51,878	55,578	–216
PROVISION FOR INCOME TAXES	71,646	–1,518	6,335	6,125	6,335	2,764	3,874	–557	–557	16,673	15,563	16,673	–65
NET INCOME (—LOSS)	167,163	–3,542	14,782	14,292	14,782	6,448	9,038	–1,300	–1,300	38,905	36,315	38,905	–151

SEE ACCOMPANYING SUMMARY OF SIGNIFICANT PROJECTION ASSUMPTIONS AND SUMMARY OF SIGNIFICANT ACCOUNTING POLICIES.

PRELIMINARY DRAFT
For discussion purposes only; all exhibits are tentative and subject to change.

345

EXHIBIT 3 (continued)

HEATHER EVANS INCORPORATED

EXHIBIT III

Projected Schedule of Operating Expenses
Year Ended May 31, 1985

	TOTAL	JUNE	JULY	AUG.	SEPT.	OCT.	NOV.	DEC.	JAN.	FEB.	MAR.	APRIL	MAY
PRODUCTION EXPENSES:													
DESIGNER'S SALARY	30,000	2,500	2,500	2,500	2,500	2,500	2,500	2,500	2,500	2,500	2,500	2,500	2,500
ASSISTANT DESIGNER AND SAMPLEHAND'S SALARIES	60,000	5,000	5,000	5,000	5,000	5,000	5,000	5,000	5,000	5,000	5,000	5,000	5,000
PATTERN MAKER SALARY	39,600	3,300	3,300	3,300	3,300	3,300	3,300	3,300	3,300	3,300	3,300	3,300	3,300
DESIGN ROOM SUPPLIES	24,000	2,000	2,000	2,000	2,000	2,000	2,000	2,000	2,000	2,000	2,000	2,000	2,000
TOTAL	153,600	12,800	12,800	12,800	12,800	12,800	12,800	12,800	12,800	12,800	12,800	12,800	12,800
SELLING AND SHIPPING:													
SALESMEN'S COMMISSIONS	85,625	2,875	7,250	7,250	7,250	6,000	6,000	3,750	3,750	12,500	12,500	12,500	4,000
TRAVEL AND ENTERTAINMENT	20,100	1,000	1,000	1,700	1,000	4,700	1,000	1,000	1,000	1,000	4,700	1,000	1,000
FREIGHT OUT	8,563	288	725	725	725	600	600	375	375	1,250	1,250	1,250	400
TOTAL	114,288	4,163	8,975	9,675	8,975	11,300	7,600	5,125	5,125	14,750	18,450	14,750	5,400
GENERAL AND ADMINISTRATIVE:													
RENT	24,000	2,000	2,000	2,000	2,000	2,000	2,000	2,000	2,000	2,000	2,000	2,000	2,000
OFFICE SALARY	31,600	800	2,800	2,800	2,800	2,800	2,800	2,800	2,800	2,800	2,800	2,800	2,800
TELEPHONE	8,400	700	700	700	700	700	700	700	700	700	700	700	700
STATIONERY AND OFFICE	12,000	1,000	1,000	1,000	1,000	1,000	1,000	1,000	1,000	1,000	1,000	1,000	1,000
LEGAL AND AUDIT	12,000	1,000	1,000	1,000	1,000	1,000	1,000	1,000	1,000	1,000	1,000	1,000	1,000
DUES AND SUBSCRIPTIONS	3,600	300	300	300	300	300	300	300	300	300	300	300	300
DEPRECIATION AND AMORTIZATION	2,700	225	225	225	225	225	225	225	225	225	225	225	225
INSURANCE	7,200	600	600	600	600	600	600	600	600	600	600	600	600
BUSINESS AND PAYROLL TAXES	16,120	1,160	1,360	1,360	1,360	1,360	1,360	1,360	1,360	1,360	1,360	1,360	1,360
UTILITIES	4,500	375	375	375	375	375	375	375	375	375	375	375	375
EMPLOYEE BENEFITS	27,404	1,972	2,312	2,312	2,312	2,312	2,312	2,312	2,312	2,312	2,312	2,312	2,312
TOTAL	149,524	10,132	12,672	12,672	12,672	12,672	12,672	12,672	12,672	12,672	12,672	12,672	12,672

SEE ACCOMPANYING SUMMARY OF SIGNIFICANT PROJECTION ASSUMPTIONS AND SUMMARY OF SIGNIFICANT ACCOUNTING POLICIES.

PRELIMINARY DRAFT
For discussion purposes only; all exhibits are tentative and subject to change.

Exhibit 3 *(continued)*

HEATHER EVANS INCORPORATED EXHIBIT III

Forecasted Balance Sheets
June 1984 through May 1985

	1984							1985				
ASSETS	JUNE	JULY	AUG.	SEPT.	OCT.	NOV.	DEC.	JAN.	FEB.	MAR.	APRIL	MAY
CURRENT ASSETS:												
CASH AND DUE FROM FACTOR	104,309	132,776	153,418	179,135	188,572	209,584	207,952	175,695	231,498	283,601	369,154	373,163
MERCHANDISE INVENTORIES	113,750	113,750	105,625	93,125	78,500	56,000	112,875	200,375	200,375	145,125	81,250	98,375
TOTAL CURRENT ASSETS	218,059	246,526	259,043	272,260	267,072	265,584	320,827	376,070	431,873	428,726	450,404	471,538
FIXED ASSETS—NET	15,075	14,850	14,625	14,400	14,175	13,950	13,725	13,500	13,275	13,050	12,825	12,600
OTHER ASSETS	6,800	6,800	6,800	6,800	6,800	6,800	6,800	6,800	6,800	6,800	6,800	6,800
TOTAL ASSETS	239,934	268,176	280,468	293,460	288,047	286,334	341,352	396,370	451,948	448,576	470,029	490,938
LIABILITIES AND STOCKHOLDERS' EQUITY												
CURRENT LIABILITIES:												
ACCOUNTS PAYABLE	87,125	94,250	86,125	78,000	63,375	48,750	105,625	162,500	162,500	107,250	73,125	94,250
INCOME TAXES PAYABLE	−1,518	4,817	10,942	17,277	20,041	23,914	23,357	22,800	39,474	53,037	71,710	71,646
TOTAL CURRENT LIABILITIES	85,607	99,067	97,067	95,277	83,416	72,664	128,982	185,300	201,974	162,287	144,835	165,896
STOCKHOLDERS' EQUITY	154,327	169,109	183,400	198,182	204,631	213,669	212,369	211,069	249,974	286,289	325,193	325,042
TOTAL LIABILITIES AND STOCKHOLDERS' EQUITY	239,934	268,176	280,468	293,460	288,047	286,334	341,352	396,370	451,948	448,576	470,029	490,938

SEE ACCOMPANYING SUMMARY OF SIGNIFICANT PROJECTION ASSUMPTIONS AND SUMMARY OF SIGNIFICANT ACCOUNTING POLICIES.

PRELIMINARY DRAFT
For discussion purposes only; all exhibits are tentative and subject to change.

347

Exhibit 3 *(continued)*

HEATHER EVANS INCORPORATED   EXHIBIT III

Projected Statements of Cash Flow
Year Ended May 31, 1985

	TOTAL	JUNE	JULY	AUG.	SEPT.	OCT.	NOV.	DEC.	JAN.	FEB.	MAR.	APRIL	MAY
CASH AND DUE FROM FACTOR—BEGINNING		125,769	104,309	132,776	153,418	179,135	188,572	209,584	207,952	175,695	231,498	283,601	369,154
RECEIPTS:													
NET SALES	1,575,500	52,900	133,400	133,400	133,400	110,400	110,400	69,000	69,000	230,000	230,000	230,000	73,600
TOTAL	1,701,269	178,669	237,709	266,176	286,818	289,535	298,972	278,584	276,952	405,695	461,498	513,601	442,754
CASH DISBURSEMENTS:													
ACCOUNTS PAYABLE—PIECE GOODS & TRIMMINGS	550,750	20,000	40,000	47,125	47,125	39,000	39,000	24,375	24,375	81,250	81,250	81,250	26,000
CONTRACTORS PAYABLE	299,625	25,375	25,375	25,375	21,000	21,000	13,125	13,125	43,750	43,750	43,750	14,000	10,000
OPERATING EXPENSES—NET	477,732	28,986	39,558	40,258	39,558	40,963	37,263	33,132	33,132	49,197	52,897	49,197	33,591
TOTAL	1,328,107	74,361	104,933	112,758	107,683	100,963	89,388	70,632	101,257	174,197	177,897	144,447	69,591
CASH AND DUE FROM FACTOR—ENDING	373,163	104,309	132,776	153,418	179,135	188,572	209,584	207,952	175,695	231,498	283,601	369,154	373,163

SEE ACCOMPANYING SUMMARY OF SIGNIFICANT PROJECTION ASSUMPTIONS AND SUMMARY OF SIGNIFICANT ACCOUNTING POLICIES.

PRELIMINARY DRAFT
For discussion purposes only; all exhibits are tentative and subject to change.

EXHIBIT 3   *(continued)*

EXHIBIT IV

Assumptions for Pro Forma Financial Statements

Income Statement
1. Sales: See Exhibit I, Sales Projections
2. Discount: 8 percent (assume discount taken on all sales)
3. Cost of goods sold:
   - Inventory—see Balance Sheet below
   - Piece goods and trimmings—65 percent of COGS
   - Contracting costs—35 percent of COGS
4. Gross profit: 50 percent of gross sales (42 percent of net sales)
5. Operating expenses—see below
6. Factor's charge—4 percent net of sales (actual charges will be commission equal to a fixed percentage of sales plus interest charge for advances against uncollected receivables)

Operating Expenses
1. Production expenses:
   - Salaries
     Designer—$2,500 per month, starting June 1983
     Assistant designer—$2,000 per month, starting June 1983
     Samplehands—$1,000 each per month, starting June 1983, another starting September 1983
     Pattern maker—$3,300 per month, starting June 1983
2. Selling and shipping:
   - Salesmen's commission—10 percent on all specialty store sales, based on standard independent representative commission rate
   - Travel and entertainment—
     General travel and entertainment—$1,000 per month
     Announcements—$700 each holiday, spring, and fall market period
     Trunk shows—$3,000 each spring and fall market period
   - Freight out—0.5 percent of sales
3. General and administrative:
   - Rent—$2,000 per month
   - Office salary—
     Part-time bookkeeper—2 days per week, at $100 per day, starting June 1983
     Office manager—$2,000 per month
   - Telephone—$700 per month
   - Stationery and office—$1,000 per month
   - Legal and audit—$1,000 per month
   - Dues and subscriptions—$300 per month
   - Depreciation and amortization—$225 per month, based on $18,000 investment in equipment, furniture, and lease improvements, depreciated on a straight-line basis over an average life of 7 years.
   - Insurance—$600 per month
   - Business and payroll taxes—10 percent of full-time payroll
   - Employee benefits—18 percent of full-time payroll

EXHIBIT 3   *(continued)*

EXHIBIT IV

<u>Assumptions for Pro Forma Financial Statements</u>

<u>Balance Sheets</u>
1. Cash and due from factor—includes 100 percent of invoices for goods shipped in each month
2. Merchandise inventories—includes piece goods and trim received 60 days in advance of sale; finished goods shipped within month
3. Fixed assets—net—depreciated straight-line over 7-year average life, from $18,000 base, as follows:

Sample room equipment	$ 7,000
Office and showroom furnishing	6,000
Remodeling	5,000
	$18,000

4. Other assets—includes lease deposit of $6,000 (3 months) and telephone deposit of $800
5. Accounts payable—includes piece goods and trimming payable within 60 days; contractors paid within 30 days; all other expenses assumed paid within month
6. Stockholders' equity—$250,000 initial capital

Exhibit 3   *(continued)*

APPENDIXES

Résumé of
HEATHER H. EVANS

Education

1981–1983
HARVARD GRADUATE SCHOOL OF BUSINESS ADMINISTRATION
Candidate for the degree of Master of Business Administration in June 1983. Awarded First Year Honors (top 15 percent of class).
Resident Business Tutor, South House, Harvard College: supervised pre-business program and oversaw student activities in residential unit of 350 undergraduate students. Instructor, Economics Department, Harvard College: designed and taught full-credit undergraduate course in managerial economics and decision analysis.

1976–1979
HARVARD COLLEGE
Bachelor of Arts degree, *cum laude*. Philosophy major. Phi Beta Kappa. Dean's list all semesters. Completed undergraduate course requirements in three years.

Publisher and Executive Committee member, *The Harvard Advocate* magazine. Vice Chairman, South House Committee.

Work Experience

Summer 1982
JACKIE HAYMAN, INC.
Assistant to President. Aided president of young firm that manufactures designer clothing under Catherine Hipp label. Involved in all areas of business, including sales, public relations, working capital management, credit, design, production, and shipping.

1979–1981
MORGAN STANLEY & CO. INCORPORATED
Financial Analyst.

Mergers and Acquisitions: Identified possible acquisition targets, recommended prices for those companies, and formulated strategies to locate buyers. Analyzed financial and market data to determine the target's long-range earning potential and the effect of the acquisition on the buyer.

Corporate Finance: Supervised preparation of debt financings for 10 clients. Negotiated terms of security documents and coordinated the activities of teams inside and outside Morgan Stanley.

1975–1979
FASHION MODEL
Managed own career as a fashion model. Represented by Ford Models, Inc., New York, N.Y.; The Model's Group, Boston, Mass.; and L'Agence Pauline, Paris, France. Credits include: *Mademoiselle, Seventeen, GQ, LeMonde, Boston,* and *The Boston Globe.*

Summer 1978
RESOURCE PLANNING ASSOCIATES
Research Associate. Planned and executed study that led RPA to add antitrust economic support work to its services. Worked on projects in oil price forecasting and U.S. mineral reliance.

Personal Background

Attended The Spence School, New York, N.Y., and Lycée Montaigne, Paris, France. Speaks fluent French and conversational Greek.

EXHIBIT 3   *(concluded)*

Background of
Belinda Hughes

Belinda Hughes received her Bachelor of Fine Arts Degree in fashion design from Parsons School of Design in May 1981. After graduation, she worked as Assistant Designer to Kasper at Kasper for J. L. Sports. She designed pants, blouses, and jackets for the Kasper line and prepared sketches and maintained records of fabrication and styles for the company's Japanese licensee. In May 1982, Ms. Hughes became head designer for Creations by Aria, a moderate-price dress house. She covered layout of the dressy dress line, from selection of fabrics to preparation of dresses, and oversaw the sample room staff. Recently, Ms. Hughes has been working as a free-lance designer for several lines, including Choo-Chee, Elan Shoe Corp., Roslyn Harte, and College Town, for which she has designed collections ranging from shoes to loungewear.

Ms. Hughes's design talent has been recognized by many academic and industry awards, including: Recognition in Design Citation from Levis (1979), scholarship award from St. John's University (1979), scholarship award from the Switzer Foundation (1980), ILGWU Design Merit Award (1980), ILGWU Design Creativity Award (1981).

Eхнвіт 4 Timing of Cycles in the Garment Industry

	March	April	May	June	July	August	September	October
Holiday line	Order sample fabrics	Sketch and design line		Make samples and order production quantities of fabric		Market weeks—take orders	Contract out cutting and sewing	Deliver garments to stores
Early spring line					Early spring line cycle begins			
Spring line					Spring cycle begins			
Transition line							Transition line begins	
Fall line	Fall line finishes up							

353

EXHIBIT 5   Heather Evans's Notes on Preliminary Discussions with Potential Private Investors

---

1. <u>David Ellis</u>, attorney, family friend (excerpt from April 28, 1983, letter):

From an investor's point of view, one would expect at least a 50 percent equity share, and probably substantially more although in nonvoting stock. The investors' stock would be convertible into voting (and indeed, control) stock in case certain minimum standards of solvency and cash flow and performance weren't met. Additional stock would be made available to management if certain performance goals were exceeded. Thus management might start with 25 percent, plus an option on a second 25 percent if the company proves to be a world-beater.

That of course may sound too complicated; but if it's to be an arm's-length <u>minimally</u> attractive proposal, I think you have to offer investors at least 50 percent or 60 percent, albeit in nonvoting shares.

If it were a proposal such as that, I would be thinking in terms of a $20,000 or $25,000 participation for myself (i.e., an investment).

But if you can get 70 percent for yourself, with only 30 percent to investors—<u>take it!</u> If that's the way it goes, I would want to make a gesture of support and encouragement—thus a $5,000 unit.

2. <u>Paul Hood</u>, classmate, HBS:
   - Says he is interested in investing for three reasons:
     —Heather Evans: trusts intelligence, dedication, design sense, and business judgment.
     —Concept: gut feel that there is a market need, has spoken with women in business about idea.
     —Upside: mentioned Liz Claiborne deal.
   - Key needs in a deal:
     —<u>No</u> limit to upside via forced call on equity.
     —Wants company to own "Heather Evans" name rather than licensing; if Heather Evans can walk after business established, this limits upside.
   - Willing to invest $25,000 to $40,000.

3. <u>Herbert Greene</u>, president, Greene Textiles:
   - I felt that Greene was a good contact with potential fabric, textile suppliers.
   - Name (especially if on board) adds credibility on Seventh Avenue/Garment Business.
   - Was in on Liz Claiborne deal, made *very* big dollars.
   - Wants in deal terms:
     —Right to force registration/issue in public market in five to seven years.
     —Low limit on my salary with incentive compensation.
     —Investors get board control until minimum performance criteria met.
   - Willing to invest $35,000–$55,000.

4. <u>John Merrill</u>, old friend, HBS classmate:
   - Wants company to own name: says if company does very well, main value created will be in name, company should own this.
   - Liquidation protection (i.e., if company goes bust, investors get what's left before I get anything).
   - Three- to five-year employment contract with three-year noncompete clause at termination of employment contract.
   - Right to sell equity, pro rata, on same terms as Heather Evans in any offering.

liz claiborne, inc.
Common Stock
(Par Value $1 Per Share)

Of the shares of Common Stock offered hereby, 345,000 shares are being sold by the Company and 805,000 shares are being sold by certain stockholders. The Company will not receive any proceeds from the sale of shares by the Selling Stockholders. See "Principal and Selling Stockholders."

Prior to this offering there has been no public market for the Company's Common Stock. See "Underwriting" for information relating to the method of determining the initial public offering price.

**THESE SECURITIES HAVE NOT BEEN APPROVED OR DISAPPROVED BY THE
SECURITIES AND EXCHANGE COMMISSION NOR HAS THE COMMISSION
PASSED UPON THE ACCURACY OR ADEQUACY OF THIS PROSPECTUS.
ANY REPRESENTATION TO THE CONTRARY IS A CRIMINAL OFFENSE.**

	Price to Public	Underwriting Discounts (1)	Proceeds to the Company (2)	Proceeds to the Selling Stockholders (2) (3)
Per Share	$19.00	$1.28	$17.72	$17.72
Total	$21,850,000	$1,472,000	$6,113,400	$14,264,600

(1) See "Underwriting" for a description of indemnification and insurance arrangements among the Underwriters, the Company and the Selling Stockholders.

(2) Before deducting expenses estimated at $356,201 payable by the Company and $168,369 payable by the Selling Stockholders.

(3) The Selling Stockholders have granted the Underwriters an option to purchase up to an additional 115,000 shares to cover over-allotments. If all such shares are purchased, the total Price to Public, Underwriting Discounts and Proceeds to the Selling Stockholders will be increased by $2,185,000, $147,200 and $2,037,800, respectively.

The Common Stock is being offered subject to prior sale, when, as and if delivered to and accepted by the several Underwriters and subject to approval of certain legal matters by counsel and to certain other conditions. It is expected that certificates for the shares of Common Stock offered hereby will be available on or about June 16, 1981. The Underwriters reserve the right to withdraw, cancel or modify such offer and to reject orders in whole or in part.

Merrill Lynch White Weld Capital Markets Group
Merrill Lynch, Pierce, Fenner & Smith Incorporated

June 9, 1981

EXHIBIT 6   *(continued)*

PROSPECTUS SUMMARY

The following information is qualified in its entirety by reference to the detailed information and financial statements (including the Notes thereto) appearing elsewhere in the Prospectus.

Liz Claiborne, Inc.

Liz Claiborne, Inc. (the "Company") designs, contracts for the manufacture of and markets an extensive range of women's clothing under the LIZ CLAIBORNE and LIZ trademarks. Since the Company's founding in 1976, it has concentrated on identifying and furnishing the wardrobe requirements of the business and professional woman. Although the Company's products are conceived and marketed as "designer" apparel, they are priced to sell in the "better sportswear" range. The Company's products are sold to over 900 customers operating over 3,000 department and specialty stores throughout the United States. Products are manufactured pursuant to the Company's specifications by independent suppliers in the United States and abroad. See "Business."

The Offering

Common Stock to be sold by:

Company	345,000 shares
Selling Stockholders	805,000 shares (1)
Common Stock to be outstanding after the offering	3,479,560 shares
Estimated net proceeds to the Company	$5,757,199
Use of net proceeds by the Company	To reduce indebtedness and for certain capital expenditures. See "Use of Proceeds."
Dividends.	None. See "Dividend Policy."
Proposed NASDAQ Symbol	LIZC

---

(1) Assumes the Underwriters' 115,000 share over-allotment option is not exercised.

Selected Consolidated Financial Data
(in thousands of dollars except per share amounts)

		Fiscal Year Ended				*Three Months Ended*	
	Jan. 19, 1976 (Inc.) through Dec. 31, 1976	*Dec. 31, 1977*	*Dec. 31, 1978*	*Dec. 29, 1979*	*Dec. 27, 1980*	*March 29, 1980*	*March 28, 1981*
							(unaudited)
Net sales	$2,060	$7,396	$23,279	$47,630	$79,492	$20,747	$26,523
Net income	50	342	1,189	3,497	6,220	1,953	2,687
Earnings per common share (1)	$.02	$.12	$.38	$1.12	$1.98	$.62	$.86

EXHIBIT 6   *(continued)*

| | March 28, 1981 (unaudited) | |
	Actual	*As Adjusted (2)*
Working capital	$11,854	$16,307
Total assets.	27,918	32,613
Long-term debt, including current portion	63	—
Short-term debt	3,884	2,884
Stockholders' equity	13,589	19,346

(1) Adjusted to reflect the issuance of 65 shares of the Company's Common Stock for each share of its predecessor company's common stock pursuant to a merger effected on April 21, 1981. See Notes 1 and 5 of Notes to Consolidated Financial Statements.

(2) Adjusted to reflect the sale of the shares offered by the Company hereby and the anticipated use of the net proceeds therefrom as well as the repayment of long-term debt in April, 1981. See ''Use of Proceeds'' and ''Capitalization.''

See ''Dilution'' and ''Shares Eligible for Future Sale'' with respect to the availability of shares for sale after this offering and the immediate dilution in net tangible book value per share to be incurred by the public investors.

IN CONNECTION WITH THIS OFFERING, THE UNDERWRITERS MAY OVER-ALLOT OR EFFECT TRANSACTIONS WHICH STABILIZE OR MAINTAIN THE MARKET PRICE OF THE COMMON STOCK OF THE COMPANY AT A LEVEL ABOVE THAT WHICH MIGHT OTHERWISE PREVAIL IN THE OPEN MARKET. SUCH STABILIZING, IF COMMENCED, MAY BE DISCONTINUED AT ANY TIME.

SELECTED FINANCIAL DATA

The following tables set forth information regarding the Company's operating results and financial position and are qualified in their entirety by the more detailed Consolidated Financial Statements included elsewhere in the Prospectus.

EXHIBIT 6 (continued)

SELECTED INCOME STATEMENT DATA:

		Fiscal Year Ended				Three Months Ended	
	Jan. 19, 1976 (inc.) through Dec. 31, 1976	Dec. 1, 1977 (unaudited)	Dec. 31, 1978	Dec. 29, 1979	Dec. 27, 1980	March 29, 1980	March 28, 1981
Net sales	$2,060,118	$7,395,898	$23,279,304	$47,630,227	$79,492,035	$20,747,500	$26,523,023
Net income	49,862	342,489	1,188,857	3,496,575	6,219,592	1,952,998	2,686,670
Earnings per common share (1)	$.02	$.12	$.38	$1.12	$1.98	$.62	$.86
Dividends declared per common share (1)(2)	—	$.007	$.023	$.046	$.077	—	—

SELECTED BALANCE SHEET DATA:

	Dec. 31, 1976	Dec. 31, 1977	Dec. 31, 1978	Dec. 29, 1979	Dec. 27, 1980	March 28, 1981 (unaudited)
Working capital	$246,471	$ 454,196	$1,179,071	$ 4,456,954	$ 9,302,745	$11,854,311
Total assets	674,806	1,901,492	5,144,142	10,786,982	19,281,718	27,918,402
Long-term debt, including current portion (3)	170,000	173,333	173,333	134,815	77,037	62,593
Short-term debt (4)	—	—	—	—	—	3,883,676
Advances from factor (4)	330,696	666,077	2,782,863	—	3,546,098	—
Stockholders' equity	135,029	455,128	1,571,649	4,923,551	10,902,023	13,588,693

(1) Adjusted to reflect the issuance of 65 shares of the Company's Common Stock for each share of its predecessor company's common stock pursuant to a merger effected on April 21, 1981. See Notes 1 and 5 of Notes to Consolidated Financial Statements.

(2) The Company has no present plan to continue to pay dividends. See "Dividend Policy."

(3) The Company repaid its long-term debt in April 1981.

(4) Factoring advances were replaced by a line of credit in March 1981. See Notes 2 and 10 of Notes to Consolidated Financial Statements.

EXHIBIT 6   *(continued)*

BUSINESS

Introduction and Background

The Company designs, contracts for the manufacture of and markets an extensive range of women's clothing under the LIZ CLAIBORNE and LIZ trademarks. Organized in 1976 by its present management, the Company has concentrated primarily on identifying and furnishing the wardrobe requirements of the working woman, providing apparel appropriate in a business or professional environment as well as apparel suitable for leisure wear. The Company offers its customers a broad selection of related separates (referred to in the apparel industry as *sportswear*) consisting of blouses, skirts, jackets, sweaters, and tailored pants, as well as more casual apparel such as jeans, knit tops, and shirts. The Company believes that the increasing number of business and professional women has contributed both to the Company's own growth and to the growth of the market for women's sportswear in general.

LIZ CLAIBORNE products are conceived and marketed as designer apparel, employing a consistent approach to design and quality, which is intended to develop and maintain consumer recognition and loyalty across product lines and from season to season. The Company defines its clothing as "updated," combining traditional or classic design with contemporary fashion influences. While the Company maintains a "designer" image, its products are priced in the better sportswear range, which is generally less expensive than many designer lines. Although no comprehensive trade statistics are available, the Company believes, based on its knowledge of the market and such trade information as is available, that measured by sales of women's better sportswear, it is the second largest producer of such merchandise in the United States.

In 1980, LIZ CLAIBORNE products were sold to over 900 customers operating over 3,000 department and specialty stores throughout the United States. Measured by their purchases of LIZ CLAIBORNE apparel, the Company's largest customers during 1980 included Saks Fifth Avenue, Lord & Taylor, Bamberger's, J. L. Hudson, Bloomingdale's and Macy's—New York. A great many retail outlets that carry the Company's products maintain separate LIZ CLAIBORNE areas in which a range of the Company's products are sold. Approximately 25 percent of the Company's 1980 sales was made to the Company's 10 largest customers; approximately 71 percent of 1980 sales was made to the Company's 100 largest customers. Certain of these customers are under common ownership. For example, 16 different department store customers owned by Federated Department Stores, Inc. (which include Bloomingdale's, Abraham & Straus, and Burdine's) accounted for approximately 12 percent of the Company's 1980 sales. The Company believes that each of these department store customers makes its own decisions regarding purchases of the Company's products.

EXHIBIT 6 *(continued)*

Although the Company expects that sales to its 100 largest customers will continue to account for a majority of its sales, increasing emphasis is being placed on sales to local specialty stores and direct-mail catalog companies. The Company began licensing its trademarks in 1978 and presently receives royalties under arrangements with three licensees that sell various products under the LIZ CLAIBORNE and LIZ trademarks.

The Company's products are designed by its own staff and are manufactured in accordance with its specifications by independent suppliers in the United States and abroad. Domestically produced merchandise accounted for approximately 55 percent of the Company's sales during 1980; the remaining approximately 45 percent consisted of merchandise produced abroad, almost entirely in the Far East. Company personnel in the United States and abroad regularly monitor production at facilities that manufacture its products.

PRINCIPAL AND SELLING STOCKHOLDERS

The following table sets forth certain information, as of March 28, 1981, with respect to the number of shares of Common Stock owned, to be offered for sale, and to be beneficially owned after this offering, by all persons who were known by the Company to own beneficially more than 5 percent of the then outstanding Common Stock, all Selling Stockholders, each of the Directors of the Company, and the Company's officers and Directors, as a group:

| Name and Address | Ownership of Common Stock prior to Offering (1) | | Shares to be Sold (2) | Ownership of Common Stock after Offering (1)(2) | |
	Number of Shares	*Percent*		*Number of Shares*	*Percent*
Elisabeth Claiborne Ortenberg (3) 1441 Broadway New York, NY	523,640	16.71	134,478	389,162	11.18
Arthur Ortenberg (3) 1441 Broadway New York, NY	523,640	16.71	134,478	389,162	11.18
Leonard Boxer 4 Emerson Lane Secaucus, NJ	523,640	16.71	134,478	389,162	11.18
Jerome A. Chazen 1441 Broadway New York, NY	523,640	16.71	134,478	389,162	11.18
J. James Gordon 1101 Park Ave. New York, NY	65,000	2.07	16,693	48,307	1.39

(1) All shares listed are owned of record and, to the Company's knowledge, beneficially.

(2) Assumes the Underwriters' 115,000 share over-allotment option is not exercised. Percentage is based on total shares to be outstanding after this offering.

(3) Arthur Ortenberg and Elisabeth Claiborne Ortenberg are husband and wife; each disclaims beneficial ownership of all shares owned by the other.

Exhibit 6   *(concluded)*

Name and Address	Ownership of Common Stock prior to Offering (1)		Shares to be Sold (2)	Ownership of Common Stock after Offering (1)(2)	
	Number of Shares	*Percent*		*Number of Shares*	*Percent*
Joseph Gaumont 200 E. 57th Street New York, NY	227,500	7.26	58,425	169,075	4.86
Charness Family Investments Ltd. 2 St. Clair Avenue, East Toronto, Canada	162,500	5.18	41,733	120,767	3.47
Catway Investments Ltd.	97,500	3.11	25,040	72,460	2.08
Albert Fink Milton	97,500	3.11	25,040	72,460	2.08
Elizabeth Fenner Milton	65,000	2.07	16,693	48,307	1.39
Albert Fenner Milton, Custodian, F/B/O Elizabeth Hunt Milton under the Uniform Gifts to Minors Act	9,750	0.31	8,346	1,404	0.04
Jerome Gold	65,000	2.07	16,693	48,307	1.39
Martin J. Tandler	65,000	2.07	16,693	48,307	1.39
Jacob Rosenbaum	40,625	1.30	10,433	30,192	0.87
Belle Rosenbaum	40,625	1.30	10,433	30,192	0.87
Theodore Brodie	40,625	1.30	10,433	30,192	0.87
Simmi Brodie	40,625	1.30	10,433	30,192	0.87
All officers and directors as a group (7 persons)	2,159,560	68.90	554,605	1,604,955	46.13

2–5 PARENTING MAGAZINE

Robin Wolaner was distracted as the waiter at the Rue Lepic restaurant in downtown San Francisco, California, asked what she wanted to order. Wolaner, her husband, and a legal advisor had just terminated negotiations with a team representing Time Inc. about a much-needed $5 million investment in her plan to launch a new magazine called *Parenting*. Negotiations had reached an impasse, with both sides digging in their heels. The Time team members had left the all-day negotiating session remarking that they thought a deal would be impossible, given the bargaining intransigence of the Wolaner group. They were headed to the airport to take the "red-eye" back to New York. It was March 27, 1986.

The particular negotiating impasse between the Time representatives and Wolaner concerned the terms under which Time might buy Wolaner's ownership in the magazine venture. Basically, Time wanted to have the option to purchase Wolaner's stake at a point three years from the signing of the contract for a price that would be capped, no matter how well the magazine was doing at that time or what the fair market value would be. Wolaner's advisors were adamant: there should be no cap. Time could buy Wolaner out, but the purchase price should be related to the then-current market value of the magazine.

Wolaner had acceded to her advisors during the meeting, but was now having second thoughts. If the project worked, the buyout price would still yield a substantial sum, particularly for someone who had spent the previous five years working as publisher of *Mother Jones,* a nonprofit magazine based in San Francisco. Did it really matter if the price wasn't "fair market value"? Moreover, raising money from venture capitalists would surely entail giving up a substantial piece of the pie, even if there were no cap on the ultimate value.

The probable consequences of losing the Time deal were disconcerting: Wolaner and her partners had exhausted their funds and were confronted with limited options for raising the requisite amount of money in the near future. Some venture capital firms and at least one other publishing company had expressed interest in investing, but no one was as close to a deal as Time. Nor were other investors as knowledgeable about publishing as Time. To make matters worse, Wolaner had a bad case of the flu, but at least that would pass: whether or not she could find a way to launch *Parenting* was another matter.

It wasn't easy for Wolaner to collect her thoughts, but she would have to decide quickly: if not, her dream of starting *Parenting* might go for nought.

Professor William A. Sahlman prepared this case.
Copyright © 1990 by the President and Fellows of Harvard College
Harvard Business School Case 9–291–015

Background Information

Robin Wolaner's search for a new venture began in late November of 1984. From 1980 to 1985, she had been publisher of *Mother Jones,* a monthly magazine with a left-leaning editorial bent. Wolaner had joined *Mother Jones* as general manager and circulation director. Two years later, she was promoted to publisher and oversaw all the business aspects of the magazine, including circulation, financial planning, operations, and advertising. (Additional biographical information on Wolaner is included in **Exhibit 1**.)

While Wolaner had enjoyed her years at *Mother Jones,* there were frustrations, including her lack of input on the editorial side. Moreover, the business challenges of *Mother Jones* were circumscribed: almost all the magazine's revenues came from circulation, with advertising and other revenues modest in comparison. Though Wolaner had helped improve the operations of the magazine, the company was consistently unprofitable, with losses being subsidized by one wealthy patron. Wolaner was ready to move, and she gave three months notice in November of 1984.

The idea that Wolaner might launch a magazine on parenting was somewhat improbable: Wolaner did not have children. However, many of her friends did, and she had often wondered what magazine they read. After discussions with a number of new parents in her peer group and several visits to the local newsstand, Wolaner came to the conclusion that the existing magazines were not appropriate. The leading magazine, *Parents,* was too lowbrow: the writing was pedestrian and the apparent target audience was not one that would include Wolaner or her friends.

Wolaner's early investigations evolved into a full-blown project to create a new kind of magazine for new parents, one that would be targeted at an upscale audience and would be characterized by great writing. Wolaner believed the time was ripe to introduce such a magazine, given the attractive demographic outlook and the perceived mismatch between the existing magazine offerings and the new wave of affluent, well-educated parents. If such a magazine were successfully introduced, total circulation could exceed 500,000, which would yield substantial profits.

Having selected what she thought was an attractive opportunity, Wolaner set out to find financing for the initial stages of the project. She had modest resources herself—her *Mother Jones* salary was under $40,000—and planned to raise approximately $100,000 for the research phase. Ultimately, she thought, the total capital required would be over $5 million. With the rudiments of a business plan in hand, Wolaner began making calls to friends and then to friends of friends.

Wolaner was beginning to pile up charges on her credit cards, so it was imperative that she get outside financing as soon as possible. One of her early meetings was with Arthur Dubow, a financier from New York, who was visiting San Francisco to look at a possible publishing acquisition. Dubow was impressed with Wolaner and the business concept. He wrote her a check for $5,000, which he described as "walking around money." That was February 5, 1985. Dubow also committed to help assemble the financing group Wolaner hoped to put together.

Dubow recommended that Wolaner contact Gil Kaplan, publisher of *Institutional Investor* magazine. Kaplan in turn recommended that Wolaner conduct a direct-mail test of the idea. Though Wolaner was not enthusiastic about direct-mail market research—her experience had shown the results to be somewhat unreliable—she eventually accepted Kaplan's advice. As a result, she raised her initial budget to $175,000, and began to design the direct-mail test.

Raising capital was not the only task occupying Wolaner's attention. She was also talking to her various contacts in the publishing world, getting advice on how to create *Parenting*. There were a myriad of challenges including designing the direct-mail campaign, assembling a team, including an editor, and building an editorial advisory board. Of course, without money, these efforts would be pointless.

Raising Capital

After meeting over 70 potential investors, Wolaner managed to line up commitments for $125,000. Included in the investor group were Arthur Dubow, who had increased his commitment to $25,000, and Playboy Enterprises, which agreed to invest $12,500. However, the $125,000 was $50,000 less than Wolaner's target. At the reduced level of funding, Wolaner would not be able to draw a salary and there was no contingency funding: any slippage or overruns in the budget would jeopardize the project.

More problematic was the fact that Wolaner could not gain access to the $125,000 without the approval of the limited partners because she fell short of the target. After extensive negotiations with the investor group, which took place during June of 1985, Wolaner reached an agreement to modify the terms of the investment. Originally, the investors were to receive a 3.5 percent stake in a limited partnership in return for each $25,000 invested. Under the revised terms, the investors would receive at least 5 percent for each $25,000, with the actual percentage dependent on how much capital was eventually raised. If $150,000 were raised on or before October 31, 1985, the equity share would be 5.5 percent; if no additional capital were raised, then the share would be 6 percent for each $25,000. As a result of the agreement, Wolaner was able to spend the $125,000 she had already raised and had strong incentives to raise the additional $50,000 before October. If she were able to raise the full amount, then she would be entitled to a salary of $27,000 during the first six months of the partnership.

Having secured sufficient financing for the market test, Wolaner proceeded on all fronts. By late August of 1985, the test was almost ready for mailing. A copy of the original package is included as **Exhibit 2.** Wolaner had also succeeded in raising an additional $37,500, bringing the total to $162,500. At that level, at least she would be able to draw some salary.

The August 30, 1985, Mailing

The actual mailing took place on August 30, exactly on plan. Some 130,000 pieces were mailed to names culled from 27 lists, mostly parents who bought books, educational toys, magazine subscriptions, or apparel for their children. Of the total sample, 90,000 were sent an identical package; 10,000 received an offering with a $15 subscription price (higher than the $12 price in most of the mailings); 10,000 received a package with a "hard" offering (implying a firmer commitment on the part of the respondent to subscribe); and the remaining packages represented variations on other aspects of the mailing (e.g., the envelope used or the text of the letter). Wolaner hoped to receive a 5 percent positive response rate to her mailing, though any rate higher than 3.5 percent would be considered a success.

As it turned out, Wolaner's diminutive mailbox was inundated with responses: the final tally showed a 5.7 percent response rate. The figure was even more impressive when the weaker mailing lists were eliminated from the base. The remaining lists, which contained the names of over 4.5 million potential subscribers, had a response rate of 7.2 percent. Wolaner had clearly identified a market segment not being adequately served. Further analysis of the market test revealed that there was modest price sensitivity—the response rate at the $15 price was 95 percent of the rate at the $12 price—and that the respondents were strongly committed to buying a magazine like *Parenting*. The project was off and running.

Refining the Plan and Raising Capital

The market test results were encouraging, but many formidable and potentially insuperable hurdles remained. Chief among these was Wolaner's estimate that she would need at least $5 million to launch *Parenting,* which she hoped to do in February 1986, a scant six months after the market test. No one in the current investor group was capable of investing that amount of money, but most were willing to help in the process. Among the possible new investors were venture capital firms, wealthy private investors, a private placement by an investment banking firm, and publishing companies. Wolaner's first choice was to raise money from noncorporate sources because of concerns about control.

As a first step in the process of raising capital, Wolaner worked hard on preparing a business plan that reflected what she had learned from the market tests. A table of contents from the business plan is included as **Exhibit 3.**

Briefly told, the plan was to create a magazine with two important constituencies: parents and advertisers. By establishing high editorial standards and attracting a well-educated, high-income readership, the magazine would become the vehicle of choice for advertisers.

Wolaner's research had revealed that the demographics of the target readership were very attractive. A follow-up questionnaire mailed in November of 1985 to the test market respondents indicated a median household income in excess of $40,000, almost a third larger than the comparable figure for her primary competitors (*Parents, Working Mother,* and *American Baby*). More than half of the respondents were college educated. These characteristics were highly valued by potential advertisers.

The total potential market for a magazine like *Parenting* was very large. There were an estimated 20 million women in the 20-to-30-year age group. Fully 16 million couples were expected to become parents during the 1980s. There were approximately 1.5 million first-child births each year. By 1990, there were expected to be almost 20 million children under five years old. Finally, many of the women having children in the 80s and beyond were bearing children later in their lives and were likely to return to the workplace during the child-raising period.

Wolaner had decided to focus on the latter segment of the parenting population. Specifically, the magazine would be targeted at women who were active in the work force and who were engaged in many activities of which parenting was one. Moreover, the marketing strategy would concentrate on the nine-year period of planning and conception, birth, toddlerhood, and early schooling. Magazines like *Parents* were targeted at broader constituencies (e.g., parents of children of all ages) and, in Wolaner's view, lost much of their editorial impact because of this lack of focus. An overview of the content of *Parenting* and a proposed outline for the inaugural issue are contained in **Exhibit 4** and **Exhibit 5.**

Wolaner planned to use a number of methods to attract subscribers to *Parenting*. Chief among these was direct mail. Wolaner planned to send out over 3 million pieces of mail in the first year of operation, which would result in approximately 126,000 subscriptions if her assumptions were correct. Gradually, the amount of mail sent out each year would decline as subscription renewals became a more important source of circulation.

In addition to direct mail, *Parenting* would be marketed through a number of other channels. For example, each issue would contain the ubiquitous insert cards. These cards were often an important source of subscriptions. Also, *Parenting* would be made available on newsstands as well as through agents like Publishers Clearing House. Finally, particularly in the early years, a certain number of free copies of the magazine would be sent to obstetricians' offices, birthing centers, and other similar outlets. Once again, the goal was to get women to read the magazine and subscribe.

The ultimate purpose of these efforts to gain readership was to create an attractive medium for advertisers. Most mature consumer magazines received at least half of their revenues from advertising rather than from circulation. However, attracting advertisers to a new magazine was very difficult, and represented a classic "chicken and egg" problem. Wolaner believed that she would be able to overcome the reluctance of advertisers to commit to a new magazine by offering a cost-effective means of reaching an upscale audience. She intended to charge approximately $5,000 per four-color page of advertising, which translated to a $25 CPM[1] rate. For early advertisers in the magazine, Wolaner planned to offer incentives, including the opportunity to receive 3 ads for the price of 2, or 10 ads for the price of 8 less 5 percent. Thus, one of the early adopters could place a page of advertising in each of *Parenting's* first-year issues for a total cost of under $40,000. By contrast, the cost of a page in *Parents* was $38,000 (which represented a CPM of slightly less than $23). Over time, as the circulation of the magazine increased, Wolaner believed she could increase dramatically the revenue generated from each page of advertising.

In the long run, there were other ways to generate revenues from a magazine like *Parenting*. For example, one possibility was introducing a monthly newsletter that

---

[1]CPM refers to the cost to the advertiser for a page of advertising divided by every 1,000 in circulation rate base. For example, if the rate base is 200,000 and the CPM is $25, then the cost of a page of advertising is $5,000.

would be targeted at specific subgroups in the *Parenting* population. Such a newsletter venture would require modest additional investment in editorial resources, but would generate substantial subscription revenues. Also, as with most mass-market publications, Wolaner believed that mailing list rentals would be a very profitable source of income in the future.

According to Wolaner's projections, the payoff from a successful launch of *Parenting* would be high: by 1991, total revenues were expected to exceed $23 million with pretax income of over $6 million. The magazine would break even in the third full year of operations. Wolaner's assumptions and related financial forecasts are summarized in **Exhibit 6.**

In order to accomplish her plans, Wolaner projected a cash need of over $4 million. She intended to raise $5 million in order to have some safety margin in the event her projections proved optimistic. Wolaner contacted a number of venture capital firms that had previously made investments in consumer marketing companies. She also began the process of contacting various publishing companies that might have an interest in financing a magazine like *Parenting*.

The response from the venture capital community was positive but excruciatingly slow. Few venture capitalists had experience with magazines, which resulted in a protracted period of due diligence. Moreover, it was difficult to get the senior partners of the funds to make definitive commitments: most of the background work on the *Parenting* project was handled by associates within the venture capital firm.

The possibility of raising money from existing publishing companies was complicated because few companies were willing to hold minority stakes in ventures. Indeed, these companies were more likely to want to own 100 percent of the project. On the other hand, there were exceptions to the general rule, and Wolaner began to explore options with companies like Times Mirror and Field Publications.

Wolaner had also considered contacting Time Inc., which was known to be considering a new magazine in the same general area. In late December of 1985, one of the venture capitalists who had looked at the *Parenting* deal suggested that Wolaner contact a man named Don Spurdle, a senior executive in the magazine development group at Time.

In January of 1986, Spurdle called Wolaner and suggested she come to New York for a meeting. When Wolaner arrived at Spurdle's office, she was immediately confronted with a dilemma: Spurdle's secretary handed her a release form that she would have to sign before her meeting. The document released Time from any obligations to Wolaner and her magazine and allowed Time to use any and all information Time might receive during discussions. Wolaner immediately headed for the elevators. She called her attorneys back in San Francisco (who had also invested in the partnership) and asked their advice. The attorneys suggested she sign the release noting that it would probably be cheaper in the long run for Time to buy the magazine than to steal from it.

Wolaner returned to Spurdle's office and proceeded to lay out her plans. She and Spurdle had a very cordial meeting at the end of which Spurdle said it was very unlikely that Time would ever invest in a venture like *Parenting* under terms that would be acceptable to Wolaner. He wished Wolaner luck, joking that Time would probably end up buying her out in five years at some exorbitant price. Wolaner left the office impressed with Spurdle's publishing acumen, but convinced Time would not back her project. She made sure to take all of her direct-mail materials with her as she left.

She returned to San Francisco to explore other financing options. The pressure to make progress was enormous. Wolaner had almost exhausted the seed capital, which had lasted well beyond the original October 1985 forecast. In early February 1986, she had sent out an appeal for an additional $50,000 (with each $25,000 receiving a 1.25 percent stake in the partnership equity). She had already succeeded in raising the full $175,000 targeted seed capital.

In spite of the pressures, progress was modest. Three different venture capital groups were continuing their due diligence. Discussions were also under way with Field Publications about possible participation. However, no one seemed close to a final decision.

Then, in late February, Wolaner received a phone call from someone at Time Inc. who was a member of the team trying to put together the new magazine project. She said that her boss was interested in talking to Wolaner about a possible joint venture. Out of courtesy, Wolaner then called Don Spurdle who suggested she come back to New York for further discussions. Unbeknownst to Wolaner, Time had come to the conclusion that Wolaner was much further along with her magazine project than Time was internally.

In mid-March, Wolaner flew back to New York for a meeting with a number of Time executives including Spurdle and Chris Meigher, executive vice president of the Magazine Group. The subsequent discussion lasted through lunch and well into the afternoon. Wolaner was peppered with questions by Meigher, Spurdle, Marshall Loeb (managing editor of *Fortune*), and a number of members of the Time group investigating the parenting field. The meeting was tough, but Wolaner felt she had more than held her own. Wolaner had made her points forcefully, including insisting that she own 51 percent of the venture initially, and she had fielded the publishing questions well. She was also convinced that Time would be a good partner, one that could truly add value and increase the likelihood of success.

In late March, Wolaner was asked to come back to New York for a meeting that would include Henry Grunwald, the legendary editor-in-chief of the Time Inc. Magazine Group. Once again, Wolaner was able to respond effectively to the questions posed by Grunwald and his fellow Time executives. As a result, Don Spurdle and a lawyer for Time agreed to come to California to work on the terms of a potential deal. That meeting was scheduled for March 27.

The Stanford Court Meeting

Early on the morning of March 27, 1986, Wolaner, her husband, and a lawyer met with Don Spurdle and Tom McEnerney, a Time Inc. lawyer. The negotiations were difficult, but substantive progress was made at each point. Some key negotiating issues that were resolved included a provision for each party to be able to buy the other party out. Some progress was also made on Time's insistence that Time buy out the interests of all the limited partners who had invested in the venture. Essentially, Time agreed to offer this group an amount equal to three times their original investment, but this proposal was subject to approval by the limited partners.

Wolaner also accepted the principle that Time would be entitled to a higher percentage of the equity in the event the venture failed to meet its financial projections. Time would also have the option to truncate its commitment at $3.2 million should certain hurdles not be surpassed.

However, one point that could not be resolved related to granting Time the option to purchase Wolaner's stake in the venture at some point in the future. Time wanted to cap the price that it would pay. Wolaner and her advisors knew that successful publishing ventures were very valuable in the market, with typical valuations of 10 times normalized pretax income. If Time were to cap the amount that Wolaner would receive for her interest, then the actual price might be far less than fair market value.

After working for several hours on the buyout issue, the meeting broke up. Spurdle stated that he believed Time would insist on a cap and that further negotiations were fruitless unless Wolaner and her advisors relented on this issue. Spurdle and McEnerney left for the airport to take the "red-eye" back to New York. Meanwhile, Wolaner, her husband, and her lawyer left for the restaurant to discuss their options.

Wolaner was exhausted. The all-day negotiations had been tense in addition to which she had a temperature of 103 degrees. While she understood the issue related to Time's right to buy her share in the venture, she was not sure that the position she and her advisors had taken was appropriate. After all, their terms would still result in a handsome payoff if the magazine were successful. And, considering the traditionally conservative posture taken by Time, much progress had been made. (**Exhibit 7** contains a brief outline of the Time proposal.)

As Wolaner considered the menu at Rue Lepic, she wondered what to do next. She was totally committed to the creation of *Parenting*. Yet her financing options were limited, and she was desperately short of cash. Moreover, she thought the people at Time could make a substantive contribution to the effort in addition to their capital. On the other hand, did it make sense to accept a contract that was potentially less lucrative?

EXHIBIT 1   **Background Information on Robin Wolaner***

Robin Wolaner, the publisher and founder, was the publisher of *Mother Jones* (an award-winning, national consumer magazine with a paid circulation of 170,000) from 1982 to February 1985.

Every summer since 1982, Robin has taught at the Radcliffe Publishing Procedures Course at Harvard University where she directs 100 students working on 10 magazine launches, each requiring a 3-year business plan, a dummy issue, etc. She was the winner of a 1984 Gold Award from *Folio,* the Magazine of Magazine Management, for excellence in circulation direct marketing. Her writing has appeared in *Working Woman* and *Glamour* magazines and she is a frequent publishing industry speaker.

Her previous positions were:

General Manager/Circulation Director, *Mother Jones,* 1980–1981.
Publishing Consultant, Ladd Associates, 1979–1980, working with clients such as *Quest, Food & Wine,* and *Newsweek* International.
Circulation Manager (top circulation executive), *Runner's World* Magazine, 1977–1979, during which time the magazine was launched nationally and grew from 90,000 to 360,000.
Editor, *Impact,* a newsstand trade magazine, 1976–1977.
Features Editor, *Viva* magazine, 1975–1976.
Promotion Copywriter, *Penthouse* magazine, 1975.

In the winter and spring of 1985, she served as a direct-marketing consultant to Banana Republic, the clothing catalog company owned by the Gap. She graduated from Cornell University with a B.S. in Industrial and Labor Relations. Profiles of Robin have appeared in *Newsday, the Boston Globe,* and *USA Today,* and her biography is included in *Who's Who in America.*

---

*This information was included in the business plan prepared by Robin Wolaner in late 1985.

PARENTING:

The Growth of Excellence

THE PREMIER ISSUE
CAN BE YOURS

FREE

Your
Charter
Invitation is Enclosed...

47 Alpine, San Francisco, CA 94117

BULK RATE
U.S. POSTAGE
PAID
PARENTING
MAGAZINE

Front of Envelope

EXHIBIT 2 *(concluded)*

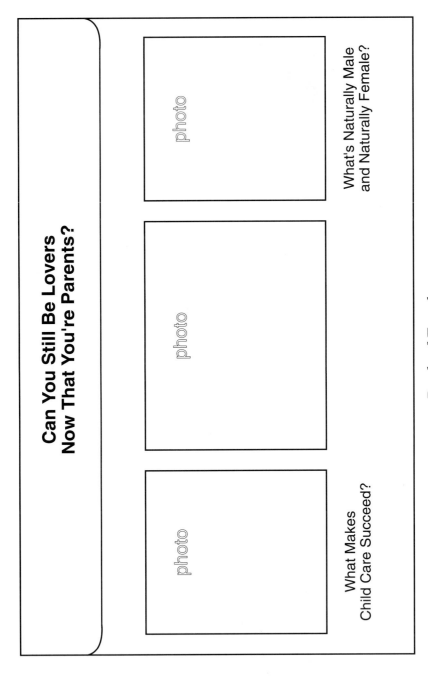

**Can You Still Be Lovers
Now That You're Parents?**

photo

photo

photo

What Makes
Child Care Succeed?

What's Naturally Male
and Naturally Female?

Back of Envelope

EXHIBIT 3

Business Plan Table of Contents

Appendixes

Tables

Exhibit 4

Editorial Overview

Parenting will help its readers make their own choices about what's best for their children by providing the most up-to-date information on children's psychological and physical development. It will also address parents' emotional and physical needs in major articles about such touchy issues as restoring intimacy to a relationship after the arrival of children. PARENTING will treat tough topics in an accessible yet authoritative way.

The brochure used in the direct mail test shows the general design of the magazine and many typical articles (see Appendix A). The following section is a description of the regular columns, departments, and features in PARENTING. Then outlines of two sample issues present the departments and features in the order they'd appear in the magazine.

COLUMNS

A column appears in every issue and is usually one page. The headline is the same each issue, anchoring the magazine for readers by providing a familiar landmark. PARENTING's every-issue columns will be:

The Editor's View. Rather than retelling the stories behind the stories, as with most magazine editor's columns, this will be intensely personal. The column will set the tone, the ethic, and the theme of the magazine. It will demonstrate, through its perspective and human touch, that there is no dry approach to life, no surefire answers on these pages; that in the sensitive business of being a mother or a father, only caring, hanging in there, and paying attention count.

Expert Opinions. Rather than simply printing our readers' letters, our column will offer a real give-and-take. Readers will voice their opinions on subjects covered in PARENTING, and our writers and editors will respond.

NewsBriefs. Up-to-the-minute news in medicine, psychology, law, education, the economy, etc. that affect our readers' lives.

First Choice. What's new and worth recommending for parents and children to read, watch, and listen to. Our video, film, book, software, television, and music reviews will help parents make educated entertainment choices.

What's In. This monthly underground report will give you an insider's understanding of what your child is saying, why she is straightening only one side of her hair, why he won't put shoelaces in his sneakers, and, in general, where he or she is at.

Kidstuff. Our illustrated best-buys page. Our staff will comb American and European specialty catalogs and stores for unique products for parents and children.

PARENTING's Puzzle. On the last page of the magazine will be a challenge for the whole family—an illustrated puzzle for children to solve with or without coaching from their parents.

CARTOONS

The subject of parenting lends itself to witty, provocative treatment by the nation's best cartoonists. Their cartoons will appear throughout PARENTING, breaking up solid pages of text and enlivening even the most serious writing.

DEPARTMENTS

Departments appear regularly in a magazine, though not every one appears in every issue and the length can vary: usually one or two pages, sometimes a department is important enough to expand to three or four pages, with photos and/or illustrations. Some run in the back, with the "editorial well" (major features) dividing the front and back. The following are regular headings; each department will also have a headline about the specific coverage in that issue.

EXHIBIT 4   *(continued)*

Great Expectations. Every pregnancy is like a first pregnancy since no two gestations are predictably alike, and scientific advances made between one birth and the next can make the recommended prenatal care, delivery procedure, and postpartum care different for each child. Expecting parents—whether for the first or the fourth time—will find the information they need to make pregnancy as safe and satisfying an experience as possible.

Childhood Profile and American Family Journal. People like to read about people, and these regular departments will showcase fine journalism. Childhood Profile will consist of excerpts from new biographies covering the early years of achievers like Georgia O'Keefe, Saul Bellow, and Henry Kissinger. American Family Journal will be vivid reporting by gifted writers on little-known, but richly interesting, American families.

Single Parenting. Whether single by choice or circumstance, the sole parent of one or more children is faced with a job that can seem overwhelming. No other magazine addresses the special needs and problems of single parents such as the financial strain of parenting alone, the need for setting personal time aside, and how to help children adjust to a single parent's social life.

Child Care. To whom do you give the ultimate responsibility of caring for your children while you're unavailable? How can parents choose and evaluate private nannies, small home play groups, and preschool programs for their children?

The Ethical Parent. This department deals thoughtfully with questions of the intelligent and ambitious parent. For example, the ultimate success in many fields means moving to a large city. But are parents sacrificing their young families on the altars of ambition? Is The Big City right for toddlers or adolescents?

Interaction. Is your praise loaded with future expectations? Is your discipline an effective deterrent or an unproductive punishment? When is giving your child what he or she wants giving in? When is it an affirmation of your child's autonomy? How do you shape the parent-child dynamic so that all family members feel respected and loved?

The PARENTING Interview. PARENTING will feature (in both question-and-answer interviews and profiles) those celebrities who make interesting observations about raising children or those who have made real efforts to raise healthy families. One or two magazine covers per year will feature famous faces (with their children when possible). The kinds of people PARENTING would cover include Meryl Streep, John Irving, Steve Wozniak, Sam Shepherd and Jessica Lange, Jane Pauley and Garry Trudeau, etc.

Kids Fashion. Shot on location, photographs of children in wonderful clothes can be visually stunning. PARENTING will examine style and material as well as practicality.

Learning. Too often parents are given a (or impose their own) schedule of normal development against which to judge their children's acquisition of skills. PARENTING will approach learning from a different perspective: Parents will gain insight into what a milestone in intellectual development means to their newborn, toddler, and preschooler at whatever age that milestone is achieved.

Family Fitness. What feels like a good workout for one member of the family is a strain for another and barely an exertion for a third. How does one plan active outings that are healthy for the whole family? What physical fitness objectives should parents keep in mind for themselves? Their partner? Their children?

The Law. Family law is one of the fastest changing legal fields, and this department will bring human interest as well as guidance for readers. For example, one of the first things expectant or new parents do is start to write their wills—but then the process grinds to a halt: choosing a guardian is much more difficult than dividing the property. Some other topics that will be covered include the legal and tax aspects of child care, employment rights of pregnant executives, post-divorce custody and support, etc.

Family Finances. Today's household income has to be allocated and invested wisely to meet the high expenses of raising children now and building up funds for future education expenses and retirement needs. Investment and tax planning strategies will help readers make their income work hard to reach their financial goals.

EXHIBIT 4   *(concluded)*

Interior Design. Becoming a parent doesn't necessitate living in disarray and eating off "Sesame Street" plasticware. Children's furniture can be a welcome addition to the home and break-resistant dishes can grace the table. Parents can display their good taste even when their children are bent on destruction.

En Route. When is it safe to take an infant abroad? When is it *sane* to take an infant abroad? How to evaluate baby-sitting services offered by hotels, cruise ships, or tourist bureaus. The best travel guides for parents. The least traumatic ways to leave the children behind while going on a business trip or away for a romantic weekend.

Family Business. Parenting is a growth industry, and this department will offer likely business reporting about the companies and people making the products PARENTING's reader's buy.

Food. Parents don't have to live on fish sticks, bologna, and frozen french toast until their children reach the age of majority. Cultivating young tastes, building menus around flexible foods that can be dressed down or up, and sharing kitchen duties with young children.

FEATURES

Usually four or five pages in length, features include illustrations or photographs and cover varied topics. They form the center, or "editorial well," of the magazine, in recognition of readers' limited time and desire for quick, accessible information.

If PARENTING were now being published, it would run many of the departments and features in the following sample issue.

EXHIBIT 5 **February** *Parenting*

The Editor's View

Expert Opinions

Newsbriefs New child care options being considered by companies all over the world.... The Missouri study that indicates that parents can be taught how to rear their babies—and those babies will be smarter and better-adjusted as a result.... The crisis of skyrocketing insurance costs for child care providers.

Great Expectations

"When Drugs Are Necessary During Pregnancy." For some women, the ideal of totally restricting intake of drugs during pregnancy is unrealistic. How women with such chronic health problems as diabetes, head, neck or back pain, or hypertension can have a healthy pregnancy despite their need for medication.

Single Parenting

"The Courting Dilemma." What happens when two single parents find each other in a romantic way, and things get personal and, well, intimate? How do you get intimate, or should you, when there are small children in the house?

Child Care

"English As a Second Language." Baby-sitters often harken from the far corners of the earth and feel most comfortable speaking their native tongue. Does exposure to two languages delay or retard speech development? Does it have beneficial effects?

The Ethical Parent

"Do As We Say, Not As We Did." The almost universal desire of parents to keep their children from experimenting with drugs conflicts with the experience of many people who grew up during the 60s: how do you set a drug-free example for your children when, in fact, your college years were filled with marijuana smoke? What do you say to your child when his or her favorite sports hero is hauled into court on a cocaine charge?

Interaction

"Friends for Life." Theorists of the last generation held that children didn't really socialize until they were three or four years old. Many parents of toddlers disagree. They say friendships can begin as far back as 18 months of age. According to the latest research, the parents are right. Does that mean that social calendars for two-year-olds are in order?

Law

"Scientific Advances that Pressure Doctors to Pressure Mothers." Chorionic villus sampling, the new alternative to amniocentesis, is an extremely accurate pregnancy test for birth defects—so accurate that its effect is to impose a strict liability standard on physicians, that is, it's the doctor's fault if an unhealthy baby is born. Some doctors react by unnecessary testing.

Learning

"Not in Front of the Children." Most parents act as if their toddlers are deaf—talking about sensitive issues in front of them just as they did when the toddlers were newborns with no language skills. Then one day, the habit catches up with them and the mention of school provokes an anxious crying fit, or a reference to ice cream results in a temper tantrum because none is available. How much more language can toddlers understand than they can speak? When should parents start to edit their conversation?

EXHIBIT 5   *(continued)*

FEATURES

(COVER) "First Love—Fathers and Daughters: Mothers and Sons"
It's conventional wisdom that our style of loving a person of the opposite sex is shaped by our first relationship with that sex—our mothers and fathers. If a man has a good relationship with his mother, he'll probably make a stable husband, and likewise for fathers and daughters. But *what* is a good relationship? What makes a bad one? The cover story profiles people willing to speak candidly and insightfully about their parents—and their partners.

"The Pregnant Pause: When is Infertility Counseling Necessary?"
Infertility counseling is available for a reasonable cost to just about every couple. But that doesn't mean that every couple will benefit from this sometimes traumatic medical intervention. Who should seek infertility counseling? Who should not?

"Forum: Child Care"
Periodically, PARENTING will sponsor discussions to address child-rearing issues. Members of the editorial advisory board, other specialists, and noted parents will meet to discuss questions such as "Is quality time a myth?" The focus of this forum will be a survey conducted among PARENTING's readers on how they are solving child care problems. This original research will be newsworthy, and the forum should have room for ground-breaking clashes of opinion as well as valuable information.

"The Art of Announcing"
PARENTING scours the country for a portfolio of the most beautiful, most original, and most outrageous birth announcements.

"Five Years at Sea"
Vicky and Sy Carkhuff were tired of fighting the rat race, tired of the stockbroker trade and the parties and suburbia. So they fulfilled many readers' fantasy: they pulled five-year-old David out of kindergarten and began an amazing odyssey, a five-year sail around the world by themselves. David's education became correspondence courses taught by his mother in the belly of the boat. Now that they've re-entered the "real world," Vicki writes candidly of the experience.

"Left-Handedness: More Than a One-Sided Preference"
New findings about left-handedness suggest that being a southpaw may have far-reaching effects much more significant than having trouble finding scissors that fit. From the structure of his brain to the effectiveness of his immune system, the lefty may have a make-up different from his right-handed counterpart.

"Growing Up Funny"
A noted television-comedy writer's journal of his attempts to instill a sense of humor in his daughter.

"Discipline for Different Ages"
Yelling at a one-year-old, reasoning with an 18-month-old, and threatening a two-year-old don't work. What does? Psychologists and educators give their opinions about fashioning discipline for effectiveness at different ages.

Exhibit 5   *(concluded)*

"Short in the Tooth"

Your family dentist may say that brushing habits and dental checkups can wait three or four years until your baby is more mature. However, today's specialists in pedodontics (childhood dental care) disagree. They believe that good oral hygiene—like good personal hygiene—is a habit that should start right after birth to protect emerging teeth. What kind of dental hygiene is important for infants and toddlers?

BACK-OF-THE-MAGAZINE COLUMNS AND DEPARTMENTS

First Choice A round-up of the best new books—memoirs of well-known parents and children: Yael Dayan on her father, Moshe; Wilfred Sheed's *Frank and Maisie: A Memoir with Parents*; John Cheever in his daughter Susan's words.

Family Finance

"Options for Tuition Savings." Tax revisions being considered by Congress this year threaten two of the most common tuition savings plans: Clifford Trusts and UGMA (uniform gifts to minors accounts). Both of these investment funds offer parents tax advantages because the money contributed to them is taxed at the lower rate of the child. If both of these savings plans are disallowed, what investment strategies could parents use to replace them?

Interior Design

"Two Kids in One Room: Variations on a Theme." How to split up the space in one room to accommodate two children depends on the temperaments, ages, and interests of the children. Design prototypes that can be mixed and matched according to a family's individual needs are pictured here.

En Route

"Ski Resorts That Welcome Young Children." "Children under 12 not allowed" is frequently the last phrase in a brochure about an elegant vacation resort. A review of resorts that do cater to small children while maintaining an atmosphere appreciated by the parents.

Family Fitness

"Avoiding Mountain Sickness." If our readers are moved by the En Route column to take a ski vacation, this column will help them protect their families against high altitude sickness.

Food

"Noodles for Them; Pasta for You." Recipes for turning their plain spaghetti and tomato sauce into your sophisticated pasta dinner for two.

What's In

Kidstuff

PARENTING's Puzzle

Exhibit 6   Financial Projections

Profit & Loss Summary	1986	1987	1988	1989	1990	1991
Revenue						
Advertising	0	$ 1,154,105	$ 3,036,966	$ 6,086,650	$ 9,460,943	$13,128,416
Subscription	0	1,841,821	2,875,630	4,927,862	5,992,461	7,293,739
Single-copy	0	578,125	681,875	905,438	994,125	1,084,500
List	0	233,625	297,084	383,173	491,761	590,168
Newsletter	0	0	0	921,827	1,115,036	1,265,426
Total revenue	0	$ 3,807,676	$ 6,873,555	$13,224,950	$18,054,326	$23,362,249
Expenses						
Circulation	898,383	1,569,809	1,705,831	3,118,509	3,126,235	3,084,839
Advertising	373,009	1,023,741	1,293,293	1,667,168	2,021,419	2,231,950
Production	0	1,762,417	2,504,081	4,340,396	5,817,752	7,790,608
Editorial	385,193	1,444,274	1,400,016	1,785,791	2,031,584	2,051,961
Art	78,777	306,888	328,896	397,462	450,516	476,760
Administration	437,300	570,040	588,928	620,711	655,073	691,487
Newsletter	0	0	0	598,515	755,378	752,953
Total expenses	$ 2,172,662	$ 6,677,169	$ 7,821,045	$12,528,552	$14,857,957	$17,080,558
Income (loss)	(2,172,662)	(2,869,493)	(947,490)	696,398	3,196,369	6,281,691
Cumulative net income (loss)	(2,172,662)	(5,042,155)	(5,989,645)	(5,293,247)	(2,096,878)	4,184,813
Cash flow summary						
Receipts						
Advertising	0	1,142,020	2,999,677	5,921,798	9,360,232	13,047,308
Subscription	0	2,864,803	3,926,836	5,793,966	6,770,542	8,058,000
Single-copy	0	550,891	675,805	859,912	987,104	1,076,695
List	0	202,540	285,388	371,727	484,096	585,621
Newsletter	0	0	0	921,827	1,115,036	1,265,426
Total receipts	0	$ 4,760,254	$ 7,887,706	$13,869,230	$18,717,010	$24,033,050
Disbursements						
Circulation	898,383	1,569,809	1,705,831	3,118,509	3,126,235	3,084,839
Advertising	373,009	1,023,741	1,293,293	1,667,168	2,021,419	2,231,950
Production	0	1,762,417	2,504,081	4,340,396	5,817,752	7,790,608
Editorial	385,193	1,444,274	1,400,016	1,785,791	2,031,584	2,051,961
Art	78,777	306,888	328,896	397,462	450,516	476,760
Administration	437,300	570,040	588,928	620,711	655,073	691,487
Newsletter	0	0	0	598,515	755,378	752,953
Total disbursements	$ 2,172,662	$ 6,677,169	$ 7,821,045	$12,528,552	$14,857,957	$17,080,558
Operating cash flow (deficit)	(2,172,662)	(1,916,915)	66,661	1,340,678	3,859,053	6,952,492
Cumulative net cash flow	(2,172,662)	(4,089,577)	(4,022,916)	(2,682,238)	1,176,815	8,129,307

EXHIBIT 6   Assumptions for the Financial Projections

Major Publishing Assumptions		1987	1988	1989	1990	1991
Number of issues/year		10	10	12	12	12
Average circulation		262,000	326,000	408,000	494,000	551,000
Circulation pricing						
1-year introductory rate		12	1 2/15*	15	15	17
Newsstand cover price		2.5	2.5	2.75	2.75	3
Direct mail†						
Volume (millions)		3.2	1.4	2.1	1.9	1.8
Average response‡		5.4%	6.2%	5.6%	5.6%	5.7%
Pay-up		75.0%	67.5%	67.5%	67.5%	67.5%
First-time renewal rate			40.0%	40;0%	40.0%	40.0%
2nd & subsequent renewal				65.0%	65.0%	65.0%
Production costs/per copy						
Printing		$0.38	$0.44	$0.52	$0.59	$0.74
Postage		$0.16	$0.21	$0.26	$0.27	$0.29
Total per copy		$0.54	$0.65	$0.78	$0.86	$1.03
Average total pages/issue		102	115	135	167	182
Average ad pages/issue		30	50	65	80	89
Four-color ad rate 1,000 circulation		$25.09	$26.60	$28.19	$29.88	$31.68
Ad rate base	Sept.86–	Feb.87–	Jan.88–	Jan.89–	Jan.90–	Sept.90–
	Jan.87	Dec.87	Dec.88	Dec.89	Aug.90	Aug.91
	200,000	300,000	350,000	430,000	500,000	550,000
Number of employees						
Editorial		9	9	10	11	11
Art and production		4	4	4	4	4
Advertising		7	7	9	10	10
Circulation		4	4	4	4	4
Administration		6	6	6	6	6
Newsletter				2	2	2
Total		30	30	35	37	37
Annual inflation rate§						
Postage		0%	15%	10%	0%	10%
Phone		10%	10%	10%	10%	10%
All other		5%	5%	5%	5%	5%

---

*The first price increase is scheduled for the middle of the second year.

†See pages 12–13 and 14 for a complete description of the direct-mail assumptions used in the business plan.

‡As a magazine matures, the overall direct-mail responsiveness declines so the business plan projections are based on a decreased percentage after the first year. However, because a lower amount of direct mail is planned after the launch, only the best performing lists will be utilized. This more selective mailing strategy results in a higher weighted average.

§If paper, printing, postage rates, or other expenses increase beyond the expectations of this plan, all magazines would be faced with the necessity of raising subscription and advertising prices. So PARENTING could compensate for any unexpected inflation without losing competitive ground.

EXHIBIT 6   Comparisons with other Magazines

	Parents	Working Mother	Parenting Year 1	Parenting Year 5
Subscriptions	1,604,000	504,000	209,000	482,000
Single-copy sales (newsstand)	90,000	16,000	53,000	69,000
Advertising pages				
per year	1,131	945	302	1,062
per issue	94	79	30	89
Cover price	$1.95	$1.95	$2.50	$3.00
Subscription price	$11.95	$11.95	$12.00	$17.00
Advertising price (CPM)	$22.81	$29.07	$25.09	$31.68

NOTE: Circulation figures for *Parents* and *Working Mother* are from the December 1984 Audit Bureau of Circulation Publisher's Statement. The figures for *Parenting* are averages from the business plan. The 1985 advertising figures for *Parents* and *Working Mother* are according to *Advertising Age*. Subscription and cover prices for *Parents* and *Working Mother* are as of January 1986. *Parenting's* 1986 CPM was set to equal that of *Parents'* 1986 CPM, plus 10%.

EXHIBIT 7 *Parenting* **Deal Structure Outline of Terms**

A. Investment.
   1. Original Limited Partners. The Original Limited Partners have contributed $175,000 and own an aggregate of approximately 34.5% of the equity. Time is to invest $5 million in the business in exchange for 45% of the equity. In addition, Time will offer to buy out the Limited Partners at three times their investment or a total of $525,000. Thus, Wolaner and Time will approach all 10 Limited Partners with an offer from Time to buy them out at three times their investment. Rationale is that Time thinks it is preferable to have only the publisher as a partner. Upon the buyout, Time will own an additional 4% or a total of 49%.
      Limited Partners to agree in writing to be bought out at the time the agreement in principle is reached between Wolaner and Time and prior to:
      (i) Time putting any money in the venture; and
      (ii) any publicity or announcement regarding the venture.
   2. Capital Advance.
      Upon resolution of the Limited Partners and execution of agreement in principle among Wolaner and Time, Time will make a $500,000 advance available to Wolaner for start-up expenses. These will be documented to Time as spent.
      Wolaner and Associates will sign a nonrecourse, interest-free, promissory note that will provide that if the Wolaner-Time deal falls through, the note is repaid with first money invested by any third party in the "Parenting" venture. The note would be a lien on that venture.
      Wolaner draws money monthly based upon budgeted cash needs for the succeeding month.
      Parties proceed diligently to sign definitive partnership agreement as quickly as practicable, estimated to be mid-May.
   3. Time Capital Contributions.
      Upon signing definitive partnership agreement, Time is committed to finance venture up to $3.2 million through July 31, 1987, when the benchmarks are to be met. If the benchmarks are met, Time is committed to fund the venture up to an additional $1.8 million or a total of $5 million. The $500,000 advance described in paragraph 2 is included in the $5 million. However, whatever Time spends to buy out the Limited Partners will be in addition to the $5 million that goes into the venture.
      Wolaner draws money monthly based upon budgeted cash needs for the following month.
   4. Failure to Meet Benchmarks.
      If the venture fails to meet one or more benchmarks, then Time has the choice of whether or not to invest the additional $1.8 million.
      If Time decides not to invest any additional money, then Wolaner has 30 days to find a new investor and if she does, then Time gets bought out for a nominal payment. If Wolaner can't find an additional investor, then Time can sell its interest to a third party or cause the venture to liquidate. Wolaner retains ownership of the Parenting trademark and the idea for the magazine and the other assets are sold and the proceeds are distributed to partners pro rata based on invested capital.
      If Time decides to invest the $1.8 million even if the venture fails to meet the benchmarks, then Time assumes control of the day-to-day operations of the business and control of the management committee or other governing body. Time's equity is increased by 20 percentage points (to 65% or more) and Wolaner's equity is reduced proportionately.
B. Benchmarks.
   Benchmarks are designed to measure the performance of the venture through July 31, 1987, as follows:
   1. For the period from January 1, 1987, through July 31, 1987, average monthly overhead cost shall not exceed $_____ (number is 10% higher than budget).
   2. For the period from commencement of the venture through July 31, 1987, aggregate advertising sales revenue of the venture shall be not less than $_____ (number is 20% less than budget). (Should be bookings plus actual for six or seven issues.)

EXHIBIT 7   *Parenting* **Deal Structure Outline of Terms**—*(continued)*

3. For the period from commencement of the venture through July 31, 1987, certain circulation benchmarks, including subscription response rates, newsstand sales, and payment rates must be met (numbers are within 15%).

C. Management.

Partnership Agreement to provide that day-to-day operation of the business is to be handled by Wolaner and Associates. There will be a five-member Management Committee to oversee the business with three members being appointed by Wolaner and two by Time. The Committee will act by majority vote except for certain significant items that will require unanimous approval. Examples of these are as follows:

1. Borrowing money by the venture.
2. Admission of new partners.
3. Sale of Assets.
4. Approval of annual Business Plan and Budget but only so long as the venture has a negative cash flow for the prior 12 consecutive months.
5. Approval of contracts that have a term in excess of 12 months, unless cancelable without penalty on no more than 60 days' notice.
6. Contracts in excess of $25,000 unless the expenditure is provided for in the annual Business Plan or Budget.
7. Distributions of cash from the venture to the partners.
8. Removal or appointment of auditors or legal counsel.
9. Commencement or settlement of legal proceedings.
10. Partnership elections under the Internal Revenue Code.

D. Financials.

The venture will operate on a calendar year and will have annual audited financial statements. The venture will provide the partners with unaudited quarterly and monthly financial information, including comparisons to budget.

Profits and losses will be divided according to the equity interest of the partners in the venture except that:

1. For tax purposes, Time may, if it desires, receive a special allocation of losses (e.g., 99% of all venture losses). Similarly, Time would then later receive a special allocation of profits, for tax purposes, that matches the special loss allocation.
2. Time will receive a larger share of profits and distributions (e.g., 80%) until such time as the capital investment of Time has been returned to it.

E. Divorce.

Except as otherwise specifically provided, neither Time nor Wolaner can sell, transfer, or otherwise dispose of their partnership interests prior to December 31, 1987. In addition, Wolaner cannot resign as Publisher prior to this date. This is the critical initial period when Time's financial commitment and Wolaner's entrepreneurial expertise will be most needed.

After December 31, 1987 (September 1, 1987, if benchmarks are not met), Time may dispose of its interest to a third party, provided Wolaner shall have a right of first refusal.

After December 31, 1987, Wolaner may resign as Publisher in the following circumstances:

1. Time has acquired 51% or more ownership of the venture and has begun exercising day-to-day control of the business.
2. In the good faith judgment of Wolaner, Time's treatment of Wolaner shall be intolerable to her or irreconcilable business differences shall exist on material business matters affecting the venture, provided, however, that at least 45 days prior to any such resignation, Wolaner shall deliver to Time a written notice of her pending resignation, describing the nature of the problems or differences and the parties shall use all reasonable efforts to resolve the problem or differences prior to the end of the 45 days.

In the event Wolaner resigns, Time shall assume control of the Management Committee and the day-to-day operation of the business and Wolaner shall receive a lump-sum severance

---

EXHIBIT 7   ***Parenting* Deal Structure Outline of Terms**—*(concluded)*

---

payment equal to 18 months' salary. Time shall also have the right for a period of 90 days after the date of such resignation to purchase from Wolaner a portion of her equity interest in the venture so that Time would have 51% equity ownership. The purchase price would be $150,000 per percentage point of equity in the venture sold by Wolaner to Time.

F. Buyout.

1. Time shall have the option to purchase Wolaner's interest in the venture during the period July 1, 1989, through December 31, 1989, at a price equal to her equity interest in the venture multiplied by the fair market value of the venture. For these purposes, fair market values shall equal (a) $XXX (amount to be determined) million minus (b) .75 multiplied by (i) the amount of money invested Time in the venture less (ii) the amount of such investment that has been returned to it prior to the date the option is exercised.

2. During the period March 1, 1990, through April 30, 1990, Time shall have the right to initiate the "shotgun" procedure.

3. During the period May 1, 1990, through June 30, 1990, either Time or Wolaner shall have the right to initiate the "shotgun" procedure.

4. During the period March 1, 1991, and April 30, 1991, (and each such two-month period in each succeeding year), either party shall have the right to initiate the "shotgun" procedure.

5. The "shotgun" procedure.
   - The party initiating the procedure does so by delivering written notice to the other party setting forth a value for the venture.
   - The receiving party has 30 days to decide whether to sell her or its interest or whether to buy the initiating party's interest.
   - The purchasing party must purchase the selling party's interest for cash within 120 days of the date the initiating party delivered the first notice.
   - Failure to pay such purchase price within said 120-day period shall be a default and shall (a) entitle the other party to reimbursement of legal, accounting and other expenses incurred in connection with the proposed buyout and (b) give such party an option to purchase the defaulting party's interest in the venture at 80% of the price set in the initiating party's notice.

G. Miscellaneous.

1. Upon a buyout by Time on or before December 31, 1989, Wolaner will remain as publisher for 18 months. For a buyout by Time in 1990 and beyond, Wolaner will remain as publisher for 12 months.

2. Upon Wolaner's resignation as publisher or a purchase by Time of Wolaner's equity interest in the venture, Wolaner will be subject to a 5-year noncompete agreement in the area of magazines relating to parents and/or children and related fields [to be refined further].

2–6   NATIONAL DEMOGRAPHICS & LIFESTYLES (A)

It was early January of 1982, and the co-founders of National Demographics & Lifestyles (NDL) were meeting with their venture capital backers to discuss the firm's need for roughly $1 million of additional financing. Jock Bickert, president and founder of the Denver-based company, described the situation:

> Although we have failed to meet our revenue projections, my faith in the company and the concept is unshaken. We have a good understanding of the challenges ahead and a clear sense of the steps required for the company to turn the corner.

Rob Johnson, NDL's vice president, added:

> We've taken the company as far as possible with the financing we've had. We underestimated the time and resources necessary to make NDL profitable. In this coming year, in addition to funding normal operating losses, we need to build our own data processing center, hire a direct sales force, and add three new people to middle management. The issue is simple: Jock and I have to convince our venture backers to inject enough capital to offset the firm's operational losses and finance our proposed expansion. Without this new money, NDL cannot survive.

Tom Claflin, a member of NDL's board and a venture capital backer of the firm, offered his perspective:

> All the venture capitalists believe in the company, and in Jock and Rob. Yet this is their fourth time back to the well for capital, when the money raised in each of the previous rounds was supposed to have been sufficient. The company has consistently fallen short of its revenue projections. Although there has been definite progress, the company is once again coming back to the well, at a time when we are a long way from turning the corner. Before the venture group puts in another $1 or $1.5 million, we must address the key issue: Is it just taking longer to prime the pump than we expected or is there something fundamentally wrong with the concept?

The NDL Concept

The concept behind NDL was simple, but revolutionary: NDL would administer the "product registration card" programs that virtually all consumer hard goods

---

Professor Michael J. Roberts and Research Associate Ennis J. Walton prepared this case.
Copyright © 1987 by the President and Fellows of Harvard College
Harvard Business School Case 9–388–043

manufacturers employed and would provide the manufacturers with marketing information derived from the cards (see **Exhibit 1**). Moreover, NDL would perform this service for a nominal charge using specially designed questionnaires that requested demographic and lifestyle information about consumers. In exchange, NDL would get the right to build a data base with the demographic and lifestyle information contained on the cards that consumers returned. In time, once its data base reached a critical mass, NDL hoped to build revenues by renting targeted mailing lists that it could generate from its data base.

In explaining his inspiration for the company, Bickert recalled:

> I became extremely interested in the idea of forming a large data base with broad application because it seemed to be an inexpensive and less time-consuming way to do research. In my survey research and consulting work, by comparison, I was continually writing questionnaires and doing field research for one-time-only use. With a demographic and lifestyle questionnaire, I thought I had finally figured out an approach to building a data base that could be used over and over again.
>
> I first tried the idea out to help the Denver Junior League identify its members in terms of their special interests and abilities. They had a problem utilizing their volunteers because the organization couldn't identify them according to what they enjoyed doing. When I built the data base that contained special interest, activity, and demographic information, the Junior League was able to more accurately target specific members for certain projects. Once I saw that the idea worked, I decided to look for a way to expand the concept to a large consumer data base.
>
> I came across the idea of using "product registration cards" to build the data base when I discovered that manufacturers weren't getting value from their warranty programs. Since consumers weren't legally required to return the cards to be covered by a warranty, many of the manufacturing clients that I consulted with simply kept the cards that they received in shoe boxes or storerooms. At that point, no one seemed to realize that the cards could provide an important source of consumer information if the data they contained was entered into a computer data file. Also, such a data base would be an excellent source of targeted mailing lists. If you think about it, the people who return these cards aren't just passive consumers; they've taken the time to fill out the card, put their own stamp on it, and send it back to the manufacturer.
>
> Our idea was to create a questionnaire that captured the purchase data that manufacturers were already collecting. We also added detailed, standard, lifestyle and demographic questions on all cards. For a nominal charge to the manufacturers, we ran market analyses of their consumers that could identify the demographic segments they were serving, and the other interests of their customers. And in return for absorbing all the costs associated with entering the data into a computer and producing various analyses of their consumers, we obtained the ownership rights to the demographic and lifestyle information contained on the cards.
>
> With this information, we could build a massive data base—the only one like it in the United States. Once the data base reached a certain size, we could use the individual lifestyle and demographic data to develop highly targeted lists of consumers. For example, we could provide *Golf* magazine with a list of specific active golfers segmented by age, income, and geography. Think of it! We were certain that a list of this kind would be far more valuable than other lists available, and that mailers would pay a premium for this kind of information.

The List Industry

NDL's main source of revenue involved renting targeted mailing lists to direct-marketing firms. This industry had grown rapidly prior to NDL's founding in 1976. In 1970, for instance, over $2.8 billion had been spent on direct-mail advertising, and the sales attributed to direct mail had exceeded $35 billion. By 1973, these figures had increased to $5.4 billion and $50 billion, respectively. Market analysts explained this increase by pointing to the ever-increasing costs of traditional advertising media (i.e., the costs of mass media coverage had skyrocketed to the point where a 30-second television commercial in prime time during the 1977–78 season ranged from $35,000 to $50,000, while a half page in the Sunday *New York Times* was priced at $7,500). Analysts also believed that advertisers were turning to direct marketing because it allowed them to utilize more refined market segmentation techniques, as well as a more exact way to track the effectiveness of their advertising expenditures.

At the heart of any successful mailing was the selection of the correct mailing lists. Typically, direct-mail firms would supplement their own "house file" (i.e., current customers or subscribers) by using a number of outside mailing lists. To assist in selecting the "right" outside lists, mailers would employ one or more list brokers who attempted to select lists that contained consumers with the greatest likelihood of responding to the mailer's offer. Ultimately, the broker would select two types of lists: (1) continuations: lists that had been tested in the past and found to meet the mailer's responsiveness criteria and from which names had been ordered in large volumes; and (2) tests: new lists that, in the broker's opinion, would likely match the mailer's potential market, and from which names could be ordered in smaller volumes to test the list's effectiveness. All of those lists were sent to the mailer's service bureau, where they went through a process known as "merge-purge" to eliminate duplicate names prior to mailing.

The effectiveness of a list was measured in terms of cost per response. Typically, the rental of a name constituted only 10 percent of the cost of a mailing, while other costs, including such items as printing and postage, constituted the remainder. The total costs of a mailing divided by the total number of responses (e.g., people who decided to accept a magazine solicitation) was the cost per response. It is important to note that a list did not have to be "the best" to be successful; all it had to do was be a money maker, which meant that the cost per response was less than the contribution margin the mailer earned from that response.

Lists were priced for one-time use. A mailer was not permitted to use a name again (unless the individual responded with an order). List owners regularly seeded control names in each rental order to detect improper usage. Prices varied widely, from $10 to $100 per 1,000 names, depending on the relative quality, market demand, and specificity of the lists; $40 per 1,000 was an average. Where more than two selector characteristics were available, premiums were usually charged for each additional characteristic. Initially, NDL management believed that the average price for a specialized consumer list with three demographic characteristics (e.g., ZIP code, income, and sex) was approximately $40 per thousand names. Related services, such as response tabulations and analyses, could also be purchased from some list renters for additional costs.

In 1977, most of the direct-mail business was based on using mailing lists that only approximated the marketers' requirements. Prior to NDL, if a manufacturer of high-priced tennis apparel wanted to mail to prospective buyers, the manufacturer had only two alternatives: (1) obtain subscription lists from tennis magazines and/or tennis clubs, which identified people who were interested in tennis but who were *not* qualified by income; or (2) select certain high-income lists (e.g., American Express cardholders), which identified the prospect's purchasing power but *not* the individual's interest in tennis. From NDL's perspective, however, both alternatives resulted in mailings of less than optimum efficiency, since those lists included a number of individuals who did not fit both the targeted demographic and interest characteristics. NDL's list permitted the manufacturer to mail to people who indicated an interest in tennis and whose incomes exceeded a certain level.

NDL estimated that there were approximately 20,000 direct-mail lists that fell within two categories:

Compiled Lists.   These lists were compiled primarily from large master lists such as telephone listings, motor vehicle registrations, and voter registrations. These lists were typically lower priced because they forced marketers to make decisions based on very general information such as automobile ownership. Unlike the NDL list, these lists had no detailed demographic characteristics such as income, type of residence (house versus apartment), length of residence, age, etc., not to mention detailed lifestyle data.

These lists were insufficient for two other reasons: First, many key demographic characteristics (e.g., income) were derived from census data and were only median figures for an entire area (e.g., census tract or ZIP code), which meant that the lists would include a number of consumers who would fall below the median; second, there was no indication of the consumers' specific interests (e.g., lifestyles) to enable marketers to target their mass mailings.

Response Lists.   These lists were made up of consumers who had made a purchase by mail or taken some other action by mail and were a by-product of a direct mailer's business. Examples of such lists included *Newsweek* subscribes, L.L. Bean catalog buyers, donors to Sierra Club, and American Express cardholders. Traditionally, direct marketers held response lists as most desirable for direct-mail programs because of the known ''direct-mail responsiveness'' of those consumers.

NDL believed that while these lists offered specificity of interest, they were often lacking in their coverage of the specific interests. For example, of the 32 million tennis players in the United States, only 315,000 subscribed to *Tennis* magazine, the most popular tennis magazine. Obviously, from NDL's perspective, the marketing firm that used the *Tennis* magazine subscriber list missed a very large proportion of its potential market. Moreover, NDL argued that these lists were also insufficient because the little demographic information that they provided represented only median figures for the entire list. In effect, such lists were basically one- or two-dimensional in terms of targeting capabilities.

NDL's Opportunity

NDL's management believed that there was an opportunity to add new value to the industry. NDL believed that the following example accurately portrayed the problem faced by the marketing arm of a company planning to introduce a new product or a service on a nationwide basis:

- A company could determine, following extensive research, that the market for the product in question was roughly 10 percent of the adult consumers in the United States.
- The company could then identify the most likely purchasers of its product based on demographic and activity characteristics.
- Once it understood its market, the company still had to determine the most effective way to reach those high potential customers.

Remarking on the process, Jock Bickert said:

It's amazing to think that a company would spend all that time and money and still leave the biggest question of all unanswered: they didn't know how to reach their high-potential customers. Our approach allows marketers to pinpoint their most likely customers.

In addition to providing a new approach to the list business, Bickert believed that his company's data base strategy provided it with a competitive advantage in an industry where there were no patents or proprietary technology to protect a firm's market position. Bickert described the leverage behind the NDL concept:

The key to our business is being able to rent your data as many times as possible. Once you build the data base, the costs associated with producing 12 lists versus 60 lists from that data is relatively insignificant.

A tremendous advantage for our firm is that the numerous information categories in our data base allow us to rent a particular name in numerous lists. For example, each name in our data base has, on average, seven interest areas associated with it in addition to the normal eight demographic categories. By comparison, most of our competitors have only one or two variables associated with the names on their lists.

As a result, we have a competitive advantage because each one of our names can potentially appear on 15 separate lists. This alone multiples the rental potential of our firm's data base by a factor of 15.

The Early Days

Bickert had been active in survey research for 14 years prior to forming NDL. A clinical psychologist by training, Bickert worked at the University Hospital in Iowa City, Iowa, and Denver General Hospital early in his career.

Later in his career, Bickert had been in charge of survey research at the University of Denver's Research Institute where he conducted numerous studies for government agencies including the National Science Foundation, the National Bureau of Standards, the U.S. Weather Bureau, the National Aeronautics and Space Administration, as well as commercial businesses. During this time, Bickert developed expertise in survey methods and market research and analysis. In one study, for example, Bickert analyzed how citizens responded to the idea of government-sponsored weather modification. Bickert's research interests had also led him to found Bickert, Browne, Coddington & Associates (BBC). A successful economic and market research firm, BBC specialized in market research for banks and other financial services institutions.

By 1975, Bickert had become bored with the "cookie-cutter" surveys BBC was doing and was excited about the concept of using questionnaires as a basis for building a data base. Thus, he and two friends contributed $500 each, and Bruce Ducker, a local lawyer who later served as NDL's attorney, added $222 to help incorporate and "start" NDL. But due to these limited resources, the firm was unable to begin its data base operations or pursue its primary expected businesses during the early years.

To finance NDL, Jock Bickert ran a one-man consulting agency. As he recalled:

> The firm was little more than an idea. We didn't have any particular office space—the firm merely shared space in the office I used to coordinate my independent research work. The NDL idea didn't get much attention, because I was busy doing analysis and writing reports for the government contracts. That work was profitable, but NDL wasn't going anywhere.
>
> Whenever I had any free time, I went around the local business community to try to recruit a few "manufacturing clients" [the manufacturing firms that would put NDL's cards in with their products]. The Colorado manufacturers that I talked to liked the idea. However, they were concentrated in the outdoor recreation industry and produced in relatively small unit volumes. I had no idea how we'd be accepted by the higher volume manufacturers, the ones we would need for the company to be successful. Still, I believed in the concept and was convinced we just needed to put more effort behind it. I knew Rob Johnson through some work we had done together and thought that he would make a good partner.

In May of 1977, Bickert convinced Rob Johnson to join him at NDL. Johnson had earned his MBA from the University of Virginia in 1970 and had worked in a number of marketing positions before joining NDL. Between 1970 and 1977, Johnson had worked for IBM selling computer products and services to large system users in Denver, a local investor's real estate concern, and a nationwide real estate development firm based in Dallas. Johnson remembered the events leading up to his decision:

> Jock and I had known each other for some time; he knew that my real estate development job was challenging, but he didn't know that I had decided to leave it to look for a position that provided me with an equity stake.
>
> When Jock mentioned the idea for NDL to me, I thought it was a promising opportunity; and when I ran some numbers on the company, I was amazed by the potential profitability of the business. At first I wasn't sure that my assumptions were correct, so I divided the revenue figures to give me more realistic results. After a few trial calculations, I was sold on the company's potential, and I bought $3,000 worth of stock in the company. This gave me an ownership position equivalent to Jock and the other two major shareholders.

Once Johnson joined NDL, he began traveling to promote the company and developed a business plan to raise the capital NDL would need to finance its growth. Bickert and Johnson decided that $450,000 would be sufficient capital to get the business to positive cash flow. They wrote a business plan that explained the concept and its potential as well as the financing required to bring manufacturing clients on board and to build the data processing capacity to enter data and process lists.

When they finished the business plan, they distributed it to a number of friends and acquaintances in the Denver area, including Lucien Wulsin, chairman of Baldwin-United. Baldwin-United was an old-line manufacturer of pianos that had embarked on a dramatic series of acquisitions in order to diversify. Baldwin's new president was not overly fond of the idea, but Wulsin convinced him the idea had merit and they went ahead, financing the company to the tune of $476,000 in January of 1978. (See **Exhibit 2** for financing history.)

The Baldwin-United Financing

Lucien Wulsin, chairman of the board of Baldwin-United, recalled his decision to support NDL:

> I was intrigued with the concept and the people. In addition, at Baldwin we marketed musical instruments and insurance products, and I thought NDL could help us.

The Baldwin-United financing paved the way for NDL to begin building its consumer information data base. In addition to providing capital, the relationship with Baldwin-United gave NDL access to Baldwin's computer services firm, Baldwin DECO. NDL contracted with DECO to perform the computer processing required to analyze data for manufacturing clients. Baldwin-United also encouraged NDL to perform its data entry function in Barbados, where Baldwin owned the local power company.

The Baldwin-United financing also allowed NDL to add a small management staff that freed Bickert and Johnson to concentrate their energies on selling the NDL concept to manufacturing clients (companies that could include the warranty/questionnaire with their product).

Jock Bickert had vivid memories of the challenges he and Rob faced launching NDL:

> In the early days, we underestimated the basic lead time it would take to generate significant card flow. At first, we thought it would be a relatively quick process. We learned, however, that it could take over a year to get things moving.
>
> First, Rob and I had to isolate the right contact person. No matter how we tried, we kept getting delayed by the bureaucracy at many of these firms. For example, if we went to the marketing division of a company, we could sell them on the value of our services. But in most cases, the marketing departments couldn't give us clearance to go ahead with the program without the concurrence of other senior management. Invariably we had to make multiple presentations and wait while a company engaged in a lengthy internal debate. Then, once we had an agreement with the marketing folks, we would have to work with the legal department, a process which slowed things up again. Furthermore, many of our potential clients were Japanese, and then they had to send everything back to Japan for final approval. It was a nightmare.
>
> Unfortunately, things didn't move much faster once a company agreed to use our questionnaire; the task simply shifted to getting the company's manufacturing divisions to put the cards in their products.

Once inserted into a manufacturer's products, we again had to wait a lengthy period, sometimes nearly a year, before the product with our cards moved from the manufacturer's warehouse, through the retail system to the consumer, and ultimately back to us. Once we get a good base of names, acquisition is still an ongoing process; because people move quite frequently in our society, a name is considered "good" for about two years. Thus, names become obsolete after that time. Once we get the pipeline full and build our cash flow, however, we will have no problem replacing the names that become obsolete each year.

Throughout the first phase of our operations, our focus was on recruiting manufacturing clients and building card flow. Without this critical mass of names, it was difficult to really be a player on the list side of the business.

For example, in the fall of 1978, we had an exhibit at a direct-marketing convention in Washington, D.C. The people at the conference were excited about our company's promotional booth. "You can do what? All that! Tell me more," they would say. Rob and I managed to impress most industry experts until it came to one question: "How many names can you supply?" At that point we only had about 65,000 names in the data base. When we told one person the actual size of our base, he laughed and told us, "Come back when you have a million names."

In addition to building our data base, we also faced other problems with the list side of the business. During the early days, many people in the direct-response industry lumped our lists together with other compiled lists, which traditionally had not been used successfully by most response-oriented mailers. Rob and I had to do a great deal of missionary work to explain the advantages of the NDL approach and convince the industry that our lists were different from compiled lists and that they would prove effective for mailers in situations where compiled lists had failed.

It took a long time, but our missionary work started to pay off and we began to get more test list orders. Most direct-response companies tested lists using a small number of names at least twice before they decided to use a larger quantity in a "rollout." Converting those tests into rollout orders was a long process because many companies in the direct-response industry only mailed twice yearly. Thus, even though the success rate of our tests was two times greater than the industry average, we still had to wait nearly 12 to 18 months from the test phase before we would recognize any appreciable orders.

Another problem was that we expected our list customers to have a good idea of who their customers were. In fact, they often didn't know. This meant that when we used the lifestyle and demographic data that they *thought* corresponded to their customer segment, our tests often performed poorly. Fortunately, most customers stayed with us as we worked out the problem by analyzing the characteristics of the respondents of the mailings, but some customers just wouldn't talk with us further.

The Search for New Capital

NDL's early activities quickly consumed the firm's finances and forced Bickert and Johnson to go back to Baldwin-United for more money. As Johnson pointed out:

Lucien Wulsin provided great moral support and guidance, but it was clear that Baldwin-United wouldn't put any more money in our company. This put us in a precarious position because we were spending cash at an alarming rate, and we had no revenue to offset our expenses. Moreover, we didn't even have any new capital sources identified.

By late 1978, NDL was scrambling to talk to venture capitalists. Desperate for an infusion of new funds, NDL mailed numerous copies of its business plan out to prospective backers hoping to get a positive reaction. As Johnson recalled:

> There were points when we were willing to drop everything to visit any venture company that showed interest. On one follow-up trip to Boston, we talked for three hours about the company, answering every difficult question they could offer, or so we thought. Finally, just before the end of the meeting, one partner asked: "What's your fallback position if the lists don't work?" We had never even considered a fallback option, and that question killed the deal instantly. Maybe we were naive, but we never thought that the company wouldn't make it.
>
> With another venture firm, we had handled all of the meetings well, but the venture capitalists never seemed to understand our business. We weren't high tech and we didn't have any proprietary technology. NDL just didn't have anything that he could comprehend. After what was to be our final meeting, Jock and I left to go to the airport while the VCs made a decision. While we were waiting, we were paged over the airport intercom system. When we arrived at the phone, we didn't know what to expect. As it turned out, it was the young venture capitalist who was the "lead" on our case. We braced ourselves, expecting the worst—they had turned us down. What he asked us, however, was more alarming: "Please explain again the way mailing lists work." Well, right then we both knew that deal was over.
>
> Finally, following a number of discussions, an investment consortium led by a major Wall Street investment banking firm indicated that it wanted to do the deal and suggested that we come to New York to finalize the details. To make sure all the bases were covered for the New York trip, we developed a fallback position that we hoped would impress the VCs. We also decided to get our corporate attorney, Bruce Ducker, to come with us, since he had experience with a number of financings.
>
> When Jock, Bruce, and I got to New York, the venture group took us to a cocktail party and then dinner on the Upper East side. At first things seemed fine, but as the night went on Jock, Bruce, and I became anxious wondering when we would start talking shop.
>
> At around 9 p.m., the banker handed us a financial document and told us to look it over and make a decision: "I have a 9:30 train to catch—take this deal or leave it," he told us. Once we looked over the terms of the agreement, we were shocked. They proposed a deal that was radically different from the one we had been discussing; essentially, they wanted to dilute our financial stake in the company down to nothing.
>
> At that point, we didn't have any other prospects, and we knew that the company wouldn't survive much longer without new funds. But we still said "no deal" because we knew that we'd rather see the company die before we sold it and ourselves, too. I think that meeting was a turning point for us. After the meeting, we went to the bar at the Plaza and talked about the future of the company until 4 in the morning. While we didn't accomplish much and had no other active leads for additional capital, we agreed that we had made the right decision. I knew that somehow we would find the financing.

Picking up the story where Johnson left off, Bickert went on:

> The very next day I called John Kidde, an old friend who liked to invest in new venture situations. He was busy so I couldn't explain our situation to him over the phone, but he invited me to come see him at a meeting he would be attending in Connecticut the next afternoon. He told me to catch a ride with a friend of his named Jerry Hardy. "Hardy's

limousine," he said, "will be leaving from the General Motors building at 8 A.M. tomorrow morning. Be there if you want to come see me."

When I went to sleep that night, I wasn't sure if I wanted to travel three hours with a stranger just to talk to Kidde. I didn't have anything to lose, but the trip didn't seem to make much sense.

The next morning, I was introduced to James Michener (the novelist) while I was checking out of my hotel room. He and I hit it off instantly, and he invited me to join him for breakfast. Quite frankly, the prospect of having a one-on-one breakfast with James Michener was intriguing; certainly as appealing as sharing a limousine with a guy I'd never heard of. I decided, however, that I should go visit Kidde.

On the way to Connecticut, Jerry Hardy and I started talking about my business. I learned that he was president of Dreyfus, the huge money management firm. Not knowing what to expect, I gave him a brief introduction to the company. To my surprise, Hardy also turned out to have been the founder and president of Time-Life books and a real direct-mail guru. His background in publishing made him extremely interested in the NDL concept; during the rest of the trip, he quizzed me about the company.

Time went by quickly, and when we arrived at Kidde's place, we exchanged cards and vowed to continue the conversation. I know Hardy put in a good word for us with Kidde. He said NDL was the most exciting direct-mail concept he'd seen in 30 years, and he wanted to introduce us to a lot of key players in the direct-mail business. About a week later, Kidde introduced me to Tom Claflin, the president of Claflin Capital, a Boston-based venture fund. That introduction saved the company.

Bickert recalled another incident that happened shortly after Tom Claflin began to review NDL as a possible investment:

I got a call from a friend who ran a major list brokerage firm in New York. She said someone had called asking about NDL, and she had given him 20 minutes of pure venom on the company and the people associated with it. After she hung up, she realized that she'd confused NDL with NLS, National List Systems. When she told me the story, my heart jumped up into my throat. I knew it was a venture capitalist who had called her, and I knew that she'd just destroyed our chances. After a few minutes, she remembered he had said he was from Boston. I figured it must be Claflin, gave her his number, and she called him back with a positive evaluation. Most people would have felt embarrassed about making such a mistake and would never have bothered to call. What a fragile process it is!

Recalling his impressions of NDL, Tom Claflin said:

NDL looked like a money-making business. The potential operating leverage was tremendous, even allowing for a certain degree of optimism on their part. Their business plan called for sales of $3 million (worst case) to $6 million (best case) in five years and profits of $700,000 (worst) to $2 million (best case). Our investigation of the industry suggested that the concept had merit. Jerry Hardy's comment probably summed it up best: He said if the NDL concept worked, it would be the most significant innovation in the direct-mail industry since the ZIP code. Given the promise of the company and the very positive feelings I had for Jock and Rob, this seemed a bet worth making.

At roughly the same time as the venture capital financing, Bickert and Johnson purchased the holdings of two early passive investors.

Once Claflin had made the decision to invest, he pulled a group of investors together, including Don Christensen of Greater Washington Investors in Washington, D.C., and several smaller venture firms. NDL, in turn, created two new seats on its board of directors for the lead venture capitalists (see **Exhibit 3**).

With the $1.2 million raised in this first venture round in December 1979, NDL entered a new phase of development. NDL management allocated most of its time and resources to four basic tasks:

- Marketing the questionnaire program to large national manufacturers. This process included calling on prospective clients and making presentations, preparing card layouts, and helping to expedite the implementation of the program.
- Improving the firm's computer software to eliminate unnecessary program steps and keep pace with innovations in the list industry.
- Building the consumer data base. This process included keypunching, data entry, data analysis, purging, and updating the data.
- Marketing the company's lists to brokers and list users to help the firm's list manager (outside sales agent) generate interest in the NDL concept.

The Need for More New Capital

By mid-1980, however, it was clear that NDL would need still more capital; the firm estimated that it would need $1.6 million or so to get to positive cash flow. The cycle of events required to build the data base and go through the list testing phase was still taking longer than expected. Another round of financing required that other venture firms be brought in. Claflin and Greater Washington were small- to medium-sized funds and although they could — and would — participate in this round, they believed that it was essential for the company to broaden its investor base in view of the amount of capital required.

Based on their prior experience in the venture market, and with the help of Claflin and Christensen, Johnson and Bickert sent a new business plan to a new group of venture firms. Several venture capitalists were interested in NDL, including Bill Egan of Burr, Egan, Deleage in Boston, Citicorp Venture Capital, Continental Illinois' venture fund, Wood River, and Fleet Ventures. Rob Johnson recalled:

> Bill Egan became the opinion leader of this group of new investors, probably because of his being in Boston and his long-standing friendship with Tom Claflin. Bill had serious doubts and was getting very mixed signals from the industry when he began his research. So before he made any decisions, he met me in New York to go on a "cold" list sales call. As those things go, the call was OK but inconclusive. A week later Tom Claflin and I had dinner with Bill in Boston to make one last pitch to him. Following that dinner, both Tom and I feared that Bill was going to pass, in which case NDL would have been dead.

Ultimately, however, Egan decided to invest along with Greater Washington and Claflin, and the rest of the group came together behind him. He discussed this decision:

> I spent more time on this investment decision than any I've ever made. On one hand, the logic was absolutely compelling. The information that NDL was pulling together was so

obviously superior to the classic demographic data other lists contained. Yet, there were two factors that suggested it would be difficult to realize this potential. First, the process of collecting data by signing up manufacturing clients seemed more difficult than first imagined. It was important enough for companies that they wouldn't just turn it over to NDL lightly, but it wasn't so important that they were in any rush to make a decision. Once you had the names, the obvious superiority of NDL's lists was not at all obvious to list brokers. To them, someone who bought *Time* magazine by direct mail was a better potential candidate for *Tennis* magazine than someone who had indicated an interest in tennis on one of NDL's questionnaires. I talked to 10 of the 20 big players in the industry, and they just did not believe in the concept. It was clear that if NDL could prove the superiority of its lists in tests, they would have no choice but to buy. And, in the final analysis, I just had faith that it would work.

Rob Johnson recalled his reaction:

Jock and I were both extremely pleased to have this additional set of venture investors behind us. Naturally, every round of financing meant more dilution for us, but we didn't seem to have any alternatives. Also, the venture capitalists had promised us options to get our positions back up at some point in the future.

During 1981, NDL was more successful in obtaining list clients. But again, the issue became one of generating real cash flow.

As Tom Claflin reflected:

Most of us had confidence in NDL, but we worried about the cash flow problem that stemmed from NDL's inability to generate any significant revenues. I remember a number of visits where we discussed ways to increase the firm's meager revenues.

Rob Johnson offered his perspective on the cash flow problem:

We are really in two very different businesses. Our "client services" business involves signing up manufacturing clients—businesses who will put *our* cards in with their products. The marketing of this service, the collection, input and maintenance of this data in the data base and the preparation of reports for manufacturing clients is an expensive proposition. But, this is really the up-front investment in the data base that is required in order to have a list product to sell.

Despite its revenue problem, NDL's management wanted to expand the firm's operations in three areas: building its own in-house computer system, adding a New York-based sales force, and hiring three new managers.

NDL had been experiencing continually rising costs with Baldwin DECO, and NDL's management felt that the company would never become cash positive unless it was able to transform this large variable cost into a fixed expense. As NDL's head of computer operations recalled:

NDL's data processing arrangement was not working out well. Baldwin DECO's major customers were the financial institutions owned by its parent company, Baldwin-United. As a result, NDL got the short end when those institutions needed something done.

In addition, the costs were becoming a serious problem. The DECO rates didn't go down enough as the time on the system went up, and NDL's use on the system was growing rapidly, mainly due to two factors: (1) the company was providing more reports back to the manufacturers as the number of clients and the card flow grew, and (2) the production of lists was becoming increasingly data processing intensive as NDL performed more and more "cuts" on the data.

We negotiated with DECO and with several other service bureaus, pointing out that NDL had to begin achieving significant economies of scale as the volumes increased; but we simply could not get the rates down to levels that made any long-term sense. Finally, after receiving a one-month bill for $70,000, I said enough is enough and told Jock that we needed to bring the data processing function in-house.

NDL also wanted to add a New York-based direct list sales force. As Bickert described:

> We had concerns about our list sales agent, a New York list management firm that provided us with sales support for the industry standard commission of 20 percent. They were well respected, but they couldn't provide the time and energy we believed was necessary to sell our concept.

On one occasion, Rob and I decided to go visit an important potential client that our list manager couldn't seem to get in to visit. After a four-hour meeting with this client, they told us that they would test our list because they liked the idea. Later that week, we got a call from our list manager regarding this same client: "I just got off the phone with a big customer that I was able to talk to for 15 minutes just about NDL's list product. It sounds like they like the company's concept," he said. When I heard this, I knew we couldn't rely on them to sell our rather revolutionary product as well as we could ourselves.

Rob Johnson added his perspective:

> Although they can't give us their total attention, they still offer NDL value because they have contacts in the list industry that we don't have. However, we can build our own direct sales force to work in tandem with them. Sure it would duplicate some of our costs, but right now we need all the exposure we can get.

Finally, NDL wanted to add a layer of senior and middle managers: a marketing representative to handle manufacturing clients, a sales manager in charge of list sales, and a person to coordinate the firm's finances. Rationalizing the additions, Bickert pointed out:

> We need a few more good people to help manage the various sides of our business. It's difficult to integrate our operations because the people on the list side of our business are completely different from those on the manufacturing side. In essence, they just don't speak the same language. We need some more people to help integrate those lines of communication. We also need someone to add some stability to the management of the firm's resources. Rob and I can't do all of this alone. The task is simply more difficult than we had imagined, and we need a larger organization to accomplish our objectives.

The Decision

In early January 1982, NDL and its venture backers met to determine the fate of the company. The firm's preliminary financials for the previous year had just come in, and

NDL's loss was the largest ever (see **Exhibit 4**). NDL had projected a break-even year for 1982, and healthy profits in 1983 and beyond (see **Exhibit 5** for recent projections, and **Exhibit 6** for historical perspective on projections and actual results).

Johnson described the situation by saying:

> Unfortunately, we keep missing our revenue projections, and now we're asking for our "fourth and last round." I think we've lost some credibility with the VCs, especially the larger ones. Just how much, I'm not sure.
>
> While we have confidence in our business concept, results to date are mixed. Some of our feedback suggests that our lists are working well (see **Exhibit 7**), but in some areas, we haven't had any big orders. In addition, its difficult to get mailers to share their marketing results with us—and in those cases we can't tell how well our lists are working.

The venture capitalists had mixed feelings about the investment. One of the second-round investors commented:

> We've already put a good deal of money in, and I'm inclined to go one more round. I question, however, whether we really need to fund the additional investment required to build the organization, the direct sales force, and the computer system. Can't we wait until the jury is in on the concept before we ante up for these projects?

Tom Claflin commented further on these thoughts:

> I think all of the VCs understand the importance of bringing the computer system in-house. Unfortunately, this will require an additional capital investment in a venture that has yet to approach its projections and is a long way from positive cash flow.

One venture capitalist thought that this might be the last window for getting out "whole":

> The names in the data base definitely have real value. If we sold the company now, at least we could recoup our investment and get back to even.

Another venture capitalist offered his perspective:

> I believe in Jock and Rob, and I don't know if I'll be able to convince the investment committee at my firm to go along. If NDL attempts this financing at the same price as the last round, I know my partners will question that.

As founder, Bickert had a different perspective on the situation:

> Things have looked bleak before, and we've made it. NDL represents the culmination of all the marketing acumen that I've accumulated throughout my professional life. I won't let it die now. We're too close.
>
> Claflin and I have talked about the firm's problems quite a bit, and I think he's very supportive. Egan and the other VCs are more difficult to predict. But some way or another, we'll keep the firm going.

EXHIBIT 1 Sample Questionnaire

Moe & Larry's
Ice Cream Machines, Inc.

IMPORTANT!   IMPORTANT!
Please complete and return within the next 10 days!

6-4-6

1. ☐ Mr.   2. ☐ Mrs.   3. ☐ Ms.   4. ☐ Miss
First Name   Initial   Last Name

Street   Apt. No.

City   State   ZIP Code

Could you tell us about your new product?

① **Model number:**

② **Date of purchase:** Month Date Year

③ **Excluding sales tax, what price did you pay for this product?**
$ _____ .00

④ **Name of store where purchased:**

⑤ **What factors most influenced this purchase?** (check up to 3)
1. ☐ Received as a gift
2. ☐ Only brand available
3. ☐ Brand reputation
4. ☐ Delivery
5. ☐ Made in the U.S.A.
6. ☐ Friend's/Relative's recommendation
7. ☐ Salesperson's/Dealer's recommendation
8. ☐ Price
9. ☐ Product features
10. ☐ Selection of accessories
11. ☐ Service availability
12. ☐ Warranty
13. ☐ Other

⑥ **What features most influenced this purchase?** (check up to 3)
1. ☐ Received as a gift   6. ☐ Quality construction
2. ☐ Compact size   7. ☐ Durability
3. ☐ Ease of installation   8. ☐ Style/Appearance
4. ☐ Ease of operation   9. ☐ Other _____
5. ☐ Portability

⑦ **What media source(s) most influenced this purchase?**
(check up to 3)
1. ☐ Received as a gift
2. ☐ Purchase not influenced by media
3. ☐ TV advertisement
4. ☐ Radio advertisement
5. ☐ Newspaper advertisement
6. ☐ Magazine advertisement
7. ☐ Magazine article/review
8. ☐ Product brochure
9. ☐ Store display
10. ☐ Information through the mail
11. ☐ Other

Could you tell us about yourself?

⑧ **Date of birth of person whose name appears above:**
Month 1 9 Year

⑨ **Not including yourself, what is the GENDER and AGE (in years) of children and other adults living in your household?**
Male Female Age   Male Female Age
1. ☐ No one else in household
1. ☐ 2. ☐ _____ years   1. ☐ 2. ☐ _____ years
1. ☐ 2. ☐ _____ years   1. ☐ 2. ☐ _____ years

⑩ **Marital Status:**
1. ☐ Married   3. ☐ Widowed
2. ☐ Divorced/Separated   4. ☐ Never Married (Single)

⑪ **Occupation:**
Homemaker
Professional/Technical
Upper Management/Executive
Middle Management
Sales/Marketing
Clerical/Service Worker
Tradesman/Machine Operator/Laborer
Retired
Student
Self Employed/Business Owner
Work from Home Office

⑫ **Which group describes your annual family income?**
1. ☐ Under $15,000   8. ☐ $45,000-$49,999
2. ☐ $15,000-$19,999   9. ☐ $50,000-$59,999
3. ☐ $20,000-$24,999   10. ☐ $60,000-$74,999
4. ☐ $25,000-$29,999   11. ☐ $75,000-$99,999
5. ☐ $30,000-$34,999   12. ☐ $100,000-$124,999
6. ☐ $35,000-$39,999   13. ☐ $125,000-$149,999
7. ☐ $40,000-$44,999   14. ☐ $150,000 & over

⑬ **Level of Education:** (check highest level completed)
Some High School or Less
Completed High School
Some College
Completed College
Some Graduate School
Completed Graduate School
Have Attended Vocational/Technical School _____

⑭ **Which credit cards do you use regularly?**
1. ☐ American Express, Diners Club
2. ☐ MasterCard, Visa, Discover
3. ☐ Department Store, Oil Company, etc.
4. ☐ Do not use credit cards

⑮ **For your primary residence, do you:**
1. ☐ Own a House?
2. ☐ Own a Townhouse/Condominium?
3. ☐ Rent a House?
4. ☐ Rent an Apartment/Townhouse/Condominium?

⑯ **Which of the following do you plan to do within the next 6 or 12 months?**
                           1-6 Months 7-12 Months
Get Married   ☐   ☐
Have a Baby   ☐   ☐
Buy a House   ☐   ☐
Remodel a Home   ☐   ☐
Move to a New Residence   ☐   ☐
Change Jobs   ☐   ☐
Retire   ☐   ☐

(please continue on back!)

⑰ **To help us understand our customers' lifestyles, please indicate the interests and activities in which you or your spouse enjoy participating on a regular basis.**

Home Life
01. ☐ Flower Gardening
02. ☐ Grandchildren
03. ☐ Home Decorating/Furnishing
04. ☐ Home Workshop/Do-It-Yourself
05. ☐ House Plants
06. ☐ Home Video Games
07. ☐ Home Video Recording
08. ☐ Vegetable Gardening

Good Life
09. ☐ Attending Cultural/Arts Events
10. ☐ Fashion Clothing
11. ☐ Fine Art/Antiques
12. ☐ Foreign Travel
13. ☐ Gourmet Cooking
14. ☐ Travel for Pleasure/Vacation
15. ☐ Travel in the USA
16. ☐ Wines

Investing & Money
17. ☐ Entering Sweepstakes
18. ☐ Casino Gambling
19. ☐ Moneymaking Opportunities
20. ☐ Real Estate Investments
21. ☐ Stock/Bond Investments

Sports, Fitness & Health
22. ☐ Bicycling Frequently
23. ☐ Dieting/Weight Control
24. ☐ Golf
25. ☐ Health/Natural Foods
26. ☐ Improving Your Health
27. ☐ Physical Fitness/Exercise
28. ☐ Running/Jogging
29. ☐ Snow Skiing Frequently
30. ☐ Tennis Frequently
31. ☐ Walking for Health
32. ☐ Watching Sports on TV

Great Outdoors
33. ☐ Camping/Hiking
34. ☐ Fishing Frequently
35. ☐ Hunting/Shooting
36. ☐ Motorcycles
37. ☐ Power Boating
38. ☐ Recreational Vehicles
39. ☐ Sailing

World & Environment
40. ☐ Community/Civic Activities
41. ☐ Current Affairs/Politics
42. ☐ Environmental Issues
43. ☐ Wildlife/Animal Protection

Hobbies & Interests
44. ☐ Automotive Work
45. ☐ Avid Book Reading
46. ☐ Bible/Devotional Reading
47. ☐ Buy Pre-Recorded Videos
48. ☐ Career-Oriented Activities
49. ☐ Coin/Stamp Collecting
50. ☐ Collectibles/Collections
51. ☐ Crafts
52. ☐ Electronics
53. ☐ Listen to Records/Tapes/CDs
54. ☐ Needlework/Knitting
55. ☐ Our Nation's Heritage
56. ☐ Photography
57. ☐ Science Fiction
58. ☐ Science/New Technology
59. ☐ Self-Improvement
60. ☐ Sewing

You Spouse

⑱ **To help us understand our customers' lifestyles, please indicate the interests and activities in which you or your spouse enjoy participating on a regular basis.**

⑲ **Please check all that apply to your household.**
1. ☐ Shop by Catalog/Mail Order
2. ☐ Military Veteran in Household
3. ☐ Member of Frequent Flyer Program
4. ☐ Travel for Business
5. ☐ Support Health Charities
6. ☐ Wear Women's Large/Tall Sizes
7. ☐ Wear Men's Large/Tall Sizes
8. ☐ Wear Petite Sizes (5'4" or Under)
9. ☐ Wear Classic/Traditional Fashions
10. ☐ Wear Easy Care Fashions
11. ☐ Wear Stylish/Trend-Setting Fashions
12. ☐ Subscribe to Cable TV
13. ☐ Have a CD Player
14. ☐ Have a Camcorder
15. ☐ Have a Dog
16. ☐ Have a Cat
17. ☐ Own a Vacation Home/Property
18. ☐ Own a Cellular Telephone
19. ☐ Use an IBM or Compatible PC
20. ☐ Use an Apple/Macintosh Computer

⑳ **Using the numbers in the above list, please indicate the 3 most important activities for:**
You _____   Spouse _____

Thanks for taking the time to fill out this questionnaire. Your answers will be used for market research studies and reports. They will also allow you to receive important mailings and special offers from a number of fine companies whose products and services relate directly to the specific interests, hobbies, and other information indicated above. Through this selective program, you will be able to obtain more information about activities in which you are involved and less about those in which you are not. Please check here ☐ if you would prefer not to participate in this opportunity.
If you have comments or suggestions about our product, please write to: Customer Service • Moe & Larry's Inc. • 123 Road Ave • Anywhere, USA 12345

© 1993 National Demographics & Lifestyles, Inc. All Rights Reserved.

Please seal with tape. Do not staple.

Exнiвiт 2 **Financing History**

	Initial Capitalization May 1976			Rob Johnson Joins May 1977			Baldwin-United January 1978			Venture Round I December 1979			Venture Round II December 1980		
	%	Shares	$ (in thousands)	%	Shares	$ (in thousands)	%	Shares	$ (in thousands)	%	Shares	$ (in thousands)	%	Shares	$ (in thousands)
Bickert	29	3,375	.500	22.5	3,375	—	11.3	3,375	—	7.2	6,750	—	3.9	6,750	—
Franklin	29	3,375	.500	22.5	3,375	—	11.3	3,375	—	—*	—*	—	—	—	—
Thomas	29	3,375	.500	22.5	3,375	—	11.3	3,375	—	—*	—*	—	—	—	—
Ducker	13	1,500	.222	10.0	1,500	—	4.8	1,500	—	1.6	1,500	—	0.9	1,500	—
Johnson				22.5	3,375	3	11.3	3,375	—	7.2	6,750	—	3.9	6,750	—
Baldwin-United							50.0	15,000	476	16.0	15,000	—	8.8	15,000	—
Claflin Capital										16.0	15,000	300	10.7	18,400	75
G. Washington										16.0	15,000	300	10.7	18,400	75
Transatlantic										16.0	15,000	300	8.8	15,000	—
6 Others										19.8	18,500	370	10.8	18,500	—
Burr, Egan, Deleage													12.2	21,000	462
Citicorp													7.7	13,200	290
Continental Ill.													7.2	12,300	271
Fleet													3.3	5,600	123
Wood River													5.8	10,000	220
Others													5.3	9,100	200
Total	100%	11,625	$1.722	100%	15,000	$ 3	100%	30,000	$476	100%	93,500	$1,270	100%	171,500	1,716

*Franklin and Thomas shares purchased by Bickert and Johnson.

EXHIBIT 3   NDL's Board of Directors

In addition to Bickert and Johnson, the following individuals served on NDL's board of directors in 1981:
- Lucien Wulsin, chairman of the board, Baldwin-United Corporation
- Jerome Hardy, chairman—Harpers Atlantic and former president of The Dreyfus Corporation and Time-Life Books
- Thomas M. Claflin II, president of Claflin Capital Management Inc.
- William P. Egan, partner in Burr, Egan, Deleage & Co.
- Don Christensen, president of Greater Washington Investors, Inc.

EXHIBIT 4   NDL Operating Statistics Summary

	1979	1980	1981
Revenue (thousands)	$363*	$ 488	$ 1,738
Pretax profit	$ 0	$(1,093)	$(1,104)
Number of manufacturing clients	10	25	57
Cards received (millions)	1.0	3.5	4.6
Data base size (millions)	0.8	2.8	5.4
Number names ordered by list clients (millions)	2	9	32
Total file turn rate	3.1	5.2	8.2
Number list orders	132	520	1,166
Number tests	121	380	807
Average test order (thousands)	9.4	11.3	15.4
Average continuation order (thousands)	28.2	34.5	48.5
Average list price per 1,000	41.20	44.98	49.50
Number U.S. employees	13	25	57

*Includes income from Bickert's Consulting

Historical Income Statements

	1977	1978	1979	1980	1981
Revenues					
Research	$ 29,700	$ 297,894	300,000	—	—
Client services	—	1,307	14,721	$ 109,472	$ 219,577
List rentals	—	390	48,634	378,320	1,518,260
Total	$ 29,700	299,591	$ 363,355	$ 487,792	$ 1,737,837
Expenses					
Research	28,436	207,581	249,185	0	0
List sales and commissions	0	28,679	96,060	217,232	742,761
Client services marketing	14,121	20,814	22,089	43,952	44,882
Data collection/entry/ file maintenance	0	27,308	292,633	556,228	715,876
Data processing/client services	0	7,675	32,693	143,772	205,714
Data processing/list services	0	7,196	30,711	139,544	211,764
G&A	21,976	203,127	285,675	320,982	529,149
Research and development	0	0	19,106	159,454	392,477
Total	$ 64,533	$ 502,380	$1,028,152	$ 1,581,164	$ 2,842,623
Net profit (loss)	($34,833)	($202,789)	($ 664,797)	($1,093,372)	($1,104,786)

EXHIBIT 4   *(continued)*

Historical Balance Sheets (year ended December 31)

	1977	1978	1979	1980	1981
Assets					
Cash and securities	$ 2,915	$ 183,904	$ 246,306	$ 253,269	$ 342,876
Accounts receivable	—	40,999	88,264	208,311	202,406
Other	—	—	500,000*	1,000,000*	—
Total current assets	$ 2,915	$ 224,903	$ 834,570	$ 1,461,580	$ 545,282
Property, plant, equipment (net)	—	29,605	62,290	71,648	70,248
Total assets	$ 2,915	$ 254,508	$ 896,860	$ 1,533,228	$ 615,530
Liabilities and Shareholders' Equity					
Accounts payable	$ 29,339	$ 7,730	$ 39,718	$ 78,211	$ 219,518
Accrued liabilities	—	—	2,101	52,465	96,988
Other	—	—	3,060	2,943	4,201
Total current liabilities	$ 29,339	$ 7,730	$ 44,879	$ 133,619	$ 320,707
Long-term debt	—	—	—	—	—
Shareholders' equity	4,722	480,722	1,750,722	3,391,722	3,391,722
Accumulated deficit	(31,146)	(233,944)	(898,741)	(1,992,113)	(3,096,899)
Net capital (deficiency)	(26,424)	246,778	851,981	1,399,609	294,823
Total liabilities and equity	$ 2,915	$ 254,508	$ 896,860	$ 1,533,228	$ 615,530

*Venture financing receivable.

Explanation of Revenue and Expense categories:

Revenues
- Research: revenues from Bickert's consulting business
- Client services: revenue from sale of services to manufacturing clients
- List rentals: revenue from sale of lists

Expenses
- Research: cost of Bickert's consulting
- List sales and commissions: cost of list sales and marketing effort and brokers' 20% commission for selling lists
- Client services marketing: cost of marketing service to manufacturing clients
- Data collection/entry/file maintenance: cost of collecting, and inputting data from cards, and maintaining data base
- Data processing/client services: cost of preparing reports for manufacturing clients
- Data processing/list services: cost of preparing lists for direct-mail clients
- G&A: General and administrative overhead
- Research and development: Cost of developing new services for manufacturing and list clients

EXHIBIT 5   Projections from November 1981 Business Plan ($000)

	1982					1983	1984
	IQ	*IIQ*	*IIIQ*	*IVQ*	*Year*	*1983*	*1984*
Revenues	$ 497	$754	$973	$1,032	$3,256	$9,250	$16,500
Operating expenses	918	816	818	974	3,526	8,100	13,200
Pretax profit	(421)	(62)	155	58	(270)	1,150	3,300

EXHIBIT 6   Projections vs. Actual Performance ($ in millions)

Projections from Business Plan Used in Financing (Date)	*1978*	*1979*	*1980*	*1981*	*1982*	*1983*	*1984*
Baldwin-United (June 1977)							
List size (millions of names)	2.4	11.9	19.2				
PBT	(.3)	0.2	2.1				
Venture I (March 1979)							
List size	—	1.1	3.8	8.4	14.6	22.4	
Gross sales	—	1.9	10.9	24.0	32.5	32.5	
PBT	—	0.6	6.0	14.3	19.6	19.6	
Venture II (September 1980)							
List size	—	—	—	6.0	12.0	12.0	12.0
Gross sales	—	—	—	2.2	11.8	23.5	47.0
PBT	—	—	—	0.3	4.4	11.1	24.4
Current (November 1981)							
List size	—	—	—	—	7.0	10.0	12.0
Gross sales	—	—	—	—	3.3	9.3	16.5
PBT	—	—	—	—	—	1.2	2.8
Actual Results							
List size	0	0	2.8	5.4			
Gross Sales	0.1	0.4	0.5	1.7			
PBT	0	0	(1.1)	(1.1)			

Exhibit 7   MEMORANDUM

TO: NDL Board Members

FROM: Jock Bickert & Rob Johnson

RE: Analysis of NDL Client List

DATE: November 26, 1981

    We have taken two separate lists of test and continuation orders and merged them in chronological order. This analysis shows that a large portion (80%) of the customers who placed their initial test order during 1979 have placed subsequent continuation orders. The "test to continuation conversion ratio" for the 1980 time frame drops to 55%. Finally, for 1981, this conversion ratio is roughly 7%. The *absolute number* of test orders had increased, however, quite dramatically during this time frame.

    This analysis suggests two things. First, the time cycle to reordering is several months, confirming the notion that the industry operates on mailing schedules that are spaced several months apart. Second, if the experience with the first-time users from 1979 becomes valid for subsequent months as we move forward in time, then we should soon begin to see a substantial pick up in continuations sometime this winter from the 1981 first-time customer group.

2–7 CVD INCORPORATED VERSUS A. S. MARKHAM CORPORATION (A)

It was 2 A.M. on April 10, 1984, and Bob Donadio and Joe Connolly sat in a small Boston coffeehouse thinking about their trial against A. S. Markham Corporation, a billion-dollar defense contractor. The two founders of CVD Inc. had sued their former employer—Markham—for relief from what they believed to be an onerous licensing contract. Markham, in turn, had sued them and their small company for a series of alleged infractions including breach of employment contracts, misappropriation of trade secrets, and misuse of confidential information.

The testimony in the trial had ended earlier that afternoon and the two men had spent five hours preparing their side's closing arguments with their lawyer. They would make those arguments tomorrow, the trial would end, and the jury would begin its deliberations—a process that was expected to take several days.

As Donadio and Connolly sat in the coffeehouse, they knew that if they lost the trial, the judgment against them would likely bankrupt the company. On the other hand, if they won, Markham could appeal the decision to a higher court and prolong the dispute even further. Perhaps, they wondered, they should try to settle the case with Markham before the jury returned with its verdict.

Background

Bob Donadio and Joe Connolly met in 1972, when Donadio recruited Connolly to work for Markham's Advanced Materials Department (AMD). In the seven years that followed, they both had satisfying careers working on Markham's research and development projects sponsored by various agencies of the United States government (see **Exhibit 1**).

Despite their good feelings about Markham, however, by 1979 both Donadio and Connolly wanted to explore new options. Thinking back, Donadio recalled:

This case was prepared by Research Associate Ennis J. Walton under the direction of Professor Michael J. Roberts.

Copyright © 1987 by the President and Fellows of Harvard College

Harvard Business School Case 9–388–042

It wasn't an easy decision to leave Markham. I had put in 20 damn good years with them, and I had obtained all the perks that a person with my seniority could expect to receive. I also had a family to think about: With a wife and three children, two of whom were of college age, I couldn't just leave the company without thinking about the possible impact my decision would have on the rest of my family. In time, I discussed things with my family, and they supported my desire. They weren't completely thrilled at first, but they eventually agreed with me.

Donadio's basic idea for CVD Inc. was to use his knowledge of the chemical vapor deposition (cvd) manufacturing process to become a supplier of infrared materials. Explaining the core technology, Donadio said:

The cvd process is an extremely useful way to combine different chemical compounds. First, gases or vapors of the compounds are brought together in a specially designed furnace. While in the furnace, the gases will react with one another to form a solid metal-like material that deposits on a substrate and then hardens as it cools. There are many different ways to form these vapors—we simply heat blocks of material in the furnace.

Following this, the solid is polished until it resembles a glasslike material capable of transmitting infrared light and high energy lasers. Once the material reaches this glasslike state, it must be subjected to a battery of tests in order to verify its purity—if it isn't pure, it won't transmit infrared light or lasers properly.

In most cases, materials manufactured by this process have properties that make them better than the same materials produced by another manufacturing process. This is particularly true for zinc selenide (ZnSe/cvd) and zinc sulfide (ZnS/cvd)—the two materials most frequently manufactured in this manner.

Donadio's original plan for the new company was to supply ZnSe/cvd to optical fabricators that used it to make output windows for commercial high energy laser (HEL) applications such as automobile body welding, steel plate cutting, and "bloodless" surgery. "We had suggested these commercial applications to Markham," said Donadio, "but they seemed uninterested." As the company grew, Donadio also expected to manufacture both ZnSe/cvd and ZnS/cvd to create infrared optical lenses used for thermal imaging in military applications that required night vision and thermal sensing in weapons.

Recalling his reasons for joining Donadio, Connolly said:

Bob first mentioned his idea for a new company to me one day after work in Markham's parking lot. This came as a welcome surprise to me since I was quietly looking around for a new job anyway. I really didn't have much to lose—I knew I could work well with Bob, so I decided to join him instead of joining a different company.

A few days after Donadio and Connolly decided to leave Markham, Donadio advised his supervisor, Dr. Smith, of their decision. During the meeting, Dr. Smith told Donadio that he and Connolly would have to appear before Markham's lawyers if they were serious about starting a cvd processing company. Reflecting on the meeting, Donadio said:

At the time, talking to Smith seemed like the right thing to do. I had consulted with him on many issues before—including this one. At one time, we even entertained the idea of combining our vast knowledge of cvd processes to form the new company. It only seemed right to let him know first.

During that meeting, however, Smith seemed to forget about all that. Instead, he told me that I would have to go before Markham's legal staff if I was serious about leaving to start a cvd processing company. A few hours later, he called Joe in his office to say the same thing.

Connolly added his perspective on being called into Markham's legal department for questioning:

For a scientist like me, it was quite bizarre to get summoned by Markham's lawyers. The entire atmosphere was different from everything that I knew about the company. Unlike the lab where I worked, the law department seemed cold and impersonal.

After the meeting with Markham's lawyers, it was obvious to Donadio and Connolly that they needed to hire a lawyer to protect their rights. As Donadio recalled:

We hadn't done anything wrong, but Markham didn't see it that way. Instead, they claimed that we were planning to steal and use its "proprietary information."

We tried to point out that because Markham's cvd research was funded under government contract, it was part of the public domain. I knew this because I'd spent the better part of my career preparing reports for the government that illustrated the cvd process.

From our perspective, Markham didn't have any proprietary information regarding the chemical vapor deposition process. They certainly didn't have any patents on the process. Moreover, Joe and I had enough expertise with the cvd processes to start a company that purposefully avoided everything that Markham considered "proprietary" or a "trade secret." Had they told us exactly what they considered to be trade secrets, we could have worked around them. But they just kept claiming that the entire process was proprietary.

After the meetings with Dr. Smith and the lawyers, I worked at Markham for about another month. During that time I was restricted to my desk and no one bothered to talk to me—for a researcher, that's like professional death. In our business, you live off the flow of information between your colleagues. I'm not naive and I'm certainly not a romantic, but I don't understand how stable personal and professional friendships could be lost in one day. I cannot understand why my friends and colleagues decided to ostracize me. Maybe they were under pressure to follow the company line—I don't know.

Initial Negotiations

Taking Markham's threats seriously, Donadio and Connolly hired Jerry Cohen, an attorney specializing in intellectual property issues, to serve as their lawyer. As their attorney, Cohen maintained a spirited debate with Markham's legal counsel, Len Davis, in an attempt to clarify Markham's case.

On one occasion, Cohen, Donadio, and Connolly met with Len Davis to discuss the alleged proprietary information. In that meeting, Cohen provided evidence from publicly available government documents to dispute Markham's proprietary claims. However, despite that information, the two sides were unable to reach a mutually acceptable agreement. Instead, Markham threatened to sue Donadio and Connolly for breaching their employment contracts (see excerpts, **Exhibit 2**) if they formed a new firm that used any of Markham's alleged proprietary information or trade secrets without a license from the company.

In January 1980, Donadio and Connolly formed CVD Incorporated. Without the benefit of salaries and with the threat of a long and costly lawsuit, Donadio and Connolly worked out of their homes during the first few months until they could design the company's manufacturing facility, finish their business plan, and raise capital.

In writing their business plan, Donadio used his knowledge to list 18 different domestic and international commercial companies that might purchase CVD's products. CVD's business plan also included a list of 35 government agencies that might purchase ZnSe/cvd and ZnS/cvd within the next five years. In all, CVD's business plan estimated that its company would generate before-tax profits of approximately $310,000 on sales of $1,400,000 during its third year of manufacturing operations. After that time, the company estimated that its overall sales would increase at an annual rate of 20 percent.

Despite a completed engineering design and optimistic figures, the process of attracting money for their venture was more difficult than they had initially expected. CVD's attempts were mired from the beginning by investors' fears that the company would be caught in an acrimonious and protracted legal fight. Prospective investors were also concerned that Markham would lower its prices and use its established position to maintain its hold on the market.

The License

Thus, after many frustrated attempts to raise capital in the spring of 1980, Donadio and Connolly, with advice from Jerry Cohen, decided to sign a licensing agreement with Markham (see **Exhibit 3**). The terms of the license called for CVD to pay Markham 15 percent and 8 percent on the net selling price for ZnSe/cvd and ZnS/cvd, respectively, for a 10-year period. Once under license, Donadio and Connolly lowered their business plan's projections to reflect the terms of the Markham license.

The license quieted investors' fears, and Donadio and Connolly were successful in raising the funds. The two men received $450,000 by mid-June 1980 from the following sources: $300,000 from a loan from the Small Business Administration; $80,000 from a prospective customer; and the remainder from the men's family and friends.

Beginning Operations

Donadio and Connolly put the firm's money to work immediately purchasing equipment and signing a lease for a 4,500-square-foot facility in Woburn. By February 1981, the firm had made significant progress: net sales had reached $751,000. Despite this progress, Donadio and Connolly still worried about the firm's $109,000 licensing fee, which when added to the company's costs and expenses produced net earnings before taxes of negative $99,000. Remembering his thoughts, Donadio said:

> Our revenues and costs were in good shape for a start-up, but it was clear that CVD couldn't survive with the original terms of the license—it was like having a tax on our gross revenues.

Based on an important clause in its license with Markham (see Exhibit 3), CVD informed Markham that it wanted to exercise its right to renegotiate the terms of the license. Markham, however, refused to alter the terms of the contract. In all, the company tried and failed to renegotiate on three separate occasions. Finally, Donadio and Connolly decided not to pay Markham until the company honored CVD's right to renegotiate the terms of the license.

In June 1981, Markham informed CVD that it was in default. Markham also advised CVD that if all obligations were not immediately paid in full, it would cancel the agreement and seek legal action. CVD responded to Markham's notices by seeking new counsel. With little time, Donadio and Connolly, aided by Jerry Cohen, identified Blair L. Perry—a high-technology and antitrust specialist—as a good attorney to handle their case.

The Suit

After a short period of negotiations, Perry agreed to handle the case. In exchange, CVD agreed to pay Perry's firm $6,000 on a monthly basis for its legal representation.

In August 1981, CVD filed a complaint against Markham in federal court, arguing that the license was invalid because it represented a violation of the Sherman Antitrust Act, which restricts illegal attempts to maintain a monopoly and restrain competition.

Blair Perry recalled his strategy:

> We filed an antitrust claim for several reasons. First, we wanted to claim the high ground by being the plaintiff. Second, an antitrust violation was the only means of getting the case heard in the federal court system. Here, you can get to trial in two years instead of the five it takes in the state courts. The federal judges are also more used to dealing with the sort of complex issues this case presents.

A few days later, Markham responded with a counterclaim, arguing that the license was valid and enforceable. Markham also claimed that Donadio, Connolly, and CVD Inc. had engaged in unfair and deceptive business practices to obtain Markham's proprietary information. As a result, Markham claimed monetary losses in excess of $4 million as well as other damages. The basis of the dispute was as follows.

CVD argued that the license was invalid because:

- Markham did not have any trade secrets related to the production of ZnSe/cvd and ZnS/cvd.
- Markham acted in bad faith when it compelled CVD to sign the license because it knew that it didn't have any trade secrets.
- The license was signed under duress.
- And the license was counter to public policy objectives in that it restrained competition and helped sustain Markham's monopoly in this market.

Markham disputed CVD's claims arguing instead that the license was valid and enforceable because:

- Markham had trade secrets and confidential business information related to the production of ZnSe/cvd and ZnS/cvd.
- Donadio and Connolly had learned Markham's trade secrets and confidential business information while employed by Markham.
- Donadio and Connolly had signed employment contracts that prevented any employee from using or disclosing any of Markham's proprietary information unless expressly authorized by Markham.
- The license agreement was a valid legal document—irrespective of whether or not Markham actually had trade secrets or proprietary information—which granted CVD the right to use Markham's knowledge related to the production of ZnSe/cvd and ZnS/cvd.
- Donadio and Connolly signed the license willingly and with a competent attorney protecting their legal rights.
- Donadio and Connolly had breached contracts and duties of good faith outlined in their employment contracts.
- Donadio, Connolly, and CVD had misappropriated Markham's proprietary information relating to the production of ZnSe/cvd and ZnS/cvd.
- And CVD had breached fiduciary duties mandated by the license.

Pretrial Actions

After reviewing the claims of each party, the court urged CVD Inc. and Markham to attempt to settle the matter out of court. In extensive pretrial settlement discussions, CVD offered to pay approximately $450,000 to Markham in return for freedom from the royalty obligations and from trade secret claims. Markham refused that offer and in exchange proposed that it would end its legal claims if CVD paid $3 million to Markham. Unable to compromise beyond this point, both sides began the lengthy pretrial preparation process. Recalling some of the reasons why it took so long to make it to court, Blair Perry said:

> The most difficult part of the pretrial process started when we tried to demystify Markham's trade secret claims. No matter what we did, we couldn't get a comprehensive list of what they were claiming as trade secrets. We eventually had to prepare our own list of possible trade secrets in order to be ready for trial—a process that was very time consuming and full of frustrations.
>
> For example, Markham told us that its trade secrets could be found in some of its engineering drawings that we were going to inspect. When I got to Markham's offices, they took me to a room and showed me a stack of about 2,000 drawings. I was simply amazed!
>
> After a cursory look at the evidence, I tried to get the court to force Markham to be more specific. To my dismay, however, the court ruled in Markham's favor, and so I spent a number of days sorting through all those drawings trying to determine which ones were really relevant.

After two years of preparations, the opposing attorneys entered court to empanel a jury. This process was important because each side expected the case to turn on the testimony of the witnesses. In the end, a 12-person jury was selected that featured a chemical engineer as the foreman.

The Trial

On March 5, 1984, the case of *CVD Inc.* v. *Markham* went to trial before Justice Stevenson of the United States District Court, District of Massachusetts. Sparing no expense, Markham appeared in court with five lawyers while Blair Perry alone represented CVD.

After hearing each side's opening statements, Justice Stevenson made two important decisions that affected the way the issues were argued. First, he ruled that Markham could not use the term proprietary because it was unclear and not well grounded in legal precedent. The court also ruled that in order for CVD to obtain relief from the license, it had to show by "clear and convincing" evidence that Markham knew it didn't have trade secrets when it enacted the licensing agreement with CVD.

The information presented during the trial focused on the following topics:

I. The CVD Process. Markham submitted the following testimony regarding the cvd process:

- The Advanced Materials Division, where Donadio and Connolly were employed, had engaged in the development of unique and sophisticated methods and equipment used to produce ZnSe/cvd and ZnS/cvd since 1959.

- An expert witness testified that there is an art or skill required to produce ZnSe/cvd and ZnS/cvd that could only be obtained through years of skilled experience.

- When asked what he would need to design, build, and operate a cvd furnace to make ZnSe/cvd and ZnS/cvd, an expert witness claimed that he would need "an experienced staff."

- Markham claimed that in 1980, it was the only company with an experienced staff (seven people) capable of producing ZnSe/cvd and ZnS/cvd.

- Markham asserted that Donadio and Connolly had acquired their knowledge of the specific processes, equipment, and methods used by Markham during their employment with Markham.

- Markham argued that no detailed information about the cvd process had been disclosed, and it claimed that CVD had misappropriated the following trade secrets:

  a. Passivation Gas Mixture: This gaseous mixture was used by Markham to scrub out the discharge lines from the cvd furnace before it was opened to prevent fires or explosions when fine zinc dust mixed with normal air. Markham's officials testified that the company had had three fires and two explosions before it discovered that a mixture of 97 percent nitrogen and 3 percent oxygen would stabilize the zinc dust and prevent fires and explosions.

     One expert witness testified that during the jury's visit to CVD's facilities, he had noticed that CVD had tried to hide its own passivation gas tank (by covering it with brown paper) to prevent Markham and the court from knowing that it used the same passivation gas mixture that Markham employed.

b. Alumina Insert Hydrogen Sulfide Injector: This was an insert that was placed over the tip of the hydrogen sulfide injector to prevent the corrosion of the stainless steel mixing chamber where gases were mixed. By using this, Markham was able to prevent hydrogen sulfide gas from reacting with and corroding the injector tip.

One of Markham's expert witnesses testified that the composition and exact positioning of the alumina insert was critical because corrosion would make it impossible to complete the long furnace phase of the cvd process (usually one to two days) necessary to produce high-quality materials. He also testified that there were other ceramic materials that could be used instead of alumina.

c. Hexagonal Graphite Nut: This piece fit inside Markham's sulfide injector assembly to allow argon gas to be distributed uniformly thereby making it possible for the company to manufacture high-quality zinc sulfide.

- Markham asserted that it always denied public access to its furnace facilities to protect its trade secrets.

The following points regarding the chemical vapor deposition process were made by CVD during the trial:

- The cvd process was well known to scientists in general and chemical engineers in particular.
- The cvd process was taught throughout the education system from grade school to college chemistry courses.
- Donadio and Connolly testified that they acquired knowledge about the process before, after, and during their employment with Markham.
- Donadio and Connolly testified that they returned all documents belonging to Markham at the end of their employment with the company; and, they stressed that their employment contracts did not contain noncompete clauses.
- CVD produced evidence that a U.S. patent on certain aspects of the cvd process had been issued to another individual in 1964 (see **Exhibit 4**).
- Markham's patent attorney testified (under cross-examination) that he had learned of this patent when Markham tried to patent ZnSe/cvd and ZnS/cvd, and therefore, he had stopped the patent process. He explained that Markham had stopped the patent process because Markham believed that there were no commercial applications of the process. Because the government was the only likely customer, and because it already held a royalty-free license on the process, it didn't make sense to proceed with the patent. Moreover, he admitted that he had informed both Donadio and Dr. Smith in a memo that Markham would not seek a patent on these products.
- Markham's patent attorney admitted that Markham had a computer system that listed all information that the company officially protected as trade secrets, and

CVD produced evidence that showed the cvd process, ZnSe/cvd and ZnS/cvd, had not been protected by this system.

- Markham's patent attorney testified that Markham had a company policy that required all protected engineering drawings to be marked or stamped secret and placed in a special drawer. And Connolly testified that he had made hundreds of detailed engineering drawings, and he had never been told to mark them *secret*.

- CVD provided evidence that Markham had disclosed elements of the cvd process in government reports, lectures, and films. These disclosures included information about Markham's hexagonal graphite nut.

- One of Markham's expert witnesses testified (under cross-examination) that a "component" engineer could construct Markham's manufacturing process from the information disclosed in the government reports.

- One of Markham's witnesses admitted that many of Markham's alleged trade secrets were known in the industry. For example, the expert witness admitted (under cross-examination) that it was well known in the industry that zinc dust would ignite if exposed to oxygen. He also acknowledged that any undergraduate engineer would recognize that a passivation gas containing less oxygen than normal air would slow the rate of oxidation, which caused fires and explosions.

- Another one of Markham's expert witnesses admitted (under cross-examination) that it would be obvious to any engineer that a corrosion-resistant material would be needed to prevent the corrosion of the stainless steel injector tip. He further admitted that it made logical sense to use an alumina insert over the stainless steel injector tip because alumina was inert and had a high melting point.

II. The Products: The following points regarding the ZnSe/cvd and ZnS/cvd products were made by CVD:

- Due to their unique light transmission properties, ZnSe/cvd and ZnS/cvd were extremely popular among military and commercial customers, and these customers used the products, rather than other infrared materials made by different manufacturing processes.

- Markham's ZnSe/cvd and ZnS/cvd had outstripped Eastman Kodak's ZnSe and ZnS made by the "hot pressing process"; Kodak had discontinued its ZnSe production.

- Before 1980, Markham produced and sold 65 percent and 98 percent of the ZnSe/cvd and ZnS/cvd, respectively.

- Markham had imposed a "price squeeze" by reducing its prices in situations where it knew it was in direct competition with CVD. Markham knew CVD could not reduce its prices, pay exorbitant royalties, and still operate on a profitable basis.

- Markham reduced its prices 20 percent on January 21, 1980, with the intent of preventing CVD from competing.

- Markham had maintained its prices at the January 21, 1980, rate despite inflation and increasing production costs.

- Markham had falsely represented to various potential customers that CVD was in violation of its contract obligations and was thus an unsuitable supplier.

Markham disputed CVD's claims arguing:

- ZnSe and ZnS, irrespective of the manufacturing process, along with 40 other materials can be used for their optical, infrared, and electrical properties.
- Markham only has a 9 percent market share of all 42 infrared materials sold in the United States.
- Donadio admitted that before leaving Markham, he had participated in the formation of the company's prices, which became effective on January 21, 1980.
- Markham claimed that its prices never fell below the average costs necessary to produce ZnSe/cvd and ZnS/cvd.

III. The License: CVD made the following claims about the license:

- Donadio and Connolly testified that Markham threatened to sue them unless they signed a license; this action, they claimed, left them with no other viable alternatives.
- Markham had never listed its "trade secrets" in its negotiations with CVD; therefore, no specific information had been granted by the license.
- Jerry Cohen testified that he had tried and failed to get Markham to limit the terms of license.
- Markham's lawyer, Len Davis, acknowledged that he had implied to Donadio, Connolly, and Cohen that the terms of the licensing agreement were less than equitable before they signed the agreement.

Markham took exception to CVD's argument:

- Markham claimed that the processes, methods, and techniques that were used by Markham represented trade secret and confidential business information.
- Donadio and Connolly testified that they had been offered new jobs inside Markham, but they turned them down to start CVD.
- Markham claimed that Donadio and Connolly voluntarily, with aid of a lawyer of their own selection, executed an agreement that recognized the authenticity of Markham's trade secrets and confidential business information.

IV. The Employment Contract: Markham argued that Donadio and Connolly had broken their employment contracts:

- Markham provided evidence that Donadio and Connolly, along with all other Markham employees, had signed employment contracts that prohibited them from using or disclosing any of the information that they had learned or practiced while they were Markham's employees for their own benefit at any time unless they were specifically authorized by Markham.
- Markham provided evidence, described earlier, that Donadio and Connolly had indeed misappropriated proprietary information and were therefore in violation of their employment contracts.

CVD presented evidence, discussed earlier, that the information that Markham claimed to be proprietary was, in fact, well known in the industry.

After 26 days of testimony, each side presented the judge with its own Suggested Instructions to the Jury (see **Exhibits 5** and **6**).

Conclusion

As the two men reviewed the past month of testimony, they were optimistic about the outcome. Yet they also knew that with a jury, anything could happen. Blair Perry felt good about the way the case was going, but he too had urged caution. As Donadio and Connolly contemplated the future, it was the consequences of this uncertainty that loomed before them. Donadio commented:

> I feel confident, but if we lose, we're out of business. Even if we win, Markham can keep us in court on appeal for years. Perhaps the testimony has convinced Markham that their chances of winning are not very good. Maybe they'd be willing to settle for a reasonable amount, or even renegotiate the license.

While the possibility of resolving this uncertainty was attractive, the two men were also cognizant of the fact that they had spent tremendous time and nearly a quarter of a million dollars in legal fees ($156,000 of which they had yet to pay). While they felt they could afford some settlement (see **Exhibit 7** for financials), to back down now seemed not only wrong, but also an admission of guilt that neither man truly felt.

Exhibit 1   The Plaintiffs

Name: Robert Donadio

Title: President, CVD Inc.

Education: BS and MS degrees in Mechanical Engineering from Northeastern University 1958 and 1963, respectively.

Work Experience: Served as principal scientist for Markham's Advanced Materials Department (AMD); managed Markham's domestic and international infrared materials marketing programs.

Special Recognition: Invented Markham's CVD Zinc Selenide and Zinc Sulfo-Selenide with Dr. Smith, B. Henderson, and W. Jung in 1973 (patent was not pursued by Markham); known as an international expert in the area of chemical vapor deposition.

Personal: Married with three children whose ages ranged from 15 to 21.

Name: Joseph Connolly

Title: Vice President, Operations, CVD Inc.

Education: AE degree in Mechanical Engineering from Wentworth Institute in 1969; BS and MS degrees in Mechanical Engineering from Northeastern University in 1972 and 1976, respectively.

Work Experience: Joined Markham's Advanced Materials Department in 1972; eventually served as senior scientist for Markham's AMD and lead engineer on the production of infrared windows for a number of government and commercial contracts.

Personal: Separated with three children whose ages ranged from 3 to 15.

Exhibit 2   The Employment Contract Signed by Donadio and Connolly

In consideration of the employment of _____ by the employer, Markham Corporation (Markham), in the course of which employment is contemplated that the Employee may make/create products and/or compose subject inventions and/or proprietary information, and the trust and confidence responded in the Employee by Markham with respect thereto, it is agreed as follows:

1. *Subject Invention* means any invention, improvement, or discovery of the Employee, whether or not patentable, other than those identified below, which during the period of his employment by Markham is (*a*) conceived by the employer, or (*b*) first actually reduced to practice by or for Markham, and which arises out of or is related to any of the business activities of Markham or any other company, which is owned or controlled by Markham.

2. *Proprietary Information* means secret or private information concerning Markham's design, manufacture, use, purchase, or sale of its products or materials, such as may be contained in but not limited to, Markham's manufacturing methods, processes or techniques, treatment or chemical composition of material, and plant layout or tooling, all to the extent that (*a*) such information is not readily disclosed by inspection or analysis of the products or materials sold, leased or otherwise disposed of by Markham, and (*b*) Markham has protected such information from unrestricted use by others.

3. All Subject Inventions and Proprietary Information are and shall remain the sole and exclusive property of Markham, subject only to any prior encumbrances attaching thereto. The Employee agrees to disclose all Subject Inventions, and all Proprietary Information generated by the Employee, promptly, completely and in writing to Markham and such others and under such conditions as may be designated by Markham.

4. The Employee agrees (*a*) to execute all documents requested by Markham for vesting in Markham the entire right, title and interest in; and to (*i*) all Subject Inventions, (*ii*) all Proprietary Information generated by the Employee, and (*iii*) all patent applications filed and all patents issuing on such Subject Inventions; (*b*) to execute all documents requested by Markham for filing and prosecutions and such applications for patents as Markham may desire covering such Subject Inventions; and (*c*) to give to Markham all assistance it reasonably requires in order to process Markham's rights in its Subject Inventions and Proprietary Information.

5. The Employee agrees that his obligation to perform the acts specified in paragraph 4 above shall not expire with termination of his employment. However, the period during which Markham's rights to Subject Inventions, and Proprietary Information generated by the Employee are created shall not be extended by virtue of the previous sentence. Markham agrees to pay the Employee at a reasonable rate for any time that the Employee actually spends in the performance of the acts specified in paragraph 4 above at Markham's written request after termination of the Employee's employment and to reimburse the Employee for expenses necessarily incurred by him in connection with such acts.

6. All documents, records, models, prototypes, and other tangible evidence of Subject Inventions and Proprietary Information, which shall at any time come into the possession of the Employee, shall be the sole and exclusive property of Markham and shall be surrendered to Markham upon the termination of the Employee's employment by Markham, or upon request at any other time.

7. The Employee agrees that, unless duly authorized in writing by an Officer of Markham, he will not either during his employment by Markham, or thereafter as long as the Employee is unable reasonably to demonstrate that Markham Proprietary Information has passed into the public domain other than as a consequence of the Employee's own acts, divulge, or use for his own or another's benefit, any of said Proprietary Information.

8. The Employee represents and warrants that he has not entered and will not enter into any agreement inconsistent herewith.

EXHIBIT 3   **Excerpts from License Agreement**

The license signed between CVD Inc. and Markham had the following important clauses:

1. Markham's cvd process used to manufacture zinc selenide and zinc sulfide, trademarked *Martran,* represents proprietary trade secrets.
2. Markham grants CVD Inc. the nonexclusive right to use its proprietary process for which CVD Inc. agrees to pay Markham royalties of 15 percent and 8 percent on the net selling prices of its ZnSe/cvd and ZnS/cvd products produced pursuant to this agreement.
3. Markham agrees to allow CVD Inc. to renegotiate the terms of this original agreement if they prove inequitable.
4. Markham retains the right to cancel the agreement at any time if CVD Inc. fails to pay the royalties.
5. No termination of the license shall release any party from the royalty obligations that have incurred.
6. This license shall be construed under the laws of the Commonwealth of Massachusetts.
7. This license is effective retroactively from January 1, 1980, until December 31, 1990.

EXHIBIT 4   Vapor Phase Crystallization Patent, Dated February 11, 1964, Granted to H. J. Gould

---

(Excerpts from U.S. Government Patent Filing)

This invention has to do with the crystallization from the vapor phase of crystals at least one component of which is a metal that is solid at normal temperature.

The invention has to do, more particularly, with improved methods and apparatus for supplying to a furnace chamber the vapor of a metallic component that is solid at normal temperature.

This invention is particularly useful in, but is not limited to, the production of semiconductive crystals such, for example, as cadmium and zinc sulphide, selenide, and telluride, and mixtures of such components. It is well known that crystals of that type can be produced in good purity by vapor phase crystallization.

In producing such illustrative crystals, the nonmetallic component is ordinarily supplied to the furnace as a continuous stream of gas, typically as hydrogen sulphide, selenide, or telluride. The rate of supply of such a gaseous component is accurately and conveniently controllable by known methods.

The metallic component is ordinarily supplied by inserting in the furnace in the gas stream a boat containing the metal in solid or liquid form. The metal then evaporates into the gas stream at a rate that is roughly controllable by variation of such factors as temperature, the rate of gas flow, and the area of the exposed metal surface.

Such control, however, is less accurate than is often desirable and is unsatisfactory for many other reasons. Even rough control of the vaporizing temperature usually requires a special furnace zone for that purpose. The rate of gas flow that is most suitable for metal vaporization may be undesirable for other reasons. And the area of metal surface usually decreases in an uncontrollable way as the initial charge is exhausted. Moreover, the rate of evaporation from a given surface area is very sensitive to contamination of the surface, which typically increases as the metal charge is consumed.

The present invention avoids all of those difficulties in a remarkably economical and convenient manner. In accordance with one aspect of the invention, the metallic component is supplied in the form of a fine wire, and is fed to the furnace at a definite velocity. The described method has the further great advantage that under equilibrium conditions of operation, the rate of vapor supply is essentially or completely independent of virtually all other variable factors. Hence, those factors may be adjusted arbitrarily as required to meet other conditions.

In accordance with a further aspect of the invention, the metal wire is fed to the furnace chamber through a capillary passage formed of suitable inert material such as quartz, for example. The passage is so arranged that the advancing metal reaches vaporizing temperature at a point spaced from the exit mouth of the passage. Vaporization then occurs within the capillary passage, and the metal leaves the passage mouth as a continuous and uniform stream of vapor. A further advantage of that structure is that, by suitable form and placement of the passage, the metal vapor can be delivered accurately to any desired point of the furnace chamber.

A further aspect of the invention provides means for surface cleaning of the metal wire immediately prior to melting and vaporization. That may be accomplished by passing the wire through a reducing chamber, which is continuously washed by a reducing gas, such as hydrogen, for example. The reducing chamber is preferably maintained at an elevated temperature, which may be only slightly less than the melting point of the metal.

A full understanding of the invention, and of its further objects and advantages, will be had from the following description of certain illustrative manners in which it may be carried out, of which description the accompanying drawings form a part. The particulars of that description are intended only as illustration, and not as a limitation upon the scope of the invention, which is defined in the appended claims.

[Drawings and explanations have been omitted for brevity.]

I Claim the Following as Patented:

1. The method of supplying vapor of a metal at a controlled rate to a furnace for production of a crystal by vapor crystallization, said method comprising providing a capillary passage communicating with the chamber, feeding a wire consisting essentially of the metal into the passage toward the chamber at such a temperature that the wire is vaporized within the passage.

2. The method of supplying vapor of a metal at a controlled rate to a furnace chamber for production of a crystal by vapor phase crystallization, said method comprising providing a capillary passage that opens into the chamber, maintaining in the passage at a point spaced from said opening a longitudinal temperature gradient that is steeper than the gradient in the chamber adjacent to the passage and that embraces the melting temperature and the vaporizing temperature of the metal, and feeding a wire consisting essentially of the metal into the passage toward the chamber at a controlled velocity.

3. The method of supplying vapor of a metal at a controlled rate to a furnace chamber for production of a crystal by vapor phase crystallization, said method comprising providing a passage communicating at one end with the chamber, feeding wire consisting essentially of the metal into the passage toward the chamber at a controlled velocity, maintaining the passage at such

---

EXHIBIT 4   *(concluded)*

---

temperature that the wire is vaporized therein adjacent said passage end, and contacting the wire in the passage prior to said vaporization with a gas that is substantially inert with respect to the metal and that chemically reacts with impurities carried by the wire.

4. The method of producing a semiconductive crystal comprising a metallic component and containing a substantially uniform relative concentration comprising providing a solid wire which consists essentially of the metallic component and doping agent in said relative concentration, feeding the wire at a controlled velocity into a capillary tube, maintaining a temperature gradient along the tube to vaporize the wire, and crystallizing the resulting vapor to form said semiconductor crystal.

5. The method of producing a semiconductive crystal containing substantially uniformly distributed therein a minor proportion a doping agent, said method comprising providing a solid wire composed primarily of metal selected from the group consisting of cadmium and zinc and containing said doping agent in a concentration corresponding to said propiration, feeding the wire at controlled velocity into a capillary tube, maintaining a temperature gradient along the tube to vaporize the wire, combining the resulting vapors in substantially constant ratio with gas selected from the group consisting of hydrogen sulphide, hydrogen selenide, and hydrogen telluride, and crystallizing said semiconductive crystal from the resulting vapor phase.

EXHIBIT 5   Excerpts from CVD's Suggested Instructions to Jury

---

[Note: Included in these instructions were legal citations that mentioned specific cases where these points of law were made or reaffirmed. These citations have been omitted in the interest of brevity.]

Donadio and Connolly's Rights as Employees

1. An employee of a company has the right to quit his job and engage in a competing business unless he has a contract of employment that forbids him to do so. In this case there was no evidence that either Mr. Donadio or Mr. Connolly had such a contract with Markham.
2. Mr. Donadio and Mr. Connolly had the right to use the general knowledge, experience, and skill they had acquired while working for Markham for the purpose of engaging in a competing business.
3. If a contract between an employer and an employee or former employee provides that the employee will not use his general knowledge, experience, and skill for the benefit of a new employer, or for the benefit of himself, such a provision is contrary to public policy and is unenforceable.
4. Although an employee has the right to leave his employment and to use his general knowledge, skill, and experience for the benefit of a new employer, he has an obligation not to use trade secrets of the old employer for the benefit of the new one.

No Trade Secrets

5. A *trade secret* may be any information that is used in a business and gives the company that uses it an advantage over competitors who do not know it. For example, a secret manufacturing process or a secret machine of unique design could be a trade secret.
6. However, information that is generally known in an industry cannot be a trade secret.
7. Information cannot qualify for protection as a trade secret unless it is information that gives to the company that knows it an advantage over competitors or potential competitors who do not have the information. Information that would be obvious to a competent engineer experienced in the particular field, or which easily could be determined by a competent engineer by means other than obtaining it from the company which has it, cannot be protected as a trade secret.
8. You must determine in this case whether the information that Markham claims as trade secrets in fact was secret and not generally known outside Markham.
9. A United States patent is a matter of public record and is available for inspection by any member of the public. Information that is disclosed in a United States patent cannot be a trade secret after that patent has been issued, even if it was a trade secret before the patent was issued.
10. If you find that information about the chemical vapor deposition process used by Markham was disclosed in reports made to government agencies and other companies, without restriction on the use of such information, then you should find that such information was not trade secret information.
11. An employer who wishes to preserve information as a trade secret must inform the employees who know the information that it is to be treated as secret and must take all proper and reasonable precautions to keep the information secret. If the company fails to do so, it cannot later prevent use of the information on the theory that it is a trade secret.
12. You have heard testimony of Markham's lawyer, Mr. Davis, to the effect that he was unable to deliver a list of the items that Markham claimed to be its trade secrets to Mr Cohen, the lawyer for the plaintiffs, because it was impossible to make a detailed and complete list of the claimed trade secrets. If you find that as of February 15, 1980, Markham was unable to identify what it claimed to be its trade secrets, then you would be justified in finding that Mr. Donadio and Mr. Connolly had not been put on notice while they were employees of Markham as to what it was that Markham claimed to be its trade secrets, and accordingly that Markham cannot now assert a right to trade secret protection for the information.

The License

13. In *some* circumstances a contract may be binding upon the parties *even if* it later is found that the contract was based on an invalid claim when the person who asserted the claim upon which the contract was based did so in good faith. However, in the case of a contract regarding the use of trade secrets, another principle of law must be considered. Some types of agreements are unenforceable because they are considered to be contrary to public policy, even if they are signed voluntarily by the parties.

EXHIBIT 5   *(concluded)*

---

14. A contract that is signed under what the law regards as unreasonable coercion or ''duress'' cannot be enforced by the party responsible for such coercion or duress. If you find that Markham threatened to sue Mr. Donadio and Mr. Connolly and their new company for alleged use of trade secrets, and that Markham made such threats in bad faith, knowing that it had no legitimate basis for the claims that it threatened to assert, and that the plaintiffs signed the license agreement because of such threats, then you should find that the license agreement was signed under what the law calls economic duress and is not enforceable. Also, threats to prevent a person from earning a living or engaging in a lawful business may constitute duress.

15. In deciding whether the license agreement was signed under duress, you may consider the following:
    a. The relative bargaining power of the parties.
    b. Whether the license required CVD Incorporated to pay royalties at excessive or unreasonable rates.
    c. Whether the plaintiffs could have obtained a judicial decision on the Markham trade secrets claims in time to save their proposed new business.

16. Under Section 1 of the Sherman Act, which is part of the antitrust laws of the United States, any contract that unreasonably restrains interstate commerce within the United States or foreign commerce of the United States is illegal.

17. It is also a violation of Section 2 of the Sherman Antitrust Act for a company to use illegal or unreasonable means to preserve or maintain ''monopoly power'' in a ''relevant product market'' for a ''relevant geographical market,'' even if that ''monopoly power'' has been acquired by lawful and proper means or simply historical accident.

18. A company can have monopoly power without having 100 percent of a market, so long as it has the power either to exclude competition or to set its own prices without regard for competitive pricing.

19. A particular type of product may constitute a relevant product market for antitrust purposes if a major customer has specified that the particular material must be used for a particular purpose, and has selected its suppliers accordingly.

20. Even if two products have the same chemical composition, like a diamond and lead in a pencil, they are not the same relevant product market if one of them has physical characteristics and those characteristics lead customers to prefer one over the other for certain purposes.

21. If two companies compete in selling a product to customers located throughout the United States, then the entire country can be the relevant geographical market.

22. You may find that the February 1980 license agreement was a contract that unreasonably restrained trade if you find *either* (1) that the license agreement required CVD Incorporated to pay royalties for the use of information which in fact was not trade secret information, *or* (2) that the license agreement required CVD Incorporated to pay royalties which were unreasonably high in amount and thus unreasonably restrained CVD Incorporated in its ability to compete with Markham.

EXHIBIT 6   Excerpts from Markham's Suggested Instructions to the Jury

---

[Note: Included in these instructions were legal citations that mentioned specific cases where these points of law were made or reaffirmed. These citations have been omitted in the interest of brevity.]

An Employer's Rights

 1. The employee agreements signed by Donadio and Connolly with respect to Markham inventions and proprietary information are valid and binding. These agreements prevent Donadio and Connolly, upon termination of their employment, from using for their own advantage, confidential information gained by them during their employment.
 2. An agreement not to use or disclose methods and procedures involved in manufacturing processes is binding on an employee and is a reasonable restraint.
 3. Donadio and Connolly, who occupied positions of trust as Markham, owed a duty of loyalty to Markham, a duty that includes not using and disclosing Markham's trade secrets and confidential information even after the termination of employment.
 4. The duty of loyalty owed to Markham by Donadio and Connolly preclude them from using, for their advantage, or that of a rival and to the harm of Markham, trade secrets or confidential information gained during the course of their employment at Markham.
 5. The confidential information that Donadio and Connolly were under a duty to Markham not to disclose, including not only particular information that Markham told them constituted Markham trade secrets and confidential information, but also any information they knew Markham would not want revealed to others. Their duty of nonuse and nondisclosure applies to unique business information and methods of Markham, trade secrets, customer lists, and the like.

Trade Secrets

 6. A trade secret may consist of any formula, pattern, device, or compilation of information that is used in one's business, and that gives him an opportunity to obtain an advantage over competitors who do not know or use it. It may be a formula for a chemical compound, a process of manufacturing, treating or preserving materials, a pattern for a machine or other device. . . . A trade secret is a process or device for use over time in the operation of the business.
 7. Manufacturing processes specifically are entitled to protection as trade secrets.
 8. Because it is the policy of the law to encourage and protect invention and commercial enterprise, the law protects processes of manufacture invented or discovered by an employer against employees who—in violation of their employment contracts and in breach of the duty of trust and confidence that the law also imposes—seek to apply such processes for their own use or to disclose them to third persons.
 9. The fact that Markham's process of manufacturing and producing zinc sulfide and zinc selenide by chemical vapor deposition may to some extent be a combination and adaptation of known principles to new purposes does not prevent that process from being a trade secret, if you find that the process as distilled or parts of it accomplish a result that gives Markham a competitive advantage due to its efforts, ingenuity, research, and development.
10. Even if you determine that general information regarding the technology of chemical vapor deposition and furnaces used in conjunction therewith may be known elsewhere, it does not follow that Markham's detailed engineering drawings, the configuration of its furnaces, apparatus and equipment, the precise materials, techniques, and procedures—which Markham claims are trade secrets and confidential information—have been disclosed.
11. General descriptions or explanations of a process or manufacturing apparatus do not constitute disclosures of detailed manufacturing drawings and designs particularly if the equipment cannot be reproduced by others absent such detail.
12. Detailed manufacturing drawings are prima facie trade secrets.
13. Only reasonable steps are required to preserve the secrecy of the information embodied in the process, machinery, and manufacturing techniques for the production of zinc sulfide and zinc selenide by chemical vapor deposition. Although there is no general rule to determine whether the security precautions taken by the possessor of a trade secret are reasonable, the existence or absence of an express agreement restricting disclosure is an important reasonable step.
14. Markham did not have to stamp *confidential* or *proprietary* on its drawings or tell Donadio and Connolly that any component of the furnaces were confidential and proprietary. Such specificity is not required to put employees on notice that their work involves access to trade secrets and confidential information.

Confidential Business Information

15. Confidential information acquired by an employee in the course of his employment is the property of the employer, which the employee holds in trust for the employer and cannot use in violation of his trust.

16. Donadio and Connolly's contractual and fiduciary obligations to Markham also include their agreement and an obligation in law not to use confidential information regarding customer lists and sources of supply to Markham's detriment upon termination of their employment with Markham.

17. It does not matter that Donadio and Connolly could have obtained some knowledge of Markham's manufacturing processes and techniques from public treatises or documents. For if you find that they obtained their knowledge through their confidential relationship with Markham, they incurred a duty not to use that information to Markham's detriment.

The License

18. Agreements for the licensing of trade secrets are commonplace and enforceable by courts of law. Through a licensing agreement, a company may protect itself from the wrongful use or disclosure of trade secrets and the preservation of confidential information by reaching mutually acceptable terms for payment and confidentiality with a licensee.

19. Payment of royalties for the right to use other parties' trade secrets is consistent with the Massachusetts law of contracts and does not conflict with federal laws and the policy of the patent laws. All agreements, including a licensing agreement, in order to be enforceable must have consideration. That is, for example, a bargained for exchange of rights, promises, or payments. In the license agreement at issue in this case, the defendant granted the plaintiffs a license to use its information to make ZnS/cvd and ZnSe/cvd in exchange for the payment of royalties.

20. In deciding whether the license agreement was premised upon sufficient consideration to be binding and enforceable, you must also consider that our law requires a duty of good faith and fair dealing in business transactions. If you find that Donadio and Connolly occupied positions of trust at Markham and that through their employment they became aware of trade secrets and confidential or proprietary information, then you must find that they had a continuing duty not to use and disclose these secrets and this information after they left the employ of the defendant. The protection of trade secret law is against breaches of trust.

21. In Massachusetts law, duress generally means that one party acted in such a way so as to have made the other party enter an agreement under such fear that would preclude the exercise of his free will and judgment. If the plaintiffs entered this agreement freely and voluntarily, you cannot find that there was duress.

22. In a business context such as the one presented in this case, the elements necessary for you to find that the plaintiffs only entered the agreement under duress are that:
    i. The plaintiffs accepted the terms of the defendant involuntarily;
    ii. The circumstances did not permit them any other alternative; and,
    iii. Those circumstances were the result of coercive acts of the defendant.

23. It is not duress sufficient to avoid a contract for a party to threaten that it will exercise its legal rights, because the enforcement of legal rights by legal means is not evidence of duress.

24. In considering the circumstances that form the basis of the plaintiffs' claim of duress, you shall also consider whether there can be duress when the plaintiffs consulted with legal counsel throughout their negotiations and that their counsel who negotiated the terms was competent and experienced. You shall also consider the parties themselves and their knowledge and understanding of the terms of agreement and their obligations thereunder.

25. Section 2 of the Sherman Antitrust Act provides: Every person who shall monopolize, or attempt to monopolize, or combine or conspire with any other person or persons, to monopolize any part of the trade or commerce among the several states, or with foreign nations, shall be deemed guilty of a misdemeanor.

26. Monopolization violative of Section 2 of the Sherman Act has two elements: first, the "possession of monopoly power in the relevant market" and, second, the "acquisition or maintenance of the power" by other than such legitimate means as patents, "superior product, business acumen, or historical accident."

27. Monopoly power is the power to control prices or to exclude competition in the relevant market. Your first task, therefore, is to ascertain the relevant product market. The relevant product market is that area of goods in which the product or products offered by Markham effectively compete.

EXHIBIT 6   *(concluded)*

28. There are two related tests for determining whether two products are actually competitive with each other: (1) reasonable interchangeability of use and (2) cross-elasticity of demand. Thus, if the product and its substitutes are reasonably interchangeable by consumers for the same purposes, or if they have a high cross-elasticity of demand in the trade, they are to be included in the same market for the purpose of determining the existence of monopoly power.

29. The test of reasonable interchangeability emphasizes two factors. They are (1) use or uses, and (2) physical characteristics. If the substitutes have essentially the same end uses as the product, they are deemed to be interchangeable with each other and may, therefore, be included in the same product market. Similarly, if the physical characteristics of the substitutes are essentially the same as those of the product, so that customers may practically switch from one commodity to another, they are part of the same market.

30. Once you have ascertained the relevant product market, you must decide whether Markham possesses monopoly power in that market (i.e., whether Markham has the power to control prices or exclude competition).

31. The antitrust laws do not prohibit monopoly in and of itself. Thus, it does not condemn one who merely by superior skill and intelligence got the whole business because nobody could do it as well.

32. If Markham's conduct was reasonable in light of its business needs and in accordance with ordinary business dealings and competition, it cannot be found to have used improper means in competing with CVD.

33. If you find that Markham's prices exceeded its total average cost of producing the goods, you must conclude that its pricing practices are lawful and do not constitute an act of monopolization in violation of Section 2. This is because the purpose of the Sherman Act is to encourage a competitive market price and lower prices to consumers.

34. Even if you find that Markham had monopoly power in the relevant market and even if you find that its prices fell below its total average cost, you must determine whether those price reductions by Markham, if any, were in response to price cuts made by CVD. If the prices charged by Markham were made in good faith to meet lower prices charged by CVD, then Markham's prices would be lawful under Section 13(b) of the antitrust laws. That Section provides for the so-called meeting the competition defense. To avail itself of the defense, Markham need not show that its prices were in fact equal to CVD's, but only that facts led Markham, as a reasonable and prudent person, to believe that the granting of the lower prices would meet the equally low prices of another.

EXHIBIT 7   **CVD Incorporated Financials**

Income Statement
(dollars in thousands)

	1984	1983	1982	1981
Revenues:				
Net sales	$2,840	$2,387	$1,547	$751
Contract research	417	342	160	—
	$3,258	$2,729	$1,707	$751
Costs and expenses:				
Cost of goods sold and cost of contract research	$1,538	$1,451	$ 805	$460
Selling, general, and administrative	835	837	508	229
Research and development	193	52	—	—
Interest	75	89	88	51
Markham royalties (set aside)	—	—	86	109
	$2,642	$2,429	$1,487	$849
Earnings before income taxes and extraordinary items	616	300	220	(99)
Income taxes	252	37	42	—
Income (loss) before extraordinary items	364	264	178	(99)
Extraordinary items	—	—	27*	—
Net income (loss)	$ 364	$ 264	$ 205	$(99)

Note: Figures may not add due to rounding.
*Utilization of net operating loss carryforward.

EXHIBIT 7   *(concluded)*

	Balance Sheets	
	Feb. 28, 1984	*Feb. 28, 1983*
Assets		
Current assets:		
Cash	$ 30,334	$ 154,407
Accounts receivable	548,463	379,307
Unbilled progress receivables on		
contract research	—	26,826
Notes receivable — officers	73,821	—
Inventories	710,189	506,922
Prepaid expenses and deposits	37,127	23,915
Deferred income taxes	—	112,000
Total current assets	$1,399,934	$1,203,377
Equipment and improvements,		
net	594,701	649,419
Other assets:	—	3,119
	$1,994,635	$1,855,915
Liabilities and Stockholders' Equity		
Current liabilities:		
Notes payable	$ 70,000	$ 80,000
Accounts payable	170,281	249,013
Accrued salaries and related		
expenses	48,275	48,601
Accrued expenses	159,874	139,719
Accrued royalties	—	194,825
Income taxes	47,761	24,187
Current maturities of long-term		
debt	111,804	111,804
Deferred revenues	221,100	—
Customers' advances	—	25,000
Total current liabilities	829,095	873,149
Deferred accounts payable	86,340	166,340
Deferred income taxes	199,200	43,500
Long-term debt, less current		
maturities	182,482	314,286
Stockholders' equity	697,518	458,640
	$1,994,635	$1,855,915

2–8 CHRIS MILLER

Chris Miller turned down the radio and began to concentrate on a pressing dilemma. Chris was 10 minutes away from the downtown office building where the second board meeting of the newly formed Boston Benefits Group (BBG) was about to be held. Chris was a member of the board and had advised the two founders—Linda Gibbons and Ellen Ravisson—on the start-up of their benefits consulting firm.

Linda and Ellen had met at a larger firm in the benefits consulting business where they both worked as benefits consultants, helping large firms purchase and provide benefit plans for their employees. The two had both quit when the management of this firm had demanded that everyone sign a noncompete agreement, forbidding them from going into the benefits consulting business on their own or from trying to woo any existing clients. While Linda and Ellen had no thoughts of doing so, they felt that the noncompete was overly restrictive. They refused to sign it and had been fired as a result. Thus, they decided that they would go into business on their own. The women had—with Chris's considerable help—developed a business plan that indicated that the business could be quite successful.

Chris had been involved in the venture because Linda was a close friend and because Chris's experience as a financial consultant was valued by the two founders. All had gone smoothly until two weeks ago, when—in a conversation about the business—Linda related that Ellen had just discovered that she was two months pregnant.

Over the past month, Chris had helped the two develop their business plan and projections and had negotiated the start-up financing they would need. At this afternoon's meeting, the closing would occur, and BBG would receive $80,000 in start-up financing from John Blackwell, a local and wealthy physician, who happened to be Drew Gibbons's partner in a cardiology practice. (Drew was Linda Gibbons's husband.) Linda and Ellen had decided that they did not want to tell Blackwell of Ellen's pregnancy:

> He's a male chauvinist, and he'll think that Ellen won't be able to be actively involved in the business. He'll back out of his financing commitment. Ellen will just take two months off, and while she's home, she'll work.

Indeed, Chris was inclined to agree with their assessment of Blackwell. At an early meeting to hammer out the details of the financing, Blackwell had flatly stated: "Be sure you girls get life insurance in case you get hit by a bus or get pregnant or something."

Professor Michael J. Roberts prepared this case.
Copyright © 1992 by the President and Fellows of Harvard College School
Harvard Business School Case 9–393–076

Yet, for all his blustering, Blackwell was giving the two women the money on extremely favorable terms. The $80,000 was essentially a loan that could be paid out of profits; Blackwell wasn't really participating in the business's upside. Chris was sure that Blackwell was being so generous on account of his relationship with Linda and her husband. Blackwell was also a member of the board, yet his involvement in the business seemed destined to be extremely passive.

Chris had asked Linda and Ellen to be available half an hour before the scheduled start of the board meeting so that the three could discuss the situation. Chris intended to offer the two strong advice to tell Blackwell of Ellen's condition, yet, as the hour approached, things seemed more and more confusing. Chris wondered what the right thing to do was, how strongly those views should be presented to Ellen and Linda, and also whether the board membership that Chris held imposed any additional obligations with respect to fellow board member Blackwell.

Chris guided the Volvo into the underground garage and immediately spotted Linda and Ellen exiting from their car. They waved expectantly, and Chris walked over to meet them.

III   ACQUIRING AN EXISTING BUSINESS

In this part of the book, we examine an alternative approach to an entrepreneurial career: purchasing an existing business. This approach has allure for many would-be entrepreneurs who think they don't have a creative idea for ''a better mousetrap,'' but who nonetheless would like to be in business for themselves.

Chapter 11 describes the search process for a company: potential sources of leads and how to assess, value, and finance the purchase. Unlike the start-up process—which is more or less in control of the entrepreneur—purchasing a business involves a critical relationship with the seller, and that relationship must be managed carefully. Chapter 12 describes the various legal forms of organization a business can choose from.

The Cases

Allen Lane describes one man's search for a business. After many false starts and close calls, he has finally found an opportunity that appears attractive. Is it too good to be true? How can he structure a deal to purchase the business on attractive terms?

Karen Vincent focuses on a woman who has the chance to purchase her family's garment manufacturing business from the LBO firm that had recently purchased it. Should she pursue this opportunity?

Tom Fisher revolves around an entrepreneur's attempt to purchase the company where he is employed. Is a last-minute ''deal-breaker'' a problem or a blessing in disguise?

11 PURCHASING A BUSINESS: THE SEARCH PROCESS

Purchasing an existing business is an excellent alternative for individuals interested in running a small- to medium-sized company. While not usually considered as "entrepreneurial" as developing the next generation of personal computers in a tiny garage, purchasing a company demands making many of the same difficult decisions required of a successful entrepreneur. In addition, it provides an opportunity for the purchaser to leverage his or her financial resources and concentrate sooner on "value adding" issues that are traditionally taught in business school management courses.

Buying a business is an informal process. No one has yet written a book that successfully defines the correct steps and best alternatives for every situation. Hence, there is no substitute for personal commitment, good business sense, and a cautiously optimistic exploration of every opportunity. Success in this process may occur randomly and can often depend on serendipity—being the right person in the right place at the right time. It is a mistake, however, to depend on good luck rather than good work.

This chapter will provide a framework that outlines many of the steps necessary to identify, evaluate, and negotiate a successful buyout. It is important to note, however, that this framework is not exhaustive. Rather, it provides a starting point that can be tailored to suit the particular nature of your search.

The areas discussed in this chapter are as follows:

- *Self-Assessment:* Understanding your motives, expectations, risk profile, and financial and professional resources, and determining the seriousness of your search process.
- *Deal Criteria:* Clarifying the dimensions of the project and characteristics that you find attractive.
- *Deal Sources:* Learning how to differentiate between the various deal sources in order to find a source that best fits your personal needs and established criteria.
- *Resources:* Evaluating and garnering the additional cash, credibility, personal and professional contacts, and information necessary to begin the deal process.

This note was prepared by Research Associate Ennis J. Walton under the direction of Professor Michael J. Roberts.
Harvard Business School Note 9–388–044

- *Deal Process:* Recognizing the sequential, often random, search process; establishing a deal timing schedule and work plan that allows you to evaluate deals that do not occur in parallel; understanding how to start the process, keep it moving, and establish initial contact with prospective sellers; and assessing the sellers' motives, weaknesses, strengths, and special nonfinancial requirements.
- *Evaluation Process:* Understanding the various analytical methods used by sellers, requesting or obtaining the key financial indicators, and analyzing the important financial dimensions of the deal.
- *Negotiating the Deal:* Identifying potential deal killers, learning from the collapsed deal, and pursuing attractive deals.
- *Adding Value:* Applying your managerial skills to add new value to the enterprise and understanding important harvesting options for the new enterprise.

Self-Assessment

The first step in buying an existing business is a personal assessment. This step is crucial because it will help you identify, articulate, and evaluate your hidden motives, expectations, risk profile, and ultimately, the seriousness of your search. Without a good sense of these personal values, the search process can become unfocused and unrewarding, causing you to waste time, resources, and energy.

The problems that could materialize in the absence of a thorough self-evaluation are intensified if you are attempting to purchase a company with another individual. In such cases, it is absolutely essential that all parties understand and agree on their motives and goals. Proceeding with a false sense of those aspirations will more than likely lead to problems—disagreements that impact on the efficiency and effectiveness of the group during the later stages of the process when clear vision and communication are important to make important decisions.

A good self-assessment will probably place you in one of three broad categories.

Serious

The serious and realistic search involves the following:

- A high level of commitment to the search.
- An ambitious set of expectations consistent with the degree of effort and commitment.
- A willingness to:

  — Risk at least some personal wealth/security.
  — Deeply research the target industry.
  — Be patient and wait for the "right" opportunity.
  — Move quickly and decisively as needed.
  — Pursue the search full time, if needed.

Casual

The casual and realistic search involves:

- A set of expectations that is consistent with this lessened degree of commitment and effort.
- Less willingness to move quickly or decisively on opportunities.
- No specified time horizon for search.
- Not being overly hungry to control one's own firm.

Unrealistic

The unrealistic search involves:

- Objectives that are inconsistent with level of commitment.
- Waiting for a ''great deal'' to fall in place.
- Looking for bargains and shortcuts.

While there is nothing wrong with either of the first two categories, the number and quality of opportunities discovered is proportional to the intensity of the search. This is not to say, however, that one cannot find excellent deals by ''shopping'' the market casually, but only that the process may take quite a while.

Another aspect of the self-assessment process that many people deal too lightly with is the listing of any and all business or personal relationships that can be called upon to add credibility or offer advice. Since the search process is lengthy and filled with important decision points, it is of great value to have others whose opinion you trust to call upon for advice.

The most important reason for the self-assessment, however, is tactical. Throughout the search process, you will have to deal with sellers or their intermediaries to get a sense of the deal. Because these individuals are often reluctant to invest their time with individuals unless they sense a degree of rational forethought and commitment, it's important to have a clear and convincing sense of what it is you're looking for. Thus, the better you have assessed yourself, the easier it will be to persuade others to take you seriously or work productively on your behalf.

Deal Criteria

A consistent and thorough screening method is essential for the successful completion of the acquisition process. Consistency is required so that analyses performed on one company are more readily comparable with those of other candidates. Thoroughness is required because all relevant aspects of a potential acquisition must be identified and analyzed. While thoroughness is critical, the screening method should have a clear focus and be kept fairly simple.

There are numerous ways to define the desired target company profile. At a minimum, one should think along such dimensions as:

- Size of deal (purchase price) desired.
- Preferred industry.
- Key factors for success (logistics, marketing, technology, etc.).
- Type of customer base (i.e., industrial versus consumer, national versus regional, etc.).
- Geographic preference.
- Profile of current ownership (i.e., how many, willingness to sell, reputation).

The mechanical dimensions highlighted above establish a preliminary framework for identifying deals that are appropriate for the particular search being undertaken. The screening process must then tackle the issue of distinguishing *good* deals from *bad* deals. Though there are several intangible and intuitive issues involved in this process, as a rule of thumb, an ideal buyout target should include:

- Potential for improving earnings and sales.
- Predictable cash flow.
- Minimum existing debt.
- An asset base to support substantial new borrowings.

When searching for a business, the buyout candidate will most likely not fit in a "nice, neat, little box;" so flexibility is important. One must constantly rethink and reassess the criteria developed. Do they fit? Are they appropriate? Is this the best way to examine this company? Will the criteria help to achieve the objective in mind?

Deal Sources

Initiating and sustaining the deal flow is one of the most challenging tasks in buying a business. In general, expect to look at dozens of deals for every one that might appear worth pursuing; there are simply a lot of poor deals out there. A seemingly endless amount of groundwork is often necessary to initiate a deal, and a targeted effort is far more likely to result in a high percentage of attractive candidates. Thus, one of the first orders of business when starting out to locate a company is to know where to look.

Depending on what size deal is sought, there are a number of potential deal sources, and each has its own approach to acquisitions. The chart that follows is a subjective assessment of the various sources of deals and the territory they cover.

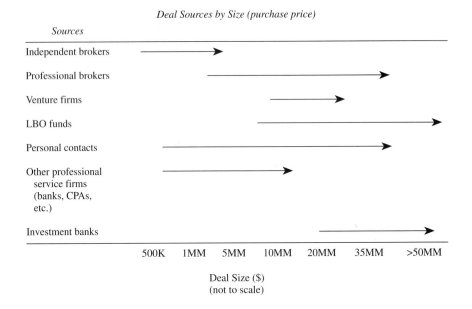

Deal Sources by Size (purchase price)

Deal Size ($)
(not to scale)

The number of deals in the lower ranges—particularly in the $1 million to $50 million category—is on the rise. Geneva Business Services, Inc., a leading national broker of small businesses, estimates that more than 15,000 deals involving companies valued in this range will close in 1987. Mainstream investment banks, on the other hand, are rarely interested in any deal valued less than $10 to $20 million. Recognizing the particular niches these players inhabit will help to minimize lost time and unnecessary frustration chasing deals where they are not likely to be found. The paragraphs below will help identify sources according to the size of deal handled.

Business brokers—independent and professional alike—are the most readily available resource; they are listed individually in the Yellow Pages of most phone directories and advertise in the business sections of many newspapers. The broker's primary function is to work on behalf of sellers to find appropriate buyers for their clients' businesses, and he or she is compensated by the seller for closing a deal based on a percentage of the price basis. Occasionally, a broker will work for a buyer to search for a business in return for a retainer fee and/or a percentage of the ultimate purchase price. It should be emphasized, though, that the broker's motivation is to close each transaction; he or she should not necessarily be considered a business consultant in the search process.

Business brokers obtain listings through cold calls and advertising. Because these listings are actively marketed, it is safe to assume that you are probably not the first prospective buyer to see the business. More reputable brokers tend to regulate how "shopped" a business becomes in order to preserve its value and may not even list properties that the seller himself has already tried to market.

At your initial meeting with the broker, you should be prepared to describe your financial constraints and industry preference. It is also valuable to indicate that you have a well-defined time horizon for a search and some knowledge of the target industry. You might want to touch base occasionally with each broker whom you meet, but it is a safe bet that you will be notified if there is an interesting opportunity and if you are a qualified buyer.

Some attention should be focused on the role of independent brokers since they are often the first place people turn for deal flow. Independent brokers are almost entirely unregulated. Because no license is required, and anyone can claim to be one, it is essential to check references (should the broker not supply them) and reputation with other intermediaries and past clients. Fourteen states require brokers to have a real estate broker's license, but, for the most part, anyone with a telephone can call himself or herself a business broker. The largest network of independent brokers is VR Business Brokers, headquartered in Boston, Massachusetts. VR has 10 franchised brokerages operating offices in 500 cities. VR claims to close up to 7,500 deals per annum, 80 percent of which are companies with sales below $800,000. On the other end of the spectrum, one can find a seemingly endless supply of one-person brokerage services in most any city. As such, one must be exceedingly cautious when trying to land a deal via this route. First of all, the deals are going to be small, less than $500,000 in sales. Second, they are most likely to be owned by entrepreneurs who have an unrealistic impression of the value of their businesses, an impression often fueled by the brokers themselves.

As for professional brokers, a few prominent ones are worth noting here:

- Geneva Business Services in Costa Mesa, California.
- W. T. Grimm & Co. in Chicago, Illinois.
- First Main Capital Corp. in Plano, Texas.
- Nation-List Network of Business Brokers, Inc., in Denver, Colorado, is a co-operative exchange of some 50 independent brokers.

These organizations tend to operate on a far more professional basis than the independents, but keep track of the fact that they still represent the seller. Their interest is in getting the highest possible price for the company, thereby ensuring high commission fees (usually around 10 percent to 12 percent at closing). Also, note that deals coming via professional brokers are very likely to be highly ''shopped.'' The deals' legitimacy are often prescreened, but count on paying a premium for businesses carried by professional brokers.

Venture capital firms will most likely be looking for liquidity on investments they made three to five years earlier. Venture-backed companies that have reached this stage are generally beyond many of the risks associated with start-ups and may pose a solid acquisition opportunity. Several points should be noted, however. First, venture capitalists are highly sophisticated investors and will likely extract the highest possible price for the company. Second, they want liquidity for their investment and will be less interested in earn-outs and other creative financing than a deal that is primarily financed with cash. Finally, existing management will likely be highly entrepreneurial and will be wary of the control issues introduced by new owners in the company.

Leveraged buyout (LBO) funds in some sense pose competition to the buyout effort. As a potential deal source, however, there may be opportunity to pick up on deals that are of no interest to the LBO fund. Such deals may still be attractive candidates if they were passed over simply because the deal did not match the particular focus of the LBO fund.

Personal contacts, although often overlooked, may be helpful. Self-initiated contacts with people who have successfully completed the search process for their own businesses may be a good source of both information and moral support. Depending on your specific situation and their area of expertise, they may be able to suggest specific contacts and strategies or allow you to tap their network. Additionally, you may be able to learn some of the common pitfalls they encountered and some rules of thumb they use. These resources may be located through your network or by tracking recently completed deals.

On occasion, combing prominent business periodicals will identify opportunities. Indications that a company will be spinning off subsidiary operations are frequently mentioned in articles in some level of detail. Nationally, *The Wall Street Journal* and publications such as *Inc.* and *Venture* routinely list business opportunities. On the local or regional level, there are business journals, franchise fairs, classified ads, and notices of bankruptcies and deaths. Newspapers and the offices of the county clerk and court clerks are good sources, as are computer data bases, available on a time-sharing basis that provide lists of prospective buyers and sellers of businesses. Academic and commercial institutions in some communities sponsor industry forums or trade association meetings. Industry and phone directories (Yellow Pages, Dun & Bradstreet, *Million Dollar Directory,* Thomas' *Register of American Manufacturers,* etc.) may be useful for a cold call or letter writing campaign and as a possible screen for industry, size, and location. You can run this process in reverse by placing your own advertisement in newspapers or journals stating your desire and criteria for purchasing a business.

Local banks represent a broad range of local businesses and have in-depth knowledge of their finances and managerial situations. Like business brokers, the M&A-type departments of banks are primarily interested in closing transactions. Their inventory of deals may include both banking clients that may be for sale or other firms that have engaged the bank to help them find a suitable buyer. A bank may also be amenable to helping you conduct a search on a success-fee basis. A good banker will also be instrumental in structuring the financial arrangements of the newly acquired business. As with lawyers and accountants, the bank may often expect to become the new firm's principal banker.

Trust departments of banks often are the executors of estate business. In cases where there is a need to dispose of such a business, a bank trust officer may serve the same role as an estate lawyer. However, the trust officer has a fiduciary responsibility to the beneficiaries of the estate and will seek the highest price for the business consistent with keeping the transaction clean, fast, and, to the greatest extent, in cash.

Bank work-out departments are another potential source of ''bargain'' opportunities. While the bank certainly has a strong interest in not disclosing credit problems, it may be a confidential go-between for a potential buyer and the owners of a deeply troubled client if a mutually satisfactory offer were presented. However, bankers indicate that because of pressures within the bank to reschedule the debt and the willingness of owners to personally collateralize additional loans, most troubled loans are in fact worked out.

Traditional, mainline investment banks pose both a problem and an opportunity for buyers seeking a midsized deal. The problem is that investment banks are rarely interested in deals below, say, $20 million. Attracting their attention can be troublesome and getting them to spend time moving on a relatively small deal requires patience and tenacity. The opportunity, for nearly the same grounds, exists because small deals carried by the investment banks are unlikely to have been widely shopped. Owners who rely exclusively on an investment bank to market their company will probably not receive extraordinary service. A buyer who works this route may find a fairly responsive seller on the other end of this inattentive deal pipeline.

No matter where the deal comes from, there will be a seller to contend with. Whether the seller is a single individual, a group of investors, or the shareholders of a small public company one will have to evaluate their motivations. Issues of timing, types of financing, credibility, desire to remain with the company after acquisition, and the like, are all relevant points of thought when approaching the seller. Fairly early on, conversations should focus on the seller's motives for selling the business and his or her expectations as to the value and form of deal. A cautious investor will also use this opportunity to gauge the character and integrity of the seller, as such traits will likely have influenced how the business has been managed in the past.

Resources

Aside from tireless energy and a wealth of patience, resources critical to the buyout project are cash, credibility, and contacts. These three factors, more than anything else, govern the success of the effort. How much will be required is simply a question of deal size. Purchasing a $300,000 business certainly requires fewer resources than putting together a $20 million buyout. As deals get larger, one is competing with a more sophisticated group of potential buyers. Larger deals are more complex, and sellers of larger companies will demand of the potential buyer those credentials they believe are necessary to put the deal together. Lacking the resources necessary to pull off the deal, the potential buyer may not even be successful in establishing an initial meeting with the seller. To get farther than the first phone call with larger deals, one should be prepared to satisfactorily respond to such inquiries as:

- How much cash do you have available?
- Who are your backers?
- What other deals have you done?
- What kind of management talent do you bring?
- What do you plan to do with the company?

Sellers value their time as much as the prospective buyer does. Neither wants to spend fruitless energy on meetings where there is an obvious mismatch between what the buyer brings to the table and what the target company will require. No amount of debt leverage will compensate for a lack of the equity capital and demonstrated personal background needed to purchase and operate the target company. Take stock of the resources available for the buyout project, and then target deals that can be reasonably snared with the resources at hand.

If buyers plan to employ the resources of backers, they must realize the extent to which they are dependent upon the backers and gauge how committed the backers are to the project. All the backers' cash and contacts are absolutely useless if they are unwilling to spend the time and energy needed to pursue the deal. Evaluate the backers' incentives. How important is the project to them? How much time have they agreed to set aside? Do their timing considerations match those of the group? Some backers are quite willing to employ the free efforts of a buyout group simply hoping they will luck into a treasure chest. Be cautious of working like a neglected employee, rather than a respected partner. Such characteristics may prove difficult to evaluate, particularly early on when enthusiasm runs high for the project. Make a critical and even skeptical assessment of the backers' sincerity, interest, and ability to follow through on their part of the bargain before relying on them for the resources critical to the effort's success.

In addition, an experienced lawyer is absolutely essential to the prudent buyer. An attorney's principal role in the search process is usually to review documents with the aim of protecting the client with adequate contractual conditions and to ensure proper disclosure and legal and regulatory compliance. An attorney can also provide tax advice and may be able to identify potential risks and liabilities in a transaction. In many cases, more experienced lawyers turn out to be cheaper because they know the appropriate safeguards and can create good standard documents without extensive new research. In addition, as established members of the local professional community, attorneys may have access to a wider network of contacts than the buyer. For example, they sometimes sit on the boards of local businesses and may have a variety of contacts in the target industry. While tapping into this network might not generate a deal, it may provide you with opportunities to learn about the target industry and to gain credibility therein.

Occasionally, in larger law firms, there may also be an ''inventory'' of business acquisition opportunities. The buyer must usually compensate the lawyer for time and effort, and if the deal is successful, he or she generally expects to become the newly acquired firm's corporate counsel. As for selecting a business lawyer, there are issues to consider. For instance, you should determine whether or not the lawyer has a potential conflict of interest (e.g., if he is representing the seller). Although no reputable attorney would pursue an engagement while conflict exists without full disclosure, it is still up to you to determine the services she or he might provide. Another issue is the lawyer's reputation. It is wise to do some background or information checks of individual attorneys or their firms. Finally, your choice of lawyer should reflect your perceived legal and other professional needs at various stages of the search and deal process.[1]

---

[1] For example, a lawyer with the technical knowledge to structure the deal from a tax perspective may not be the most skilled negotiator.

The Deal Process

Once you have specified the characteristics that you are looking for in a company, understood the best ways to generate deal flow, and have garnered the resources necessary to successfully purchase an existing company, you should prepare to enter the deal market. At this phase, it is important to recognize and prepare for the random nature of the process.

There are two important timing issues to be concerned with when you enter the deal market. First, the sequential nature of the search process makes it difficult to compare deals in parallel. Rarely will you be able to view two deals within a time frame that allows you to evaluate them comparatively. Given that fact, it is important to realize that if you let one deal pass, you will probably encounter another one in the near future. An analytical framework to help you screen businesses (see Figure 11–1) will better equip you to track and compare various deals as you interface with sellers, deal sources, and other active parties at different points throughout the deal process (see also Chapter 2, "The Start-up Process").

The second critical issue concerns the timing of the approach: before it hits the market, as soon as it hits the market, or after it has been "shopped." There are advantages and disadvantages to entering at each stage. In some cases, being the first person to see a deal (before it is on the market) may give you the inside track or first right to refuse. Yet, at this early stage, the seller will not have developed a realistic perspective on his or her demands (asking price, terms, inclination to provide desired information, willingness to actually part with the business, etc.). In such a case, discussions might be futile or you may end up paying a relatively high price. In a later stage, the seller may be more eager to sell, but you should be concerned about the health or the attractiveness of the business that has been on the market for a lengthy period.

Once you understand these basic timing issues and prepare a schedule and work plan, you should begin your search. Most of the search resources are amenable to a free introductory meeting even on the basis of a cold call. A persuasive presentation at this first meeting might include a demonstration of your industry research or experience, a well-thought-out preliminary business plan, a realistic assessment of your financial resources, and suitable dress and demeanor. Academic credentials help your chances of getting in the door, as does the referral of a mutual acquaintance. This meeting should not necessarily result in a commitment; in fact, you might consider meeting with many attorneys, CPAs and bankers, or others you deem helpful before committing to work with anyone in particular. You might also schedule some "warm-up" sessions with some of these professionals before meeting with your highest priority contacts.

The preliminary meeting should serve several purposes: Resources will be interested in qualifying you both as a realistic, potential buyer and as someone they will want to work with. You should attempt to determine their expertise and willingness to help, along with any conditions on your relationship with them. With regard to establishing fees, practice ranges from hourly fees to contingent fees; the arrangement of one lawyer may be substantially different from another. This is another reason to meet

FIGURE 11–1   **Purchasing a Business: The Search Process**

Business Screening Analyses

---

1. General
   Company, business strategy, age and history, trends.
2. Product
   Description/technical specifications, function, volume, prices, value added/commodity, patents.
3. Management Team
   Key employees—names, positions, education, track record, skills.
   Organization chart.
   Is management team complete? Efforts/ability to hire new management?
   Willingness to remain after purchase?
   Characterization of management team (i.e., aggressive/passive, young/old, etc.).
4. Market Position
   Market size ($, units).
   Market growth and growth drivers.
   Segmentation of the market (geographic, functional).
   Who, how, and why does the buyer buy (identification of buyer)?
   Relationship with customers (number, loyalty, concentration).
   Distribution channels (types, support/training required, advertisement strategy).
   Market share of major players.
   Company's major differentiating factors (price, quality, service, features, brand identity).
5. Competition
   Barriers to entry/exit—economies of scale, proprietary technology, switching cost, capital requirements, access to distribution, cost advantages, government policy, expected retaliation, brand identity, exit cost.
   Competitive factors—number, strength, characterization, product differences, concentration, diversity, management, financial/ration analysis, industry capacity, competitive advantages, corporate stakes.
   Substitution threat—relative price/performance of substitutes, switching cost, buyer propensity to substitute.
   Suppliers' power—relationship, concentration, manufacturing/marketing process, presence of substitute inputs, importance of volume to supplier, switching cost of supplier, cost relative to total purchases, impact of inputs on cost or differentiation, threat of forward integration, supplier profitability.
   Buyers' power—bargaining leverage, buying patterns, concentration, volume, switching cost, ability to backward integrate, substitute products, price sensitivity, price/total purchases, product differences, brand identity, impact on quality/performance, buyer profitability, decision-making units' incentives and complexity.
   Trends—technology, economic, changes in tax law.
6. Operations
   Work force—seize, union/nonunion, work rules, contract expiration, age and skill level, match with developing technology, attrition, attitude, manufacturing engineering staff competence.
   Manufacturing flow and scheduling—job shop/batch continuous, systems, process flow, material handling, multiplant strategy/logistics, cost accounting, work discipline, work order tracking, percent dead time.
   Capacity—percent of total capacity, bottlenecks current and projected.
   Purchasing—opportunities for redesign, fewer parts, add/subtract vendors, larger discounts, incoming material sampling, out-sourcing policies.
   Quality control—attitude/priority, problem areas, methodology.
   Capital equipment—age/maintenance, sophistication, general versus special purpose, level of automation, trends.
   R&D—percent of sales compared to industry, type, technical strengths/weaknesses, organization, importance, trends.
   Information systems—importance, competitive advantage, level of sophistication, systems under development.
7. Financials
   Sales/profitability
      Income statement.
      Historical and two-, three-, five-year pro formas.
      Growth—sales, costs, profits, EPS, sustainable growth rates.

FIGURE 11–1   *(concluded)*

Quality of earnings—accounting, pension funding, depreciation, write-offs, earnings segments, earnings patterns, earnings sensitivity.
Ratio analysis—compared to competitors and industry averages, gross margins, ROS, ROE, P/E comparables.
Leverage and liquidity
Balance sheet.
Historical and pro formas.
Examination of equity and debt composition.
Ratio analysis—current and quick ratios, debt as percentage of total capitalization, assets/equity, days receivable, days payable, days inventory.
Funds flow
Statement of changes.
Historical and pro formas.
Analysis of sources and uses of cash.
Assets
Composition and type, quality, bankability, book and market values, obsolescence, age.
8. Valuation
Terminal value—FCF perpetuity/annuity, book value, liquidation value, P/E value.
Components of value (i.e., investment tax credits, depreciation, energy cost savings, etc.).
Sensitivity analysis.
Expected returns analysis.
9. Risk/Reality Check
Industry.
Technology.
Financial.
Product/company liability.
Employee/supplier/customer response.
Seller's desire to do the deal.
Is value appropriate?
Prohibitive terms?
Value to be added.

with many professionals before committing to work exclusively with any one in particular.

In most of these preliminary discussions, the issue of what to tell and what to hide arises. While this is a personal decision, a perspective on your financial resources, level of commitment, and objectives is probably best expressed frankly. You may want to be more vague if you are dealing with an intermediary who represents a potential seller or if you have reservations about the person with whom you are meeting. The fact that your backers may want their identities shielded will also push you to be somewhat guarded. Checking out the reputations of such individuals before divulging any of your private information is the only prudent course of action.

The average time required to find the right business runs about one year—significantly longer if your search is more casual or if your target is more elusive. Therefore, depending on your degree of commitment, your financial flexibility, and your time schedule, you may elect to manage your own search by calling on the search resources periodically, or you may choose to retain a search resource to conduct the search for you.

An attorney, for instance, could make cold calls and write letters to industry sources on your behalf. While his personal and professional contacts may unearth your dream business, much of the research you pay him for could be easily done yourself from industry directories, Yellow Pages, etc. Thus, if time permits or your budget requires and you are sophisticated enough about basic business and legal issues, you may choose to undertake many of the basic research tasks yourself. This also provides first-hand contact with the marketplace.

The industry-specific knowledge you pick up may be invaluable to you later on, when you need to demonstrate expertise or commitment to financing sources or to a seller. In some industries, acquisition opportunities rarely reach the marketplace because the industry is essentially closed. Therefore, if you are interested in entering such an area, you must "network" your way in. This might include meeting owners or executives of any firms in that industry whether or not they are interested in selling their own businesses. Industry association meetings or trade meetings can be good places to meet people and become more of an insider.

You might consider periodically touching base with some of the individuals in your new network to see if they have any ideas for you and to reiterate your degree of interest. But be sensitive to the demands you are making: A short phone call every three or four weeks is appropriate—more frequent contact may be annoying. You might also update them on your progress, especially because they may be able to help you more at different phases in your search. Keep in mind that they would more likely readily share information or leads with you if you exchange any ideas or intelligence with them.

Once underway, you may come across a potential acquisition candidate. An inexpensive way to obtain financial and operating information on the company and biographical background on the owners or officers is through a Dun & Bradstreet report or by other background checks. Note that the D&B report is based upon information provided by the subject company and is not independently verified.

In addition to doing some preliminary investigative research, it is important to meet the owner(s) and visit the business. An aspect of this evaluation is to understand the "seller's psychology," for it is critical to appreciate the seller's needs—financial and psychological. There are cases in which the owner has no emotional attachment to the business, and he or she would willingly sell to the highest bidder. More likely, especially in small operations, much of the seller's life is tied up in the business, resulting in a high degree of emotional involvement. There may be other significant psychological considerations, you could identify, such as the seller's age, marital situation, illness, or family situation. Usually, a deal structure will need to reflect these factors in the form and terms of the consideration. In these cases, you may need to "sell" the seller.

Selling the seller does not simply include a generous financial package (e.g., insurance, providing for his family, etc.), but may require demonstrating your commitment to preserve the character, quality, and spirit of the enterprise he worked long and hard to build. Occasionally, even when an owner indicates a willingness to sell, he or she may in fact be unwilling to part with the firm when it comes to closing the deal and transferring control. Reading the owner's psyche ahead of time may avoid such fruitless discussions or may provide insight into a more mutually satisfying deal structure.

In this respect, your professional resources may be able to provide a great deal of insight and advice because they may either know the seller or have dealt with similar situations previously. It also may be helpful to have your agent negotiate on your behalf for a variety of reasons: to preserve your rapport with the seller, to neutralize personality clashes, and to preserve and improve decision options.

The Evaluation Process

After preliminary research and introductory meetings with the prospective seller, you may decide to pursue the opportunity, which would involve reviewing confidential operating and financial statements and interviewing key employees and customers.

''Getting the numbers'' can be more easily said than done. Generally, small-business owners are reluctant to share any operating and financial data with outsiders, often for tax and competitive reasons. Typically a buyer does not receive any meaningful financials until after signing a purchase agreement and putting down a deposit. Thus, a good understanding of the business and the industry may give you increased credibility and leverage with the seller. A seller with a distressed business may be more willing to provide numbers earlier in the process, and for bankrupt firms, the numbers may be part of the public domain. In most cases, confidentiality agreements must be signed before reviewing any financials.

While not necessary, you are well advised at this point to retain your own counsel to ensure that you are protected and are covering all bases, especially if you are signing any documents or agreements. An accountant might also be very useful depending on the complexity of the situation (financial reports, taxes, inventory, etc.). Other experts may help investigate leases and contracts. To the extent that these are people with whom you have already worked, you will be more comfortable dealing with them and trusting them.

It is often useful to collect a ''thumbnail'' sketch of the deal's financial attractiveness prior to performing any detailed analysis. As some preliminary checks, one can screen against company size, profitability, and attractiveness of the balance sheet. Some deals may be thrown out on this basis, while others will merit a more thorough examination of ''the numbers.''

There are several ways to reasonably estimate the value of a company, and it is most often useful to employ more than one method when performing a valuation analysis. How much to pay, how much debt and from what source, and potential harvest values are going to be valued differently. Each plays an important role in the assessment of the opportunity at hand. Below are types of analysis that can prove useful in establishing an estimate of the deal's price (see Chapter 4, ''Valuation Techniques''):

Method Used	*What the Results Indicate*
Discounted cash flow	Underlying operating value of the business and ability to service debt.
Asset valuation	Liquidation value and/or adjusted book value of assets.
Multiples	Multiples of cash flow, P/E, sales, or EBIT are useful to establish some sense for market value relative to other firms in the same industry and offer some indication of harvest potential. Each type of multiple has its own merit; what is critical is that one be consistent in applying them.

Both cash flow analysis and multiples analysis estimate the opportunity's value based upon future events, either operating results or market reaction to public offering. When trying to place a value on a business in this manner, there are a multitude of assumptions that must be made. Some of the most prominent include:

- Level of risk: How volatile are the company's cash flows?
- Competition: How fiercely contested is the market for the company's products?
- Industry: Is this a growing or declining industry, and what profitability trends exist?
- Organizational stability: How well established is this company in the intended line of business?
- Management: Is a competent and complete team in place?
- Company growth: Historically, has the company been growing or shrinking, and how fast?
- General desirability: To what degree does the marketplace find this line of business attractive?

A cautionary note on valuations: Many deal proposals are put together with ''recast financial statements.'' In theory, such a practice is legitimate and endeavors to reflect true operating results possible in the business. In reality, assumptions implicit in the recast are not always reasonably attainable and can be downright misleading. Always ask whether or not the financials shown have been recast, and, if so, understand all adjustments that have been made to the statements. No assumption should be left unchallenged. This will be particularly true for smaller companies whose owners will often have previously operated with numerous adjustments to minimize their tax burden.

Once a general idea on price is established, the deal will have to be structured with attractive returns to one's equity investment. There are two fundamental considerations. First, is the overall financeability of the deal, which includes:

- Assets to secure bank financing.
- Cash flow to support further debt instruments (i.e., company-issued debentures).
- Personal collateral, if any.

Second, one must consider (possibly in conjunction with the above analysis) the actual structure of the financing. What is desired here is a structure that caters to the interest of all parties involved. The buyer might, for example, establish financing ''strips'' of debt and equity to provide both secured fixed income and participation in potential capital appreciation. Tax losses may be scrutinized and sold to investors who will find such items attractive (see Chapter 8, ''Deal Structure'').

Negotiating the Deal

When you discover a company whose purchase is financially feasible and meets your other criteria, it is important to recognize any situations that could prevent you from closing the deal successfully. The following represent a few important obstacles:

- Forcing the deal: One must be responsive to timing issues inherent in a less than perfect process. This may be the area of greatest difficulty due to the lack of control associated in timing the buying of a company. Patience and persistence go a long way toward managing one's expectations in this area. One's attitude plays a role here, as well. While the deal should not be forced, one must recognize there are always reasons *not* to do a deal. Buying a company is an emotional as well as intellectual process, and there are times when the cynical outlook should be tempered with a bit of positive thinking.
- Competition: One should expect to run into competition from other buyout firms or larger companies in the same industry, perhaps with greater resources. A professional buyout firm will typically have the resources, capital, time, and sophistication to move quickly and expertly on a deal. In particular, with the great mergers and acquisitions activity of the mid- to late-1980s, many buyout firms who in the past would have sought relatively larger deals have begun searching for small- and medium-sized deals ($10 to $20 million). Larger companies in the same industry may be willing to pay a higher premium due to operating synergies in common with the target acquisition candidate. This makes for a challenging search process and means that if deals can be found that have not been shopped around, then one's chances of success improve dramatically.
- Poor communication: This pertains to all parties involved—backer, target company, project team, and the many professionals required to complete a deal. There is plenty of opportunity for communications to either drag out or break down entirely. Demonstration of commitment is again prominent, as frequent and regular discussion will sustain each party's involvement and better move a deal to completion.

Such obstacles do not necessarily have to get in the way, but one should be prepared to meet them if they do appear. Indeed, you may have to walk away from your share of deals. While having to walk away from a business you wanted can be disappointing, you should learn several important lessons. For example, you should become a better judge of character and business situations. This is knowledge that will be invaluable to you as you continue the deal process. Also, the firsthand experience and knowledge you gain about the industry in the collapsed deal may result in greater credibility in the future with sellers or their intermediaries.

Adding Value

Before you purchase a company, you can begin to concentrate on ways to improve the firm's performance. Indeed, such plans are a vital component of understanding a business's potential and your willingness to pay. Adding value to a new firm can be accomplished in many ways:

- Making operational changes: You should give a good deal of thought up front as to what you plan to do with the company after the acquisition. You may recognize opportunity to broaden distribution, open new markets, and otherwise make operational changes that boost sales and/or margins. In evaluating such possibilities, be realistic. Chances are the easy things have already been tried, so exercise some creative thought in defining positive operating improvements. This also requires an assessment of the management team and personnel in place. In short, are they reliable, competent, honest, and are they the right people for the challenge that lies ahead for the business?

- Changing the financial structure of the business: In many small businesses, the very essence of the company can be improved if the underlying financial structure is modified. For example, negotiating a longer payment schedule with your creditors, creating incentives for your customers to pay bills sooner, and obtaining lines of credit from commercial banks can help change the dynamics of the business and improve cash flow.

Conclusion

Searching for a small business to buy can be difficult; not only is there no established marketplace for these firms, but you are trying to purchase an entity created and cultivated by another individual, and you are attempting to meld it with your own style, character, and interests. This process can be extremely time consuming, expensive, and frustrating. And although available research indicates the good acquisition candidates are few and far between, sound search techniques and a realistic personal assessment can significantly improve your chances of success and allow you to achieve some measure of control over some of the more random elements of the process.

Finally, remember that this process is also an investment decision. Even a superb company is of little value to an investor if nobody is willing to pay for it. Identifying an appropriate "exit" strategy to make one's investment liquid will define the project's monetary returns. This can include running the company in perpetuity, getting out in a secondary public offering, liquidating the assets, or selling out to another organization.

12 THE LEGAL FORMS OF ORGANIZATION

One of the key issues an entrepreneur must resolve when considering a new venture is what legal form of organization the enterprise should adopt. The most prevalent forms are:

- The individual proprietorship.
- The partnership.

  - General partnership.
  - Limited partnership.

- The corporation.

  - The S corporation (formerly Subchapter S).
  - The "regular" corporation.

Each of these forms of organization differs from the others along several dimensions. The characteristics of the business entity will determine its tax status. It is important to note that merely claiming partnership or corporate status *will not* result in the tax treatment accorded that form of organization. The IRS (see Internal Revenue Code Sec. 7701(a)(3)) has elaborated four factors that determine the classification and resulting tax status of an organization:

1. Continuity of life—An organization possesses continuity of life when the death, insanity, or retirement of an owner will not cause the organization's dissolution.
2. Centralized management—Management is centralized when continuing, exclusive authority to make managerial decisions is constituted in some subgroup of the organization's ownership.
3. Limited liability—The liability of an organization is limited when no member of the organization is personally liable for debts or claims against the business.
4. Free transferability of interest—Interest can be freely transferred only when each member of the organization can transfer all attributes and benefits of ownership without the consent of other members.

This note was prepared by Michael J. Roberts under the direction of Howard H. Stevenson.
Copyright © 1984 by the President and Fellows of Harvard College
Harvard Business School Note 9–384–184

As the table below indicates, the proprietorship and partnership occupy one end of the spectrum with regard to each of these criteria while the corporation occupies the other; the limited partnership form falls in the middle.

	Corporation, including S Corporation	*Limited Partnership*	*Proprietorship/ Partnership*
Continuity of life	Yes	No	No
Centralized management	Yes	Yes	No
Limited liability	Yes	Yes/No	No
Free transferability of interest	Yes	No	No

It is also important to note that *any* business that seeks tax treatment under any of the legal forms of organization *must* have as its objective the carrying on of a trade or business *for profit*. An individual cannot engage in a hobby, such as travel or purchasing books or stamps, and then claim tax deductions for expenses involved in pursuing these activities.

In most cases, the IRS has an incentive to tax as corporations entities that have claimed *not* to be corporations, but which, in fact, possess the characteristics of corporations.

In general, tax courts have found that:

- If the organization claims to be a corporation, and it possesses at least two of the four characteristics, it will be taxed as a corporation.
- If an organization claims to be a partnership, but in fact possesses three of the four characteristics of a corporation, it will be taxed as a corporation.

The remainder of this chapter will discuss each of the forms of organization mentioned above. Figure 12–1 lists several important aspects of the various legal forms of organization.

Individual Proprietorship

The individual or sole proprietorship is the oldest form of organization: a person who undertakes a business without any of the formalities associated with other forms of organization. The individual and the business are one and the same.

Classification

A proprietorship is legally defined as follows:

- Continuity of life: The proprietorship ceases to exist upon the death, insanity, or retirement of the proprietor.
- Centralized management: A proprietorship is deemed not to have centralized management because the proprietor is viewed as the legal decision-making authority. Therefore, management is not centralized in any subgroup of the ownership.

Figure 12-1 Comparison of Various Legal Forms of Organization

	Proprietorship	Partnership	Regular Corporation	Subchapter S Corporation
Taxable year	Usually calendar year	Usually calendar year; however, September, October, or November can be elected	Any year-end is permissible	Calendar year, unless a valid business purpose can be demonstrated for another choice
Expensing of depreciable business assets	Limited to $10,000 in 1986	Limited to $10,000 in 1986	Limited to $10,000 in 1986	Limited to $10,000 in 1986
Ordinary distributions to owners	Drawings from the business are not taxable; the net profits are taxable; and the proprietor is subject to the tax on self-employment income	Generally not taxable	Payments of salaries are deductible by corporation and taxable to recipient; payments of dividends are not deductible by corporation and generally are taxable to recipient shareholders	Same as regular corporation
Limitations on losses deductible by owners	Amount "at risk," except with respect to real estate activities	Partner's investment plus his or her share of the partnership recourse liabilities except for real estate partnerships	No losses allowed to individual except upon sale of stock or liquidation of corporation	The shareholder's investment plus his or her loans to the corporation; basis of loans reduced by losses and distributions
Dividends received	$100 dividend exclusion ($200 on joint tax return)	Conduit	70% dividend-received deduction	Treated as ordinary income; no exclusion or deduction
Formal election required	No	No	Must incorporate under state law	Yes
Capital gain	Taxed at individual level; 28%, except 33% on certain amounts	Conduit	Taxed at corporate level, 34%	Amounts flow through to extent of shareholder's portion of corporation's taxable income, but (unlike partnership) ordinary losses and capital gains are netted at corporate level
Capital losses	Carried forward indefinitely	Conduit	Carry back three years and carry over five years as short-term capital loss, offsetting only capital gains	Carry over five years as short-term capital loss, offsetting only capital gains

FIGURE 12–1 (Continued)

	Proprietorship	Partnership	Regular Corporation	Subchapter S Corporation
Section 1231 gains and losses	Taxed at individual level, combined with other Section 1231 gains or losses of individual; net gains are capital gains for individual; net losses are ordinary losses for individual	Conduit	Taxable, or deductible at the corporate level	Net gain is a capital gain to the shareholder; net loss is an ordinary loss to the shareholder; however, corporation's Section 1231 losses are not netted with shareholder's Section 1231 gains
Basis of allocating income to owners	All income and deductible expense picked up on owner's return	Profit and loss agreement (may have "special allocations" of income and deductions if they reflect economic reality)	No income allocated to stockholders	Number of shares owned on the last day of the corporation's tax year
Basis for allocating a net operating loss	All losses flow through to owner's return	Profit and loss agreement (may have "special allocations" of income and deductions if they reflect economic reality)	No losses allocated to stockholders	Prorated among shareholders on a daily basis, based on actual ownership
Group hospitalization and life insurance premiums and medical reimbursement plans	Itemized deductions: for medical expenses, half of insurance premiums up to $150, medicine and drugs in excess of 1% of adjusted gross income, other bills over 3% of AGI; no deduction for life insurance premiums	Cost of partners' benefits are not deductible as a business expense; may be treated as distribution to individual partners, eligible for some possible deduction as if paid by individual	Cost of shareholder-employee's coverage is generally deductible as a business expense if plan is "for the benefit of employees"	Same as regular corporation
Retirement benefits	Limited to H.R.-10 plan benefits, normally 15% of income up to $15,000; however, some defined-benefit H.R.-10 plans may provide more. Limitation increases to essentially same as regular corporation.	Same as individual	Normal corporate employee benefits up to $115,000 after which a 5% excise tax is owed	Corporation can deduct normal corporate employee contribution; however, owner-employee must add income contribution in excess of $15,000 to taxable income. Limitation increases to essentially same as regular corporation
Organization costs	Not amortizable	Amortizable over 60 months	Amortizable over 60 months	Same as regular corporation

Figure 12–1 (Continued)

	Proprietorship	Partnership	Regular Corporation	Subchapter S Corporation
Partner's or shareholder's "reasonable" salary	Not applicable	Treated as an allocation of partnership profits and a conduit	Expense to the corporation taxable to the shareholder-employee, subject to FICA	Same as regular corporation
Charitable contribution	Subject to limits for individual; gifts for the use of private foundation, 20% of AGI; gifts to public charity, cash 50% of AGI; appreciated property, 30% of AGI. Other limitations for specific items contributed	Conduit	Limited to 10% of taxable income before special deductions	Same as regular corporation
Liability	Individually liable on all liabilities of business	General partners individually liable on partnership's liabilities; limited partner liable only up to amount of his or her capital contribution	Capital contribution is limit of liability of shareholder	Same as regular corporation
Qualified owners	Individual ownership	No limitation	No limitation	Only individuals, estates, and certain trusts may be shareholders
Type of ownership interests	Individual ownership	More than one class of partner permitted	More than one class of stock permitted	Only one class of stock permitted
Transfer of ownership	Assets of business transferable rather than business itself	New partnership usually created; consent of other partners normally required if partnership interest is to be transferred	Ready transfer of ownership through the use of stock certificates; restrictions may be imposed by shareholders' agreement	Shares can be transferred only to individuals, certain types of trusts, or estates; no consent by new shareholders to Subchapter S election is needed
Capital requirements	Capital raised only by loan or increased contribution by proprietor	Loans or contributions from partners (original, or newly created by remaking partnership)	Met by sale of stock or bonds or other corporate debt	Met by sale of stock or bonds, but corporation has only one class of stock and is limited to 35 shareholders
Business action	Sole proprietor makes decisions and can act immediately	Action usually dependent upon the unanimous agreement of partners or general partners	Unity of action based on authority of board of directors	Same as regular corporation except unanimous consent is required to elect or revoke Subchapter S status

Figure 12–1 *(Concluded)*

	Proprietorship	Partnership	Regular Corporation	Subchapter S Corporation
Management	Proprietor responsible and receives all profits or losses	Except for limited or silent partners, investment in partnership involves responsibility for management decisions	Shareholder can receive income without sharing in responsibility for management	Same as regular corporation
Flexibility	No restrictions	Partnership is contractual arrangement, within which members can do in business what individuals can, subject to the partnership agreement and applicable state laws	Corporation is a creature of the state functioning within powers granted explicitly or necessarily implied and subject to judicial construction and decision	Same as regular corporation
Investment credit	None	Conduit	None	Conduit
Tax preferences (minimum tax)	All preference items are subject to an expanded alternative minimum tax	Conduit	Taxed at corporate level; 20% on preferences in excess of either $10,000 or tax liability, whichever is greater. Certain other items based on complex calculation for which professional guidance is needed	Conduit
Character of income and deductions	Taxed at individual level; long-term capital gains deduction; limitation on investment interest deductions	Conduit	Taxed at corporate level	Except as to long-term capital gains, income and profits are computed at corporate level, so that characteristics are determined at corporate level and do not flow to shareholder

SOURCE: S. Jones and M. B. Cohen, *The Emerging Business* (New York: Coopers & Lybrand, 1983).

- Limited liability: The individual proprietor is personally liable for all liabilities of the business.
- Free transferability of interest: The proprietor cannot freely transfer his interest; once she or he does, the proprietorship is dissolved.

Tax Status

The proprietorship does not pay taxes as a separate entity. The individual reports all income and deductible expenses from both the business and any other sources on the personal income tax return. Note that the earnings (as reported on the company's income statement) of the business are taxed at the individual level whether or not they are actually distributed in cash. There is no vehicle for sheltering income. Moreover, the sole proprietor cannot deduct as a business expense the costs of medical or life insurance.

The Partnership

The General Partnership

A partnership is defined as ''a voluntary association of two or more persons to carry on as co-owners of a business for profit.'' A partnership is more complicated than merely a collection of individuals. The partners must resolve and should set down in writing their agreement on a number of issues:

- The amount and nature of their respective capital contributions. One partner might contribute cash, another a patent, and a third property and cash.
- The allocation of the business's profits and losses.
- Salaries and drawings against profits.
- Management responsibilities.
- Consequences of withdrawal, retirement, disability, or death of a partner.
- Means of dissolution and liquidation of the partnership.

The Limited Partnership

A limited partnership is a partnership that has both limited *and* general partners.

- The general partner assumes the management responsibility *and* unlimited liability for the obligations of the business, and must have at least a 1 percent interest in profits and losses.
- The limited partner has no voice in management and is legally liable only for the amount of the capital contribution plus any other debt specifically accepted.

In a limited partnership, the general partner may be a corporation (a corporate general partner). In situations where a corporation is the sole general partner, in order to ensure that there are sufficient assets to cover the unlimited liability that the general partner must assume, the corporate general partner must have a net worth equal to $250,000 or 10 percent of the total capitalization of the partnership, whichever is less.

Classification

A partnership is treated much like a proprietorship.

- Continuity of life: The partnership will cease to exist upon the death, insanity, or retirement of any of the partners, unless specifically reconstituted according to the governing law and documents of the partnership.
- Centralized management:
  - In a general partnership, management is not centralized because *all* of the partners have decision-making authority.
  - In a limited partnership, a subgroup of the owners—the general partners—has decision-making authority, and therefore, management is centralized.
- Limited liability: The nature of a partnership is such that someone, or some group, must accept unlimited liability.
  - In a general partnership, all of the partners have full, unlimited liability.
  - In a limited partnership, the limited partner's liability is limited to the capital contributed plus any other liability the limited partner agrees to accept. The general partners in a limited partnership *still* have full, unlimited liability.
- Free transferability of interest: Partnership interests are generally not freely transferable.

Tax Status

For tax purposes neither a general nor a limited partnership is considered a separate tax entity (although the partnership does file a return) but is merely a conduit through which income (or losses) is passed to the partners.

- Profit and losses are allocated to individuals in accordance with the partnership agreement, as long as that distribution has some basis in economic reality.
- Cash distributions are allocated in a manner that may or may not parallel profits and losses.

Generally, the following tax rules apply:

- The apportionment of profits and losses must have some economic substance; it may not be designed solely to avoid taxes.
- Generally, the amount of losses that a partner may deduct is limited to the amount of capital at risk (i.e., equity contributed plus debt assumed). (Note: Real estate partnerships are an exception to this ''at risk'' rule.)
- The income of the partnership is taxed at the personal level of the individual whether or not any cash is actually distributed.

- The distribution of cash out of income or retained earnings is not itself a taxable event. The only time when cash distributions are a taxable event is when the cash distribution exceeds the partners' basis in the partnership.
- The basis is equal to the amount of capital originally contributed, plus the amount of income on which tax is paid, less any cash distributions. (Example: An individual invests $100 in a partnership, and his share of income in Year 1 equals $30. He must pay tax on this $30 at the personal rate. His basis is now $130. If he receives a $20 cash distribution, his basis drops to $110.)

The Corporation

Both the "regular" corporation and the S corporation are creatures of the law. The S corporation technically refers to an election that corporate shareholders may make to receive "Subchapter S tax treatment."

Classification

A corporation is defined according to the following criteria:

- Continuity of life: The death or divestiture of interest by any shareholder, or group, will not cause a dissolution of the corporation.
- Centralized management: The decision-making authority of a corporation is legally constituted in the corporation's board of directors, rather than in the shareholders.
- Limited liability: The "corporate veil" protects the shareholder from personal liability (exception: owners and managers of a corporation may be personally liable for certain liabilities that result from fraud or violations of the tax code or securities laws).
- Free transferability of interest: Shareholders are usually free to sell their interest in the corporation without the consent of other shareholders. They may bargain this right away in the original shareholders' agreement. In the case of an S corporation, however, the sale of shares to any entity *except* an individual U.S. citizen or testamentary trust will automatically trigger the loss of S corporation status.

Legally, the organization of a corporation requires a charter, bylaws, a board of directors, and corporate officers (president, treasurer, clerk). The precise legal requirements are a function of the specific state law where the firm is incorporated.

Tax Status: S Corporation

The S corporation is a vehicle of Congress specifically targeted to give certain advantages to the small business. Essentially, an S corporation is treated like a partnership for tax purposes (i.e., it functions as a conduit through which income is allocated). However, the S corporation owners are afforded the same protection from unlimited liability as the owners of a corporation.

In order to qualify for S corporation status, the organization must meet a number of rather restrictive conditions. It must:

- Have only one class of stock, although differences in voting rights are allowed.
- Be a domestic corporation, owned wholly by U.S. citizens and derive no more than 80 percent of its revenues from non-U.S. sources.
- Have 35 or fewer stockholders.
- Derive no more than 25 percent of revenues from passive sources (i.e., interest, dividends, rents, and royalties).
- Have only individuals, estates, and certain trusts as shareholders (i.e., no corporations).

The election of S corporation tax status requires the unanimous, timely consent of all shareholders. This status may be terminated by unanimous election, or if one of the above-mentioned conditions is broken.

Tax Status: Regular Corporation

Corporations do not receive a deduction for dividends paid to shareholders. Further, shareholders are taxed on the receipt of dividend income. Hence, shareholders are taxed twice on the same earnings. This "double taxation" is the main disadvantage of a corporation. (The exceptions to this rule are qualified investment companies and real estate investment trusts that qualify under Sections 856–858 of the tax code.)

In order to avoid this double taxation, the principals of closely held corporations (especially wholly owned companies) often resort to the tactic of attempting to structure the return of earnings in a form that is deductible to the corporation (i.e., interest or salary). The IRS has a number of rules that deal explicitly with these issues.

- Salary: By raising his salary to a very high level, the owner of a corporation could effectively reduce earnings to zero and pay tax only once, at a personal level, on salary received.

    - Federal Tax Code Section 162, paragraph (A) states that the IRS will permit "... a reasonable allowance for salaries or other compensation for personal services actually rendered."
    - The IRS can, upon audit, reclassify a portion of salary as dividends, and thus create both a corporate and a personal tax liability.

- Interest: By initially capitalizing the business with debt (rather than equity) the owners can receive some of their cash distributions in the form of interest rather than dividends. Interest expense is deductible by the corporation and is therefore a "cheaper" way to get money out of the business.

    - Federal Tax Code Section 385 deals with the issue of "thinly capitalized" corporations (i.e., where the IRS believes that the capital structure of the business is too heavily weighted in favor of debt).
    - In essence, the IRS can, upon audit, reclassify debt as equity and reclassify interest as dividends when:

- The debt does not have the characteristics of debt (i.e., is held in proportion to stock, payment of interest is contingent upon certain conditions, or interest is unreasonable).
- The corporation has "excessive" debt (i.e., a debt to equity ratio of greater than 10:1).

Another disadvantage of the corporate form of organization is the inability to flow through losses. In a proprietorship, partnership, or Sub S corporation, losses will flow through to the owners of the firm for deduction that year on their personal tax return. A corporation accumulates tax losses for its own use in later years.

One exception in this area involves "Section 1244 stock." This is a special creature of the tax code. If a new business is formed and elects 1244 treatment rather than regular treatment, and if the business goes bankrupt, owners of the stock can claim an ordinary income loss up to the amount of their investment. Had the company been formed with regular shares, the loss would have been a capital loss.

There are, however, several tax advantages to the corporate form of organization. These include:

- Deductibility of certain personal fringe benefits, such as medical and health insurance.
- The ability to shelter earnings (i.e., keep earnings within the company and transfer them out, as dividends, at a later date when the recipients may be in a more tax advantageous situation).

Summary

Each of the various legal forms of organization is distinguished from the others in a variety of ways. Often the decision about which legal form to elect is made solely in an attempt to minimize taxes. While this is a legitimate economic aim, the forms of organization differ along many other important dimensions. It is important to have a full understanding of *all* of these differences before electing the legal form. The counsel of a competent attorney is usually called for.

3–1 ALLEN LANE

It was March 1982, and Allen Lane sat at his desk pondering a confusing array of issues relative to his bid for Plas-Tek Industries (PTI). Allen had been trying to buy a company for almost two years. On a number of occasions he had come quite close, only to have one circumstance or another block his way. Would his bid for PTI meet the same fate, or would his search for a business finally be over?

Background

Allen Lane, 45, had had a variety of experiences since his graduation from business school in 1965 (see **Exhibit 1** for résumé). He spent several years with Wagner Electric Co. in Springfield, Massachusetts, eventually filling the role of vice president of operations for this relatively small manufacturer of electronic parts.

Allen left the firm in 1972 to become an independent consultant to industry. He focused primarily on operations-oriented work: inventory control systems, manufacturing methods, material control, etc.

After three years of relative success, Allen disbanded his efforts in order to join James & Co. in New York.

> I enjoyed working for myself and was making a comfortable living. I grew tired, however, of working on the same kind of problems. James offered the opportunity to get involved with more general management issues and strategic problems. I was also excited about working with some people whom I considered to be extremely bright and interesting.

Allen joined James in January of 1975 and worked with a varied roster of clients and industries. By 1980, however, Allen reached the conclusion that it was time to leave.

> I was becoming frustrated with the cumbersome and generally bureaucratic processes at the very large companies that are the base of James's clientele. James really did expand my horizons and my point of view. My experience there built a lot of general management perspective and honed important general management skills (I thought) that I was eager to use. I wanted to run my own company.

In June 1980, Allen informed James of his intentions to leave. It was important to Allen that James was generous enough to offer the continued resources of the firm,

This case was prepared by Michael J. Roberts under the direction of Howard H. Stevenson.
Copyright © 1983 by the President and Fellows of Harvard College
Harvard Business School Case 9–384–007

including office space and secretarial services, while he looked for an opportunity. Allen began thinking about how to get into his own business.

Laying the Groundwork

Allen had once before thought about buying a company but had no idea where to begin and did not have any close friends who had tried. His experience at James had given him numerous contacts and some credibility, as well as modest financial resources (i.e., roughly $100,000 in liquid assets that he felt he could afford to invest in a company). He described the thought process behind his plan of action and his progress.

First, I was sure that I wanted to purchase a going concern rather than start up a business:

- The start-up process is a lot riskier, takes longer to pay out, and requires a more single-minded commitment to the process than does purchasing a going concern.
- I never felt I had a "better mousetrap" around which to start a business.
- I enjoy being a fixer, a consultant, more than being a creator.
- Finally, I had the time and resources to wait until I found a good deal.

Next, I decided that in order to have a shot at finding something you needed to have a *focus:* "If you don't know where you're going, any path will get you there." Even if you change your focus later on, at least people have a sense that you know what you want. I decided to look for an industrial distribution business.

- I specifically excluded high-tech and software-type businesses:
    - There is a lot of growth, which makes these businesses attractive, but they are "faddish" and as a result there is an incredible amount of competition for deals from large corporations with very deep pockets.
    - I felt that I had to understand and be able to manage the key aspects of the technology in order to minimize risk and successfully run the business.
    - I wanted it to be a business where the decisions *I* would make would have a major influence and make the difference—not the research engineer down the hall.
- I decided to focus on a distribution business:
    - I had done a lot of work in the industry as a consultant.
    - Distribution businesses are typically very undermanaged.
    - One of the key factors for success is excellent systems—a good fit for my skills.
    - In any given segment (like electronics components distribution) the firms are typically spread over a wide range in terms of their profitability. If you can buy a company in the bottom third of that range, and manage its margin up into the upper third, you can make *a lot* of money. And the skills required to do this are all basic general management skills.
    - These businesses lend themselves to asset-based financing (i.e., they have heavy current assets).
    - There are lots of small, owner-managed distributors around, and the competition for deals is less (to a large extent because they are not, historically, favored corporate acquisition targets).

About this time, I started talking with contacts who were in the deal flow, who encouraged me and suggested I look into electronics distribution. They also told me that I wouldn't *really* understand the acquisition process until I actually went through the process of trying to buy a company.

Early that fall (1980), I spoke with another guy, Dan Ray, who was also leaving James, and who had some experience in the electronics distribution business. We decided to work together.

We had just started making contacts in an attempt to look at deals when we heard through an accounting firm that Spectronics might be for sale. We called the president, Bert Spec, and sure enough, it was for real.

We had only been at it for only a short time, and we were ready to chase our first deal.

Spectronics

Spectronics was a $165 million (sales) distributor of electronic components, located in Newark, New Jersey. It was a publicly traded company, but Burt Spec owned a controlling interest of about 55 percent.

We looked at the numbers and, in the price range he was talking, about $20/share or $15 million, the deal made good economic sense. Spectronics also seemed to offer the potential for improvement in rate of return that we were looking for. (See **Exhibit 2**.) We put together a 200-page business plan that outlined the industry, our credentials, the company, our plans for it—the works. After six or eight weeks, we managed to pull together an $11 million package of financing that included $1 million in equity, $8 million in secured debt, and $2 million of "mezzanine debt" (i.e., a higher risk unsecured loan with a higher return to the lender). We offered $21.50 a share. By now, it was the middle of December, and we had been working on the deal for about three months.

We found out a week later that the company was sold for $2/share *less* than our offer. The other group had offered $19.50 plus a huge "consulting contract" for Bert Spec. We were livid and wanted to sue, but this would have required revealing our equity backer who was anxious to protect his anonymity. So—there went our first deal.

A Reflection

Looking back two years later, it was probably a good thing that we didn't get the first deal that came down the pike. We learned an incredible amount, and it cost us nothing but our time. The valuable lessons included:

- Don't go after a public company unless you have a backer willing to underwrite the process. The lawyers and accounting fees required to put a public deal together are far higher than for a private company. This is a sunk cost, and if the deal falls apart—as they often do—you've lost these fees.
- The acquisition business is a rough-and-tumble one. We were advised not to tell potential investors the name of a company until we absolutely had to. We heard horror stories about guys like us getting squeezed out by the people who had the money and who went around the entrepreneurs and bought the company themselves.
- It is a lucrative business. If you find a deal, *and* hold on to it, you can extract 10 to 20 percent just for finding it and packaging the deal. If you put some money in or are actually going to manage the venture, your share can go up to 50 percent or so with a limited investment in even a large deal.

Back to the Drawing Board

So Dan and I put our heads together to decide where to go. We came to the conclusion that all of our initial thoughts on the industry were correct. Moreover, we knew a lot more about the industry, had some contacts, and we thought we could keep our backers together. So we decided to maintain our focus on the electronics distribution industry.

We called every company—about 60 or so—that met our criteria:

- Northeast corridor location.
- Sales of $5 to $50 million.

We looked for any way in other than a cold call—a lawyer, accountant, friend, anything. We talked to industry observers, customers, suppliers, and banks in an attempt to plug into the grapevine.

We had heard that 5 percent of *all* businesses are "for sale" and that 2 percent are *very actively* for sale. Well, out of our 60 calls, we found 8 that seemed interested enough to warrant a meeting. Of these, we had second meetings with 4, a third meeting with 2, and pursued 1, Ace Electronics, very aggressively.

Ace Electronics

By now it was March of 1981, and we had been looking at the industry for about six months. Ace was a little different—it focused on very low tech and together with current inventories had a large stock of almost obsolete parts. Ace was owned by Abe Fox, who had started the business 25 years ago and was now retiring. He was typically one of the only sources in the *country* for some old condensers, vacuum tubes, and electromechanical parts. You can imagine that his margins were *very* good.

We spent two months haggling and finally shook on a deal. He went away to California for a vacation, and when he came back, he declared that the deal was off.

Another Reflection

Ace really opened my eyes to the world of small business. Most small businesses that we looked at, and of which Ace was the first, have "undervalued inventory." Ace, for instance, had its inventory on the books for $600,000, although the owner claimed (and after some careful checking we concurred) that it was worth at least $4 million. (See **Exhibit 3** for two sets of financial statements.)

This understatement is done because of *taxes*. If you overstate your cost of goods sold, you reduce your stated profit, and hence your taxes. Over time the stated book value of inventory becomes small relative to the actual value.

This is not a problem to the buyer, of course, if you are going to continue this practice. However, I had decided early on that I did not want to play such games.

This can create a problem in a small company acquisition. If you keep the inventory on the books at its understated amount, the IRS is very unlikely to see any potential issue. However, if you mark the inventory up to its "fair market value," the IRS may catch on and can (fairly) claim that the company had been underpaying its taxes all along.

So, then you come up against two issues:

- Sale of stock versus assets: The liabilities of a company always remain attached to the stock. If you buy the assets of a firm, the seller maintains the potential tax liability. However, if you buy the stock, as most sellers prefer, then *you* are stuck with the potential liability.

- Tax on ''discovered inventory'': Once the inventory is discovered, of course, this item has to be run through the income statement and shows up as profit, which must be taxed. My view, of course, was that Ace should pay this tax since it had been underpaying all along, and that it had, in effect, accrued taxes. Naturally, Ace would think that if I am ''stupid enough'' to be honest and declare this to the IRS, I should pay the tax.

Perhaps at this point, I should comment on what I perceive as my own style. There is a large gray area between what is ethically right and wrong. There are many opportunities to ''play games'' in the process of looking for a deal: exaggerating net worth, experience, the numbers on a deal, and so forth. These things may be ethically ''wrong,'' or perhaps they are borderline. Whatever the case, I had decided early on that they just didn't make good business sense for me. One of the critical things I had going for me was my reputation. People ''calibrate you'' based on the veracity of your total presentation. If they detect that you are being less than totally honest about *anything,* then they discount *everything* that you say—I couldn't afford to let that happen. Thus, I decided that the right style for me was to be very open and straightforward with sellers, financial sources, and others.

Gardenpro

Gardenpro was a distributor of garden products, hardware, and paint, located in New Jersey. I heard about the deal from a business broker who showed me financials (with the name of the company deleted) and I was interested. He set us up to meet Chuck Stamen, Gardenpro's owner/manager.

It was an attractive business in a good location and was a distributor—just the kind of company I was looking for.

I met Chuck, and after the preliminary chat and tour, we started talking price. Pretty soon, Chuck mentioned that ''the financials didn't fairly reflect the earning power of the business.'' Why was that so? Well, it seems that Chuck had a little scheme going where he pulled about $500,000 in cash out of the business—off the books and tax free.

It worked roughly like this: he would take an order for products from one of his ''friendly'' customers and give the order to his employees to load in the truck. Then Chuck would announce that he had to do some business with the fellow anyway, and he would drive the truck over. His friend would pay about 80 cents on the dollar—in cash—for the goods, and then Chuck would just rip up the order. No one would ever know.

Of course, he wanted me to value this off-the-books amount in making my bid. My position was that I wasn't going to play these games, and further, I was likely to lose these customers altogether, because I wasn't going to accept 80 cents on the dollar for my products if I was selling them.

I did submit a bid and knew that I could obtain financing. By this point, I was familiar with the approximate formula that secured lenders use to calculate the ''financibility'' of a company.

- 85 percent of the receivables under 90 days old (to solid accounts), plus

- 40 percent to 60 percent of the inventory, depending on its salability, and to some extent on how good the deal is.

In addition, you can usually also borrow one quarter to one third of the appraised value of the plant and equipment; real estate assets can be mortgaged up to 80 percent or 90 percent. This is a very straightforward approach to calculate how much you can borrow on an asset-financed deal.

As you might expect, I lost Gardenpro to someone with a higher bid. But I later found out that the company was never sold.

Hydrapress

A few months later, in October of 1981, I came across Hydrapress, a manufacturer of hydraulic presses for making refractories and special bricks for use in high-temperature processes, such as furnaces for molten metal and glass. I heard about this deal from another business broker. He was hesitant to refer me to Morris Golden, president of Hydrapress, because I did not have the $3 or $4 million in hard cash required to do the deal. But he did set me up with an investment banker who had appraised Hydrapress and who was representing the seller.

We got together, and I learned that it was a fairly typical selling situation. Golden was 68 and had decided it was "time to retire and enjoy life." His wife wanted to go to Florida, and all his friends were telling him to sell the company and tidy up his estate.

The investment banker told me that there were two very serious buyers lined up who clearly had the cash and were interested in purchasing the company as an investment. They would need a management team; perhaps I could work a joint deal with one of them. I did speak with each of these groups, but told them I was also working to raise the capital to make a bid on my own. In any event, under the banker's auspices, I was able to visit Hydrapress and meet with its principals.

After visiting numerous banks, I finally did get an oral commitment for the money from the Fiduciary Bank and wrote my proposal letter. I bid $3.4 million, but lost out by a small margin to a NYSE company.

Six months later, the investment banker called to ask if I was still interested. It seems that when push came to shove, Golden had balked at selling the company. According to the banker, he kept finding little nits with the deal until the buyer got so exasperated that he finally walked away.

By this time, I was chasing Plas-Tek and didn't have the time to get involved. More importantly, I had learned a lesson about buying a company from the founding owner: It's *tough*. No one wants to sell "his or her baby."

A Perspective

Allen commented on a few other aspects of the deal business he had learned about over the past several years.

"Ham and Egging"

One of the real "arts" to the process of trying to buy a company is called *ham and egging*. It refers to the delicate process of trying to get the financing secured before you have the company locked up and trying to get the company committed before you have the financing.

Naturally, potential backers don't want to spend the time evaluating the deal or commit to financing unless they are fairly certain that you have an acceptable deal worked out with the company. The company, on the other hand, feels it is wasting its time talking to you unless you have the money.

I was always very straightforward with companies; I would describe the deal to different financial backers, get an oral commitment of interest, and tell the company that I had this oral commitment. Naturally, I projected the attitude that I was sure that financing would be available.

The process does get much easier as you go along. The first time is always the hardest. On subsequent deals, even if the previous deals have fallen apart, you can talk about having raised money before, and you have a portfolio of backers to deal with. After people know you, and have seen you in action on one deal and have come to trust you, they are far quicker to make a commitment on financing.

A Hierarchy of Buyers

All this leads one to talk about what I call ''a hierarchy of buyers.'' None of the companies would even be talking to me if they could have sold to a NYSE company in an all-cash deal, or a tax-free exchange of stock. From a seller's perspective it appears that there are several classes of buyers doing deals:

- Class A: Another company who views the seller as a business with ''strategic fit.'' They are willing to pay cash, and pay a premium price for the company.
- Class B: Investment bankers representing some company looking for a deal, often a conglomerate. Generally they won't pay the premiums that a strategic buyer will, but in either case, as a seller you don't have to worry about the money being there.
- Class C_1: A leveraged buyout specialist who will in all probability pay even less, but who has done deals before and who has a track record in raising the cash.
- Class C_2: An individual who doesn't have the cash, hasn't done a deal, but knows what he's doing and can probably raise the money. I felt that I was a C_2 given my contacts and experience.
- Class C_3: An individual with nothing but desire; this was me when I started out, before the Spectronics deal.

Plas-Tek

In March of 1982, I ran into Jeff Brewster, an accountant with a Big 8 firm, with whom I had spoken around the time of the Spectronics deal. He thought he might have a few companies I'd be interested in, and we scheduled a lunch for the following week. One of the companies was Plas-Tek.

Background

Harry Elson had founded Plas-Tek, a manufacturer of specialty plastic components, in 1954. When he died in November of 1981, he left an estate that was valued at $7 million or so to a half-dozen well-known charities. Plas-Tek was part of the estate, and the trustee/executor, a big New York bank, had decided to sell it. In fact, PTI was actually two companies: HE Manufacturing and its sister company, Plas-Tek Sales Company. PTI refers to both companies.

The bank had a valuation of the business performed (see **Exhibit 4** for a description of PTI's business and the valuation report) and then contacted customers, suppliers, and competitors to see if any were interested in purchasing Plas-Tek. When none expressed interest, the bank quietly put Plas-Tek on the market.

By the time I heard about the business, it had been on the market for a month or so, and the bank told me that unless I were going to bid $600,000 or more not to bother. They told me that they wanted to close off bidding later that week, but I figured that I could stall them for a little while. When Elson died, all of his estate went into a charitable trust. The bank's trust and estate department had a fiduciary obligation to get the highest price for the business. They would not look good if they refused to let me submit a bid.

So, during the next few days, I raced around trying to put together a deal and submit my bid. I had the valuation and the banks' ". . . beat $600,000" as a starting point.

Strategy

My strategy was to first *value* the business, and then *price* it. They are two different things. Obviously, I wanted my price to be lower than the business's value but high enough for the bid to get *me* to the bargaining table with the bank.

The Business: Fit with Allen Lane

First, I had to evaluate the business and how it fit with my skills and objectives. Clearly, it wasn't in the distribution area, but they did have some things in common, including the importance of customer service. Further, it was *definitely* going to require a lot of hands-on management. With Elson dead, there was really a management vacuum at Plas-Tek.

The Business Itself

Obviously, a crucial issue was the business itself. I was amazed to see that Plas-Tek had gross margins in excess of 50 percent for a nonproprietary product. Harry was pulling down over half a million a year from a business with a million dollars in sales! Was this a legitimate profit, and, more important, would it continue if I bought the business?

Key Employees

Plas-Tek had the equivalent of eight full-time shop workers as well as a bookkeeper and a customer service/order entry clerk. I spent a day walking around the shop and was convinced that I could learn the manufacturing end of the business. As an engineer, I felt comfortable with the basic molding and machining operations. Still, there were several key employees whose efforts would be crucial to getting off to a good start.

- Bernie, the shop foreman, had been with PTI for 18 years. I talked with him and was convinced of his desire to stay on. He was about 55 and was making almost $50,000 a year, so he seemed to have little incentive to move. Unfortunately, he was in failing health, and if something did happen, we would be in tough shape.
- Sarah, the bookkeeper, knew the financial side of the business as well as Harry's pricing policies.

- Eleanor, the customer service/order entry clerk, knew a little bookkeeping as well as who the key customers were, what they ordered, and how it was priced. She also knew where all of the finished goods inventory was stored.

Harry had been clever in having a lot of part-time people on board, so there were often two people who knew the same job.

A Partner

Since the Spectronics deal, I had looked at doing things both on my own and with a variety of partners. Generally, I am the verbal type and do my best thinking in a teamlike atmosphere. I also wanted someone to mind the store while I was away and vice versa. I didn't want to be tied to the business night and day, every day.

I thought it was important that a partner and I each be able to handle key aspects of the business, but still have a clear enough division of responsibilities that we not get in each other's way. I was also looking for someone with flexibility and a set of values, goals, and expectations that was compatible with mine.

I also knew that if I brought in a partner, I wanted it to be a full 50 percent partner. I had been involved with some less-than-equal partnerships before, and such a partner feels that he is doing more than his share of the work. The individual I chose as a partner was capable of matching my $100,000 equity contribution in order to buy his half of the equity. Dan Ray had joined a semiconductor firm after the Spectronics deal fell through, but we had kept in touch. I knew he was still interested in doing something with me, and I still thought he would make a good partner.

Financing

Because I had the experience of putting together the described deals (and others), I had a portfolio of equity backers, asset-secured financiers, and other lenders to draw on for financing.

I did have about $100,000 in equity, and ideally, I hoped to finance the remainder so that my partner and I could control 100 percent of the equity.

I thought we might be able to get the estate (represented by the bank) to take back a note if we could get a reputable bank to guarantee this debt. I did have excellent relationships with a few banks that I had worked with on other deals, and they seemed eager to work with me.

I also knew that if we borrowed on the business itself, that we would have to personally guarantee at least a portion of the note, and that the interest rate would be about 2 percent over prime (i.e., in the 17 percent to 19 percent range).

A Lawyer

I had worked with a variety of lawyers. Some were good negotiators, others good on tax or securities issues. I had developed a list of criteria to aid in the selection of an attorney (see **Exhibit 5**). We had to pick one and get him up to speed fast.

Stock versus Assets

The purchase of stock versus the purchase of assets was a major issue in the deal structure, and we knew we had to make a decision on this point early on. I would have preferred a simple purchase of assets. In this way, we would not have to assume *any* of the liabilities associated with the old company.

The bank, however, wanted to clean up and settle the estate. They were strongly in favor of a purchase of stock, which would saddle me with all liabilities, including contingent liabilities.

Contingent Liabilities

Contingent liabilities are real or potential liabilities that do not exist on the balance sheet. For instance, if an employee had lost an arm in an industrial accident, but had not sued the company, there was a contingent liability in that he *might* sue later and *might* win some *unknown* amount of money. We thought that the following contingent liabilities might exist for Plas-Tek and checked them out thoroughly:

- Existing lawsuit.
- Potential lawsuit.
- Potential tax liability.

We interviewed employees in an attempt to discover any potential problems (i.e., injuries or customer problems). As best we could determine, there were no existing lawsuits against the company, and we checked the literature to unearth the possibility of potential product liability suits. We made a list of all the major substances the company used and ran computer searches to determine whether any of these was suspected of causing cancer or other diseases. Fortunately, they checked OK.

On the tax issue, however, we were not so lucky. There were two areas of potential liability:

- Unreasonable compensation: Harry had been pulling out *a lot* of money as salary, and hence deducting it on the corporate tax return. If the IRS stepped in, they could declare that some amount of this "salary" was excessive compensation, and reclassify it as a dividend. (See **Exhibit 6** for tax code and explanation.) Then the company would be liable for an income tax on this amount. This issue was complicated by the fact that Harry was operating PTI as two separate companies: HE Manufacturing was a straight corporation, and Plas-Tek Sales was a Sub S. If the IRS questioned the transfer-pricing policies of the company, the potential tax liability could increase to an even greater amount. (See **Exhibit 7** for a full explanation of the potential tax liabilities.)
- Accumulated earnings: HE Manufacturing, the straight corporation, had a substantial amount of interest-earning current assets on its books. (See Exhibit 4 for balance sheet.) The IRS could, on examination, claim that these assets were earnings that Elson had accumulated in HE Manufacturing rather than distributing them as dividends. (Again, see Exhibit 7 for full explanation.)

The Decision

Allen and his partner put a pot of coffee on the stove and prepared themselves for a long evening. They knew that it would not be easy to resolve these issues and value the business, but they had to submit their bid the following morning.

EXHIBIT 1   Résumé of Allen Lane

Allen Lane

Experience

1975 to 1980   NEW YORK, NEW YORK
JAMES & COMPANY, INC.
Engagement Manager. As consultant to top management of large manufacturing and distribution companies, led teams of several consultants and up to 50 client personnel to formulate strategies, and to identify and implement opportunities to increase profitability and improve functional performance.

Served clients in electronics (telecommunications equipment, computers, components), machinery (business equipment), consumer products (sanitary paper, pharmaceuticals) and process (paper, packaging) industries ranging in annual revenues from $150 million to $9 billion.

Developed and presented consultant training in techniques for assisting manufacturers and distributors to reduce costs and improve delivery performance.

1972 to 1975   CAMBRIDGE, MASSACHUSETTS
LANE AND ASSOCIATES
As Principal, designed and implemented management systems to enhance competitive performance and improve profitability of manufacturing and distribution clients. Applications included inventory management, order entry, billing, accounts receivable, sales analysis, purchasing, accounts payable. Industries served included automotive parts and pharmaceuticals.

1965 to 1972   SPRINGFIELD, MASSACHUSETTS
WAGNER ELECTRIC CO.
As Vice President, Operations, for this $30 million manufacturer, responsible for planning and scheduling factory operations and managing inventories (raw material, work in process, finished goods). As Manager, System and Planning, responsible for developing capacity plans to support company's rapid growth. Also developed production planning and scheduling, labor control, budgeting, and other operational and accounting systems.

1958 to 1963   BOSTON, MASSACHUSETTS
ACME STEEL FABRICATORS, INC.
Purchasing Agent and Assistant to Vice President, Manufacturing, for this $5 million manufacturer of steel tanks, pressure vessels, and other weldments.

Education

1965   BOSTON, MASSACHUSETTS
EASTERN BUSINESS SCHOOL
MBA; concentrated in manufacturing and control.

1958   TROY, NEW YORK
RENSSELAER POLYTECHNIC INSTITUTE
Bachelor in Mechanical Engineering; elected member of Tau Beta Pi, Pi Tau Sigma honorary societies.

Exhibit 2   Profitability of 15 Largest Publicly Held Electronic Components Distributors

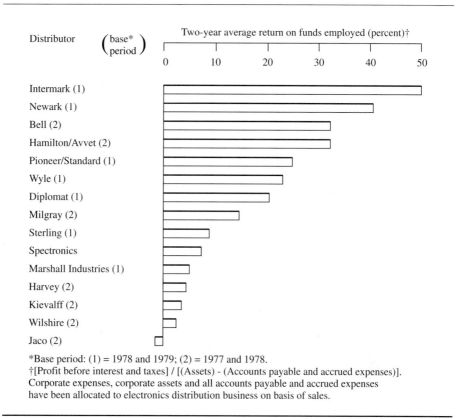

*Base period: (1) = 1978 and 1979; (2) = 1977 and 1978.
†[Profit before interest and taxes] / [(Assets) - (Accounts payable and accrued expenses)].
Corporate expenses, corporate assets and all accounts payable and accrued expenses
have been allocated to electronics distribution business on basis of sales.

Source: Annual Reports (line of business data for electronics distribution).

Exhibit 3   Two Sets of Ace Financial Statements, Fiscal 1979 (in thousands of dollars)

	Income Statement #1 *(as reported to IRS)*	*Income Statement #2* *(as "estimated" by Fox)*
Sales	$4,000	$4,000
Cost of goods sold	3,050	2,250
Gross margin	950	1,750
Expenses	750	750
EBIT	200	1,000
Interest	0	0
Taxes	100	100
Net profit	$ 100	$ 900

	Balance Sheet #1 *(as reported to IRS)*	*Balance Sheet #2* *(as "estimated" by Fox)*
Assets		
Cash	$ 30	$ 30
Accounts receivable	500	500
Inventory	600	600
Fixed/other	20	20
Additional inventories	—	4,900
Total	$1,150	$6,050
Liabilities and Net Worth		
Accounts payable	$ 250	$ 250
Accrued expenses	50	50
Accrued taxes	25	25
Bank loan	100	100
Net worth	725	725
Additional net worth	—	4,900
Total net worth	725	$5,625
Total	$1,150	$6,050

<hr>

Exhibit 4 **Introductory Letter and Valuation Report**

March 16, 1982

Dear Mr. Lane:

Enclosed is the evaluation report that we had prepared to guide us in the sale of Plas-Tek, Inc. Based on this report and our own preliminary analysis, we have now set the asking price for the sale of the companies at $750,000, and are so advising all of the parties who have met our preliminary requirements for establishing serious interest in the acquisition.

Please let us know within the next ten (10) days (*a*) if you are willing to pay our asking price, (*b*) the terms of your proposal, and (*c*) if you wish to make a counterproposal.

At this time we will only give serious consideration to offers to purchase at a price in excess of $600,000.

As you were previously advised, we intend to sell the corporation's entire stock (after removal of cash and marketable securities). We will only consider offers on terms if the purchase price is adequately secured by satisfactory collateral security other than the assets of the business itself.

Our plan is to proceed as follows: We will immediately enter into negotiations with qualified buyers in order of the magnitude of their initial offer. We anticipate, based on the interest expressed to date by a number of apparently serious and qualified prospective purchasers, that we can settle within our proposed price range. If we find that we are unable to do so, we intend to broaden the base of prospective purchasers by announcing the availability of the companies to a wide variety of customary sources of prospective purchasers.

We trust that it will be apparent to you that we consider this to be the most expeditious way for us to attain the highest price we can, consistent with our responsibilities as executors of the estate of Harold Elson.

Accordingly, if you wish to be the successful purchaser, it will certainly be in your interest to make the highest offer in response to this request as soon as you can do so, as we intend to complete this transaction as quickly as we can.

Sincerely yours,

Senior Trust Officer
New York Bank

PLAS-TEK INDUSTRIES (PTI)

We have been asked to determine the fair market value of PTI. All of the outstanding common stock of the company is presently held in the estate of Harold Elson. The purpose of this appraisal is to assist the executors of the estate in determining the value of the business in order to sell it.

Conclusion

Based on our analysis of the relevant facts, it is our opinion that the current fair market value, in an all-cash transaction, of the operating assets and business of PTI is $600,000.

Description of Business

The business will be referred to in this report as PTI. HE Manufacturing is a corporation, and Plas-Tek Sales is a Subchapter S company; PTI refers to both companies.

The business was founded some 25 or more years ago by Harold Elson and was operated by Mr. Elson until his death on November 20, 1981, at age 72.

EXHIBIT 4   *(continued)*

PTI, located in Patterson, New Jersey, is in the business of manufacturing and distributing gaskets, washers, "O" rings, and similar items made of plastic. PTI makes parts out of fluoroplastic resins as well as other materials, including nylon, polyethylene, and acrylic resins.

Products are generally made to industry standards or customer specifications. Approximately 90 percent of sales are made to distributors and original equipment manufacturers (OEM) with the balance sold to end users. PTI's customers come from a variety of industries, the most important being the food and chemical industries.

Sales are made primarily in response to requests for quotations and to repeat customers. PTI has no salesmen. Advertising is confined primarily to a small listing in *Thomas' Register.* The company has about 300 active customer accounts. Listed below are the sales figures for the five largest customers, which accounted, in the aggregate, for 35.3 percent of 1981 sales.

	1981 Sales	*Percent of Total Sales*
Customer A	$98,487	10.5%
Customer B	72,377	7.7
Customer C	61,615	6.5
Customer D	51,599	5.5
Customer E	48,362	5.1
		35.3%

Income Statements

Shown following is a summary of income statements of the company for the five-year period ended August 31, 1981.

PTI Income Statement (in thousands of dollars)

	Fiscal Years Ended August 31				
	1981	*1980*	*1979*	*1978*	*1977*
Net sales	$942	$1,050	$894	$709	$652
Gross profit	551	640	495	427	369
Operating and overhead expense	97	92	78	76	67
Profit before officer salary, investment income and income taxes .	454	548	417	351	302
Investment income*	93	92	65	66	18
Profit before officer salary and income taxes	547	640	482	407	320
Officer salary	480	505	415	360	280
New Jersey sales tax	20	23	18	19	6
Profit before federal income tax	$ 47	$ 12	$ 49	$ 28	$ 34

*Interest and dividends on cash and securities.

Manufacturing

Gaskets and washers are machined principally from cylinders or other shapes molded by PTI itself and also from plastic purchased from outside vendors. The company's facilities occupy a 3,700-square-foot building owned by it in Patterson, New Jersey. Principal items of production equipment

EXHIBIT 4   *(continued)*

include a press, a sintering oven, and a number of lathes and other machine tools. The company has five full-time production employees and four part-time employees. The company is nonunion. Hourly wage rates range from $5 to $9. The office staff consists of a manager and a bookkeeper-secretary-receptionist.

Management

The success of PTI has essentially been based on, and dependent on, the management efforts of Harold Elson. The company built a reputation of fulfilling orders quickly. Mr. Elson put a great deal of personal effort into providing responsive service to his customers, often working on weekends to do so.

Approach to Value

The definition of *fair market value* employed in this appraisal is the price at which the property would change hands between a willing buyer and a willing seller when the former is not under any compulsion to buy and the latter is not under any compulsion to sell, both having reasonable knowledge of relevant facts.

In establishing a value for PTI, we have taken into account a variety of factors, including the nature and history of the company, the economic outlook, the book value, financial condition and earnings capacity of the company, its dividend capacity and intangible values, past sales of securities of the company, and comparisons with public companies in the same or similar industry.

It is assumed for the purpose of this valuation that PTI will be purchased exclusive of its excess cash or investment assets. The excess cash and investments would either be removed from the company prior to sale or would be compensated for with an additional dollar-for-dollar payment by the purchaser of the business.

Balance Sheet

Exhibit A shows a combined balance sheet for the business with the excess cash and investments set forth.

It can be seen that, with the excess cash investments removed, the net worth of the operating assets of the business is $200,000. If the land and buildings were carried at their current appraised value of $92,000, the adjusted net worth of the company would be $292,000.

Earnings Capability

In 1981 PTI earned $454,000 before officer salary, investment income, and income tax. Clearly, a buyer would be attracted to the acquisition of PTI for its earnings capability rather than for its asset base. The estimate of fair market value, then, must begin with an analysis of the earnings history and capability of the company.

Set forth below is a summary of the earnings of the company.

Year	Operating Profit* before Officer Salary ($000)
1981	$454
1980	548
1979	417
1978	351
1977	302

*Before investment income and federal and New Jersey income taxes.

EXHIBIT 4   *(continued)*

A key question is how much of the earnings ability of the company was due to the personal efforts of Mr. Elson and, accordingly, how much of such earnings ability is likely to remain in the future in his absence. The months since his death, in November 1981, have seen a decline in sales as illustrated below. It is the feeling of those presently running the business, however, that a good part of this decline is attributable to softness in the economy in general rather than to the absence of Mr. Elson. Some of the softness had already begun to make itself felt in the months prior to Mr. Elson's death. No customer is known to have ceased doing business with the company because of Mr. Elson's death. We understand that the executors have communicated with all the major customers and these customers have assured the executors of their satisfaction and that they anticipate continuing to do business with PTI.

PTI Sales
(in thousands of dollars)

	3 Months Sept.–Nov.		2 Months Dec.–Jan.*		5 Months Sept.–Jan.*	
	Amount	*% Chg. from Prev. Yr.*	*Amount*	*% Chg. from Prev. Yr.*	*Amount*	*% Chg. from Prev. Yr.*
1981	$214	− 3.2%	$111	− 24.0%	$325	− 11.4%
1980	211	+ .5	146	− 17.0	367	− 7.3
1979	220	+ 25.0	176	0.0	396	+ 12.5
1978	176	+ 10.0	176	+ 58.6	352	+ 29.9
1977	160	+ 3.2	111	+ 6.7	271	+ 4.6
1976	155		104		259	

*Of following year.

We have taken the view that the current decline in sales volume is temporary, being related to the currrent soft economy and possibly to the uncertainty related to a prospective change in ownership of the company. With new capable ownership in place, there is no reason that the business should not be able to continue at least in the levels of the recent past. Accordingly, we have elected to employ the 1981 levels of profit before taxes and owner compensation as the best available indication of future profitability, and the one on which buyer and seller might be most likely to base a sale price.

Staffing

In view of Mr. Elson's heavy personal involvement in the business and the long hours that he put in, a new owner might well be required to staff the company with more than one person to replace Mr. Elson.

We have assumed that the functions formerly performed by Mr. Elson could be replaced at a cost of $150,000.

Future Earnings Capability

Using this estimate of management cost, and the 1981 level of pretax income before owner compensation, produces the following estimate of the earnings capability of PTI.

EXHIBIT 4   *(continued)*

Pro Forma Earnings (in thousands of dollars)

Profit before owner compensation and increased taxes....	$454
Management compensation................................	150
Profit before income taxes	304
New Jersey income tax (10%)............................	30
Profit before federal income tax..........................	274
Federal income tax (1982 rates).........................	106
Net income after taxes	$168

We have concluded, then, that a party acquiring PTI and staffing it at the annual cost shown above, would be buying a business capable of generating net income after taxes at the annual rate of $168,000.

Capitalization Rate

The capitalized earnings approach to value is based on the premise that a potential investor in a going concern will base the purchase price he is willing to pay on some multiple of the earnings power of the company. The approach consists of applying an appropriate price/earnings multiple (P/E) to the earnings of the company in question. It becomes necessary, then, to determine the appropriate P/E. The most reasonable way to do so is to determine what earnings multiple investors have been willing to pay for stocks of other companies engaged in similar lines of business.

Ideally, in selecting comparable companies, we look for companies not only in the same general line of business, but with a similarity that extends as far as possible into all areas of corporate circumstances, including capital structure, specific services performed, areas and intensity of competition, growth rates, and, if possible, size in terms of assets held, and the volume of sales. Only in the most unusual circumstances, however, will there be available even one publicly traded company that would begin to satisfy these multifarious requirements.

Since PTI is a fabricator of plastic products, we have conducted our search for comparable companies from the industry group of plastic products manufacturers. After examining a large number of companies, we have selected four as comprising a representative group for purposes of this appraisal. Key facts on the companies in this group are set forth in Exhibit B.

Exhibit B shows a range of price/earnings ratios for plastic parts fabricators of from 3.6X to 6.4X with an average of 5.4X. The comparable companies are, of course, considerably larger than PTI. In the case of some of the companies, there is a proprietary element to their product offerings, which is lacking with PTI. They are also possessed of more management depth.

For the above reasons, we have selected a price/earnings ratio of 4.5X for PTI, which is below the average of the group.

Applying the 4.5X multiplier to the previously calculated earnings level of PTI produces a preliminary value for PTI of $750,000.

$168,000 × 4.5 = $756,000, say $750,000.

This, in effect, represents the hypothetical value at which PTI would trade if it were a public company. It is acknowledged that it is unlikely that a company as small as PTI would trade as a public company. Nonetheless, this approach to value corresponds with that which would be taken by many prospective buyers.

Adjustment for Illiquidity and Control

The valuation procedure above compares PTI to a group of companies whose securities are traded in the public market. The result produced, then, is the hypothetical price at which shares of PTI would trade if it were a public company. Since PTI is not a public company, it is necessary to make

Exhibit 4   *(continued)*

an adjustment in the price to reflect the fact that a holder of stock in PTI would not be able to sell his shares without considerable effort or delay. This adjustment is normally made by applying a discount to the price, called a discount for illiquidity.

A further adjustment must be made to reflect the fact that we are valuing PTI as a whole, rather than valuing a minority holding in the company. The market prices that we used to establish value were based upon transactions in minority interests in companies. It is necessary to reflect this difference. This is normally done by applying a premium called a control premium to the price paid on minority transactions.

It is our opinion that in the case of PTI, the appropriate discount for illiquidity and premium for control would approximately cancel each other out, leaving the value, based upon market prices, at what it would be without such adjustment, $750,000.

Dividends

With the exception of Subchapter S distributions, PTI does not have a history of paying dividends to its shareholders. For this reason, the dividend approach to value is not apposite in this case.

Prior Transactions

There are no known prior transactions in the stock of PTI. Therefore, this approach to value is not relevant.

Book Value

As stated earlier, the book value of the operating assets of PTI is $200,000, or $292,000, if the current appraised value of the real estate is taken into account. Since this value is considerably below the value based on earnings, it has little relevance in this case.

Adjustment for Cash Sale

The executors of the estate that owns PTI wish to sell the company in a transaction that will permit a winding up of the estate shortly thereafter. Accordingly, they are not in a position to offer extended payment terms to prospective buyers.

Ordinarily, if a business of this size were sold, particularly to an individual, it would be customary for the seller to permit the payment of a significant portion of the purchase price over time.

Since an extended payment sale is not possible in this case, two effects will be produced, (*i*) the number of willing buyers with means available to consummate a purchase will be reduced, and (*ii*) the remaining buyers, in the absence of the availability of seller financing, will not be willing to pay as much for the company.

Because of these two effects, we have adjusted downward our assessment of the value of PTI by 20 percent, producing a value of $600,000.

Contingent Liabilities

The value determined in this appraisal presumes that a buyer of PTI would, in purchasing the business, assume no liabilities, real or contingent, other than the trade payables and other similar accrued liabilities arising from operations in the ordinary course of business. To the extent that the form of the transaction would require him to become actually or potentially obligated for other liabilities, the appraised value would have to be correspondingly adjusted.

Conclusion

Based on our analysis of the relevant facts, it is our opinion that the current fair market value, in a cash transaction, of the operating assets and business of PTI is $600,000.

Exhibit 4   (concluded)

Exhibit A
Combined Balance Sheets
(in thousands of dollars)

	HE Manufacturing	Plas-Tek Sales	Eliminations	Combined	Investment Assets and Liabilities	Operating Assets and Liabilities
Assets						
Cash........................	$170	$133		$ 303	$ 290	
Securities.....................	507	234		741	750	
Accounts receivable	41*	150	$41*	150		$148
Inventory	60			60		60
Loans receivable	19	20		39	45	
Prepaid expenses...............	6	—		6		6
Total current assets	803	537	41	1,299	1,085	214
Fixed assets—net						
Equipment	5	6		11		11
Building.....................	10	—		10		10
Land........................	10	—		10		10
Total assets....................	$828	$543	$ 41	$1,330	$1,085	$245
Liabilities and Capital						
Accounts payable	$ 36	$ 50	$ 41	$ 45		$ 45
Taxes payable	10	7		17	17	
Accrued salary—officers	164	318		482	482	
Accrued expenses	10	—		10	10	
Total liabilities...............	220	375	41	554	509	45
Capital	608	168		776	576	200
Total liabilities and capital	$828	$543	$ 41	$1,330	$1,085	$245

*All HE accounts receivable are due from Plas-Tek sales.

Exhibit B

Earnings per Share Latest 12 Months

Company (market)	Fiscal Year	Revenues ($millions— 1980 FY)	Amount	Period Ended	Book Value per Share (1980 FY)	Stock Price 2/18/82	Price/Earnings Ratio
Kleer-Vu Industries, Inc. (ASE)........	Dec.	$13.5	$1.48	9/81	$5.16	5 1/4	3.5
Liqui-Box Corp. (OTC)	Dec.	43.8	1.28	9/81	9.64	8 1/4	6.4
Plymouth Rubber Co. Cl.B (ASE)	Nov.	63.8	.38*	11/81	6.75	2	5.3
Star-Glo Industries, Inc. (OTC)........	Dec.	8.3	.57*	9/81	2.73	3 5/8	6.4
Average							6.4
Range...........................							5.4
							3.5–6.4

*Excluding extraordinary items.

EXHIBIT 5   Criteria for Selection of Attorney

1. Strong professional orientation—possess strong character, high degree of integrity and honesty, and general business competence.
2. Creative deal maker—ability to spot opportunities for mutual benefit in structuring deal terms.
3. Interest in working with entrepreneurs on a relatively small deal—enthusiasm for working on interesting issues with substantial creativity rather than mega-deal.
4. Caliber of corporate and tax skills—ability to integrate full range of corporate and tax issues into deal structure.
5. Strength as "hands-on" negotiator—ability to achieve goals at the bargaining table; good speaker, fast on feet.
6. Understanding of business issues—ability to craft deal in light of overall business goals, not merely tax and financing considerations.

EXHIBIT 6   Business Expenses—Unreasonable Compensation

TAX CODE SEC. 162. TRADE OR BUSINESS EXPENSES (paragraph a)

(a) In general, business expenses deductible from gross income include the ordinary and necessary expenditures, paid or incurred during the taxable year, directly connected with or pertaining to the taxpayer's trade or business, including

- cost of goods sold, including a proper adjustment for opening and closing inventories,
- a reasonable allowance for salaries or other compensation for personal services actually rendered,
- traveling expenses (including amounts expended for meals and lodging other than amounts which are lavish or extravagant under the circumstances) while away from home in the pursuit of a trade or business; and
- rentals or other payments made as a condition of the use or possession, for purposes of the trade or business, of property to which the taxpayer has not taken or is not taking title or in which he has no equity.

Explanation: Unreasonable Compensation

Compensation deductions are usually questioned by the IRS only in closely held corporations. The usual reason for disallowance is that the compensation paid is "unreasonable." Factors that are generally considered in establishing reasonableness include: the work actually performed by the individuals; their training and experience; the time and effort devoted to the work; the results that have been achieved; the requirement for ability and skill; the inadequacy of compensation in earlier years; and compensation paid for comparable services by similar businesses.

Compensation payments that are based on profits are subject to the same rules as amounts paid as straight salary. Thus, a legitimate bonus arrangement is recognized as an allowable deduction, even though in years of high profits, the amounts paid may be larger than would ordinarily be paid on a straight salary basis.

In all cases, the IRS carefully checks any compensation arrangement that distributes compensation in a way that is proportional to stockholdings. The IRS may reclassify some or all of such compensation payments as dividends.

The wrongful deduction of business expenses, including unreasonable compensation, may be grounds for criminal action.

Exhibit 7   Letter from Accountants on Contingent Liabilities

---

April 14, 1982

Dear Mr. Lane:

A review has been made of the federal income tax returns and financial statements of HE Manufacturing Corporation and its related company, Plas-Tek Sales Company, for their fiscal years ending in 1979, 1980, and 1981. The purpose of the review was to estimate the magnitude of tax deficiencies from certain adjustments which may result from an examination of their federal returns by the Internal Revenue Service. Our findings were made taking into account certain assumptions regarding reasonable compensation and other matters which were discussed at a meeting last week among ourselves and counsel.

Background

The capital stock of each of the companies was owned entirely by Harold Elson, who died in late 1981. Plas-Tek Sales is a Subchapter S corporation which reports on a fiscal year ended August 31. HE Manufacturing Corporation reports its income on a June 30 fiscal year. The business consists of the manufacture of gaskets, washers, and other plastic products.

Operations over the years have been quite profitable. In each of the three years prior to his death Mr. Elson's salary from both companies amounted to more than $400,000. The balance sheet of HE Manufacturing discloses substantial amounts of cash and investments and relatively small liabilities. For these reasons, concern has been expressed that the Internal Revenue Service could assert an unreasonable compensation and/or accumulated earnings issue if the tax returns of the companies were to be examined.

Since Plas-Tek Sales has a Subchapter S election in effect, the accumulated earnings issue would not result in a tax deficiency unless the company's Subchapter S status could be involuntarily terminated. We believe the prospect of that situation to be extremely remote. While unreasonable compensation is not generally considered in a Subchapter S situation because all earnings are taxed currently to the shareholders, a net deficiency could result if compensation, taxed at a minimum rate of 50 percent, were converted to dividend income taxable (before 1982) at a maximum rate of 70 percent by changing its character to passive income. Since such as assessment would be at the individual level it has not been considered in our review of corporate matters.

Unreasonable Compensation

Based upon our discussions and the valuation appraisal it is believed that compensation of $150,000 per year for PTI could be sustained if the issue were to be challenged by Internal Revenue Service. Using that number as a bench mark, we have calculated the deficiency to HE Manufacturing which would result using three different approaches:

1. Disallow amounts in excess of $75,000 per company.
2. Disallow compensation in excess of $75,000 and allocate the taxable income earned between the companies on an equal basis. This results in allocating income from Plas-Tek Sales to HE Manufacturing.
3. Disallow compensation in excess of $75,000 per company and allow Plas-Tek Sales a return of 5 percent on sales plus its reported expenses. Allocate excess income to HE Manufacturing.

The federal income tax deficiency before interest which would result from adjustments described above, as summarized in Exhibit A, would be as follows:

Alternative 1 — $ 86,768
Alternative 2 — $196,280
Alternative 3 — $369,773

EXHIBIT 7   *(continued)*

We are not aware that Internal Revenue Service has ever challenged the intercompany pricing of products sold by HE to Plas-Tek. However, considering the structure of the related companies, i.e., HE being taxable but Plas-Tek electing Subchapter S status, the Service could maximize the tax revenue by allocating income back to HE Manufacturing. The fact that the cash ultimately resides in Plas-Tek may be reconciled by the Service by claiming that HE paid a dividend of the excess income to Elson which was then reinvested by him in Plas-Tek, a common position when dealing with related corporations. The result would then be additional income tax to HE with no corresponding reduction of tax at the individual level.

We are not in a position to conclude as to the reasonableness of the profit rate that should be realized by each of the companies, i.e., manufacturing by HE and sales by Plas-Tek. The gross profit reported by Plas-Tek for each of the three years was exactly 40 percent, whereas the gross profit realized by HE ranged from 27 percent to 35 percent. Accordingly, Alternative 2 was predicated upon an equal splitting of the combined net profit between the two companies. It is conceivable, however, that the Service may take the position that Plas-Tek is nothing more than an agency and is entitled only to a reasonable commission on sales plus its actual selling expenses and officer's compensation of $75,000. If the Service were to take such a position, substantial income would be allocated to HE.

Accumulated Earnings Tax

If it were to be assessed, the accumulated earnings tax would be imposed only upon HE since all of the taxable income of Plas-Tek is taxed currently to its shareholder under the provisions of Subchapter S. The balance sheet of HE at June 30, 1981, included $507,000 of securities on total assets of $828,000 and shows a ratio of current assets to current liabilities after excluding unpaid salary to shareholder of more than 12 to 1. Based upon those statistics, it is reasonable to assume that an accumulated earnings question would be raised upon examination.

If assessed, the accumulated earnings tax is calculated on an annual basis on the "accumulated taxable income" of the corporation. In simplified terms, the tax base is equal to the taxable income for the year less federal income taxes on income and any dividends paid for the year. Because HE paid out substantial salaries to its shareholder, the reported taxable income in the three years in question was relatively modest. Thus, tax for all three years would only amount to approximately $20,000. Of course, the Service could attempt to impose the tax on the income of the corporation after a substantial increase due to disallowed compensation deductions. If that were to happen, however, we believe a successful argument could be made that the excessive compensation should be treated as a constructive dividend to the shareholder, thus reducing the "accumulated income" tax base back to an amount approximately equal to the taxable income reported on the returns. Accordingly, the accumulated earnings tax issue does not appear to be especially troublesome.

Statute of Limitations

It was represented to us that the Internal Revenue Service has examined the returns of PTI through fiscal 1978. While it was stated that the examination resulted in a "no change" report, we have yet to see a copy of the letter. Returns for the three fiscal years since 1978 remain open under the statue of limitations.

While specific representations have not been made, we believe the companies followed the practice of filing returns on or before the original due date, without extension. On that basis, the normal three-year statute of limitations would run as follows:

EXHIBIT 7   *(concluded)*

	Fiscal Year Ending		
	1979	*1980*	*1981*
HE	9/15/82	9/15/83	9/15/84
Plas-Tek	11/15/82	11/15/83	11/15/84

Normally the statute of limitations is not a major consideration to a Subchapter S corporation, unless it has capital gains taxable at the corporate level or loses its qualification, since an adjustment to the corporation's income would be reflected as an assessment to its shareholders. While the matter is somewhat unclear, one case has held that an assessment may be made by reference to the statute as it applies to the shareholders, a point which should be considered in the case of fiscal year corporations.

We will be pleased to provide further services in this area if required.

Sincerely,

3–2 KAREN VINCENT AND ZODIAC CORPORATION

It was a Friday night, and by the following Wednesday, Karen Vincent would have to decide whether or not to leave her consulting job and buy her father's company. If she did want to buy it, she would have to piece together a convincing plan of attack for reversing the firm's poor performance in recent years. Zodiac Corporation, a children's apparel company in western Massachusetts, had lost over $500,000 in 1987 following an almost break-even year in 1986.

Karen had worked for Zodiac when she graduated from college; back then, the company was making money. (See **Exhibit 1** for financial data.) It was now February of 1988 and West Point Pepperell (WPP), Zodiac's main supplier, had just called to say that it was withholding shipment of cloth for credit reasons. Zodiac was $700,000 in arrears on accounts payable, and WPP had serious doubts about its chances for a recovery. Karen tried to convince WPP that she and her father were in the process of restructuring the company. The supplier agreed to make that week's shipment but said it would hold the following week's shipment unless Karen and her father, Zach, could regain control of Zodiac, which had been acquired in October 1986 by the LBO Group ("the Group") from New York.

The Group had bought Zodiac Corporation in 1985; it put up $150,000 in equity, and the balance was comprised of debt held by Zach, bank debt, and its own debt capital. Should Karen buy the company back and take over this mess? And if she did, how could she convince the bank to lend her the $500,000 it would take to get the creditors off her back and avoid filing for Chapter 11?

Background

Karen Vincent graduated from Brandeis University in 1977 and then went to work at Zodiac. By 1981, Karen was unhappy because of conflicts with her father over the direction of the company.

> I really wanted to quit in 1981. My father and I were having all kinds of disagreements, but two major conflicts in particular. The first was a question of management philosophy—I

Research Associate Susan Harmeling prepared this case under the supervision of Professor Howard H. Stevenson.

wanted to try to foster a more participative style while he had an authoritarian management approach. The other disagreement had to do with future plans for the company—I wanted to see Zodiac expand and go into new areas, and he was basically not interested in taking risks. So I decided to leave. Right after I made this decision, my father offered to sell me the business. He said he had heard of this idea where you could buy a company with no money—it was called an LBO. It seems funny now that an LBO was such a radical notion back then, but it was a relatively new thing. Anyway, I came back and said, "Great, I'll do it," and Dad said he would work for me.

This fell through for a number of reasons. My sister wasn't thrilled that Dad was going to sell the company to me, and Dad really wasn't ready to part with it at the time. In addition, we didn't have the foggiest idea of how to structure an LBO. I kept working during the next couple of years. I decided to leave in six months, and then it became nine months, and then a year. Finally, in September of 1983, I decided to go to business school, and I enrolled at Harvard in September of 1984.

Upon graduation, Karen couldn't decide what to do. She had worked for Pantheon Consultants during the summer between her first and second years at business school and was offered a position there after she graduated.

I wanted to start an apparel business or maybe work with a start-up retail company. I interviewed with firms in both the apparel and retail industries, but nothing appealed to me. One of the partners at Pantheon was interested in doing research in the apparel and retail industries, so I decided to go back. Much to my surprise, I loved it there. I was able to gain a lot of insight into the "big picture" of the apparel industry after having a number of years' experience working in a small company within that industry.

In October of 1986, Karen's father decided to sell Zodiac Corporation to the LBO Group for $4.2 million. Karen was surprised at the terms of the deal.

The projections that the buyout was based on were ridiculous given the history of the company. In addition, the LBO Group was only putting in $150,000 of equity. My father agreed to these terms for three reasons: First, he figured that the Group had deep pockets and that it would keep pouring money into the company if needed. Second, he thought that they had good connections in the banking world and could handle this type of transaction better than he could; and third, he was ready to get out and go on to something else. He didn't want an employment contract, but in the end, the Group insisted that he be president and stay with the company for at least five years.

I thought there might be problems, but I had just started my new job a month earlier and was too busy to concern myself with Zodiac at that time.

A year later, in November of 1987, Scott Kohen, a partner of the LBO Group, called Karen to ask her to come back to Zodiac:

Scott called me and said, "We want you to come back and we'd be willing to give you equity." I told him that I liked New York and my job and that I didn't want to work for my father again—he was still president at the time. So Scott said that they would pay for me to commute back and forth from New York to Springfield and that my Dad had agreed to step down if I would come back. I still said no, but I started to think about it more seriously.

Then I went down to see my parents in Florida, and my Mom put a lot of pressure on me to come back to Zodiac. The company was close to bankruptcy and things were only getting worse. She was worried because my Dad was so fed up with the whole thing, she thought it was affecting his health.

So what I decided to do was to take a two-month leave of absence from Pantheon to evaluate the whole situation. I should point out that the only reason Pantheon let me do this was because it was a family business and what they considered to be an unusual situation given my background and the circumstances at the time. My leave of absence began in February of 1988.

The Evaluation

So Karen went up to Springfield to see if the opportunity (*a*) was a good one for her, and (*b*) if not, if it was good for anyone, or was it time to dissolve the corporation? She explained her preliminary findings:

> The first day of my leave of absence was weird—it was emotionally very tough for me. Here were all these people I had hired a few years earlier. Nothing much had changed except that things had really gone downhill.
>
> Jim Fenson, the plant manager who replaced me when I left in 1984, was a pretty good manager. But he had resigned and was replaced by a guy named Steve Zubek who was hopelessly incompetent. As a result, production efficiency had declined and there were all kinds of problems with the workers and the union. Basically, this guy was a problem definer, not a problem solver.
>
> That was only the tip of the iceberg. Zodiac's operating earnings were getting lower and lower. With sky-high debt service, the transaction costs from the LBO, my father's higher salary (because he was now an employee, not an owner), and the LBO Group's monthly management fees, the operating earnings were nowhere near sufficient.
>
> It didn't take a genius to see that there was a big problem. The company was steadily losing volume, while both operating costs and SGA were going up.
>
> But I went forward with my plans to do a full-scale evaluation of the state of the company. My experience at Pantheon proved to be very helpful—I approached this project much like a consulting study. I interviewed actual customers and potential customers. I did a basic year-to-year financial comparison, which had never been done. I looked at the way marketing was being approached, analyzed production and payroll records, talked with the managers and got their input on where the problems were, etc., etc.

Karen's Findings

At this point, the company was largely a subcontractor. The bulk of its sales were to three customers, with one accounting for over 50 percent of sales. Karen quickly discovered that the bulk of Zodiac's problems centered around production. In 1986 and 1987, plant production dropped seriously and the size of the stitching work force fell substantially. Volume declined due to a loss of stitchers and poor management on the sewing floor, costs were not cut in proportion to the decline in volume, and prices remained flat. Karen was careful to explain, however, that only about half of the decline was caused by a loss of stitchers. The balance was the result of excess "labor losses" and fewer hours worked. Karen explained what "labor losses" are:

Labor losses occur when production workers produce at less than 100 percent efficiency. Most labor losses happen at Zodiac when a stitcher is asked to go from his or her normal task—which is done on piecework—to another task. This other task is performed on hourly rate, so incentive to produce quickly and effectively goes way down. People end up spending a lot of time walking around or talking to their friends on the phone.

Karen saw labor losses as the company's worst problem, and noted in her study that little effort had been made toward developing a solution to this problem. (See **Exhibit 2** for Karen's analyses of Zodiac's performance.) Materials costs were fairly standard across the industry.

The Union

Karen realized that change would be difficult to effect because of the union rules:

The work rules system under the union contract is very limiting and cumbersome. The irony of it is that we're having trouble working this out even though the union is dissatisfied with the system, too. This is just a very complicated situation.

It is common in the apparel industry for most production workers to be compensated according to a piecework system. This system worked well when the industry manufactured mostly long production runs of basic products. As the industry began to change toward shorter runs and higher complexity, many companies became dissatisfied with the straight piecework system and began to search for a new system. Few viable alternatives have been found.

Zodiac has a standard piecework system. In addition, it has a system of job seniority that is more restrictive than the industry norm. This system is complicated and cumbersome to administer. (See **Exhibit 3**.) It allows the more experienced workers to claim the easier jobs like shoulders and collars, leaving the more difficult jobs like smocking and side seams for the new people. It also discourages cooperation and limits the flexibility of supervisors to respond to changes in the schedule.

To make matters worse, Zodiac's starting wages are low compared to other companies in the area. And stitching wages are below those of other departments within the company plant. That's a real problem because the plant is completely dependent on stitchers. They are the heart of Zodiac.

Mary Smith, the union steward for the plant, had this to say about the problems:

This plant used to be a Carter's plant, and people got accustomed to doing one thing all the time. There would be one style of shirt or pants and that was what you would do from one year to the next. Then when Zach, Karen's father came in and bought the company, things changed. You had the Carter's people on one side, wanting to do things their way, and the Zodiac people on the other side, new people who were more willing to change. That caused problems. And to add to that, people have for a long time thought of Zach as more of an outside person. Production was just not his thing. When Karen was here before, she was more hands-on. I think things would improve around here if she came back. Anyone with a big stake in the company would try to work harder to see it survive.

The union members don't know the extent of the crisis, but Karen's coming back would make them take a long, hard look at the ways things are done around here. She has come in and uncovered the problems, and now if she comes back, maybe some of them could be corrected.

As for this other operation, the LBO Group, well they just don't seem to care what happens around here. A company like that just isn't going to get involved on a day-to-day basis.

I think there are two things that my people want. They want more money, of course, but they also want supervisors who are properly trained. They want to see the manager involved in the system. And they want to see one unified system, one consistent way of doing things that simply doesn't exist right now. We do quality work here, and we have effective quality control checks on all our garments. We take pride in that and if some of these problems can get straightened out, Zodiac has a chance at surviving.

The Industry

Zodiac was operating in a competitive industry, and the competition was coming both from the domestic front and from overseas. But, as one of the few plants of its type in the Northeast (most were in the southern states), Zodiac enjoyed an advantageous proximity to New York designers, which allowed the company to be more responsive to its customers. Zodiac was known for its high quality standards, and as a result it was able to gain the support of loyal customers like Oshkosh and Polly Flinders. In addition, stricter import quota systems made children's apparel one of the least import-affected segments of the entire apparel industry. Furthermore, children's apparel had seen a dramatic shift toward more fashion-oriented styles, and Zodiac had been working to accommodate this change. New equipment and more advanced information systems for controlling inventory and production had all been put in place.

Running Out of Time

In mid-March, at the end of the first month of Karen's two-month leave from Pantheon, Zodiac received a call from the West Point Pepperell Corporation saying it was holding shipment on cloth for credit reasons. So Karen's decision became a little more urgent.

I didn't have as much time as I would have liked. Basically, I had to decide in a few days what to do. We were $700,000 in arrears on accounts payable, and things were a real mess. I flew down to New York and told West Point Pepperell that they just couldn't hold shipment on us, that we were really making an effort to turn things around. They said OK, but only for that shipment. They didn't trust the LBO Group, and they wanted to see my father and/or me take complete control. I pretty much had to decide then and there what I was going to do.

We entered into negotiations with the LBO Group to see what sort of deal could be worked out. They owned the company, but had put very little in. Still, they wouldn't just walk away with nothing. Dad wasn't willing to forgive the $1.7 million that the company owed him, and quite frankly, he was a bit angry with the Group as well.

I went to see Midlantic Bank (which held all the bank debt) to ask if they would give us the $500,000 we needed to get the creditors off our backs and give us a moratorium on principal payments for the balance of 1988. They were in shock as to the state of affairs at Zodiac at this point. The lending officer who was in charge of our account had quit, and his replacement had died on January 1. The bank had received no follow-up reports for quite a while. No one had kept the bank informed, so unfortunately, I had to fill them in on all the bad news while I was telling them that I was thinking of buying the company and that I needed $500,000 to survive.

I spent a full day giving a presentation on how I was going to turn Zodiac around. The loan officer who was handling our account, her supervisor, and a senior vice president in charge of the bank's asset-based lending group were all there.

At first, they said they'd put up the money, but they wanted it fully guaranteed by my father, and they also insisted that he forgive half of his debt. After a week of negotiations, they agreed to do it if $150,000 of it was guaranteed. They agreed to accept another guarantor, but I had to sign an employment contract and agree to stay around and liquidate the company if it didn't make it.

My father refused to put up any personal guarantees, and he wouldn't forgive any of his share of the debt if the LBO Group remained involved. The Group wouldn't put up the money to secure the loan unless they were still part owners of the company. It was a catch-22.

It may or may not have been rational, but my father was *very* reluctant to go through with this deal. He refused to risk one penny of his own money. He felt that since he had not taken his salary for over a year, he had sacrificed enough.

In the end, Karen went to her father and told him that if he and the LBO Group couldn't work something out soon, then she would no longer consider being a part of the deal. There was a new project waiting for her at Pantheon, she said, and she was prepared to get on the first plane back to New York.

So Mr. Vincent called Andre, the director of the LBO Group, and finally the two of them worked out a deal where the Group would keep a 40 percent stake in the company and would put up the $150,000 guarantee provided Mr. Vincent forgive half his debt and the Group would forgive half of its debt. Terms of the deal were:

a. LBO Group will convert its existing $250,000 debt into an unsecured note, which shall provide for a (*i*) $125,000 principal amount, bearing no interest, subordinate to all other debt and obligations and contingent on meeting certain financial thresholds and (*ii*) $125,000 principal amount, payable in full in 15 years, bearing no interest during the first 12 months after issuance and 9 percent annually thereafter.

b. Mr. Vincent will convert his existing $1.7 million subordinated note into an unsecured note, which shall provide for a (*i*) $850,000 principal amount, bearing no interest, subordinate to all other debt and obligations and (*ii*) $850,000 principal amount, payable in full in 15 years, bearing no interest during the first 12 months after issuance and 9 percent annually thereafter, subordinate to other debt and obligations, including obligations to trade creditors, and guaranteed as to payment by Zodiac.

Mr. Vincent will agree that in lieu of his existing employment arrangements (which will be canceled), he will act as the principal sales consultant of Zodiac, devoting sufficient time and using his reasonable efforts to sell merchandise of Zodiac for an annual fee of $80,000 plus reimbursement of reasonable expenses. The Group will, or will cause its affiliates to, pay Mr. Vincent, concurrent with the closing of the transactions contemplated herein, consulting fees in the aggregate amount of $39,000 for Mr. Vincent's services in reviewing a variety of businesses for the Group during the preceding 13 months. Mr. Vincent shall be held harmless from and against any and all claims arising out of events occurring while Mr. Vincent was the president and chief operating office of Zodiac.

Arrangements with Ms. Vincent

c. Ms. Vincent will agree to become employed for a period of two years as the chief executive officer of Zodiac for an annual salary of $80,000 plus bonus to be determined by the board of directors of Zodiac. In addition, Ms. Vincent will be reimbursed for all reasonable expenses incurred by her as chief executive officer of Zodiac, including, but not limited to, her automobile expenses and her living expenses in Massachusetts.

d. Ms. Vincent will purchase 60 percent of the stock of the company for $10. Ms. Vincent also will receive as additional compensation from the sale or partial sale, in one or more transactions, of the capital stock or assets of Zodiac, 30 percent of the first $1 million of all distributions and proceeds from such sale or sales remaining after the payment of such obligations to Midlantic and 70 percent of the second $1 million of all such distributions and proceeds. Such payments to Ms. Vincent will be made prior to any distribution or payment with respect to any subordinated debt held by the LBO Group or Mr. Vincent. Proceeds above $2 million will be split according to stock ownership after payment of all subordinated debt and capital notes.

The Possibilities

If she could turn Zodiac around, Karen saw a number of opportunities for expansion and diversification in the future. Among these were developing a private-label business selling direct to retail (see **Exhibit 4** for excerpts from Karen's *Harvard Business Review* article), acquiring other manufacturing plants, wholesaling Zodiac's own brand of children's wear, and retailing in either retail outlets or catalogues.

Karen was well aware from her prior research that successful apparel companies such as Oshkosh and Liz Claiborne earn returns of 5 percent to 6 percent on sales while catalog companies like Lands' End and L. L. Bean earn up to 15 percent. She had in the back of her mind plans for Zodiac in these areas.

The Decision

All that was left was for Karen to decide if this was what she wanted. Should she sign the letter of agreement, go through with the bank loan, and try to run this company?

Zodiac had lost over $500,000 in 1987, and $200,000 so far in the first quarter of 1988. She would be responsible for 300 employees and for turning around a slew of problems that had been mounting for the past three years. She had a great job and had made a life for herself in New York. Was she crazy to even think of going through with this? Was she only considering this opportunity out of loyalty to her family? Was the challenge of turning things around exciting enough for her to risk having to liquidate their business? Did this opportunity have real long-term potential? Karen had before her the chance to buy a company for nothing but an employment contract she would be asked to sign. The terms of the contract were indeed attractive, but before she signed it, Karen would have to ask herself all these questions, and, unfortunately, she didn't have the luxury of time on her side. It was mid-April, and the end of her two-month leave from Pantheon was near. They had called her to say there was an interesting study waiting for her if she came back to New York. Karen was well aware that Pantheon had been very generous to give her this leave, and she couldn't press them anymore. In a few days she would have to go to the bank to give them her decision—what was it going to be?

EXHIBIT 1   Effect on Fixed Charges

1988 Fixed Charges ($000)	*Before Reacquisition*	*After Reacquisition*
Projected 1988 gross profit before depreciation	$1,020	$1,020
"Normal" SGA	371	371
Fees to LBO Group	23	
Interest	483	300
Profit before tax and depreciation	139	345
Depreciation/amortization	387	387
Profit before tax (= profit after tax)	(248)	(42)
Principal payments	300	0
Plus depreciation	387	387
Cash for reduction of accounts payable	(161)	345

EXHIBIT 1   **Effect of Proposed Transaction on Balance Sheet** *(continued)*

January Balance Sheet ($000)	1988 Pro Forma	Pro Forma after Proposed Transaction
Cash	$ 21	$ 21
Accounts receivable	1,370	1,370
Inventories	2,203	2,203
Prepaid expenses (insurance)	23	23
Total current assets	$3,617	$3,617
Real estate	$1,077	$1,077
Furniture and fixtures	181	181
Machinery and equipment	1,857	1,857
Leasehold improvements	137	137
Less: accumulated depreciation	($1,058)	($1,058)
Total fixed assets	$2,194	$2,194
Investment in oil[a]	$ 200	
Intangible assets	58	58
Cash value life insurance	3	3
Total other assets	$ 261	$ 61
Total assets	$6,072	$5,872
Accounts payable	$1,669	$1,069
Note payable current[b]	300	—
Accrued wages/taxes	278	278
Total current liabilities	$2,247	$1,347
Long-term debt (bank)[b]	$ 850	$1,150
Revolving credit	1,278	1,778
Subordinated notes payable[c]	1,950	975
Deferred taxes	98	—
Accrued acquisition expenses	44	44
Total other liabilties	$4,220	$3,947
Capital notes[c]	—	$ 975
Common stock	200	200
Retained earnings	(595)	(597)
Total equity	($ 395)	$ 578
Total liabilities plus equity	$6,072	$5,872

[a]Hold Oil owned by LBO Group sold for $100 cash (used to pay down payables) plus contingent note for $150 not on balance sheet.
[b]Moratorium on principal payments.
[c]One half of debt to Zach and LBO Group converted to capital notes—noninteresting bearing.

EXHIBIT 1   ZODIAC Corporation Operating Pro Forma— 1988 *(concluded)*

Pro Forma Profit and Loss Statement
(1988 by quarter)

	1	2	3	4	Total	1987
Sales	$3,091	$3,464	$2,736	$3,259	$12,549	$12,302
Direct labor	475	532	454	540	2,001	2,068
Indirect/direct	81	90	77	92	340	334
Indirect labor	256	256	256	256	1,025	1,225
Exec	60	60	60	60	238	220
Fringe	235	253	229	256	973	1,042
Factory costs	127	127	127	127	509	480
Materials	1,174	1,316	1,040	1,239	4,769	4,535
Contract labor	471	528	308	367	1,675	1,856
Increase in inventory	—	—	—	—	—	(151)
Cost of goods sold	$2,880	$3,163	$2,550	$2,937	$11,529	$11,609
Gross profit before depreciation	211	300	186	323	1,020	693
SGA	93	93	93	93	372	374
Depreciation	97	97	97	97	388	372
Other income	—	—	—	—	—	—
Other expenses	—	—	—	—	—	83
Profit before interest and taxes	22	111	(3)	133	262	(136)
Depreciation/amortization	97	97	97	97	388	372
Cash flow before interest and tax	$ 118	$ 208	$ 94	$ 230	$ 650	$ 234

ZODIAC Profit and Loss (1983–87)

	1983	1984	1985	1986[a]	1987[b]
Sales	$11,559	$16,511	$13,522	$14,531	$12,302
Gross profit before depreciation	609	1,006	1,014	748	693
SGA	449	358	364	308	374
Interest	6	58	5	148	475
Other income					
Profit before tax, depreciation, and nonrecurring expenditures	$ 154	$ 590	$ 645	$ 292	$ (156)
Depreciation/amortization	80	110	151	220	372
Nonrecurring	—	—	—	68	85
Profit before tax	74	480	494	4	(613)
Depreciation	80	110	151	216	372
Other noncash	—	—	—	4	15
Cash flow from operations[c]	$ 154	$ 590	$ 645	$ 224	$ (226)

[a]LBO took place October 1986.

[b]1987 figures are preliminary.

[c]Cash flow is before capital expenditure.

Exhibit 2   Working Capital Needs—1980–87

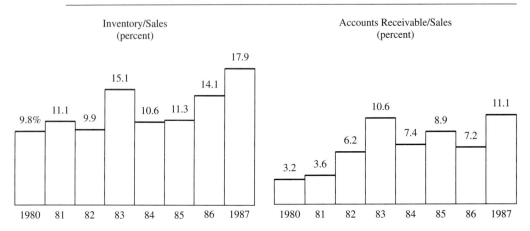

Inventory/Sales (percent)

Accounts Receivable/Sales (percent)

Sales and Gross Profit—1980–87

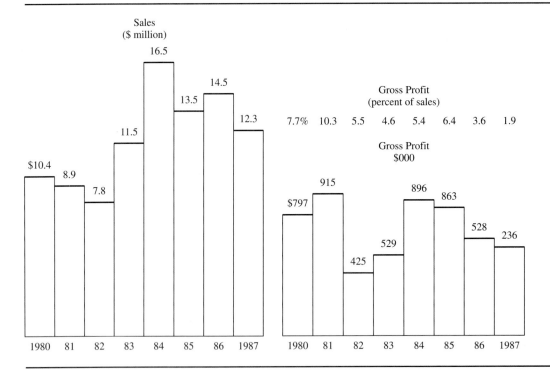

Sales ($ million)

Gross Profit (percent of sales)

Gross Profit $000

EXHIBIT 2   Factory Expenditures— 1983–87 ($ million) *(continued)*

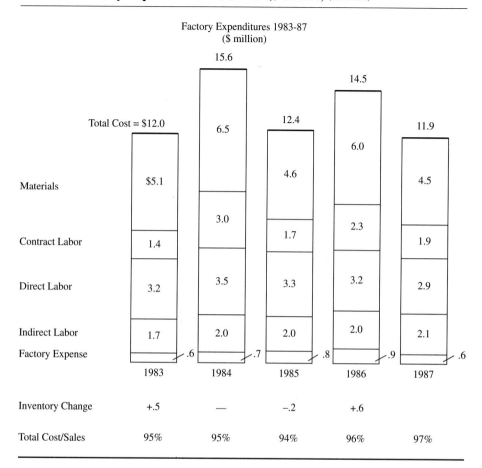

Factory Expenditures 1983-87
($ million)

Exhibit 2   Factory Costs—1983–87 ($ million) *(continued)*

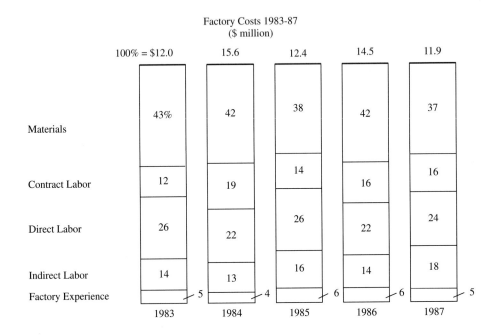

Factory Costs 1983-87
($ million)

EXHIBIT 2   1987 Ms* and Stitcher Count *(continued)*

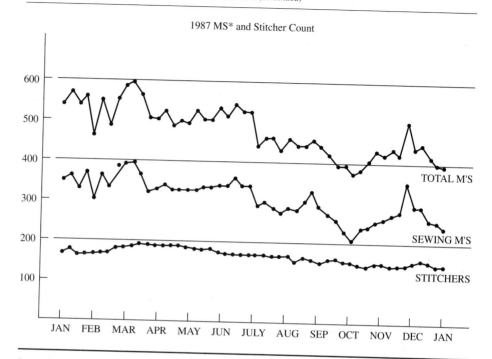

1987 MS* and Stitcher Count

SOURCE: Weekly Factory Performance Summary.

*Ms are standard minutes of work.

EXHIBIT 2   **Total Plant Production— 1983–87
(millions of standard minutes of work)** *(continued)*

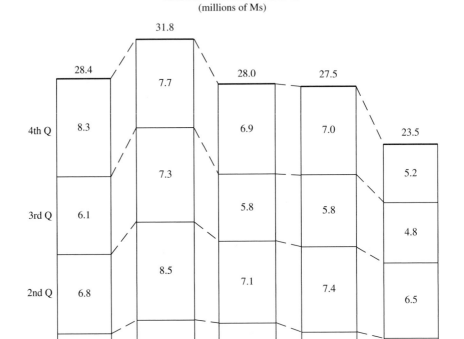

Total Plant Production—1983-87
(millions of Ms)

SOURCE: Payroll records.

**Exhibit 2   Causes of Lost Ms* — 1986–87
(Total plant Ms/week)** *(continued)*

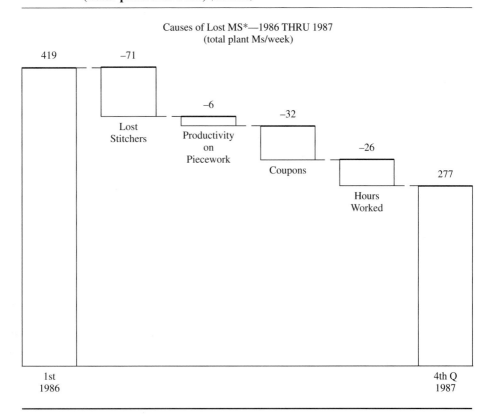

Causes of Lost MS*—1986 THRU 1987
(total plant Ms/week)

419   −71

                    Lost
                    Stitchers   −6
                                Productivity   −32
                                on
                                Piecework   Coupons   −26
                                                                Hours   277
                                                                Worked

1st   4th Q
1986   1987

*Ms are standard minutes of work.

EXHIBIT 2   **Hourly Starting Wages for Zodiac vs. Other West Massachusetts Companies** *(continued)*

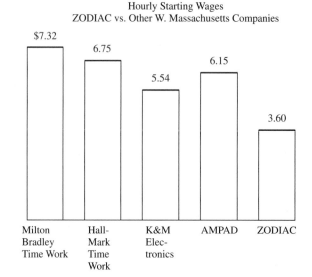

Hourly Starting Wages
ZODIAC vs. Other W. Massachusetts Companies

SOURCE: Phone survey.

Zodiac Average Wages by Department vs. all Nondurable Manufacturing in the West Massachusetts Area

ZODIAC Average Wages by Dept vs. all Non-durable Manufacturing in the W.Massachusetts Area

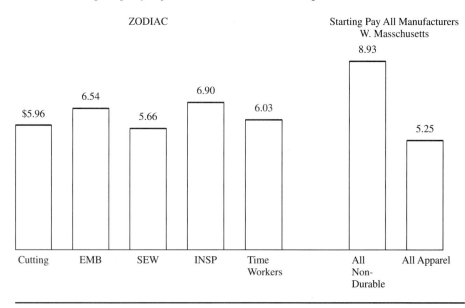

Exhibit 2   Causes of Lost Ms by Quarter — 1986–87 (Average per week) *(continued)*

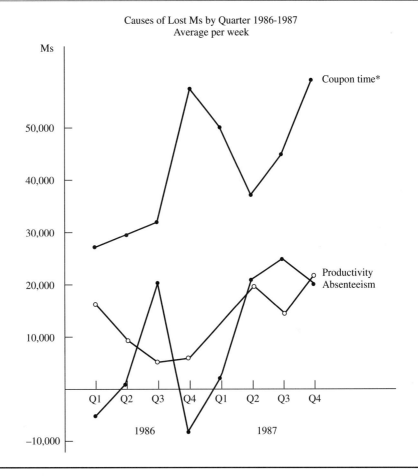

Causes of Lost Ms by Quarter 1986-1987
Average per week

Source: Payroll records.

*Given for hours not on piecework over a certain period of time.

EXHIBIT 3   **Draft Write-Up of Past Practices Regarding Job and Cluster Seniority**

Definition of Job Seniority

1. Job seniority entitles an operator to work on her regular (primary) job when there is work available. If the supervisor wants her to do anything else, the operator gets a white coupon.[a] The supervisor may give an operator other work in her cluster on piecework (with appropriate training time) if she "tables" her regular work.

2. If there is not enough work for all operators assigned to a regular (primary) job, the supervisor may remove the least senior operator and put her on other work in her cluster. If there is not enough work in the cluster, the least senior operator in the cluster is given work in another cluster or another area on pink coupon.[b] If the shortage of work continues, the operator is reassigned at the next cluster assignment period (see *Assignment of Operators,* below).

3. If there is too much work on a job, the supervisor may put other operators on the job from the same or another department either temporarily or permanently. There is no obligation to save work.

4. The supervisor should *try* to distribute work among all the operators assigned to a specific job, so that each operator gets an equal share of each style, even if it requires operators to change machines. However, in Departments 4 and 5, if training time is involved, the supervisor may call it a new job, and put the least senior operator on that job.

How You Get Job Seniority

1. You have to be assigned to a job for four months to hold seniority on that job. You lose your seniority when you qualify for seniority on another job. (In other words, after four months on another job.)

Definition of Cluster Seniority

1. Cluster seniority entitles an operator to bump a less senior operator off a job in her cluster when there is no other work in the cluster.

How You Get Cluster Seniority

1. You must be assigned to a cluster for four months in order to hold cluster seniority. You lose cluster seniority when you qualify for seniority in another cluster (in other words, after four months in another cluster).

Assignment of Operators

1. If there is not enough continuous work for all operators on a job, the least senior operator on the job can be assigned to another job in her cluster,

   If no other job in her cluster is available, the supervisor may put her on a red coupon until the next cluster assignment sheet comes out, at which time she can either:

   a. Transfer the operator to another department where there is an opening in the same or similar cluster. (She will not have seniority until she has been in that department for four months.)

   b. Transfer her to a new cluster (with appropriate training time).

   c. Keep her on a red coupon until a opening comes up on her type of machine. When an opening arises in a cluster, the operator who has been unassigned the longest is entitled to the job.

   d. Bring work in her cluster from another department.

---

[a]Entitles operator to hourly pay based on last month's average earnings.
[b]Entitles operator to plant minimum hourly rate.

Combat between manufacturer and private brands in the same product categories is as much a feature of modern marketing as combat among manufacturer brands. Now the battle between manufacturer and private brands has taken a new turn. Strong brand names and private labels, originally confined mainly to packaged-goods businesses, have become immensely important in the fashion industry. The reactions of retailers and manufacturers have implications that transcend the boundaries of the soft-goods trade.

Ralph Lauren, Benetton, and Liz Claiborne are now brands as well as fashions. Brands once associated only with function like Jockey underwear and Sperry Top-Siders also have introduced style and color into their products and now stand for fashion as well as function.

The ascension of manufacturer brands in the fashion world has stimulated other important developments. Ralph Lauren and Coach, and a number of European retailers including Burberry, Benetton, and Laura Ashley, have opened their own or franchised stores that sell only merchandise of their own labels.

Confronted suddenly by manufacturers that as a result of the acceptance or cachet of their brand names possess ''consumer power,'' traditional retailers have reacted decisively:

- Macy's has boosted its private-label sales from 6% of volume in 1980 to more than 20% in 1986 and currently has more than 50 in-house labels. In some categories, private-label merchandise represents as much as 50% of sales.
- The Limited, one of the fastest growing fashion specialty chains, has made private-label merchandise a cornerstone of its strategy. Such goods represent 70% of its sales. The Limited's private brand Forenza and Outback Red combined are the third largest in sales of women's apparel in the country.
- Sears Roebuck and J. C. Penney, in contrast, are adding national brands to what were assortments of almost entirely private-label merchandise. Safeway and Kroger, the nation's two largest food chains, are also reemphasizing national brands at the expense of private labeling.

The explanation of these apparently contradictory developments is complex. It involves:

Changing consumer shopping habits.

The impact of sophisticated management information systems on the technology and scale of retailing.

New relationships between retailers and manufacturers.

Shifting consumer merchandise tastes.

Waning dedication of several chains to private labels.

Consequences for manufacturers

The success of private labels in the fashion business has implications for apparel manufacturers as well as producers of other merchandise. They face four issues: whether to become private-label suppliers, how to defend their own brands from encroachment by private labels, whether to integrate vertically, and what distribution opportunities will emerge out of shifting emphasis onto private-label products.

Becoming a private-label supplier often produces higher immediate profits, but they are not always sustainable. Although enlightened retailers recognize that their suppliers must be profitable, part of the reason for going into private label is to capture manufacturing profits in excess of the cost of capital. So from a manufacturer's point of view, big profits for the supplier of private-label goods are unlikely, and even sustained profitability at a level equal to the cost of capital may demand exceptional production efficiency and superior service to customers.

Manufacturers that opt out of the private-label supply business have to devise a plan for defending their own brands against attack. They must:

1. Be sure that the fashion, features, quality, retail price, and overall appeal of their own brands represent at least fair value for the consumer compared with private labels.

2. If this value is in doubt, accept some immediate profit sacrifice for restoration of a favorable value comparison.

3. Encourage retailers to use a fair yardstick for comparing private-label with national-brand profitability. Direct product profit, rather than initial markup or gross margin, is such a yardstick. When it is used, the purported profit advantage of private-label merchandise often declines or even disappears.

4. Develop relationships with store executives that simulate the information sharing that occurs between retailers and their private-label suppliers.

*Note: Author's name has been disguised.

EXHIBIT 4   *(concluded)*

For some manufacturers, the best defense (as well as a powerful marketing strategy) may be to integrate vertically in addition to or in lieu of selling through the usual channels. This course of action is wise, however, only if the product line is important enough to the target market to warrant the effort consumers must make to shop in a specialty store; if the ambience, service, and selection the manufacturer can offer fit the target market's interests better than what is available elsewhere; and if the manufacturer is prepared to sacrifice support or even distribution through existing channels.

The most difficult element of this assessment is the selection of a fair price for transferring merchandise from production to retailing. The transfer price should represent the same amount at which the goods are sold to arm's-length channels, plus or minus any costs or savings in dealing with owned or franchised outlets. By these criteria, few manufacturers facing private-label competition will find distribution through owned or franchised stores attractive.

The final issue for manufacturers in the shift toward private label is the impact on their distribution strategy. Many manufacturers of fashion goods have had mixed feelings regarding the emerging interest of J. C. Penney and Sears Roebuck in selling branded merchandise. They have feared retaliation from traditional department and specialty stores. Given the growing infatuation of such stores with private-label merchandise, however, manufacturers of certain branded fashion items may find good reasons for exploring new alliances with national chains.

The consequences of the new penchant for private labels in fashion portend changes in the marketing of all consumer goods. Today, wearing apparel is not the only fashion category. Industries as diverse as food, electronics, and financial services are seeing themselves as purveyors of fashion products. Manufacturers of all consumer products must begin to think more broadly about branding and the role it plays in their relationship with consumers and with retail channels. Manufacturers and retailers need to assess whether these changes call for strategies of defense or offer an opportunity for aggressive marketing.

SOURCE: Walter J. Salmon and Karen A. Vincent. Walter Salmon is the Stanley Roth, Senior professor of retailing at the Harvard Business School. He is the author of several books and articles on retailing and a director of several companies, including Carter Hawley Hale Corporation, the Quaker Oats Company, and Zayre, Inc.

Karen Vincent is an associate in the New York City office of the consulting firm of Pantheon ⑬ Company, where she specializes in assisting consumer products and retailing companies.

3–3 TOM FISHER

Tom was stunned. After negotiating for four months to purchase the Frank Foster Walnut Lumber Co., it now looked as if the deal might collapse on the day of the closing.

Tom Fisher had decided in September of 1984 to purchase the company at which he was employed, Foster Lumber Company, a division of Atlantic Paper Company. In August of 1984, Atlantic had indicated it would liquidate the division. Tom believed that the company could succeed on its own, and he offered to purchase the division through a leveraged buyout. After months of tense negotiations with both Atlantic Paper and the lending institutions, Tom constructed an agreement suitable to all parties. Included in the agreement was a $600,000 loan guarantee from Atlantic Paper to the bank supplying the debt for the purchase.

Now, on March 28, 1985, as Atlantic Paper's attorney reviewed the final agreement, he said, ''We need to make a note here that our guarantee will be reduced on a pro-rata basis as Tom pays down the loan—right?'' Tom looked at his banker for guidance; the banker said, ''Well that's a shame. I guess we don't have a deal.'' In order to save the purchase, Tom needed to act quickly since the money transfer lines were to close in 1 1/2 hours. Tom considered what, if anything, he could do. On the one hand, he wanted to complete the purchase, but on the other hand, the company had been allowed to deteriorate so much over the last six months that perhaps Tom was experiencing a blessing in disguise.

Tom Fisher

Tom Fisher graduated in 1975 from the University of Vermont with a B.A. degree in art. After two years as a medical technician, he returned to school at the University of Minnesota to receive a B.S. in forestry in 1980 (**Exhibit 1**).

From the University of Minnesota, Tom went to work for Amadeo Box Co., a hardwood mill in Arkansas with sales of $6 million. The family-owned mill was losing money, and in an effort to turn the mill around, after six months Tom was promoted from shift supervisor to mill manager. Within two years, Tom had successfully established

This case was prepared by David M. Dodson under the supervision of H. I. Grousbeck. Development of this case was funded by the Robert Denzil Alexander Fund. Reprinted with permission of Stanford University Graduate School of Business,
Stanford Business School Case S–SB–105

the beginnings of a solid earnings record. However, in 1984 Tom collided with one of the sons of the founder and decided to resign.

The Frank Foster Walnut Lumber Company

After leaving Amadeo Box Co., Tom joined Frank Foster Walnut Lumber Co., a subsidiary of Atlantic Paper Co. (sales $1.6 billion). Foster Lumber Co. had been founded in 1897 in Kansas City, Kansas, by its namesake, Frank Foster. Kansas City is in the western edge of the eastern hardwood stands, and the company was situated near the finest walnut forests in North America.

Foster Lumber began as a log yard where woodmen stacked freshly cut logs prior to transport to a lumber mill. In 1914, Frank Foster moved his company from downtown Kansas City to 10 acres of land on the banks of the Kaw River—four miles from downtown. In 1917, Foster installed a lumber mill and began to concentrate on walnut.

Business grew steadily until the "Flood of '51" wiped out the entire company. While Frank Foster watched his company float down the Kaw river, he made plans to rebuild the business. He did so and in 1955 sold the company to Lehigh Industries, a $230 million conglomerate.

Between 1955 and 1975, the Frank Foster Walnut Lumber Co. was sold to three other large corporations before eventually being acquired in 1975 by Atlantic Paper. Atlantic acquired Foster Lumber through the acquisition of Rosen-Thomas (of which Foster Lumber was a wholly owned subsidiary). In 1982, Atlantic sold Rosen-Thomas, but the buyer did not want Foster Lumber, so Atlantic continued to operate the company as one of its divisions.

The Walnut Lumber Industry

Walnut is considered a specialty hardwood, used principally for furniture, trophy plaques, and architectural millwork. In 1987, the United States produced 12 billion board feet of hardwood. Of the more than 15 varieties, walnut accounted for only 143 million board feet, or 1.2 percent **(Exhibit 2)**. Foster Lumber sold all of its lumber domestically. The walnut lumber industry was highly fragmented, with Foster Lumber, the dominant producer, estimated to have only 2.3 percent of the total market.

A walnut tree is typically cut down when the diameter of the log becomes "chest height," or 14 inches or more. At this point, the tree may be as many as 100 to 150 years old. On occasion, a bullet from the Civil War era is found deeply imbedded in the trunk of a walnut tree. Tom Fisher offered, "We give the tree a second life—the walnut chair you are sitting in may have come from a tree that General Robert E. Lee or Daniel Boone once leaned up against."

A buyer purchases logs from local landowners by walking through the walnut forests and marking trees. Of the trees, 80 percent are purchased within 100 miles of the mill and 100 percent are purchased within 250 miles of the mill. The buyer and landowner work together to make sure that the cutting is done in a way that preserves the long-term viability of the forest. Typically, landowners take extreme care in harvesting their walnut since the trees being cut may have been planted by their great-great-grandparents, and the trees they plant may benefit their great-great-grandchildren.

After marking, the trees are cut down and transported by truck to the log yard located at the mill. From the log yard, the logs are lifted by heavy machinery into the mill. The first operation debarks the log by scraping it against rotating tungsten carbide teeth. The log is then sawed using a carriage on tracks and a band saw remotely controlled by an operator referred to as a ''sawer.'' The sawer must cut the log in a way that maximizes both the yield from the log (the board footage of finished lumber divided by the board footage of log) and the quality of the grain of the wood. The value per board foot of the walnut lumber is determined by quality of the material, and the sawer must make continuous trade-offs between increasing the yield from the log and cutting the log in a way that maximizes the quality.

After the logs are cut, the boards are trimmed to widths of 3 1/2 inches to 20 inches and lengths of 4 feet to 16 feet. They are then steamed to bring out the color of the wood and then stacked outside for a period of one week to one year before being kiln dried. The kiln is the bottleneck of the operation and is why lumber may remain as unfinished inventory for up to one year.

Once dried, the boards are inspected individually and accepted, trimmed, or rejected according to the judgment of the inspector. The inspector, an employee of the company, makes sure that the boards meet industry standards for length and width.

Joining Frank Foster Walnut Lumber Co.

Tom joined Foster Lumber in February of 1984 as plant manager. The company had made a small amount of money in 1983 and was projected to lose money in 1984 (**Exhibit 3**). Tom believed that he had been hired to turn the mill around — similar to the task he performed at Amadeo Box Co. However, he found that his suggestions for improving the operations were not well received. In April, after making a suggestion to invest $5,000 to replace the company's natural gas boiler with one fueled by wood chips, Tom was told by the division vice president of Atlantic, ''Son, you need to understand something — we don't work for you; you work for us. Now just do your job and we'll get along fine.''

Matters deteriorated further when in May Tom did not receive the raise that he felt he had been promised. He went to Durham, North Carolina, to discuss the matter with the division president. After demonstrating to him that the raise had indeed been promised, Tom watched the president lean across the desk and say, ''Tom, you've quit your job at Amadeo, moved your wife and kids to Kansas City, and bought a house. We're not giving you the raise, and what are you going to do about it?''

At the same time, the president of Atlantic made several public comments indicating that Atlantic might be selling or liquidating selected divisions. By August, when Tom was told that his ability to authorize spending was reduced from $5,000 to $500, all capital expenditures canceled, and inventory levels were to be reduced significantly, he realized that Foster Lumber had been chosen for sale or liquidation.

Tom approached his immediate supervisor, the division controller, who confirmed that the company was to be liquidated unless a buyer could be found. Tom was also instructed not to tell any of the employees of the decision.

Tom's Offer to Atlantic Paper Co.

By September of 1984, Tom had decided to attempt the purchase of Foster Lumber, but he chose not to act at that time. Instead, he tried to support the value of the assets by making sure that the equipment was well maintained and that the inventory of supplies was not decreased below minimum levels.

Tom felt that with a series of operational changes, and by taking advantage of recent events, he could improve the performance of the mill and return it to profitability. Specifically, Tom planned to take the following steps:

- Increase the mix of higher-grade lumber resulting in a higher average unit selling price with no increase in product costs.
- Take advantage of recent declines in the cost of unprocessed logs to reduce raw material costs.
- Improve profitability over a three-year period through several bargain purchases the mill had recently made.
- Convert from natural gas to wood chip fuel for many of the operations.

In late November of 1984, Tom met with the controller to discuss the potential closing of the mill. During this meeting, in which the controller did not know of Tom's intention to buy the company, the controller told Tom that they would probably close the mill because they doubted a buyer would come forward. Tom asked the controller, "If Atlantic were to sell the company, how much do you think it would go for?" The controller guessed that Atlantic would accept $1 million just to get the company off the books.

The next day Tom told the controller that he was interested in buying the company and would like to talk to the division vice president. The division vice president liked Tom and liked the idea of a management buyout. Not only would it save Atlantic from the problems associated with a mill closing, but a management buyout also would foster good public relations. Both the controller and the division vice president suggested that Tom submit an offer to Bud Granger, division president.

Tom knew that he needed to act quickly before the company was decimated through the depletion of inventory and lack of capital commitments. He contacted an attorney, Sy Peterson, whom he knew through his father. Sy Peterson had recently worked on a well-publicized LBO involving a $300 million retailing company. Sy agreed to help Tom structure an agreement to purchase Foster Lumber, and the two crafted a letter of intent. They offered Atlantic Paper $1 million, of which $500,000 would be in the form of a seller note.

Tom mailed the letter of intent to Bud Granger on December 6. On December 9, Tom contacted the president by phone to discuss the offer. To Tom's surprise, the president told him that he questioned Tom's ability to raise $500,000 and that they had a ''large corporate buyer offering $1.5 million cash.''

After discussing the situation with Sy, Tom wrote back to Granger asking for a ''last look'' at whatever offer Atlantic was prepared to accept. Both Tom and Sy believed that Granger would accept this proposal since it could only improve the offer for Atlantic, and it would demonstrate a good faith effort on Atlantic's part in trying to sell the company to management.

Again to Tom's surprise, when he contacted Granger by phone the president told him to ''quit bothering me.''

Tom's Trip to Durham

Tom and Sy agreed that the only move left was to circumvent the division president and contact the senior vice president of Atlantic Paper, Stan Blackstone. To protect Tom, Sy made the phone call so that, if necessary, Tom could claim that he was unaware of Sy's actions. In the call, Sy stressed Atlantic's responsibility to its shareholders to discuss the sale of the division with all qualified buyers and Atlantic's responsibility to its employees to offer them an opportunity to purchase the company. Soon after Sy's call, Granger called Sy to invite him and Tom to Durham.

Both Tom and Sy believed they could structure an agreement at this meeting, and they looked forward to a long day of negotiations. When they arrived at Atlantic, they were greeted by Granger and Granger's personal attorney (both Tom and Sy were surprised to see Granger's personal attorney at the meeting). Unfortunately, their plane to Durham had been four hours late, and as they arrived Granger and his attorney were preparing to leave for lunch.

Rather than a working lunch—which Sy suggested—Granger insisted on taking Tom and Sy to the executive dining room for a ''real Southern lunch.'' As they walked to the dining room, they passed by a fashion show that was being sponsored by Atlantic Paper. To Tom's dismay, Granger invited them to enjoy the show for a moment. Only after 45 minutes and Tom's obvious impatience did the group finally adjourn to the dining room.

By the time the meeting began, Tom had become visibly upset, and when Granger started the meeting by accusing him of a conflict of interest through some of his recent purchases for the mill, Tom lost his temper and initiated a boisterous argument with Granger. Sy saw the deal falling apart and called for a break to discuss the situation with his client. ''Sy told me I was about five seconds away from blowing the whole deal,'' Tom recalled.

From that point forward, Sy took over the negotiations and asked about the status of Tom's request for a last look. Granger told Sy that they could not offer Tom a last look because they had a firm deal in place. Giving Tom a last look could be interpreted as interfering with a contractual arrangement.

Sy agreed with the need to protect any prior contract but asked for details of the agreement. Granger, on advice from his attorney, discussed the agreement with Sy for the all-cash purchase of Foster Lumber Co. for $1.5 million. After reviewing the details, Sy determined that the agreement was not a firm commitment because the buyers had not yet performed any due diligence on the mill. This, Sy noted, presented a ''seed of doubt'' in the agreement and suggested that Atlantic Paper should properly consider Fisher's offer.

The meeting ended with Granger's promise to take Tom and Sy's comments ''under advisement.''

When Tom returned to Kansas City, he found a phone message from Granger. Tom had a good feeling about the call and contacted Granger immediately. However, Granger had called to inform Tom that he was to lay off 50 percent of the work force effective that day—it was December 23, one day before Christmas Eve.

Tom asked Granger not to lay people off before Christmas Eve and that he would comply with the layoffs following the New Year's holiday. Granger told Tom, ''Either you lay off those workers or I'll add one more name to the list.''

Soon thereafter, Tom decided that the purchase of Foster Lumber was no longer viable. With half the work force gone, the inventory of logs well below normal operating levels, the depletion of the best-selling lumber inventory, and both landowners and buyers switching to other mills, Tom felt it was too late to save the company.

Letter of Intent

As a result, Tom did not know what to do when Granger called him on January 3, 1985, to request a letter of intent from Tom for the purchase of the Frank Foster Walnut Lumber Co. Apparently the other buyer had backed away from the deal when Atlantic refused to supply it with a certified audit of the inventory.

Tom discussed the matter with Sy, who suggested that he contact Norm Peck, Sy's client who had purchased the $300 million retail operation. Tom discussed the matter with Norm, who encouraged Tom to do the deal. In Norm's view, you seldom find an opportunity to purchase a company that you have so much information on—if Tom really wanted to get into business for himself, this would be his best opportunity.

Energized by Norm's advice, Tom met in Chicago the next day with Sy to draft a letter of intent. The offering price for the company would be $1.5 million cash. However, Atlantic would be required to assist in the purchase by guaranteeing $600,000 of the required bank debt. In this way, Tom could offer Atlantic an all-cash deal and still have a high likelihood of securing the bank financing. Tom and Sy believed that the purchase could take place with $100,000 of equity and the balance in the form of debt. Tom wanted to include his management team in the buyout as long as he maintained 51 percent of the company. Tom felt that between him and the management they could raise the $100,000.

While Tom was prepared to put the team of managers together immediately, Sy advised him to buy the company personally, and then to split the equity among the managers after the deal was completed. Sy was concerned that adding multiple equity participants might jeopardize the closing.

Tom sent the letter to Granger by overnight mail, and on January 10, 1985, he received a signed copy from Atlantic Paper (**Exhibit 4**).

Bank Financing

Tom met with several local bankers to arrange financing. While he was able to explain the operations of the mill, his minimal understanding of accounting and lack of financial documentation left the bankers unenthused with the deal. Tom, therefore, contacted a prominent Big Eight accounting firm to assist him in the due diligence and forecasting of future earnings. With its help, Tom projected earnings through 1989 (**Exhibit 5**). He believed that sales would increase dramatically over the first two years as the company liquidated inventory and then resume a steady state of $4 million in 1987 with modest growth thereafter.

Using this data, Tom resumed his search for a debt source. Through his connections with Sy, his CPA, and acquaintances in the local business community, he received introductions to 14 banks: 9 in Kansas City and 5 money-center banks. For three weeks, Tom met with bankers constantly, and each time they would either request additional information or decline Tom's request. Tom remembers that time as "the most humiliating experience of my life. These guys wake up every morning and for two hours practice saying 'no' in front of the mirror." Tom was surprised at the difficulty of securing the loan given Atlantic's $600,000 guarantee. Tom also found some of the local banks very inexperienced in LBO transactions. Upon returning to one local bank, he was handed a loan document to review that was in fact a standard auto loan application with "auto" crossed out and "company" inserted.

By the third week of January, Tom saw no imminent bank financing, while at the same time Frank Foster Walnut Lumber Co. was slowly being liquidated. His prior concerns about buying a "dead" company with no inventory, employees, or customers returned. After discussing the matter with six of his key employees, he decided to call the deal off. However, he would wait until the end of the day before notifying Atlantic Paper.

During this time, he called Norm Peck to inform him of his decision. Peck's reaction was strong and to the point. Peck told Tom, "Don't call me for a shoulder to cry on! You can get the deal done if you want to—just go do it and don't waste any more of my time." While Tom poured himself a cup of coffee to consider Peck's candid advice, Granger called.

The division president expressed his concern that Tom would not be able to complete the purchase if Atlantic continued to slowly liquidate the company. Therefore, Atlantic offered Tom the following concession: the purchase price would remain at $1.5 million: however, any pretax profit or loss that occurred between January 1, 1985, and the time of closing would be Tom's. During this period, Atlantic would not charge Foster Lumber any corporate overhead.

This significantly improved the deal for Tom. During the liquidation, the company was earning windfall profits. It maintained its inventory under LIFO, and since no new purchases were being made, inventory booked at low historical costs was being consumed. Tom believed the company might earn as much as $200,000 to $350,000 between January and March.

Tom fatalistically decided that Granger's phone call, only two hours before he was to call the deal off, and his talk with Peck signaled that he should continue his efforts to purchase Foster Lumber. Tom authorized his log buyer to purchase $40,000 in inventory, which Tom paid for personally. Upon buying Foster Lumber, the company would reimburse Tom for the purchase—if he did not buy Foster Lumber, Tom would be personally responsible for the inventory. For Tom, it was now all-or-nothing.

A New Strategy with the Banks

Tom reflected on his discussions with the banks and discovered a common theme to the banks' reluctance to finance the venture—Tom's age. The banks he negotiated with usually talked to older, more experienced managers and while they probably liked the structure of the deal, they viewed Tom's inexperience as too great a risk.

Based on this information, Tom decided to form a board of directors composed of "gray hair." Each board member would fill a specific role within the board: entrepreneurship, product innovation, market research, marketing, legal, and finance. Tom realized that he could address the assembly of the board in two different ways: (1) find the "best" people in the industry in order to showcase their experience; or (2) find individuals whom Tom personally respected and on whom he could count to make a serious commitment to the board. Deciding that commitment was more important than "face value," Tom chose to go with the latter option. He tapped a network of contacts that included family friends, his father's business associates, and various "friend of a friend" connections to assemble the following board:

- Norm Peck (entrepreneurship), president of Tasco Stores, a $300 million retail chain. Peck purchased Tasco Stores from The McFadden Company. Peck was a member of the board of directors of the First City Bank of Oklahoma.
- Thomas Williams (product innovation), vice president of innovation management, Clark Robbins Company, a $5.2 billion consumer goods company. Williams was responsible for many of Clark Robbins' new products including the invention of the disposable diaper.
- Jerry K. Barston (market research), chairman, Jerry K. Barston. Barston had a wide reputation in the United States and internationally as a respected market research firm.
- Franklin Fadden (marketing), partner, Fadden/Doolittle. Fadden had extensive experience in strategic planning, business plans, and developing market strategies for new product lines.
- Sy Peterson (legal), partner, Hendricks & Cooley. Peterson, a partner at Hendricks & Cooley, a medium-sized corporate law firm with extensive experience in LBOs and management-led purchases.

· Stan Overholser (finance), CEO, Kips Grocery Company, a $3.5 billion grocery chain. Overholser's background was in finance, and he would serve as an excellent resource for banking relationships and accounting requirements.

By mid-February, Tom returned to the banks and laid out for them the recent developments: Atlantic's new offer, the personal purchase of $40,000 of inventory, and the establishment of a board of directors. The banks responded favorably to the first two developments, but they did not react as well as Tom expected to the new board. When Tom asked them about their response, they told him that they doubted the sincerity of the directors and their ability to devote much time to the company. Tom then supplied the banks with a list of the directors' phone numbers and asked the banks to call them and discuss the matter directly.

In the meantime, Atlantic had grown impatient and told Tom that he would need to have financing in place by March 5, 1985, or Atlantic would liquidate the company. Tom took the ultimatum back to the banks and used it as a wedge to force them into a decision. On March 5, three banks telefaxed letters to Tom offering to provide the debt financing. Tom had a deal (see **Exhibit 6** for sample letter).

Closing the Transaction

The deal was scheduled to close on March 28 in Chicago. By the time of closing, Foster Lumber had earned $300,000, effectively reducing the price to $1.2 million. Of the purchase price, $200,000 was to be allocated to land, building, and equipment and $1 million to inventory. Tom would be purchasing only the assets of the company and therefore would not assume any of Atlantic's obligations or liabilities.

The bank that Tom chose would provide a $1.2 million loan, of which $600,000 would be guaranteed by Atlantic. Terms of the bank debt called for a floating interest rate of prime plus 2 percent (prime was 11 percent) and repayment of the balance within five years. The bank would also make available a $500,000 line of credit at 14 percent for working capital requirements. Tom and selected managers would provide $100,000 in equity, which would be used for working capital.

Tom chose to keep 70 percent of the company but did not have $70,000 to invest. Therefore, he set the price per share such that $30,000 would purchase 70 percent of the company. This meant that the remaining 30 percent of the company would cost $12,857, leaving them $57,143 short of the required $100,000 equity. To make up the shortfall, Tom required each manager to purchase subordinated debt on a pro-rata basis such that $57,143 of subordinated debt was raised. Since the debt was subordinated, the banks found this arrangement acceptable.

When Tom arrived at the Chicago offices of Hendricks & Cooley on March 28, 1985, he found three rooms with 20 stacks of documents and over 15 people present. He mused about the converted auto loan form that he had been asked to sign at one point!

A spirited mood prevailed as documents were being passed out. But that mood passed quickly when Atlantic's attorney demanded that its $600,000 guarantee be reduced on a pro-rata basis as the loan balance was reduced. Since Atlantic was guaranteeing $600,000 of the $1.2 million note, or 50 percent, it wanted its guarantee to be reduced by 50 cents for every dollar repaid. For example, if the loan had been repaid such that the balance was reduced from $1.2 million to $1 million, Atlantic Paper's guarantee would be reduced from $600,000 to $500,000 — 50 percent of the $1 million balance.

The bank, on the other hand, interpreted the agreement such that Atlantic was guaranteeing $600,000 of the note throughout the life of the note. In the above example, even though the balance on the note had been reduced to $1 million, Atlantic would still be responsible for $600,000.

Tom could not believe what he was hearing—he had just assumed that Atlantic had interpreted the agreement as a fixed $600,000 guarantee with no pro-rata reduction. It was Friday and the wire transfer lines were to shut down in 1 1/2 hours and would not reopen until Monday. Sy believed that more than a weekend was at stake: if Tom wanted to complete the purchase he would have to act quickly.

Tom needed to consider two things. First, should he use this as an ''out'' for not doing the deal? After all, the payroll of the company had been reduced to only 50 percent of previous levels, inventories were well below normal, and in spite of Tom's best efforts, customer and landowner relations had deteriorated. Had Peck ''shamed'' Tom into doing the deal and had this evolved into an issue of pride instead of solid economics? While Tom understood the company and the industry well, did it make sense for him to embark on a turnaround situation? And would the company have enough ''dry powder'' capital to sustain a turnaround? Tom knew that it would take upwards of six months to restore the company to profitability.

Second, if Tom decided to save the purchase, what response should he give to Atlantic or to the bank? Was this a bluff on Atlantic's part that would disappear, or had it truly misunderstood the terms of the deal?

EXHIBIT 1

Thomas H. Fisher
4900 West 69th Street
Prairie Village, Kansas 66208

Vocational Experience

2/84–3/85:
Atlantic Paper Company
Foster Lumber Company, Kansas City, Kansas

Plant Manager. Responsible for coordination of log purchasing over five-state area; sawmill production of lumber and quality control. Oversaw sales of lumber and veneer logs. Coordination of three areas: purchasing, production, and sales. Plant facilities include log yard, sawmill, boiler, warehouses, remanufacture, inspection, rail facility, and shipping. Managed five supervisors, two log buyers, and forty employees.

6/80–1/84:
Amadeo Box Company
Chriqui Forest Products, Fandango, Arkansas

Mill Manager: 11/80–1/84. Responsible for the scheduling of and mill production; inventory levels and rotation of logs; inventory levels of lumber, ties, cants, chips; marketing lumber and chips; supervision of log purchasing, training of supervisors; facility planning and expansion; equipment selection and purchase.

Second Shift Supervisor: 6/80–11/80. Responsible for mill production including manufacture of lumber, cants, chips, oversaw inventorying of these materials. Reorganized methods of accounting for, and storage of, cants and lumber. Hired and trained mill hands. Supervised eight persons.

Education

B.S., Production Management, College of Forestry University of Minnesota, 1980

B.A., Art, University of Vermont, 1975

National Hardwood Lumber Association, 1981
Memphis, Tennessee
14-Week Hardwood Lumber Grading Course

EXHIBIT 2   **End Uses of Walnut, 1987 (100% = 143 million board feet)**

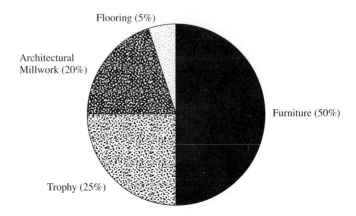

Annual Production of U.S. Hardwoods, 1987 (100% = 12 billion board feet)

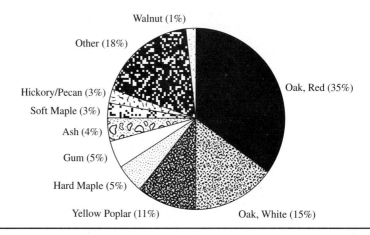

Exhibit 3   Frank Foster Walnut Lumber Co. Income Statements (1982–84)

	1982	*1983*	*1984*
Sales			
Board feet (thousands)	2,959	3,257	3,396
Average selling price per foot ($)	1.07	1.12	1.07
Total Sales	$3,166,130	$3,647,840	$3,633,720
Cost of goods sold			
Material	1,371,774	1,854,061	1,968,761
Operations			
Log buying	135,718	133,557	147,217
Sawmill	605,533	517,826	567,185
Yard storage and handling	195,118	178,930	203,981
Kiln drying	118,178	88,691	104,044
Dressing and shipping	294,249	220,286	243,342
Total operations	1,348,796	1,139,290	1,265,769
Supervisory and Administrative	121,347	120,816	150,391
Insurance	24,884	36,846	24,256
Property taxes [a]	87,009	100,556	124,307
Depreciation	88,730	90,478	84,017
Total cost of goods sold	$3,042,540	$3,342,047	$3,617,501
Gross profit	123,590	305,793	16,219
Selling and administrative	87,319	41,883	76,431
Income (loss) from operations	36,271	263,910	(60,212)
Charges by Atlantic	98,367	131,367	294,229
Other income	(10,994)	(16,728)	(3,107)
Net income (loss)	$ (51,102)	$ 149,271	$ (351,334)

[a]Includes taxes on real property and personal property such as inventory.

EXHIBIT 3   *(concluded)*

Frank Foster Walnut Lumber Co.
Balance Sheets (1983–85)

	December 31, 1983	December 31, 1984	March 31, 1985[a]
Assets			
Current assets			
Cash	740	1,600	0
Receivables	1,400	1,118	0
Inventory			
Logs	159,923	177,069	100,000
Lumber	1,706,325	1,799,924	1,050,000
Total inventory	1,866,248	1,976,993	1,150,000
Total current assets	$1,868,388	$1,979,711	$1,150,000
Property, plant, and equipment			
Land	16,449	16,449	16,449
Buildings	140,035	140,035	140,035
(Less: Depreciation)	(44,333)	(49,403)	(50,689)
Net land and buildings	112,151	107,081	105,795
Equipment	1,068,162	1,078,762	1,078,762
(Less: Depreciation)	(575,707)	(641,870)	(658,250)
Net Equipment	492,455	436,892	420,512
Total property, plant, and equipment	$ 604,606	543,973	526,307
Total assets	$2,472,994	$2,523,684	$1,676,307
Liabilities			
Current liabilities			
Accounts payable	21,446	3,166	0
Accrued expenses	68,115	49,068	0
Total current liabilities	$ 89,561	$ 52,234	0
Net worth	$2,383,433	$2,471,450	$1,676,307

[a]Estimated assets to be acquired.

Exhibit 4   Letter of Intent, January 10, 1985

Atlantic Paper Co.   January 10, 1985

Augusta, Georgia

Attention: Mr. Bud Granger

Gentlemen:

It is the intent of a management group consisting of myself and other personnel of your Kansas City, Kansas, Walnut Lumbermill ("Lumbermill"), to cause the purchase of the business and all of the fixed assets and inventory of the Lumbermill, on the following general terms and conditions:

1. The buyers will be an entity organized by the management group.
2. The assets purchased will consist of all of the Lumbermill's fixed assets, inventory, and the following leased vehicles and pickups (free of Leases): Three 1984 Cutlass Sierra automobiles and one 1984 Chevrolet pickup truck.
3. Subject to adjustment because of the last sentence of paragraph 5 below, the purchase price will be $1,500,000 plus 50% of the lease buyout price of the four leased vehicles listed in paragraph 2 above, payable in full, in cash at the closing.
4. The purchaser shall not assume any of your liabilities.
5. The purchaser will use its best effort to close the transaction as soon as possible, but, in any event not later than February 28, 1985. When closed, the transaction shall be deemed to have been closed, for all economic purposes, as of January 1, 1985.
6. A detailed formal agreement by the parties will be prepared for this transaction ("Asset Purchase Agreement"). The Asset Purchase Agreement will be the binding agreement between the parties with respect to the subject matter of this letter of intent. The Asset Purchase Agreement will contain the customary covenants, representations, warranties and conditions for a transaction of this type. Until the Asset Purchase Agreement is entered into no party shall have any liability to the other except that paragraph 7 will be binding on the parties regardless of whether the Asset Purchase Agreement is entered into.
7. You shall not negotiate with, or take any action which might lead to the sale of the assets being sold hereunder to any party other than purchaser and its representatives during the period you and purchaser negotiate the Asset Purchase Agreement.
8. You will guarantee a $500,000 portion of the loan which the purchaser will obtain in order to consummate the transaction, described in this letter. If required by purchaser's lender, such guarantee shall be increased but in no event will it be more than $600,000.
9. Between the date hereof and the closing, you shall not make any further employee dismissals. At closing, you shall deliver the assets purchased in their current condition.
10. This letter shall constitute our entire letter of intent to date with respect to this transaction.

If this letter is acceptable to you, please so indicate by signing and returning the enclosed copy. Upon our receipt of an accepted letter, I will instruct my attorneys to begin to draft the Asset Purchase Agreement.

Very Truly Yours,

Tomas H. Fisher

Thomas H. Fisher

Accepted:
Atlantic Paper Co.
By:_____

EXHIBIT 5   **Frank Foster Walnut Lumber Co.**
Income Statement Projections (1985–89)[a]

	9 Months Ended Dec. 31, 1985	1986	1987	1988	1989
Sales					
Board feet (thousands)	2,840	3,720	3,310	3,200	3,200
Average selling price per foot	$0.89	$1.17	$1.23	$1.29	$1.32
Total sales	$2,527,600	$4,352,400	$4,071,300	$4,128,000	$4,224,000
Cost of goods sold					
Material	1,240,000	2,100,000	2,030,000	2,069,000	2,085,000
Operations					
Log buying	89,050	121,250	127,500	135,000	142,000
Sawmill	216,009	405,816	433,543	450,000	473,000
Yard storage and handling	78,091	206,985	214,670	220,000	231,000
Kiln drying	179,789	121,063	124,195	130,000	137,000
Dressing and shipping	172,832	246,259	257,979	265,000	278,000
Total operations	735,771	1,101,373	1,157,887	1,200,000	1,261,000
Maintenance	52,000	53,500	56,500	60,000	63,000
Insurance	30,000	30,000	35,000	35,000	40,000
Property taxes[b]	50,000	35,000	20,000	15,000	18,000
Depreciation	36,000	36,000	36,000	36,000	36,000
Total cost of goods sold	$2,143,771	$3,355,873	$3,335,387	$3,415,000	$3,503,000
Gross profit	383,829	996,527	735,913	713,000	721,000
Selling and administrative	293,000	320,000	331,000	351,000	375,000
EBIT	90,829	676,527	404,913	362,000	346,000
Interest expense	225,000	125,000	35,000	0	0
Income from operations	(134,171)	551,527	369,913	362,000	346,000
Less: Taxes (35%)[c]	0	146,075[d]	129,470	126,700	121,100
Net income (loss)	$ (134,171)	$ 405,452	$ 240,443	$ 235,300	$ 224,900

[a]Projections by Tom Fisher.

[b]Includes taxes on real property and personal property such as inventory.

[c]Includes state taxes.

[d]Includes net operating losses from 1985.

Exhibit 6 **Conditional Commitment to Finance Acquisition (March 5, 1985)**

Farmer's Branch Bank and Trust Company
4800 S. Cornhusk Avenue
Backwater Bend, Kansas 66322
(913) 873-9800

March 5, 1985

Mr. Thomas H. Fisher
P.O. Box 242
Kaw River Road
Kansas City, Kansas 66119

Dear Tom:

The purpose of this letter is to set forth a proposal to you regarding your loan requests for the following:
(1) purchase all fixed assets and inventory of Atlantic's Kansas City, Kansas, walnut lumber mill, and
(2) working capital line of credit. The following are terms and conditions which we propose:

1. *Amount:*	$1,200,000 — purchase of assets
	$500,000 — Line of credit
2. *Terms:*	$1.2 million note — 5-year amortization.
	$500,000 note — demand basis; interest paid monthly; reviewed annually.
3. *Rate:*	Farmer's Branch Bank's base rate plus two percent floating.
4. *Collateral:*	All accounts receivable, inventory, furniture, fixtures, equipment, machinery and first mortgage on real estate.
5. *Guarantees:*	$600,000 unconditional by Atlantic Paper Company; Mr. and Mrs. Thomas Fisher.
6. *Financial Statements:*	
	Monthly balance sheet and income statements; annual audit; monthly accounts receivable aging; quarterly physical inventory schedule.
7. *Fees:*	1% annually for line of credit.
8. *Capital:*	$100,000 by outside investors in form of stock and subordinated debt.
9. *Life Insurance:*	
	$1,000,000 on Thomas Fisher.
10. *Property/Casualty Insurance:*	
	Maintain insurance coverage at all times in amounts satisfactory to Farmer's Branch Bank.
11. *Title Insurance:*	
	Provide clear title to real estate property.
12. *Loan Agreement:*	
	Covers such items as dividend payments, limitation on capital expenditures, and the normal representations, warranties and covenants.
13. *Legal Fees:*	Maximum of $2,000 to be paid by applicant.

The above items are outlined as a proposal to you, and they should not be interpreted by you as a commitment by the Farmer's Branch Bank. Tom, after you have reviewed these terms and conditions, please let me know if you have questions.

Sincerely,

Stephen F. Gallagher

Stephen F. Gallagher
Sr. Commercial Loan Officer

SFG:cso

IV   MANAGING THE ENTERPRISE AND HARVESTING VALUE

In this final section, we look at what happens after the start-up. Managing a venture in an entrepreneurial manner involves a constant search for new opportunities. Yet growth and wealth often create bureaucracy, specialization, and a desire to protect assets rather than to seek growth. This last part provides a good opportunity to review Chapter 1; the ideas therein are useful for existing companies that want to remain entrepreneurial. Chapter 13, ''Managing Growth,'' describes the administrative challenges that growth engenders and how they can be successfully managed.

Sometimes the period after the start-up brings not growth and success, but problems. Chapter 14, ''Bankruptcy: A Debtor's Perspective,'' describes how to deal with the unhappy and final stage in the life of some businesses.

Chapter 15 looks at a firm's decision to become a public company. ''Securities Law and Public Offerings'' describes the legal and business considerations in going public.

The Cases

Gordon Biersch Brewing Company focuses on a team of entrepreneurs who have successfully started and grown a restaurant and brewing business. An ambitious growth plan calls for more restaurants and retail distribution of their beer. Is their plan *too* ambitious?

Vinod Khosla and Sun Microsystems explores the challenges of running a young company in the rapidly changing computer industry. Khosla must make a decision upon which the company's future might hinge. What should he do?

Image Presentations considers a small and growing company in search of management talent for a new business opportunity. Why does the firm seem unable to hire the people it needs?

Dragonfly Corporation looks at a business with grave financial and legal problems. Is bankruptcy the answer?

SSS examines a company that has decided to become a public entity. Is this the right action? What are the criteria for selecting an underwriter? What are the key items to negotiate? Which investment banker should SSS choose?

Glenn DeKraker considers a successful entrepreneur's options for exiting from a business he has built. Which alternative will best meet Glenn's needs?

Finally, Howard Head and Prince Manufacturing provides insight into the life of a famous entrepreneur and the companies he has started. The case looks at the issue of when, if, and how value should be harvested.

13 MANAGING GROWTH

The set of changes that smaller, younger firms need to make as they grow is often termed *the transition from entrepreneurial to professional management*. This chapter addresses the issues that firms must deal with in making the transition:

- What is entrepreneurial management and how does it differ from professional management?
- What pressures force the firm to make the transition?
- How can entrepreneurs and their firms make the transition with a greater chance of success?

Entrepreneurial and Professional Management

The terms *entrepreneurial* and *professional management* mean very different things to different people. To some, *entrepreneurial management* suggests creative people and an innovative and successful organization, while *professional management* implies a stifling bureaucracy. To others, entrepreneurs are associated with disorganization, and professional management offers efficiency and effectiveness. For the sake of this note, however, *entrepreneurial and professional management* are merely descriptive terms and imply nothing about the creativity, innovation, or success of the organization.

Entrepreneurial Management

Entrepreneurial management is a style of management that is typically used when the firm is young and small. It is characterized by a number of features, including:

- *Centralized decision making:* In a small organization, the general manager can usually make most of the decisions required to manage the firm. The business is sufficiently small and simple enough that one person can comprehend all the information required for decision making.
- *Informal control:* The entrepreneurial firm is typically informal. There is little need for formal procedures, systems, and structures because the firm is small

This note was prepared by Michael J. Roberts.
Copyright © 1986 by the President and Fellows of Harvard College
Harvard Business School Note 9–387–054

enough that activity can be monitored via the personal supervision of the entrepreneur. Moreover, the firm is young and inexperienced and has not yet learned the routines required for success.

The entrepreneur's own ability to collect information, make decisions, and monitor their implementation reduces the need for formal structure, policies, and procedures.

Professional Management

Professional management is characterized by:

- *Delegation of decision-making responsibility:* Larger firms are sufficiently complex that one individual cannot make all of the decisions required to manage the firm. Therefore, the general manager must delegate responsibility to a hierarchy of middle managers. This pattern of delegation both determines and is determined by the firm's structure.
- *Use of formal control systems:* In response to the delegation of decision-making responsibility, formal systems are introduced. Because the general manager does not *personally* make all of the firm's decisions, there is a need for systems to guide and evaluate the performance of those who *are* making those decisions. These systems usually include a mechanism for setting objectives, monitoring performance against those objectives, and rewarding desired performance. In addition, general managers also develop policies and standard procedures to guide the actions of those below.

The "Strategy of Coordination"

Just as the firm has an (explicit or implicit) strategy for its actions in the competitive marketplace, it also has an internal strategy for coordinating its efforts. Essentially, the dimensions of organization that we have been discussing are all elements of the way in which the firm chooses to coordinate its efforts.

There are two key dimensions to the strategy of coordination:

- The delegation of responsibility: whether the general manager makes the day-to-day operating decisions personally or delegates that decision-making responsibility to a hierarchy of middle managers.
- The use of formal control systems: whether the firm uses formal systems to set objectives, monitor performance, and control the activities of organization members.

These two dimensions describe a broad range of approaches to coordinating the firm's efforts. If we simply think in terms of the two-by-two matrix defined by these two dimensions, we can see that there are four archetypical strategies of coordination:

- Entrepreneurial management, which relies on centralized decision making and informal, personal control.

- Professional management, which utilizes the delegation of responsibility and extensive formal controls.
- Laissez-faire management, in which responsibilities are delegated, but control remains informal.
- Bureaucratic management, in which centralized decision making is supplemented with formal control.

		Use of Formal Control Mechanisms	
		Low	**High**
	High	Laissez-faire management	Professional management
Delegation of responsibility			
	Low	Entrepreneurial management	Bureaucratic management

A *fundamental proposition* that underlies these ideas is that decisions regarding delegation and control have a strong influence on the firm's performance along two critical dimensions:

- Efficiency: the firm's ability to achieve its goals with a minimum of resources.
- Effectiveness: the firm's ability to adapt its goals and innovate to meet the changing needs of its environment.

Moreover, these two performance dimensions—and the decisions regarding delegation and control that underlie them—are *fundamentally in opposition*. Broadly speaking, choices that favor delegation have the potential to increase effectiveness, but simultaneously decrease efficiency; and the use of formal controls increases efficiency while reducing effectiveness. *Thus, the general manager's choices regarding delegation and control determine how these critical trade-offs are made.*

Making the Transition to Professional Management

When properly implemented, professional management offers an approach to coordinating the activities of a larger, more complex organization while avoiding the problems inherent in laissez-faire or bureaucratic management. There are several steps required for a successful transition to professional management.

Recognizing the Need for Change

The first step in the transition process is a recognition of the need for change. This is often extremely difficult because it is a by-product of success. Success reinforces beliefs and behavior that are appropriate to the entrepreneurial mode but that may not fit the needs of a larger, more complex firm.

Frequently, it is a crisis of some sort that highlights the need for change. Fortunately, knowledgeable outsiders can often help the entrepreneur see the need for such change before a crisis. Experienced board members or consultants can spot the early warning signs: lack of follow-up on details, incredible stress on the individual entrepreneur, and a sense of organizational disarray.

Once the entrepreneur has recognized the need for change, it is often difficult to know what to change *to*. Those who have successfully made the transition report that it requires a fundamental change in orientation: the manager must shift from getting personal satisfaction from direct action to a mode where that sense of accomplishment comes from achieving results *through others*.

Developing the Human Resources

Given this change of personal role in the organization, the entrepreneur needs to develop the human resources required to implement that model. Often, individuals who can accept and execute responsibility are not present in the entrepreneurial organization. The entrepreneur's style has made it difficult for aggressive, independent, employees to survive. Moreover, many young firms simply lack the resources to attract and hire managerial talent.

In order to develop a competent managerial team, the entrepreneur must overcome personal loyalties that threaten the organization. In virtually every firm, the entrepreneur has a "right-hand person" without whom the business would not have survived in the early years. Unfortunately, many of these employees are unable to develop the more specialized skills needed to grow with the company. Entrepreneurs must overcome their personal loyalties and find more suitable employees for critical positions.

Delegating Responsibility

Once the entrepreneur has perceived the need for change and developed a management team, real delegation of responsibility can begin. The power of professional management lies in placing the responsibility close to the source of information required for sound decision making. Typically, this means delegating responsibility to managers who are close to customers, suppliers, and competitors. In the process of delegating, the general manager must be careful *not* to give up responsibility for key policy issues that require personal perspective. Moreover, delegation does not mean that the entrepreneur loses the opportunity to have *input* into the decision-making process; surely, the benefit of that experience should not be lost.

Developing Formal Controls

A final step in the transition process is the development of formal control mechanisms. Successful entrepreneurs realize that, with the onset of delegation, they can no longer control the behavior of individuals in the organization. It is important that the focus of the control system shifts to performance rather than behavior. In addition, successful firms realize the danger in simply adapting policies and procedures that are used at other firms. Firms that customize policies ensure that the practice makes sense for the organization. The process of devoting time and effort often inspires creative solutions, and builds commitment.

Conclusion

The reason why the transition to professional management is often so difficult is that it requires *far more* than changes in organizational systems and structures. It requires a *fundamental change in the attitudes and behaviors of the entrepreneur.* Merely creating organizational structures and systems accomplishes little if the entrepreneur is unwilling to truly delegate. Control systems are meaningless if the entrepreneur fails to use them. It is this need to fundamentally change the individual general manager's self-concept behavior that makes the transition process so difficult.

14 BANKRUPTCY: A DEBTOR'S PERSPECTIVE

For the most part, government in America treats the private sector with cautious noninterference. Direct public participation in the economic affairs of an individual or a corporation is limited to a monitoring function through such bodies as the Internal Revenue Service, the Securities and Exchange Commission, and the Federal Trade Commission. Only when things go wrong does the government step in to take action. In the case of financial failure, public policy has dictated that the legal system act as a buffer between debtors and creditors, seeking to maximize both economic efficiency and equity. Thus, bankruptcy laws have been passed to help ensure that resolutions to situations of financial adversity maximize the present and future value of the "estate" and deal fairly with all debtors and creditors.

Bankruptcy is by no means the obvious result of financial trouble. There are many types of financial adversity and many solutions other than resorting to bankruptcy proceedings. An individual or a firm that becomes insolvent, without cash to pay the bills, may simply stall creditors until the situation improves. They may also default on loan payments, negotiate reduced schedules, or liquidate inventory to generate funds. The notion of bankruptcy implies a sense of direct cause. Someone, either debtor or creditor, decides that the individual or firm should not continue in its present financial incarnation. Then bankruptcy becomes an option for either the debtors or creditors to utilize the law to amend the situation.

For the debtor, bankruptcy provides a chance to bail out from under an impossible burden of debts, to wipe the slate clean and start again. Often it provides an alternative to years of struggling to pay off angry and impatient creditors with an income—personal or corporate—that is insufficient to meet all obligations as they come due. For creditors, bankruptcy provides a chance to get back some portion of their claims on an equitable basis with all other creditors. Often it provides an alternative to continuously postponed payments and the fear of being treated unfairly vis-à-vis other creditors. No one wants to see his debt go unpaid while another creditor is paid in full. Bankruptcy provides a means for creditors to hedge their bets: it gives them a guarantee of partial payment, rather than a gamble for full payment at a cost of entering into the timing uncertainty inherent in the legal system.

This chapter will discuss bankruptcy from the point of view of the individual or corporate debtor. First, it will describe the new Bankruptcy Reform Act of 1978 and

This note was prepared by Martha Gershun under the direction of Howard H. Stevenson.
Copyright © 1983 by the President and Fellows of Harvard College
Harvard Business School Note 9–384–119

the legal jurisdiction for bankruptcy law in the United States today. Then, it will examine bankruptcy in general and three forms of bankruptcy in particular: liquidation, corporation reorganization, and the adjustment of debts of an individual with a regular income. Finally, it will talk about some of the ways debtors can protect themselves before taking this final step and will discuss what actions are prohibited under the new law.

The New Law

Until a few years ago, the prevailing code for bankruptcy law in the United States was the Bankruptcy Act of 1898, also known as the Nelson Act. While this act was amended some 50 times, including a major overhaul under the Chandler Act of 1938, it remained in effect for 80 years until Congress passed the Bankruptcy Reform Act of 1978. The new code, Public Law 95-958, has eight odd-numbered substantive chapters. The first three are administrative rules that are relevant to *all* bankruptcy proceedings, and the remainder deal with specific types of bankruptcy. Note that the election of any type of bankruptcy triggers an automatic stop of all lawsuits against the company:

- Chapter 1 sets forth general definitions and rules.
- Chapter 3 deals with case administration.
- Chapter 5 deals with such issues as creditors' claims, debtors' duties and advantages, exemptions, and trustees' powers.
- Chapter 7 deals with liquidations.
- Chapter 9 deals with municipal debts.
- Chapter 11 deals with reorganizations for businesses including railroads.
- Chapter 13 deals with debts of a person with a regular income.
- Chapter 15 contains the necessary provisions to set up a new United States Trustee Pilot Program.

Under the new act, bankruptcy courts are established as adjuncts of each U.S. District Court. Bankruptcy judges are appointed by the president, with the advice and consent of the Senate. This situation prevailed until early 1983 when the Supreme Court determined that bankruptcy judges were members of the judicial branch of the government just like all other judges and, as such, had to be given certain guarantees of independence, including lifetime tenure.

Total bankruptcy proceedings of all types increased from slightly more than 10,000 cases commenced in the fiscal year ending June 30, 1946, to more than 254,000 in fiscal 1975. They declined during the next three years to just under 203,000 in fiscal 1978 before soaring to approximately 298,500 for the fiscal year ending September 30, 1980, the first year of operations under the Bankruptcy Code of 1978, and then continuing to soar to reach 561,000 in fiscal 1987.

A final note: not all companies can elect to go bankrupt. Banks, including savings and loans, insurance companies, and all foreign companies are prohibited from doing so.

Getting into Trouble

For an individual, the path to bankruptcy is often clearly discernible in retrospect; through hindsight, it is easy to see where a person made a bad decision, when they became overextended, how they misjudged their financial situation. There are two ways individuals accumulate sufficient unpaid debts to contemplate bankruptcy. The first is painfully simple: they purchase more on credit than they can afford to buy. This happens because they underestimate the amount of money they will have to pay for their accumulated credit purchases or because they overestimate the amount of income they will earn. Thus, the incidence of individual bankruptcies has increased with rises of easy consumer credit and in periods of unemployment, when people may lose their jobs unexpectedly or be unable to find new work if they are laid off. The second road to individual bankruptcy is more complex. It occurs when an individual's personal finances are in order, but he or she chooses to act as guarantor for a business or for another individual whose situation may not be as fortunate. When an individual agrees to accept the burden of another's debts (either for an individual or a corporation), then that person becomes legally responsible if the first entity defaults on payments. Sometimes, this additional financial requirement is more than the individual's personal budget can accommodate. Bankruptcy then becomes a way of eliminating these added debts, leaving the individual free to begin again.

For corporations, the path to bankruptcy is considerably more complicated. Ray Barrickman outlines 18 potential causes of business failure: excessive competition, the general business cycle, changes in public demand, governmental acts, adverse acts of labor, acts of God, poor overall management, unwise promotion, unwise expansion, inefficient selling, overextension of inventories, poor financial management, excessive fixed charges, excessive funded debt, excessive floating debt, overextension of credit, unwise dividend policies, and inadequate maintenance and depreciation.[1]

John Argenti, studying corporate failures in Great Britain, posits a chain of events, beginning with poor management, which usually precipitates a firm's slide into bankruptcy:

> If the management of a company is poor then two things will be neglected: the system of accountancy information will be deficient, and the company will not respond to change. (Some companies, even well-managed ones, may be damaged because powerful constraints prevent the managers making the responses they wish to make.) Poor managers will also make at least one of three other mistakes: they will overtrade; or they will launch a big project that goes wrong; or they will allow the company's gearing [financial leverage] to rise so that even normal business hazards become constant threats. These are the chief causes, neither fraud nor bad luck deserve more than a passing mention. The following symptoms will appear: certain financial ratios will deteriorate but, as soon as they do, the managers will start creative accounting that reduces the predictive value of these ratios and so lends greater importance to nonfinancial symptoms. Finally the company enters a characteristic period in its last few months.[2]

---

[1] Ray E. Barrickman, *Business Failure, Causes, Remedies, and Cures* (Washington, D.C.: University Press of America, 1979), p. 28.

[2] John Argenti, *Corporate Collapse: The Causes and Symptoms* (London: McGraw-Hill, 1976), p. 108.

These are not all root causes of bankruptcy, of course. The direct catalyst for bankruptcy proceedings is a person or company's inability to pay debts on time. When this situation occurs, the individual or company may begin voluntary bankruptcy proceedings or their creditors may try to force them into involuntary bankruptcy. Any person, partnership, or corporation can file for voluntary relief under the bankruptcy code. Even solvent entities can file for bankruptcy as long as there is no intent to defraud.

For example, Manville Corporation filed for bankruptcy in late 1982, even though the company had a book net worth of nearly $1.2 billion. The manufacturer was seeking protection from an anticipated 32,000 lawsuits relating to the injury or death of workers who used Manville's asbestos products. Assuming an average settlement of $40,000 per lawsuit, Manville calculated that it could not afford to stay in business and sought bankruptcy relief from these "creditors."

Sometimes the resort to bankruptcy is motivated more by strategic than financial issues. Wilson Foods, a producer of meat and food products, recently sought Chapter 11 protection in order to force union officials to reduce labor wages. Wilson's chairman announced publicly that the firm did not intend to close any of its plants or lay off any workers. He further stated that Wilson had sufficient cash, receivables, and available credit to meet its short-term obligations. The bankrupt can apply to the court to nullify a union contract that would otherwise have lasted until 1985. The court must decide such cases based upon what is in the best interest of the estate. Thus, the move allowed Wilson to put in place sharply reduced hourly wages. A similar case—Bildisco—has been decided by the Supreme Court. The outcome of this case, involving the issue of whether or not bankruptcy allows a firm to change contract terms with union employees, determined that firms may use Chapter 11 protection in this manner. Unions are currently lobbying for congressional relief from this decision.

In order to seek relief from their debts, a person or corporation must file in the office of the Clerk of the United States District Court in which the domicile, residence, principal place of business, or principal assets of the entity have been located for the preceding 180 days. The filing fee is $60 for parties commencing a bankruptcy case under Chapter 7 (liquidation) or Chapter 13 (adjustment of debts for an individual with regular income). The filing fee for businesses seeking relief under Chapter 11 (business reorganizations) is $200; railroads must pay a filing fee of $500. *A person or corporation can only file for bankruptcy protection once every six years.*

In certain situations, creditors can force debtors to go bankrupt. An involuntary bankruptcy case can be commenced by:

- Three or more creditors whose aggregated claims amount to more than $5,000 over the value of any assets securing those claims; or
- One or more such creditors if there are less than 12 claim holders; or
- Fewer than all the general partners in a limited partnership.

Creditors do not have to prove that the debtor is unable to pay his or her bills; mere failure to pay on time, regardless of ability to pay, is sufficient grounds for creditors to seek involuntary bankruptcy. However, in an involuntary bankruptcy proceeding, the court can require petitioners to post a bond to cover the debtor's costs if the court finds in the debtor's favor. Furthermore, if the creditors are found to have petitioned in bad faith, the court may award the debtor any damages caused by the proceedings, including punitive compensation. In practice, involuntary bankruptcy is uncommon. For the year ending June 30, 1979, only 926 involuntary bankruptcy cases were filed out of a total of 226,476 cases.[3]

Choosing Your Poison: Which Chapter?

There are three distinct chapters of the bankruptcy code that can shape the outcome of the bankruptcy proceedings: Chapter 7 (liquidation), Chapter 11 (reorganization), and Chapter 13 (adjustment of an individual's debts).

In theory, bankruptcy procedures can be concluded very quickly. In practice, however, they are often long, drawn-out affairs. Corporate reorganizations, in particular, can take many years to reach completion. Speaking before the 94th Congress, Representative Elizabeth Holtzman noted that "it is reported that the average corporate reorganization case in the Seventh District of New York takes eight years to resolve."[4]

In a Chapter 7 bankruptcy, the assets of the individual or corporation are liquidated and distributed to creditors. In a Chapter 11 or Chapter 13 bankruptcy, the debtors keep their assets with some arrangement to pay off their debts over time. Since the outcomes of these types of bankruptcy are radically different, affecting the form of the assets that the debtor keeps as well as the timing and amount of payments that the creditors receive, both groups have some ability to influence the choice of prevailing chapters.

When the creditor files for an involuntary bankruptcy case under Chapter 7 or 11, the debtor can convert the case to a bankruptcy under any of the other chapters. When a debtor files for voluntary bankruptcy under any chapter, the creditors can request that the trustee convert the case to a Chapter 7 or a Chapter 11 bankruptcy. Only a Chapter 13 bankruptcy cannot be commenced without the debtor's consent. Before choosing a chapter for bankruptcy, debtors should carefully consider whether they would prefer to liquidate their assets or continue their business with personal finances, attempting with reorganization or adjustment to pay off their debts over time.

Chapter 7: Liquidation

Chapter 7 of the Bankruptcy Act provides for either voluntary or involuntary liquidation of the assets of the debtor or distribution to the creditors. When a petition is filed under Chapter 7 it constitutes an Order for Relief. The debtor now has a legal obligation to:

---

[3]Table of Bankruptcy Statistics with reference to bankruptcy cases commenced and terminated in the United States District Courts during the period July 1, 1978, through June 30, 1979. Administrative Office of the United States Courts.

[4]House Report #686, p. 56.

1. File a list of creditors, assets and liabilities, and a statement of financial affairs.
2. Cooperate with the trustee appointed to the case.
3. Give the trustee all property of the estate and all records relating to the property.
4. Appear at any hearing dealing with a discharge.
5. Attend all meetings of creditors.

As soon as possible after the Order for Relief, an interim trustee will be appointed. If creditors holding at least 30 percent of the specified claims request one, an election will be held to choose one person to serve as trustee in the case. This can be the debtor serving as trustee while debtor in possession. If no trustee is elected in this manner, the interim trustee will continue to serve. The duties of the trustee include:

1. Reducing the property of the debtor's estate to cash and closing up the estate as expeditiously as possible.
2. Accounting for all property received.
3. Investigating the financial affairs of the debtor and examining all claims for validity.
4. Providing information about the estate to any interested party, furnishing reports on the debtor's business if it is authorized to be operated, and filing a final report of the disposition of the estate with the court.

Portions of the debtor's estate will be exempt from liquidation; that is, they may not be distributed to the creditors. In many states, the debtor can choose between the federal exemptions or the relevant state exemptions. However, states can require their residents to adhere to the state exemptions; Florida and Virginia have passed such laws, and South Carolina, Delaware, and Ohio are considering similar statutes. Under the current federal exemptions, a debtor gets to keep:

1. The debtor's interest, not to exceed $7,500, in the debtor's (or a dependent's) residence; in a cooperative that owns property used by the debtor (or a dependent) as a residence; and in a burial plot for the debtor or a dependent.
2. The debtor's interest, not to exceed $1,200, in a motor vehicle.
3. The debtor's interest, not to exceed $200 in value for any particular item, in household furnishings, clothing, appliances, books, animals, crops, or musical instruments, that are kept for the personal, family, or household use of the debtor or a dependent.
4. The debtor's interest, not to exceed $500, in jewelry held for personal, family, or household use of the debtor or a dependent.
5. The debtor's interest, not to exceed $400, in any property in addition to Item 1 exemptions.
6. The debtor's interest, not to exceed $750, in any implements, professional books, or tools of the trade of the debtor or a dependent.

7. Any insurance contract that is not mature other than a credit contract.

8. The debtor's interest, not to exceed $4,000, in any accrued dividends or interest or loan value or any nonmature life insurance contract under which the debtor or a dependent is insured.

9. Prescribed health aids for the debtor or a dependent.

10. The debtor's right to receive Social Security benefits, unemployment compensation benefits, local public assistance benefits, veterans' benefits, and illness or disability benefits.

11. The debtor's right to receive alimony, support, or separate maintenance.

12. The debtor's right to receive a payment, stock bonus, pension, profit sharing annuity, or similar plan on account of illness, disability, debt, age, or want of service.

13. The debtor's right to receive an award under a crime victim's reparation law; a payment on account of a wrongful death of an individual of whom the debtor was a dependent; a payment under a life insurance contract that insured the life of an individual of whom the debtor was a dependent; a payment not to exceed $7,500 on account of personal bodily injury, not including pain and suffering or compensation for actual pecuniary loss, of the debtor or an individual of whom the debtor is a dependent; or a payment in compensation of loss of future earnings of the debtor or an individual of whom the debtor is or was a dependent.

The rest of the debtor's estate is distributed first to secured creditors and then to priority claimants. These claims include, in order: administrative expenses and filing fees assessed against the debtor's estate; certain unsecured claims arising before the appointment of a trustee in involuntary cases; wages, salaries, or commissions, including vacation, severance, and sick leave pay to the extent of $2,000 per individual earned within 90 days of the date of filing or the date of cessation of business, whichever occurred first; contributions to employee benefit plans up to $2,000 per employee earned within 180 days; claims of individuals, up to $900 each, arising from the deposit of money in connection with purchases of property or services that are not delivered; claims of governmental units of taxes and custom duties.

Next come the general unsecured creditors and the general unsecured creditors who filed late claims. Punitive penalties are next in distribution, followed by claims for interest accruing during the bankruptcy case. Interest is paid at the legal rate on the date the petition was filed. If there is any surplus after these six classes are paid, it goes to the debtor. If there aren't enough funds to pay a class in full, claims within the class are paid pro rata. The table below shows how assets are distributed in cases closed during 1977. It is interesting to note that fully 22.9 percent of the assets in bankruptcy cases were used to pay administrative expenses. (Note: These figures were the results of bankruptcies under the Bankruptcy Act, *not* the current code.)

Distribution of Assets in Cases Closed in 1977

	Payment	*Percent of Total*
Paid priority creditors	$ 27,799,506	12.1
Paid secured creditors	77,479,621	33.8
Paid unsecured creditors	61,109,352	26.6
Other payments	10,612,376	4.6
All administrative expenses	52,534,678	22.9
Total distribution	$229,535,533	100.0

Source: Table of Bankruptcy Statistics with reference to bankruptcy cases commenced and terminated in the United States District Courts during the period July 1, 1976, through June 30, 1977. Administrative Office of the United States Courts.

When the debtor is an individual, the court will usually grant *discharge*. This means the debtor is discharged from all past debts except certain debts arising from alimony, child support, and taxes, or debts that were not listed on the debtor's financial statements when bankruptcy was filed.

Chapter 11: Reorganization

The purpose of Chapter 11 of the new Bankruptcy Code is to provide a mechanism of reorganizing a firm's finances so it can continue to operate, pay its creditors, provide jobs, and produce a return to its investors. Usually debtors and creditors will opt for this form of bankruptcy if they think a business or estate has more value as a going concern than as a pile of liquidated assets. The objective of the reorganization is to develop a plan that determines how much creditors will be paid and in what form the business will continue. Any individual, partnership, or corporation that can file for liquidation under Chapter 7 can file for reorganization under Chapter 11, except stockbrokers and commodity brokers. Furthermore, railroads can proceed under Chapter 11, while they are prohibited from seeking liquidation.

Like a Chapter 7 case, a reorganization can be either voluntary or involuntary. After the entry for an Order for Relief, the creditors and debtor must meet within 30 days to discuss the organization of the business. Under the new Bankruptcy Code, the court may not attend a creditor's meeting. Rather, the interim trustee or the U.S. trustee will preside. This follows from the new code's attempt to correct previous problems caused by having bankruptcy judges serve as both judge and administrator in bankruptcy cases.

After the Order for Relief, the court will appoint a committee of general unsecured creditors. This committee is usually comprised of those creditors holding the seven largest claims; however the court has great latitude in composing the committee to make it representative of the different kinds of interests in the case. This committee is primarily responsible for formulating a plan for the business and collecting and filing with the court acceptances of the plan. The debtor keeps possession of the business unless any of the creditors can show the debtor is guilty of fraud, dishonesty, incompetence, or gross mismanagement, or otherwise proves such an arrangement is not in the interests of the creditors. If the court upholds that either of these conditions exists, a trustee will be appointed. Unlike a Chapter 7 trustee, a Chapter 11 trustee is not elected and cannot be a creditor or an equity holder of the debtor or the debtor's business. The duties of a Chapter 11 trustee include being accountable for all of the information and records necessary to formulate the reorganization plan and filing the plan with the court or recommending conversion to a Chapter 7 or a Chapter 13 case or dismissing the case altogether.

If a trustee is not appointed, the debtor possesses these powers. No court order is necessary for the debtor to continue to run the firm; rather, the business is to remain in operation unless the court orders otherwise.

The debtor has 120 days to file the reorganization plan and 60 more days to obtain acceptances. The plan must designate the various classes of creditors and show how they will be treated. The plan can be a liquidation. Thus, a business could be liquidated under Chapter 11 rather than Chapter 7. The plan must be accepted by half of the creditors in number who are affected by the plan and two thirds of the creditors in dollar amount. Creditors must vote to accept or reject the plan, and the plan must obtain the endorsement of a simple majority of those who vote. If the court confirms a reorganization plan, the debtor is discharged from any past debts except as they are handled under the new plan.

Chapter 13: Adjustment of Debts of an Individual with Regular Income

Chapter 13 of the new Bankruptcy Code covers individuals with regular income whose unsecured debts are less than $100,000 and whose secured debts are less than $350,000. This includes individuals who own or operate businesses. It does not include partnerships or corporations. There cannot be an involuntary Chapter 13 bankruptcy case.

The purpose of Chapter 13 is to allow an individual to pay off debts with future earnings while the court protects him or her from harassment by creditors. Furthermore, it allows the debtor to continue to own and operate a business while Chapter 13 is pending. A plan under Chapter 13 can be an extension—creditors paid in full—or a composition—creditors paid in part—and is payable over three years, with a two-year extension allowed for cause.

In a Chapter 13 case, the property of the estate includes property and earnings acquired after the commencement of the case but before it is closed. The court will appoint a Chapter 13 trustee to administer the case but not to take possession of the estate.

Chapter 13 has several major advantages for the debtor:

1. Once it is filed, all of the debtor's property and future income are under the court's jurisdiction. An automatic stay order is issued against litigation and collection efforts.

2. Unlike Chapter 7, the trustee does not take possession of the debtor's property. The debtor can increase his or her estate while on the plan.

3. Chapter 13 can help preserve the debtor's credit. Also, the six-year ban on filing for bankruptcy can be avoided in an extension plan and some compensation plans.

4. Since only the debtor can file a plan, there are no competing proposals.
5. The court can still convert a Chapter 13 case to a Chapter 11 case or a Chapter 7 case if it determines it is in the best interests of the creditors or the estate.

The court will hold a confirmation hearing on the plan. Secured creditors can stop confirmation if one of the following is violated: (*a*) they keep the lien securing their claims or (*b*) they receive the property securing their claims. Unsecured creditors have no voice in the confirmation process. The court will grant the debtor a discharge after all payments under the plans are completed.

Powers of Trustee

In addition to the responsibilities enumerated in Chapters 7, 11, and 13, the trustee in a bankruptcy case has a great deal of power that can determine how assets are allocated and debt restructured. Note that in some instances, the debtor himself (debtor-in-possession) is functioning as the trustee. Chapters 3 and 5 of the Bankruptcy Code set forth such powers as the ability to employ professionals to help carry out the duties of trustee; the power to use, sell, or lease property; the power to obtain credits secured by priority claims and new liens; the power to reject or assume contracts and unexpired leases; and the power to avoid preferences and fraudulent transfers, known as *the avoiding powers*. These powers can change the status of certain classes of creditors, depending on how they are applied. For instance, by rejecting an unexpired lease, the trustee can convert a long-term leaseholder into just another unsecured creditor. If a trustee is not appointed, then the debtor in possession of the estate assumes these powers.

Negotiations and Settlements

While they may feel persecuted and helpless, debtors actually have a great deal of power to negotiate with their creditors for arrangements that will leave the firm intact, either before or after bankruptcy is declared. This power stems from several sources: the incentive for all creditors to reach a speedy and workable solution to the debtor's financial problems; the differing interests of various classes of creditors; and the ultimate protection of the bankruptcy laws.

A debtor in serious financial shape may find he or she has a lot of leverage with creditors who fear the recourse of bankruptcy. These creditors may be willing to undertake voluntary arrangements to restructure loans, postpone payments, relinquish lease obligations, or ignore accrued interest, as a way of helping the debtor avoid bankruptcy. Creditors have several motivations for such voluntary arrangements. If the debtor is threatening to seek bankruptcy relief under Chapter 7, the creditors might determine they have a better long-run chance of repayment if the firm continues to exist than if it is dissolved and the assets are sold at low liquidation values. Creditors might also fear the high administrative and legal costs of bankruptcy proceedings, particularly in a complicated case. These costs might be incurred by the creditors directly or they might be incurred by the debtor's estate, thus reducing the amount of money for distribution to creditors. When Itel Corp., the computer leasing company, filed for bankruptcy in January 1981, it took two years for the company to be reorganized under Chapter 11. The first four months of administrative and legal expenses cost the estate $6.7 million. Creditors might also prefer a voluntary arrangement because it avoids the adverse publicity of a liquidation; they want the prospect of future business with the debtor; or such an arrangement appears faster than a court-supervised settlement. Sometimes creditors who want a voluntary arrangement will pay off the debtor's liabilities to other creditors just to avoid legal proceedings.

Debtors also derive power from the differing interests of creditors. As noted above, a creditor for whom speed of settlement is more important than full payment might negotiate with another creditor whose interest lies in full payment rather than a quick solution. In such an instance, both groups of creditors can be satisfied if the first pays the second's claims in order to expedite a settlement. Trade creditors and money creditors might have varying interests too, with trade creditors preferring a settlement that leaves the firm intact to do business in the future, and money creditors preferring a liquidation that provides as much cash as possible. Debtors can use this dichotomy to their advantage, using available cash to pay off money creditors while asking trade creditors to forbear in the hope of putting the firm back on solid financial ground rather than driving it into bankruptcy.

Of course, creditors do not have to be conciliatory. In 1978, Food Fair, Inc., ran into cash shortages, and its suppliers refused to extend credit beyond their normal terms. Angered by what they perceived as preferential treatment to suppliers with family connections to Food Fair's management, the supermarket's other suppliers refused to extend trade credit terms, even after the company significantly reduced its outstanding obligations. The firm was forced to seek bankrutpcy protection under Chapter 11.

In his book, *Corporations in Crisis*, Philip Nelson notes that the measures available to debtors and creditors short of filing for bankruptcy can lead to economic inefficiencies on the macro level:

> Focusing for the moment on the triggering decision, it appears that, because bankruptcy is only triggered when economic actors perceive that bankruptcy promotes their interests, social losses may easily accumulate as a firm struggles on outside the court's protection. In most sample cases, no economic actor had the incentive and the knowledge to trigger bankruptcy when it was needed. Executive preference for continued salaries, the distaste for the stigma of bankruptcy, inadequate information flows, and ignorance of the advantages offered by bankruptcy combine to encourage delays. Only at the few firms where the controlling executives associated relatively little stigma with bankruptcy and understood its advantages was bankruptcy triggered promptly. As a result, bankruptcy often comes after the resources of the firm are largely expended.

Despite this point of view, the debtor in each individual case certainly has the right and considerable power to cut the best possible deal.

Debtors also derive power within the framework of formal bankruptcy proceedings. Removed from a position of turmoil and harassment, where every unpaid creditor can hound the individual or corporation for immediate payment, the debtor who has filed for bankruptcy is suddenly in a position to bargain with creditors. Further, the automatic stay against all lawsuits that is provided by the bankruptcy law is an additional incentive for creditors to work out an acceptable plan. As with settlements that occur short of the bankruptcy proceeding, the debtor's leverage lies in the creditor's wish for a speedy, efficient plan that maximizes the wealth of the debtor for distribution or future payment. If the creditors retain some faith in the firm, there is usually a strong incentive to seek Chapter 11 relief. The debtor in this position can often negotiate a deal that will get the firm back on its feet. When Itel Corp. filed for bankruptcy, the firm received four 60-day extensions from the Bankruptcy Court to work out a reorganization package that would be acceptable to creditors. In the final deal, Itel's Eurobond holders were allowed $110 million of claims, although that class of creditors only had $91 million in principal and accrued interest outstanding when Itel filed for reorganization.

The distribution to Eurobond holders per $10,000 of claim was estimated by Itel's reorganization plan as follows:

Security	Face Amount	Market Value
Cash	$3,690	$3,690
14% secured notes	2,035	1,689–1,780
10% notes	1,032	443–501
New preferred stock	11.5 shares	259–305
New common stock	124.3 shares	186–311

Itel said one of the main reasons for increasing the amount of these creditors' claims was to avoid possible delays in the reorganization plan from pending litigation involving the Eurobonds.

The Bankruptcy Code was not intended to shift the balance of power away from creditors; it was designed to give both debtors and creditors motivation for seeking a solution that will maximize the settlement for both parties.

Debtor's Options

While the new Bankruptcy Code deals generously with debtors, providing a chance to discharge debts and begin again, no debtor wants to be thrown into bankruptcy proceedings against his or her will. There are several steps a debtor can take to ensure against involuntary bankruptcy. These include being sure that the number of creditors exceeds 12 and that no 3 creditors' claims amount to more than $5,000. Sometimes, this could mean paying off some creditors in full while not paying others all that they are due. If there are more than 12 creditors in a case, 1 or 2 claimants cannot force an individual or a corporation into involuntary bankruptcy.

There are many steps a debtor can take to maximize the amount of exempt assets that can be retained in a bankruptcy case. In contemplating bankruptcy, the debtor should examine exemptions closely and arrange his or her affairs in such a way as to give the best possible start following declaration. These measures should not be considered cheating or violating the law. The regulations were set to give debtors the best possible chance of regaining financial stability, while treating all creditors fairly.

There are also many actions a debtor *cannot* take under the law. Besides the obvious violation of hiding assets or hiding liabilities, the most important prohibition placed on debtors is that of preferential treatment. Once a debtor has filed for bankruptcy, the trustee has the power to disallow any payment to a creditor that enables that creditor to receive more than others in the same class. A preferential payment is one made 90 days prior to the bankruptcy. If the creditor was an insider, this limit extends to one year if the insider has cause to believe the debtor was insolvent. This provision ensures the bankruptcy policy of equality of distribution among creditors. Any creditor who manages to extort a larger share than others of the same class prior to the bankruptcy is forced to return it to the general pot for fair allocation. This provision also limits the debtor's ability to play one creditor off against others in an attempt to avoid bankruptcy, since creditors know such settlements could be disallowed if bankruptcy is declared within three months.

There are many avenues available for the savvy debtor to pursue, either before filing for bankruptcy or after such proceedings have been initiated. Debtors in financial trouble would be wise to seek competent legal counsel early so as to carve the best path out of their predicament.

References

Argenti, John. *Corporate Collapse: The Causes and Symptoms*. London: McGraw-Hill, 1976.

"Asbestosis: Manville Seeks Chapter 11." *Fortune*, September 20, 1982.

"Bankruptcy." Harvard Business School 9–376–221, prepared by Laurence H. Stone, copyright 1976.

Bankruptcy Reform. Washington, D.C.: American Enterprise Institute for Public Policy Research, 1978.

Barrickman, Ray E. *Business Failure: Causes, Remedies, and Cures*. Washington, D.C.: University Press of America, 1979.

Bluestein, Paul. "A $2.5 Billion Tale of Woe." *Forbes*, October 30, 1978, p. 51.

"A Brief Note on Arrangements, Bankruptcy, and Reorganization in Bankruptcy." Harvard Business School 9–272–148, rev. 7/75, written by Jasper H. Arnold, Research Assistant, under the supervision of Associate Professor Michael L. Tennican.

Disclosure Statement for Itel Corporation's Amended Plan of Reorganization, Case No. 3–81–00111, December 8, 1982.

Drinkhall, Jim. "Fees Charged by Itel's Overseers Suggest Bankruptcy Can Be Enriching Experience." *The Wall Street Journal*, June 5, 1981, p. 27.

"Food Fair Inc. Seeks Protection under Chapter 11." *The Wall Street Journal*, October 3, 1978, p. 2.

"Itel Corp. Plans to Amend Plan for Reorganization." *The Wall Street Journal*, January 20, 1982, p. 33.

"Itel Corp. Receives More Time to Submit Reorganization Plan." *The Wall Street Journal*, November 16, 1981, p. 23.

"Itel Files Petition for Protection of Chapter 11." *The Wall Street Journal,* January 20, 1981, p. 4.

"Manville's Costs Could Exceed $5 Billion in Asbestos Suits, Study It Ordered Shows." *The Wall Street Journal,* September 15, 1982, p. 7.

Nelson, Philip B. *Corporations in Crisis: Behavioral Observations for Bankrupt Policy.* New York: Praeger Publishers, 1981.

Quittner, Arnold M. *Current Developments in Bankruptcy and Reorganization.* Practicing Law Institute, 1980.

Schnepper, Jeff A. *The New Bankruptcy Law: A Professional's Handbook.* New York: Addison-Wesley Publishing, 1981.

Table of Bankruptcy Statistics with reference to bankruptcy cases commenced and terminated in the United States District Courts during the period July 1, 1978, through June 30, 1979. Administrative Office of the United States Courts. See also July 1, 1976, through June 30, 1977.

"Unpaid Bills: Itel Goes Bust." *Fortune,* February 23, 1981, p. 19.

"Wilson Foods Seeks Chapter 11 Protection Citing Labor Costs, Cuts Wages Up to 50%." *The Wall Street Journal,* April 24, 1983, p. 16.

15 SECURITIES LAW AND PUBLIC OFFERINGS

In "Securities Law and Private Financing," we looked at the process and laws that affected private financings. In this piece, we will look at similar issues as they relate to public offerings.

Why "Go Public"?

For many companies, the decision on whether or not to become a public company is a difficult one. For some, the "glamour and prestige" of becoming a public company are the deciding factors. For others, the scrutiny and lack of privacy that go along with being publicly held clearly outweigh the advantages.

The Advantages

There are some significant advantages that go along with being a public company. They include,

- A vast continuing source of capital: The public equity markets do represent a vast pool of capital. A healthy, growing firm can often tap this source more cheaply than other private sources of equity. And, as the company continues to grow, the public equity market will be available as long as investors have confidence in the company's prospects.
- Liquidity: A public market for the company's securities makes them far more liquid. The company can give employees stock or options as an incentive to lure talented individuals. And the principals of the firm can (subject to certain SEC regulations) sell their stock as they desire.
- Wealth creation: Taking a company public establishes its value in the market. In addition, through a "secondary offering" of securities, the principals can often sell a portion of their interest at the time of the initial public offering. This creates wealth for both the founders and the financial backers—such as venture capital firms—who invested in the business.

This note was prepared by Michael J. Roberts, Howard H. Stevenson and Richard E. Floor, of Goodwin, Procter & Hoar, Boston.

- Glamour and prestige: For many individuals, "taking their company public" is an important goal. It certainly is one measure of success, as a certain minimum size is generally required in order to take a firm public. Being a public concern may also enhance the company's image with customers, suppliers, and employees.

For some entrepreneurs, these advantages are outweighed by the disadvantages of being a public concern.

The Disadvantages

The disadvantages include:

- Cost: Going public is expensive; estimates run from $100,000 to over $300,000 for an "average" public offering. In addition, there is an underwriters' commission of 7 to 10 percent, which goes to compensate the investment bank for selling the securities. Finally, there is an annual expense associated with the added accounting and record-keeping required for a public company.
- Public scrutiny: A public company must file, and make available to the public, its financial statements, as well as certain information about stockholders, customers, business plans, and officers. A company might prefer that its suppliers, customers, and competitors not know how profitable it is, or be aware of some aspect of its business. Finally, certain business practices, such as officers' salaries and business expenses, also come under public scrutiny.
- Pressures on management: Being a public concern also puts certain pressures on top management. The stock market likes to see constant earnings growth, and the faster the better. There has been a great deal of publicity lately that this "short-term earnings focus" is the cause of serious longer-term competitive problems for many American industries. Finally, management must spend a good deal of time dealing with the financial community, keeping bankers and analysts up to date and interested in the stock.
- Loss of independence: As a sole owner or small group of principals, management could feel securely in control. But public ownership brings with it a larger constituency. Managers must now manage the company for the good of all the shareholders. Previously borderline "business expenses" may now be totally inappropriate. In addition, there is always the possibility that some outside group may actually try to take over the company. As a public concern, management is far more vulnerable.

These disadvantages are accentuated by the close relationship that usually exists between ownership and management in the entrepreneurial concern. In large public companies, these "disadvantages" have been accepted as a way of life by a management team, which typically controls very little of the stock. In entrepreneurial firms, where the founder(s) may still hold a majority of the shares, the distinction between management and ownership may easily blur. This can lead to management that manages for itself rather than the entire group of stockholders. While this can happen in large companies, minority shareholders in small firms have less chance of successfully combating this practice.

The Decision

The decision to go public is an important one and should be made with the counsel of experienced accountants, lawyers, and bankers. Remember, though, that these people have their own stakes: the investment banker stands to gain a good deal on the sale of the company's securities; a local accountant often loses out to a Big Eight firm when a company goes public and seeks an accounting firm with a national reputation.

In general, it does seem that many entrepreneurs overestimate some of the benefits of being a public company. Liquidity, for instance, is often seen as a major advantage. But it is a very difficult task indeed for a president to explain at an analysts meeting why he ''dumped'' some of his holdings in the market.

Clearly, the need for equity capital must be at the heart of the firm's decision to go public. And, before wandering down this path, the firm would be well advised to consider other options, such as a private placement of debt or equity.

Selecting an Underwriter

Once a company has made a decision to seriously consider going public, it is time to choose an underwriter. Underwriters, or investment bankers, are required both to sell the securities and lead the company through this complex process.

Choosing an Underwriter

The process of selecting an underwriter is not easy. Many investment banks will be anxious to serve the company and will make convincing arguments about why their firms are well suited to execute the company's public offering. When choosing a firm, the following criteria are important.

- Reputation: The underwriter's name will appear at the bottom of the prospectus, often in letters as large as the company's name. The underwriter's reputation will affect its ability to sell the stock both to other investment banks and to institutional and retail customers.
- Distribution: Investment banks have certain strengths and weaknesses in terms of their ability to distribute the stock. Some have a strong institutional network selling to large pension funds and money managers. Others sell primarily to retail accounts—private investors.
- It is often desirable to have a mix of stockholders. Institutions have deep pockets, but can be unfaithful, deserting and selling a stock on the first sign of bad news. Retail accounts tend to be more stable, but are not as big a force in the stock market.

- Aftermarket support: It is important that a bank support a company after the public offering. This support includes:

  - Research—to sustain interest in the stock on the part of investors.
  - Market-making—committing capital to buying and selling the stock, to provide investors with liquidity.
  - Financial advice—bankers can provide valuable advice on the subject of dividends, new financing, or mergers and acquisitions.

Recently, underwriters have become more competitive, and investment banking is not the "gentlemanly business" it was considered to be years ago. The entrepreneur would be wise to consider and negotiate with a variety of firms.

What about Stock Price?

Note that we have not mentioned price as one of the criteria. Clearly, you would prefer to sell stock in your company to the underwriters who thought it was worth the most in the market. During the negotiation process, underwriters will often "estimate" the price at which the stock will be sold in the public offering.

- First, they make projections of the company's earnings per share.
- Then, they attempt to place a price/earnings multiple on this figure to arrive at a per share value.

In theory, this approach should work just fine. But the price/earnings multiple is a very subjective judgment, based on an assessment of what multiples "similar" companies are trading at.

The night before the offering, after many months of work and after spending a good deal of money, the market will in all likelihood appear quite different than it did at the time of the initial negotiations. The underwriter may suggest an offering price that is substantially different from the price discussed during negotiations. The company has little choice save to cancel the offering entirely.

This fact is *not* lost on the underwriters.

Other Issues

Once a company has decided to go public, and chosen an underwriter, several other important issues remain.

- Listing: The company must decide where its shares will be listed and traded. The New York and American Stock Exchanges, as well as other exchanges, all have certain requirements that must be met in order for the firm to obtain a listing.
- Amount of primary offering: The firm must decide how much money it wishes to raise.
- Amount of secondary offering: In addition to selling its "own shares"—the primary offering—the principals of the firm may sell some of their own stock.

This is called a *secondary offering,* and the owners of the stock, *not* the company, get to keep the money that is raised from sale of secondary stock.

Registered Offerings

All public offerings must be registered with the SEC under the Securities Act of 1933.

The Registration Process

The registration process for a company that is not yet publicly traded involves the preparation by management of a carefully worded and organized disclosure document called a *registration statement.* This includes a "prospectus," which will be provided to the potential investor. The registration statement is filed with the appropriate securities agency, which, for federal registrations, is the SEC. The various items of disclosure that must be discussed in a registration statement are fixed by law. In addition, there must be set forth any other material matter that affects or may affect the company.

The SEC staff reviews the disclosure documents and (unless a special "cursory review" procedure is used) makes detailed comments on the disclosure, and the documents are revised as a result of these comments. If the staff is satisfied with the revisions, the SEC enters an order declaring the registration statement "effective," and sale of the offering may commence. The SEC order in no way constitutes an approval by the SEC of the accuracy of the disclosures or the merits of the offering, and any representation to that effect violates the securities laws. At the time of the effectiveness of the registration statement, the underwriters will usually place a "tombstone" advertisement in the financial press announcing the offering. A copy of the final prospectus in an initial public offering must be distributed to persons purchasing company securities of the type sold in the offering for 25 days after the effective date, or until the offering is sold or terminated, whichever occurs last. During this period, if any material event affecting the company occurs, it must be disclosed by a sticker "supplement" to the prospectus. In general, the disclosure documents become outdated after approximately nine months from the effective date and may not be used thereafter unless updated by posteffective amendment to the registration statement.

Cost

Federal registration is expensive and time consuming. An initial public offering using an underwriter frequently takes four months to accomplish and costs from $150,000 to $300,000, exclusive of underwriting commissions. A typical cost breakdown is as follows: printing, $75,000; legal fees, $100,000; accounting fees, $50,000; and Blue Sky and miscellaneous costs, $25,000. (These figures are rough and may vary considerably from offering to offering.) In view of the amount of the costs involved, federal registration of a first offering using an underwriter is generally not feasible unless in excess of $2 million is involved in the financing.

The cost of a public offering depends as much upon whether or not an underwriter is used as upon whether or not federal registration is required. This is true because the agreement between the company and the underwriter usually requires the company's attorneys and accountants to undertake at the company's expense detailed and costly verification of the disclosures in the prospectus. Underwriting commissions typically run from 7 1/2 percent to 10 percent of the gross amount of the offering in first equity offerings. The underwriter may also require warrants to purchase an amount of stock equal to 10 percent of the shares sold at the offering at a small premium over the offering price as additional compensation. Because placement of a large amount of securities often involves market price stabilization and other sophisticated and highly regulated techniques, an attempt by a company to place a large amount of securities without a professional underwriter or selling agent usually involves an unacceptable amount of risk. Also, it may be extremely difficult for a large amount of securities to be placed without the assistance of a professional underwriter or selling agent with a number of investor customers that rely upon his or her investment advice.

Underwriters

Underwriters essentially agree to sell the company's securities for a fixed percentage of the underwriting. Underwritings are of two types—''firm-commitment'' underwritings in which the sale of the entire offering at an established price is guaranteed by the underwriters and ''best-efforts'' underwritings in which the underwriter uses his best efforts to sell as much as he can of the offering at the offering price. Best-efforts underwritings may also include a provision requiring that either all or a minimum amount of the securities must be sold as a condition of any of the securities being sold. The type of underwriting used is usually determined by the size and strength of the company and of the underwriter.

The first step in an underwritten offering is usually the execution of a nonbinding ''letter of intent'' between the company (or selling stockholder) and the managing underwriter. Although not a legally binding document, the letter of intent is one of the most important documents in the offering, as it establishes the basic terms of the underwriting, usually including the price range—perhaps as a range of multiples of the company's most recent earnings. (If multiples of per share earnings are used, it should be made clear whether the per share figures are to be calculated using the number of outstanding shares before or those after the offering.) After the letter of intent has been signed, the disclosure documents (including the prospectus) are prepared for filing with the SEC.

From the outset of an underwritten offering, the managing underwriter and the company (or selling stockholder) commence subtle negotiation of the price of the offering, which is usually culminated by the setting of the price on the evening before the offering. During the course of the registration, the company incurs substantial offering expenses, which (as both parties well realize) will be to a large extent unrecoverable if the financing is postponed or aborted. In addition to the problems a firm-commitment underwriter has in guaranteeing sale of the entire offering when the price is at a high level, a managing underwriter has an incentive to negotiate a low price for his or her own customers and for those of the members of his or her underwriting and selling syndicate, with which she or he usually has an established business relationship. (A broker with unhappy customers soon has no customers.) She or he often does this by subtly threatening to abandon the deal after the company has expended substantial unrecoverable funds in preparation for the offering and after it has terminated negotiations with competing underwriters. It is thus important for the company, if possible, to require the underwriter to bear his or her own expenses (including attorneys' fees) so that any abandonment will result in some loss (although a lesser one) for the underwriter. This arrangement should be set forth in the letter of intent. On the other hand, the offering price should not be set too high or the price of the securities may suffer in the aftermarket, thereby reducing the value of the remaining securities holdings of the principal owners and diminishing the company's ability to raise capital in the future.

Throughout the period of registration, including the prospectus delivery period following the effective date, the company must carefully monitor the public statements of its management, its public relations advisors, and its advertising program to assure that no optimistic disclosures concerning the company's condition or prospects are disseminated to the investing public. If, for example, an article on the company appears in *Forbes* or *Business Week* during registration, it may be deemed to be part of the company's selling effort (to the extent it is based upon information supplied by management) and thus subject to the rigid standards of the securities laws. Disclosure during the period preceding the initial filing of the registration statement with the SEC (the "prefiling period") is particularly sensitive, as such disclosure might be considered to be an attempt to precondition the market ("gun-jumping"). Even the information to be contained in an announcement of the filing of the registration statement is regulated by SEC rule. After the effective date, however, certain types of supplementary selling literature may be used if preceded or accompanied by a final prospectus.

The registration statement as initially filed contains a preliminary prospectus with a "red herring" legend printed in red sideways on the cover page. While the SEC staff is reviewing the registration statement and preparing its comments (the "waiting period"), the preliminary prospectus will be used by the underwriter in the formation of its underwriting and selling syndicate. Although the various members of the underwriting and selling syndicate often have an established business relationship with the managing underwriter, a new syndicate is formed for each deal. The preliminary prospectus will be used by syndicate members during the waiting period to solicit "indications of interest" from the investing public. The reception of the investing public to the preliminary prospectus will affect the price of the offering, which, as noted above, is usually established immediately prior to the effective date.

As a result of registration with the SEC, a company becomes subject to the periodic reporting requirements of the SEC. In the case of a first public offering, the company must report the actual use of proceeds to the SEC three months after the offering so the SEC can compare this with the disclosures in the prospectus. If there is a discrepancy, the company can expect SEC inquiry.

Offerings registered with the SEC generally must also be registered with the securities administrators of each of the states in which the offering is to be made. A simplified registration by "coordination" with the federal registration is usually allowed under state law. Many states do exempt from registration offerings of securities that will be listed on the New York or American Stock Exchange. If an underwriter or selling agent that is a member of the NASD is used, the terms of the underwriters' or sales agents' compensation must be reviewed by the NASD.

Form SB-2

In 1992, the SEC adopted a new form to simplify public offerings for smaller companies. The new form replaced Form S-18, which allowed expedited filing procedures and simplified disclosure requirements for companies engaged in small initial public offerings. Under Form SB-2, these advantages are now available to small business issuers, defined as companies with under $25 million in revenues and a public float of under $25 million, making any form of public offering.

The principal features of Form SB-2 are (*a*) the filing is made in the local SEC regional office (nine offices around the country) rather than in Washington; (*b*) an audited balance sheet is required for only the most recent fiscal year, and audited statements of income, cash flows, and changes in stockholders' equity are required for only the two most recent years; (*c*) the general disclosures are significantly simpler and are tailored for smaller and less mature companies. The primary advantage of Form SB-2 is dealing with the lighter workloads and geographical proximity of the regional offices. These, coupled with the reduced disclosure requirements, could be expected to reduce by 25 percent or more both the amount of time and the expenses involved in an offering.

The use of Form SB-2 is limited to offerings by domestic or Canadian issuers that are not investment companies or the subsidiaries of companies that are not small business issuers. If Form SB-2 is used to register an initial public offering, the offering may not be expected to result in a public float of greater than $25 million. The company must also report the use of the proceeds of an initial public offering to the SEC within 10 days after the first three-month period following the effective date of the registration statement, and within 10 days after the application of the offering proceeds of the termination of the offering.

Regulation A Offerings

If the financing involves a public offering on behalf of the company of $5 million or less, and if the company's management, principal equity owners, and other persons whose securities require registration before resale seek to publicly offer not more than $1.5 million as part of that offering, the offering may be made under SEC Regulation A rather than pursuant to full registration. When considering such an offering, an issuer must be aware of several potential obstacles. For example, a company may not issue more than $5 million of its securities under Regulation A during any 12-month period, and for purposes of calculating that limitation, any offerings made pursuant to an exemption or in violation of the registration requirements are included. Further, insiders and affiliates may sell pursuant to Regulation A only if the company has had profitable operations during one of its last two fiscal years. Finally, the exemption is totally unavailable to issuers that have been *inter alia,* convicted of violating the securities laws or subjected to an SEC refusal or stop order, post office fraud order or injunction within the previous five years, or whose directors, officers, principal security holders, or underwriters have been convicted of violating the securities laws within the previous 10 years or enjoined from violating the same.

Assuming availability of the exemption, the Regulation A offering procedure is similar to that used with Form SB-2 and is similarly less complex. The primary difference between Form SB-2 and the use of Regulation A is that the latter has no requirement for audited financials. In addition, issuers contemplating a Regulation A offering may "test the waters" before preceding if they file the solicitation materials with the SEC before use and then allow a 20-day cooling-off period before the first sale.

A 90-day prospectus delivery period exists for Regulation A offerings. After each six-month period following the date of the original offering circular and within 30 days following the completion of the offering, the company must report the use of proceeds to the SEC.

Like fully registered offerings, Regulation A offerings must be registered (usually by "coordination") with the securities administrators for the states in which the offering is to be made. Use of an underwriter that is a member of the NASD requires NASD review. In practice, the "Reg. A" offering is little used.

State-Registered (Intrastate) Offerings (Rule 147)

If a local business seeks local financing exclusively, registration under the federal securities laws is not required. More accurately, if all of the "offerees" and purchasers in the offering are bona fide residents of the state under the laws of which the company is organized (e.g., the state of incorporation, if the company is a corporation), if the company's business is principally conducted and the company's properties principally located in that state, and if the proceeds of the offering are to be used in the state, the issuer may avail itself of exemption under SEC Rule 147. In such instances, the financing may be made pursuant to a long form ("qualification") registration under the state securities laws.

As a matter of practice, exclusive reliance upon the Rule 147 exemption is a somewhat perilous course. In order to satisfy Rule 147, the issuer must meet various technical requirements as to "residence," some of which are included in Rule 147 and some of which relate to common law standards. At the time of sale, for example, the issuer must obtain from the purchaser a written representation of his residence. Yet there is no provision in the rule that will protect the issuer from a good faith mistake in determining the residence of a purchaser. Moreover, should even a single purchaser resell to a nonresident within nine months of the offering, the exemption will be lost. To prevent this latter problem, certificates evidencing the securities offered under Rule 147 must bear a legend reflecting these transfer restrictions and a "stop transfer" order must be entered.

Rule 147 also provides a means for segregating an intrastate offering from other discrete offerings pursuant to other exemptive provisions of the act. In order to have

Rule 147 available, an issuer must not have sold any similar securities to purchasers outside the state in the prior six months and may not make any such sales in the subsequent six months. Rule 147 does not require the filing of any documents.

Because registration-by-qualification requirements vary widely from state to state, it is impossible to estimate the costs of a Rule 147 offering. Such costs are generally somewhat less than are those for Regulation A offerings, however. As in the case of other offerings, NASD review is required if a NASD member serves as underwriter or sales agent.

Acquisitions

Like any other securities, securities issued by a company in the acquisition of another company must be registered under federal and state securities laws unless an exemption from registration applies. Most state securities laws provide registration exemptions for acquisitions by statutory merger or stock for assets. Under federal law, however, full registration is required unless either the intrastate or private offering exemption is available. Thus, regardless of the form of the transaction and the number of separate steps it may involve, the company must consider its overall effect and the identity of ultimate recipients of the securities in determining the availability of an exemption.

Under present law, solicitation of the target company's shareholders requesting the execution of proxies to vote on the acquisition is deemed to constitute an offering of the acquirer's securities. If the private or intrastate offering exemptions are unavailable, the acquirer must therefore register. A registration procedure is available under SEC Form S-4, which requires information about both the acquirer and the target. Form S-4 permits the incorporation by reference of material previously filed under the SEC's annual reporting requirements for companies that are already public. The prospectus under a Form S-4 registration statement is often made up of a proxy statement conforming to SEC rules, to which a cover sheet setting forth the terms of the offering has been added — the combination sometimes being referred to as a "wrap-around" prospectus. As with other offerings, the various state securities laws must also be reviewed.

Securities received by the acquired company's management or principal equity owners as a result of an acquisition are restricted and can be resold only if the resale is registered, exempt, or permitted under Rule 145 (which is similar to Rule 144 but without a holding period or filing requirement). Resales pursuant to a registration statement are particularly hazardous, however, because management may be held personally liable for misstatements in the prospectus concerning the acquiring company as well as any concerning their own company. The risk of liability in this situation is great, as the target company's management rarely has access to information concerning the sometimes unfriendly acquirer.

Acquisitions of equity securities of public companies for either cash or securities is further discussed below in connection with tender offers and takeover bids. See also "Investment Companies" for regulation under certain circumstances.

Disclosure of Material Inside Information

In any purchase or sale of a security, whether public or private, if one of the parties has any nonpublic material inside information that relates to the present or future condition of the company's business or its properties, he must disclose it to the person on the opposite side of the transaction or be personally liable under the antifraud provisions of the securities laws for any damages that may result. Similar liability will accrue to any person who aids and abets the misuse of inside information by tipping others or otherwise even if that person does not actually trade. In this regard, both ''tippers'' and ''tippees'' are liable under the law.

This simple principle is at the heart of all securities laws and yet is perhaps the most abused. The courts' necessarily amorphous definition of *materiality* is partially responsible for this abuse: any fact which, under the circumstances, would likely have assumed actual significance to a reasonable investor is deemed material. The liabilities can be enormous in scope, and prudent companies and their management should either disclose significant information or, if such information is particularly sensitive, refrain from trading.

One emerging area of securities law deserves special mention because of the magnitude of the exposure involved and the ease in which violations may occur. If any public pronouncement by a public company (whether by press release, report to stockholders, or otherwise) contains a statement concerning the company's condition or prospects that is erroneous or misleading in a way that is material to an investor, so that the price of the company's securities in the securities markets is affected (either up or down), the company, its management, and its principal owners may be personally liable for any ensuing loss to *all* persons who trade in the company's securities to their disadvantage in the open market, regardless of whether or not management, the company's owners, or the company are concurrently trading in the company's securities in the market. Cases decided in this area so far indicate that management must have some ulterior purpose for the misinformation in order to be held liable; however, this purpose need not include any intention to violate the securities laws.

Manipulation

The securities laws broadly prohibit use of fraudulent or manipulative devices of any type in the purchase or sale of securities, whether in private transactions or in the securities markets. Specifically, market manipulation of securities prices up or down or at any level (except in connection with stabilization in a public offering, as to which special rules apply) or falsely creating the appearance of security trading activity—by the use of fictitious orders, wash sales, or other devices—is prohibited. Again, violation can lead to substantial personal as well as company liability.

Regulation of Public Companies

Companies of significant size that have a larger number of security holders, and companies that are listed on a national securities exchange, are regulated under the

Securities Exchange Act of 1934. The filing reporting requirements of this statute attach when the company files a registration statement under the Exchange Act as a result of being listed on a national securities exchange or of having in excess of $5 million in total assets and in excess of 500 holders of a class of its equity securities at the end of one of its fiscal years, or following the effectiveness of a Securities Act Registration statement. (A registration statement under the Securities Exchange Act of 1934 should not be confused with a public offering registration statement under the Securities Act of 1933.) Registration under the Exchange Act submits the company to the periodic reporting, proxy, tender offer, and insider trading provisions of that act. Once registered, the number of equity security holders must drop below 500 and its assets must have been below $5 million for three years before the company may be deregistered.

Periodic Reports

In order to maintain a constant flow of reliable information to the SEC and the financial community, companies registered under the Exchange Act and those that have previously undertaken full registration under the Securities Act are subject to the periodic reporting requirements of the SEC. Under these requirements, the company must file with the SEC annual reports (containing audited financial statements) on Form 10-K, quarterly reports on Form 10-Q, and current reports on Form 8-K. These reports are generally available to the public through the SEC.

Subsequent Offerings

The "continuous disclosure" effect of the periodic reporting requirements has led the SEC to adopt two simplified forms (Form S-2 and Form S-3) for the registration of sales of securities by public companies and their affiliates (secondary offerings). These forms permit the incorporation by reference of material previously filed as periodic reports and may therefore be shorter and simpler. In many cases, the SEC will permit such registrations to become effective immediately without subjecting them to the SEC review and comment process.

Proxy Solicitations

To ensure that security holders of companies registered under the Exchange Act are advised of proposals (including the election of directors) to be acted upon at meetings of security holders, such companies must use proxy or information statements that conform to SEC rules. Such proxy statements are reviewed by the SEC staff prior to distribution to security holders. They must be transmitted at least annually and upon each proxy solicitation to the company's voting security holders. The form of the proxy itself is also regulated.

Tender Offers and Takeover Bids

Tender offers to acquire the securities of a company whose securities registered under the Exchange Act (other than offers by a company to repurchase its own shares, which are regulated separately) must conform to the SEC tender offer rules. These require the filing of certain information with the target company and the SEC not later than the date the tender offer is first made. Securities tendered are recoverable by the tenderer while the offer is open. Acceptance of less than all of the shares in a tender offer must be on a pro rata basis. Of course, if the tender is being made using securities of the acquiring company rather than cash, they must be registered under the Securities Act prior to the offering.

In order to alert the SEC and the management of a target company to an acquisition of securities that could lead to a change of control, any person acquiring any equity security of an Exchange Act–registered company, which results in his owning in excess of 5 percent of the outstanding securities of that class, must file with the SEC within 10 days after the acquisition. He must also transmit to the company certain information concerning the acquiring person, his purpose in making the acquisition, and his method of financing the acquisition. This requirement applies even if the shares were received as a result of an acquisition in which the acquirer exchanged some of its equity securities in return for securities of the acquired company. If two or more persons who together own in excess of 5 percent of a class of equity securities of an Exchange Act–registered company enter into a mutual arrangement, they too must file Form 13 D within 10 days after entering of the arrangement.

If either of the above transactions results in an appointment of a majority of directors for the company other than by vote of security holders, there must be transmitted to all security holders eligible to vote for the election of such directors if elected at a meeting of security holders, at least 10 days prior to the appointment, information equivalent to that contained in a proxy or information statement under the proxy rules.

The securities laws of some states contain tender offer provisions designed to discourage takeover of corporations based in those states or whose principal business and substantial assets are within the state. The federal laws, however, do not purport to discourage tender offers directly but rather seek to ensure full disclosure of information concerning such offers.

Insider Reporting and Trading

Management and 10 percent equity security holders are deemed *insiders* of an Exchange Act–registered company and must report their transactions in the company's equity securities to the SEC on forms 3 and 4. An annual report on Form 5 is also required to catch up with any transactions during the year that may have been exempt from the monthly filings. The SEC publishes these transactions quarterly.

The insider trading provisions of the Exchange Act contain a section, 16 b(3), which includes an absolute six-month trading rule designed to preclude any incentive for insiders to make use of insider information to gain for themselves short-term profits by trading in the company's securities.

If both a purchase and a sale or a sale and purchase of such securities by an insider falls within any six-month period, any security holder of the company may sue on behalf of the company to recover for the company the "profits" thereby obtained. The word *profits* has a technical meaning in this context and does not necessarily refer to any benefit obtained by the insider—in fact, the insider may have incurred a net overall loss in a series of such transactions and still be liable to the company for substantial sums. The formula used by the courts in measuring the recovery is to match the highest sale with the lowest purchase in any six-month period, then to match the next highest sale with the next lowest purchase, and so on, so that the largest possible amount of profits from any given set of trades is thereby computed. Since theoretical losses incurred are not offset against theoretical profits, the liability to the insider can be substantial even though he sustains an overall loss.

That an insider, in fact, is not trading on inside information is no defense to an insider trading suit. In fact, if an insider purchase and sale have both occurred within six months, there is virtually no defense to a timely and properly prosecuted insider trading suit, and the best course of action is usually to pay the profits to the company as quickly as possible to minimize the ample legal fees that are usually awarded by the courts to plaintiff's counsel in such actions. These suits may be brought by anyone with standing.

Investment Companies

A company whose principal business is investing or trading in securities is subject to regulation under the Investment Company Act of 1940, unless it has not made and is not making a public offering and has fewer than 100 security holders. Although this act is primarily directed toward mutual funds, it also regulates companies that inadvertently fall within the statutory definition of *investment company*. Thus, if a public company sells a major portion of its assets, and, rather than distributing the proceeds to its security holders, holds and invests the proceeds in other than government or commercial paper while exploring alternate business activities, it may be deemed to have become an investment company. "Hedge funds" and investment clubs that rely upon the private offering exemption become investment companies when the exemption is lost and the offering becomes public, or when they have more than 100 participants.

Summary

We have attempted to describe the factors that influence an entrepreneur's decision on whether or not to take a company public. We have also tried to describe the complex process of raising equity through the public markets.

Our placement of this piece in the section on "Managing and Harvesting the Venture" bears explaining. We do not mean to imply that going public is a clean exit route for the entrepreneur to take his or her money and move on. While the entrepreneur can often get some money out of the business in a public offering, a large portion of his or her equity will undoubtedly still be tied up in the venture. Rather, we mean to imply that the decision relative to going public is one that is made after the business's start-up. It is a decision about where to obtain capital for growth.

4–1 GORDON BIERSCH BREWING COMPANY

It was January 1992. The San Francisco restaurant was three months behind schedule and now was not expected to open until March 1992. As a result, it was consuming most of management's time. The duo had just finished the 1991 fiscal year and had reported revenues of over $5.9 million and net profit of over $570,000. Meanwhile, the two founders of Gordon Biersch Brewing Company, Dan Gordon and Dean Biersch, were determined to expand beyond their three existing restaurants in Palo Alto, San Jose, and San Francisco, and they were in the process of pursuing the funds to finance these plans. The plans had two parts: to engage in retail distribution of their Märzen and Export beers and to open more restaurant/breweries based on the same concept as their established restaurants. To them, these ideas seemed a logical extension of their success. Thus, their most pressing decision was not whether or not to pursue these plans. Instead, they wanted to know from whom they should obtain their financing and whether they had the appropriate organizational structure in place to accomplish their goals successfully.

Gordon and Biersch Meet

Gordon Biersch Brewing Company was the brainchild of two individuals, Dan Gordon and Dean Biersch, each of whom independently developed the concept of a micro-brewery/restaurant in response to a 1983 change in California law. The new law allowed the brewing and serving of beer in the same locale. The previous law had existed to regulate national brewers, as an enforcement of antitrust laws. The "three-tier laws" separated the producer, the distributor, and the retailer, dictating that businesses with liquor licenses could own no more than 10 percent of a brewery. When this changed in 1983, brewpubs started appearing. By 1991, brewpubs accounted for 25 percent of microbrewery production. Many of these microbrewery/restaurants emulated English pubs by serving heavy fried food like french fries and hamburgers, while offering recreation in the form of darts. Both Gordon and Biersch had a different idea.

This case was prepared by L. A. Snedeker under the supervision of H. Irving Grousbeck. All figures have been disguised.

Development of this case was funded by the James G. Shennan (MBA '65) Teaching Fund.

Stanford Business School Case S–SB–130

Dan Gordon, a likable guy with a relaxed outward demeanor that belied his quick mind and acuity, grew up in Los Altos, California. As an economics major at U.C. Berkeley, Gordon spent his junior year as an exchange student in Germany, learning the language and immersing himself in the beer-drinking culture. He graduated the following year, 1982, and worked during the summer as a union laborer for Budweiser. He then returned to Germany to enter the Technical University of Munich. The university's brewing program was rigorous and intense, taught entirely in German and composed of courses in microbiology, chemistry, process engineering, and business. The entire program was five years long, and only 18 percent ultimately graduated. Gordon did, receiving his Dpl. Br. Ing. degree in 1987. This degree was considered the highest technical degree in brewing engineering. Moreover, Gordon was the first American to receive the degree in 30 years. Gordon returned the following summer with plans to open his own German brewery restaurant. He proceeded to write a business plan for a restaurant in Sunnyvale, California, to be known as Gordon's Beer Clinic.

Dean Biersch, a man with high energy and a flair for quality of life, grew up in Southern California. His career was structured around his attraction to food service and his desire to surf and ski. At 15, he began cooking burgers in the evenings to finance his athletic pursuits. After that, he worked as the manager of a liquor store while participating on his high school ski team. At Mammoth Mountain one day, he met a man who promised him a job if he moved up there. He did, but when he got there, he discovered there was in fact no job. Biersch had deferred his college plans, so he decided to stay anyway (since, after all, he could ski every day). Undeterred, he visited an employment agency that got him a job cooking in a little restaurant at night. This left his days free to ski, and he stayed there for a year. Next, at age 20, Biersch went to Portugal for a year to surf with some friends.

He then began college, San Francisco State University, from which he graduated in 1982 (at age 26) with a B.A. in international relations. During summers, between 1979 and 1982, he worked at the Beverly Hills Hilton, first as a server and then eventually as catering manager, maitre d', and office manager. From there, he worked as catering manager and food and beverage manager for Hornblower Yachts, Inc., in San Francisco. This company organized parties on cruises around the San Francisco Bay. While employed there, Biersch established management systems for the "City of San Francisco," a vessel in the Hornblower fleet, and was responsible for all of its food and beverage-related services.

Biersch's idea to combine a fine restaurant with a microbrewery dated back to 1983, when he and a girlfriend wrote a business plan for one in Mendocino, California. Despite his efforts to obtain financing, even attending a microbrewery convention on one occasion, he was unable to do it alone. A family friend, Robert Carrau, a very successful real estate developer, read a business plan from a different brewery/restaurant group and decided to pursue the idea with Biersch. Biersch left Hornblower to work with Carrau, and eight months later, in July of 1987, Biersch and Gordon met. The duo soon decided to enter into a partnership to bring their individual concepts to fruition as a team.

The Plan

That summer, the two budding entrepreneurs spent a week lying around the pool at Gordon's parents' home, discussing their ideas for the venture. They were encouraged to find that their ideas and vision were similar. Biersch's sister loaned them her Macintosh, and they proceeded to combine their two business plans. Gordon's sister's boyfriend, who had his own sophisticated Macintosh equipment, did the page layout. The conception of their partnership was simple: Dean Biersch had the food-service experience and thus would be responsible for conceiving and managing the restaurant half of the business, including running the day-to-day operations. Dan Gordon had the microbrewery experience and thus would be responsible for producing the beer. He also had more business education and thus could handle the financing and accounting issues. As one employee described (although later admitting it was a bit of a simplification), "Dan gets the money and Dean spends it." Each was happy to defer to the strengths of the other, and each half of the business—the restaurant and the beer—was viewed as equally important.

After completing their plan, they initially decided they needed $950,000 to begin the company. After getting some hard numbers, they increased their estimate to $1.1 million. They found that this funding was fairly easy to come by. Gordon's sister, one of the first employees at Silicon Graphics, introduced Dan to several of the founding engineers there. These four people, "beer freaks" by Gordon's description, were immediately interested in investing in the venture. Also interested was a founder of Oracle, a Dutch brewing colleague of Gordon's, a local physician, and Carrau (the largest stockholder). Together, they contributed $720,000 in equity. The ultimate capital needed proved to be about $1.12 million. Fortunately, Gordon and Biersch were able to obtain from Security Pacific a $400,000 line of credit, which Robert Carrau guaranteed. These funds allowed them to start their restaurant, to be known as Gordon Biersch.

The concept they envisioned was "to provide high quality, moderately priced dining and professional service in a lively atmosphere featuring exceptional German-style lagers in on-site breweries." The atmosphere—trendy but upscale—was meant to appeal as much to older generations as young. The distinguishing characteristics were Gordon Biersch's emphasis on fine dining and German beers. The nearest competition, the Tied House in Mountain View, California, was a good 10 miles away and served English ales in a decidedly casual atmosphere. (English ales used a less expensive production process with a different yeast strain and a different fermentation process.) (See **Exhibit 1** for an explanation of the brewing process.)

The brewing received just as much attention as the design of the restaurant. Gordon chose to brew and serve three lager beers. The three beers included the *Export,* a smooth beer light in color but not "light" in alcohol content; *Märzen,* an Oktoberfest style beer; and *Dunkles,* a malty, yeasty Bavarian dark beer. Because of the intricate nature of brewing and the pride Gordon took in his beer, Gordon Biersch espoused a philosophy of offering no other beers in its restaurant. This was a business strategy as well; they would base their identity on their premium, very high quality beers, and it made sense to effect a monopoly. They did, however, offer wine and a number of nonalcoholic beverages.

The Restaurant Realized

The next step for Gordon and Biersch was to locate the appropriate space. Location was crucial in the restaurant business, and they were able to find a good one. The site was two blocks from Palo Alto's University Avenue, a busy street with many restaurants, stores, and movie theaters. The surrounding area, although not as populated with foot traffic, contained a number of retail outfits and office buildings as well. The location in which Gordon Biersch opened had previously been used as a movie theater, the Bijou, and consisted of 5,200 square feet of floor space with 25-foot ceilings. Dean Biersch designed the restaurant to take advantage of the airy feeling within. For example, the dining area, although elevated a few feet above the bar section, was not separated by walls, and the entire space was visible to anyone in it. When the restaurant/brewery was filled with people, the effect was of a huge, boisterous party. Artwork by local artists adorned the walls. The brewery equipment was located in the back but was visible to the guests through glass windows. This was important, in order to establish Gordon Biersch's identity as a microbrewery. The restaurant and bar accommodated 185 people.

To set up his brewery, Gordon used some secondhand equipment that he had bought in his second year of graduate school in 1984 from a friend in Germany; the rest he bought new. The capacity of the brewery was 1,500 barrels per year (or 46,500 gallons per year). He didn't expect to use all of this capacity at first, until he observed the success of the Tied House, which had opened six months earlier. The food Biersch chose to serve was California cuisine, offering elaborate salads, entrees, and decadent desserts. (See **Exhibit 2** for a sample menu.) Meanwhile, delays caused by city hearings consumed four months, as the brewery/restaurant was considered controversial (due to noise and the potential odor). Ultimately, Gordon and Biersch obtained clearance for the project.

The target market was the fairly sophisticated Palo Alto population as well as the Stanford University faculty, staff, and graduate student body. This market appeared open to new concepts. For example, the members of this college town sustained several movie theaters featuring foreign and independent films, a number of health food restaurants, a multitude of coffeehouses, and a variety of frozen yogurt vendors. Certainly, Palo Alto had its share of mainstream eateries too: a Burger King, several Chinese and Japanese restaurants, and several pizza parlors (although many offered "gourmet" selections or a whole wheat crust). Within this market, Gordon Biersch opened in July of 1988.

The Opening

The restaurant was an immediate success. First-year sales were projected at $1.5 million, but actually topped $2.2 million. The following year's sales grew to $2.8 million. Sales stayed at that level during the next year as well, although pretax profit increased from 7 percent to 12 percent. (See **Exhibit 3** for Gordon Biersch Brewing Company financial statements.) The owners paid back their $300,000 loan in six months. The pair learned from their mistakes (they forgot to buy the soup spoons) and slowly began to assimilate this knowledge into a smooth-running operation. As expected, Gordon Biersch derived a larger percentage of its revenues from beverage sales (38 percent) than the restaurant industry average (22 percent). Their income before taxes was double the industry norm (11.3 percent versus 5.6 percent).

However, with a 90 percent failure rate in the industry, this may have been what it took to survive as a restaurant. The industry is very much focused on the moment of service; there is no second chance to "perform" (as Biersch described it). If a guest has a bad experience the first time around, there is little likelihood of return patronage. Thus, a significant expense of the business entails cultivating the appropriate image, in both subtle and overt ways. Upkeep of the physical space, including upgrades, accounts for 2 percent of sales in the industry, although at Gordon Biersch, it accounted for 2.5 percent. This upkeep includes replacing broken or pilfered items (the Gordon Biersch glasses were often stolen), laundering and replacing linens, and repairing and cleaning the physical plant. Employee turnover is another given in the restaurant industry. Servers and bussers tend to quit regularly, thus adding hiring and training costs. Gordon Biersch, however found its turnover quite low, as the restaurant soon came to be considered a desirable place to work.

Gordon Biersch encouraged repeat business by developing a core clientele. Gordon offered his regular guests a beer stein with his or her name on it and a polished wood locker in which to keep it. The duo kept their prices in a moderate range (entrees hovered between $10 and $15) and offered souvenir beer steins and T-shirts for sale. (These items accounted for less than 1 percent of revenue.) They advertised very little, focusing their attention on public relations and customer referrals to attract new business. These public relations efforts included sponsorship of charity events, attendance at local beer festivals, supplying free beer at Stanford parties, and participation in local alcohol safety campaigns. The partners aspired to an image of "gourmet without pretension," and it seemed to work.

They soon began thinking about expansion. Although San Jose was ultimately chosen as the location of the second restaurant; it was not their first choice. Indeed, Gordon later asserted, "If we had had to pay market rates for that location, we would never have built in San Jose." However, another brewery/restaurant in San Jose (Biers Brasserie) went bankrupt within six months, and the landlord, stuck with the facility, approached Gordon and Biersch with an offer to sell the $1.4 million of fixed assets for $400,000. The two decided to do it.

Expansion to San Jose

The location in San Jose was a 10,800-square-foot space. Despite the failure of the previous microbrewery/restaurant, Gordon and Biersch were confident they would succeed. They attributed the failure of Biers Brasserie to its high-priced menu and its decision to serve beers other than those brewed on the premises. This conclusion further reinforced Gordon Biersch's strategy to serve only its own beers and did nothing to discourage the owners from opening their second restaurant on the site. With $600,000 from internal cash flow and a line of credit, plus a landlord note of $350,000, they were able to lease the facility, make the necessary improvements, and open Gordon Biersch San Jose in April of 1990.

In opening a second restaurant, Gordon and Biersch were introduced to several new issues. One of these was city regulations, which vary from town to town; for instance, San Jose was considering a nonsmoking ordinance. San Jose itself was encouraging new business, however, and Gordon Biersch's decision to expand to the city was welcomed. As the *San Jose Mercury News* reported, "Gordon Biersch's arrival was hailed as a healthy sign that the city can attract glitzy restaurants to a downtown that has about 110 mostly low-profile eateries." The building they were in was a designated historical landmark within the city's downtown redevelopment zone. It was close to the Fairmont Hotel and the San Jose Convention Center.

The concept behind the second restaurant was almost identical to the first, with a few minor differences. The menu, although still the same California cuisine style, offered many new items. (See **Exhibit 4** for a sample menu.) The space was much bigger, with a second floor/loft and an outdoor garden area that featured jazz musicians six months a year. (Gordon plays trombone.) The capacity of the brewery was 2,400 barrels per year versus 1,500 per year in Palo Alto. With the establishment of the Tied House and Winchester Brewing Company in San Jose, the challenge of competition had been introduced to the market. However, according to Louis Jemison, the president of Redwood Coast Brewing Company (the Tied House's parent company), "Gordon Biersch is more of a fine dining experience. We are a beer hall and that's what we do." Similarly, Winchester Brewing Company offered simple finger foods and sandwiches.

The type of servers reflected the difference in the market demographics. Whereas patrons in Palo Alto consisted of the Stanford community and an upscale native population, San Jose's consisted of Silicon Valley professionals. Accordingly, the servers were "less pretentious," as one manager described, and more homey than those in Palo Alto. The restaurant also derived more of its revenues from corporate parties (both catered and on site) than in Palo Alto. For example, in the summer of 1991, San Jose Gordon Biersch hosted 60 events versus 30 in Palo Alto. The new facility became an immediate success: sales reached $3.1 million in the first year, more than twice the budgeted level.

Meanwhile, the partnership between Dan Gordon and Dean Biersch proceeded smoothly. Although the two spent little time together outside of the restaurant, their business relationship was a positive one according not only to the duo, but also to their employees. It thrived by nature of their distinct strengths and duties. Each had individual quirks, but because of respect for one another's expertise, tension was uncommon. For example, Gordon recalled, "During our first five months, we were cooped up together in an office the size of a closet, and honestly, we disagreed maybe once." Biersch, obviously, knew little about brewing and Gordon was unfamiliar with restaurant operations, so each stayed clear of the other's area of interest and expertise. The two communicated in weekly management meetings, which also included the general managers from the two restaurants and the director of operations, Mack Tilling. Tilling, a Stanford graduate in his late 20s, had joined Gordon Biersch in its first week as a server and had quickly assumed managerial duties as the restaurant grew. He was considered a crucial member of the senior management team. Decisions were made by all involved in the meetings, as Gordon and Biersch strove for informality, creativity, and decentralized decision making. Even disagreement was usually painless. As Gordon described:

> Sometimes Dean would want to make capital improvements to the restaurants, and I would feel there wasn't enough money to do it. I'd just tell him, "Dean, there's not enough money; we have to wait." And he'd say "OK, we'll wait."

Gordon remembered only a few occasions when miscommunication had caused problems:

> When we first opened, Jaime, our chef, asked me who was going to do the bookkeeping for the previous night's receipts. This took me by surprise; I figured we just made a deposit and that was that. I thought that Dean, with his restaurant experience, would know if we should be doing anything different. He didn't. So, after we figured that one out, we had to go get a bookkeeper in our first week.

Gordon continued:

> The worst it really gets is me saying, "I told you so." For instance, we had trouble getting delivery for some special Mexican tile for our San Francisco restaurant. Finally we got it, after waiting three months. Then, Dean wanted to order more tile from the same place for the area around the pizza oven. I warned him that they had screwed up delivery before, so it wouldn't be a good idea to reorder. But we went ahead, and sure enough now they can't deliver on time. So we have to find new tile before the opening.

The general observation among employees was that while they were two very different people, with individual personality quirks, the combination mixed well. The low rate of turnover attested to the fact that the staff was happy. As one server observed:

> The management will do anything to accommodate our schedules, and they respect our abilities. Our newest bartender has been here for 13 months! Although there's some turnover in the wait staff, it's because of going back to school or something, not because of a better job.

While Dan and Dean possessed the necessary individual skills to create and execute the Gordon Biersch concept, Mack Tilling was viewed as the "glue that held the restaurant together." By 1991, Tilling was responsible for day-to-day management of both restaurants; in fact, the general managers of each of the restaurants reported to him (see **Exhibit 5** for an organization chart). He had devoted himself to the business since the beginning, deferring his graduation with a B.A. from Stanford until 1990, at age 26. Employees found Mack to be very talented, hardworking, and intelligent. According to several, he straddled both the technical requirements of his job (he managed the computer systems) and administrative requirements quite well.

The two founders and Tilling spent most of their time at the Palo Alto restaurant or at their office across the street, with most of their communication with San Jose occurring at the weekly management meetings. Gordon kept on top of the San Jose brewery by means of faxes detailing daily production. This approach was in line with their decentralized philosophy; both Gordon and Biersch wished to encourage personal initiative. Compensation for management even included stock options, an unheard-of benefit in the restaurant industry. (See **Exhibit 6** for equity distribution.)

By 1991, Gordon Biersch brewery/restaurants ranked as the first (San Jose) and fourth (Palo Alto) largest in the United States. An estimated 45,000 patrons entered

Gordon Biersch's two restaurants each month. Furthermore, it was ranked as the best brewery restaurant in *Focus magazine* and one of the top 100 restaurants in California in *California* magazine. Thus, with the concept successfully replicated once, they began planning for the "big time."

San Francisco

San Francisco was considered the ultimate challenge for Gordon Biersch. The potential clientele was much more sophisticated even than Palo Alto and expected both style and exceptional food. With over 3,200 restaurants competing in the city, it would be difficult for a mediocre restaurant to stay in business. As Biersch saw it, "It's like moving from off Broadway to Broadway."

The restaurant was projected to require capital of $3.3 million, including developer contributions of $1.7 million. Gordon and Biersch were pleased with their location, 15,000 square feet on three levels in the Hills Brothers building. The facility was in a redeveloping area near the financial district; it also housed the headquarters of The Gap. Gordon and Biersch expected to get excellent lunchtime traffic in that location.

The competition would be intense, although again, Gordon and Biersch felt there were no other restaurant/microbreweries with quite the same concept as theirs. The most successful of the already-established brewpubs was 20 Tank. 20 Tank was described in the *Guide to the Good Life at Stanford* (a student guide to the Bay Area published in 1991) as follows:

> This newcomer to SoMa [the South of Market area of San Francisco, known for its trendy clubs and funky nighttime inhabitants] has quickly become a hot spot for singles and all variety of trendily garbed San Franciscans (if you're lucky you might see one particularly stylish patron who sports waist-length dreadlocks and a black leather biker's outfit). The interior recalls an ancient beer hall, complete with sawdusted floor, tin ceiling, and dark, Teutonic tables and chairs. Sandwiches are cheap and excellent, and the handcrafted brews are so enthusiastically appreciated by the crowd that the bartender sometimes runs out of glasses.

Another well-known brewpub was the San Francisco Brewing Company, which featured a menu of very simple fare: hamburgers, fries, and club sandwiches in a pub-like atmosphere; however, it did a low-volume business. Furthermore, Gordon and Biersch felt that their success in the South Bay would produce favorable word-of-mouth publicity.

In order to minimize risk, Gordon and Biersch moved the general manager of the Palo Alto restaurant to San Francisco. Tilling, too, planned to devote his energies to the opening and indeed hoped to move into the city to avoid a 45-minute commute from Palo Alto.

Despite the frenzied activity that preceded the opening (now delayed until March 1992), they were confident of their concept. They planned to replicate it once more by the end of 1993, in Pasadena, California, and again in 1994, in San Diego. The Pasadena site had already been selected, located on Colorado Boulevard in the heart of the city. They planned to build a 180-seat brewery restaurant at a cost of $1.5 million.

First full-year revenues were expected to be $3.2 million. Gordon and Biersch intended to expand into several metropolitan areas of the western United States in the coming five years. (See **Exhibit 7** for pro forma income statements.)

The Wheels Keep Spinning

Meanwhile, Gordon and Biersch continued to generate new ideas for expanding their business. One obvious thought was to leverage the local reputation of their beer by bottling it for retail distribution to restaurants, grocery stores, liquor stores, and bars in the San Francisco Bay Area. Outside the northern California market, Gordon and Biersch planned to first establish one or more brewery restaurants, then follow with retail distribution. The brewery restaurants would introduce the consumer to the company's beers, creating brand awareness and spurring retail demand. The retail demand, in turn, would reinforce the consumer's decision to frequent the Gordon Biersch brewery restaurants. They believed this integrated approach would create marketing synergy through strengthening brand awareness and increasing demand for the restaurants and retail beers. Any surplus beer would be used in the brewery restaurants, which sometimes could not keep up with customer demand.

Bottling and retail distribution would present a number of challenges. For one, it would be run entirely by Gordon; Biersch would not be involved managerially. Gordon did not know how much of his time the new brewery would take and whether too much of his attention would be diverted from the restaurants. However, because Gordon and Biersch had espoused a management style of decentralization, lessened involvement might not be a problem. As far as the product itself, the most obvious difference would be the freshness of the beer. Bottled beer would never taste as good as that served fresh from the keg, but Gordon had made provisions to optimize the flavor by imposing on his retailers a maximum shelf life approximately three months.

Perhaps the most exciting challenge was the head-to-head competition (no pun intended) with other microbreweries and other premium beers.[1] Northern California was considered a key geographic market for microbrewed specialty beer, growing 22 percent between 1990 and 1991. (Microbreweries were defined as those with production of less than 35,000 barrels per year.) The total northern California market in 1991 was approximately 181,500 barrels of beer. Three manufacturers comprised the bulk of the market: Anchor Brewing Company, Boston Brewing Co. (Samuel Adams beer), and Sierra Nevada Brewing Co., which together owned 68 percent of the market. (Anchor and Boston Brewing technically brewed more than 35,000 barrels per year, but they competed in the target market.) Pete's Brewing Co., Mendocino Brewing Co. (Redtail Ale), and Redhook Brewing Co. accounted for 22 percent of the total market. Nevertheless, Gordon felt that he would be able to capture 11 percent of the market by 1996. (See **Exhibit 8** for U.S. brewing industry market analysis.)

---

[1]The author is indebted to a project by Peter Cooley, Barry Eggers, Omid Kordestani, and Wini Welch (all Stanford MBA class of 1991) for much of the industry information on retail distribution.

There were several options for distribution: through a master distributor, direct to the distribution network, direct to retailers, or through a wine/spirits distributor. *Master distributors* provided warehousing, transportation, and sales/distributors management. In particular, the master distributor would manage relationships with the distribution network (approximately 10 distributors, given Gordon Biersch's expected production level of 22,000 barrels). A prime benefit of this arrangement was that Gordon Biersch would not have to worry about receivables; it would simply be issued one check per month. In exchange, the master distributor received a fee of 3 to 5 percent of cost. Additionally, Gordon Biersch would be responsible for creating customer "pull" and providing profit incentives for the master distributors. If Gordon Biersch chose to bypass the master distributor and market directly to the distributors, each one would be required to hold two to three weeks of inventory (as opposed to one to two days). This option, however, would allow Gordon Biersch to maintain more control over sales and distribution, since the brewer would be in direct contact with the people who actually supplied the beer to the retail stores. A third option would be to market beyond the distribution network directly to the *retailers* (bars, liquor stores, restaurants, and grocery stores), but the complexity of dealing with a large number of retailers made it economically infeasible for a microbrewery. The final option would be to go through a *wine/spirits distributor or a major brand network*. These distributors offered excellent retail penetration, but since they carried several brands, their ability to devote attention to Gordon Biersch would be questionable. Furthermore, a wine/spirits distributor might not have the appropriate expertise in beer. With a major brand network (e.g., Budweiser), Gordon Biersch faced the distinct possibility of conflict of interest and a resulting lack of attention.

Gordon planned to market the product as a superpremium microbrewed beer. A six-pack of 12-ounce bottles would retail for about $6.50. This would place Gordon Biersch beer in the same price range as Anchor Steam, Samuel Adams, and Sierra Nevada. A six-pack retailing at $6.50 assumed that Gordon Biersch would sell it at $3.81 (or $15.26 per case), with a 5 percent markup for the master distributor, 30 percent for the distributor, and a retail markup of approximately 25 percent. Gordon planned to structure his pricing so the final retail price would be competitive in the target market.

In July of 1991, Gordon Biersch had been contacted by Markstein Companies, who offered to act as master distributor. Markstein also distributed Miller beer and several imports (e.g., Corona and EKU). However, Gordon Biersch would be its only microbrewed beer. In return, Markstein would receive a 5 percent fee based on the wholesale price (e.g., $0.76 on a $15.26 case). Gordon had made no decision as of December of 1991.

Meanwhile, Gordon had signed a letter of intent with the property owners for the option to lease 30,000 square feet of production space at the former San Martin Winery facility. Of note, the property owners included the San Jose restaurant's landlord, with whom Gordon and Biersch had a good relationship. Even better, construction costs for the site would be minimized since the facility had previously been used as a winery. For example, the refrigeration warehouse would be ideal for fermentation. Gordon planned a capacity of 100,000 barrels per year, with an expectation of brewing 22,000 barrels in the first year. He would divide this evenly between the Märzen and the Export beers, varying the mix as time went on to satisfy customer demand.

The project would require an investment of $3.75 million: $2.5 million for brewing equipment and $1.25 million for preopening expenses and initial inventory. Gordon hoped to be able to have his brewery in operation by early 1994. (See **Exhibit 9** for pro forma income statements.)

Financing

Gordon and Biersch were seeking $5.5 million (the rest would come from developer contributions) and were considering three alternatives for financing. (See **Exhibit 10** for pro forma income statements for the entire expansion.) The first was a venture capital firm in the northern California area. Gordon Biersch would benefit from the management experience of the firm, and its proximity would ease communication.

The second alternative was a French investment banking concern. Although it offered an attractive entrance into international distribution (Asahi beer in Japan would handle Japanese distribution, for example), its European location might create communication problems. On the other hand, it might allow Gordon and Biersch to operate more freely.

The final option was to try to finance the expansion entirely from cash flow. This would require the plans to proceed much more slowly, but would allow Gordon Biersch to retain control over both the equity and the expansion plans. Because the San Francisco restaurant had consumed much of management's time, no solid deals had been negotiated. Along with these options, too, Gordon Biersch had "expressions of interest" from friends and associates totaling $500,000.

The expansion would require not only financing, but also hiring a number of new people. Key personnel would include a development director, responsible for site development, and a chief financial officer. In late 1991, Gordon Biersch employed 85 full-time and 95 part-time employees and expected to hire 50 to 70 full-time-equivalent employees as each new restaurant opened. Fifteen people (11 full-time and 4 part-time) would be hired for the brewery. (See **Exhibit 11** for a postexpansion organization chart.)

Conclusion

Gordon Biersch's hope was to increase revenues to over $54 million annually by 1997, with operating earnings before interest and taxes of over $7.8 million. At that point, according to Gordon, they could reach "Phase 3," which would include either going public or selling to a larger brewery or food/restaurant group.

Although they were excited about these prospects, they were consumed with preparations for the San Francisco opening. By mid-1992, they hoped to turn their attention back to the broader expansion plans and carefully consider the financing options available to them. They were confident that they would be successful in these new efforts. Gordon and Biersch had worked hard to ensure that the present restaurants could be operated independently by encouraging decentralized management. This self-sufficiency would be crucial in the coming years, as the founders' attentions became further dispersed.

Certainly, the growth they anticipated would put to the test their organizational theories.

Exhibit 1   Brewing Beer

The process of making beer is complicated, involving six exacting processes—milling, mashing, lautering, boiling, fermenting, and filtering—and four ingredients—malted barley, hops, yeast, and water.

Each ingredient serves an important function. Malted barley allows the yeast to metabolize, which in turn ferments the beer by converting the carbohydrates into alcohol. There are hundreds of different yeast strains, each one imparting a different flavor on the finished beer. Hops give beer its slightly bitter flavor, without which beer would taste sweet. Water is used throughout the brewing process and needs to be of drinking quality.

The first step of brewing is *milling* the malted barley to an appropriate degree of fineness. After milling is completed, *mashing* converts the carbohydrates and proteins in the malt to simple sugars and amino acids. Mashing begins when the malt is mixed with warm water. The mixture is then gradually taken to temperature levels that activate specific enzymes. Typically, the brewer will take the mixture to a given temperature level (e.g., 62 degrees Celsius) and hold it there for a specific length of time (e.g., 30 minutes), and then proceed to the next higher temperature level, holding again for a specific period of time. This routine proceeds until the mashing is completed and all enzyme groups have been activated. This usually takes about three hours. From there, the substance is pumped to a lauter tun for *lautering*. Lautering is a two-step process, consisting of the first run-off (*Vorderwürze* in German) and three rounds of sparging (defined below). The lauter tun contains a sieve, through which the mashing liquid is drained into pipes leading to a wort receiver. (This liquid extract is called "wort.") This process of draining is the *Vorderwürze*. When the top of the grain bed is dry, the solid matter is "sparged" with hot water, and the water is allowed to flow through the grain bed and into the wort receiver. This is repeated for a total of three times, with the amount of liquid used for sparging equalling the amount of water used for mashing. The process is not unlike brewing coffee through a filter.

After the liquid from the *Vorderwürze* and the sparging is all collected in the wort receiver, the wort is *boiled*. The hops are added during the process. Hops are of two primary types: bitter and aroma hops. Usually, bitter hops are added at the beginning of the boil, aroma hops at the end. However, Gordon used imported aroma hops at the beginning of the boil, a more expensive process. The boiling process serves several functions, including sterilizing the product, increasing the concentration of the extract to its desired level through evaporation, and coagulating the protein. The wort is boiled for 100 to 120 minutes, depending on the desired final extract concentration.

From there, the hopped wort is pumped into a tank called the whirlpool. In the whirlpool, the sediment from the coagulated protein and the hop particles is allowed to settle at the bottom of the tank. This takes about 25 minutes. The clear hot wort is then fed into the heat exchanger, where the wort is cooled to 6 degrees Celsius. Exiting the heat exchanger, the cold hopped wort is injected with sterile air, which allows the yeast to reproduce. The wort is then pumped into a yeast-lined flotation tank; the turbulence from pumping allows the yeast to blend with the wort.

The beer sits in the flotation tank for 8 to 12 hours, allowing the "cold break" to rise to the top of the tank. This "cold break" is removed, as it leads to an unnatural bitterness and harsh flavor. The beer is then pumped to the fermentation tank. The goal of fermentation is to convert the sugars to ethyl-alcohol and carbon dioxide. Temperature control during fermentation is vital. Lagers ferment best at 9 degrees Celsius. Colder temperatures inhibit the yeast from fermenting; higher temperatures cause the yeast to "sweat," producing undesirable compounds that either affect the taste or result in a higher likelihood of headaches and hangovers. At the end of the primary fermentation, the yeast sinks to the bottom and is removed, although some yeast cells remain suspended in the beer. Next, the fermentation tank is chilled to 4 degrees Celsius. The secondary fermentation, which makes use of these yeast cells, produces carbon dioxide in the beer to absorb or break down chemicals produced during the primary fermentation that adversely affect the flavor of the beer. At least four weeks total is required for proper aging.

Finally, the beer is *filtered* to remove any yeast that hasn't settled during the fermenting process. This is accomplished with sheets of cellulose or metal that are coated with diatomaceous earth. The beer is then ready for packaging and consumption.

EXHIBIT 2   Sample Menu, Palo Alto

LUNCH MENU

APPETIZERS

QUESADILLA OF BBQ CHICKEN AND CHEDDAR CHEESE
WITH AVOCADO SALSA, SOURCREAM AND ROASTED RED BELL PEPPER 5.95
QUICKLY FRIED CALAMARI TOSSED WITH FRESH GARLIC, LEMON AND PARSLEY 5.75
GRILLED PRAWN SKEWERS WITH SPICY CORAL ISLAND SAUCE 7.95
BAVARIAN PLATE OF ASSORTED SLICED MEATS AND CHEESE 8.50
THAI CHICKEN SKEWERS WITH SPICY PEANUT SAUCE 4.95
MAUI ONION RINGS 3.75
GARLIC FRIES 2.50

SANDWICHES

CHEESE BURGER WITH GARLIC FRIES 6.50
WITH GRILLED ONIONS AND MUSHROOMS ADD .75
PASTRAMI WITH GRILLED ONIONS, MUENSTER CHEESE AND DIJON 6.95
GRILLED CHICKEN BREAST WITH PROSCIUTTO AND PROVOLONE ON SOURDOUGH 6.50
CALIFORNIA RIBEYE CHEESESTEAK WITH RED ONION, GUACAMOLE AND JACK CHEESE 7.50
MESQUITE SMOKED TURKEY CLUB WITH APPLEWOOD BACON ON 9-GRAIN TOAST 6.95
BUFFALO MOZZARELLA, TOMATO, BASIL AND GRILLED EGGPLANT
WITH GAETA OLIVE AIOLI ON SWEET FRENCH BREAD 5.95

SALADS

HOUSE SALAD WITH BALSAMIC VINAIGRETTE 3.75 WITH DANISH BLUE CHEESE 4.50
CHICKEN BREAST WITH BLUE CHEESE, WALNUTS, APPLE AND CREAMY VINAIGRETTE 8.95
SPICY SESAME BEEF SALAD WITH A SESAME-SOY DRESSING, OVER A BED OF MIXED GREENS
TOPPED WITH SHREDDED CUCUMBER, CARROT, RADISH AND GREEN ONIONS 7.95
SOUTHWEST MARINATED CHICKEN WITH BELL PEPPER, RED ONION, TOMATO, CILANTRO,
GUACAMOLE AND SOURCREAM OVER MIX GREENS WITH TOASTED TORTILLA CHIPS 7.95
POACHED SALMON OVER MIX GREENS WITH TOMATO, RED ONION, GAETA OLIVES
AND LEMON WITH A RASPBERRY-WALNUT VINAIGRETTE 9.50
CAESAR SALAD WITH GARLIC CROUTONS AND PARMESAN CHEESE 7.50

ENTREES

BAKED PASILLA PEPPERS STUFFED WITH CHICKEN, RICE AND
JALAPENO JACK CHEESE SERVED OVER A BED
OF RICE, BLACK BEANS AND CURRY SAUCE AND GARNISHED WITH ROASTED RED PEPPERS 7.95
WARM SPINACH WITH PINEAPPLE, OYSTER MUSHROOMS, RED BELL PEPPERS, RED ONION
AND TOASTED MACADAMIA NUTS IN GINGER-SCALLION DRESSING OVER TOMATO LINGUINE 9.95
SAUTEED GARLIC-FENNEL SAUSAGE WITH BELL PEPPERS AND MUSHROOMS
TOSSED WITH A TOMATO-BASIL PESTO SAUCE OVER LINGUINE 9.95
GRILLED CHICKEN BREAST WITH A FETA CHEESE, ARTICHOKE
HEART, TOMATO AND DILL SAUCE 10.95
PENNE PASTA WITH SAUTEED MUSHROOMS, TOMATOES, BASIL,
GARLIC, OLIVE OIL AND GOAT CHEESE 8.95
CHEESE TORTELLINI WITH PROSCIUTTO, MUSHROOMS AND
BABY SPINACH IN A LEMON BUTTER SAUCE 9.95

EXHIBIT 2   *(concluded)*

FILET MIGNON OVER SPINACH, MUSHROOMS AND
SAUTEED ONIONS WITH GORGONZOLA SAUCE 15.95
SAUTEED BABY SCALLOPS, TIGER PRAWNS, RED PEPPERS, MUSHROOMS AND SCALLIONS
WITH INDONESIAN RED CURRY OVER BLACK FETTUCINE 13.95

DESSERTS

CHOCOLATE PECAN TART WITH FRENCH VANILLA ICE CREAM 4.50
FLORENTINE ICE CREAM SANDWICH WITH JAMOCA ALMOND FUDGE ICE CREAM 4.50
IRISH CREAM TRIFLE WITH LADYFINGERS, FRESH
BERRIES, MASCARPONE, AND CREME ANGLAISE 4.95
FUDGE BROWNIE SUNDAE WITH WHITE CHOCOLATE CHIPS,
MACADAMIA NUTS AND CARAMEL SAUCE 4.50
HAZELNUT CHEESECAKE IN A CHOCOLATE CRUMB CRUST WITH A FRANGELICO SAUCE 4.95

EXHIBIT 3

Palo Alto and San Jose
Income Statements
(Year ended November 30)

	1988[a]	*1989*	*1990*[b]	*1991*
Revenues	$719,608	$2,406,770	$4,986,310	$5,926,907
Cost of sales	392,329	1,386,158	3,023,001	3,180,666
Gross profit	327,279	1,020,612	1,963,309	2,746,241
General and administrative expenses	215,297	666,642	1,470,276	1,971,328
Net operating income	111,982	353,970	493,033	774,913
Depreciation	34,982	90,738	110,184	138,503
Interest expense	0	104,541	35,971	50,621
Profit before tax	$ 77,000	$ 158,691	$ 346,878	$ 585,789
Provision for income taxes[c]	15,943	55,500	59,293	12,000
Net income	$ 61,057	$ 103,191	$ 287,585	$ 573,789

[a]Includes five months of operations.

[b]San Jose restaurant opened in April 1990.

[c]Gordon Biersch was incorporated as a C corporation from 1988–1990 and changed to an S corporation in 1991.

EXHIBIT 3   *(continued)*

Palo Alto and San Jose
Balance Sheets
(Year ended November 30)

	1988	*1989*	*1990*	*1991*
Assets				
Current assets				
Cash	$ 36,930	$ 0	$ 0	$ 51,106
Accounts receivable	14,759	38,148	41,193	26,354
Inventory	21,777	42,774	104,640	135,109
Prepaid expenses	12,225	14,379	50,342	78,912
Employee receivables	0	4,552	15,109	12,787
Receivable from ltd. partnership	0	0	63,967	0
Total current assets	$ 85,691	$ 99,853	$ 275,251	$ 304,268
Fixed assets				
Leasehold improvements	413,713	479,734	798,509	892,926
Furniture, fixtures, and equipment	226,881	403,909	586,178	634,623
Brewing equipment	233,046	250,863	444,218	462,285
Automobiles	37,661	22,862	24,612	37,930
Total fixed assets	911,301	1,157,368	1,853,517	2,027,764
Less: accumulated depreciation	(35,235)	(124,381)	(239,418)	(409,941)
Net fixed assets	$ 876,066	$1,032,987	$1,614,099	$1,617,823
Other assets				
Start-up costs	172,144	172,144	172,144	172,144
Less: accumulated amortization	(14,345)	(48,774)	(83,203)	(117,632)
Receivables from ltd. partnership	0	0	88,828	550,427
Net other assets	$ 157,799	$ 123,370	$ 177,769	$ 604,939
Total assets	$1,119,556	$1,256,210	$2,067,119	$2,527,030

EXHIBIT 3   *(concluded)*

**Palo Alto and San Jose
Balance Sheets**
(Year ended November 30)

	1988	1989	1990	1991
Liabilities and stockholders' equity				
Current liabilities				
Bank overdraft	$ 0	$ 743	$ 0	$ 0
Accounts payable	1,108	60,525	338,615	256,398
Accrued liabilities	0	0	0	154,173
Interest payable	2,879	109,161	0	0
Payroll and sales tax payable	13,570	24,483	146,145	0
Income taxes payable	11,963	8,800	59,610	10,000
Bank line of credit	303,789	106,326	300,961	100,837
Current portion of notes payable	0	4,891	7,414	121,085
Note payable-stockholder	0	0	116,000	0
Total current liabilities	$ 333,309	$ 314,929	$ 968,745	$ 642,493
Notes payable—less amounts classified as current	0	57,452	52,531	264,905
deferred taxes	3,980	25,571	0	0
Total liabilities	$ 337,289	$ 397,952	$1,021,276	$ 907,398
Stockholders' equity				
Subordinated debentures[a]	720,000	720,000	0	0
Common stock[bcd]	100	100	620,100	620,100
Retained earnings	62,167	138,158	425,743	999,532
Total stockholders' equity	$ 782,267	$ 858,258	$1,045,843	$1,619,632
Total liabilities and				
stockholders' equity	$1,119,556	$1,256,210	$2,067,119	$2,527,030

[a]Subordinated debentures redeemed for common stock in 1990.

[b]1 for 100 stock split in 1989.

[c]In 1989, 1,000,000 shares of no par value common stock authorized, 90,000 shares issued and outstanding.

[d]In 1990, 1,000,000 shares of no par value common stock authorized, 167,500 shares issued and outstanding.

APPETIZERS

THAI CHICKEN WITH SPICY PEANUT SAUCE 4.95
GRILLED JERK PRAWNS WITH SPICY HONEY MUSTARD 7.95
QUICKLY FRIED CALAMARI TOSSED WITH FRESH GARLIC, LEMON AND PARSLEY 5.75
HAWAIIAN AHI CARPACCIO WITH TAMARI GLAZE AND EXTRA VIRGIN OLIVE OIL 6.95
BAVARIAN PLATE OF ASSORTED SLICED SAUSAGES, MEATS AND CHEESE 8.50
SMOKED SALMON QUESADILLA WITH CREAM CHEESE,
SAUTEED ONIONS AND BLACK BEAN SALSA 7.50
GARLIC FRIES 2.50

SANDWICHES

CHEESEBURGER WITH GARLIC FRIES 6.50
SPICY BBQ CHICKEN SANDWICH WITH GRUYERE CHEESE ON WHOLE WHEAT 6.95
NEW YORK STEAK SANDWICH WITH CARMELIZED RED ONIONS, HORSERADISH AND SAGE 7.95
MESQUITE SMOKED TURKEY WITH TOMATO, BACON AND GUACAMOLE 6.50

INDIVIDUAL PIZZAS

PROSCIUTTO, GOAT CHEESE, THYME AND OREGANO 7.95
MARINATED ARTICHOKES, GORGONZOLA, JULIENNE VEGETABLES AND MARINARI 7.50
HUNTERS SAUSAGE, LINGUICA, SAUTEED PEPPERS AND SMOKED GOUDA 8.25
CHORIZO, TOMATILLO, MASCARPONE, JALAPENO AND CILANTRO 7.75
FRESH TOMATO, FONTINA, MOZZARELLA, FETA AND BASIL 6.25

SALADS

HOUSE SALAD WITH MUSTARD VINAIGRETTE 4.00 WITH DANISH BLUE CHEESE 4.50
GREEK SALAD WITH FETA, CALAMATA OLIVES, CUCUMBER, TOMATO AND ONIONS 7.95
NICOISE SALAD WITH FRESH TUNA AND A GINGER-TAMARI GLAZE 8.95
SMOKED DUCK OVER MIXED GREENS IN LIGHT SESAME VINAIGRETTE
WITH PAPAYA, BLACK PLUMS, RED ONIONS AND MANDARIN ORANGES 9.95
CAESAR STYLE SALAD WITH FRESH BAY SHRIMP AND CROUTONS 8.95

ENTREES

LOBSTER ENCHILADAS WITH JALAPENO JACK AND FONTINA OVER PAINTED RED BEANS
WITH SALSA FRESCA, TOMATILLO SALSA WITH BASMATI RICE 13.95
TORTELLONI CARBONARA WITH PANCETTA, PEAS, CRACKED BLACK PEPPER AND CREAM 12.95
SINGAPORE STYLE VERMICELLI WITH SHRIMP, PROSCUITTO,
PEPPERS AND BERMUDA ONIONS 13.95
GRILLED CHICKEN BREAST WITH CHIPOTLE, CORN SAUCE,
BLACK BEAN CHILI AND GUACAMOLE 11.95
LEMON BASIL LINGUINE WITH SHITAKE MUSHROOMS, SUN-DRIED AND
YELLOW TOMATOES WITH BALSAMIC VINEGAR AND OLIVE OIL 9.95
BEEF, GINGER, AND ORANGE STIRFRY WITH LEEKS, PEPPERS
AND RED CABBAGE OVER BASMATI RICE 12.95
MEDALLIONS OF FILET MIGNON WITH PRESERVED
MUSHROOM AND PORT SAUCE, TEMPURA EGGPLANT,
AND HERB ROASTED POTATOES 15.95
SEAFOOD AND SAUSAGE ETOUFFEE WITH FLORIDA SCALLOPS, PRAWNS, ONIONS AND PEPPERS,
ENGULFED IN CLAMS AND MUSSELS OVER BASMATI RICE 14.95

EXHIBIT 4   *(concluded)*

CHICKEN BREAST SA-TE WITH PEANUTS, COCONUT MILK, SUGAR
SNAPS AND PEPPERS OVER BASMATI RICE 12.95
MARINATED FLANK STEAK OVER BLACK BEANS WITH ROASTED
TOMATILLO SALSA, SOUR CREAM AND FLOUR TORTILLAS 12.95

DESSERTS

CHOCOLATE DECADENCE WITH RASPBERRY SAUCE 3.95
FLORENTINE ICE CREAM SANDWICH WITH JAMOCA ALMOND FUDGE 4.50
FRUIT CRISP WITH APPLES, PEACHES, PEARS AND FRENCH VANILLA ICE CREAM 4.50
CHOCOLATE, PECAN TORTE WITH FRENCH VANILLA ICE CREAM 4.50
THREE-LAYER MUD PIE WITH OREO COOKIE CRUST 4.95
FRESH FRUIT CHEESECAKE 4.25

EXHIBIT 5   Organization Chart (October 1991)

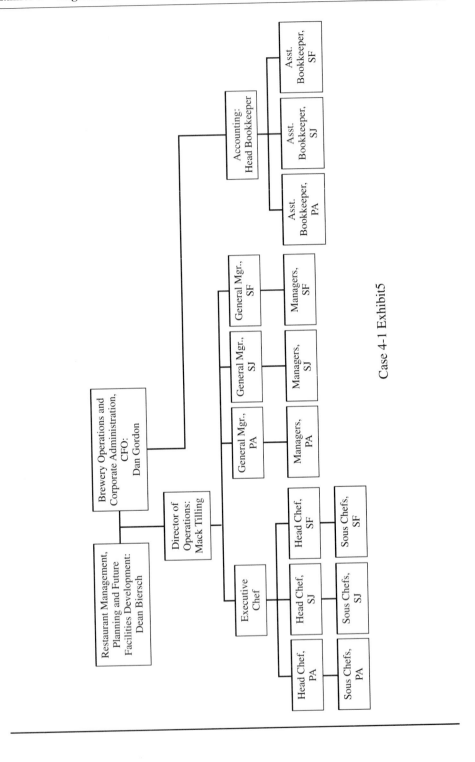

Case 4-1 Exhibit5

Exhibit 6   Equity Distribution

Investor	Shares	Percentage of Shares Issued	Options	Percentage of Fully Diluted Ownership
Dean Biersch	40,500	24.18%	5,000	22.91%
Dan Gordon	40,500	24.18%	5,000	22.91%
Executive chef	0	0.00%	3,524	1.77%
Head chef, San Jose	0	0.00%	2,114	1.06%
Head brewer, San Jose	0	0.00%	1,762	0.89%
General manager, San Jose	0	0.00%	1,762	0.89%
General manager, Palo Alto	0	0.00%	1,762	0.89%
Mack Tilling	0	0.00%	10,180	5.13%
#1	35,714	21.32%	0	17.98%
#2	12,500	7.46%	0	6.29%
#3	12,500	7.46%	0	6.29%
#4	3,518	2.10%	0	1.77%
#5	3,518	2.10%	0	1.77%
#6	3,125	1.87%	0	1.57%
#7	3,125	1.87%	0	1.57%
#8	3,125	1.87%	0	1.57%
#9	3,125	1.87%	0	1.57%
#10	3,125	1.87%	0	1.57%
#11	834	0.50%	0	0.42%
#12	833	0.50%	0	0.42%
#13	833	0.50%	0	0.42%
#14	625	0.37%	0	0.31%
Subtotal	167,500		31,104	
Total shares allocated	198,604			

Exhibit 7

New Restaurant Operations
Pro Forma Income Statements
(Years ended November 30)

	1993	1994	1995	1996	1997
Revenues	$1,067,000	$4,800,000	$9,600,000	$16,000,000	$24,800,000
Cost of sales	576,180	2,592,000	5,184,000	8,640,000	13,392,000
Gross profit	490,820	2,208,000	4,416,000	7,360,000	11,408,000
General and administrative expenses	317,820	1,321,000	2,550,000	4,176,000	6,385,000
Net operating profit	173,000	887,000	1,866,000	3,184,000	5,023,000
Depreciation	50,000	225,000	450,000	750,000	1,163,000
Interest expense	0	0	0	0	0
Profit before tax	$ 123,000	$ 662,000	$1,416,000	$ 2,434,000	$ 3,860,000
Provision for income taxes	43,050	231,700	495,600	851,900	1,351,000
Net profit	$ 79,950	$ 430,300	$ 920,400	$ 1,582,100	$ 2,509,000

Total number of restaurants (year end)	4	5	7	9	12
Number of operating months—new units	4	18	36	60	93

Exhibit 8   U.S. Brewing Industry

Total U.S. beer sales were 188.5 million barrels in 1991. Overall, beer production in the U.S. has increased 1 to 3% annually over the last several years, but declined by about 2% in 1991. The decline is attributed primarily to the increase in federal excise tax enacted in 1991. The U.S. brewing industry is comprised of three types of manufacturers: major national breweries, regional breweries, and microbreweries (defined as breweries with production less than 35,000 barrels per year). The majors account for approximately 94% for all production in the United States. Economies of scale in advertising, production and distribution have benefited the national breweries at the expense of the regional producers, whose output has dropped at rates of 15 to 20% per year. Chapter 11 filings have plagued the regionals, which currently account for 6% of production. Several regional breweries, in order to use excess capacity, also produce specialty brands under contract. Examples of contract brewed brands include Samuel Adams and Pete's Wicked Ale. Microbreweries account for only 0.4% of total production but are the fastest growing segment of the beer industry. During the last four years, microbrewery sales have increased 35 to 40% annually. As the larger microbrewers such as Sierra Nevada and Anchor increase output and geographic distribution, the differences between regional brewers and microbrewers are becoming less distinct. As a result, brewers are better defined by beer styles and price positioning of their brands. Specialty brewers are defined as those marketing high quality, full-bodied ales or lagers priced higher than mass-market brands.

Imports, which enjoyed double-digit growth in the United States during the late 1970s and early 1980s, have more recently faced flat sales growth and saw a 7.6% decline in 1991. Importers attribute the decline to increased excise taxes and competition from U.S. specialty brands. Although imports currently account for only 4% of all beer sold in the United States, they account for nearly 30% of beer consumed in restaurants and bars. Similarly, domestic specialty beer sales account for greater restaurant and bar sales than are represented by total market sales. Fifty-four percent of microbrewery production is sold at bars and restaurants.

The substantial growth in the specialty beer segment has been fueled by an increase in the number of new breweries. Between 1988 and 1991, the number of microbreweries and brewpubs grew from 123 to over 250. Although microbreweries face higher production costs than large brewers, their beers command a premium price. In addition, microbreweries enjoy favorable tax considerations compared to large brewers. Microbrewers pay $7 per barrel for the first 60,000 barrels produced, compared to $18 per barrel paid by large brewers.

Microbreweries are segmented into brewpubs and micros. Brewpubs sell beer for on-premises consumption, typically provide food, and generally produce less than 4,000 barrels per year. Brewpubs, which significantly outnumber micros, account for 25% of microbrewery production. Micros bottle or keg beer primarily for off-premises consumption and produce from 2,000 to 35,000 barrels or more per year. On average, micros keg 54% of their production and bottle the remaining 46%.

Exhibit 9

Brewery Project
Pro Forma Income Statements
(Years ended November 30)

	1993	1994	1995	1996	1997
Revenues	$0	$4,408,477	$8,870,286	$13,772,093	$18,218,733
Cost of sales	0	2,465,628	4,793,488	7,490,036	10,000,119
Gross profit	0	1,942,849	4,076,798	6,282,057	8,218,614
General and administrative expenses	0	1,059,607	1,768,611	2,670,541	3,459,315
Net operating profit	0	883,242	2,308,187	3,611,516	4,759,299
Depreciation	0	310,431	310,431	327,098	343,764
Interest expense	0	0	0	0	0
Profit before tax	0	$ 572,811	$1,997,756	$ 3,284,418	$ 4,415,535
Provision for income taxes	0	200,484	699,215	1,149,546	1,545,437
Net profit	$0	$ 372,327	$1,298,541	$ 2,134,872	$ 2,870,098

EXHIBIT 10

All Operations
Pro Forma Income Statements
(Years ended November 30)

	1992	1993	1994	1995	1996	1997
Revenues	$9,021,000	$11,767,000	$20,176,000	$29,712,000	$41,239,000	$54,715,000
Cost of sales	4,871,340	6,354,180	10,979,808	16,048,168	22,322,216	29,707,959
Gross profit	4,149,660	5,412,820	9,196,192	13,663,832	18,916,784	25,007,041
General and administrative expenses	3,061,660	3,939,820	6,276,192	8,489,832	11,346,784	14,799,041
Net operating profit	1,088,000	1,473,000	2,920,000	5,174,000	7,570,000	10,208,000
Preopening expenses[a]	0	1,129,000	400,000	320,000	480,000	325,000
Depreciation	379,000	593,000	1,035,000	1,260,000	1,602,000	2,032,000
Interest expense	122,000	(10,000)	(80,000)	(60,000)	(35,000)	(90,000)
Profit before tax	$ 587,000	$ (239,000)	$ 1,565,000	$ 3,654,000	$ 5,523,000	$ 7,941,000
Provision for income taxes	0	0	531,000	1,462,000	2,209,000	3,176,000
Net profit	$ 587,000	($ 239,000)	$ 1,034,000	$ 2,192,000	$ 3,314,000	$ 4,765,000

[a]Consists of preopening expenses for new restaurants and $660,000 in 1993 and $250,000 in 1994 for the brewery.

EXHIBIT 11   Proposed Organization Chart after Expansion

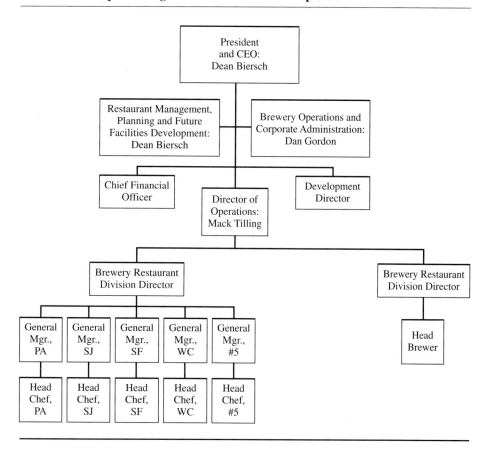

4–2   VINOD KHOSLA AND SUN MICROSYSTEMS (A)

The president of Computervision was on the line. "We like your workstation," he said, "but the deal with Apollo really is done. I don't see how you could change our minds."

It was July 1983. The future of Sun Microsystems, Vinod Khosla thought, lay in the balance. He had to stop Computervision from signing a contract with Apollo. But how could he? Sun was a 40-employee enterprise, started just over a year ago by a team of 26- and 27-year-olds, that had just posted its first million-dollar sales month. Apollo, on the other hand, owned the engineering workstation business. Founded by industry veterans in 1980, Apollo provided high-performance workstations to Computervision's key competitors. Could Computervision bet its future on Sun?

The Workstation Market

Workstations, like personal computers (PCs), were designed to provide users with dedicated computing power. Historically, many users had shared the computing power of a single minicomputer or mainframe computer through more or less "dumb" terminals. Workstations and PCs, on the other hand, gave individuals their own CPUs (central processing units—the "brains" of a computer) at their own desks.

There were, however, two important differences between workstations and PCs. First, workstations were designed to provide more computing power (close to a minicomputer's) and a greater variety of functions than were PCs. Bitmapped screens and graphics displays, for example, were considered standard in a workstation, but not in a personal computer. Correspondingly, a workstation sold for about $20,000 compared to a $5,000 to $7,000 unit cost for a PC. Second, while a PC system was entirely self-contained, workstations were usually attached to a network in order to share devices like printers and file servers.

The concept of a workstation—a high-performance desktop computer linked to a network—was developed at Xerox PARC (Palo Alto Research Center) in California. Xerox defined the hardware specifications and the network's operating systems. It also designed the network, which it called Ethernet. Xerox first had a functioning workstation in 1976. By 1982, it was running sophisticated applications, like desktop

---

Professor Amar Bhide prepared this case.
Harvard Business School Case 9–390–049

publishing, on workstation networks. Xerox PARC was, however, ahead of its time. Its workstations were expensive and could not compete against traditional, centralized computer systems.[1]

By 1982, though, declining microprocessor and memory costs had turned the economics around. According to Khosla:

> You could buy a microprocessor with half a MIP of computing power for $100 and memory for a few hundred dollars. Yet most existing computing environments caused 30 to 50 engineers to share that amount of processing and memory. Here you were paying $60,000 to $70,000 total burden cost for an engineer, and you were having them share their principal tool, memory and processors, 30 to 50 ways. The reason was because the memory and processors were attached to disks and tapes and printers that cost a few hundred thousand dollars.
>
> But now, this technology called Ethernet networks coming out of Xerox PARC in Stanford gave you the ability to separate those two resources. If you look inside a computer, it has a bus; on it is the processor, memory, and the disks and tapes and all that. Ethernet sort of stretches the bus over hundreds of meters so that the cheap stuff can be dedicated and you only need to share what's expensive. So fundamentally, the rapid drop in the cost of memory and microprocessors and the availability of Ethernet changed the economic model.

Not surprisingly, workstations and PCs served different customer bases. Typical PC users were light users, in terms of time spent and performance demanded; computing was peripheral to their jobs, and before the advent of PCs, most had not been active computer users. In contrast, the typical workstation customer—often a scientist or engineer—was a "power user" who relied heavily on computers.

Computer science departments of universities constituted an important customer segment. Student enrollment in computer science boomed, but departmental mainframes and minis were stretched to their limits. Rather than adding new centralized CPUs, many universities installed networked workstations.

In industry, workstations were used in computer-aided design (CAD) and computer-aided engineering (CAE). CAD and CAE took off in the 70s when applying computers to the design of mechanical parts, buildings, and even electronic circuits proved a major success. Initially, CAD/CAE software was tied to minicomputer hardware, but now workstation-based systems were gaining popularity, especially at the low end.

CAD and CAE users like GM and Boeing either bought hardware and CAD and CAE software separately or bought turnkey systems from the so-called OEMs (original equipment manufacturers).[2] OEMs, in turn, exhibited varying levels of vertical integration. Computervision, Daisy, and Intergraph, who were market leaders in their respective segments, produced their own hardware and software. Almost all the other OEMs, however, were "system integrators": they concentrated on developing CAD/CAE software and bought the hardware they needed from one or more vendors.

---

[1] Sometimes referred to as "timesharing" architectures.

[2] Since many OEMs did not build their own hardware at all, the term is a confusing misnomer. It has, however, been firmly established in the industry jargon.

Apollo's workstations were adopted by the three major OEMs that were not vertically integrated—Mentor Graphics, Calma, and Autotrol—as well as by most of the smaller OEMs.

Apollo faced little competition. (See **Exhibit 2** for Apollo financials.) Digital, IBM, Prime, and other vendors of minicomputers and mainframes—the traditional hardware "platforms" for CAD and CAE applications—did not offer workstations. According to Apollo's marketing director, mainframe and minicomputer manufacturers were too wedded to their existing lines of business: "Anything that they may want to incorporate has to be made compatible with their existing timesharing system, and this takes the edge off their price and performance." The only established player that had announced its intention to compete was Hewlett-Packard; in the meantime, the only firms that Apollo saw in the marketplace in 1983 were scores of small start-ups, the largest of which was Sun. These start-ups were thinly capitalized and offered workstations whose broad design specifications were all drawn from the work at Xerox PARC; they were therefore very similar.

Background

Before Sun, Khosla had been a founder of Daisy Systems, an integrated vendor of CAE systems. Khosla recalled how he got involved with Daisy:

> Since I was 15, I had wanted to start a company in Silicon Valley. When I finished my bachelor's in electrical engineering at the Indian Institute of Technology, I had tried to start a company in New Delhi to produce synthetic milk out of soy extract. This ran into utter frustration. I was 20 and very impatient. So I decided to come here and find my way to Silicon Valley. I first went to Carnegie-Mellon and got my master's in biomedical engineering. The reason was purely economic—they agreed to fund me.

Khosla then joined the Stanford MBA program. He worked for a small electronics company in the summer after his first year and, as he prepared to graduate, sought a position in a small company.

> I established a set of criteria. I would only work with companies started after 1976, and this was in 1979. I would only work with companies that had less than a hundred employees. So I went through the American Electronics Association directory and wrote a letter to every company that met these criteria. There were 400 letters I wrote, which was a big burden for me. Four hundred letters was about $400.
>
> It didn't pay off. But there is a small business club at Stanford, and I had a little team that was helping high-tech companies write business plans. One of the guys on my team said his dad was talking to some guys who wanted to start a company out of Intel. I called them, met them for about an hour, and accepted the job. This was early in 1980.

Daisy was a pioneer in the computer-aided engineering business. Its goal was to provide engineers with the means to do circuit design on computers. Khosla began to question its hardware strategy.

> We invested 80 percent of our resources in the first 18 months building the computer hardware needed for CAE and about 20 percent developing the CAE tools (the software).

I thought that was ridiculous. If you are building a general-purpose computer, you might make a $10 million investment in semiconductor technology to build gate arrays or something like that, because you know that cost will be amortized. But if you are building hardware for one application and you know your volume is going to be 500 units a year, not 50,000 or 100,000 units a year, your economics are very different. You end up with a very much more expensive machine and with much more limited capability.

Yet nobody was building a computer that Daisy could use, because the CAE market was so new. There were fundamentally no CAE tools available. There was a chicken and egg problem.

Apollo had just introduced a workstation, but it didn't fit Daisy's needs. So the company developed its own hardware from scratch.

We bought a microprocessor from Intel and built a whole machine around it that was appropriate for our CAD applications. It was clear that it had a lot of limitations. The day after we delivered our first machine, and I personally went and delivered it, the customer said, "Can I have a Pascal compiler for it?" A day after they got this complete tool set, which they paid a lot of money for, they wanted to start changing it and adding programs to it. That basically said to me that there really was a market for a general-purpose machine.

Khosla investigated whether Daisy could modify and market the hardware it had developed, but

It never seemed to make sense, because there were too many other things to do in their primary business. This was a different business requiring a different set of criteria, a different set of support and business infrastructure.

Therefore, Khosla decided to leave Daisy in December 1981 to pursue this new opportunity.

From Concept to Prototype

Finding a Collaborator.   Khosla drew up a specification form a workstation that was influenced strongly by the work at Xerox PARC. The workstation would use a Motorola 68000 microprocessor, have a bitmapped display, run the UNIX operating system, and plug into the Ethernet network. These were, according to Khosla, "the only reasonable specs," as evidenced by the fact that by 1983 "there were maybe 30 companies implementing exactly that same spec." As *Datamation* noted in March 1983: "The new venture uniform of UNIX and the Motorola 68000 is getting as fashionable as IBM's blue and white stripes."

Notwithstanding his engineering training, Khosla looked for a collaborator:

I'm probably more of a conceptual engineer, and I can draw block diagrams for almost anything I can think of, but I can almost never implement them. So I started looking for someone who had done this kind of stuff before. I heard of a project at Stanford called the Stanford University Network, or Sun workstation project. I called the computer science department, and some secretary who did not want to bother a professor gave me the name of a graduate student from Germany, Andy Bechtolsheim.

Apparently, Andy, who was also at Carnegie at the same time I was, but I did not know him there, had come to Stanford to do his Ph.D. in CAD tools. I think he realized there was no appropriate machine to develop CAD tools, following the same discovery process I had gone through, so he decided to build one himself. His specs fit mine almost to a T.

Andy had developed the workstation concept in a fair amount of detail and had a prototype implementation of it. Stanford had assigned the technology to him because, in their great wisdom, and after calling DEC and Prime, they had decided it had no value.

So, for over a year he had been licensing the technology to six or seven companies. He had invested $25,000 of his own money into building prototypes, and as a grad student licensing it at $10,000 a pop, he thought that was just wonderful.

Bechtolsheim offered Khosla his usual $10,000 license. Instead, Khosla tried to persuade Bechtolsheim to join forces to start a company to build workstations based on his designs.

I said to him, ''I want the goose that laid the golden egg, and I don't want the golden egg.'' I thought that kind of resource is very rare to get. So I would rather have him than any one design he would come up with. I had nothing very concrete to offer. I told him we could build a big company, that we could raise a few million dollars. He would be a founder of the company.

It was not a tough sell.

Andy is just a very easy person to work with. He is terribly nice, very bright, very, very accommodating. His only concern was, should he drop his Ph.D. at this point? He claimed to be about three or four months away from finishing his Ph.D. I thought he was nine months away. I finally convinced him he could come back and finish his Ph.D. six months later. If he thought, in fact, that it was that short a distance, he could do it in parallel.

That was the tough part of the sell, and that was very tough I think. But the rest of it was not. He had had enough frustration with these other guys who he had licensed to, not understanding his concepts even though they had all the details. These people had seen some sophisticated technology, grabbed it, but did not know what to do with it. It was almost like they had a design for a Lamborghini engine and they put it in a Volkswagen chassis, so you couldn't corner more than 50 miles an hour. They had this incredible performance design, but anything they added to it to complete it limited it rather than enhanced it.

You really have to conceptually understand something. It's got to be in your gut. Intuition. Otherwise almost all technology licenses fail to work. In fact, if you look at the history of technology licensing, by and large, it has failed. People never, never believe how important it is to have that understanding. They just fundamentally don't believe it!

Obtaining Seed Money.   Andy Bechtolsheim agreed to participate by late January 1982. The two started working out of Andy's office at Stanford and in a couple of weeks had produced a brief plan (see **Exhibit 3**).

It was a real concise statement of the reasons for making an investment: how the economics had changed, what the product would be, when it would be out, and how big it could be and why the market made sense.

The next day, February 12, we met with two venture capitalists, one of whom, Bob Sackman, had helped me write the Daisy business plan. Within three or four days, they agreed to give us $300,000 in equity. They gave us a $100,000 check right away and said,

''You can get going and let's work on the paperwork.'' On February 22, we formally incorporated the company and received the remaining $200,000. The price of the stock was $2.75 a share. We also gave them an option to put an additional $2.2 million for a total of $2.5 million at $5.60 a share, that option to expire on June 30, 1982. By that date we were supposed to hire a marketing person, write a business plan, and demonstrate a prototype.

Bob Sackman led the thing, and he trusted me. It was really on trust. There was very little due diligence on their part—they just believed in the concept and said, ''Yes, we think you can do it.''

Getting Started.   Sun failed to recruit a marketing manager by June 30. Khosla explained:

I made organization charts for every major company I could think of, and I made over a hundred phone calls. Most of them just hung up on me. When you are 26 years old, look like a little kid, talk with a funny accent, and have two people in your company, and you're calling the vice president at DEC or HP, you don't get very far. . . . Besides, you can't hire someone until you have the money to pay them. Nobody wants to leave established companies to join someplace where they can't even see six months of salary.

Progress on other fronts, however, was rapid. Within days of obtaining seed financing, Khosla had persuaded Scott McNealy, a friend from his MBA class, to leave his job as director of operations at a small high-tech firm called Onyx and run manufacturing for Sun. By May 20, Sun not only had produced a prototype, but it had also made its first sale.

We had to procure power supplies, procure monitors, select our vendors, design the housing, and design sheet metal. Andy and I designed the sheet metal. So we became industrial designers for a while, and I became the purchasing agent to buy all these components, do component selection and all that. Then there was a bunch of software to be developed, because these things are worthless without software, so what we did was develop some terminal emulation software. You could at least do a terminal emulation and appear to a computer as a terminal with some graphics capabilities. And we promised our customers that we would soon have UNIX [an operating system] running on it.

Our first customer was another start-up called Solo Systems. They had requirements for a box just like ours for reasons similar to why Daisy needed such a box. They didn't really need much software from us since they were going to develop their own operating system and applications software.

Recruiting Bill Joy.   Unlike Solo, other customers demanded that Sun provide an operating system with its hardware. The original specifications had called for the UNIX operating system; Sun now needed to decide which kind of UNIX to provide. As a stopgap, the company contracted with a software house, Unisoft, to produce a quick version of UNIX. For the longer term, Sun appeared to have two choices: AT&T UNIX or Berkeley UNIX.

It was the biggest decision I had to make last year. AT&T had developed UNIX, but they didn't take it seriously; nobody did. Their version matched the old 16-bit minicomputer hardware but not the new 32-bit machines. The Berkeley UNIX, on the other hand, had been optimized for 32-bit hardware. Berkeley's UNIX also came with a wide range of utilities, contributed by a variety of universities, that enhanced its power and usefulness. But while Berkeley UNIX was technically superior, AT&T was the industry standard, to the extent that there was a standard.

There was no question in Andy's mind that Berkeley UNIX was the right thing to do, but in my mind, I had to play out the business issues. Everybody else was going with AT&T. Everybody.

Khosla picked the Berkeley version.

As he did with Andy Bechtolsheim, Khosla tried to recruit the resident UNIX guru at Berkeley, Bill Joy, rather than merely license the software. At age 26, Bill Joy was a UNIX star.

When he called DEC and said, "I need a VAX," they used to say they'd deliver a six-pack of VAXes, free. DEC knew that Bill was responsible for a lot of their university sales. Berkeley UNIX was getting to be very popular in the universities, DARPA,[3] and the defense community, so Digital really wanted this work at Berkeley to continue, and so I think he had 10 to 12 VAXes in that one room all to himself.

By June, Bill Joy had been persuaded to join Sun. His reasons, speculates Khosla, were similar to Bechtolsheim's.

I think he joined mostly to make the Berkeley system a commercial product. Andy didn't have a lot of software interest or expertise or didn't want to do anything about it. When Bill Joy saw the hardware, he saw a way to influence the hardware to match his operating system and to bring the two together. The financial issues were not small, but I think his ego played a big role.

The participation of Bechtolsheim and Joy enabled Sun in the months ahead to build top-notch engineering and software teams.

Most of the engineers came because they wanted to work with Bill Joy and Andy, who were leaders in the field. They also wanted to work on commercial products that could be leadership products. They were all excited about this kind of stuff because it was well publicized in the research community by Xerox PARC.

These "worker bees" weren't as conservative as the senior managers who wouldn't talk to us. In fact, the worker bees considered management in their existing companies a problem. It was the same managers that didn't want to come to work for us.

The Business Plan

Key Strategic Principles.   In parallel with his other tasks, Khosla began writing the business plan. In this endeavor, he had little help.

Anybody you really tried to talk to outside started with "You are foolish." Inside, Scott, who had never used a computer before, knew nothing of the technology or the market or the strategies. Andy and Bill didn't either, except they understood what things could be used

---

[3]Defense Advanced Research Projects Agency.

for very, very well. Bill and Andy really had a very great perspective on what was usable and what wasn't. Bill and Andy are the best marketing people in terms of specifying the marketing requirements, because they know what technology can do and know what people need to do. They are dealing with technical scientific people whose needs are similar to their own. That was a big help, because I knew it globally but not quite as intuitively and in as much depth as these two guys did. But they had no interest in the business end of things. The business selection of technologies was my responsibility. As I sat down to write the business plan, I was sort of the marketer, the marketing strategist, sort of the technology person.

By the end of June, Khosla had completed the business plan. While much of it described the operational plans, it also laid out Sun's key strategic principles.

We said, "We want to take on IBM and DEC." And not only do we want to take on IBM and DEC, we want to take them in the mainstream business, not in the little niches that most companies had positioned themselves in the Valley.

We had big dreams. When I was hang gliding, I remember seeing this motto: "Success comes to those that dare to dream dreams and are foolish enough to try and make them come true." You have to try doing something extraordinary, because unless you try something extraordinary, you won't ever do anything extraordinary.

We were going after a general business. We wouldn't develop any applications software. We would not specialize in any one narrow function—whenever we had a trade-off we'd go after the general computing environment. For example, should we use our resources to build better compilers in the UNIX development environment, or should we build a fast graphics thing like Silicon Graphics was doing? We'd pick the general one, which we'd need to compete against DEC, as opposed to the one we'd need to compete against Megatek or Lexidata. We chose DEC as the target even though we knew it was a much harder target to get than Lexidata or Megatek.

Sun's ambitions led to the choice of a direct sales force.

There was discussion on distributors or direct: how do you sell and support it, how about advertising? All the little things which we had no money for. I made the decision that I only wanted to do a direct sales force, because that was what all the successful computer companies had. I did not know anybody who had been successful through third-party distribution and third-party support.

It was very hard, because you didn't know how you were going to get revenue with a direct sales force, and you knew on the distribution side you could probably pick up revenue fairly quickly and not have to make investments with money you did not have in the first place. But "the moon or bust" was our motto. As Scott said, "If we are going to flop, we might as well be controversial and be a big belly flop."

Our calculations showed we would not have money for anything besides a direct sales force and direct support. So marketing went out of the window at Sun. We couldn't afford any promotion, we couldn't afford a PR firm and all those things, so we did without those. If we did not get money to put a color brochure together, that was OK. Because we weren't going to compromise the key fundamentals that were going to make us successful.

The business plan reaffirmed Sun's commitment to standard components. Andy Bechtolsheim's prototype and initial design had employed off-the-shelf building blocks because he had no choice.

Stanford had paid for some very early development, but once Andy got past the bread-boarding stage they did not want to pay for it and he funded it out of his own pocket. So he picked what was available: Ethernet cards from 3-Com, memory and disk controller cards for the multibus, and the like.

Khosla believed that Sun should continue this strategy.

I looked at what Sun needed to be competitive and I knew I wouldn't have the resources. I picked the smallest successful entity I could find, which was Hewlett-Packard, which was developing some entries in the technical side of the computing arena. I said I need to have development resources comparable to this operation, because that has to be critical mass. Since they are stable and everybody below them I don't consider stable, my fundamental objective is going to be to get as close to them in resources as quickly as possible.

They had 200 engineers and were going to spend $300 million on their workstations. I figured, if I got 80 or so engineers I could do the same work as 200 HP engineers could. But I could find no way to raise even those 80 engineers.

The only way was to convince other people to do your development for you. The only way to get people to do development for this hole-in-the-wall, five-person operation would be if they were doing the development anyway for somebody else. And the whole idea of standards came because there were other people doing other things: multibus disk control-lers, multibus serial I/O cards, standard memories, standard Ethernet chips. Ten people here, 5 people here, and I could add up to 80 people that I could get relatively quickly working on my project.

It was absolutely counter to any business principle in any computer company. We were severely criticized for being so standard. Everybody said that with this standard product with a bunch of things thrown together, you will never have a proprietary advantage.

Apollo, the industry leader, had taken the opposite tack. Whereas Sun had adopted Xerox's Ethernet, Apollo had developed its own Domain network. Whereas Sun had adopted Berkeley UNIX, Apollo had invested in its own operating system.

They took the conventional view and chose not to have standards. In fact, I talked to their marketing guy who I was trying to recruit about using standards and he said, "What a stupid idea." He said, "I have just finished going through my literature and eliminating all references to the Motorola 68000 chip because people might perceive it as a standard."

Manufacturing Strategy.   Sun would depend on outside resources for manufactur-ing.

We would do as little as possible because of resource constraints. And our costs would be lower because whoever was doing our board manufacturing would amortize 2 percent or 3 percent of the overhead of managing such a facility to us, while if you were doing it yourself you amortized 100 percent. Even after you added in a 10 percent or 15 percent profit margin we were still better off than doing it on our own.

The company would rely on the network of suppliers in Silicon Valley.

There is a lot of infrastructure here. You can get PC boards turned around in a week. There are a lot of companies here that only support small companies. You can get almost anything you want. You get more than you can get internally in a large company: In terms of resources, facilities, turnaround on components, pricing on components, response time on bids, range of services—from mechanical design to custom fabric machining to PC board fabrication to component loading. If there's an expensive piece of equipment like a $2 million tester, somebody probably has it and is amortizing it across 20 companies. And all these guys are used to dealing with small companies, used to being responsive, because their business depends on it.

In contrast, Apollo, which was located on the East Coast and designed its own proprietary components, was much more vertically integrated in manufacturing.

Target Customers. Sun's long-term goals for obtaining customers had to be tempered by short-term realities.

> The issue was, who would buy these things, half-baked as they were, and yet be important customers? We did not want just revenue. We wanted strategic revenue.
>
> There were two classes of people who could use a not-fully-developed machine. Universities could use it, because they did all kinds of kludgy stuff themselves and they did not mind putting in resources. Typically, they were trying something new so they did not have to rely on the whole hardware as much. Second, OEMs could use it. Daisy, Computervision, and others could essentially develop a machine from scratch, and they could definitely develop it from halfway on.
>
> It was clear that not many OEMs would buy it. We had no credibility. So we were only left with the universities as a realistic customer set for our first year.
>
> Prior to us, DEC had been successful in establishing itself primarily through the technical credibility they gained with universities. Whenever a commercial customer went to a university for consulting help, they talked about DEC, because those were the state-of-the-art machines. So in the first year I decided to set a sales target of the top 50 computer science departments in the United States. The next year we would go after OEMs.

Venture Capital. As June 30 approached, Sun's founders decided to broaden their base of funding. They persuaded the two firms that had provided the seed capital not to exercise their option to put $2.3 million of stock while Sun sought to raise funds from three highly regarded venture capitalist firms—Kleiner Perkins, TVI, and TA Associates.

> The original venture capitalists were very cooperative in not exercising their option. They said if the other firms, which were real brand name firms, were involved, it would add a lot to the credibility of the company.

TA, a Boston firm, refused to participate.

> They had just opened their office, and the guy who started the office had been in the same MBA class with Scott and me. And there was this real paranoia, a concern with perceptions.

The other two firms were attracted to the concept but had reservations about the team.

> They thought the business plan was very good. Experts in universities they checked with were enthusiastic about the future of workstations. And we had found customers for our early units. We had generated revenue.
>
> On the other hand, none of us really had any meaningful work experience. Andy and Bill had been grad students. Scott had worked at FMC for a year and had managed a

manufacturing operation for a small high-tech firm thereafter. I had never really worked at a serious job. I had been in one start-up for a year and a half, but that was it. I understood the technologies, but I didn't understand a lot of things about doing business.

One of the venture capitalists at TVI insisted that Sun add more experienced members to the team. The founders, whose earlier efforts at recruiting had not been successful, balked. The disagreement caused the financing to be delayed until September, although some funds were made available earlier. Sun raised $4.5 million— $2.3 million from the seed investors and $2.2 million from Kleiner Perkins and TVI. The seed investors got slightly cheaper stock.

The First Year: June 1982 to June 1983

The University Market.   In the first year of full operations, Sun succeeded in developing a strong presence in the university market.

> We all worked hard to sell to universities. Our rule was, if anyone was traveling, they had to call on a university. That was very, very fortunate, because universities were really looking for a machine like this. They could really play with it because it was standard, and they could buy standard pieces of hardware and interfaces, and they liked that a lot. And nobody else had anything close. The universities weren't interested in Apollo, and Apollo wasn't interested in the universities. It was small peanuts revenue.
>
> Stanford, Berkeley, and Carnegie-Mellon were our early breaks. They were three of the top four computer science schools in the country, and that counted for a lot. All the other computer science departments— 42 out of our target 50 — then picked it up around the country. So in our first fiscal year starting July 1, 1982, we have been able to do $8 million of business, 80 percent of it at universities.
>
> Universities have become our mechanism for credibility. It had worked for DEC, and it is working like a charm for us. Whenever Berkeley or Stanford talks about computing in the future, they talk about Sun, and it is the gospel message coming from an impartial source. Suddenly, every OEM is calling on us because they are hearing from the top research departments around the country that we are the next generation. Although we do not have business credibility, we have technological credibility.

Sales and Support.   Success in the university market allowed Sun to recruit a small sales force of three to five salespeople. Recruiting them was easy.

> They don't have career loyalties, long career plans. Several came out of XYZ Computers.[4] XYZ doesn't have a corporate philosophy of long-term relationships with customers. It is, "get as much from the customer, screw him and move on." So their salespeople were really mobile.
>
> And they thought they could make a buck at Sun. The product was hot, and, unlike Digital's or IBM's, our salespeople were highly commissioned. If they did well, they could make $200,000 to $300,000 in commissions. Anyplace where there are a few stories of

---

[4]Disguised name of a minicomputer company.

people making in the hundreds of thousands of dollars selling, people just run to it. The next year they can move to another company.

Since the salespeople were "process people and not information contact people," they worked in tandem with presales support engineers, who answered most of the questions. Sun's support engineers were UNIX specialists, hired out of universities and from "forgotten groups" who had been hacking away at UNIX at large corporations like Amdahl, National Semiconductor, and Intel. "We had a pretty competitive UNIX support function from the beginning," Khosla said. "Since UNIX wasn't popular, nobody else had anything."

Khosla considered Sun's sales support engineers to be a critical resource.

This is very much a salesman support-oriented company. The system, and especially our UNIX, is too sophisticated to hand out to somebody and walk away. Every field office has technical support people who are really UNIX programmers. That's helped a lot.

Engineering: Hardware and Software.

The hardware engineering team led by Andy Bechtolsheim had its hands full in Sun's first year. Not only did it have to work on completing features Sun had promised its customers would be provided later, but it also began work on a next-generation product, the Sun 2, in October 1982. Sun 2 was scheduled to be shipped in fall 1983.

Bill Joy's software engineering team went to work adapting Berkeley UNIX to Sun's hardware as well as enhancing its capabilities.

Initially, anybody could have been our equal, but now we are way ahead. We have 50 man-years of software invested in it. We've added a network file system and all kinds of other stuff. We have taken the utilities that were contributed by various universities and significantly improved them. So when someone buys a Sun they get what appears to be a standard operating system, but it is in fact pretty significantly added to.

Our UNIX is making Sun attractive to software developers. They develop their software on our machine and then port it to other hardware. . . . When the UNIX trade show was held early this year [1983], one of the most important sessions was "News from AT&T, DEC, and Sun." That was the absolute vindication that, in the UNIX marketplace, we are going to be very important.

Financial Performance.

Sun turned profitable in the first quarter, starting July 1982, and stayed profitable for the rest of the fiscal year. Khosla ran a tight ship.

We didn't have a big overhead structure, because we didn't have any money to spend. We matched our expenses to our revenue real tight. You might ascribe this to my Indian heritage—$100K was a huge sum of money. I insist on daily cash flow reports. On the first anniversary, they presented me with a sharp pencil, because, one, I needed it, and two, that was all they could afford, they said. But that is pretty much the culture of the company. We really have tight controls. Accounting, inventory control, auto management, MRP, general ledger, accounts payable, accounts receivable: All this was computerized by Scott and me almost from day one.

We were unlike most start-ups. Most start-ups have everything—marketing, sales, support, advertising, and PR—in place even before they have a product to sell. They get up to

$600,000 to $800,000 a month of expenses before they've really started selling anything. In that range, given you're starting out with low gross margins because your product costs are high, you've got to start selling $1.5 million worth just to break even in a month.

Sun's profitability began to help it attract some experienced managers.

Since we've finished the first year, have gotten to a million dollars a month, and are profitable, people have started to look at us seriously, started to consider us viable. People feel a lot more comfortable with something there and running and profitable and operating, even if it is small relative to nothing there. There's a radical nonlinear function between those two.

The OEM Market.   One area in which Sun did not make much progress in its first year was the OEM market. Sun considered gaining share in the OEM market to be a major, long-term goal and adapted its product and pricing strategies accordingly.

One fundamental part of our strategy is to get as many CPUs out there as possible, and get them popularized. Market share is very important to us and revenue is not. Even though we did really good in revenue last year, our goal was not revenue.

So if somebody is better off buying our CPU and putting his own disk drives and tape drives, because they can't afford ours, we will let them. We have created sort of an airline pricing structure. People who want full support and service and don't want to hassle with it pay full price. People who are sort of willing to book two weeks in advance and sort of leave on Thursday evenings get a price break. Everybody puts in their level of pain to get their price point. Our goal is to skim as much of the money and also get as many of our CPUs and operating systems out there as we can. We can capture the rest of the system revenue later. And if our co-developers—all these other guys who put in the other 70 or 80 engineers in various companies—get a lot of revenue, they will invest more in Sun.

In spite of Sun's efforts, and even with the endorsement of computer science departments, OEMs had proven a very tough nut to crack.

Daisy is the leader in its market segment, and Computervision and Integraph are leaders in their market segments. These three have decided that they are going to build their own computers. Calma, Autorol, and Mentor Graphics are the second tier, but the most important second tier after the top three, and Apollo has them all. Calma, Autorol, and Mentor account for 60 percent to 70 percent of Apollo sales. Mentor, I think, accounts for 40 percent of Apollo and is really catching up on Daisy, and its growth has been very good for Apollo. Apollo has been going through the roof because of these customers. And because of that, all the smaller people in the business are picking Apollo.

Apollo is the successful platform. They have this huge momentum. They have $20 million or $30 million of financing versus our $4 million. They have well-connected senior management.[5] We have diddly squat. We clearly have the better technology, and people recognize it, but. . . .

Apollo's customers were, apparently, satisfied customers. As Mentor Graphics, Apollo's first OEM customer, noted in its prospectus:

---

[5] Apollo's chairman Poduska had been a co-founder of Prime; four of the seven founders were "repeaters"—they had previously founded another venture.

The use of Apollo hardware enables the company to concentrate on applications software and special-purpose hardware development, while benefiting from Apollo's research and development efforts in general-purpose hardware and operating systems software. The company believes this strategy enables it to stay at the leading edge of technology in computer hardware, operating systems, and applications software. In addition, the company has benefited from market acceptance of the Apollo computer for general applications, as well as rapid improvements in the price and performance of Apollo's hardware.

As *Datamation* had noted: "Everything seems to be going like clockwork for young Apollo; the original business plan [which] called for launch in 1980, sales in 1981, profits in 1982, and a public offering in 1983 [is] right on schedule."[6]

The Computervision Order

In December 1982, Sun saw an opening into the OEM business. Computervision announced that it was considering buying a workstation instead of building its own.

Computervision was a company in transition. From the time it was founded in 1969, it had followed an ambitious strategy. It offered complete "turnkey systems"— all the hardware, software, and training that users needed. Instead of designing specialized systems for one or two industries, Computervision aimed for a wide range of domestic and international customers. And unlike most of its competitors, who added software to Digital's or IBM's minicomputers, Computervision designed and built its own.

In the 70s, according to a *New England Business* article, "Computervision was a high-tech company on a roll. Everything was in superlatives. It was *the* fastest growth, *the* newest technology, *the* highest income."[7]

Although Computervision was still the market leader, the CAD pioneer's position had begun to erode by 1983. IBM, Digital, Prime, Perkin Elmer, and several other minicomputer manufacturers had entered the market with software from third-party vendors, and they were enjoying some success. IBM had become the number two player, almost overnight, with the help of Lockheed's popular software. And the effectiveness of Computervision's response had been undermined by delays in the development of its next generation (32-bit) minicomputer.

In addition, dozens of start-up companies were gnawing at the low end of the market with cheap workstation-based systems aimed at specific niches. Using hardware from companies like Apollo and Sun, these start-up companies were able to sell CAD systems for under $100,000, compared to the $500,000 typical of Computervision's systems.

Computervision was taking several actions to shore up its position. In August 1982, founder Martin Allen gave up the titles of president and CEO to James Berret, formerly a group vice president at Honeywell. Allen said that he had "wanted

---

[6]*Datamation*, March 1983, p. 79.

[7]*New England Business*, April 18, 1983, p. 46.

someone who came from a multibillion-dollar environment and who had experience competing against IBM.''[8]

The company also seemed to be edging away from its commitment to vertical integration: it had bought Cambridge Interactive Systems, which sold CAD software to go with other vendors' hardware; it was negotiating to buy IBM's System 4300 computer line, as a backup to its own 32-bit minicomputer development; and, to respond to its new low-end rivals, it was planning to buy a workstation platform instead of developing one.

To gear up for the Computervision contract, Sun hired a veteran executive and group operations manager, Owen Brown, away from Digital.

> We needed credibility. The East Coast establishment didn't take me or Sun too seriously. They thought we were quirky . . . because of things like . . . I hated smokers, and for the first 20 people we didn't hire a smoker or anyone who drank coffee.
>
> Besides there was a real crunch on my time. I was chief salesman, CEO, and everything. Engineering was reporting to me. Finance was reporting to me. So we asked Owen to be VP of sales and marketing. He said, ''Give me the title of president so I can deal with these Computervision guys and do big corporate account selling and go play golf with them.'' I didn't play golf, and in some situations it is very important. So we hired him and formed an office of the president.

In the months that followed, competition for the Computervision order narrowed to Apollo and Sun. ''We had our friends in Computervision,'' said Khosla, ''who were mostly the technologists, and Apollo had theirs, who were mostly the businesspeople and all the senior executives. And there were some people who wanted Computervision not to go outside at all.''

At 4 one afternoon in July, Khosla received an ominous call.

> It was from a purchasing guy from Computervision and that was terrible. You never want to hear from a purchasing guy, because that means you are getting a rejection. He thanked us very much for bidding on the contract but said they had chosen another vendor.
>
> I was livid. Had smoke coming out of my ears. Owen Brown, who was supposed to be running that account, was off for two weeks on his Navy reserve training. How could he be off on Navy reserve training or anywhere else when the future of the company depended on this one deal and he didn't even know the deal is happening in this two-week period?
>
> I took over. By 6 p.m. I had sent off a letter, Federal Express, to about 30 or 40 people at Computervision. I said we would do anything for their business.
>
> I didn't go home; I had my wife bring my clothes to the office, and I caught a red-eye to Boston.
>
> The next morning, I was in the Computervision lobby, making phone calls, trying to see someone. Nobody would talk to me.
>
> After four hours and over 50 phone calls, I got through to the VP of sales and marketing, who was a Sun friend. Apparently, Computervision had made the decision long ago. By now, there were Computervision technical people from Europe who had arrived here for technical training, at Apollo. It had gone that far. They were on crossing the Ts and dotting the Is on the contract. So people were avoiding me for political reasons.

---

[8]*Business Week,* December 20, 1982, p. 76C.

The sales VP said that, "If you go back to the Sun office in Boston, I will make sure somebody calls you and talks to you." With that promise, since I wasn't getting anywhere, I went back to the Sun office there. I showered and shaved there and waited.

The Call. Finally, the president called.

He was saying, "We have decided, and here is why." He was giving me all the good reasons. "You are a 40-person company, and you have an incomplete product. We love your technology, but there is no way you can supply it. Apollo is the standard in the industry, well financed and well managed."

Exhibit 1   Selected Financial Data (in thousands, except per share amounts)

Operating Data	*January 2–June 30, 1983*	*February 24–June 30, 1982*
Net revenues	$ 8,657	$ 86
Cost and expenses		
Cost of sales	4,486	56
Research and development	1,868	99
Selling, general and administrative	1,715	61
Total costs	$ 8,069	$ 216
Operating income (loss)	588	(130)
Interest income (expense), net	136	—
Income (loss) before taxes	724	(130)
Provision for income taxes	70	—
Net income (loss)	654	(130)
Net income (loss) per share	0.04	(0.02)
Weighted average common and common equivalent shares outstanding	$14,660	$5,619
Balance Sheet Data		
Working capital	$ 3,357	$ (14)
Total assets	7,733	405
Short-term borrowings	111	—
Long-term obligation, less current maturities	749	—
Shareholders' equity	$ 4,849	$ 158

EXHIBIT 2   Apollo: Selected Financial Data

The following table summarizes certain selected consolidated financial data and is qualified in its entirety by a more detailed Consolidated Financial Statement included elsewhere in this Prospectus. The information as of July 2, 1983, and for the six months ended July 3, 1982, and July 2, 1983, is unaudited but, in the opinion of the management of the Company, reflects all adjustments (consisting only of normal recurring adjustments) necessary to a fair presentation. The operating results for the six months ended July 2, 1983, are not necessarily indicative of the results to be expected for the full fiscal year.

Consolidated Statements of Operations

	February 13, 1980, (inception) to January 3, 1981	Fiscal Year Ended		Six Months Ended	
		January 2, 1982	January 1, 1983	July 3, 1982	July 2, 1983
Net sales	—	$ 3,400,000	$18,099,000	$ 5,281,000	$31,728,000
Costs and expenses					
Cost of sales	—	2,244,000	8,047,000	2,705,000	12,940,000
Research and development	$ 582,000	1,674,000	3,005,000	1,250,000	3,407,000
Selling, general, and administrative	644,000	2,889,000	6,842,000	2,412,000	9,688,000
Total costs and expenses	1,226,000	6,807,000	17,894,000	6,367,000	26,035,000
Operating income (loss)	(1,226,000)	(3,407,000)	205,000	(1,086,000)	5,693,000
Interest income, net	149,000	415,000	102,000	60,000	1,222,000
Income (loss) before provision for income taxes	$(1,077,000)	$(2,992,000)	$ 307,000	$(1,026,000)	$ 6,915,000
Provision for income taxes	—	—	—	—	2,490,000
Income (loss) before extraordinary tax benefit	(1,077,000)	(2,992,000)	307,000	(1,026,000)	4,425,000
Extraordinary tax benefit from prior year net operating loss carryforwards	—	—	—	—	1,950,000
Net income (loss)	$(1,077,000)	$(2,922,000)	$ 307,000	$(1,026,000)	$ 6,375,000
Earnings (loss) per common and common equivalent share:					
Income (loss) before extraordinary tax benefit	(.38)	(.69)	.02	(.24)	.23
Net income (loss)	(.38)	(.69)	.02	(.24)	.32
Weighted average number of common and common equivalent shares outstanding	2,819,000	4,349,000	17,100,000	4,299,000	19,651,000

Consolidated Balance Sheet Data

	January 3, 1981	January 2, 1982	January 1, 1983	July 2, 1983
Working capital	$3,178,000	$5,093,000	$ 8,176,000	$62,278,000
Total assets	3,743,000	8,579,000	19,450,000	80,247,000
Long-term capital lease obligations	226,000	914,000	2,092,000	1,838,000
Stakeholders' investment	3,332,000	6,427,000	11,761,000	69,574,000

SOURCE: Apollo Prospectus

EXHIBIT 3   **Preliminary Business Plan**

VLSI SYSTEMS INC.   **CONFIDENTIAL**

Mission

Develop, manufacture, market, and support graphics workstations for OEM CAD/CAM marketplace. Evolve a family of compatible graphics workstations. Maintain lead with the best cost/performance product on the market.

Objectives over Next Four Months: February 1982 — May 1982

1. PRODUCT. Bring product to market. Make first customer shipments of the SUN workstation by May 31, 1982.
2. DEVELOPMENT. Define a product family for the OEM market, including enhancements, options, and software for OEMs. Begin development of distributed UNIX operating system.
3. PEOPLE. Assemble a team of people to lead the company through its rapid growth. Recruit high-level marketing and software expertise.
4. PLANNING. The following pages contain a preliminary business plan designed to present the overall picture. A full operating plan and budget will be worked out by May 31, 1982.
5. FINANCING. Estimates for seed financing are outlined in Appendix B. Objective is to obtain seed money in February 1982 and full funding by May 31, 1982.

Tentative 2-Year Plan

Following the launch in June 1982 we plan to achieve the following objectives:

1. SALES. Deliver 500 units in the first year at an ASP of $8,000 for total sales of $4M in fiscal 1983. Ship 1,500 units in the second year for sales of $10M.
2. OPERATIONS. Set up an operating company with 50 employees by the end of the first year and 150 employees by the end of the second year. Implement proper manufacturing and testing procedures, financial and accounting controls, and an international marketing and customer support organization.
3. FINANCING. Manage company growth to produce break-even cash flow by the end of the first year. At that time it is expected that $750,000 will be required to finance inventory, $1,000,000 to finance accounts receivables, and $500,000 to finance cumulative losses and capital equipment. The balance of the expected $2,500,000 financing together with receivables financing will provide working capital. Appendixes C and D list the development and staffing requirements over the next year.

Product: The SUN Workstation

SYSTEM. The SUN workstation is a powerful modular network-based graphics workstation. Its primary use is as a single-user computer with high-resolution, high-performance graphics capabilities and substantial local processing power. Its modularity permits it to be reconfigured for a variety of applications, including support for networks of SUN workstations in the form of printer servers, file servers, terminal concentrators, and gateways. Such a system provides a suitable hardware base to support design automation, advanced text processing, office automation, distributed systems, computer-aided manufacturing, robotics, and many other interactive graphical computing tasks.

Adhering to popular industry standards—the Motorola 68000, the Intel Multibus, the Xerox Ethernet, Bell Lab's UNIX operating system, the C, PASCAL and ADA programming languages—the SUN workstation makes it as simple as possible for an OEM to integrate the SUN workstation into its system.

HARDWARE. The SUN workstation consists of a bitmap display, keyboard, network connection, and processor. A "mouse" pointing device may be connected to the keyboard. The display has 1024 by 800 pixel resolution and can show arbitrary raster images, thus permitting variable width fonts, foreign alphabets, mathematical symbols, vectors, curves, shaded regions, and even photographic

EXHIBIT 3   *(continued)*

pictures. The processor is based on the Motorola 68000 CPU and provides full virtual memory management hardware. The design allows a 10 MHz 68000 to operate at full speed without wait states. The SUN workstation uses Ethernet as its local network. The Ethernet connection allows many SUN workstations to be tied together to exchange messages and electronic mail and to share services such as file storage and printing.

SOFTWARE. Three commercial versions of the Bell Lab UNIX operating system are available for the SUN workstation: Microsoft Xenix, Unisoft UNIX, and Lucasfilm UNIX. Commercially available PASCAL, FORTRAN, and ADA compilers have been demonstrated on the system.

Summary of Key Competitive Advantages

- Lowest cost graphics workstation for scientific-engineering-CAD marketplace.
- High-resolution, high-speed graphics capability for text and lines.
- Design based on emerging industry standards: 68000, Multibus, Ethernet, UNIX.
- Lowest chip-count, therefore high reliability.
- Proven hardware design, available today.

Market: OEM Workstations

The company intends to focus initially on the OEM market for high-performance graphics workstations with computational and networking capabilities. Target customers are all companies serving the turnkey CAD/CAM, robotics, process control, simulation and modeling, and other specialized industrial markets.

Currently most CAD/CAM workstations are priced in the $40,000 to $200,000 range. At this price, it is difficult to justify one workstation per engineer or professional. The SUN workstation breaks new cost/performance barriers with a hardware price of $5,000 to $7,000 in OEM quantities. This will enable OEMs to sell their workstations at an end-user price of $10,000 to $15,000.

The SUN workstation has been reviewed and acclaimed by the scientific community. Literally hundreds of inquiries have been received without any active marketing. Cadlinc, a company licensed to manufacture the SUN workstation for its turnkey CAD system, has expressed a strong interest in entering the OEM market and projected sales of 1,500 workstations at $7,500 ASP in the first year.

This tremendous interest is prompting us to launch a new company whose specific mission is to exploit this market. The proposed company, led by the original designers, is in the best position to take this product immediately to market. Concurrently, a family of hardware configurations and support software will be developed to provide the OEM with a range of options. Support software will be targeted to aid OEM software development. A cost-reduction effort is planned to introduce a lower cost product by November 1982.

Summary of Marketing Approach

- Focus on OEM sales for maximum growth.
- Target initial production at OEM customers for software development.
- Put SUN workstations into selected universities to gain visibility.
- Develop options/cost reductions as market requires.

Competitors

There is external and internal competition. External competitors are:

- Workstation manufacturers: Apollo, Three Rivers, and Xerox.
- Graphics system manufacturers: Megatek, Lexidata, RamTek, Aydin.
- Minicomputer manufacturers: Data General, DEC, HP.
- Personal computer manufacturers: Apple, Fortune, Tandy.

EXHIBIT 3   *(continued)*

Primary competition is the workstation manufacturers.

Apollo Computers Inc. The Apollo Domain product has similar capabilities to the SUN workstation: 68000, high-resolution graphics, networking. Compared to the SUN workstation, the Apollo has the disadvantage of a nonstandard operating system (DOMAIN), nonstandard network technology, and a retail price of $25,000 per workstation.

Three-Rivers Computer Corp. The PERQ workstation product again has similar capabilities to the SUN workstation. It is based on a bit-slice computer architecture and is difficult to use because of the limited software available. Unit price is in excess of $30,000, with pricing flexibility limited by high manufacturing costs.

Xerox Corp. The Xerox Star workstation has very similar capabilities to a SUN workstation, with identical networking and graphics capabilities. Xerox is targetting the Star to the office automation market but might also begin selling into the OEM market. However, the Star system is based on a bit-slice, microcoded processor that is difficult to use for an OEM. Also, the only software Xerox offers is a proprietary programming language called MESA.

Internal competitors are companies that have been licensed to build SUN workstations or SUN workstation components, usually for a special turnkey application. These companies are: Cadlinc, Codata, Forward, Imagen, and Pacific Microcomputer.

Cadlinc is a Chicago-based start-up CAD company. The license agreement with Cadlinc was entered with its intention to use the design solely for a turnkey CAD workstation. With the publicity surrounding the SUN workstation, and Cadlinc being the only manufacturer of the workstation so far, Cadlinc is now planning to enter the OEM workstation market since it sees an opportunity of selling 1,500 SUN workstations in its fiscal 1983. Cadlinc has currently no marketing, sales, or manufacturing in place for this market. It is believed that Cadlinc can be legally delayed from entering the OEM market.

Codata is a $3 million Sunnyvale company selling stand-alone UNIX systems based on the SUN 68000 board. It has no license to other parts of the system.

Forward Technology is a start-up Santa Clara company currently selling the SUN 68000 board and the graphics board, but intending to move into the workstation marketplace.

Imagen builds the SUN 68000 board as its laser printer controller. It is not selling the board.

Pacific Microcomputer is a very small San Diego company selling the SUN 68000 board.

Patents and Other Rights

The original SUN workstation design has been performed by Andy Bechtolsheim while being a student at Stanford University. Subsequently, Stanford has released all its rights to the design to Andy's company, VLSI Systems Inc.

The SUN workstation design includes sufficiently novel ideas that we have filed invention disclosures on two aspects of its design: the graphics subsystem and the processor memory management.

No patent applications have been filed yet. Patents need to be filed before April 30, 1982, since the concepts were first published one year ago that day (publication bar).

The design itself has been copyrighted, and the engineering documentation is maintained as a trade secret by VLSI Systems.

Current Team

1. Andreas Bechtolsheim, Ph.D. student at Stanford University, the principal designer of the SUN workstation while at Stanford. Responsibilities: engineering and development, production engineering, system engineering, new product definition.
2. Vinod Khosla, M.S., MBA Stanford University, was a member of the founding team of a successful CAD start-up (Daisy Systems). Responsibilities: overall management, finance, strategic planning.

EXHIBIT 3   *(continued)*

---

3. Scott McNealy, MBA Stanford University, is currently director of operations at Onyx Systems. Responsibilities: Operations.

The team will be expanded over the next few months, concentrating on the areas of marketing and software. In addition, the company can draw on consultants that are currently with VLSI Systems:

1. Vaughan Pratt, professor of computer science, Stanford University, has managed the SUN project at Stanford over the last year and was the main implementor of the SUN software environment.
2. Forest Baskett, professor of computer science, Stanford University, started the SUN workstation project and defined some of its key architectural features. Forest is currently with Xerox Corporation.

Appendix A: Costs

Product:

SUN-1: Current SUN workstation.
SUN-2: Single board version of SUN-1.
SUN-3: Custom LSI version of SUN-2.

Direct material costs (qty 1,000/year):

	SUN-1	**SUN-2**	**SUN-3**
Electronics (ICs)	$1,100	$1,000	$ 800
Other parts			
Monitor	$ 400	$ 350	$ 300
Keyboard	$ 120	$ 100	$ 70
Mouse	$ 180	100	$ 80
Power supply	$ 100	$ 50	$ 50
Packaging	$ 600	$ 200	$ 200
Subtotal	$1,400	$ 800	$ 700
Total material cost	$2,500	$1,800	$1,500
Direct labor (10%)	$ 250	$ 180	$ 150
Indirect labor (10%)	$ 250	$ 180	$ 150
Total manufacturing cost	$3,000	$2,240	$1,800
Average selling price	$7,000	$5,000	$4,000

Appendix B: Financial Requirements February 1982 — May 1982

Salaries (6 people at $ 2,000/month + benefits)	$ 60,000
Marketing, advertising, and sales	15,000
Hardware development	25,000
Software development (UNIX license fees)	60,000
General and administrative (including travel and legal)	15,000
Rent and utilities	5,000
Total expenses	$180,000
Inventory (20 systems at $3,500)	70,000
Total cash requirement	$250,000

Exhibit 3   *(continued)*

Appendix C: Engineering Development Required

Mouse and Keyboard	Start Date	Responsible Individuals	Collaborating With
Hardware (HW)			
Foreign version of SUN-1	5/1	HW2	
10 MB Ethernet and Transceive	5/1	HW1	
Single disk workstation integration	•2/15	HW1	SW1
Color graphics	•8/1	HW3	HW1/MK2
Product family (cost reduction, options etc.)	7/1	HW1	HW2/MK2
File server/gateway hardware	3/1	HW1	SW2
Floating point processor	7/1	HW2	HW1
Patent filing	3/1	HW1	
Ongoing debug and maintenance	5/1	•HW2	HW1
Manufacturing Engineering			
EMI/RFI and safety requirements	5/1	ME1	Consultant
Acceptance tests (at all levels)	4/1	ME1	HW2
Primary and secondary sources, "Vendor Selections"	2/15	ME1	HW1
Diagnostics	3/1	HW2	ME1
Documentation	•3/1	HW2/ME1	HW1
Parts list and standard costs	3/1	ME1	HW1
Packaging	•2/15	ME1	HW1/MK1
Software (SW)			
Mouse Programming			
Single user UNIX	•2/15	SW1	SW2/HW4
Distributed UNIX	•2/15	SW2	SW1/HW1
Software development aids (PWB)	•6/1	SW5	SW1/SW2
Text editor	•5/1	SW4	AE1/MS2
Graphics editor	5/1	SW4	AE1/MS2
Benchmarks	•6/1	AE1	MS2
File server/gateway software	3/15	SW1	HW1/SW2
Documentation	•5/1	TW1	
Programming languages	•4/1	SW3	
Software configuration management	•10/1	SW6	

HW = Hardware engineer
ME = Manufacturing engineer
SW = Software engineer
TW = Technical writer
AE = Applications engineer
MS = Marketing
GA = General and administrative
MO = Manufacturing operations
•   = Earliest required

Exhibit 3   *(continued)*

Organizational Developments Required

General and Administrative (GA)	Start Date	Responsible Individual	Collaborating With
Form corporation (select names, lawyers, auditors, bankers, sort licenses)	•2/8	GA1/HW1	
Seed financing	2/15	GA1/HW1	
Full financing	4/15	GA1/HW1	
Business licenses (county, state, federal, sales) and filings (taxes etc).	2/15	GA1	Consultant
Establish payroll, benefit, and insurance programs	3/1	GA—	GA1
Investor relations/reports	2/8	GA1/HW1	
Recruiting	2/8	GA1/HW1	
Accounting system (cost/general)	•3/1	GA—	GA1/MO1
Budgets, controls, and planning (cash flows, forecasts, staffing)	2/15	GA—	All others
Facilities	2/15	GA1	MO
Banking (cash management, credit lines, etc.)	2/15	GA1	
Marketing and Sales (MS)			
Sell sample evaluation and development units	•3/15	MS1	
Brochures and advertising material	3/15	MS1	Consultant
OEM, research and university sales	5/1	MS—	
Sales training and tools (slide presentation etc.)	4/1	MS	MS2
Competitive analysis (pricing, new products etc.)	6/1	MS3	MS1
Public relations and exposure (announcements, articles, conferences)	6/1	MS3	Consultant
Sales program (OEM contracts, licenses, sales compensation plan etc.)	4/1	MS1	
Trade shows	4/1	MS3/MS1	
Establish sales offices (national, European, Japan trading Co.)	7/1	MS1	MS—
Order administration (schedule, credit check, etc.)	7/1	MS1	GA1/MS1
Manufacturing Operations			
Production line organization (work orders, assembly flow, scheduling etc.)	3/1	MO1	ME1
Vendor qualification	3/1	MO1	ME1
Quality assurance (test and accep. procedures, ECO's etc.)	5/1	MO1	ME1
Materials systems (part no., inventory control and stockroom orgz., returns etc.)	4/1	MO1/MO2	GA1
MRP	4/1	MO1/MO2	
Purchasing procedures and operations	4/1	MO1/MO3	GA1
Shipping/receiving procedures and operations	5/1	MO1/MO4	
Board debug/repair			
System assembly			

EXHIBIT 3 *(concluded)*

Appendix D

Staffing Plan 1982–83

	Jan.	Feb.	March	April	May	June	July	Aug.	Sept.	Oct.	Nov.	Dec.	Jan.	Feb.	March	April	May	June
Software																		
Engineers	2	2	3	4	5	5	5	5	5	5	5	5	7	7	7	10	10	10
Support	0	0	1	1	1	1	1	1	1	2	2	2	2	2	2	2	2	2
Hardware																		
Engineers	1	1	1	2	3	3	3	3	3	3	3	3	3	3	3	3	3	3
Manufacturing Engineering Engineers	1	1	1	1	1	1	1	1	1	1	1	1	1	1	2	2	2	2
Marketing and sales																		
Management	0	1	1	1	2	2	2	2	2	2	2	3	3	3	5	5	5	5
Sales	0	0	0	0	2	2	2	3	3	3	3	4	4	4	7	7	7	7
Application Engineers	0	0	0	0	1	1	1	2	2	2	2	2	2	2	3	3	3	3
Support	0	0	0	1	1	1	1	1	1	2	2	3	3	3	4	4	4	4
General and Administrative																		
Management	1	1	1	1	1	1	1	1	2	2	2	2	2	2	2	2	2	2
Finance/Accounting	0	0	0	0	1	1	1	1	1	1	1	2	2	2	2	2	2	2
Personnel	0	0	0	0	0	0	0	1	1	1	1	1	1	1	1	1	1	1
Support	0	1	1	1	1	1	1	3	3	3	3	4	4	4	5	5	5	5
Manufacturing Operations																		
Management	0	0	0	1	2	2	2	2	3	3	3	3	3	3	3	3	3	3
Buyer/Planner	0	0	0	1	1	1	1	2	2	2	2	2	3	3	3	3	3	3
Technicians	0	1	1	1	1	1	2	2	2	2	2	4	4	4	5	5	5	5
Hourly	0	0	0	0	1	2	3	3	4	4	4	4	4	5	5	5	5	5
Clerical	0	0	0	0	1	1	1	1	1	1	2	2	2	2	3	3	3	3
QA Engineers	0	0	0	1	1	1	1	1	1	1	1	1	1	1	1	1	1	1
Total Employees	5	7	9	11	17	26	27	27	38	40	40	40	50	50	51	66	66	66
Number of units produced	–	–	–	–	5	15	25	30	35	40	45	50	55	60	65	75		

Annotations: "new projects" (near Software Support, mid-1982); "start European operations" (near General and Administrative, late 1982).

4–3 IMAGE PRESENTATIONS, INC.

"I'm really disappointed," said Mark Edwards. "Lisa Johnson has just turned down our job offer, and we don't have any other candidates. Got any ideas?"

Mark was president of Image Presentations, Inc. (IPI), which designed and produced videos, films, slides, and multimedia shows for educational institutions and large corporations. (See **Exhibits 1** and **2** for financial statements.) Their work was used for fund-raising, recruiting, product launches, employee motivation, and other public relations and communication events. Mark and his partner, Jonathan Spring, were determined to start a subsidiary—Recruiting Arts—that focused on working with companies to recruit top candidates through the use of media advertising. It would offer a broader range of products and services than IPI did. Recruiting Arts appeared to be an exciting growth opportunity. Lisa, a second-year MBA student at the Harvard Business School, seemed just the right person to take charge of this new venture. But she had just accepted a position with the *New York Times*.

IPI faced recruiting challenges in its existing business as well, particularly in hiring producers. The company looked for individuals who could perform both creative and client management tasks and who would fit into an organization that strove to be more professional and "buttoned down" than was usual in the industry. IPI's failure to attract such individuals was proving to be a major obstacle to its growth.

Brief History

Image Presentations grew out of Jonathan Spring's high school interest in filmmaking. Jonathan took courses in film and art as a student at the Phillips Exeter Academy in New Hampshire.

Jonathan did not expect to make a career of filmmaking. He enrolled at the Massachusetts Institute of Technology (MIT) because be believed that "engineering, unlike filmmaking, was something that real people did in real life." At MIT, however, his interest in film was rekindled.

> What I did not know when I applied to MIT . . . was that it had an excellent filmmaking program, taught by Richard Leacock, the father of American cinema verite, and by Ed Pincus. Besides great teachers, it also had unbelievable equipment. I started taking courses,

Research Associate Kevin Hinton prepared this case under the supervision of Professor Amar V. Bhide.
Copyright © 1990 by the President and Fellows of Harvard College
Harvard Business School Case 9–390–140

and, before long, I had sort of finagled my way in among the graduate students in the film program.[1]

During his sophomore year at MIT, Exeter asked him to produce a film to commemorate its bicentennial. Mark Edwards, an Exeter senior who had enrolled in the same course that had sparked Jonathan's film interest, was assigned to help him. Working with a $40,000 budget, the duo wrote, shot, and edited a highly praised documentary history of Exeter.[2]

Word of the Exeter documentary eventually reached MIT's president, who later asked Jonathan to produce a fund-raising video for MIT's art programs. Jonathan accepted the project and collaborated on it with Mark, then a freshman at Harvard College.

After Jonathan and Mark completed the MIT video, word of their work spread throughout the Boston area. Other schools in the area began to request their services, and the two began a filmmaking business from their college dorm rooms. In addition to producing videos for educational institutions, they began organizing and producing shows, product promotions, and sales meetings for corporations. Balancing their studies and production, Mark recalls, was hectic.

I was doing a big shoot down in New York during the day. . . . My government junior tutorial was at seven o'clock at night. . . . I was living a lot of days like that.[3]

After Mark's graduation in 1983, the duo pursued media production full time. "I think I was the happiest person at commencement," Mark said. "Finishing college meant I could work 14 hours a day instead of the usual 18."[4] By then, IPI's clients had included several Ivy League colleges, IBM, Gillette, and Westinghouse. Concerning their college business, Mark added,

In 1978, few people were thinking about doing media for recruiting. However, we entered the market just as the bottom started to drop out of everyone's applications pools. Schools started scrambling for new ways to get people to apply, and they began to seize upon media as a way to differentiate themselves. We were right there, in position, and we were lucky enough to have worked with the most prestigious schools early.

IPI in 1989

IPI grew rapidly, doubling its revenues almost every year after 1977. In 1989, the firm booked annual revenues of about $2.5 million, on which it earned about $240,000 in profits.

---

[1]Desiree Baynes, "Taking Care of Business: Script to Screen Success, Film Production Company Projects a Strong Image," *Essence,* November 1985, p. 19.

[2]Theresa Pease, "Capturing the MIT Experience: Alumnus Filmmaker Thinks About the Future," *MIT Spectrum,* Summer 1988, p. 3.

[3]E. S., "Videoman," John Harvard's Journal, *Harvard Magazine,* November–December 1985, p. 103.

[4]Ibid.

The company continued to serve two types of clients: universities, which accounted for 58 percent of total revenues, and corporations, which accounted for 42 percent of revenues. IPI had become, according to its president, the preeminent firm in education.

> Image Presentations is the national leader in media for schools. For over 10 years, we have expertly crafted videotapes, slide shows, and films for many of the country's leading educational institutions. Image Presentations has garnered 17 CASE [Council for Advancement and Support of Education] awards for our clients.

Jonathan explained why he thought IPI had done so well in this market.

> Our ability to make videos that differentiate has been the cornerstone of our business. There are about a dozen firms doing college videos. About a half dozen are regionally based mom-and-pop-type operations staffed by two or three people, and we also compete with some other audiovisual companies who do work in-house. However, if you take a look at five of any of our competitors' videos, you will notice that they all look alike. Schools realize that unless students see things that are different, then they aren't going to be able to use that information as part of their decision-making process. Our ability to meet this need is really the key to our success. We are about 50 percent to 100 percent more expensive than our competitors. If colleges budget sufficiently, then chances are that we'll win 19 out of 20 jobs.

Jonathan contrasted the company's success in the educational market to its position in the corporate market. (See **Exhibit 3** for corporate marketing brochure.)

> There are many organizations that are bigger than us in (the corporate) market, and they have been around longer than us. We have four competitors in Boston, and they too are larger (in terms of the amount of business they do) and older. The corporate market is more mature, and much more competitive. In addition, consumers are much more brand loyal to their production companies. We are not the market leader, but we try to deliver the same kind of tailored product to our corporate clients that we deliver to our educational clients.

Jonathan outlined the company's broad range of capabilities. (See **Exhibit 4** for list of recent projects.)

> Image Presentations is a full-service production company with the know-how, facilities, and personnel to bring a presentation from script to screen. While each project is a cooperative effort between our company and our client. Image Presentations takes ultimate responsibility for directing, scriptwriting, photographing, mixing the soundtrack, and delivering the final viewing format.
>
> [Image Presentations] now occupies an entire building on Newbury Street in Boston. It has an impressive production facility. It was designed from the ground up to be very functional for us and very comfortable for our customers. We offer one of the best sound studios of any production company in New England; video, film, and slide interface; complete in-house design facilities; screening and meeting rehearsal rooms.
>
> Image Presentations has an exceptional full-time staff of producers, designers, production and technical professionals. Their creativity and dedication make our clients return again and again.

The Organization.   By 1989, the organization had grown to comprise 16 employees. Although no formal organizational chart existed, IPI's employees were organized into four functions—sales, production, art, and administration. Mark supervised the sales department:

> The sales force is my direct responsibility. It consists of four people, including myself. We have two telemarketers, Don and Betsy, who generate appointments for me and Matt, our new sales manager. Don works with the schools, and Betsy with the corporations. Sometimes Don and Betsy sell our services, but they're not directly responsible for bringing in clients. That responsibility belongs to me and to Matt. Matt is the newest member of the sales team, but he has a lot of prior experience in advertising sales.

Jonathan supervised the production staff and the art department.

> We have on staff four producers—Laura, Steve, Ken, and Bill. They are responsible for the talent, script, photography, soundtrack, staging, everything. They are responsible for creating the vision. Producers are also responsible for the profitability of the show. They have to design the budget and work within it. They hire free-lancers. They design the production schedule.
>
> The producers also deal directly with clients—we don't have an account executive position. Our product has to represent and complement the mood and the personality of the company. You might lose something if you had to go through a third party.
>
> The art department supports the production staff in that they will design artistically the entire show. They will design logos and graphically enhance the shows through slides we generate. A producer will come to the art staff with a concept, and it will work with him to discern which elements will work and which ones are inconsistent.
>
> There are three people in the art department: Lori, designer; Don, traffic coordinator; and Jackie, camera operator. Don is responsible for getting the shows through the different levels of production, for scheduling, and for ensuring that facilities are coordinated with the timing of the production. Jackie does opticals.
>
> Artistic design is something that, up until three years ago, we did completely out-of-house. We brought art design in-house, to try to fix our costs and keep some continuity as far as the design sense of all our shows is concerned.

The administrative staff comprised a bookkeeper, a word processor, a receptionist, "gofer," and general manager Jack Garrity.

Hiring Jack Garrity.   Despite IPI's rapid growth, its profits had not kept pace with revenues. In fact, IPI had incurred a loss in fiscal year 1988. This led Mark to believe that IPI needed somebody "from outside of the production or audiovisual community" to come in and manage. As a test, they hired a Harvard Business School student for the summer of 1988. The experience convinced them of the value of and need for a full-time professional manager. With the help of a headhunter, they recruited Jack Garrity that fall.

Jack recalled:

> I spent six years with Touche Ross as a certified public accountant, and I started with them right after college. I had become a manager, and I was just two steps away from partner when I started to doubt whether I wanted to stay in public accounting. I was at a crossroads in my career, and I didn't know whether I really wanted to sell my soul to them for the next six years—without any guarantees. I did some real soul-searching, and finally in May of 1988 decided to get out of public accounting and into something more creative.

I set my sights on advertising, public relations, and communications. Many people said that it would be tough for me to find a job, given my background as a CPA, and that I would have to give up everything I'd learned and start from scratch. I didn't want to do this. I wanted to use everything I'd learned and yet not "sell out" to anyone.

I finally decided to go through an executive placement firm. I didn't want to do this initially, because I figured that I would be pigeonholed. A fellow at a search firm introduced me to IPI. He introduced the position as that of an office manager, and I said, "No! I don't want to be an office manager!" I think he just had a hard time describing the position.

Jack interviewed with Mark and Jonathan late in the summer.

I remember asking them, "If this is not an office manager position, what is it going to be?" They said they had a tough time coming up with a title because it would involve so much. That interested me. They then said that they would call it the general manager. I said that that could be a lot of things, and they replied, "Well, it is a lot of things."

We talked first about the financial management aspect, which was the strongest part of the position. I would be at the helm, literally steering the financial direction of the company. I would be in some respects the financial historian of the company; but I would also institute some kind of cash management, do budgeting, and make financial projections.

This aspect fascinated me. At Touche Ross, as part of my audit function, I would come in at the end of the fiscal year to tell clients what had happened and to make recommendations as to what they should do the next year. I was never the one to establish goals and guidelines or to implement them.

Secondly, we talked about the operations side of the position. I would work with each producer, and with each production, to monitor and hopefully ensure its profitability. They had just started to implement a budgeting system for each producer, which I thought was very unique in such a creative arena. Fine-tuning that system would be my job. Also, there was the element of taking a production and changing it to make it more profitable. Being involved in this would give me the creative crossover I wanted.

Then [the position] became more open-ended. I would do some human resource work, some physical plant work—basically, anything that had a financial implication would become my responsibility.

Jack's Role

Finance/Operations.   When Jack started in September 1988, he was surprised at the breadth of his responsibilities.

I didn't realize until I got here the amount of responsibility I was given. That, initially, was frightening. Although most decisions are made in unison, my "vote," so to speak, is given as much weight as those of Jonathan and Mark, the owners of the business. Although I'm not in an equity position, they've relinquished almost a third of the responsibility for the company. This was both good and bad. It was good, in a sense, because I began to think like an owner. But I wasn't an owner, and I had to remind myself often that I was just an employee.

Jack described his financial and operational roles.

Although Mark and Jonathan maintained direct contact with the staff, they were not around much. So I came in to try to maintain [staff members'] productivity and flow. I began by looking at their utilization rate. Were they chargeable to clients, and were they bringing in enough revenue to cover their expenses? Their utilization rate is now a part of their evaluation; if they aren't chargeable to their clients, then they won't be on staff any more.

I met with the producers on a monthly basis—not only to monitor their profitability and spending, but also to get a sense of where we are in each production and whether we needed to make any changes. If we spend too much money on graphics, then something else—to stay within our profitability guidelines—has to give. So we may not be able to have as interesting a soundtrack, or we may not be able to have a free-lance scriptwriter. We may have to do this in-house. Or photography may have to . . . not suffer, but be compromised. If production strayed from its initial path, and we spent beyond our guidelines, then we'd regroup and figure out another way to do things.

[Producers] needed to be more sensitive to our external service expenditures. With a school show, we rely minimally on external services—they account for between 20 percent and 30 percent of the costs of goods. But with a corporate video, it's closer to 50 percent, and we need to see how much more we can do in-house. In the winter, we purchased a computer graphics systems because so much was being done outside. We spent $35,000 on the system. We had spent more than that before on these services.

To be more effective in his financial role, Jack began participating in the creative process.

Jonathan maintained monthly producers' meetings to stimulate the creativity of the producing group. When I first started, I suggested that I sit in on one in order to learn the elements of production. After the first one, I said to him that I would not learn as much by sitting and listening; I had to take an active role. He said fine, and so afterwards I had to contribute just as much as the producers. For example, if a meeting was held about graphics, then I needed to do research, to bring examples, to be able to critique and analyze why things are graphically correct, and to be able to say what makes things work from a creative point of view. That was the only way I would be able to voice an opinion on anything. I only helped myself by crossing that boundary and stepping into their world, so to speak. It was a difficult step for me to make, but it's the part of the job I have enjoyed the most.

Human Resource Management.   In addition to his financial responsibilities, Jack became concerned with human resource management.

There was really no human resource function here. There were no formal review structures, evaluation forms, or formal meetings with staff. People didn't have compensation plans, and they were rewarded only sporadically. They were given vacation time, and they would use it, but they didn't know how they were earning it. They were awarded a pay-out every time they were reviewed, which was very bad. You need to give people immediate feedback, but you shouldn't open up the wallet every time to do it.

Further, nothing tied in any way to the cycle of the fiscal year. For example, producers would only be evaluated during the month each year that marked the start date of each individual. I couldn't project a year knowing that I've got salary increases coming up in March, salary increases in September, and so on.

We began to change some of these things after we designed an evaluation form. We ask [employees] to sign it after they've seen it—not to show that they agree with it, but only to mean that they've seen it. We had to tell everyone: "You will be reviewed more often, and you will not get a salary increase every time you are reviewed. You will get an increase once a year." We've designed compensation plans which tie directly with the results of these evaluation forms. They now know what elements they're being evaluated on, and they know that if they get a low grade that—well, it's going to hit them where it counts. I'd hate to think that money is the only motivating factor, but we know that it is a motivating factor—and we've designed our most recent compensation plans with this in mind.

I've helped with terminations. Mark and Jonathan had never fired anyone before I came, and they had not considered how it should be handled. Neither had they considered the additional liabilities that can be associated with discharge. We have fired only one person since I arrived, but she came back at us with a lawsuit. However, my background at Touche enabled us to handle that situation more smoothly than they would have before. I was involved in human resource management at Touche, and I worked very closely with the human resource director there. A lot of people get fired in public accounting. There is a lot of attrition. You need to manage that attrition, or else you're going to get caught up in it. This didn't mean that I had all the answers for IPI's problems, but at least I knew people who I could turn to for help.

One of my major crusades has been developing professionalism. I was surprised at the lack of professionalism I saw in some of these people. I shocked me to see that some of these people were at times childish, or concerned only with themselves and their role in production, or abusive to one another. I couldn't believe that people would react in certain ways to one another.

The older employees, the ones that came in before me, would say: "Jack, we can't operate like you want us to—we don't need to. We can wear jeans every day to work, and that doesn't mean anything. We can treat our peers almost to the point of being rude to get something done." I'd say: "No, we don't have to be like that. And I think that we are going to be able to go a lot more places if we have a new professional work ethic instilled in us!"

Accounting firms don't have rights on professionalism. There's this whole stigma concerning "creative types." They say that creative types can't be fiscally responsible, and they can't be professional; they must be earthy. I don't buy that, and I don't think this industry is as unprofessional as our employees have been allowed to think. I don't care what we're doing—there's a certain level of professionalism that we always need to maintain. We need to maintain professionalism more so with clients, but also amongst fellow employees. We should be professional in the way we dress and present ourselves to peers, the way we manage people and get work out of them, and in the way we handle ourselves on the phone.

We are trying to get everyone to become more professional. How do we do this? I think that communicating to everybody how these changes are taking place, why these changes are taking place, and what they're doing for us is the only way to buy them into it. If people still resist after we have done this, then we don't think this will be the right place for them.

We have made professionalism an element of their evaluations. We've even had to tell some people to "shape up or ship out." We had two people on staff whose personalities clash violently. Clients witnessed outbursts between them, and we had to sit down with them to say, "One more outburst like that, and you will be fired." In general, we haven't been that firm, but in a year or so we're going to have to. If everybody doesn't share this vision, then they won't be able to come along for the ride. And we can't have people just coming along for the ride; they'd better be contributing.

Looking Ahead

In May 1989, Jack assessed IPI's performance and its short-term needs.

I'm pleased with our financial performance last year. We grew, and we were more successful profit-wise—but not revenue-wise. Last year, the company increased its revenues by

50 percent to 60 percent, but it did not make any money. This is not surprising, because Image [Presentations] was going through a phase of growth. This year, after we instituted our budgeting system, we maintained the same level of revenue as last year. However, our profitability has swung around by 300 percent, from being negative to being close to 10 percent to 11 percent of revenue. We have proven that you can grow and be profitable without revenue growth when you put the right people in the right places and monitor things. We showed that we could pull back on the reins financially without sacrificing quality and creativity.

Our goals for next year are to resume the revenue growth we once had while maintaining our profitability. We brought on Matt to increase our revenues, and Mark and Matt have set out a very aggressive sales plan for next year. But, to meet this plan, we will need two additional producers. The production staff is strapped. They are doing as much as they possibly can, and we need to add another producer immediately and one in the fall.

Staffing to meet current production needs is the most important issue we face. We've been looking for new producers for eight months, ever since I started, but we haven't found anyone. I've been told that the talent pool is limited, but I just can't believe it. We have been very selective—maybe a little too selective. I also don't think our network is strong enough, and I don't think our pool of resources has developed enough with the people we have on staff. So developing this pool has become my responsibility. It might be helpful if we created an account executive position. Then we could hire skilled producers without having to worry about their ability to manage clients.

We have had problems with our art staff, too. We just hired a new art director and another designer. We've had an art director before, but we fired her in December because she was not managing the department. The new people are coming on staff in July. We hope that the new designer will work out, because our present designers have had a difficult time addressing themselves to our clients' needs. There has to be a marriage between what the designer wants to create and what the client wants to see. The designer cannot create just for the sake of creation. We are learning that the designers we hire have to be able to understand what our clients—and especially our corporate clients—need.

Space is another issue. It has recently become my responsibility to determine how much longer we can last in this building. We've grown at an alarming rate, but I think that we could last here another three to five years by redesigning our space. This has already started. We're redesigning the second floor to accommodate five to six more people. At some point, we will need even more space—that's given. The principal constraint on that happening will be our ability to hire more people to increase business.

On the marketing side, our school business is booming. Schools are coming to us. On the corporate side, it is more difficult. We are selling two different products. We sell corporate meetings, which are the first things to get cut out of corporate budgets when companies are not doing well. We also do product-introduction and corporate-identity videos. We do more corporate meetings than corporate videos, but I think we can do more of a rising business in the latter than we realize.

Although Jack was concerned with immediate staffing needs, Mark and Jonathan were keen on pursuing growth opportunities.

Jonathan and I want to grow. We have always been interested in having a larger creative organization than the one we have now. We could have easily established a small, boutique-like shop, but we rejected that idea long ago. We don't want to grow because we feel we could make more money that way. To be frank, we could probably make more money by ourselves than we do now! We are just interested in having a large organization with many people—that's all. It's much more of a personal matter than it is a business matter.

We want to do more of our present work, but we don't see how Image Presentations as it exists today will support the growth we want to achieve. Colleges are not spending big, big dollars for the kind of work that we're doing now, and we're in the top end of the market right now. College work makes up about 50 percent of our work, but it isn't going to be the ticket for growth. On the corporate side, too, we don't feel the things we now do—mainly audiovisual support for corporate meetings—will support the growth we want.

We talked to some people about starting a company that focused on recruiting. We went to some schools, to find out what people thought, and we were encouraged by what we heard. At one school, we went even farther. We redesigned a tour that guides used at Simmons College. They used our version, and it worked out well. We haven't done any research on the corporate side, but we think that the opportunity is there.

Our school background has given us expertise in the uses of media for recruiting. And we've thought about the fact that organizations other than colleges, like investment banks, have recruiting needs. We are thinking about starting another company to take care of those organizations' needs.

Now, the reason we need to start another company is that we want to do things outside of film, video, and slides. Image Presentations is synonymous with those things. For example, we have wanted to do brochures for colleges, but people have reacted by saying "Image Presentations? You're the film and slide guys!" and going elsewhere. In the corporate market, Image Presentations is known as the corporate meeting company or the product introduction company. Only directors of advertising and marketing want to talk to Image Presentations.

Maybe it's a marketing problem, but we're being defined by the media we use. And so, we thought about starting another company that focuses on recruiting—not on media, not on film. I think also that we are establishing this company in recognition of the fact that things will change. We won't always be a film and media company. It's been clear to us for a long time that the types of media we've specialized in won't be around forever. When we first broke into the business, people were enthusiastic about filmstrips. Since then, filmstrips have gone the way of the eight-track. In 15 years, we may not even be using film and video—we'll be using computers.

Recruiting Arts

In early 1989, Mark and Jonathan decided to create a subsidiary they called Recruiting Arts. Recruiting Arts would focus on helping educational institutions and companies recruit the best students and employees through sophisticated marketing, advertising, and image enhancement techniques.

We figured that, initially, Recruiting Arts would bank off our existing client list and share production resources with IPI. This way, we think that Recruiting Arts would gain the distinction needed for us to make inroads into the markets, and eventually Recruiting Arts would develop separate production capabilities. Recruiting Arts would not replace [IPI], but we think that IPI could possibly become the film/slide/print arm of Recruiting Arts. Ultimately, we think that Recruiting Arts could be a much bigger business than IPI.

The two owners decided to hire a director for the new subsidiary.

We wanted to hire a director to supervise Recruiting Arts in its start-up phase. He [or she] would redefine our business plan and then move to a marketing role. In this role, he [or she] would work off our existing client lists and use some of our sales force to generate leads for . . . products. Finally, he [or she] would move into a management role.

Late that spring, they began to recruit business school students in the Boston area.

Our experience with our HBS intern led us to believe that we could easily recruit a half-dozen good candidates from business schools. We also thought that we would stand a better chance of finding people who had already started companies in these places. We needed someone who was familiar with business plans, and we wanted someone who was highly educated. We recruited at three schools: Harvard, Babson and Boston University. We picked Harvard because of the experience the prior summer, and we had become familiar with Babson and BU because we had done work for them.

We first designed an information handout that we stuffed in student mailboxes. The flier primarily addressed Image Presentations. We tried to generate interest by talking about our prior track record, so we wrote about IPI's client base and about how Recruiting Arts would extend from this. We then held information sessions at each school. We thought it was important to establish our credibility, especially since IPI was not a household name. So we spent about half of our time talking about IPI. Quite frankly, we dropped a lot of our clients' names and talked about our bigger projects. We talked about our corporate work more than about our school work. We also brought two videos and some of our commercial literature for show.

We then told students that we were interested in someone who could participate in an entrepreneurial venture. We needed someone who would be willing to take risks, and who could take on high levels of responsibility without having to ask many questions. We knew that the only people who would work for us would be those who believed in our idea. We felt that if the concept didn't hit students in the gut and make them think, ''Hey, this seems like a good opportunity,'' then we weren't going to be able to convince anyone that it was. So we started to talk about a topic that hit close to home—recruiter briefings at business schools. We observed that you don't have to go to many financial services briefings before you discover that these don't answer all the questions that you have. We then talked about some changes that have occurred in education recruiting and about how these changes could serve as a model that could be applied to other industries. Students had an intuitive feel for these types of things, and we didn't get many blank stares about Recruiting Arts afterwards.

We didn't talk much about hard facts during the briefing. We didn't talk about our size, or our sales, or any nitty-gritty things like that. We did talk briefly about Image Presentations' history of growth, mentioning that our revenues had grown at a rate of about 40 percent to 50 percent per year. We didn't have any financial projections for Recruiting Arts, and we purposely avoided creating a formal business plan—that's what we wanted our new director to help us do.

We interviewed about 15 people at Harvard, but we could have interviewed more. Out of these 15, we came up with a candidate that we were all excited about named Lisa Johnson. Lisa was the best of the candidates we interviewed at any of the schools. (See **Exhibit 5** for resumé.) She seemed to believe in Recruiting Arts' viability, and she had expressed an interest in an entrepreneurial opportunity. She seemed genuine, and we thought that she would be committed to the opportunity. In addition, she had had some prior work experiences which I thought were interesting. . . . Jack was concerned that she had not had much experience managing people, but we were all nevertheless hopeful that she would work out.

We met with her five times over a course of about three weeks. Jack, Jonathan, and I each held separate interviews with her, and we all interviewed her together for a fourth time. Finally, we invited her out to dinner and made her an offer. We offered her a high base between $40,000 and $45,000 and a commission that we tied to revenues. We knew that we could not tie it to profitability, because Recruiting Arts would probably not make money for the first few years.

"Where Do We Go from Here?"

Despite Lisa's apparent interest and Mark, Jonathan, and Jack's recruiting efforts, Lisa refused the offer.

I think that Lisa turned us down for a number of reasons, one of which was financial. R. J. Reynolds had financed her graduate education, and she needed high up-front compensation so that she could pay them back. Meeting this need would have placed too much strain on us. We did try to address her concern, which she seemed to appreciate, by reducing her base salary and offering her a bonus between $5,000 and $7,500.

Her boyfriend may have also been a factor. He had been considering jobs in both Boston and New York, and he finally chose a New York offer, so I guess she followed him there.

We don't have any backup candidates. We didn't find anyone at Babson and BU, and she was the only Harvard applicant we considered. Aside from her, we really haven't found the type of people we were looking for—someone who is committed to an entrepreneurial venture.

We found that many of the people we interviewed were not interested in this opportunity. There didn't seem to be very many people interested in working for a company this size. And I think that many were uncomfortable with the element of risk involved—Lisa included. My sense is that many of these folks plan to enter a training program at a larger institution to get experience and then to go out on their own. I also thought that people began to lose interest in us after we started to talk about size. And I'm beginning to think that the experience we had last summer was truly exceptional, because we just haven't found the type of people we thought we would here.

Do you have any ideas about where we should go from here?

EXHIBIT 1   **Balance Sheets for 1988 and 1989**

	At June 30, 1989		At June 30, 1988	
Assets				
Current assets				
Cash and cash equivalents	$ 79,395.93	$ 145,436.88		
Prepaid insurance	11,240.00	11,240.00		
Accounts receivable	514,904.18	248,223.66		
Total current assets		$ 605,540.11		$ 404,900.54
Fixed assets				
Motor vehicles	35,783.40		35,783.40	
Equipment	136,853.14		131,602.57	
Leasehold Improvements	131,698.76		129,811.18	
Office equipment	66,916.11	17,795.24		
Other assets	10,800.00		—	
Total fixed assets		$ 382,051.41		$ 314,992.39
Less accumulated depreciation		(133,883.78)		(104,524.00)
Net fixed assets minus depreciation		$ 248,167.63		$ 210,468.39
Total assets		$ 853,707.74		$ 615,368.93
Liabilities and shareholders' equity				
Current liabilities				
Accounts payable	$159,610.27		$132,620.28	
Current portion of long-term debt	36,000.00		36,000.00	
Notes payable	19,010.29		49,457.82	
Deferred revenue	47,260.00		—	
Accrued expenses	—		3,675.00	
Withholding tax	2,368.86		2,036.20	
Federal income taxes payable	87.00		87.00	
Total current liabilities		$ 264,336.42		$ 223,876.30
Long-term debt		153,460.63		134,136.35
Shareholders' equity				
Retained earnings		435,910.69		257,356.28
Total liability and equity		$ 853,707.74		$ 615,368.93

EXHIBIT 2 Summary Income Statements

	1989		1988	
Revenues				
Fees—corporate	$1,068,617.87	—		
Fees—schools	1,465,562.29	—		
Other fees	1,916.04	—		
Other income	12,796.27	—		
Total revenue		$2,548,892.47		$2,611,672.00
Direct project costs				
Free-lance people	487,791.79		663,134.00[a]	
Production supplies	269,584.54		366,489.00[a]	
Production services	252,355.79		343,068.00[a]	
Transportation and accommodations	70,880.38		96,359.00[a]	
Other	53,714.43		73,022.00[a]	
Total direct costs		$1,134,326.93		$1,542,072.00
Gross profit		$1,414,565.54		$1,069,600.00
Indirect costs and overhead				
Salaries and benefits				
Officers' salaries	108,666.64		111,500.00	
Other salaries and benefits	524,347.97		416,811.00	
Total		$ 633,014.61		$ 528,311.00
Indirect production costs				
(not attributable to specific projects)				
Production supplies	$ 14,828.78		—	
Production services	16,781.19		—	
Equipment rental O/H	18,555.87		39,436.00	
Travel, transportation, and meals	81,069.13		161,392.00	
Conventions	31,305.38		—	
Total		$ 162,840.35		$ 200,828.00
Office overhead				
Rent	60,849.30		64,040.00	
Insurance	32,058.11		33,432.00	
Telephone	19,346.27		20,861.00	
Utilities	7,900.52		10,127.00	
Repair and maintenance	18,328.71		14,325.00	
Office and computer supply	28,444.89		34,886.00	
Postage and Xeroxing	19,066.62		25,649.00	
Depreciation	27,276.48		24,975.00	
Amortization	2,083.30		—	
Total		$ 215,354.20		$ 228,295.00
Professional services				
Promotional	8,411.04		—	
Other advertising	13,278.09		11,218.00	
Legal and accounting	20,366.67		13,991.00	
Consulting fees	27,364.45		42,576.00	
Total		$ 69,420.25		$ 67,785.00
Miscellaneous		15,360.78		—
Total SGA		$1,095,990.19		$1,025,219.00
Earnings from operations		318,575.35		44,381.00
Interest and bank charges		23,231.04		28,639.00
Earnings before taxes		295,344.31		15,742.00
Taxes		53,825.66		48,344.00
Net earnings		$ 241,518.65		$ (32,602.00)

[a]Estimates provided by Jack Garrity.

620

Exhibit 3   IPI Yellow Pages Brochure

▶ Annual Meetings

Jonathan Spring
   350 Newbury Bos 536-7089
Mark Edwards
   350 Newbury Bos 536-7089

▶ AV Programming

Kevin Hays
   350 Newbury Bos 536-7089

IMAGE PRESENTATIONS
Dynamic, creative, exciting programming of
your presentations that will move your
audience 536-7089

▶ Cinematography

Mark Edwards
   350 Newbury Bos 536-7089
Steve Mooney
   350 Newbury Bos 536-7089
IP FILMS
   350 Newbury Bos 536-7089
   see our display ad this page

▶ Collateral Materials

IMAGE PRESENTATIONS
            TOTAL SERVICE
Concept, copy, design, production, and printing
       ALL YOUR COLLATERAL NEEDS
• Brochures   • Direct Mail
• Catalogs   • Posters
350 Newbury Bos 536-7089

Maggie Sanftleben
   350 Newbury Bos 536-7089
Lori D'Aprile
   350 Newbury Bos 536-7089

▶ Confetti Canons

Betsy's Canons
   350 Newbury Bos 536-7089

CANON CITY
  ''WE'LL BLOW YOU AWAY!''
  "OUR SHREDDERS ARE STANDING BY."
       536-7089
         CALL TODAY

THE CONFETTI BIN
        Confetti for all occasions
   350 Newbury Bos 536-7089

▶ Consulting

IMAGE PRESENTATIONS
   "CAN WE TALK?"
   LET US EVALUATE YOUR
   COMMUNICATION NEEDS
350 Newbury Bos 536-7089

MARK EDWARDS
   ''YEARS OF FINDING
   CREATIVE SOLUTIONS TO
   YOUR COMMUNICATION
        PROBLEMS''
       536-7089
350 Newbury S Bos 536-7089

Ken Lehrhoff
   350 Newbury Bos 536-7089
Steve Mooney
   350 Newbury Bos 536-7089
Jonathan Spring
   350 Newbury Bos 536-7089

Laura Voss
   350 Newbury Bos 536-7089

▶ Corporate Portraits

M. Edwards
   350 Newbury Bos 536-7089
K. Lehrhoff
   350 Newbury Bos 536-7089
IMAGE PRESENTATIONS, INC.
   350 Newbury Bos 536-7089
   please see our display ad this page

▶ Design, Graphic

Lori D'Aprile 350 Newbury .. 536-7089

IMAGE PRESENTATIONS
GRAPHIC DESIGN SERVICES:
• MULTI-IMAGE • VIDEO • PRINT •
CORPORATE IDENTITY • PACKAG-
ING • PROMOTIONAL MATERIALS
"Present a consistent unified Image"
       536-7089
350 Newbury S Bos 536-7089

Maggie Sanftleben, *Art Director*
   350 Newbury Bos 536-7089

▶ Directing

Mark Edwards
   350 Newbury Bos 536-7089
Louis Gudema
   350 Newbury Bos 536-7089
Ken Lehrhoff
   350 Newbury Bos 536-7089
Jonathan Spring
   350 Newbury Bos 536-7089
Steve Mooney
   350 Newbury Bos 536-7089

▶ Extravaganzas

IMAGE PRESENTATIONS
• Corporate Theater
• Lasers
• Light Shows
• Special Effects
• Pyrotechnics
• Live Entertainment
• Set Design and Construction
Total production coordination
       536-7089
   350 Newbury St., Boston, MA

▶ Film, Production

Image Presentations
   350 Newbury Bos 536-7089
   please see our display ad this page

▶ Film and Video Transfers

IMAGE PRESENTATIONS
   350 Newbury Bos 536-7089
Laura Voss
   350 Newbury Bos 536-7089

▶ Humor

IMAGE PRESENTATIONS
   When they LAUGH they LEARN

   • Salespeople
   • Managers
   • Even Presidents!

   "FOR INFORMATION CALL"
   350 Newbury, Bos ...536-7089

▶ Interactive Media

IMAGE PRESENTATIONS
   350 Newbury Bos 536-7089
          (ask for Jonathan)

▶ Interviewing

IMAGE PRESENTATIONS
        "Testimonials
            A
         Speciality"
   350 Newbury St., Boston, MA
       536-7089

▶ Media Installations

Kevin Hays 350 Newbury 536-7089
Image Presentations
   350 Newbury Bos 536-7089

MEETINGS
Annual • Sales • Shareholder • Employee
• Planning • Theme Development
• Openers/Closers • Modules
• Product Introductions
• Speech Writing/Speaker Support
• Speaker Training • Staging
IMAGE PRESENTATIONS
Call
536-7089

Design   *"Always in good taste!"*
IMAGE PRESENTATIONS
DESIGN SERVICES
350 Newbury St.
Boston, MA   **536-7089**

FILMS
For ▪ INDUSTRY
      ▪ EDUCATION
      ▪ FINANCE
      ▪ MOTIVATION
      ▪ TRAINING
      ▪ DOCUMENTARY
      ▪ FUNDRAISING
   The Experts Agree ...
        ● ● ● ●
   Image Presentations
350 Newbury St., Boston, MA
       536-7089

CORPORATE PORTRAITS

350 Newbury Street, Boston, MA
       536-7089

Exhibit 3 *(concluded)*

► **Multi-Image**

Image Presentations
350 Newbury Bos 536-7089
see our display ad this page

► **Music**

Image Presentations
350 Newbury Bos 536-7089
please see our display ad this page

► **Optical Services**

Jackie Murtha
350 Newbury Bos 536-7089

IMAGE PRESENTATIONS
OPTICAL SPECIAL EFFECTS
• Multi-Image • Print
• Video • Film
Call for *Fast* Service • 536-7089

► **Photography**

Image Presentations
350 Newbury Bos 536-7089
Steve Mooney
350 Newbury Bos 536-7089
Ken Lacouture
350 Newbury Bos 536-7089

► **Props and Sets**

POPPY'S PROP SHOP
Props for Photography
Stills, Film, A.V.
350 Newbury St., Boston, MA
536-7089

► **Sales**

IMAGE PRESENTATIONS
• Sales Training
• Sales Meetings
• Motivational Presentations
"Everything your company needs to
generate sales."
350 Newbury St., Boston, MA
536-7089

M. Edwards
350 Newbury Bos 536-7089
IMAGE PRESENTATIONS, INC.
350 Newbury Bos 536-7089
K. Lehrhoff
350 Newbury Bos 536-7089
Steve Mooney
350 Newbury Bos 536-7089

Jonathan Spring
350 Newbury Bos 536-7089

► **Slides**

IMAGE PRESENTATIONS
• Design and Production of Slides for
Speaker Support and Multi-Image
Presentations
• Slide Duplication
• Special Effects
• Slide Shows
" No job too big or too small! "
536-7089
350 Newbury St., Boston, MA

Laura Voss
Miss All-America Slide Show
350 Newbury Bos 536-7089

► **Sound**

Mark Edwards
350 Newbury Bos 536-7089

IMAGE PRESENTATIONS
SOUNDS
GREAT!
• NARRATIONS
• SOUND EFFECTS
• CUSTOM MUSIC
• LIBRARY MUSIC
• MIXING
Complete Soundtrack Services
536-7089
350 Newbury St., Boston, MA

Steve Mooney
350 Newbury Bos 536-7089
Jonathan Spring
350 Newbury Bos 536-7089

► **Staging**

IMAGE PRESENTATIONS
• Guaranteed "without a hitch"
• One to one hundred projectors
• Lighting and set design and
construction
536-7089
350 Newbury St., Boston, MA 02215

► **Stress**

STRESS RELIEF
350 Newbury, Bos 536-7089

► **Theatre Design**

Image Presentations
*Permanent or Temporary
Installations, Home Office or
Traveling Trade Show*
350 Newbury Bos 536-7089
Kevin Hays
Technical Consultant
350 Newbury Bos 536-7089

► **Thinking**

BOB'S SURPLUS
"MORE IDEAS THAN WE KNOW WHAT
TO DO WITH"
• IDEAS THAT SELL
• IDEAS THAT MOTIVATE
• IDEAS THAT MAKE MONEY FOR YOU

JACKIE'S
OPTICAL
SERVICES 4 U
350 Newbury St.
LOWER LEVEL
536-7089

► **Trade Shows**

Image Presentations
Media for Trade Shows
350 Newbury Bos 536-7089

► **Video**

Image Presentations
Complete Video Service
350 Newbury Bos 536-7089
see our display ad this page

► **Wrap Shows**

IMAGE PRESENTATIONS
"Be yourself—See yourself!"
350 Newbury, Bos . 536-7089

PHOTOGRAPHY
• STUDIO
• LOCATION
• STYLING
• CASTING
• DIRECTING

PHONE:
536-7089
350 Newbury St., Boston, MA 02215

Multi Image Multi Image Multi Image Multi Image Multi Image Multi Image
Multi Image Multi Image Multi Image Multi Image Multi Image Multi Image
Award Winning Multi-Image Presentations
350 Newbury Street, Boston MA 02215
536-7089
IMAGE PRESENTATIONS

YOUR ONE SOURCE
FOR ALL YOUR
VIDEO
COMMUNICATION
NEEDS

Video
• Corporate Video
• Off-line Editing
• On-line Editing
• Video Dubs
• Video Discs
• Video Conversions
• Video Walls
• Videography
536-7089

Image Presentations
350 Newbury St., Boston, MA

Music
• **Custom Sound
Tracks,** Composed,
Performed and
Recorded by
Professionals
• **Extensive Music
Library** From
Around the World.
Thousands of Cuts
Available

IMAGE PRESENTATIONS

WE
DELIVER

COAST TO COAST

Image
Presentations
350
Newbury
Street
Boston, MA 02215
536-7089

EXHIBIT 4   IPI Recent Project List

Recent Projects

- Spalding Sports Worldwide
  A recent sales conference, staged in Florida, featured a theatrical presentation which integrated actors playing colorful sports figures of the past, slide modules introducing new products, a real astronaut as the host, and a cameo by a golf-playing robot.
  RESULT: Documented increase in sales.

- Parker Brothers
  To introduce 16 new products to the trade, Image Presentations wrote, produced and staged in New York City, a two-hour game show which, with the aid of an interactive computer system, engaged, informed, and entertained the audience.
  RESULT: Most successful product introduction ever.

- Ocean Spray Cranberries
  Corporate I.D. which portrays the history, accomplishments, and aggressive marketing position of this industry leader.
  RESULT: First comprehensive overview of the company to be widely distributed.

- Boston Whaler
  Produced entire dealer meeting including awards presentation, product introductions, extensive speaker support, and original music to accompany laser show and fireworks display.
  RESULT: Sold 40% of entire yearly sales goal in two days.

- Con Edison of New York
  Created a training tape about the safe handling of hazardous materials in the work place. Produced in five days, the tape was necessary to successfully thwart court action against Con Ed.
  RESULT: Injunction reversed.

- Bank of Boston
  Designed a presentation to celebrate employees' induction into the Bank's "Quarter Century Club."
  RESULT: Best received presentation in the history of the Club.

- Shearman and Sterling
  Produced a revealing portrait of what goes on at one of New York City's largest and most prominent law firms. The presentation is shown to clients and has been distributed to nearly every law school in the country.
  RESULT: Documented increase in client interest and in applications by law students to work at the firm.

Exhibit 5

LISA JOHNSON

Education

1987–1989	HARVARD GRADUATE SCHOOL OF BUSINESS ADMINISTRATION BOSTON, MA

Candidate for Master in Business Administration degree, June 1989. General management curriculum. Elected Chairman of Eminent Speakers Committee. Manager of 25th Reunion of HBS Class of 1963. Non-resident business tutor for Winthrop House, Harvard College. Member of Real Estate Club.

1982–1983   BOSTON UNIVERSITY SCHOOL OF LAW   BOSTON, MA

Completed first year of JD program in good standing. Core curriculum included courses in real property, contracts, torts, civil procedure, and constitutional law.

1977–1981   SMITH COLLEGE   NORTHAMPTON, MA

Earned AB degree in Government, May 1981. Named to Dean's List. Selected for Junior Year in France and Jean Picker Washington, D.C., intern programs. Awarded Dare foreign study scholarship. Elected representative to Student Government Association. Staff writer for college magazine and newspaper.

Work Experience

RUSSELL REYNOLDS ASSOCIATES, INC.   BOSTON, MA

summer 1988   Associate, Venture Practice

Executive recruiter with leading client-retained search firm. Worked with venture capitalists and entrepreneurs to recruit managers and technical specialists for start-up companies.

1985–1987   Associate   LOS ANGELES, CA

Youngest person in firm to hold Associate title. Planned and executed senior management recruiting projects for client companies in the real estate, financial services, and health care industries. Brought in new client business, built key relationships with savings & loan and health insurance clients.

1983–1985   Consultant   LOS ANGELES, CA

Managed research group responsible for compiling industry and company information in support of recruiting projects. Identified and screened prospective candidates for client companies.

summer 1983   FIRST INTERSTATE BANCORP   LOS ANGELES, CA

Associate, Office of the General Counsel

Prepared report for senior management on legal restrictions on bank securities activities. Drafted compliance manual for investment management subsidiaries.

1981–1982   COVINGTON & BURLING   WASHINGTON, DC

Legal Assistant, Banking Department

Monitored federal legislation and regulations affecting banking clients.

Personal

Participated in urban planning program at Harvard Graduate School of Design. Strong interest in art and architecture. Fluent in French. Active member of Smith College Alumnae Association. Enjoy most sports, particularly running and tennis.

4–4 DRAGONFLY CORPORATION

On December 20, 1991, with the close of the Christmas season just a week away, Janet and Michael Thompson received yet another call from their attorney: It was time to make some difficult decisions about their fledgling business. For the past three and one-half years, the couple had been operating their Dragonfly teenage clothing stores in Seattle, trying to earn a living and keep the business alive despite continuing losses. Now their angry landlord was threatening legal action if Dragonfly did not deliver on its overdue lease payments. The Thompsons' attorney was pushing them for an answer: What did they want to do?

The financial picture was not rosy. Dragonfly had lost money since it opened, with the accumulated deficit from both stores near the end of 1991 reaching over $100,000. (See **Exhibits 1** and **2**.) While the owners believed the business had gone more smoothly over the past year, the numbers were ambiguous. The Thompsons' best calculation to date still showed Dragonfly losing money (**Exhibit 3**.) But the couple believed they were managing the business more wisely and felt they had corrected many of their early operating problems. They weren't sure why their dream child still wasn't profitable. Was it the slowing U.S. economy, which affected Seattle? Was there still something wrong with the way they were running the business?

The Thompsons felt they had several possible courses of action. They could try to buy time with the landlord and hope the economy and their business turned around. They could turn to Janet's parents for additional financial help to see them through this crisis. Or they could admit the project wasn't working and begin bankruptcy proceedings.

The Thompsons felt their decision was complicated by the substantial investment Janet's parents had already made in the business. Could they admit defeat to their family and close up the stores? Even worse, could they ask the family to increase their investment in an endeavor that might fail sooner or later?

There was also the problem of timing. While the Thompsons knew that Christmas was the peak sales season for retail operators, they also knew that January was the peak season for refunds. How should they interpret their recent financial figures in the face of such unevenness? Janet and Michael were inclined to think the entire situation was somehow unfair. Just when they felt the stores were turning around, the issue of the lease payments was raising the specter of bankruptcy and forcing them to make a decision about Dragonfly before all the facts were in.

This case was prepared by Martha Gershun under the direction of Howard H. Stevenson.

Copyright © 1993 by the President and Fellows of Harvard College

Harvard Business School Case 9–393–118

Background

Janet Hepburn and Michael Thompson met in Seattle as assistant buyers for Bon Marché, a full-line department store chain, and were married in 1979. Three years later, they quit their jobs at Bon Marché—Michael took a job as store manager for the Lerner's chain, and Janet decided to stay at home in anticipation of the birth of their first child. In 1984, the couple moved to Arizona where Michael took a job working for Kidder Peabody in commercial sales. He hated the environment and found the work boring. He quit in 1985 to return to retailing with a job for a local women's clothing store. Meanwhile, the couple's second child was born. In 1988, the Thompsons returned to Seattle and began looking into franchising a store with the Lady Madonna chain, a successful group of stores offering maternity clothes at the upper end of the pricing scale. Janet was tired of staying home and wanted to get back into the work force. Both the Thompsons liked the lifestyle of retailing. They enjoyed going on buying trips, choosing inventory, and serving customers. With the combined experience in retailing, the couple believed they could make a serious attempt to run their own business.

In the process of investigating the Lady Madonna operation, the Thompsons became intrigued with what they perceived to be an obvious market niche for an upscale store serving Seattle's teenage market. When vigorous research turned up few competitors in the local area, the Thompsons decided to abandon the Lady Madonna franchise idea and pursue opening their own store instead, selling teenage clothes and accessories at fairly high price points. They developed pro forma cash flows that showed that the business would just break even in the first year of operation (**Exhibit 4**).

Janet and Michael had friends who were successfully operating a chain of T-shirt shops. They liked the idea of opening one store now and using it later to leverage the venture into a thriving chain. Since they believed that most of the expenses involved in running retail stores were fixed on the corporate level, the Thompsons saw the long-term opportunity to generate a sizable income for themselves and a generous profit for their company. (See **Exhibit 5**.)

Dragonfly

The Thompsons were not particularly worried about financing their new venture. Janet's parents had expressed willingness earlier to finance their entry into the Lady Madonna enterprise, and the couple did not think starting up their own store would take a great deal more capital. They approached Janet's older brother, Charles, who was a corporate attorney in Chicago, and asked him to help them develop a plan to use in approaching the Hepburns for money. Based on Charles's knowledge of business and the Thompsons' retail experience, it was determined that $120,000 would be sufficient to start up the new operation, which by now had been dubbed *Dragonfly*.

Janet called her parents to discuss the prospect of underwriting the new store. She asked them for $90,000. The Hepburns offered little resistance to the idea. They were happy to see Janet so excited about the new business and felt that $90,000 was a small investment to help their daughter reach financial independence. Mr. Hepburn had recently retired from a successful career in real estate and preferred to give his children money now, rather than having them wait until after his death for an inheritance. He had only two concerns. First, the deal must be structured so that Michael was as responsible as Janet for the financial success of the venture and any obligations to the Hepburns. Second, the Hepburns must receive the tax benefits from any start-up losses.

With those caveats in mind, the family met on June 1, 1988, with Janet and Michael's attorney to set up the Dragonfly Corporation.

The Beginning

The Thompsons thought it seemed like a very informal way to begin such a serious venture. Here they were, serving coffee in their living room to Janet's parents, her older brother, and their attorney, Jeff Lawrence. When the meeting was over and the papers were signed, they would be the owners and managers of the Dragonfly Corporation. The family decided to give the company authorization to issue 50,000 shares of stock with a par value of $1. Initially, 20,000 shares were issued: 15,000 shares to the Hepburns for $15,000 in cash and 5,000 shares to Janet and Michael for their 1986 Volvo, which had a fair market value of $5,000. Jeff Lawrence explained that they would designate Dragonfly as a Subchapter S corporation for income tax purposes and allow the Hepburns to take their proportionate tax benefits that might accrue from early losses. Later, when the corporation began to make money, this could be changed so that either Janet and Michael or the company paid any tax liabilities.

The remaining capitalization was undertaken in the form of debt. In order to be sure that Michael was financially tied into the project, the Hepburns loaned the young couple $75,000 at an annual interest rate of 7.75 percent. The Thompsons, in return, loaned this money to Dragonfly, payable beginning July 1, 1988, in quarterly installments of $1,677.51, including the 7.75 annual interest. Charles felt this capital structure had the additional advantage of giving the couple leverage in any financial adversity, because they would be the store's primary debt holders. The corporation also borrowed $30,000 from Seattle Trust for leasehold improvements, payable in monthly installments of $1,000, with interest at 21 percent per year. (The debt was guaranteed personally and secured by the leasehold improvement.)

Confident that they had enough money to set up shop properly, the Thompsons began looking for a site for their store. They decided to lease a site at the Woodscross Shopping Center, near the major north/south road in that part of Seattle. Woodscross was in an old, open mall, which had recently been renovated. The Thompsons believed that the emerging character of the shopping center would appeal to their upscale customer base. Also, because the renovation made it a slightly risky location, the rents at Woodscross were roughly half (i.e., $7.50 per foot versus $15 to $17 per foot) those in the more fashionable parts of town. Janet and Michael signed a lease on behalf of

Dragonfly for 3,000 square feet at $1,875/month or 6 percent of monthly sales, whichever was greater. The lease was for slightly over four and one-half years, ending March 1, 1993. They also agreed to pay some portion of common area maintenance costs, averaging about $425/month. (See **Exhibit 6** for sample lease clauses.)

With the signing of the lease, the Thompsons went to work in earnest. Michael supervised the store setup while Janet went off to buy their beginning merchandise. One month later, on August 1, 1988, they were ready to open for business.

Early Results

The results for Dragonfly's first full year in business were not very good. Sales had been lower than expected, and much of the merchandise had been marked down significantly before it was sold. Thus, gross margins were considerably lower than the industry average. In addition, operating expenses were way out of line, bringing the annual loss at December 31, 1989, to $42,253. (**Exhibit 7** gives financial and operating data for the industry. **Exhibit 8** itemizes Dragonfly's expenses.) Faced with cash shortages, the Thompsons fell behind in their rent payments on the store.

The second year brought problems, too. While sales were up slightly and gross margins were up, Janet had clearly overbought, and inventory levels were up to $80,000. Also, the Thompsons had managed to reduce Dragonfly's expenses but had primarily done so by missing more payments to their Woodscross landlord and by reducing the amount of money they were taking out of the store. They were forced to borrow $15,000 from Janet's parents to make ends meet at home. In addition, the Hepburns lent Dragonfly $30,000.

1991: A Tough Year

Thus, the Thompsons began 1991 in a precarious position. Their personal financial situation was very tight (**Exhibit 9**). Janet had cut back on all the extras at home; the family was eating meat only twice a week. Dragonfly was saddled with $80,000 of inventory, and it looked as though only heavy markdowns would move the clothes. To make matters worse, the Woodscross mall was deteriorating rapidly. Already, 10 of the 60 tenants in the new part of the shopping center where Dragonfly was located had begun preparations to move out. It didn't look as though the renovated shopping center was going to make it.

Furthermore, the economic slowdown, which was hurting retail operations nationwide, was particularly evident in Seattle. Both Boeing and Weyerhaeuser, the two major employers in the area, had hit upon hard times. Boeing was actually laying off workers, while Weyerhaeuser was trying to make do with reduced capital spending, pay freezes, and shorter work weeks.

To counter the problems posed by the deterioration of the Woodscross Mall, the Thompsons decided to open a second Dragonfly store in one of the more prosperous sections of Seattle. The new location, in the Bellevue Strip Mall, was 1,450 square feet. The lease, beginning on July 1, 1991, was for two years at $910/month for the first year and $970/month for the second, or 7 percent of gross sales, whichever was greater. Janet and Michael believed there were a number of reasons for opening a second store, despite their precarious financial condition.

First, they hoped to recycle merchandise between the two stores, selling the clothing faster and increasing gross margins by avoiding markdowns. Opening a second store provided other merchandising advantages, too. With a larger customer base, Janet felt there was a better chance of approaching a normal curve in the distribution of sizes; she hoped this would lead to greater sales as customers began to rely on Dragonfly to have the sizes they needed. Janet also felt it was a good idea to send sale merchandise to a second location. She knew customers felt bad if they purchased an item at the regular price and then saw it on sale later. Dragonfly also had potential economies of scale in advertising. The Thompsons had developed a large mailing list of existing customers and felt they could spread this advertising cost among the possible revenues from two locations instead of just one. They were also looking for protection in case the situation at Woodscross did not improve. In a worst case scenario, the Thompsons thought they could fold the first Dragonfly store on March 1, 1993, when the lease was up, and move the merchandise to the Bellevue location. In the four months then remaining on the Bellevue lease, they could either try to make the second store successful or use it to liquidate the inventory from both stores. Most important, with many of their significant expenses fixed, the Thompsons saw the second store as a chance to generate excess revenues for the incremental cost of the second set of lease payments. Despite the problems with the Woodscross store, they were pursuing their vision of a profitable multisite operation.

Finally, near the end of 1991, the precarious financial situation forced the Hepburns to reclassify the $30,000 of debt they held as equity.

The Woodscross Situation

In the meantime, faced with increasing cash flow problems, the Thompsons fell further behind on their lease payments for the Woodscross Dragonfly store. In February, they made arrangements with the landlord to begin paying off their previous balance at the rate of $875/month. But this expense left little cash for regular monthly rental payments; these dropped off to $500/month. Thus, the balance owed to Woodscross was still increasing at $925/month.

In late June, the Thompsons talked with the Woodscross landlord again and offered to pay rent of 6 percent of gross revenues, which at the time was considerably less than the $1,875/month base fee. They would spend the differential in advertising for the store, in the hope of increasing Dragonfly's sales, as well as the shopping center's traffic. In addition, they would still be obligated for the common area maintenance charges of about $425/month. At the same time, the payments on the overdue balance would drop to $650/month (**Exhibit 10**). The landlord agreed, but the Thompsons did not receive any documentation confirming the transaction.

By early October, the Thompsons believed they had spent as much money on advertising as they could reasonably expect to be effective. Michael met with the Woodscross landlord and proposed that Dragonfly begin paying the full $2,300/month toward the rent again, with the payments on the overdue balance remaining at $650/month. He felt that the meeting went well and believed that his proposal had been accepted. Thus, the Thompsons were extremely surprised when Jeff Lawrence called on October 25, 1991, to say that he had received a very inflammatory note from the Woodscross lawyers. The letter **(Exhibit 11)** threatened to pursue further legal action if the Thompsons did not sign a confessed judgment for the entire amount overdue of $21,576.79. Jeff Lawrence responded immediately with another letter explaining the situation as the Thompsons understood it **(Exhibit 12)**, and also suggested to the Thompsons that they consider signing the note.

Battening Down the Hatches

Jeff cautioned the Thompsons that this kind of angry response from a creditor often preceded the initiation of bankruptcy proceedings. He told them to be prepared for the worst possibility. Janet was extremely upset by this news. She had known Dragonfly was in trouble, but it did not seem possible that the landlord had suddenly decided to close up their entire operation.

During this time, another distressing piece of news came to light; about six months earlier, one of Janet's vendors had insisted on subordinated credit. Lawrence had gotten the Thompsons to sign a general subordination agreement, which subordinated their debt to that of all trade creditors. While the account had been paid off, this agreement was still in the contract with that vendor. Janet spoke with her brother, and Charles was very anxious that this subordination agreement be terminated before the issue of bankruptcy was discussed further. He did not want this small creditor to destroy the careful chain he had set up, in case bankruptcy was actually triggered. As far as Charles was concerned, this was a further example of incompetence on the part of Jeff Lawrence. He should have known better than to allow Janet to sign such a contract. Thus, Charles proposed that the Thompsons make arrangements with this creditor to change the agreement immediately. As well, he suggested they start to think about the real prospects for Dragonfly and frame their response to the Woodscross landlord in this light. Perhaps there was a way to negotiate their way out of the lease, using bankruptcy as their own threat.

The Decision

By December, the Thompsons still hadn't heard from the Woodscross landlord again. Jeff cautioned them that it was unlikely the incident had been dropped. Rather, he suggested, Woodscross might be waiting to see how Dragonfly fared through the Christmas season before determining what action to take. While Woodscross had earlier mentioned bankruptcy as a final recourse, Lawrence now confirmed Charles's earlier opinion that one creditor did not have the power to force involuntary bankruptcy on either a business or an individual. Rather, bankruptcy should be viewed by the Thompsons as a way out, if they decided that the Dragonfly stores were not financially viable.

Now, on December 20, Jeff Lawrence had called again. He felt Woodscross would not wait any longer for an answer about the overdue lease payments. Did Janet and Michael want to stall and hope the after-Christmas season bore out their optimism about Dragonfly's improved performance? Did they want to strike a deal and get out of the lease? Did they want to seek more money from Janet's parents? Or did they want to file for bankruptcy and put the entire disappointing experience behind them?

The Thompsons were very torn. They believed the stores were doing better. Inventory levels were down. Existing merchandise was moving rapidly, with little or no markdowns. Their accounts payable appeared to be good. Just when the situation should be at its brightest, the Woodscross mess was threatening to blow out their light. The Thompsons were resentful and confused: Was it really time to quit?

EXHIBIT 1   Dragonfly Income Statement

DRAGONFLY CORPORATION
Income Statement
(unaudited)
For the Years Ending December 31

	1989	1990
Net sales	$246,236	$261,336
Cost of goods sold	160,148	155,562
Gross margin	86,088	105,774
Operating expenses	117,918	106,951
Interest expense	10,423	8,899
Net profit (loss)	$(42,253)	$(10,076)

Exhibit 2   **Dragonfly Balance Sheets**

DRAGONFLY CORPORATION
Balance Sheets
(unaudited)

	December 31, 1989	December 31, 1990	December 20, 1991 (est.)
Assets			
Current assets			
Cash	$ 2,560	$ 4,821	$ 4,930
Inventory	61,432	81,846	84,977
Prepaid insurance	408	0	0
Total current assets	64,400	86,667	89,907
Fixed assets			
Furniture and fixtures	25,682	26,278	46,429
Office and shop equipment	2,802	2,908	2,805
Leasehold improvements	22,540	22,540	32,321
Less accumulated depreciation	(11,319)	(15,441)	(19,206)
Total fixed assets	39,705	36,285	62,349
Other assets			
Deposits	1,970	1,970	1,970
Organization costs, net of accumulated amortization	2,023	1,463	903
Total other assets	3,993	3,433	2,873
Total assets	$108,098	$126,385	$ 155,129
Liabilities and Stockholders' Equity			
Current liabilities			
Notes payable—bank	$ 30,116	$ 33,574	$ 33,201
Notes payable—stockholders	4,776	9,901	8,623
Accounts payable—trade	55,514	48,230	90,045*
Gift certificates outstanding	284	163	210
Accrued liabilities	7,296	5,520	5,264
Deposits	0	82	0
Long-term debt due within one year	1,053	1,053	1,053
Total current liabilities	99,039	98,523	138,396
Long-term debt due after one year	71,272	70,151	69,098
Debt due Hepburns	0	30,000	0
Stockholders' equity	20,000	20,000	50,000
Accumulated deficit	(82,213)	(92,289)	(102,365)
Total liabilities and equity	$108,098	$126,385	$ 155,129

*Includes:

Trade payables	$68,468
Woodscross rent	21,577
	$90,045

Does *not* include remaining balance of lease payments due:

Woodscross, January 1992 through March 1993	$32,200
Bellevue, January 1992 through July, 1993	17,100
	$49,300

Exhibit 3   December 20, 1991, Financials

DRAGONFLY CORPORATION
Estimated Financial Condition
As of December 20, 1991
Accrual Basis

Sales—gross	$247,000
Sales tax (6.5%)	16,055
Sales—net	230,945
Cost of goods sold	143,186
Gross margin	87,759
Expenses:	
Rent*	31,360
Payroll†	36,000
Advertising	9,000
FICA	8,400
Medical insurance	1,800
Miscellaneous	1,400
Interest	10,640
Net loss	$(10,841)

*Rent breakdown:

Woodscross	$24,100
Bellevue rent	5,460
Bellevue common area payments	1,800

†Does not include $21,000 salary to Thompsons not accrued or paid.

Exhibit 4 Pro Forma Cash Flows, March 1988 – February 1989

	March	April	May	June	July	Aug.	Sept.	Oct.	Nov.	Dec.	Jan.	Feb.	TOTAL
Projected sales	$20,000	$13,000	$18,000	$20,000	$25,000	$27,000	$20,000	$16,000	$20,000	$30,000	$16,000	$17,000	$242,000
Cost of merchandise	10,000	9,000	9,000	10,000	12,500	13,500	10,000	8,000	10,000	15,000	8,000	8,500	123,500
Cost of markdowns	1,500	1,500	1,100	1,100	2,500	1,000	1,000	1,000	1,100	1,300	2,000	1,000	16,100
Totals	11,500	10,500	10,100	11,100	15,000	14,500	11,000	9,000	11,100	16,300	10,000	9,500	139,600
Gross profit	3,500	7,500	7,900	8,900	10,000	12,500	9,000	7,000	8,900	13,700	6,000	7,500	102,400
Selling expenses													
Sales salaries	1,700	1,700	1,700	1,800	1,900	2,100	1,800	1,600	1,700	2,200	1,600	1,650	21,450
Advertising	600	500	400	500	600	600	400	400	500	400	600	500	6,000
Buying trips	500	—	—	—	—	500	—	—	500	—	—	—	1,500
Selling supplies	100	1,400	100	100	100	1,400	100	100	200	200	100	100	4,000
Other	50	50	50	50	50	50	50	50	50	50	50	50	600
Total	2,950	3,650	2,250	2,450	2,650	4,650	2,350	2,150	2,950	2,850	2,350	2,300	33,550
Occupancy expenses													
Depreciation	400	400	400	400	400	400	400	400	400	400	400	400	4,800
Insurance	90	90	90	90	90	90	90	90	90	90	90	90	1,080
Maintenance	265	265	265	265	265	265	265	265	265	265	265	265	3,180
Rent	1,875	1,875	1,875	1,875	1,875	1,875	1,875	1,875	1,875	1,875	1,875	1,875	22,500
Other (merch. assn.)	150	150	150	150	150	150	150	150	150	150	150	150	1,800
Total	2,780	2,780	2,780	2,780	2,780	2,780	2,780	2,780	2,780	2,780	2,780	2,780	33,360
Administrative													
Officer's salary	1,200	1,200	1,200	1,200	1,200	1,200	1,200	1,200	1,200	1,200	1,200	1,200	14,400
Bad debt	20	20	20	20	20	20	20	20	20	20	20	20	240
Bank discount	120	110	110	120	150	162	120	100	120	130	100	110	1,502
Dues, etc	30	30	30	30	30	40	30	30	30	30	30	30	370
Employee benefits	75	75	75	75	75	75	75	75	75	75	75	75	900
Life insurance	50	50	50	50	50	50	50	50	50	50	50	50	600
Loan interest and repayment	253	253	660	660	660	660	660	660	660	660	660	660	7,106
Office supplies	10	20	20	20	20	20	20	20	20	20	20	20	230
Professional services	100	300	100	100	300	100	100	300	100	100	300	100	2,000
Taxes (payroll)	750	730	730	750	780	810	750	705	750	830	705	705	8,995
Taxes (excise)	250	250	250	250	300	325	250	225	250	350	225	225	3,150
Telephone	75	70	70	70	75	75	70	70	70	70	70	70	855
Total	$ 2,933	$ 3,108	$ 3,315	$ 3,345	$ 3,660	$ 3,537	$ 3,345	$ 3,455	$ 3,345	$ 3,585	$ 3,455	$ 3,265	$ 40,348
Profit (loss)	$ (133)	$(2,008)	$ (415)	$ 353	$ 940	$ 1,563	$ 555	$(1,355)	$ (145)	$ 4,515	$(2,555)	$ (815)	$ 500

EXHIBIT 5   Pro Forma Income Statements for the Years Ending February 28

	1989	1990	1991	1992	1993
Revenues					
Gross sales—Store 1	$247,000	$300,000	$350,000	$350,000	$ 350,000
Gross sales—Store 2	-0-	-0-	250,000	350,000	350,000
Gross sales—Store 3	-0-	-0-	-0-	250,000	350,000
Total gross sales	$247,000	$300,000	$600,000	$950,000	$1,050,000
Expenses					
Cost of goods sold	$139,600	$165,000	$330,000	$522,500	$ 577,500
Selling expenses	33,550	35,000	40,000	40,000	40,000
Administrative expenses*	25,948	30,000	75,000	100,000	100,000
Officers' salaries	14,400	20,000	40,000	60,000	60,000
Rent	22,500	22,500	47,000	71,500	73,500
Common area maintenance	3,180	4,000	8,000	12,000	12,000
Other occupancy expenses	7,320	8,000	9,000	10,000	10,000
Total expenses	$246,498	$284,500	$549,000	$816,000	$ 873,000
Profit before taxes	$ 502	$ 15,500	$ 51,000	$134,000	$ 177,000

*Includes repayments and interest; assumes new bank loans to finance opening Store 2 and Store 3.

EXHIBIT 6   Lease Excerpts

Section	Lease Index
1	Premises
2	Construction of Premises
3	Lease Term
4	Delayed Possession and Options to Terminate
5	Rent
6	Taxes and Insurance Premiums
7	Utilities
8	Common Areas
9	Common Area and Mall Maintenance
10	Conduct of Business on the Premises
11	Alterations
12	Maintenance and Repair
13	Quiet Enjoyment
14	Assignment or Sublease
15	Indemnification; Liability Insurance
16	Signs and Advertising
17	Entry by Lessor
18	Eminent Domain
19	Fire or Other Casualty
20	Waiver of Subrogation
21	Insolvency
22	Defaults
23	Liens and Encumbrances
24	Advances by Lessor for Lessee
25	Attorneys' Fees
26	Waiver
27	Other Stores
28	Notice
29	Successors or Assigns
30	Lease Consideration
31	Merchants Association
32	Change of Location
33	Subordination; Notice to Mortgagee; Attornment
34	Holding Over
35	Memorandum of Lease
36	Sale of Premises by Lessor

EXHIBIT 6   *(continued)*

Selected Excerpts from Lease

SECTION 14
ASSIGNMENT OR SUBLEASE

Lessee shall not assign, sublease or transfer this lease or any interest therein or in the premises, nor shall this lease or any interest thereunder be assignable or transferable by operation of law or by any process or proceeding of any court, or otherwise, without first obtaining the written consent of Lessor. No assignment of this lease by Lessee shall relieve Lessee of any of its duties or obligations thereunder. If Lessee is a corporation, then any merger, consolidation or liquidation to which it may be a party or any change in the ownership of or power to vote the majority of its outstanding voting stock shall constitute an assignment or transfer of this lease for the purposes of this section.

SECTION 15
INDEMNIFICATION; LIABILITY INSURANCE

Lessor shall not be liable to Lessee or to any other person, firm or corporation whatsoever for any injury to, or death of any person, or for any loss of, or damages to, property (including property of Lessee) occurring in or about the Shopping Center or the premises from any cause whatsoever. Lessee agrees to indemnify and save Lessor harmless from all loss, damage, liability, suit claim, or expense (including expense of litigation) arising out of or resulting from any actual or alleged injury to, or death of, any person, or from any actual or alleged loss of, or damage to, property caused by, or resulting from, any occurrence on or about the premises, or caused by, or resulting from, any act or omission, whether negligent or otherwise, of Lessee, or any officer, agent, employee, contractor, guest, invitee, customer, or visitor of Lessee, in or about the Shopping Center or the premises. Lessee shall, at its own expense, maintain at all times during the lease term proper liability insurance with a reputable insurance company or companies satisfactory to Lessor in the minimum limit of One Hundred Thousand Dollars ($100,000) (per accident) for property damage, and in the minimum limits of Five Hundred Thousand Dollars ($500,000) (per person) and One Million Dollars ($1,000,000) (per accident or occurrence) for bodily injuries and death, to indemnify both Lessor and Lessee against such claims, demands, losses, damages, liabilities, and expense as against which Lessee has herein agreed to indemnify and hold Lessor harmless. Such policy or policies shall name Lessor, its ground lessor and lenders as insureds, be issued by companies noted A+, AAA or better in Best's insurance guide, and shall be noncancellable as to such named insureds except upon at least ten (10) days prior written notice. Lessee shall furnish Lessor with a copy of said policy or policies or other acceptable evidence that said insurance is in effect.

SECTION 21
INSOLVENCY

Lessee agrees that it will not cause or give cause for the institution of legal proceedings seeking to have Lessee adjudicated bankrupt, reorganized or rearranged under the bankruptcy laws of the United States, or for relief under any other law for the relief of debtors, and will not cause or give cause for the appointment of a trustee or receiver for Lessee's assets, and will not cause or give cause for the commencement of proceedings to foreclose any mortgage or any other lien on Lessee's interest in the premises or on any personal property kept or maintained on the premises by Lessee; and Lessee further agrees that it will not make an assignment for the benefit of creditors, or become or be adjudicated insolvent. The allowance of any petition under the bankruptcy law, or the appointment of a trustee or receiver of Lessee's assets, or the entry of judgment of foreclosure in any proceedings to foreclose any such mortgage or other lien, or an adjudication that Lessee is insolvent shall be conclusive evidence that Lessee has violated the provisions of this section if said allowance, appointment, judgment, or adjudication or similar order or ruling remains in force or unstayed for a period of thirty (30) days. Upon the happening of any of such events, Lessor may, if it so elects, elect to terminate this lease and all rights of Lessee hereunder without prior notice to Lessee.

SECTION 22
DEFAULTS

Time is the essence hereof, and if Lessee violates or breaches or fails to keep or perform any covenant, agreement, term or condition of this lease, and if such default or violation shall continue or shall not be remedied within ten (10) days (three (3) days in the case of nonpayment of rent or other payments due hereunder) after notice in writing thereof given by Lessor to Lessee specifying the matter claimed to be in default, Lessor, at its option, may immediately declare Lessee's right under this Lease terminated, and reenter the premises, using such force as may be necessary, and repossess itself thereof, as of its former estate, removing all persons and effects therefrom. If upon the reentry of Lessor, there remains any personal property of Lessee or of any other person, firm or corporation

EXHIBIT 6   *(concluded)*

upon the premises, Lessor may, but without the obligation to do so, remove said personal property and place the same in a public warehouse or garage, as may be reasonable, at the expense and risk of the owners thereof, and Lessee shall reimburse Lessor for any expense incurred by Lessor in connection with said removal and/or storage. Notwithstanding any such reentry, the liability of Lessee for the full rent provided for herein shall not be extinguished for the balance of the term of this lease, and Lessee shall make good to Lessor each month during the balance of said term any deficiency arising from a reletting of the premises at a lesser rental than that herein agreed upon as the Minimum Rent, plus the cost of renovating the premises for the new tenant and reletting it.

SECTION 23
LIENS AND ENCUMBRANCES

Lessee shall keep the premises free and clear of any liens and encumbrances arising or growing out of the use and occupancy of the premises by Lessee hereunder. At Lessor's request, Lessee shall furnish Lessor with written proof of payment of any item which would or might constitute the basis for a lien on the premises if not paid.

SECTION 24
ADVANCES BY LESSOR FOR LESSEE

If Lessee fails to do anything required to be done by it under the terms of this lease, except to pay rent, Lessor may, at its sole option, do such act or thing on behalf of Lessee, and upon notification to Lessee of the cost thereof to the Lessor, Lessee shall promptly pay the Lessor the amount of that cost, plus interest at the rate of twelve percent (12%) per annum from the date that the cost was incurred by Lessor to the date of Lessee's payment.

SECTION 25
ATTORNEYS' FEES

Lessee agrees to pay, in addition to all other sums due hereunder, such expenses and attorneys' fees as Lessor may incur in enforcing all obligations under terms of this lease, including those fees and expenses incurred at trial and on appeal, all of which shall be included in any judgment entered therein. Such covered fees and expenses shall include those incurred in suits instituted by third parties in which Lessor must participate to protect its rights hereunder and those incurred in suits to establish and enforce rights of indemnity hereunder.

SECTION 27
OTHER STORES

Lessee agrees that neither it, nor any subsidiary or affiliate of it, nor any other person, firm or corporation using any store or business name licensed or controlled by Lessee, shall, during the term of this lease, operate a store or business which is the same as or similar to that to be conducted on the premises, or which merchandises or sells the same or similar products, merchandise or services as that to be sold or furnished from the premises, at any location within a radius of four (4) miles from the Shopping Center without the written permission of Lessor. Lessee further agrees that it will not promote or encourage the operation of any such store or business within said radius by any person, firm or corporation. In addition to any and all other remedies otherwise available to Lessor for breach of this covenant, it is agreed that Lessor may at its election either (*a*) terminate this lease or (*b*) require that any and all sales made at, in, on or from any such other store be included in the computation of the percentage rent due hereunder with the same force and effect as though such sales had actually been made at, in, on or from the premises.

SECTION 32
CHANGE OF LOCATION

Lessee shall move from the premises at Lessor's written request to any other premises and location in the Shopping Center, in which event such new location and premises shall be substituted for the premises described herein, but all other terms of this lease shall remain the same, with the exception that the Minimum Rent provided for herein shall be abated during the period that Lessee is closed for business as a result of the move to the new location; provided, however, that Lessee shall not be moved to premises of less square footage than those herein leased, and that Lessor shall bear all actual cash expenses incurred by Lessee in so moving. It is further understood and agreed, however, that in the event that Lessee shall move to any other premises and location within the Shopping Center for any reason other than to comply with a request from Lessor, then this paragraph shall be inapplicable and the Lessee shall bear all expenses of moving.

EXHIBIT 7 **Industry Operating Results 1989 Specialty Stores—Sales under $1 Million (percent figures unless otherwise noted)**

	Average	*Middle Range*
Sales data		
Credit sales	20.87	11.70 - 36.68
Sales per square foot—selling space ($)	114.90	42.61 - 137.94
Sales per square foot—total space ($)	85.68	37.60 - 126.00
Returns—% gross sales	1.82	1.00 - 3.60
Sales per employee ($)	50,643	41,194 - 68,270
Markdowns	12.15	0.90 - 15.23
Employee discounts	1.09	0.00 - 2.12
Shortages	1.90	0.96 - 2.94
Gross margin	41.47	39.66 - 43.83
Net operating expenses		
Earnings from operations	3.57	1.59 - 5.00
Other income	0.62	0.18 - 1.72
Pretax earnings	4.19	2.52 - 5.31
Management payroll	8.43	6.57 - 10.54
Selling payroll	9.13	7.48 - 9.87
Payroll total	17.56	16.30 - 20.33
Supplementary fringe benefits	0.73	0.41 - 0.99
Media costs	3.09	2.21 - 3.33
Taxes	2.11	1.80 - 2.23
Supplies	2.99	2.00 - 3.78
Credit services	0.83	0.43 - 1.84
Other	1.05	0.81 - 1.37
Travel	0.85	0.13 - 1.40
Postage and phone	0.88	0.50 - 1.20
Insurance	1.29	0.74 - 1.66
Depreciation	0.97	0.29 - 1.56
Professional services	0.53	0.18 - 0.68
Bad debts	0.41	0.09 - 0.67
Outside maintenance and equipment service	0.26	0.18 - 0.30
Real property rentals	4.35	3.09 - 4.97
Total:	37.90	36.29 - 40.60

Adapted from National Retail Merchants Assn., *Financial and Operating Results of Department and Specialty Stores 1989*, pp. 104–5.

Exhibit 8 **Dragonfly Expenses**

DRAGONFLY CORPORATION
Statement of Operating Expenses
For the Years Ending December 31

	1989	1990
Operating expenses		
Sales salaries	$22,607	$30,445
Advertising	9,317	10,726
Alteration costs	204	0
Bank card discounts	2,014	2,343
Buying trips	2,648	2,056
Delivery	149	0
Display	330	0
Selling supplies	5,559	5,864
Over/short	45	(629)
	42,873	50,805
Occupancy expenses		
Depreciation/amortization	8,964	4,683
Insurance	742	742
Maintenance	542	151
Property taxes	0	542
Rent	20,128	16,942
Utilities	101	95
	30,477	23,155
Administrative expenses		
Officer's salary	23,447	13,542
Employee benefits	874	2,169
Bank charges	187	223
Donations	25	40
Dues and subscriptions	101	50
Officer's life insurance	2,231	1,780
Bad debts	367	0
Office expense	1,645	104
Professional services	6,794	5,080
Business taxes	1,216	1,024
Payroll taxes	5,661	5,232
Telephone	854	1,172
Postage	787	712
Temporary help	154	79
Travel and entertainment	225	0
Miscellaneous	0	1,435
	$44,568	$32,642

Exhibit 9   Janet and Michael Thompson—Personal Balance Sheet, January 1, 1991

Assets

1979 VW	$ 1,000
House	140,000
Marketable securities*	20,000
Equity in Dragonfly	5,000
Note receivable—Dragonfly	75,000
	$241,000

Liabilities

First mortgage on house—Bank	$ 47,000
Second mortgage—Hepburns	35,000
Note payable—Hepburns	75,000
Note payable—Hepburns	15,000
Total liabilities	$172,000
Net worth	69,000
Total liabilities and net worth	$241,000

*While these stocks were in Janet's name, Washington is a community property state.

Exhibit 10   History of Lease Obligations and Payments for Woodscross Store

Time Period	Rent Incurred* (approx.)	Rent Paid	Payment on Old Balance	Total Remaining Unpaid Obligation†
July–Dec., 1988	$13,800	$13,800	$ 0	$ 0
Jan.–Dec., 1989	$27,600	$20,128	0	7,472
Jan.–Dec., 1990	27,600	16,942	0	18,130
Jan. 1991	2,300	878	0	19,552
Feb. 1991	2,300	500	875	20,477
March 1991	2,300	500	875	21,402
April 1991	2,300	500	875	22,327
May 1991	2,300	500	875	23,252
June 1991	2,300	500	875	24,177
July 1991‡	1,425	1,425	650	23,527
Aug. 1991	1,425	1,425	650	22,877
Sept. 1991	1,425	1,425	650	22,227
Oct. 1991	1,425	1,425	650	21,577
Nov. 1991	2,300	2,300	0	21,577
Dec. 1991	2,300	2,300	0	21,577

*Including common area maintenance assessments.

†Does not include future obligations under lease, which runs through March 1993.

‡Thompsons negotiate with landlord to pay rent of 6 percent of gross sales or $2,300 per month, *whichever is less.*

EXHIBIT 11   Correspondence from Attorney

October 25, 1991

Jeff Lawrence, Esq.
Attorney at Law
600 Seattle Trust Building
10655 NE Fourth
Bellevue, WA 98004

Re: Woodscross Properties
     <u>Janet and Michael Thompson Lease Default</u>

Dear Mr. Lawrence:

As we have discussed recently by telephone, your clients, Janet and Michael Thompson, are currently in substantial default under the terms of their lease with Woodscross Properties. Any prior understanding which may have existed with respect to payment of this default was mutually rescinded by request of your clients on or about June 1, 1991. A subsequent arrangement, which was conditioned upon execution and delivery of an installment note and deed of trust, was proffered to Mr. Thompson on or about July 14, 1991, but he never executed a note and he failed to provide a legal description for his residence so that the deed of trust could be prepared, notwithstanding his repeated assurances that it would be forthcoming. As indicated in our prior correspondence to your clients, that offer has long since lapsed.

You now indicate that the Thompsons cannot further encumber their residence, that they own no other property on which a deed of trust might be placed, that they have no other security to offer in any form, and that they are even fighting to hold off lien foreclosures on their new store. In spite of all this, you propose that Woodscross Properties should be content without even a promissory note evidencing the indebtedness or the installment terms. You further suggest that no interest should accrue on the lease indebtedness. Moreover, although you acknowledge that the Thompsons' family members are helping them financially, they are reportedly unwilling to provide a guarantee of payment for this debt.

The fact that the Thompsons desire to avoid signing a note evidencing the terms of payment suggests that they have no intention of paying the lease default. Your suggestion that Woodscross Properties should rely solely on the Thompsons' good faith is completely unrealistic and unacceptable, both as a general business practice and as a result of your clients' past failures to perform as promised. We have enclosed a promissory note, bearing interest at 15% per annum, and requiring payments of $800 per month, which you have indicated are within the Thompsons' means. We have also enclosed a confession of judgment, which is to be entered in the event of default by the Thompsons in their payments due under the note.

Kindly arrange for Mr. and Mrs. Thompson to sign the note and confession of judgment and return the fully executed documents to us by no later than 5 o'clock p.m., November 5, 1991. If we do not receive them by that date and time, Woodscross Properties reserves all rights to collect the amounts due, without further notice to you.

Very truly yours,

PELLETT & CRUTT

Andrew A. Savage

Enclosures
CC: Woodscross Properties

EXHIBIT 11   *(continued)*

PROMISSORY NOTE

$21,576.79   Seattle, Washington
                                                                    _____, 1991

   FOR VALUE RECEIVED, the undersigned ("Maker") promises to pay to the order of Woodscross Properties, a Washington corporation limited partnership, the principal sum of Twenty-One Thousand Five Hundred Seventy-Six and 79/100 Dollars ($21,576.79), together with interest thereon, all as hereinafter provided and upon the following agreements, terms, and conditions:

   Interest. All sums which are and which may become owing hereon shall bear interest from the date hereof until paid, at the rate of fifteen percent (15%) per annum.

   Payment. Maker shall pay principal and interest in consecutive monthly installments of Eight Hundred Dollars ($800.00), or more, commencing on the fifteenth day of November 1, 1991, and continuing on the fifteenth day of each succeeding calendar month thereafter until the total indebtedness herein is paid in full. Each payment shall be applied first to interest accrued to the installment payment date and then to principal. All payments shall be payable in lawful money of the United States of America which shall be the legal tender for public and private debts at the time of payments. All payments shall be made to the holder hereof at Suite D–9, Woodscross Mall, Bellevue, Washington 98008, or at such other place as the holder hereof may specify in writing from time to time.

   Prepayment. All or any part of the sums now or hereafter owing hereon may be prepaid at any time or times. Any such prepayment may be made without prior notice to the holder and shall be without premium or discount. All partial prepayments shall be applied first to interest accrued to the date of prepayment and the balance, if any, shall be credited to the last due installments of principal in the inverse order of their maturity without deferral or limitation of the intervening installments of principal or interest.

   Late Payment Charge. If any installment of principal or interest shall not be paid within five (5) days commencing with the date such installment becomes due, Marker agrees to pay a later charge equal to three percent (3%) of the delinquent installment to cover the extra expense involved in handling delinquent payments. This late payment charge is in addition to and not in lieu of any other rights or remedies the holder may have by virtue of any breach or default hereunder.

   Default; Attorneys' Fees and Other Costs and Expenses. Upon the occurrence of any Event of Default, at the option of the holder, all sums owing and to become owing hereon shall become immediately due and payable. The occurrence of any of the following shall constitute an "Event of Default": (i) Maker fails to pay any installment or other sum owing hereon when due; (ii) Maker admits in writing its inability to pay its debts, or makes a general assignment for the benefit of creditors; (iii) any proceeding is instituted by or against Maker seeking to adjudicate it a bankrupt or insolvent, or seeking reorganization, arrangement, adjustment, or composition of it or its debts under any law relating to bankruptcy, insolvency or reorganization or relief of debtors, or seeking appointment of a receiver trustee or other similar official for it or for any substantial part of its property; or (iv) any dissolution or liquidation proceeding is instituted by or against Maker, and if instituted against Maker, is consented to or acquiesced in by Maker or remains for thirty (30) days undismissed or unstayed or remains for thirty (30) days undismissed after such proceeding is no longer stayed. Maker agrees to pay all costs and expenses which the holder may incur by reason of any Event of Default, including without limitation reasonable attorneys' fees with respect to legal services relating to any Event of Default and to a determination of any rights or remedies of the

EXHIBIT 11   *(continued)*

holder under this note, and reasonable attorneys' fees relating to any actions or proceedings which the holder may institute or in which the holder may appear or participate and in any reviews of and appeals therefrom, and all such sums shall be secured hereby. Any judgment recovered by the holder hereon shall bear interest at the rate of eighteen percent (18%) per annum, not to exceed, however, the highest rate then permitted by law on such judgment. The venue of any action hereon may be laid in the Country of King, State of Washington, at the option of the holder.

No Waiver. The holder's acceptance of partial or delinquent payments or the failure of the holder to exercise any right hereunder shall not waive any obligation of Maker or right of the holder or modify this note, or waive any other similar default.

Liability. All persons signing this note as Maker thereby agree that they shall be liable hereon jointly and severally, and they hereby waive demand, presentment for payment, protest, and notice of protest and of nonpayment. Each such person agrees that any modification or extension of the terms of payment made by the holder with or without notice, at the request of any person liable hereon, or a release of any party liable for his obligation shall not diminish or impair his or their liability for the payment hereof.

Maximum Interest. Notwithstanding any other provisions of this note, interest, fees, and charges payable by reason of the indebtedness evidenced hereby shall not exceed the maximum, if any, permitted by governing law.

Applicable Law. This note shall be governed by, and construed in accordance with, the laws of the State of Washington.

Michael Thompson

Janet Thompson

DRAGONFLY CORPORATION

BY _____

Its _____

EXHIBIT 11   *(continued)*

IN THE SUPERIOR COURT OF THE STATE OF WASHINGTON FOR KING

COUNTY WOODSCROSS PROPERITES, a limited partnership consisting of DICK MALLET and GEORGE VALE, as general partners, and other persons or entities as limited partners,	)))))))	
Plaintiff,	)))	No.
v.	( ))	CONFESSION OF JUDGMENT
MICHAEL THOMPSON and JANET THOMPSON husband and wife, the marital community thereof, and DRAGONFLY CORPORATION, a Washington corporation,	))))))))	
Defendants.	))	

Michael Thompson, Janet Thompson, husband and wife, the marital community thereof, and Dragonfly Corporation, defendants, do hereby confess judgment in favor of Woodscross Properties, plaintiff, on the terms and conditions and for the sums set forth below, and do hereby authorize the above Court to enter judgment for said sum and on said terms and conditions against defendants and in favor of plaintiff.

1. Defendants agree and confess that this confession of judgment and judgment based thereon may be entered immediately herein if, at any time hereafter, an Event of Default occurs, as defined in that certain promissory note (the "Promissory Note") executed by defendants and dated _____, 1991, a copy of which is attached hereto as Exhibit A and incorporated herein by this reference.

2. In proof of the occurrence of an Event of Default as specified above, it shall be necessary and sufficient proof for plaintiff to present to the Court a writing certified by the then current holder of the Promissory Note that an Event of Default has occurred as defined in the Promissory Note.

3. Judgment may be entered in the principal amount of $21,576.79, together with interest in accordance with the terms of the Promissory Note, save and except the following: (a) any amount paid to plaintiff pursuant to the Promissory Note by defendants shall be deducted from the amount of said principal and interest specified in the Promissory Note; and (b) plaintiff's court costs, disbursements, and attorneys' fees incurred in connection with defendant's default in making payments due under the Promissory Note shall be added thereto.

4. Defendants specifically waive their right to a hearing on the merits of any issues that may arise in connection with the execution or enforcement of, or otherwise relating to, the Promissory Note, and confess and admit that the above-entitled court has full and exclusive jurisdiction over the parties and over the subject matter of any action arising from or relating to the Promissory Note, and defendants, for themselves and for all parties claiming under, by, or through them, hereby waive any and all claims or defenses, whether substantive or

---

EXHIBIT 11   *(continued)*

---

procedural, to entry of judgment in accordance with the terms and conditions of this confession of judgment.

5. Defendants state, agree, and admit that this confession of judgment is a completely voluntary and knowing act of defendants. Defendants have been fully advised by their counsel of the effects and scope of the judgment confessed herein.

6. Defendants hereby expressly waive notice of presentation of this confession of judgment to the court. If, notwithstanding defendants' waiver of any notice requirements, plaintiff elects to notify defendants of the time and place for presentation of the judgment, defendants shall have a right to be heard on the following questions only: (a) whether plaintiff has complied with the requirements set forth in paragraph 2 regarding proof that an Event of Default has occurred; and (b) the reasonableness of the attorneys' fees and costs to be included in the judgment.

7. Defendants state, admit, and believe that this confession of judgment is for money justly due and owing to plaintiff under the terms of the Promissory Note, which was executed by defendants, as their free and voluntary act, to evidence indebtedness owing by defendants to plaintiff for delinquent lease payments arising under a commercial lease between the parties.

DATED this _____day of _____, 1991.

_____

Michael Thompson

_____

Janet Thompson

_____

DRAGONFLY CORPORATION

BY_____

Its _____

STATE OF WASHINGTON)
) ss.
COUNTY OF _____)

MICHAEL THOMPSON, being first duly sworn, states: I am the defendant in the above-entitled action, and I am authorized to make this verification on its behalf. I have read the foregoing Confession of Judgment, know the contents thereof, and that the same is true in all respects; I verify that the Confession of Judgment herein contained has been voluntarily made by Michael Thompson with full knowledge.

_____

SUBSCRIBED AND SWORN TO before me this _____day of _____, 1991.

_____

NOTARY PUBLIC in and for the State of Washington, residing at

_____

EXHIBIT 11   *(continued)*

STATE OF WASHINGTON)
) ss.
COUNTY OF _____)

JANET THOMPSON, being first duly sworn, states that I am a defendant in the above-entitled action, and I am authorized to make this verification. I have read the foregoing Confession of Judgment, know the contents thereof, and that the same is true in all respects; I verify that the Confession of Judgment therein contained has been voluntarily made by Janet Thompson with full knowledge.

SUBSCRIBED AND SWORN TO before me this _____day of _____, 1991.

_____

NOTARY PUBLIC in and for the State of Washington, residing at

_____

STATE OF WASHINGTON)
) ss.
COUNTY OF_____)

_____, being first duly sworn, states: I am the _____of Dragonfly Corporation, the defendant in the above-entitled action, and I am authorized to make this verification on its behalf. I have read the foregoing Confession of Judgment, know the contents thereof, and that the same is true in all respects; I verify that the Confession of Judgment therein contained has been voluntarily made by Dragonfly Corporation with full knowledge.

SUBSCRIBED AND SWORN TO before me this _____day of _____, 1991.

_____

NOTARY PUBLIC in and for the State of Washington, residing at

_____

STATE OF WASHINGTON)
) ss.
COUNTY OF _____)

On this _____day of _____, 1991, before me, the undersigned, a Notary Public in and for the State of Washington, duly commissioned and sworn, personally appeared MICHAEL THOMPSON known to me to be the party that executed the foregoing Confession of Judgment, and acknowledged the said Confession of Judgment to be his free and voluntary act and deed for the uses and purposes therein mentioned, and on oath stated that he was authorized to execute this said Confession of Judgment.

WITNESS my hand and official seal hereto affixed the day and year in this certificate first above written.

_____

NOTARY PUBLIC in and for the State of Washington, residing at

_____

EXHIBIT 11 *(concluded)*

STATE OF WASHINGTON)
) ss.
COUNTY OF _____)

On this _____ day of _____, 1991, before, me, the undersigned, a Notary Public in and for the State of Washington, duly commissioned and sworn, personally appeared JANET THOMPSON known to me to be the party that executed the foregoing Confession of Judgment, and acknowledged the said Confession of Judgment to be her free and voluntary act and deed for the uses and purposes therein mentioned, and on oath stated that she was authorized to execute the said Confession of Judgment. WITNESS my hand and official seal hereto affixed the day and year in this certificate first above written.

                                                            ————————————————————

                                                      NOTARY PUBLIC in and for the State of Washington, residing at

                                                            ————————————————————

STATE OF WASHINGTON)
) ss.
COUNTY OF _____)

On this _____ day of _____, 1991, before me, the undersigned, a Notary Public in and for the State of Washington, duly commissioned and sworn, personally appeared _____, known to me to be the _____ of DRAGONFLY CORPORATION, the corporation that executed the foregoing Confession of Judgment, and acknowledged the said Confession of Judgment to be the free and voluntary act and deed of said corporation, for the uses and purposes therein mentioned, and on oath stated that he was authorized to execute the said Confession of Judgment and that the seal affixed (if any) is the corporate seal of said corporation.

WITNESS my hand and official seal hereto affixed the day and year in this certificate first above written.

                                                            ————————————————————

                                                      NOTARY PUBLIC in and for the State of Washington, residing at

                                                            ————————————————————

EXHIBIT 12   Correspondence from Attorney

October 27, 1991

Mr. Andrew A. Savage, Esq.
2300 The Bank of California Center
Seattle, WA 98164

RE: DRAGONFLY CORPORATION
Woodscross Shopping Center

Dear Andrew:

On October 8, 1991, we discussed Michael Thompson's and my meeting with Frank Murdock, Manager of Woodscross Properties. On that date, we proposed that the Dragonfly Corporation continue to pay the accrued lease balance in monthly payments of $649.95 with the current lease payments to revert to the pre-percentage rent amount of approximately $2,300 per month.

As you are aware, the Thompsons have paid $875 a month on the past-due balance from February through July, at which time it was reduced to the $649.95 monthly installment. Payments were made without a note and without security.

As I informed you, my clients do not have property which they can pledge to secure the unpaid lease amounts accrued and I have advised them that no note should be necessary where all parties are basically going back to their pre-July agreement.

Mr. and Mrs. Thompson have access to additional financial support from their relatives and fully intend to weather the current economic downturn. They have made a great investment in their Dragonfly stores and are excellent managers. They will be around to complete payment of the Woodscross Properties lease obligations.

On October 8, 1991, you informed me that you would be consulting with Frank Murdock and return to me with your response to our offer or alternative proposal. Please inform me of Mr. Murdock's response.

Very truly yours,

JEFF LAWRENCE

4–5 SSS

In January of 1983, Vincent Lamb, Jr., president of Scientific Systems Services (SSS), was attempting to choose an investment bank to underwrite the initial public offering of SSS stock (see **Exhibit 1** for recent financials). SSS had recently decided to become a publicly held corporation, and Lamb had mentioned this fact during a presentation at a financial conference for high-tech firms. In response, several firms had forwarded underwriting proposals to SSS. In addition, Lamb had solicited proposals from additional underwriters and had narrowed the choice down to the four that appear as exhibits in this case. (See **Exhibits 2** through **5**.)

SSS

SSS designed, marketed, and serviced integrated computer systems for monitoring and controlling industrial processes. These systems combined commercially available hardware and custom software configured to meet customer requirements. The company's principal customers were large electric utilities and automated industrial facilities.

Recent Financing History

SSS was founded in 1965 by two engineers, and the initial financing was obtained from their personal funds. One of the founders left SSS in 1971, and the other left the company in 1978; Lamb was then installed as chief executive. Lamb and a small group of officers and key employees purchased 152,000 shares from the former president, and SSS entered a period of rapid growth.

In late 1980, two vice presidents left SSS and an option was obtained to purchase their combined holdings, 500,000 shares for $500,000. SSS decided that the most appropriate way to handle this transaction was to arrange for a venture capital firm to purchase this block of stock as well as some additional shares to provide much needed working capital.

The Charles River Partnership purchased the 645,000-share block[1] for $750,000, and later that year purchased an additional 60,760 shares for $3.30 per share. With a

This case was prepared by Michael J. Roberts under the direction of Howard H. Stevenson.

Copyright © 1983 by the President and Fellows of Harvard College

Harvard Business School Case 9–384–129

[1]Note: All share figures and per share amounts have been adjusted to reflect a 5:1 stock split that occurred in February of 1983.

major venture capital firm as the largest single owner of SSS, the stage was clearly set for SSS to become a public corporation.

Eleven months later, in November of 1982, SSS was in need of funds to finance its efforts to enter the business of systems integration (i.e., packaging hardware and software). SSS sold 422,640 shares of stock for $7 per share via a private placement, which was arranged by the firm J. C. Bradford. At the time of this private placement, Bradford had also attempted to negotiate for the public offering. Lamb had been very careful to keep the two transactions separate, so that SSS would have maximum flexibility in choosing an underwriter.

In early 1983, SSS had decided that it was an appropriate time to consider the option of going public.

- SSS needed a great deal of capital to fund the expansion program (primarily via acquisitions, which it had chartered).
- The increased capitalization would help SSS gain credibility for bidding on large contracts with major utilities.
- SSS's ability to attract and hold onto high-caliber employees would be enhanced by a stock option plan and a publicly traded security.

A Secondary Offering

One issue, which had to be resolved, centered around a secondary offering of stock. All of the current institutional owners of SSS stock had the right to sell, on a pro rata basis, their own shares ("piggy-back rights"). (In a primary offering, only the company sells its own authorized but as yet unissued shares of stock—no individuals actually sell stock even though their ownership position is diluted.) Lamb and the board had to decide what portion, if any, of the total offering could be of secondary stock.

The Selection of an Underwriter

Lamb was very concerned that the chosen underwriter have the commitment not only to sell the stock, but also to support it strongly as a public issue. Lamb reasoned that, as a low capitalization stock, SSS would be unlikely to develop a strong following with large institutions. Therefore, strong research and market support would be crucial to developing a following of individual investors and eventually, to develop an institutional following as the stock became more widely traded.

Lamb was concerned with several other issues:

- Should SSS use one or two underwriters? If it used two, what additional qualities should it seek in an underwriting team?
- How important was a strong retail brokerage network?

Lamb was charged with recommending a plan of action to the board of directors at a special meeting that would be held the following week. This decision was complicated by the fact that the overall market had improved dramatically over the past several months (see **Exhibit 6**), and this made comparison of the underwriting offers more difficult.

As he looked over the proposals, Lamb knew that he needed to prepare an agenda for the board discussion and his recommendations as to the priorities of the various considerations.

EXHIBIT 1   **Scientific Systems Services Financials**

SCIENTIFIC SYSTEMS SERVICES, INC.
Balance Sheets
December 31

	1981	*1982*
Assets		
Current assets		
Cash and temporary cash investments	$ 816,766	$2,244,504
Certificates of deposit	100,067	308,067
Contract receivables	1,195,169	2,189,444
Income taxes receivable	—	247,363
Costs and estimated earnings in excess of related billings on uncompleted contracts.	345,366	994,550
Assets held in trust (current portion)	137,669	53,740
Prepaid expenses and other.	45,346	37,556
Total current assets	2,640,383	6,075,224
Assets held in trust	1,162,331	228,836
Property		
Land.	355,385	355,385
Building	—	1,147,637
Laboratory equipment.	317,783	1,025,687
Furniture and fixtures	312,917	756,705
Leasehold improvements.	45,808	85,345
Equipment held under capitalized leases	44,474	276,837
Total.	1,076,367	3,647,596
Less accumulated depreciation and amortization	275,297	478,872
Property—net	801,070	3,168,724
Other assets	74,895	88,461
Total.	$4,678,679	$9,561,245
Liabilities and Stockholders' Equity		
Current liabilities		
Current portion of long-term debt	$ 152,635	$ 180,660
Accounts payable	181,733	490,138
Billings in excess of related costs and estimated earnings on uncompleted contacts	348,547	323,456
Accrued payroll and related taxes	90,698	376,599
Accrued employee benefit plan	—	74,467
Income taxes payable	199,857	—
Deferred income taxes (current portion)	329,356	778,591
Accrued vacation benefits.	107,588	172,880
Other	14,993	10,877
Total current liabilities	1,425,407	2,407,668
Long-term liabilities		
Long-term debt	1,425,293	1,470,659
Deferred income taxes	30,536	114,723
Total long-term liabilities	1,455,829	1,585,382

EXHIBIT 1   *(concluded)*

SCIENTIFIC SYSTEMS SERVICES, INC.
Balance Sheets
December 31

	1981	1982
Stockholders' equity		
Commitments		
Common stock—$.01 par value; authorized		
10,000,000 shares;* issued 575,332 shares in 1981 and	115,066	33,379
3,337,925 in 1982; outstanding 466,532 in 1981 and		
2,773,425 in 1982..................................		
Paid-in capital	977,703	3,987,420
Retained earnings	1,239,074	2,176,446
Total..	2,331,843	6,197,245
Treasury stock—at cost 108,800 shares in 1981 and 564,500 in	(534,400)	(629,050)
1982..		
Stockholders' equity—net.............................	1,797,443	5,568,195
Total..	$4,678,679	$9,561,245

*Reflects 5:1 split.

SCIENTIFIC SYSTEMS SERVICES, INC.
Statements of Income and Retained Earnings
For the Years Ended December 31

	1980	1981	1982
Revenues	$4,992,559	$7,920,386	$15,523,134
Cost of revenues	3,244,496	4,830,694	10,314,390
Gross profit	1,748,063	3,089,692	5,208,744
Selling, general and administrative expenses	1,174,415	2,132,373	3,798,272
Operating income	573,648	957,319	1,410,472
Interest income	1,764	24,896	213,370
Interest expense....................................	(47,699)	(42,910)	(134,022)
Income before income taxes	527,713	939,305	1,487,820
Provision for income taxes............................	238,266	408,047	550,448
Net income	289,447	531,258	937,372
Retained earnings, beginning of year.....................	474,428	733,846	1,239,074
Dividends paid......................................	(30,029)	(26,030)	—
Retained earnings, beginning of year.....................	$ 733,846	$1,239,074	$ 2,176,446
Earnings per share:			
Earnings per common and common equivalent share.........	$.13	$.23	$.37
Earnings per common share assuming full dilution	$.13	$.22	$.36

EXHIBIT 2   J. C. Bradford Proposal (entire proposal attached)

May 7, 1982

Mr. Vincent Lamb
Chairman of the Board and President
Scientific Systems Services, Inc.
Box 610
Melbourne, Florida 32901

Dear Vincent:

J. C. Bradford & Co. is prepared to assist Scientific Systems Services, Inc., in its efforts to increase the firm's equity capital under either of the following options.

OPTION I: A PRIVATE PLACEMENT OF COMMON STOCK TO INSTITUTIONAL INVESTORS. Under this option, we would act as agent to assist SSS in raising $3,200,000 in new equity for the company, and as agent to assist certain shareholders in selling common stock valued at $800,000. We would propose to value the stock at around 23 times the trailing 12 months' earnings per share for the quarter ending June 30, 1982. We are prepared to act in this capacity immediately upon notification by you, and would anticipate closing such a transaction within 45 to 60 days after you have given us your approval to proceed. Our fee for this transaction would be 3 percent of the proceeds raised, payable at closing.

OPTION II: A PUBLIC OFFERING OF COMMON STOCK. We are prepared to act as manager or co-manager of a public offering of SSS common stock. We understand that you want to raise about $4,000,000 in new equity for the company and $2,000,000 for selling shareholders. We believe that the Company can justify a valuation in such an offering of between 19 times and 23 times the trailing 12 months' earnings per share for the quarter ending June 30, 1982. We would suggest an underwriting discount of no less than 7 percent under this option. This offering could take place around September 1, 1982.

Under either option, we would recommend that you have a minimum of a 2.5-for-one stock split prior to undertaking the applicable transaction.

Attached to this letter are several tables which show what could conceivably be done in a public offering at several different pricing levels ranging from a low of 18 times earnings to a high of 23 times earnings. To keep the number of total shares offered at a constant level, we have decreased the number of shares sold by the Company and increased the number of shares offered by selling shareholders at each higher price level. About 45 days prior to the offering date, the Company would fix the number of shares offered by the Company and the selling shareholders, based upon prevailing market conditions at that time. This event would occur upon entering registration with the SEC.

We look forward to further discussions with you and your board on this. Thank you so much for the fine meeting we had this week.

Yours very truly,

J. Robert Philpott, Jr.
Vice President
Corporate Finance Department

EXHIBIT 2   *(continued)*

Historical and Projected Quarterly Earnings per Share, Assuming 510,000 Shares

	1981				1982				1983			
	Q_1	Q_2	Q_3	Q_4	Q_1	Q_2	Q_3	Q_4	Q_1	Q_2	Q_3	Q_4
Quarterly earnings per share	$.225	$.247	$.273	$.296	$ .47	$ .47	$ .50	$ .49	$ .70	$ .74	$ .82	$ .78
Trailing 12 months EPS					$1.04	$1.29	$1.51	$1.74	$1.93	$ 2.16	$ 2.43	$ 2.75	$ 3.04
Trailing 12 months net income ($000)					$ 531	$ 658	$ 770	$ 887	$ 984	$1,102	$1,239	$1,402	$1,550

Assuming 510,000 Shares Outstanding

	1977	1978	1979	1980	1981	1982$^{(P)}$	1983$^{(P)}$
Annual revenues ($000)	$1,299	$2,637	$3,531	$4,992	$7,945	$16,400	$21,300
Aftertax profit ($000)	$ 72	$ 271	$ 181	$ 289	$ 531	$ 984	$ 1,550
EPS	$ .14	$ .53	$ .35	$ .57	$1.04	$ 1.93	$ 3.04
Increase in revenues		103%	34%	41%	59%	106%	30%
Increase in aftertax profit		276%	(33%)	60%	84%	85%	58%
Increase in EPS		278%	(34%)	63%	82%	85%	58%

P = projected

Historical and Projected Quarterly Earnings per Share, Assuming 1,275,000 Shares

	1981				1982				1983			
	Q_1	Q_2	Q_3	Q_4	Q_1	Q_2	Q_3	Q_4	Q_1	Q_2	Q_3	Q_4
Quarterly earnings per share	$.09	$.10	$.11	$.12	$.19	$.19	$.20	$.19	$.28	$.30	$.33	$.31
Trailing 12 months EPS				$.42	$.52	$.61	$.70	$.77	$.86	$.97	$1.10	$1.22
Trailing 12 months net income ($000)				$531	$658	$770	$887	$984	$1,102	$1,239	$1,402	$1,550

Assuming 1,275,000 Shares Outstanding

	1977	1978	1979	1980	1981	1982$^{(P)}$	1983$^{(P)}$
Annual revenues ($000)	$1,299	$2,637	$3,531	$4,994	$7,945	$16,400	$21,300
Aftertax profit ($000)	$ 72	$ 271	$ 181	$ 289	$ 531	$ 984	$ 1,550
EPS	$ .06	$ .21	$ .14	$ .23	$ .42	$ .77	$ 1.22
Increase in revenues		103%	34%	41%	59%	106%	30%
Increase in aftertax profit		276%	(33%)	60%	84%	85%	58%
Increase in EPS		250%	(33%)	64%	83%	83%	58%

EXHIBIT 2   *(continued)*

Scientific Systems Services, Inc.

Assumptions: Offering 9/1/82, off trailing 12 months' figures to 6/30/82 of $770,000 net income (or $.61 per share). At P/E multiple of 18, Company worth $13,860,000. 1,275,000 shares outstanding before offering.

$$\frac{\$13,860,000}{1,275,000} \text{ shares} = \$10.87 \text{ per share} \quad \text{Offer at } \$11 \text{ per share} \quad 7\% \text{ spread}$$

Number of shares outstanding before offering	1,275,000
Number of new shares issued by Company	370,000
Number of shares sold by selling shareholders	180,000
Total shares offered for sale	550,000
Number of shares outstanding after offering	1,645,000

$$\text{Dilution} \frac{1,645,000}{1,275,000} = 1.29 = 29\%$$

Offering P/E Multiple	Per Share	New Shares by Company	Gross Proceeds to Company	Net Proceeds to Company	Shares Sold by Selling Shareholders	Gross Proceeds to Selling Shareholders	Net Proceeds to Selling Shareholders	Gross Proceeds of Offering
18	$11	370,000	$4,070,000	$3,785,100	180,000	$1,980,000	$1,841,400	$6,050,000

Projected earnings for the Company for 12 months through 6/30/83 are $1,239,300.

$$\frac{\$1,239,300}{1,275,000} = \$.97 \quad \frac{1,239,300}{1,645,000} = \$.75$$

If 10% pretax, 5% aftertax, earned for 10 months on net proceeds to Company, add $157,712 to 6/30/83 net income and earn $1,397,012 for 12 months ending 6/30/83.

$$\frac{\$1,239,300 + \$157,712}{2/12\,(1,275,000) + 10/12\,(1,645,000)} = \frac{\$1,379,012}{212,500 + 1,370,833} = \frac{\$1,397,012}{1,583,333} \$.88 \text{ or } 44\% \text{ over } 6/30/82.$$

Assumptions: Offering 9/1/82, off trailing 12 months' figures to 6/30/82 of $770,000 net income (or $.61 per share). At P/E multiple of 20, Company worth $15,400,000. 1,275,000 shares outstanding before offering.

$$\frac{\$15,400,000}{1,275,000} \text{ shares} = \$12.08 \text{ per share} \quad \text{Offer at } \$12 \text{ per share} \quad 7\% \text{ spread}$$

Number of shares outstanding before offering	1,275,000
Number of new shares issued by Company	340,000
Number of shares sold by selling shareholders	210,000
Total shares offered for sale	550,000
Number of shares outstanding after offering	1,615,000

$$\text{Dilution} \frac{1,615,000}{1,275,000} = 1.27 = 27\%$$

EXHIBIT 2   *(continued)*

Offering P/E Multiple	Per Share	New Shares by Company	Gross Proceeds to Company	Net Proceeds to Company	Shares Sold by Selling Shareholders	Gross Proceeds to Selling Shareholders	Net Proceeds to Selling Shareholders	Gross Proceeds of Offering
20	$12	340,000	$4,080,000	$3,794,400	210,000	$2,520,000	$2,343,600	$6,600,000

Projected earnings for the Company for 12 months through 6/30/83 are $1,239,300.

$$\frac{\$1,239,300}{1,275,000} = \$.97 \quad \frac{1,239,300}{1,615,000} = \$.77$$

If 10% pretax, 5% aftertax, earned for 10 months on net proceeds to Company, add $158,100 to 6/30/83 net income and earn $1,397,400 for 12 months ending 6/30/83.

$$\frac{\$1,397,400}{2/12\ (1,275,000) + 10/12\ (1,615,000)} = \frac{\$1,379,400}{1,558,333} = \$.90 \text{ or } 48\% \text{ over } 6/30/82.$$

Scientific Systems Services, Inc.

Assumptions: Offering 9/1/82, off trailing 12 months' figures to 6/30/82 of $770,000 net income (or $.61 per share). At P/E multiple of 22, Company worth $16,940,000. 1,275,000 shares outstanding before offering.

$$\frac{\$16,940,000}{1,275,000} \text{ shares} = \$13.29 \text{ per share} \qquad \text{Offer at } \$13.25 \text{ per share} \qquad 7\% \text{ spread}$$

Number of shares outstanding before offering	1,275,000
Number of new shares issued by Company	310,000
Number of shares sold by selling shareholders	240,000
Total shares offered for sale	550,000
Number of shares outstanding after offering	1,585,000

$$\text{Dilution } \frac{1,585,000}{1,275,000} = 1.24 = 24\%$$

Offering P/E Multiple	Per Share	New Shares by Company	Gross Proceeds to Company	Net Proceeds to Company	Shares Sold by Selling Shareholders	Gross Proceeds to Selling Shareholders	Net Proceeds to Selling Shareholders	Gross Proceeds of Offering
22	$13.25	310,000	$4,107,500	$3,819,975	240,000	$3,180,000	$2,957,400	$7,287,500

Projected earnings for the Company for 12 months through 6/30/83 are $1,239,300.

$$\frac{\$1,239,300}{1,275,000} = \$.97 \quad \frac{1,239,300}{1,585,000} = \$.78$$

If 10% pretax, 5% aftertax, earned for 10 months on net proceeds to Company, add $159,166 to 6/30/83 net income and earn $1,398,466 for 12 months ending 6/30/83.

EXHIBIT 2 *(concluded)*

$$\frac{\$1,398,466}{2/12\ (1,275,000)\ +\ 10/12\ (1,585,000)} = \frac{\$1,398,466}{1,533,333} = \$.91 \text{ or } 49\% \text{ over } 6/30/82.$$

Assumptions: Offering 9/1/82, off trailing 12 months' figures to 6/30/82 of $770,000 net income (or $.61 per share). At P/E multiple of 23, Company worth $17,710,000. 1,275,000 shares outstanding before offering.

$$\frac{\$17,710,000}{1,275,000} \text{ shares} = \$13.89 \text{ per share} \qquad \text{Offer at } \$13.75 \text{ per share} \qquad 7\% \text{ spread}$$

Number of shares outstanding before offering	1,275,000
Number of new shares issued by Company	290,000
Number of shares sold by selling shareholders	260,000
Total shares offered for sale	550,000
Number of shares outstanding after offering	1,565,000

$$\text{Dilution } \frac{1,565,000}{1,275,000} = 1.23 = 23\%$$

Offering P/E Multiple	Per Share	New Shares by Company	Gross Proceeds to Company	Net Proceeds to Company	Shares Sold by Selling Shareholders	Gross Proceeds to Selling Shareholders	Net Proceeds to Selling Shareholders	Gross Proceeds of Offering
23	$13.75	290,000	$3,987,700	$3,708,561	260,000	$3,575,000	$3,324,750	$7,562,500

Projected earnings for the Company for 12 months through 6/30/83 are $1,239,300.

$$\frac{\$1,239,300}{1,275,000} = \$.97 \quad \frac{1,239,300}{1,565,000} = \$.79$$

If 10% pretax, 5% aftertax, earned for 10 months on net proceeds to Company, add $167,000 to 6/30/83 net income and earn $1,405,466 for 12 months ending 6/30/83.

$$\frac{\$1,239,300\ +\ \$154,523}{2/12\ (1,275,000)\ +\ 10/12\ (1,565,000)} = \frac{\$1,393,823}{1,516,667} = \$.92 \text{ or } 51\% \text{ over } 6/30/82.$$

Exhibit 3   Dean Witter Proposal (entire proposal)

DEAN WITTER REYNOLDS INC.
100 Peachtree St., N.W., Suite 800
Atlanta, GA 30303 Telephone (404) 658-5800

January 17, 1983

Mr. Vincent S. Lamb, Jr.
Chairman
Scientific Systems Services, Inc.
1135 John Rodes Boulevard
Melbourne, Florida 32901

Dear Vince:

As we discussed, this letter is written to summarize why Dean Witter Reynolds ("DWR") is best qualified to become Scientific Systems Services' investment banker. In your evaluation of potential investment bankers, we believe that you should consider the capabilities of each firm in light of the services you will require; of equal importance are the people in those firms who will be working with and be committed to Scientific Systems Services. The combination of the people, their degree of commitment, and the firm's resources will ultimately determine the quality of services that your Company receives, and the anticipated quality of these services could well serve as criteria for choosing your investment banker.

A key Dean Witter Reynolds strength lies in managing and co-managing public offerings. The firm's performance during 1980 and 1981 represented approximately 13 percent of all public domestic offerings of debt and equity, totaling approximately $15 billion of capital. DWR also ranks as one of the leading major bracket investment banking firms in terms of dollar volume of initial public offerings. Since January 1980, the firm has managed 17 such offerings with an aggregate dollar amount of $440.75 million. The firm offers not only outstanding syndication abilities as the lead manager, but also unexcelled distribution power. DWR has often shared this distribution strength when acting as the book-running co-manager with a specialty or regional firm as a co-manager. In the southeastern United States, we have long been the leading originator of initial public offerings among major bracket investment banking firms for companies across a wide spectrum, including technology companies.

Dean Witter Reynolds has substantial experience servicing software and related companies. Recently, DWR was the sole lead underwriter of the initial public offering of On-Line Software International, Inc. DWR sold 70.9 percent of the offering and placed a substantial percentage of the shares in 100–200 share trades. The offering was priced at $15 on September 29, 1982, and the opening bid and ask were $15.75–$16.25. Buoyed by recent interest in high-technology stocks, On-Line's common stock closed on January 14 at $26 bid.

Perhaps more impressive was our lead co-management on Friday, January 14, 1983, of the initial public offering of Quality Micro-Systems (QMS), which was offered at $17 per share and is now trading at $23 bid per share. This offering was brought to fruition in less than two months from our initial involvement, and has received tremendous national retail and institutional interest. QMS, based in Mobile, Alabama, designs, manufactures and markets intelligent graphics processors used primarily in dot-matrix and other printing systems. These processors feature extensive use of "PROM," or applications firmware which, as you know, is essentially software on a circuit board.

In addition, DWR recently completed a private placement of $8 million of convertible subordinated debentures of Applied Data Research, Inc. We will soon be filing as a manager of the initial public offering of American Software, Inc., an Atlanta-based applications software firm. All of these offerings have featured primary involvement by our Atlanta staff, as discussed below.

We believe that DWR's strengths include the following:

Exhibit 3   *(continued)*

Distribution—DWR has long been known for its outstanding retail sales force representing approximately 9 percent of all registered sales personnel working for New York Stock Exchange member firms. More than 4,600 account executives in 338 offices worldwide are in contact with over 1 million active investors making DWR the second largest retail-distribution power with similar strengths in institutional distribution.

Syndication—Your investment banker must be able to distribute securities under all market conditions. DWR's syndicate department provides effective coordination, working with the client to determine the desired distribution pattern for the security, and assembling an underwriting group to achieve this distribution. DWR's distribution strength means more than simply an outlet for the sale of securities. Sales professionals maintain close contact with investment banking officers, advising on the factors affecting the market. This close cooperation helps to ensure an effective distribution and optimal pricing in even volatile markets. As a result of our exceptional retail and institutional placement capabilities, DWR, as your book-running manager, can tailor the distribution to be placed with any desired mix of institutional and retail investors and in any geographic location to meet your objectives.

Equity Trading—DWR is one of the largest factors in equity trading in the United States. Our large capital position allows the trading department to take a leading role in the marketplace and exert market-making power even in unfavorable markets. The firm's block trading capabilities are currently considered among the best on Wall Street. In surveys of institutional investors, DWR consistently places among the top firms for research, execution of orders, block trading, and overall service. DWR's Over-the-Counter Trading Department makes markets in approximately 1,000 stocks through 42 traders, representing one of the largest such commitments.

Sensitivity—Pricing new securities requires not only an analysis of comparable companies' trading patterns but also sensitivity to the supply and demand factors of the marketplace. As one of the largest managing underwriters, DWR has consistently demonstrated intelligent pricing resulting in satisfied sellers and investors.

Technology Orientation—DWR has placed a priority on developing high-technology business and made a substantial commitment to this business. DWR's technology group is staffed with corporate finance professionals in Atlanta, New York and San Francisco, who work primarily with science and technology clients, including the undersigned. This group, which would be available to you at all times, provides a full range of investment banking services and coordinates support and sponsorship from research, trading, and syndication/distribution.

Research Coverage—DWR's research effort is recognized by independent polls as one of the top four in Wall Street. Our research group of some 50 analysts features a technology group of 8 analysts, including 3 analysts who specialize in software and software-related issues. Terry Quinn of our staff covers the leading software companies in the southeast, and has indicated a strong interest to follow your Company. Terry is also a coauthor of our Emerging Growth Stock publication, in which your Company would be included for monthly distribution to our customers and account executives.

Southeastern Presence—DWR is unique among major investment banking firms in that we have a historic commitment to regionalization. Here in Atlanta, we are the successor to Courts & Co. with a 50-year investment banking heritage, and have the largest investment banking staff of any major firm, including three technology specialists. Bill Green and John Williams would be your key account officers in Atlanta, assisted by other staff members in Atlanta and New York. These officers have extensive experience with technology issuers, including Lanier Business Products, Microdyne Corporation, On-Line Software, Quality Micro Systems, SCI Systems, and numerous others. Should you

Exhibit 3   *(continued)*

choose to work with us, we would recommend processing the transaction here in Atlanta. We would use the Atlanta law firm of Hansell, Post as underwriters' counsel. If you choose to print here, we believe you would save considerable expense versus most alternative locations. We have worked in the past with many of the leading SEC corporate lawyers in the South, and could be of assistance in your selection process in this respect if requested. In any event, we could facilitate early implementation of your SEC filing and assure that we would at no time cause you delay in the financing.

Valuation and Capitalization—In valuing your Company, we seek to be aggressive and competitive with offers you may receive from other firms of stature, but also realistic. We have reviewed certain relatively comparable software companies, including Ask Computer Systems, Tera Corporation, and others. These two companies, in particular, currently trade at price/earnings ratios (on trailing 12 months earnings) of 46.8× and 37.3×, respectively. Factors favoring SSS relative to these larger companies include your greater margin expansion potential, your evolving product mix, and other factors. We believe that Scientific Systems Services can be marketed on a basis similar to or perhaps higher than Tera, but perhaps at a discount to Ask. We could currently propose a valuation range for the offering of 37.0× possibly to 42× trailing 12 months' earnings. Based on your current 1983 earnings forecast of $1.5 million in profits after tax, this range would provide 24.5× and up to 27.5× forecast 1983 earnings of $1.5 million, or a total current value for the Company prior to the offering of about $37 million to $41.5 million.

We understand that you desire to raise approximately $8 million in new equity funds and $4 million in funds for selling shareholders, for a total offering of about $12 million. This could appropriately be accomplished by undertaking a 5 for 1 or similar split of the current shares, providing about 2,750,000 shares prior to the financing. The offering could then be composed of, say, 800,000 shares, consisting of 535,000 shares for the Company and 265,000 shares for selling shareholders, and a filing price range of perhaps $13 to $16 per share. We would suggest establishing a maximum filing price of perhaps $17 to provide initial flexibility to exceed this range if demand allows. We would also request an over-allotment option of 10 percent of the basic amount of the offering (here 80,000 shares) which could be provided by the Company, by the selling shareholders, or by both.

The above concepts would, of course, be refined more carefully in the context of an implementation.

Underwriters' Compensation—Based on present market conditions, and assuming that your shares were priced in the mid-teens, we would expect to recommend a gross spread of approximately 7 to 7.25 percent. We would be pleased to discuss the components and rationale for this spread level should you desire.

Marketing—If selected as your managing underwriter, we would undertake with you immediately the preparation of a well-written prospectus and target an early filing with the SEC as soon as your year-end numbers are available, perhaps by mid or late February. We would then orchestrate a series of institutional and retail information meetings in Atlanta, Boston, New York, Chicago, San Francisco, and other major cities.

Depending on the success of these meetings and demand for your shares, we may be able to increase the filing price range of the offering above the level set forth above. We would be delighted to do this if market conditions allow. In the Quality Micro Systems offering last week, we were in fact able to achieve a price $2 above the high end of the initial filing range and still produce a significant premium in aftermarket trading. Without question, the intensive marketing effort conducted for that company played an important role in this price improvement.

Exhibit 3   *(concluded)*

Currently our system is highly attuned to quality offerings of emerging technology companies. We are most eager to demonstrate our marketing capabilities to serve your Company.

We sincerely hope that this presentation will lead you to select DWR as your investment banker. Let us emphasize that we would view this selection as only the first step in building a relationship. We would consider this to be a commitment to work with you over a long period of time, and we hope you would view it in the same way. We are anxious to begin working with you at an early date and feel that such a relationship will be mutually rewarding. If there are any questions, please do not hesitate to call.

Sincerely yours,

DEAN WITTER REYNOLDS, INC.

William S. Green
Managing Director

John Williams
Vice President

Exhibit 4   E.F. Hutton Proposal (excerpts from proposal)

* = Included in Exhibit 4.

EXHIBIT 4   *(continued)*

E.F. Hutton
E.F. Hutton & Company Inc. One Battery Park Plaza, New York, N.Y. 10004
(212) 742-5336

Thomas G. Greig III
Senior Vice President

December 13, 1982

Mr. Vincent S. Lamb

Chairman and President
Scientific Systems Services, Inc.
2000 Commerce Drive, P.O. Box 610
Melbourne, FL 32901

Dear Mr. Lamb:

This letter will outline the terms of an underwritten public offering for Scientific Systems Services, Inc., ("SSS") for which E.F. Hutton & Company Inc. ("Hutton") proposes to act as managing underwriter.

Size of Offering: Hutton has assumed that SSS intends to raise a minimum of $9 million in a primary offering of common stock. We have assumed $9 million based on forecasts supplied to us and assume net proceeds to SSS of $8.025 million. Hutton believes that SSS would successfully market a larger issue of $12 million, combining both primary shares and shares owned by existing shareholders ("secondary stock"). Hutton recommends that no member of management be allowed to sell more than 20 percent of his holdings and that the secondary portion should amount to no more than 35 percent of the offering. It is presumed that the proceeds from the primary portion of the offering would be used for working capital.

Recapitalization: Hutton recommends SSS effect a 6.1 for 1 stock split prior to the initial filing of the registration statement, resulting in 3,642,675 shares outstanding.

Pricing: Hutton believes that initial public offerings are priced principally on future earnings and how they relate to current earnings trends, and not on the basis of current earnings. Based upon information provided by SSS to date, Hutton believes that SSS's common stock will sell at a multiple range of forecast 1983 and 1984 earnings (fully diluted, from continuing operations, before extraordinary items) of $31\times - 36/\times$ and $24\times - 27\times$, respectively. This forecast is based on estimated growth for the markets in which SSS competes, the current condition of the equity market and the new issue market, the future financial prospects for SSS, and its historical financial record which will be included in the prospectus. Given a capitalization of 3,642,675 shares (after effecting a 6.1 for 1 stock split), Hutton recommends an initial filing price range of $14–$16 per share. This is based upon a calculation of 1983 and 1984 earnings per share presented in a price/earnings analysis included in Section II, resulting in 1983 earnings per share of $0.45 and $0.59 for 1984. Hutton feels that pricing of the offering should be such that there is a reasonable expectation for the stock to trade initially at a 10 percent to 15 percent premium to the offering price. Hutton's final pricing recommendation would be based on this immediate aftermarket premium philosophy, general market conditions, initial public offering market conditions and condition of the managing underwriter's "book." An analysis of price/earnings valuations of companies perceived as comparable to SSS, in terms of either their line of business or their future prospects for growth and profitability, is included in Section II. Given the assumptions as to 1983 and 1984 earnings per share and Hutton's pricing ideas, the offering would consist of approximately 650,000 primary shares and 200,000 secondary

---

EXHIBIT 4   *(continued)*

---

shares, resulting in approximately a $12 million offering. Given 4,292,675 (primary) shares outstanding after the offering, SSS would have a market value of at least $60 million ($14 per share). Moreover, if earnings are substantially above the current forecast as a result of the award of a multiplant utility contract in 1983, Hutton believes that a market valuation of approximately $80 million ($18 per share) can be supported.

Over-Allotment Option: Hutton recommends that SSS extend to the underwriters an over-allotment option for up to 10 percent of the size of the offering. These shares would be purchased by the underwriters to cover the underwriters' short-sale position, if any, resulting from the offering, only if, in Hutton's judgment, the aftermarket performance of SSS stock would not be adversely affected.

Gross Spread: Based on an offering of 850,000 shares, Hutton's present anticipation is that the gross spread (underwriting discount) will range from 6.75 percent to 7.3 percent of the offering price for an offering range of $14–$16 per share. Section IV sets forth the gross spread information for initial public offerings of common stock in 1982. Hutton's final gross spread recommendation will depend on the condition of the general market, the new issue market, and the managing underwriter's "book" at the time of the offering.

Co-Manager: Hutton is prepared to co-manage the offering with another firm or firms of SSS's choosing. Hutton believes those firms should be selected in view of Hutton's strengths of retail distribution capability, recognition by institutions of Hutton's knowledge of the computer industry and the profitable experience of Hutton's customer base in investing in the stocks of such companies. If selected as a co-manager, Hutton believes that it should be the lead manager in order for it to effectively organize and execute a retail and institutional market distribution plan.

Timing: Hutton recommends that SSS proceed with an initial public offering during the first quarter of 1983. We believe an SSS offering based on December 31, 1982, financial statements would be readily marketable based on recent market conditions. Hutton personnel would be pleased to begin working with SSS immediately to gain in-depth knowledge of SSS and ensure that SSS is optimally postured for its initial public offering.

Syndication: Hutton recommends that a syndicate of approximately 65 underwriters be formed to distribute the offering. This syndicate would include the "major bracket" national securities firms, the larger regional underwriting firms, selected smaller regional firms, and selected foreign underwriters and would be determined according to the desired distribution mix for the offering chosen by SSS. Hutton as managing underwriter will underwrite approximately 25 percent of the offering, retain for sale through its own distribution network approximately 40 percent to 50 percent of the offering, and distribute the balance of the stock to the other syndicate members based upon SSS's choice of retail versus institutional and geographic distributional goals. After release of the stock for sale, Hutton as managing underwriter will stabilize the market for SSS's stock, if necessary, by making purchases of the stock in the open market to assure an orderly distribution and aftermarket for the stock. When, in Hutton's determination, such has been achieved, Hutton will terminate the syndicate thereby releasing the syndicate members to make a market in SSS's stock and begin normal trading activities.

Distribution Mix: Hutton recommends a specific retail/institutional mix as well as a broad geographic distribution for SSS's common stock offering. Hutton believes that the goal for the offering should be a 65 percent retail, 35 percent institutional distribution for the following reasons:

> Retail: The high percentage of retail distribution would place the stock in a large number of relatively small lots of approximately 300–500 shares each. New York Stock Exchange statistics indicate that retail investors hold twice the dollar amount of equities, and account for only one-half the trading volume as compared to institutions, thereby suggesting retail investors are better long-term holders of securities and are less likely to sell a stock after a short-term price upswing, or in the event of intermittent growth or profitability. Hutton believes that a broad shareholder base gives a company the greatest likelihood of less volatile aftermarket trading and a better forum from which to raise future equity to support rapid growth.

EXHIBIT 4   *(continued)*

Institutional: Institutional distribution is desirable since (i) it is a finite audience of approximately 150 addressable institutions who over the past several years have been the consistent purchasers of emerging growth stocks; (ii) these institutions have been price leaders in supporting high valuations through purchase in the offering and in the after market; (iii) institutional holders can also cause additional research coverage. Institutional demand for the offering will be more than 35 percent. Institutions would have their orders only partially filled and would be encouraged to purchase up to their desired holding levels through buying in the open market after the offering, thereby supporting the issue in the aftermarket.

In order to achieve this distribution mix, Hutton believes that SSS must engage managing underwriters who will address both retail and institutional securities purchasers. Section I contains charts which describe the roles of different investment banks in distributing securities. E.F. Hutton, with its 5,172 account executives managing over 800,000 accounts, is particularly well qualified to provide SSS with the retail distribution necessary for consummating a successful offering, especially in highly volatile markets.

Hutton also recommends broad geographic distribution for the offering. Hutton would tailor its own internal distribution and that of the underwriting syndicate to obtain this goal.

Marketing Program: As manager of SSS's initial public offering, Hutton will conduct a coordinated, national marketing program to educate the investment community on SSS and its business, and to generate purchase orders for the issue. This program would begin with producing a marketing oriented prospectus, the principal sales document in the offering. During the SEC review of the offering documents, Hutton will orchestrate both an institutional marketing program to expose SSS to buyers in major domestic and European financial centers, as well as an internal marketing program to generate interest in the offering within Hutton's own distribution system.

- The prospectus in the registration statement will be the most important marketing document for the offering; therefore, it must contain a detailed business description of SSS, organized to present SSS's major selling points for use by the retail sales force as well as by the institutional analyst community. Hutton will assist SSS in the final drafting of the prospectus so as to accomplish this marketing objective.
- In marketing the SSS offering to institutional purchasers, sales information meetings and "one on one" discussions will be held in various cities, the most likely being Boston, New York, Chicago, San Francisco, and Los Angeles. Similar meetings in the major European financial centers of London, Edinburgh, Geneva, and Zurich we feel is also desirable. Hutton will assist SSS in preparing a presentation geared to the needs and interests of this institutional audience. A proposed timetable for these meetings is included in Section V.
- Hutton will aggressively market the SSS offering to its 4,872 retail and 300 institutional account executives who serve over 800,000 retail and 1,500 major institutional accounts from 335 domestic and foreign offices. This program would include:
  - A wire to branch managers describing the offering and key marketing points, followed by a four-page sales memorandum to each account executive and an article in *Products and Markets,* an internal publication.
  - Interaction between corporate finance and equity research personnel and retail syndicate coordinators to explain the offering and field questions.
  - Daily communication with the 10 Hutton regions to monitor national demand during the offering.
  - Hutton's institutional sales force is kept abreast of the offering through conference calls twice daily, one of which is taped and available for replay on a toll-free 800 number. Hutton's corporate finance team will sponsor SSS management in these broadcasts to the institutional sales force.

EXHIBIT 4   *(continued)*

- Hutton corporate finance and equity research personnel on the SSS team will make themselves available to the entire sales force to answer questions about SSS or the offering.

Section VI of this presentation contains a more detailed description of the internal marketing program.

Aftermarket Sponsorship: Given SSS's importance to E.F. Hutton as a potential client and the involvement of the other senior officers in developing a relationship between the two firms, SSS will become a cornerstone in the continuing evolution of Hutton as the major factor in investment banking for technology based companies. SSS would be a client of E.F. Hutton, not of specific individuals, and would enjoy the visibility and sponsorship of the senior management of the firm. However, individuals must take responsibility for the execution of proper aftermarket sponsorship. That responsibility would belong to Tom Greig from Hutton's New York headquarters. Hutton believes that the client services provided by an investment banker between transactions are at least as important as the execution of the offering itself. Consequently, Hutton strives to offer its corporate finance clients aftermarket sponsorship unequalled by its competitors. This sponsorship will include:

- Research Coverage: E.F. Hutton will provide regular research coverage on SSS through its equity research department. Coverage will include comprehensive annual research reports on SSS, its prospects, and its industry, "all wires" releases which outline fast-breaking events concerning SSS, and an up-to-date research comment data base which brokers can access through their desk-top quote machines.
- Exposure to Financial Community: Hutton will ensure that the financial community keeps current with SSS by providing in-depth research coverage and arranging securities analyst meetings, institutional forums, and investor conferences. In particular, Hutton will sponsor SSS at forums such as the New York Society of Securities Analysts and assure that SSS be given the opportunity to participate in events staged by groups such as the American Electronics Association.
- Management Follow-Up: When not working directly with SSS on a specific transaction, Hutton's corporate finance team will keep abreast of SSS's financial progress, monitor developments in its industry, keep it informed with reports on market conditions, and provide it with financing alternatives to capitalize on specific market opportunities.
- Market Making: E.F. Hutton is the primary market maker for the securities of its investment banking clients and, in this role, will assure SSS of a liquid and stable market for its securities. Following SSS's initial public offering, Hutton will become the lead market maker for its stock.
- Special Services: As an investment banking client, SSS will receive special attention by functional areas of Hutton, other than those thus far mentioned. Special services available to SSS would include cash management consulting, lease financing, tax shelter assistance, and distribution of "Rule 144" stock.
- Long-Term Commitment: E.F. Hutton, through its Technology Group, aspires to become the preeminent investment banker to computer and electronics companies among the national securities firms. To attain this goal, Hutton must secure as clients today the industry leaders of tomorrow and then strengthen these relationships by continuing to provide the best possible service. E.F. Hutton wishes to initiate such a long-term relationship with SSS.

Financial Statements and Accountants: Hutton understands that SSS will provide annual financial statements, which will be audited by Deloitte Haskins & Sells and will meet the SEC requirements for the form S-1 Registration Statement. SSS will also provide additional financial data Hutton believes is necessary for marketing purposes. The underwriters will request Deloitte Haskins & Sells to provide "cold comfort" review of information included in the registration statement which can be traced back to the financial records of the company.

Printing: Hutton recommends that SSS select a qualified financial printer to print the registration statement, prospectus, underwriting agreement, and underwriting syndication papers. Hutton

EXHIBIT 4   *(continued)*

will request that 40,000 preliminary prospectuses and 30,000 final prospectuses be printed. SSS will assume all printing costs.

"Blue Sky" Law Qualification: The underwriters will request that SSS register varying amounts of the shares in the offering in all states in order for the stock to be sold to retail investors over a broad geographic area. The cost of registration and fees of counsel in completing the applications and in clearing the offering through the various state "Blue Sky" commissions will be paid by SSS.

Underwriters' Counsel: It is Hutton's intention to use as underwriters' counsel a law firm experienced in securities law and in offerings for technology based companies. The underwriters will request that this counsel handle all matters as to "Blue Sky" law qualification. The fees of such counsel, other than the fees incurred for "Blue Sky" qualification, will be paid by the underwriters.

Underwriting Agreement: Neither SSS nor Hutton will be obligated to proceed with the offering unless and until the underwriting agreement is executed. Such agreement will contain Hutton's usual provisions including an agreement that neither SSS nor its officers, nor directors will, without prior written consent of Hutton, sell, transfer, or otherwise dispose of any shares of common stock for a period of 90 days from the date of the offering. The execution of the underwriting agreement is subject to SSS and Hutton being satisfied with the form and substance of the preliminary, amended, and final registration statements and propectuses, and with all items and conditions of the underwriting agreement.

The following presentation contains additional information on an initial public offering of SSS common stock, as well as on Hutton's ability to manage this offering. Specifically included are financial and market data on companies in SSS's industry, a price/earnings and recapitalization analysis of SSS, a proposed underwriting syndicate, an offering timetable, and information on recent initial public offerings.

Hutton is most interested in developing a long-term investment banking relationship with SSS. We are enthusiastic about the prospects for the continued growth of SSS and will marshall Hutton's resources to help SSS meet its goals.

I look forward to discussing Hutton's interest in SSS with you at greater length.

Yours truly,

Thomas G. Greig III
Senior Vice President

EXHIBIT 4   **Segmentation of Managing Underwriters** *(continued)*

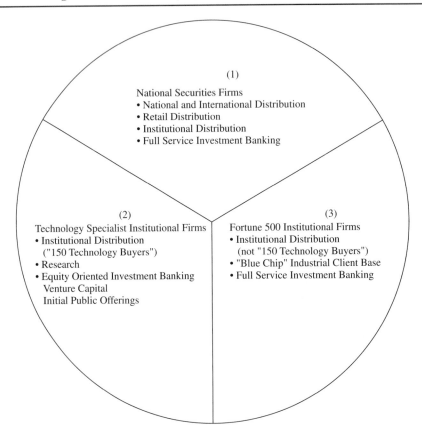

(1)

National Securities Firms
- National and International Distribution
- Retail Distribution
- Institutional Distribution
- Full Service Investment Banking

(2)
Technology Specialist Institutional Firms
- Institutional Distribution
  ("150 Technology Buyers")
- Research
- Equity Oriented Investment Banking
  Venture Capital
  Initial Public Offerings

(3)
Fortune 500 Institutional Firms
- Institutional Distribution
  (not "150 Technology Buyers")
- "Blue Chip" Industrial Client Base
- Full Service Investment Banking

(1) National Securities Firms
- E.F. Hutton
- Merrill Lynch
- Dean Witter
- Shearson/American Express
- Blyth, Paine Webber
- Smith Barney
- Bache

(2) Technology Specialist Institutional Firms
- Hambrecht & Quist
- L.F. Rothschild
- Alex Brown
- Robertson, Colman
- Montgomery Securities

(3) Fortune 500 Institutional Firms
- Morgan Stanley
- First Boston
- Goldman Sachs
- Kidder Peabody
- Lehman Brothers
- Saloman Brothers

EXHIBIT 4   *(continued)*

Price/Earnings and Recapitalization Analysis

This analysis sets forth the effect on earnings per share and the resulting range of price/earnings multiples resulting from an initial public offering of shares by Scientific Systems Services, Inc.

Assumptions:

1. SSS becomes public in the first quarter of 1983 off year end 1982 financial statements.
2. The filing range for the offering price would be $85.71 to $97.95. For computational purposes we assumed an offering of 105,000 primary shares at $85.71 per share.
3. Net proceeds to SSS from the primary portion of the offering are $8,025,000. This consists of gross proceeds of $9,000,000 less a gross spread of $630,000 (7%) and issuance expenses of $345,000.
4. 1983 revenues and net earnings from operations will be $24,000,000 and $1,680,000 (7% after tax), respectively. 1984 revenues and net earnings from operations will be $36,000,000 and $2,520,000, respectively. In addition, the valuation study (see next pages of this Section) also considers the scenario in which the Company's 1983 revenues are $30 million, with $2.1 million earnings, and its 1984 revenues are $45 million with $3.15 million earnings.
5. Net proceeds of $8,025,000 are received April 1, 1983. As a result, the Company earns additional interest income, at 5 percent after tax, on an average of $5 million during the last nine months of 1983.

SSS Forecast Operating Results

	Year Ended December 31,		
	1982	*1983*	*1984*
Net sales	$16,800,000	$24,000,000	$36,000,000
Net income before extraordinary items	1,000,000	1,867,500	2,520,000
Earnings per share	1.98	2.77	3.60
Weighted average shares outstanding	505,000	673,750	700,000
Price/Earnings Impact			
Filing price range per share		$85.71–$97.95	
Earnings per share	$1.98	$2.77	$3.60
Price/earnings range	44x–50x	31x–36x	24x–27x
Market value of SSS Post offering (millions)		$60–69	

For discussion purposes we have not incorporated any stock split in the above analysis. Prior to the initial public offering Hutton recommends SSS split its stock 6.1 for 1 so as to target an initial filing range of $14–$16 which would broaden retail investor participation in the offering.

<u>**EXHIBIT 4**</u>   *(continued)*

Recapitalization Analysis Assuming a 6.1 for 1 Stock Split

	Year Ended December 31,		
	1982	*1983*	*1984*
Net income before extraordinary items	$1,000,000	$1,867,500	$2,520,000
Earnings per share	$0.32	$0.45	$0.59
Weighted average shares outstanding	3,091,682	4,124,794	4,285,500

Price/Earnings Impact

Filing price range per share		$14–$16	
Earnings per share	$0.32	$0.45	$0.59
Price/earnings range	44x–50x	31x–36x	24x–27x
Market value of SSS Post offering (millions)		$60–69	

Increased 1983 Earnings

Management has informed Hutton that the forecast 1983 operating results could be dramatically higher ($2.1 million versus $1.68 million) if the company secures a multiplant utility contract in the first quarter of 1983. Hutton's valuation study (please see the next pages of this section) indicates that the postoffering market value of the Company could approach $80 million (approximately $18 per share) in such a case.

Comparative Market Analysis
Index of Five SSS Comparable versus the NASDAQ Industrials Index

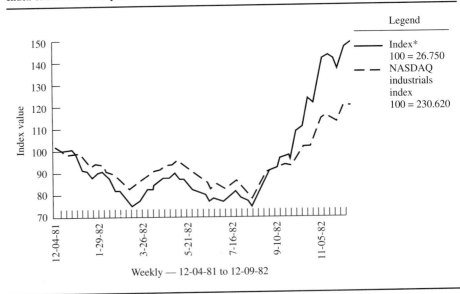

Weekly — 12-04-81 to 12-09-82

*Index includes: Shared Medical Sys. Corp., Systematics Inc., Policy Mgmt. Sys. Corp., Triad Sys. Corp., and SEI Corp.

EXHIBIT 4   *(continued)*

Valuation Study (in millions of dollars)

E.F. Hutton & Company, Inc.
Corporate Finance Department
December 10, 1982

	Scientific Systems Services			On-Line Software International	Systems & Computer Technology Corporation	Par Technology	ARGO-Systems	Dionex Corporation	Quantum Corporation
Current market value (12-10-82)	$60,000	$70.00	$80.00 (1)	$77.66	$290.61	$186.88	$96.52	$98.78	$199.60
Current market price (12-10-82)	14.00	16.00	18.00	21.875	22.75	25.00	31.50	24.50	22.50
Market value/projected revenues (dollars in millions)									
Calendar 1983 revenues-ratio	$24.00-2.5x	$24.00-2.9x	$30.00-2.7x	$24.00-3.2x	$49.00-5.9x	$44.00-4.2x	$42.00-2.3x	$22.00-4.5x	$63.00-3.2x
Calendar 1984 revenues-ratio	$36.00-1.7x	$36.00-1.9x	$45.00-1.8x	$37.00-2.1x	$74.00-3.9x	$59.00-3.2x	$53.00-1.8x	$28.00-3.5x	$78.00-2.6x
Market value/projected net income									
Calendar 1983 net income-ratio	1.87-32.1x	1.87-37.4x	2.29-34.9x	3.5-22.2x	5.9-49.3x	6.6-28.3x	3.5-27.6x	2.8-35.3x	10.0-20.0x
Calendar 1984 net income-ratio	2.52-23.8x	2.52-27.8x	3.15-25.4x	5.3-14.7x	8.9-32.7x	8.9-21.0x	4.6-21.0x	3.5-28.2x	12.5-16.0x
Growth rate valuation									
Five-year projected compound growth rate		50%	50%	50%	50%	35%	30%	25%	25%
Indicated P/E (.65x) (2)		32.5x	32.5x	32.5x	32.5x	22.75x	19.50x	16.25x	16.25x
Market valuation on 1983 net income		$60.78	$74.43	$113.75	$191.75	$150.15	$68.25	$45.50	$162.50

(1) If SSS is awarded the contract for either power plants in the first quarter of 1983, Hutton believes a $75–$80 million valuation can be defended assuming 1983 revenues and earnings (after entered income from an April 4 offering) of $30 million and $2.29 million, respectively.

(2) Under current market conditions, Hutton believes that investors capitalize common stocks at a P/E based upon forecasted earnings of 65% of a company's expected sustainable growth rate.

EXHIBIT 4   (continued)

Comparative Pricing Analysis: Selected Technology Company Initial Public Offerings

Company	Lee Data Corporation	PAR Technology	ARGO-Systems	Dionex Corporation	Quantum Corporation	Mogem Systems, Inc.
Shares filed (000)	2,207	750	606	1,200	1,700	1,290
Shares offered (000)	2,607	900	801	1,400	2,500	1,500
IPO filing date	10-18-82	10-29-82	10-27-82	11-02-82	11-09-82	11-05-82
IPO effective date	11-18-82	12-03-82	12-02-82	12-07-82	12-10-82	12-10-82
Fiscal year end	03-31-82	12-31-81	06-30-82	06-30-82	03-31-82	03-31-82
Latest 12 months for IPO	09-30-82	09-30-82	10-01-82	09-30-82	10-02-82	09-30-82

Size data: ($000)

Revenues (LTM)	$29,380	$27,574	$32,187	$16,888	$29,769	$12,896
Pretax income—margin	9,068-30.9%	7,148-25.9%	4,329-13.4%	3,648-21.6%	6,509-21.9%	3,358-26.0%
Net income						
(a)—margin	5,725-19.5%	4,162-15.1%	2,462-7.6%	1,934-11.5%	4,114-13.8%	2,316-18.0%
EPS (LTM)	$.47	$.59	$1.08	$.55	$1.02	$.49
Projected EPS (next fiscal yr.)	1.40	1.00	1.40	.65	1.00	.75
R&D expenses—% of revenues	$1,606-5.5%	$749-2.9%	$1,146-3.6% (c)	$1,078-6.4%	$2,345-7.9%	$944-7.3%
Tangible book value	13,736	7,392	9,442	7.752	13,981	1,731

Market Data:

Pro forma shares outstanding (000)	12,332	7,475	3,064	4,032	8,871	5,601
Filing price range	$14.00-16.00	$14-17	$16-18	$14-16	$15-17	$15-18
P/E range—LTM EPS	30.0x-34.0x	23.7x-28.8x	14.8x-16.7x	25.5x-29.1x	14.7x-16.7x	30.6x-36.7x
P/E range—projected EPS	10.0x-11.4x	14.0x-17.0x	11.4x-12.9x	21.5x-24.6x	15.0x-17.0x	20.0x-24.0x
Pro forma market value ($MM)	$167.0-190.9	$104.7-127.1	$49.0-55.2	$56.4-64.5	$133.1-150.8	$94.0-100.8
Offering price	$ 19.00	$ 20.00	$21.50	$19.00	$ 20.50	$ 21.00
P/E—LTM EPS	40.4x	33.9x	19.9x	34.5x	20.1x	42.9x
P/E—projected EPS	13.6x	20.0x	15.4x	29.2x	20.5x	28.0x
Pro forma market value ($MM)	$234.3	$149.5	$65.9	$76.6	$181.9	$117.6

NASDAQ Industrial Index:

On filing date	233.26	242.89	243.12	250.00	265.43	261.88
On pricing date	262.34	276.28	274.92	279.19	277.45	277.45
Percent change	12.47%	13.75%	13.08%	11.68%	4.53%	5.95%

Growth Data:

Earnings per share (a)						
LTM	$ .47	$.59	$1.08	$.55	$ 1.02	$ .49
1 year prior	.14	.41	.85	.58	.03	.24
2 years prior	(.07)	.10	.63	.43	(1.50)	.22
3 years prior	(.25)	.07	.46	.36	—	(.21)
4 years prior	—	.04	.55	.27	—	—

Exhibit 4   *(continued)*

Comparative Pricing Analysis: Selected Technology Company Initial Public Offerings

Company	Lee Data Corporation	PAR Technology	ARGO-Systems	Dionex Corporation	Quantum Corporation	Mogem Systems, Inc.
Compounded growth rate	NMF	105.0%	22.9%	24.3%	NMF	NMF
Revenue/net income (a)						
LTM ($MM)	$29.4/$5.7	$27.6/4.2	$32.2/2.5	$16.9/1.9	$29.8/4.1	$12.9/2.3
1 year prior	13.7/2.0	21.4/2.9	28.1/1.9	16.0/2.0	13.7/0.2	8.3/1.1
2 years prior	6.7/(0.4)	10.3/0.7	20.9/1.3	12.0/1.4	—/—	3.4/0.6
3 years prior	0.6/(1.4)	7.6/0.4	19.2/0.9	10.7/1.2	—/—	0.6/(0.6)
4 years prior	—/—	6.1/0.2	17.0/1.0	8.7/0.9	—/—	—/(0.8)
Compound growth rate	NMF 49.8%/112.6%		21.6%/32.3%	22.5/25.7%	235.0%/NMF	220.0%/NMF

Line of Business:

	Designs, manufactures, markets, and services multifunction interactive terminal systems.	Point-of-sale systems for restaurants, software systems for gov't/ military.	Electronic reconnaissance systems which acquire and analyze radar and military communications signals.	Develops, manufactures, and markets ion chromatography.	Designs, manufactures, and markets rigid disk drives based on Winchester technology.	Integrated line of standard banking applications software programs.

(E)—Estimate

(a)—From continuing operations before extraordinary items.

(b)—Eight month financial figures.

(c)—Excludes 8,000,000 of customer-funded research and development.

LTM = Last 12 months.

NMF = Not meaningful figure.

EXHIBIT 4 *(continued)*

1982 Initial Public Offerings*: Growth and Business Information *(July–December)*

					Latest 12 Months	
Date	Issuer	Shares (000s)	Offering Price	Total Dollar Amount (000s)	Net Sales (000s)	Net Income (000s)(1)
07-08	Tera Corp.	2,500	$16.00	$ 40,000	$ 31,015	$ 5,258
07-13	Ryan's Family Steak Houses	475	9.25	4,394	8,157	712
07-20	Super Sky International	640	13.00	8,320	27,088	3,199
07-21	Atlantic Southeast Airlines	860	6.50	5,590	9,743	1,531
07-29	CPI Corp.	750	14.00	10,500	108,899	5,302
08-05	Foster Medical	2,300	13.75	31,625	122,814	(1,376)
08-11	Environmental Testing	1,000	5.00	5,000	556(9)	867(9)
08-17	Electronic Mail Corp.	800	6.25	5,000	−(8)	−(8)
08-20	Universal Money Centers	600	5.00	3,000	NA	NA
08-26	Vicorp Restaurants	900	10.25	9,225	37,571	2,021
09-01	Family Entertainment Centers	475	10.50	4,988	5,212	(296)
09-02	North Fork Bancorp.	500	17.50	8,750	6,437	1,655
09-09	Electronic Theatre Rest.	610	8.25	5,033	5,935	(1,929)
09-15	Electronics Corp. of Israel	720	11.25	8,100	11,669	1,936
09-23	Psych Systems	700	5.00	3,500	3,429	199
09-29	Genex Corp.	2,000	9.50	19,000	5,154	(2.38)
09-29	On-Line Software	800	15.00	12,000	14,859	2,034
09-29	Rodime	1,000	8.00	8,000	4,294(10)	611(10)
10-07	TANO	515	9.25	4,764	29,888	947
10-13	Pacific Express Holding	1,300	5.00	6,500	12,291	(10,251)
10-14	University Federal Savings	400	12.00	4,800	31,376	(2,059)
10-15	Gott	635	10.75	6,826	28,623	1,633
10-18	InteCom Inc.	2,500	20.00	50,000	17,652	(3,504)
10-26	Sizzler Restaurants	900	17.00	15,300	120,927	3,376
10-27	Fidelity Federal S&L	2,798	10.00	27,976	189,321	(30,198)
10-29	Merrimac Industries	550	7.00	3,850	10,376	927
11-02	Systems & Computer Technology	2,580	16.50	42,570	26,792	3,225
11-04	Aaron Rents	1,000	15.50	15,500	52,724	4,030
11-04	Altos Computer Systems	3,300	21.00	69,300	57,351	6,360
11-04	Americana Hotels & Realty Trust	5,000	20.00	100,000	83,692	7,372
11-09	Washington Federal S&L	954	11.75	11,208	82,465	(26,701)
11-16	Taco Viva	400	9.00	3,600	12,736	605
11-18	Lee Data	2,607	19.00	49,535	29,380	5,040
11-26	Triangle Microwave, Inc.	696	6.25	4,350	4,474	799
12-01	Patient Technology, Inc.	575	6.75	3,881	676(11)	17(11)
12-01	Quality Systems, Inc.	600	17.00	10,200	8,919	948
12-02	ARGOSystems	801	21.50	17,213	32,187	2,462
12-03	PAR Technology Corp.	900	20.00	18,000	27,574	4,162

*Value of $3.0 million or more, offering price of $5.00 or more.

(1) From continuing operations before extraordinary items.

(2) Percentage difference between latest interim figure and the corresponding figure one year earlier.

(3) Based on historical E.P.S. figures. Latest 12 months.

(4) Actual book value prior to offer.

(5) Based on data for four years.

(6) Based on data for three years.

(7) Based on data for two years.

(8) Insufficient or no prior operating history.

| Five-Year Growth Rates | | | | Latest 12 Mos. | | | |
| Sales | | Net Income(1) | | | | | |
Fiscal Year	Latest Interim (2)	Fiscal Year	Latest Interim (2)	EPS	P/E (3)	Price/ Book (4)	Business Lines
57.2(5)	42.5	58.8	43.4	$0.66	24.2x	8.5x	Computer software/sys.
51.4(6)	5.9	50.7(6)	41.9	0.90	10.3x	4.7x	Operates restaurants
50.0	37.0	69.0	58.7	1.10	11.8x	3.8x	Designs & installs skylights
352.2(7)	187.7	44.2(7)	274.4	0.99	6.6x	5.2x	Regional airline
33.7(7)	31.6	102.1	52.5	1.62	8.6x	4.4x	Portrait photo studios, cleaning
11.5(6)	21.6	NA	NMF	(0.69)	NMF	NMF	Distributes medical supplies
NA	NA	NA	NA	(0.43)	NMF	6.7x	Management of chemical wastes
–(8)	–(8)	–(8)	–(8)	–(8)	NMF	NMF	Communications mgt. & special info. processing
NA	NA	NA	NA	NA	NA	NA	Markets automatic tellers
14.0	18.2	49.0	89.7	1.01	10.1x	4.6x	Operates & franchises restaurants
NMF	311.5	NMF	NMF	(0.29)	NMF	3.7x	Operates restaurants
17.4	50.5	33.0	55.0	3.93	4.5x	1.0x	Bank holding company
NMF	449.5	NMF	NMF	(0.55)	NMF	7.8x	Operates restaurants
57.0	36.8	149.2	103.0	1.09	10.3x	3.0x	Telecommunications equip.
NMF	225.0	NMF	NMF	0.29	17.2x	2.4x	Patient test equip.
495.8	104.3	NMF	NMF	(0.25)	NMF	3.7x	Genetic engineering
52.9	42.3	149.8	72.6	.67	22.4x	6.4x	IBM-compatible software
NMF	NMF	NMF	NMF	.16	50.0x	4.4x	5¼″ Winchester disk drives
26.6	47.0	34.7	140.3	1.11	8.3x	1.7x	Process control systems
135.0	438.7	NMF	NMF	(22.99)	NMF	NMF	Jet service between S.F. & L.A.
20.0	9.3	NMF	NMF	(2.92)	NMF	0.4x	Savings & loan
28.5	29.2	40.5	17.0	1.42	7.6x	3.0x	Consumer plastic products
NMF	NMF	NMF	NMF	(0.32)	NMF	42.6x	Large PBX phone systems
19.5	25.9	3.3	178.2	1.55	10.9x	1.0x	Steakhouse restaurants
28.1	6.5	NMF	NMF	(7.02)	NMF	.3x	Savings & loan
25.2	.8	28.8	367.8	.81	8.6x	2.2x	Signal processing systems-for defense
33.3	54.0	39.9	170.5	.29	55.0x	22.6x	Software for gov't./universities
32.3	14.7	24.2	40.9	1.21	12.8x	1.3x	MFG/rent/sell furniture
428.7	59.7	396.0	53.0	.55	38.2x	16.5x	Multiterminal microcomputer system
8.5	NMF	29.0	NMF	3.08	8.6x	1.1x	Real estate investment trust
9.7	8.3	NMF	NMF	(7.08)	NMF	.6x	Savings & loan
37.6	17.9	31.9	111.0	.52	17.3x	4.1x	Fast-service Mexican restaurants
365.4(6)	326.7	NMF	1,984.4	.47	40.4x	12.8x	Multifunct. interactive term. systems
NA	94.4	NA	286.0	.53	11.8x	7.2x	Microwave components
NA	NA	NA	NA	.02	NMF	21.8x	Electronic medical instruments
85.2	66.9	80.7	175.5	.52	32.7x	15.9x	Information systems for dentists
24.1	79.2	61.3	207.9	1.08	19.9x	4.8x	Electronic reconnaisance systems
53.3	42.5	106.9	68.9	.58	34.5x	18.9x	P.O.S. systems: defense/ software

NA = Not applicable.

NMF = Not meaningful figure.

(9) For the period from 12-27-81 through 4-24-82.

(10) Operating data for the 40 weeks ended July 3, 1982.

(11) For eight months ended Aug. 31, 1982.

EXHIBIT 4 *(continued)*

Date	Issuer	Shares (000s)	Offering Price	Total Dollar Amount (000s)	Gross Spread $	Gross Spread %	Management	Underwriting	Selling	EFH Commission (100 shares)	Selling Concession EFH Comm.	Aggregate Underwriting (100 shares)
07-08	Tera Corp.	2,500	16.00	40,000	1.04	6.50	.20	.19	.65	.47	1.38x	475
07-13	Ryan's Family Steak Houses	475	9.25	4,394	.79	8.50	.18	.16	.45	.35	1.29x	76
07-20	Super Sky International	640	13.00	8,320	.98	7.50	.20	.205	.57	.42	1.36x	131
07-21	Atlantic Southeast Airlines	860	6.50	5,590	.52	8.00	.08	.11	.33	.29	1.14x	95
07-29	CPI Corp.	750	14.00	10,500	1.00	7.14	.20	.25	.55	.43	1.28x	188
08-05	Foster Medical	2,300	13.75	31,625	.98	7.13	.20	.20	.58	.43	1.35x	460
08-11	Environmental Testing	1,000	5.00	5,000	.42	8.40	.08	.08	.26	.25	1.04x	80
08-17	Electronic Mail Corp.	800	6.25	5,000	.63	10.00	NA	NA	NA	.28	NA	NA
08-20	Universal Money Centers	600	5.00	3,000	.50	10.00	NA	NA	NA	.25	NA	NA
08-26	Vicorp Restaurants	900	10.25	9,225	.70	6.83	.14	.14	.42	.37	1.14x	126
09-01	Family Entertainment Centers	475	10.50	4,988	.84	8.00	.17	.17	.50	.37	1.35x	81
09-02	North Fork Bancorp.	500	17.50	8,750	1.23	7.03	NA	NA	.75	.50	1.50x	NA
09-09	Electronic Theatre Rest.	610	8.25	5,033	.70	8.49	.14	.19	.37	.31	1.19x	116
09-15	Electronics Corp. of Israel	720	11.25	8,100	.82	7.29	.22	.18	.42	.37	1.14x	130
09-23	Psych Systems	700	5.00	3,500	.50	10.00	.27	(1)	.23	.25	0.92x	189
09-29	Genex Corp.	2,000	9.50	19,000	.75	7.89	.15	.15	.45	.37	1.20x	300
09-29	On-Line Software	800	15.00	12,000	1.08	7.20	.22	.28	.58	.44	1.33x	224
09-29	Rodime	1,000	8.00	8,000	.56	7.00	.11	.15	.30	.31	0.97x	150
10-07	TANO	515	9.25	4,764	.74	8.00	.14	.20	.40	.37	1.07x	103
10-13	Pacific Express Holding	1,300	5.00	6,500	.43	8.50	.09	.085	.25	.25	1.00x	111
10-14	University Federal Savings	400	12.00	4,800	.96	8.00	.36	(1)	.60	.37	1.60x	76
10-15	Gott	635	10.75	6,826	.86	8.00	.19	.17	.50	.37	1.33x	108
10-18	InteCom Inc.	2,500	20.00	50,000	1.35	6.80	.30	.35	.70	.55	1.27x	875
10-26	Sizzler Restaurants	900	17.00	15,300	1.19	7.00	.24	.30	.65	.50	1.30x	270
10-27	Fidelity Federal S&L	2,798	10.00	27,976	.72	7.20	.14	.18	.40	.37	1.07x	504
10-29	Merrimac Industries	550	7.00	3,850	.56	8.00	.12	.16	.28	.31	.90x	88
11-02	Systems & Computers Technology	2,580	16.50	42,570	1.16	7.03	.23	.30	.63	.50	1.26x	774
11-04	Aaron Rents	1,000	15.50	15,500	1.08	6.97	.22	.26	.60	.44	1.36x	260
11-04	Altos Computer Systems	3,300	21.00	69,300	1.47	7.00	.30	.37	.80	.56	1.43x	1,221
11-04	Americana Hotels & Realty Trust	5,000	20.00	100,000	1.60	8.00	.40	.20	1.00	.56	1.79x	1,000
11-09	Washington Federal S&L	954	11.75	11,208	.82	6.98	.17	.20	.45	.37	1.20x	191
11-16	Taco Viva	400	9.00	3,600	.76	8.44	.15	.17	.44	.31	1.42x	124
11-18	Lee Data	2,607	19.00	49,535	1.33	7.00	.27	.31	.75	.50	1.50x	808
11-26	Triangle Microwave, Inc.	696	6.25	4,350	.63	10.00	.25	(1)	.37	.25	1.48x	NA
12-01	Patient Technology, Inc.	575	6.75	3,881	.68	10.00	.37	(1)	.30	.25	1.20x	NA
12-01	Quality Systems, Inc.	600	17.00	10,200	1.25	7.35	.25	.30	.70	.50	1.40x	180
12-02	ARGOSystems	801	21.50	17,213	1.52	7.07	.30	.32	.90	.56	1.61x	256
12-03	PAR Technology Corp.	900	20.00	18,000	1.45	7.25	.29	.29	.87	.56	1.55x	261

*Value of $3 million or more, offering price of $5 or more.

(1) Combined with management fee because issue was not syndicated.

EXHIBIT 4   1982 Initial Public Offerings*: Gross Spread Information (*July–December*) (concluded)

Date	Issuer	Shares (000s)	Offering Price	Total Dollar Amount (000's)	Primary as % of Shares Offered	Dilution (%)(1)	1 Day after Offer(2)	% Change	1 Week after Offer(2)	% Change	Stock Symbol
07-09	Tera Corp.	2,500	16.00	40,000	50.0	13.6	16.00	—	16.13	0.8	TRRA
07-13	Ryan's Family Steak Houses	475	9.25	4,394	86.6	33.9	10.00	8.1	10.25	10.8	RYAN
07-20	Super Sky International	640	13.00	8,320	0.0	0.0	13.00	—	13.25	1.9	SSKY
07-21	Atlantic Southeast Airlines	860	6.50	5,590	92.5	32.7	6.25	(3.8)	6.00	(7.7)	ASAI
07-29	CPI Corp.	750	14.00	10,500	56.7	11.5	13.75	(1.8)	13.75	(1.8)	CPIC
08-05	Foster Medical	2,300	13.75	31,625	100.0	45.6	13.25	(*3.6)	13.00	(5.5)	FMED
08-11	Environmental Testing	1,000	5.00	5,000	100.0	33.3	4.75	(5.0)	4.50	(10.0)	ETCC
08-17	Electronic Mail Corp.	800	6.25	5,000	100.0	50.0	6.25	—	6.25	—	EMCA
08-20	Universal Money Centers	600	5.00	3,000	100.0	NA	NA	NA	5.00	—	UMCI
08-26	Vicorp Restaurants	900	10.25	9,225	44.4	16.7	10.88	6.1	10.63	3.7	VRES
09-01	Family Entertainment Centers	475	10.50	4,988	70.6	21.5	10.75	2.4	9.75	(7.1)	FMLY
09-02	North Fork Bancorp.	500	17.50	8,750	100.0	54.3	17.50	—	17.50	—	NFBC
09-09	Electronic Theatre Rest.	610	8.25	5,033	100.0	21.7	8.25	—	8.00	(3.0)	ETRC
09-15	Electronics Corp. of Israel	720	11.25	8,100	93.1	23.5	12.00	6.7	13.25	17.8	ECILF
09-23	Psych Systems	700	5.00	3,500	100.0	49.8	6.25	25.0	6.25	25.0	PSYC
09-29	Genex Corp.	2,000	9.50	19,000	100.0	17.3	8.88	(6.6)	8,00	(5.8)	GNEX
09-29	On-Line Software	800	15.00	12,000	62.5	14.1	15.25	1.7	16.13	7.5	OSII
09-29	Rodime	1,000	8.00	8,000	100.0	20.2	7.75	(3.1)	8.25	3.1	RODMY
10-07	TANO	515	9.25	4,764	77.7	30.2	9.25	—	9.62	4.0	TANO
10-13	Pacific Express Holding	1,300	5.00	6,500	100.0	41.6	NA	NA	3.75	(25.0)	PXXP
10-14	University Federal Savings	400	12.00	4,800	100.0	77.1	13.50	12.5	13.00	8.3	UFSL
10-15	Gott	635	10.75	6,826	86.6	29.9	13.00	21.0	13.75	27.9	GOTT
10-18	InteCom Inc.	2,500	20.00	50,000	66.4	12.1	22.00	10.0	25.63	28.1	INCM
10-26	Sizzler Restaurants	900	17.00	15,300	100.0	27.3	17.00	—	20.00	17.6	SIZZ
10-27	Fidelity Federal S&L	2,798	10.00	27,976	100.0	0.0	11.00	10.0	12.75	27.5	FFED
10-29	Merrimac Industries	550	7.00	3,850	63.0	23.2	8.75	25.0	8.25	17.9	MMAC
11-02	Systems & Computers Technology	2,580	16.50	42,570	71.4	14.4	NA	NA	20.88	26.5	SCTC
11-04	Aaron Rents	1,000	15.50	15,500	15.0	4.0	20.75	33.9	21.50	38.7	ARON
11-04	Altos Computer Systems	3,300	21.00	69,300	82.0	19.1	29.75	41.7	31.75	51.9	ALTO
11-04	Americana Hotels & Realty Trust	5,000	20.00	100,000	100.0	0.0	21.25	6.3	21.00	5.0	AHRC
11-09	Washington Federal S&L	954	11.75	11,208	100.0	0.0	19.00	61.7	18.00	53.2	WFSL
11-16	Taco Viva	400	9.00	3,600	56.3	15.8	10.75	19.4	9.50	5.6	TVIV
11-18	Lee Data	2,607	19.00	49,535	69.0	14.6	28.25	48.7	28.00	47.4	LEDA
11-26	Triangle Microwave, Inc.	696	6.25	4,350	93.1	30.0	8.50	36.0	11.00	76.0	TRMW
12-01	Patient Technology, Inc.	575	6.75	3,881	100.0	35.9	8.75	29.6	9.00	33.3	PTIX
12-01	Quality Systems, Inc.	600	17.00	10,200	51.7	14.5	18.25	7.4	20.75	22.1	QSII
12-02	ARGOSystems	801	21.50	17,213	81.1	21.2	33.25	54.7	32.50	51.2	ARGI
12-03	PAR Technology Corp.	900	20.00	18,000	53.1	6.5	27.50	37.5	—	—	PARR

*Value of $3.0 million or more, offering price of $5.00 or more.

NA Not available

(1) Primary shares as a percent of shares outstanding after the offer.

(2) OTC stocks show bid price.

EXHIBIT 5   Alex Brown Proposal (entire proposal attached)

January 13, 1983

Mr. Vincent S. Lamb, Jr.
President
Scientific Systems Services, Inc.
2000 Commerce Drive
Melbourne, Florida 32901

Dear Vince:

It was a pleasure to meet with you and Mike at your office. Don and Al very much enjoyed meeting with you, Pat, and Howard in Boston. We continue to be impressed by the Scientific Systems Services, Inc. (Triple S) story and are convinced that a public offering of Triple S securities will be well received by the investment community.

To assist you in finalizing decisions regarding the offering, we have outlined below our preliminary conclusions regarding the offering, structure and timing, and Triple S's valuation.

Structure

We understand that an offering of $12 million is being contemplated, and that the offering will consist of $8 million of primary stock and $4 million of secondary stock. Such an offering could be readily accomplished.

Valuation

Our valuation of Triple S is based upon our understanding of its business, current market environment, and our assumption of projected Triple S's financial performance. Currently, we believe that your 1982 performance when finalized will show revenues of $15.7 million and net income of just under $1 million. We believe that 1983 projections call for approximately 60 percent revenue growth to a total of $25 million in revenues and $1.5 million of net income. We believe that this net income figure should be increased to reflect the net income received from the proceeds of the offering. Conservatively, we feel that the Company could estimate receiving net proceeds of $7.2 million after all deal costs and that an 8 percent pretax return could be realized on these funds for nine months of the year. Hence, we believe the offering would add at least $250,00 to net income for 1983. We estimate Triple S's market value in the initial public offering to be approximately $45 million. This valuation represents a multiple of approximately 26 times expected 1983 net income. Initial public offerings in today's market are generally being priced at a modest discount to market, although the market is currently particularly receptive to new issues even to the point of some buyers saying that "new is better." Therefore, for your planning purposes, we would estimate that the initial public offering would be priced at approximately 25 × 1983 expected earnings and would trade at approximately 26 × expected 1983 net income. The 25–26 × valuation range is one which we consider to be very supportable. It is possible, however, that Triple S could attain an even higher market value if the market remains strong and if the road show marketing effort is particularly well received.

In our phone conversation, Vince, you asked about the methodology which we use to determine valuations. As we have discussed, Alex. Brown looks at market conditions, your business, and overlays these factors on prices received by publicly traded comparable companies. These comparable companies include a large number of software and systems companies as well as turnkey systems companies. On average, this group of companies, which includes ASK, MSA, Cullinane, Computer Associates, Pansophic, Tera, and PMS, is trading at approximately 26 × expected 1983 net income.

Timing

Work on the offering should begin as soon as possible. Prompt action is desirable in order to capitalize on the existing strong market and to achieve maximum visibility for Triple S by entering

EXHIBIT 5   *(continued)*

the market ahead of the numerous filings that are expected to occur when year-end results are available.

Prospectus preparation and all legal work can be accomplished within a 4–5 week period. The first step of the process should be an all hands meeting (including underwriters and their counsel, Triple S and its counsel and auditors) during which a time and responsibility schedule is agreed upon. Alex. Brown's involvement should facilitate this entire process as a result of our considerable experience in writing computer service prospectuses and our knowledge of your Company.

Expenses

If Triple S's initial public offering is in the $12 million range, we estimate that the underwriting spread will not exceed 7.5 percent. Other expenses, consisting of printing costs, Company counsel and filing fees should total approximately $175,000. Expenses of the underwriters, including underwriters' counsel fees and their travel expenses, are borne by the underwriters.

Selection of Managing Underwriter

Alex. Brown is uniquely qualified to serve as investment banker and lead underwriter to Triple S. Our firm's emphasis has always been to concentrate our resources on aftermarket support and sponsorship, particularly in the areas of research, market making and knowledgeable institutional and retail sales support. This emphasis, combined with our strategy of focusing on specific markets within the high technology sector, has allowed Alex. Brown to achieve the leading position within its chosen markets. As you know, Alex. Brown is considered to be the leading investment banker to the computer services industry.

The cornerstone of our work in the computer services industry is our monthly research product, published by a team headed by Al Berkeley. This monthly research, sent out to over 6,000 investors, serves to educate the financial community regarding computer services, industry trends, and individual companies. Further, Alex. Brown sponsors the annual Computer Services Seminar where you spoke. In 1982 over 50 companies spoke at the seminar, addressing an audience of over 500 institutional investors.

You have mentioned that you might utilize two managing underwriters for Triple S's initial public offering. Alex. Brown would be pleased to work jointly with any of the underwriters which you have mentioned. Given our considerable knowledge of the Company and our leadership position in computer services, we are uniquely qualified to serve as Triple S's lead or book-running manager.

We hope that this letter addresses all of your questions plus conveys our enthusiasm for Triple S. Please feel free to call me, Don Hebb, or Al Berkeley if there are additional questions which we may answer. We look forward to hearing from you.

Very truly yours,

Beverly L. Wright

Schedule for Public Offering of Shares of Common Stock

January					1983		February					1983		March					1983	
S	M	T	W	T	F	S	S	M	T	W	T	F	S	S	M	T	W	T	F	S
						1			1	2	3	4	5			1	2	3	4	5
2	3	4	5	6	7	8	6	7	8	9	10	11	12	6	7	8	9	10	11	12
9	10	11	12	13	14	15	13	14	15	16	17	18	19	13	14	15	16	17	18	19
16	17	18	19	20	21	22	20	21	22	23	24	25	26	20	21	22	23	24	25	26
23	24	25	26	27	28	29	27	28						27	28	29	30	31		
30	31																			

EXHIBIT 5   *(concluded)*

CO	Scientific Systems Services, Inc.
U	Alex. Brown & Sons
CC	Peirsol, Boroughs, Grimm & Bennett
UC	Piper & Marbury
CA	Deloitte, Haskins & Sells
P	Printer

Date	Undertaking	Responsibility
January 24, 1983	Prepare and distribute time schedule and team list.	U
	Commence preparation of registration statement and O & D questionnaires; consult SEC.	CC
	Select printer.	CO
	Prepare necessary board of directors resolutions.	CC
	Commence preparation of underwriting documents and Blue Sky filings.	UC
	Deliver draft of registration statement to all parties.	CC
February 2 and 3	Meeting of team to revise draft.	All
February 5	Send out draft to team.	CC
February 9 and 10	Team meets to revise draft and review underwriting agreements, syndicate list, comfort letter.	All
February 11	Draft of all documents to printer.	CC
February 14	Printed draft to team.	P
February 16 and 17	Meet at printer's for final review of drafts.	All
February 18	File registration statement with SEC and NASD.	All
	Press release.	CO
	Syndicate invitations.	U
	Blue Sky filings.	UC
Week of March 7	Road show; due diligence meetings.	CO, U
March 16	Receive SEC comments. Team available to draft response to SEC comments.	CC
March 17 and 18	Meet at printer's to review SEC comments, revise registration statement and refile.	All
March 21	Negotiate price and spread.	CO, U
March 22	Underwriting agreement signed.	CO, U
	Price amendment filed.	CO
	Registration statement declared effective.	CO, U
	Comfort letter delivered.	CA
	Blue Sky clearances received.	UC
	Stock released for sale.	U
	Tombstone released for publication.	U
	Press release.	CO
March 28	Preclosing.	CO, U, CC, UC
March 29	Closing.	CO, U, CC, UC

Exhibit 6   1982 Stock Market Performance

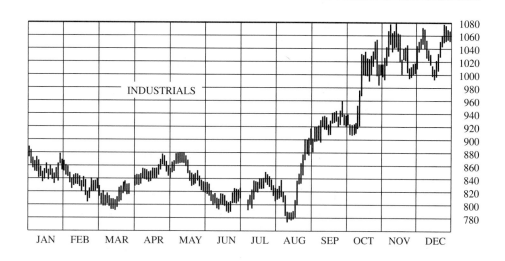

4–6   GLENN DEKRAKER

Having just returned from a Stanford University alumni gathering, Glenn DeKraker and his wife, Pauline, sat down to discuss the diverse career paths his classmates had taken and the different opinions they had offered on Glenn's current dilemma. Glenn had spent the first 19 years of his career working at a large electronics firm from which he departed at age 41 to start his first company. Unfortunately, however, he and his partners strayed from their original strategy and within two years the company had failed and had consumed Glenn's entire life savings. But his optimistic outlook and willingness to work hard soon led him into another venture that was moderately successful over the ensuing nine years. After selling that firm in 1981, he founded his third company, Media Software Technology, Inc., to meet advertising agencies' data processing needs surrounding the purchase of media time and space. The company's steady growth, excellent profit margins, and high market share had recently led several potential buyers to approach Glenn.

Deciding what was best for the company as well as for himself (since he was now 62 and owned 60 percent of the stock) was Glenn's highest priority in June 1988. The options he had to choose among included a venture capital minority investment followed by an initial public offering in two years, a merger with a data processing company to be closely followed by an initial public offering, and the outright sale of the company. Now, as he and Pauline considered each possibility, Glenn knew he had to reach a conclusion soon.

Background

After graduating from Stanford with an electrical engineering degree in 1950, Glenn joined American Electronics, Inc., a Midwest supplier to the electrical utility and defense industries. The company manufactured electrical and electronic instruments such as meters for measuring energy consumption, capacitors, modems, and sonar products for the Navy. During his 19 years with American Electronics, Glenn became a rising star among the ranks and, after gaining significant marketing experience, he was picked to head up the Electronics Systems Division in 1965. American Electronics'

This case was prepared by Marjorie H. Tillman under the supervision of H. I. Grousbeck. All numbers and names, except Glenn DeKraker's, have been disguised.

Development of this case was funded by the Robert Denzil Alexander Fund.

Stanford Business School Case S–SB–109

corporate structure with its multilayered bureaucracy was beginning to prove too rigid for the level of new product development necessary to keep the company growing. So Glenn was also appointed to oversee the firm's investments in and acquisitions of several high-technology ventures in Silicon Valley. While he was slated to become the next president of American Electronics, which had grown to $150 million in revenues, he was growing increasingly attracted to the freedom and creativity he witnessed in these start-up companies. In 1969, he gathered his nest egg and family and moved back to ''God's side of the tracks'' in northern California.

A Midlife Turn to Entrepreneurship

Joining forces with two former American Electronics executives who had also resigned, Glenn established his first company, I/O Data Corporation. Drawing from their experience, the trio aimed to develop a hardware system for input/output communications. Data processing technology at the time consisted of the punching, sorting, and reading of computer cards. By further automating this process, Glenn's team hoped to develop a system whereby one could enter and process data electronically, store it temporarily on a magnetic disk, then transmit it to the central processing unit of the computer system. While at American Electronics, they had worked on projects to develop such data entry products for companies with large data processing needs, including insurance companies and credit card companies. The team's plan for I/O Data differed in that it targeted specific vertical markets in which remote data entry devices were needed. For example, if meter readers in the electrical utility industry could input their data as they traveled from house to house, management could significantly reduce the time and cost of processing monthly bills. In the retailing industry, if employees could enter inventory information on sight while they were in the aisles of the stores or in the distribution warehouses, management could more tightly control inventory levels.

Without any seed financing, the three men each invested $50,000 and defined their individual responsibilities. Glenn (41) took on the role of president and set out to raise more money and to accomplish the logistics of setting up the company. Assuming the functional roles which they had held at American Electronics, Bill Schwartz (40) became vice president of marketing, and Frank Durham (60) stepped into the vice president of manufacturing position.

Within a month of starting I/O Data, Glenn was contacted by Charlie Zarem of Performers' Residuals, Inc. (PR). PR was in the business of representing talent unions by auditing payments to actors and actresses who were in TV commercials. While at American Electronics, Glenn had worked on a project to develop a coding system enabling PR to electronically monitor TV commercials. Given the different professional styles of PR's entertainment executives and American Electronics' engineering executives, Glenn had also served as a buffer between the two managements. Charlie was a former CPA and lawyer who had plenty of creative ideas but poor business judgment and execution capabilities.

When Glenn left American Electronics, PR had canceled its contract, and Charlie wanted Glenn to resume his work as a consultant on a very lucrative month-to-month contract, which was equivalent to a $100,000 annual salary. Glenn would also need the technical assistance of his two partners and therefore could immediately direct some business to their new company. Glenn, Bill, and Frank had not completed their strategic plan for I/O Data and questioned whether the financial benefits of the arrangement outweighed the intangible cost of temporarily interrupting their plans for I/O Data. Feeling that they could earn a nice sum within a fairly short period of time, they accepted the job.

Glenn's team set out to organize a staff, design the coding system, purchase the design and prototype equipment from American Electronics, and organize I/O Data to produce the monitors for 40 markets. The product needed was a detection system that would identify coded broadcasts and then communicate such information back to PR in Chicago. If bar codes were placed in the four corners of the film for commercials, a system could detect such codes as a digital signal and identify the commercial as a unique number. The only problem was that such a system would require millions of dollars to develop and install. With the I/O Data team as technical consultants to PR, one of the oldest venture capital firms in the United States agreed to invest $6 million in PR with the intent that the company would go public within a year.

Glenn and his colleagues received approval from the Federal Communications Commission (FCC) for a critical ruling that allowed advertising agencies to put bar codes on their commercials. After the detection system was installed and operating in 25 markets, the venture capital firm started preparing for an initial public offering. The stock market was extremely strong in 1970. In order to get stock rights in PR before the offering and to avoid a conflict of interest, Glenn was forced to resign from I/O Data and sell his shares at a total loss. Simultaneously, he invested $300,000, his total savings, to buy 5 percent of PR. All of the investors were convinced they would reap huge gains on their stock positions when PR went public. The expected market valuation was approximately $125 million.

A Scuttled IPO

What they didn't expect, however, were the third-party influence problems that suddenly began interfering with the detection system. Before a commercial was shown on TV, it passed through many hands. The advertising agency shot the film and assigned a unique number to each commercial, an optical house developed the film and applied the bar code in the corners, a film lab copied it, and then the TV broadcasters aired it. Unfortunately, the optical houses in different cities had different standards. And the broadcast industry didn't align the film in a consistent manner and often cropped out the bar code. In reality, these crucial third parties were basically opposed to the whole concept of a monitoring system. The advertising agencies feared that such controls would show that they weren't managing their clients' money very efficiently. The broadcasters feared such auditing would dispute their invoices of what commercial ran when and how many people saw it. The major forces behind the system were the talent unions and advertisers, neither of whom had a direct influence on the implementation of the monitoring system.

While technically the system worked well once the bar codes were picked up, the lack of standards in the film and broadcast industries sometimes caused the codes to go undetected. As the installations expanded beyond the largest 25 markets, which generally had cleaner standards than the smaller markets, problems with the code detection began surfacing in early 1971. These problems affected the support of advertisers and caused a severe downturn in PR's cash flow. It quickly became clear the company could not go public. The venture capitalists took control, contributed more funds, which severely diluted existing investors (Glenn's share declined to less than 1 percent), and liquidated the company in mid-1971. The institutional investors ended up taking a 50 percent write-off. Glenn, who was the largest individual investor, wrote off his entire $300,000 investment but was eventually paid $100,000 two years later for the design of the system. His former two partners in I/O Data never got paid for their technical and production work.

A Second Venture

"Poor and poverty stricken," Glenn had three options. He could put the past two years behind him and accept an offer to join another large electronics firm such as IBM, General Electric, or Westinghouse. Several of his prior industry contacts had offered him senior marketing positions with $100,000 annual salaries. Or, if he persevered, he could start another company either by returning to his original plans for I/O Data or by pursuing another niche in the advertising market. In spite of having failed with his first entrepreneurial venture, Glenn was relieved to find a number of good options open to him.

His experience at PR had convinced him of the need for an electronic media audit trail, and he became intent upon finding an inexpensive way to verify when certain commercials ran. The only way to do this was to develop a monitoring system that operated manually rather than by the electronic means he had employed at PR. This would allow him to buy time until the broadcasters embraced videotape technology or until pattern recognition technology was refined, either of which would eliminate the third-party influence problems he had encountered before. He also was convinced of his ability to persuade advertisers to put pressure on their agencies to implement such a system.

Joining forces with a PR marketing manager, Joe O'Leary, Glenn turned down the secure industry positions and launched Adtrac Corporation in 1972. Bill Schwartz went on to pursue other opportunities, and Frank Durham retired. Schering-Plough, a major pharmaceutical company with an in-house advertising agency, had been supportive of Glenn's efforts at PR and agreed to pay Adtrac $150,000 up front to monitor its commercials. Glenn and Joe devised a plan involving the installation of 24-hour audio recording equipment in handicapped persons' homes in 40 markets. Adtrac sent them prelabeled tapes that they periodically replaced in the recording equipment and then shipped back to the company. Adtrac paid each handicapped person for his or her electricity expenses and a monthly salary of $300. The equipment simultaneously recorded the sounds from eight different stations and did not interfere with the person's own viewing. The equipment also continually recorded the time and date on the tapes. These tapes provided a means for Adtrac to check the broadcasters' invoices stating the date and time each commercial ran. Schering-Plough paid $150,000 annually and on average received $800,000 as a rebate for commercials that were incorrectly aired. Such stories motivated advertisers to force their agencies to provide such audits. Due to the competitive nature of their marketplace, soft drink companies such as Seven-Up and Dr Pepper wanted close monitoring of their ads and became early customers of Adtrac.

The company only grew to about $1 million in revenues because of the limitations of manual monitoring. Glenn sold the business in 1981 to a firm that was in the comparable newspaper advertising field and wanted to get into TV monitoring. At the time of the sale, Glenn owned 30 percent of the company and had invested a total of $50,000 equity, most of which he had raised through a second mortgage. While Adtrac did little more than provide an acceptable living, it did allow him to stay in touch with the advertising market.

Other Advertising-Related Opportunities

Advertising results have always been somewhat intangible because it is difficult to measure the direct sales response after an ad runs. During the 1970s, buyers of television advertising utilized the gross rating point, or GRP, system provided by syndicated audience measurement services to determine how many households were reached by a particular TV show or commercial. Gradually the advertisers demanded to know the personal demographics (i.e., women 24 to 49 years old) of the audience watching each program. This information allowed advertisers to target their audiences better through the placement of their commercials.

Rating services such as Arbitron (owned by Control Data) and Nielsen (owned by Dun and Bradstreet) built data bases that were continuously replenished. They collected the data by electronically monitoring TV viewing patterns in over 2,000 homes across the United States. The data was gathered from 220 markets and published, in most cases, four times a year. Results from the largest markets were released seven or eight times a year. The data base suppliers contracted with advertisers, advertising agencies, and broadcasters and distributed the market statistics in book form. Unfortunately, due to the huge amount of data and poor presentation (see **Exhibit 1**), one needed an eyeshade, ruler, magnifier, and calculator to interpret the results.

Glenn recognized the need for users to be able to better understand this data and to incorporate it into their media purchase decisions. While many of the top 50 advertising agencies were utilizing time-sharing systems to manipulate the data, the needs of the firms below the top 50 had not been addressed. Viewing their data bases as ends in themselves, Nielsen and Arbitron were far from recognizing this opportunity.

Media Software Technology

In late 1981, Glenn founded his third company, Media Software Technology, Inc. (MST). His strategy was to license application software to provide advertising agencies with TV, radio, and print audience rating data in a more usable format to assist in media purchase decisions. The chart in **Exhibit 2** shows which agency needs MST aimed to meet with its value-added products. Glenn's initial financing for MST consisted of a second mortgage on his house, $10,000 of which became an equity investment. The rest was set aside to support his family so that he would not have to draw a salary. Also, certain software that Glenn had developed at Adtrac became the property of MST in return for MST's assumption of a $160,000 Small Business Administration loan that had been made to Adtrac and personally guaranteed by Glenn. This software provided the basis for MST's source code. As Glenn stated, ''In the early days, we had a champagne appetite with a beer pocketbook!''

The Product

MST employed data compression and restructuring techniques that allowed its software customers to quickly and easily access audience data. This data consisted of broadcast-oriented measurements from Nielsen (TV), Arbitron (TV/radio), and Birch (radio), and print-oriented measurements (magazines/newspapers) from MRI Simmons and Scarborough. After receiving the audience data on magnetic tape from Nielsen, for example, MST condensed and copied it onto floppy disks and had it in the customer's hands the next day. Then MST's software product allowed the agency to conduct sophisticated analyses of the data, create impressive color graphics, and produce standardized reports adhering to a consistent methodology and format. **Exhibit 3** further describes how MST interfaced with the data base suppliers and the end users. MST offered a ''cookie cutter'' product with no custom tailoring provided. However, MST did integrate its software package with the other processing needs of advertising agencies, such as the back room or ''housekeeping'' operations like accounting and billing.

MST programmed its software for use in a stand-alone microcomputer-based system in each agency. In the early 1980s, Glenn disputed people who said microcomputers were too small to deal with large data bases and felt such nay sayers were blinded by the conventional wisdom that these data bases automatically needed to involve a mainframe computer system. Nevertheless, there was a lot of data to be handled. When Nielsen surveyed all 220 markets, it created over 100 megabytes of data. By the time one seasonally adjusted, trended, and compared such data to historicals, he or she needed a system with a 600 megabyte capacity. Yet, a typical medium-sized agency with $10 million in annual billings needed only a 50 megabyte system for its other processing needs. To get around these disparate needs, Glenn determined that by breaking down the data on a market-by-market basis, it could be stored on floppy disks, MST could process it more quickly, and the agencies could utilize it more easily. It wasn't hard to convince customers that a PC-based system provided the greatest benefits in terms of cost, ease of use, and constant access.

When Glenn started the company, he was the only employee, and magnetic tape to floppy disk conversion technology was not very advanced. It actually took 1 1/2 hours per TV station per market to convert the data (instead of the 50 seconds it takes now). During the "crunch" periods following a nationwide Nielsen survey, Glenn would get up every 1 1/2 hours to change the tapes through the night. He converted the data for the largest markets first, which sometimes took up to 24 hours per market. Needless to say, as more employees and equipment were added and as conversion technology advanced, MST's turnaround time decreased dramatically and the luxury of a full night's rest was Glenn's once more.

The MST system was sold only by subscriptions of three to five years in length. Pricing was based on a fixed monthly fee, which was determined by the number of application modules and the number of markets for which data was accessed.

Customers and Competitors

The target market was initially small to medium-sized agencies to whom MST would license the software tools, allowing them to compete more effectively with the major New York firms. As **Exhibit 4** shows, this is the fastest growing segment of the advertising industry. MST sold its service through a direct sales force of seven people and had 750 customers by June 1988. The total market was approximately 5,000 users of media audience data in the United States.

As the competitive analysis in **Exhibit 5** shows, MST was by far the dominant player in providing media software to advertising agencies, and much of the market remained untapped. It may seem surprising that Nielsen and Arbitron were only minor forces in this market. In reality, by the time these data base suppliers realized the opportunity, MST already had a dominant market share and presented customers with integrated data for all forms of media, not just TV data. None of MST's competitors offered as complete a package as MST's, which covered TV, radio, and print and also addressed all four of the media purchase functions described in Exhibit 2. In addition, competitive time-sharing and on-line services were either difficult to use, more costly, or both.

Broadcast Software Technology

Launched in 1984, Broadcast Software Technology, Inc. (BST) provided TV and radio stations with an application software product similar to that that MST offered advertising agencies. Glenn decided that if he could help the buyers of media time make more informed purchase decisions, he could also assist the sellers of media time in making better sales proposals. The stations used the first of BST's software packages to access audience data and to analyze their competitive position in their marketplaces.

The second software package provided stations with the ability to manage their program inventory and to generate advertising time availability and campaign proposals. BST was merged into MST in 1987.

By June 1988, BST had 270 TV station customers and 250 radio station customers out of a total market of 750 TV stations and 7,000 radio stations. As shown in **Exhibit 6**, competitors included some of the same names that competed with MST as well as several other on-line systems. Again, BST's system was less expensive and offered greater user friendliness. BST had a direct sales force of five people and sold its system on a subscription basis with fixed licensing fees.

Financial Performance

From humble beginnings, MST grew to over $8.5 million in consolidated revenues and a 32 percent operating profit margin in 1987. This slow but steady growth of the company was financed by internally generated cash flow and in 1987 a bank revolving line of credit. The historical balance sheets, income statements, and cash flow statements of MST are found in **Exhibits 7** to **9**. The financial projections in **Exhibit 10** were based on the premise that new product development and selective acquisitions would continue to provide significant growth opportunities.

Along with revenue increases, MST's number of employees grew to 70. The key members of the management team are described in **Exhibit 11**.

The Time To Harvest

In mid-1988, Glenn was in excellent health at age 62. He continued to enjoy the challenges and demands of running MST and arrived at the office each day at 7 A.M. He was intimately involved in all of the company's operations. Nevertheless, he was conscious of the need to plan how he and a few other managers would eventually cash out of the company, of which he then owned 60 percent. Glenn had originally invested $10,000 equity, and the $160,000 SBA loan he had personally guaranteed had been paid off. He also owed MST $300,000, which he had borrowed to start a company that acted as a value-added reseller of computer hardware to complement MST's software. He did not plan to cash out of this related investment but would have to repay the loan when he exited MST.

During 1987 and 1988, several interested parties had approached Glenn regarding the recapitalization or sale of MST. The wide range of initial valuations now caused him to question if a more coordinated effort might bring an even higher price. He wondered what exit strategy would truly maximize the shareholders' value. In order not to take too much of his time away from running the company, he hired an investment banking advisor who uncovered the following three harvest options for his consideration.

A Minority Investment

A major venture capital firm in Palo Alto, California, proposed a minority investment of $8.4 million for a 37 percent ownership stake in the company. The proceeds would be divided as follows: $4.8 million to selling shareholders for 21 percent and $3.6 million to MST for 16 percent. The cash infusion into the company was for the purposes of working capital needs, debt repayment, and acquisitions. The company would then go public at the end of 1990. Assuming management's projection and a $15 \times$ price/earnings ratio, the pre-money IPO valuation could be $94 million. (Before the October 1987 stock market crash, computer services firms were trading at P/E's greater than $25 \times$. Since then, their multiples had averaged in the $15-20 \times$ range.)

Glenn had mixed feelings about the venture capital plan. On the one hand, he wanted to see his company remain independent, and a minority investment would allow him to partially cash out while growing the company faster through acquisitions. Glenn also felt that the involvement of the venture capital firm, known to be an agile and opportunistic investor, would allow MST to take advantage of consolidation opportunities in the industry. Yet, on the other hand, MST was now reaching a size where it needed a tighter organizational structure and more controls, which he was not particularly interested in devising. He also had no shortage of ideas for other companies. As he remarked, "When I feel my toes touching the mud, I know I've got to get out in deeper water!"

A Merger Partner

A second possibility involved merging with Dillingham Data Corporation (Dillingham), a firm that provided "housekeeping" systems to automate the back-room operations of broadcast stations and broadcast representatives, who sell media time in nonlocal markets. Such a combination would have great synergy with BST's business and would give each firm access to the other's client base. With revenues of $40 million and pretax income of $2.5 million in 1987, Dillingham had a much larger sales base but weaker profit margins than MST. Dillingham's products allowed more efficient running of the stations in areas such as billing, accounting, traffic control, etc. The company was the dominant provider of such services and had over 200 clients. **Exhibits 12** and **13** present financial information on Dillingham and the proposed combination.

The consideration for the merger would be distributed as follows: (1) MST would own 80 percent and Dillingham would own 20 percent of the combined entity, and (2) the combined entity would issue a $20 million subordinated note (with 8 percent coupon, 10-year bullet amortization, and prepayment allowed) to Dillingham. Both firms expected the new entity to go public in six months (January 1989), which would trigger an immediate prepayment of the subordinated note. Again, using a $15 \times$ multiple of 1988 combined earnings of $4.7 million (MST $2.8 million and Dillingham $1.9 million), the pre-money IPO valuation could total $71 million. Glenn would be chairman of the new company, and two presidents from Dillingham and MST would be named.

While the synergy was apparent and the opportunity to go public in six months had certain timing advantages over the minority investment proposal, there were other problems. First, Dillingham's management had joined the firm from Donovan, another competitor. These people were known to be vicious competitors whose tactical moves often didn't reflect sound economic strategies and represented vindictive acts against their former employer. Second, Dillingham had mostly Burroughs mainframes and IBM minicomputers that needed upgrading and didn't necessarily fit in well with MST's microcomputer strategy.

A Sale Of MST

While a number of potential buyers expressed interest in MST, Local Communications, Inc. (LCI), emerged as the leading candidate if Glenn wanted to sell the company. LCI was one of the regional telephone companies that had been formed as a result of the breakup of AT&T. LCI had two sets of operations: (1) telephone/communications businesses and (2) nonregulated operations, including the directory/Yellow Pages business in 44 states, a cellular telephone business, and financial services operations. The division that published the telephone directory and Yellow Pages had annual revenues of $960 million. This division served small to medium-sized businesses by providing them with promotional and marketing services designed to attract and maintain their customers. Since the Yellow Pages business was data base driven, LCI highly valued MST's ability to provide creative, market-driven, application software tied to an existing data base. From MST's and Glenn's perspectives, such a linkup would provide exciting new challenges and expansion potential. LCI was also fully committed to MST's own new product development plans.

LCI had proposed to structure the purchase either with or without an earnout provision as described below:

A. *With earnout:* $22 million up front with potentially $59 million more to come over five years if the company met its plan. See **Exhibit 14** for a further explanation of the earnout provision, which was tied to revenues and pretax income. The up-front payment would go directly to shareholders, while the earnout payments would be split between shareholders (75 percent) and employees (25 percent, of which Glenn would receive one fifth). In addition, LCI had committed to lend $5 million to MST over the next 2 1/2 years at favorable rates. LCI was unlikely to impose controls that would jeopardize the earnout, since MST would have strong legal recourse. This arrangement was more likely to allow MST to operate as an independent company and to maintain its own culture than the no earnout scenario was. The payments to employees and resulting recapitalization would provide additional incentives to achieve exceptional performance.

B. *Without earnout:* $37 million up-front payment, plus agreement from Glenn and other key managers to stay on 2 1/2 years. Since a recession or more competitive business conditions could decrease or negate the earnout payment above (as well as negatively impact an initial public offering in future years), this structure had less financial risk. It was also unclear whether LCI's unfamiliarity with earnouts could eventually become a problem, since it had never acquired a company under an earnout scenario.

Nevertheless, there were some nonfinancial issues to be considered. First, the cultures of these two organizations were totally different. As a regulated company, LCI had an operations/administrative orientation and was not particularly market driven. It was a multibillion-dollar company with a much more bureaucratic decision-making style than MST's. Glenn wondered whether his little company would lose its focus and direction in such a mammoth organization. Finally, he had not met very many LCI managers but had spoken mostly with the "deal people" (i.e., the president of the directory/Yellow Pages division, the controller, the strategic planner, and attorneys). It was unclear how well he and his top managers would mesh with the LCI team.

No Time To Lose

As he talked with his wife, Glenn reflected that as was usual in his business, there was never enough time or information to make the perfect decision. His choice would determine his own personal wealth, what he would devote his time to over the next few years, and the future direction of his start-up success, MST. But, decide he must, since two of his three proposals would expire in two days, June 30, 1988. As he and Pauline sat down to the dinner table, Glenn knew he had to reach a prompt conclusion.

EXHIBIT 1

Tuesday
3.00PM–8.00PM

(Left margin, vertical: TIME PERIOD)

Metro HH / DMA HH

Station	Program	Metro RTG	Metro SHR	Wk 1	Wk 2	Wk 3	Wk 4	Avg RTG	Avg SHR	Nov 87	May 87	Feb 87
	R.S.E. THRESHOLD .25-%	3		8	8	8	8					2
	(1 S.E.) 14 WK AVG 50-%	1		2	2	2	2					1
3.00PM												
KATU	ALL-CHILDREN	4	17	6	4	4	4	4	18	27X	20	22
KGW	DAYS-OUR LIVES	8	34	9	6	7	7	7	31	31X	37	33
KOAP	FOCUS-SOCIETY	<<		<<	<<	<<	<<	<<		X		2
KOIN	GERALDO	5	24	4	7	5	5	5	19	13X	10	5
KPTV	BUGS BUNNY	3	11	3	3	2	2	2	9	12	11	11
KPDX	TEDDY RUXPIN*	1	3	<<	1	<<	1	1	3	X	3	5
	HUT/PUT/TOTALS*	23		26	25	22	21	24		23	23	24
3.30PM												
KATU	ALL-CHILDREN	5	18	6	5	4	5	5	18	25X	18	20
KGW	DAYS-OUR LIVES	8	31	9	7	7	6	7	29	29X	36	33
KOAP	MR. ROGERS	1	4	1	1	1	1	1	3	X		2
KOIN	GERALDO	5	21	4	7	5	5	5	18	12X	10	5
KPTV	SMURFS	3	11	3	4	2	2	2	9	12X	17	12
KPDX	DINOSAUCERS	1	6	1	3	<<	1	1	5	X	5	7
	HUT/PUT/TOTALS*	25		27	28	23	23	25		26	25	26
4.00PM												
KATU	OPRAH WINFREY	10	32	11	12	12	9	9	28	23X	14	18
KGW	DONAHUE	5	16	5	5	7	5	6	17	23X	29	24
KOAP	SESAME STREET	2	6	2	2	1	1	2	5	6X	5	6
KOIN	LOVE CONNECTN	6	21	3	8	6	5	6	17	13X	16	18
KPTV	REAL GHOSTBSTR	4	14	4	8	2	3	4	13	13X	9	7
KPDX	BEVERLY-TEENS	1	3	1	2	<<	1	2		5	5	10
	HUT/PUT/TOTALS*	30		32	38	29	28	32		31	31	31
4.30PM												
KATU	OPRAH WINFREY	9	27	11	12	7	6	9	24	20X	10	18
KGW	DONAHUE	5	15	6	5	8	5	6	16	23X	28	21
KOAP	SESAME STREET	2	5	2	1	1	1	1	4	5X	5	7
KOIN	PEOPLE'S COURT	10	28	6	10	7	11	9	24	19X	25	24
KPTV	DUCK TALES	6	18	6	10	3	5	6	18	15X	9	8
KPDX	JETSONS	1	2	1	1	<<	1	1	2	4X	4	7
	HUT/PUT/TOTALS*	35		38	40	31	37	36		36	33	24

DMA Ratings

Program	P 2+	P 18+	P 12-34	P 18-34	P 18-49	P 25-54	W 18+	W 18-34	W 18-49	W 25-49	W 25-54	WKG	Fem 12-24	Per 12-24	M 18+	M 18-34	M 18-49	M 25-49	M 25-54	TNS 12-17	Ch 2-11	Ch 6-11
R.S.E. .25-%	1						1								1							
(1 S.E.) 50-%	1						1								1							
ALL-CHILDREN (3:00)	2	2		1	1	1	2	2	1	1	1	2		1	1	1		1	1	2	2	2
DAYS-OUR LIVES (3:00)	4	4	3	3	3	3	7	7	6	5	5	4	9	6	1	1	1	1	1			
FOCUS-SOCIETY																						
GERALDO (3:00)	2	2	1	1	1	1	2	2	1	1	1	2	1	1	2	2	2	1	1			
BUGS BUNNY	2		1										2	2						1	6	4
TEDDY RUXPIN*																				2	2	2
HUT/PUT/TOTALS* (3:00)	12	12	11	11	9	8	16	15	13	11	12	11	17	13	7	7	5	5	4	12	12	10
ALL-CHILDREN (3:30)	2	2		1	1	1	2	2	1	1	1	2	2	3	2	1	1		1	2		
DAYS-OUR LIVES (3:30)	4	4	3	4	3	2	4	6	5	5	5	4	11	7	1	1		1	1	7		3
MR. ROGERS	1	1																				
GERALDO (3:30)	2	2	1	1	1	1	2	2	1	1	1	2		2	2	2	1	1	1			
SMURFS	2		1											3						2	7	6
DINOSAUCERS	1																			1	4	4
HUT/PUT/TOTALS* (3:30)	13	12	11	11	9	7	17	16	13	11	11	11	20	15	7	6	5	5	3	14	18	13
OPRAH WINFREY (4:00)	5	5	5	6	5	5	8	8	8	8	7	6	4	4	4	4	3	3	3	1	1	
DONAHUE (4:00)	2	3	2	1	1	2	3	2	2	3	3	3	3	3	2	3	3	1	1	4		2
SESAME STREET (4:00)	1																					
LOVE CONNECTN	3	2	2	2	2	2	3	2	2	3	2	2	3	2	2	2	2	1	1	3		
REAL GHOSTBSTR	3	1	2	1	1	1	1		1	1	1	2	2	4	2	1	1	1	1	7	11	10
BEVERLY-TEENS															1	1				1	2	3
HUT/PUT/TOTALS* (4:00)	19	20	15	13	12	12	21	18	17	17	17	13	18	16	12	9	8	7	7	20	26	25
OPRAH WINFREY (4:30)	5	5	5	6	5	5	7	7	8	7	7	6	4	4	4	4	3	3	3	1		
DONAHUE (4:30)	3	3	1	1	1	2	3	2	3	3	3	3	3	2	2	1	1	1	1	1	4	1
SESAME STREET (4:30)	1																					
PEOPLE'S COURT	4	6	2	2	2	2	3	3	2	2	2	3	6	7	2	2	2	2	2	3	19	20
DUCK TALES	3	1	4	2	2	1	2	1	1	1	1	1	1	2	5	2	1	2	1	11	1	1
JETSONS															2	2	2	2	2	1	3	3
HUT/PUT/TOTALS* (4:30)	21	20	15	13	13	13	24	18	17	17	18	14	19	17	15	9	9	8	8	21	30	30

EXHIBIT 1 (continued)

Tuesday 3.00PM– 8.00PM

	Metro HH				DMA HH									DMA Ratings																					
	RTG	SHR	Station	Program	Ratings Weeks				Multi Week Avg.		Share Trend			Persons						Women								Men						Child	
					1	2	3	4	RTG	SHR	Nov 87	May 87	Feb 87	2+	18+	12-34	18-34	18-49	25-54	18+	18-34	18-49	25-49	25-54	WKG	Fem 12-24	Per 12-24	18+	18-34	18-49	25-49	25-54	TNS 12-17	2-11	6-11
	1	2			3	4	5	6	7	8	10	11	12	14	15	16	17	18	19	20	21	22	23	24	25	26	27	28	29	30	31	32	33	34	35
5.00PM	10	21	KATU	CH 2 NWS 1	15	10	9	9	11	23	21X	17	22	6	7	3	4	4	5	7	3	4	4	5	4	2	2	7	4	4	4	4	1	1	
	9	20	KGW	5.00 NWS 8	11	9	8	7	9	19	25X	25	26	5	6	2	3	4	5	6	3	4	5	5	6	2	1	6	1	3	3	4	1	1	
	3	6	KOAP	SQUARE ONE TV	2	4	2	2	2	5	4X	3	2	2	2	1											1						1	10	11
	13	29	KOIN	NWSROOM 6-E	10	12	13	13	12	26	26X	24	26	7	9	3	4	5	4	9	3	5	4	4	4	3	3	8	5	5	4	5	1	1	1
	5	11	KPTV	LITTLE HOUSE	5	6	5	6	6	12	10X	12	9	4	3	5	5	4	3	3	7	5	4	4	3	10	6	2	2	2	2	2	7	9	10
	4	8	KPDX	H DAYS AGAIN	3	3	4	2	3	6	4X	4	5	2	1	2	2	2	1	2	1	2	1	1	4	4	4	2	2	1	1	1	4	4	6
	45			HUT/PUT/TOTALS*	50	51	47	47	47		49	43	47	28	29	19	19	19	20	30	22	21	20	22	20	22	21	27	16	18	17	18	20	30	36
5.30PM	10	21	KATU	CH 2 NWS 1	17	9	8	9	11	22	20X	16	20	6	7	4	4	4	5	7	5	6	5	6	6	2	2	7	5	5	5	5	1	1	
	10	20	KGW	5.00 NWS 8	13	9	9	10	10	20	23X	26	27	6	7	3	3	3	5	7	4	5	5	5	7	2	1	7	2	4	4	5	1		
	2	5	KOAP	3-2-1 CONTACT	2	4	<<	1	2	4	3X	2	2	1	1		1			1					1			1					2	6	6
	15	31	KOIN	NWSROOM 6-E	12	13	15	13	13	27	29X	25	25	7	9	4	4	5	5	9	4	4	4	5	5	2	2	9	5	6	5	5	1	1	1
	5	10	KPTV	LITTLE HOUSE	6	5	6	7	6	12	10X	12	10	4	3	6	6	4	3	4	5	5	4	4	3	10	6	3	2	3	3	3	6	8	8
	3	7	KPDX	GIMME A BREAK	3	2	2	2	2	5	5X	4	6	2	1	2	2	1	1	2	1	2	2	1	1	2	3	1	1	1	1	1	3	3	4
	47			HUT/PUT/TOTALS*	56	49	44	47	49		50	47	50	29	31	22	22	22	22	33	21	23	23	24	23	22	22	29	20	20	20	21	21	21	27
6.00PM	10	20	KATU	ABC-WORLD NWS	14	9	8	12	11	22	19X	17	19	6	8	3	3	4	5	8	3	5	6	7	7	1	2	7	5	5	5	5	1	1	
	10	20	KGW	NBC NITELY NWS	12	9	9	10	10	19	19X	23	22	5	6	2	2	2	4	5	3	3	4	4	5	1	1	7	2	4	4	4	2		
	1	2	KOAP	FRUGAL GOURMT	1	1	1	<<	1	1	X	2	2	1	1		1	1	1	1							1	1							
	14	27	KOIN	CBS EVE NWS	12	15	15	10	13	25	29X	25	25	7	9	4	5	5	6	9	4	6	6	6	7	2	2	9	6	6	7	7	2	2	1
	8	15	KPTV	FAMILY TIES	7	6	7	8	7	14	12X	12	13	5	4	6	5	4	4	4	5	5	5	4	3	9	9	6	5	4	4	4	11	8	8
	4	8	KPDX	FACTS OF LIFE1	3	5	3	2	3	6	7	6	8	2	2	3	2	2	3	2	2	2	2	2	2	5	4	2	1	1	1	1	4	4	5
	50			HUT/PUT/TOTALS*	56	49	48	50	51		56	51	55	32	35	23	23	25	27	35	23	25	25	27	26	21	22	34	23	25	25	26	22	22	22
6.30PM	10	20	KATU	CH 2 NWS 2	13	10	8	13	11	21	19X	16	18	6	8	1	1	4	6	8	1	4	5	6	6	1	1	7	1	4	4	5	1	1	
	8	15	KGW	ON THE SPOT	11	11	6	5	8	16	11X	19	19	6	6	1	1	3	3	6	1	3	3	3	4	1	1	5	1	2	2	2	1		2
	2	4	KOAP	NITE BSNSS RPT	2	2	3	<<	2	3	3X	3	3	1	1		1	1	1							1		1							
	16	33	KOIN	MASH 1	18	14	14	17	16	31	33X	28	27	10	12	13	13	12	12	11	11	11	11	11	11	6	9	13	14	14	13	12	5	4	
	7	13	KPTV	THREE'S COMPNY	5	6	7	8	6	11	9X	11	13	4	3	5	4	3	3	4	3	3	3	2	2	7	9	4	5	3	2	2	2	6	6
	4	8	KPDX	FACTS OF LIFE2	3	4	4	3	3	7	7	5	8	2	2	4	3	2	2	2	2	2	2	2	2	5	4	1	1	1	1	1	5	6	6
	50			HUT/PUT/TOTALS*	57	52	45	52	52		57	50	56	34	36	26	26	28	29	36	24	27	28	28	28	22	26	36	27	29	27	29	24	25	25

EXHIBIT 1 (concluded)

Tuesday 3.00PM- 8.00PM

	Metro HH RTG (1)	Metro HH SHR (2)	Station	Program	Wk1 (3)	Wk2 (4)	Wk3 (5)	Wk4 (6)	Multi RTG (7)	Multi SHR (8)	Nov 87 (10)	May 87 (11)	Feb 87 (12)	Pers 2+ (14)	Pers 18+ (15)	Pers 12-34 (16)	Pers 18-34 (17)	Pers 18-49 (18)	Pers 25-54 (19)	Wom 18+ (20)	Wom 18-34 (21)	Wom 18-49 (22)	Wom 25-49 (23)	Wom 25-54 (24)	Wom WKG (25)	Fem 12-24 (26)	Per 12-24 (27)	Men 18+ (28)	Men 18-34 (29)	Men 18-49 (30)	Men 25-49 (31)	Men 25-54 (32)	TNS 12-17 (33)	Child 2-11 (34)	Child 6-11 (35)
7.00PM	11	20	KATU	WIN LOSE-DRAW	12	15	8	7	10	18	15X	10	12	8	8	7	8	7	7	8	8	7	7	7	7	6	7	8	8	7	7	7	5	7	5
	8	15	KGW	ENT TONIGHT 30	9	2	10	9	8	13	13X	14	13	4	5	5	5	4	5	5	5	5	6	6	5	3	4	5	4	5	5	5	5	5	2
	7	12	KOAP	MACNEIL&LEHR	5	5	6	6	5	9	8X	7	7	3	4	1	1	2	3	3	1	2	2	2	5			4	1	2	2	3	3	2	
	15	27	KOIN	WHEEL-FORTNE	15	19	13	13	15	27	34X	33	34	9	11	5	5	6	7	11	5	5	6	7	7	4	4	10	6	6	6	6	3	6	3
	8	14	KPTV	CHEERS	5	5	8	13	8	13	10X	10	11	6	5	8	8	7	6	6	8	7	7	7	7	9	8	5	7	6	6	6	8	6	3
	3	6	KPDX	MAGNUM	3	3	3	2	3	5	4X	6	7	2	2	2	2	2	2	2	2	2	2	2	3	3	2	2	2	2	2	2	3	2	2
	54			HUT/PUT/TOTALS*	55	56	56	60	57		56	51	59	39	42	33	35	34	37	43	35	34	36	38	36	28	28	41	34	34	35	37	28	34	35
7.30PM	9	17	KATU	HLLYWD SQUARES	10	11	8	8	9	16	10X	12	13	7	6	7	7	7	6	7	7	6	5	6	6	8	7	7	6	6	6	6	7	10	7
	11	20	KGW	PM MAGAZINE	11	4	11	13	10	17	19X	15	17	6	7	7	7	7	8	7	5	7	7	7	6	3	5	8	8	8	9	8	7	3	3
	6	12	KOAP	MACNEIL&LEHR	4	5	6	5	5	9	9X	8	8	3	3	1	1	2	3	3	1	2	2	2	1			4	1	2	2	3	1		
	16	30	KOIN	JEOPARDY	18	22	15	12	17	30	34X	29	30	10	12	6	7	8	9	13	6	8	9	9	10	4	4	12	8	8	8	9	9	4	4
	5	10	KPTV	NW NEWLYWED G	2	4	8	9	6	10	9X	10	10	4	4	4	4	4	4	5	5	4	4	4	3	5	5	4	3	3	2	2	5	4	2
	4	7	KPDX	MAGNUM	3	3	4	2	3	5	4X	6	7	4	4	2	3	2	2	2	3	2	2	2	2	2	2	2	2	2	2	2	2	2	3
	54			HUT/PUT/TOTALS*	59	52	57	58	57		55	52	61	39	42	33	33	34	37	43	32	33	36	38	36	24	27	41	34	34	36	36	29	29	29

EXHIBIT 2   **MST Value Added Analysis**

Agency Functions	Needs	Current Products	New Products
Overall Agency Management	Forecasting Profit planning Personnel Space needs		Agency management
New Business Development	Agency history Agency strengths Market trends Media goals Knowledge of competition Effective management Market approaches		New business development Adbase
Media Planning	Budget Media mix Creative Implementation guidelines Competitive position		Power planner Market rate adbase
Media Audience Analysis	Analysis of data bases Automatic lookup Accurate Use CPM/CPP Apply judgment What-if scenarios	MST audience analysis (TV, radio, print)	
Media Prebuy	Effective estimates Accurate cost data Current availability info Complete schedule timing	MST prebuy (TV, radio, print, newspaper)	Cost analyzer
Media Control	Automatic transfer of estimates Allow effective negotiation Audit results Automatically invoice Produce summary reports	MST control (TV, radio, print)	
Media Management	Transfer media info Collect/summarize media costs Produce overall summary reports	MST interface	Cost analyzer
Agency Operations	Production Traffic job summaries Automatic transfer to GL Flexible for growth		Agency operations

SOURCE: Company records.

EXHIBIT 3   **MST Base Business**

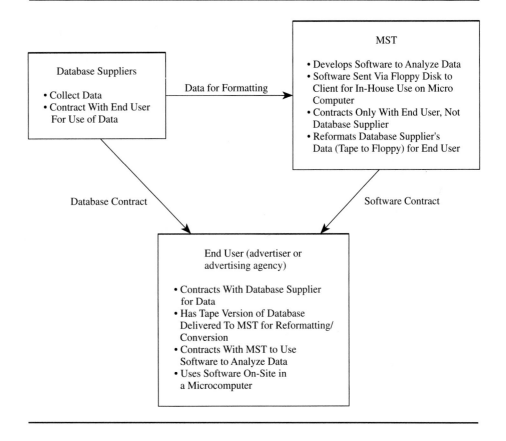

EXHIBIT 4   **Advertising Expenditures for Agencies Ranked by Size ($ in millions)**

	1985	1986	Growth
Top 25 agencies			
Newspaper	$ 1,289	$ 1,462	13.4%
Magazine	2,410	2,729	13.2%
Radio	872	1,014	16.3%
Network TV	6,126	6,582	7.4%
Spot TV	2,881	3,684	27.9%
Cable	184	241	31.0%
Other	1,340	1,452	8.4%
Total	$15,102	$17,164	13.7%
Top 100 agencies			
Newspaper	$ 1,910	$ 2,275	19.1%
Magazine	3,401	3,960	16.4%
Radio	1,485	1,691	13.9%
Network TV	7,407	8,127	9.7%
Spot TV	4,626	5,732	23.9%
Cable	256	330	28.9%
Other	2,654	3,077	15.9%
Total	$21,739	$25,192	15.9%
Top 500 agencies			
Newspaper	$ 2,740	$ 3,403	24.2%
Magazine	4,200	4,976	18.5%
Radio	2,060	2,501	21.4%
Network TV	7,746	8,579	10.8%
Spot TV	5,672	7,094	25.1%
Cable	306	431	40.8%
Other	4,173	5,210	24.9%
Total	$26,897	$32,194	19.7%

SOURCE: *Advertising Age,* March 26, 1987, p. 123.

**Exhibit 5   Media Software Technology, Inc.
Competitive Analysis as of June 1988**

Program: TV Prebuy

Product Features*	MST	Competitor			
		Nielsen	Tapscan	Donovan	On-Line
Range of applications	100	50	40	50	25
User friendliness	100	70	70	60	50
Graphics capability	100	90	80	0	30
Hardware requirements	Micro	Micro	Micro	T/Share	T/Share or Micro
Price/month	$250–4,000	$0–200	$250	Inc.	Variable
Number of clients	725	40	16	64	150

Program: Radio Prebuy

Product Features*	MST	Competitor		
		Tapscan	Marketron	On-Line
Range of applications	100	100	70	50
User friendliness	100	90	70	50
Graphics capability	100	75	60	30
Hardware requirements	Micro	Micro	T/Share	T/Share
Price/month	$150–3,600	$200	Variable	Variable
Number of clients	700	90	65	80

Program: Broadcast & Print Control

Product Features*	MST	Competitor	
		Adverse	Donovan
Range of applications	100	60	100
User friendliness	100	60	80
Graphics capability	—	—	—
Hardware requirements	Micro	Mini	Main
Price/month	$250–2,000	†	†
Number of clients	600	20	50

*Ratings of product features range 0–100.

†Prices tied to advertising billings. Estimate Donovan's annual revenues are between $30 and $35. Donovan dominant in New York City market.

Source: MST management estimates.

EXHIBIT 6   Broadcast Software Technology, Inc.
Competitive Analysis as of June 1988

Program: TV Sales Research

			Competitor			
*Product Features**	*BST*	*Marketron/ Arbitron*	*Soft Pedal*	*Nielsen*	*Tapscan*	*Katz*
Range of applications	100	75	40	40	40	20
User friendliness	100	60	85	80	70	30
Graphics capability	100	90	90	90	85	0
Hardware requirements	Micro	O-L/Micro	Micro	Micro	Micro	On-Line
Price/month	$400–925	$550	$550	$150	$400	Variable
Number of clients	180	100	72	12	5	120

Program: Avails & Proposals

			Competitor			
*Product Features**	*BST*	*Marketron/ Arbitron*	*Soft Pedal*	*Tapscan*	*Katz*	*Blair*	*Minipac*
Range of applications	100	130	60	75	140	140	140
User friendliness	100	60	85	70	30	30	30
Graphics capability	100	90	90	85	100	100	100
Hardware requirements	Micro	O-L/Micro	Micro	Micro	On-Line	On-Line	On-Line
Price/month	$400–1,050	$550	$550	$400	$1,500–1,800	$1,500–1,800	$1,500–1,800
Number of clients	210	52	78	5	120	90	260

*Ratings of product features range 0–100.
†Katz clients receive both functions together.
SOURCE: BST management estimates.

EXHIBIT 7   **Media Software Technology, Inc. Income Statement ($ in 000s)**

	1986	*1987*
Operating revenue	$5,360	$8,576
Operating expenses	4,278	5,771
Operating profit	1,082	2,805
Pension expense	(264)	(408)
Software writeoff (a)	(504)	(655)
Interest income (exp.)	(23)	4
Income before tax and extraordinary items	291	1,746
Tax expense	(186)	(637)
Cumulative effect of change in accounting (b)	0	185
Net Income	$ 105	$1,294

(a) 1986 — one time write-off of obsolete BST software. 1987 — full write-off of acquisition of perpetual rights to a facilities management software program for advertising agencies due to fraud on the seller's part.

(b) Change in timing of revenue recognition of the last month's licensing fee which is prepaid by each customer.

| | Historical Summary | | | | |
	1984	1985	1986	1987	1988(est)
MST—parent only					
Number of clients	90	170	346	600	870
Revenue	$626	$1,997	$3,769	$6,294	$9,637
BST					
Number of Clients	17	80	108	156	270
Revenue	$125	$ 924	$1,591	$2,282	$2,640

EXHIBIT 8   Media Software Technology, Inc. Balance Sheet ($ in 000s)

	1986	1987
Current assets		
Cash	$ 584	$ 612
Accounts receivable	545	1,087
Other assets	35	42
Total current assets	1,164	1,741
Other assets		
Equipment, net	265	308
Software, net	442	1,980
Due from officers		
and related parties	106	600
Other assets	29	181
Total assets	$2,006	$4,810
Current liabilities		
Notes payable	$ 0	$ 205
Accounts payable	330	332
Accrued pension expense	264	409
Current long-term debt	95	227
Current deferred taxes	151	0
Taxes payable	0	529
Due to related parties	322	182
Total current liabilities	1,162	1,884
Other liabilities		
Long-term debt	83	492
Deferred taxes	104	500
Deferred revenue	346	312
Other liabilities	78	29
Total liabilities	$1,773	$3,217
Shareholders' equity		
Common stock	1,099	1,196
Notes receivable for		
common stock repurchase	(104)	(90)
Retained earnings	(762)	487
Total stockholders' equity	233	1,593
Total liabilities and stockholders' equity	$2,006	$4,810

EXHIBIT 9   Media Software Technology, Inc. Cash Flow Statement ($ in 000s)

	1986	1987
Net income	$ 105	$1,294
Noncash charges		
Depreciation	115	134
Amortization of software	91	163
Software write-off	504	0
Deferred taxes	186	214
Other	98	(4)
Cash from operations	$1,099	$1,801
Changes in operating working capital		
Accounts receivable	(275)	(542)
Other assets	88	24
Notes payable	0	205
Accounts payable	142	2
Accrued pension expense	264	144
Taxes payable	0	529
Total	$ 219	$ 362
Increase in long-term debt	203	540
Issuance of common stock, net		
of notes receivable	(191)	53
Capital expenditures	(199)	(152)
Capitalized software development costs	(532)	(756)
Purchased software (a)	0	(971)
Increase in other assets	(106)	(661)
Decrease in due to related parties	0	(188)
Increase in cash	$ 493	$ 28

(a) 1987 — includes $1,626 purchases of new product rights and $655 write-off of facilities management program.

Exhibit 10   Media Software Technology, Inc., Financial Projections ($ in 000s)

	1988	*1989*	*1990*	*1991*	*1992*
Revenue					
MST*	$ 9,637	$16,094	$20,600	$25,750	$32,188
BST	2,640	2,983	3,222	3,351	3,384
Total	12,277	19,077	23,822	29,101	35,572
Operating profit					
MST*	3,710	6,438	8,652	10,944	14,098
BST	1,078	1,289	1,496	1,540	1,660
Total	4,788	7,726	10,148	12,484	15,758
Operating margin	39.0%	40.5%	42.6%	42.9%	44.3%
Pension expense	(480)	(480)	(480)	(480)	(480)
Pretax income	4,308	7,246	9,668	12,004	15,278
Tax expense (35%)	(1,508)	(2,536)	(3,384)	(4,201)	(5,347)
Net income	$ 2,800	$ 4,710	$ 6,284	$ 7,803	$ 9,931
Net margin	22.8%	24.7%	26.4%	26.8%	27.9%

*Parent Only

Assumptions:

MST—Revenues continue to increase for current product line. Average license fees decline over 5-year period reflecting competitive pressure. Attrition in current client base averages 5% per year. Revenue growth based primarily in new products for existing customers. Staff grows from 50 to 100 in 1991. Base salaries increase 7% and sales force grows from 7 to 10.

BST—License fees per TV broadcast client fall from $800 to $725 in 1991. Number of new clients drops off due to competitive pressures and market saturation. Sales force starts declining in 1990.

Exhibit 11   Key MST Personnel

Glenn DeKraker

Founder and chairman of MST and BST. He has devoted the past 18 years of his professional life to a series of entrepreneurial ventures. His early career was spent at an international electronics firm. He has focused his ventures in the areas of advertising and pattern recognition monitoring technology. Mr. DeKraker holds a degree in electrical engineering from Stanford University.

Roger Harris

President of BST. He was one of the original founders of Arbitron Ratings Co. and is a recognized expert in market information for the broadcast industry. He has also worked as a consultant and station manager. Mr. Harris attended Whittier College.

Dennis Martin

Executive vice president of MST. Prior to joining MST in 1986, he was an associate professor at the University of Denver Business School following an assignment as the marketing and advertising research specialist at the Federal Trade Commission. He also was president of a marketing research and consulting firm. Mr. Martin holds a PhD from the University of Florida.

Joe O'Leary

Executive vice president of MST. He is in charge of MST's sales operations. He is an experienced sales manager having served in that capacity in two previous ventures with Mr. DeKraker. Mr. O'Leary holds a degree in economics from Blackburn University.

David Warner

Executive vice president of BST. He heads up the sales and marketing effort. Prior to joining BST, he spent 14 years as a general sales manager of TV stations. He is a graduate of Penn State University.

EXHIBIT 12   **Dillingham Data Corporation Financial Statements**
($ in 000s)

1987 Income Statement

Revenue	$ 39,853
Cost of sales	(13,400)
Gross profit	26,453
Operating expenses	(19,561)
Operating profit	6,892
Depreciation	(3,509)
Amortization of noncompete agreements	(422)
Other	148
EBIT	3,109
Interest income	46
Goodwill amortization	(614)
Pretax income	$ 2,541

1987 Balance Sheet

Cash	$ 2,989	Accounts payable	$ 1,862
Accounts receivable	5,651	Notes payable	1,333
Inventory	610	Other	1,064
Other	251		
		Current liabilities	4,259
Current assets	9,501		
		Long-term debt	3,418
Investments and other	1,579	Deferred taxes	0
PPE, net	10,734		
Goodwill	13,525	Equity	27,662
Total assets	$35,339	Total liabilities and equity	$35,339

EXHIBIT 13   MST / Dillingham Merger Financial Projections ($ in 000s)

	6 Months 1988	1989	1990	1991	1992
Revenue					
MST	$ 7,059	$19,077	$23,822	$29,101	$35,572
Dillingham	20,138	42,120	42,120	42,120	42,120
Total	$27,197	$61,197	$65,942	$71,221	$77,692
EBIT					
MST	2,826	7,246	9,668	12,004	15,278
Dillingham	1,745	4,978	6,094	7,433	9,040
Total	$ 4,571	$12,224	$15,762	$19,437	$24,318
Interest income	82	179	0	158	1,099
Interest expense	(858)	(1,385)	(665)	(185)	(89)
Pretax income	3,795	11,018	15,097	19,410	25,328
Tax expense (35%)	(1,328)	(3,856)	(5,284)	(6,794)	(8,865)
Goodwill amortization	(338)	(678)	(678)	(678)	(678)
Net income	$ 2,129	$ 6,484	$ 9,135	$11,939	$15,785
Depreciation and amortization	2,334	4,246	4,367	4,475	4,518
Capital expenditures	(1,398)	(2,899)	(2,935)	(2,832)	(2,767)
Required working capital	(642)	(1,609)	(1,181)	(1,321)	(1,633)
Cash flow available for debt service	2,423	6,222	9,386	12,261	15,903
Subordinated debt repayment	(2,423)	(6,222)	(9,386)	(2,369)	0
Net cash flow	$ 0	$ 0	$ 0	$ 9,891	$15,903

EXHIBIT 14   LCI Earnout Provision ($ in 000s)

In each year an earnout payment will be made only if the cumulative earnings before tax (EBT) threshold for such year as set forth below has been met. Such payments will be calculated as percentages of revenue above and below the revenue trigger amount for such year. The aggregate earnout payment in any given year when added to all prior earnout payments will not exceed the maximum cumulative payment amount applicable to such year as set forth below.

Year	Cumulative EBT Threshold	Revenue Trigger	Payment as % of Revenue at or below Trigger	Additional Payment as % of Revenue above Trigger	Maximum Cumulative Payment
1988	$ 3,840	$ 9,840	8.0%	32.0%	$ 2,280
1989	9,480	17,640	8.0%	32.0%	8,160
1990	17,040	21,960	12.0%	30.0%	19,800
1991	26,280	26,640	12.0%	30.0%	36,120
1992	38,160	31,680	12.0%	30.0%	58,800

4–7 HOWARD HEAD AND PRINCE MANUFACTURING INC.

"We can own the tennis world," Howard Head told Prince Company President Jack Murray and Jim Baugh, director of marketing. Unfortunately, Mr. Head was not sure that these key people shared his dramatic vision. They were quite satisfied with Prince's recent 100 percent growth rate, and they were not inclined to risk change.

In the spring of 1982, Head had begun to think seriously about the future of Prince. Having already achieved success with his oversized Prince Classic tennis racket, he now envisioned an empire greater than any the industry had ever seen. A small company called Kennex had just approached Mr. Head to ask if Prince would consider promoting its rackets. Although Head found the Kennex racket to be an "excellent and aesthetically beautiful product," he declined the offer. As he put it:

> I was afraid to accept Kennex's offer for fear that word would get out that I was promoting a midsize racket that wasn't mine. Unfortunately, Prince company management didn't want to listen to my ideas for an expanded line of Prince tennis rackets. I had written about 80 pages of company objectives which laid it all out very clearly. However, Prince's director of marketing was afraid that plans for promotion of the 110 would falter unless the company ruled out consideration of any size other than the 110. He felt that a leak concerning the possible consideration of any other size would be detrimental to Prince's marketing plans. That was why he thought we should tell Kennex no. I, on the other hand, declined their offer mainly because I had no interest in marketing any racket other than one designed by, built by, and carrying the name of Prince.

Mr. Head's company objectives included plans for aggressive experimentation with a series of 93- and 100-square-inch rackets to go along with the original 110-size Prince. With the standard racket size of 70 square inches on one end and Head's successful 110-square-inch Prince on the other, Head felt sure that there was a market for these midsize versions, and he didn't want to miss out on an obvious opportunity. Head's objectives told of his "growing feeling that Prince should expand to a full line of 93s and 100s." He saw the possibility for Prince to "move at once to blanket the entire tennis market, simply taking over and making all other rackets obsolete and unnecessary." This was Head's plan, but he felt that his own company was getting in the way.

This case was prepared by Susan Harmeling under the direction of Howard H. Stevenson.
Harvard Business School Case 9–388–079

Howard Head also felt that Prince's officers were taking an overcautious stance with regard to his plans for expanding the company's telephone-answering force to include computerized information on every dealer. In addition, he envisioned other improvements that involved Prince's public relations and customer service departments. He wanted to fine-tune Prince to the very limits, but his own people were stopping him.

Head's now famous oversized racket had taken his young company from $1 million to $35 million sales in just five years, and 1982 projections were for gross sales of close to $60 million. (See **Exhibit 1** for Prince Financial Summary). Should he, at the age of 68, set forth to implement these ambitious goals, or should he sell while the value of his business was on the rise? Should he finally ''give up the 'thing' world and move into the 'people' world,'' breaking his addiction to the ''powerful drug of creativity''?

Head certainly wasn't thinking of going into business again when the Head Ski Company and its famous name were sold to AMF, Inc., in 1969 for $16 million. On the contrary, he was ready to throw in the towel, for success was sweet, but it was not without its strains. ''If a logo had to be designed,'' Head explained, ''I did it. If a selling tour had to be made, I did it. If the factory floor had to be swept, I did it. You can't run a frantically expanding business that way.'' Maybe not, but the inventor had done something right, for ''when AMF took the broom out of Head's hands in 1969, he personally realized more than $4 million in cash.''[1] The opening chapter of his amazing story was complete, and Howard Head's sometimes frustrating experience with his first company was history. Or was it? Actually, this initial business experience with Head Ski Company proved to be a valuable asset as Mr. Head set out a few years later to create yet another superior sporting implement. But did he really want to invest the time and energy in Prince Manufacturing Inc. to take it to the heights he knew were possible?

Prince Company History

Howard Head came to the tennis industry largely by accident. He initially made himself known in recreational circles in the early 50s when he designed the first metal ski. As an aircraft engineer during World War II, he had become an expert on the various uses of aluminum. Using this knowledge, he produced a metal sandwich ski in 1950, which, by the 1960s, had all but crushed its wooden competitors. As Head described it,

> This success had nothing to do with promotion, but stemmed from the fact that the product was almost magically easier to use, making the sport accessible to millions of skiers. Heretofore the extreme difficulty of skiing on the laminated hickory skis of the prior era had limited the sport to the hearty elite. The Head ski was later credited as a key factor in the growth of the sport from perhaps a total of 10,000 U.S. skiers in the 1940s to millions in the 1960s.

---

[1]Walter McQuade, ''Prince Triumphant,'' *Fortune,* February 22, 1982.

Head retired in 1970, a year after selling Head Ski Company to AMF, but his retirement didn't last very long. As he told the story:

I put in a court and decided to take up tennis, but I found that it wasn't as easy as I thought. Even after I took a lot of lessons, I still had trouble. . . .

My tennis pro must have gotten tired of trying to hit against me, because in the summer of 1971 he suggested that I get a tennis ball machine to practice against. He put me in touch with a little company called Prince up in Princeton, New Jersey. I called them up and told them I wanted to buy one of their machines. They said it would cost $285.00. I said, "All right, you put a machine on the truck today, and I'll put a check in the mail today." That's the way we got started.

They sent a machine down, and I recognized almost immediately that it was a carefully thought-through and well-designed piece of equipment, but about as crude as the first Head ski. Everything went wrong with it: the ball would jam, the ball would glunk, the ball would drop. *Everything* went wrong—I spoke with them over the phone and within two months I joined the company as chairman of the board and de facto chief engineer. I had gotten into a thing I loved, which was debugging and perfecting a piece of equipment. A year and a half later, Prince had captured half the ball machine business.

One indication of Howard Head's ongoing devotion to innovation and quality was illustrated by this initial contact with the Prince Manufacturing Company. He did it the service of fixing its flawed product before he had invested in the business. In October of 1971, after Head had successfully "debugged" the Prince ball machine, he bought 27 percent of the company for $27,000. (See **Exhibit 2** for Chronological Outline and 1971 Balance Sheet.) The company averaged a 15 percent net profit for the first three years from 1972 to 1974. Head explained:

The reason we were able to do that was because our business was based on the ultrasimple process of someone calling up and saying, "Can I buy a machine?" and we would say, "Sure, put a check in the mail, and when it hits our mailbox we will ship you a machine." We basically had no distributors and no advertising. We just waited for checks and then shipped the machines so we could market the machines at low cost and make a whopping profit.

That ball machine company taught me how to run a profitable business because it was so simple. Furthermore, I was just sitting down in Baltimore smiling and saying, "Well done, fellows; it's great to see this money piling up. . . ."

Mr. Head explained that he had not been particularly anxious to get back into business, and it was clearly not a financial necessity. Rather, it was the result of his own personal struggle with existing sports equipment. This was the crux of Howard Head's whole motivation . . . to fine-tune the existing equipment for each individual user. Head's first invention transformed the ski world, and Prince rackets opened up the same possibilities in the tennis world. As Head put it, "God had smiled on two occasions."

Mal Bash, who came to Prince in 1974 as quality control manager and who was later promoted to chief engineer and chief of manufacturing, had this to say about Howard Head's early role with the company:

We had this fellow, Howard Head, who came up once in a while and looked around and helped with the company. He offered suggestions on how to improve our product, our ball machine. He came up from Baltimore at least once a month and spent a day or two. I remember we had a lot of discussions about the ball-throwing machine and the ways he thought it could be improved. He was always asking us to try different things. He would never accept a no. If I said I couldn't do something, he'd ask why? I'd say it wouldn't work, and he'd ask why? again. I found it quite challenging, and it often led to accomplishing things I didn't think could be accomplished.

Mr. Bash went on to tell of Prince's later attempts to develop a more advanced model of the ball machine. It was to be called the Professional and was to have a greater ball capacity. There were problems with the design of this model—the balls constantly jammed as they were feeding into the machine, and as Bash pointed out, it was the "eleventh hour." The company had presold these machines and were now ready to go into production before the jamming problem was fixed. Bash recalled that Howard Head averted the crisis.

> There was a little part of the machine called the spring pin, which kept more than one ball at a time from feeding into the machine. One of Howard's suggestions was to take a couple of spring pins and bolt them into the top of the rotor. He thought it would stir everything up enough to prevent the jamming. I didn't think it would work, but Howard insisted that it would. Sure enough, it solved the problem, and we went into production the next day.

Howard Head's enthusiasm for fixing things, for creating a better product, had started a generation earlier when a different sport caught his fancy. From skis to ball machines to rackets, Head explained that his success was the result of an obsession with performance. He said:

> Sports-minded people will simply gravitate toward a product that works better. Give them a better piece of fly casting equipment, and they will buy that fishing rod. Give them a better ski-down-the-hill design, and they will buy that ski. A better tennis ball hitting implement, and they'll buy that racket when it becomes available. It's performance that counts, and word of mouth that sells the product. No amount of promotion or advertising or other pizazz will alter this fundamental truth.

Tennis—The Industry

During the late 1960s and the early 1970s, another revolution was taking place in tennis, which had nothing to do with equipment. Gone were the days when the sport was synonymous with country clubs, white garb, strawberries and champagne; tennis was no longer reserved for the elite. Courts were springing up everywhere, and amateur athletes from all walks of life were heading out in droves with rackets in hand. Tennis was starting to sell, and as the sport moved from exclusive circles into the mass market, the possibilities for innovation were endless. As early as the mid-1960s, tennis was clearly "in." Courts were being built in record numbers, especially indoor courts made to accommodate the serious, year-round player. A 1965 *Business Week* article noted the trend:

> Tennis, anyone? This winter, the answer has been a resounding "yes." From its traditional home in grim and drafty armories scarred by National Guard drills, indoor tennis has moved

into plush, well-lighted clubs and has attracted thousands of new players. ''The demand is so great the new courts aren't even coming close to taking care of all the people who want to play,'' says an official of the U.S. Lawn Tennis Association. A spokesman for Wilson Sporting Goods estimates that there are some 200 indoor courts in the country, most of them built in the last five years, and about one third of them in the last 12 months.

By 1966, *Newsweek* estimated that there were 8.5 million tennis players in the United States, and among this group, the population of ''insiders'' was growing rapidly.

This was just the beginning of the craze. The long-standing tradition of ''tennis whites'' was made obsolete in the late 1960s. ''I'm a progressive,'' claimed Arthur Ashe when he showed up at a January 1968 exhibition match wearing snazzy powder blue shorts and shirt. And though many U.S. clubs were still sticking to the old belief that ''whites were right,'' even some of the most traditional members of the tennis community had decided to jump on the bandwagon, as *Time* reported in February of 1968:

> Said Walter Elcock, president of Brookline's Longwood Cricket Club where players have worn only whites since 1877, ''So many changes are being made in tennis, I can't see that a few more will hurt the game. I might even try a colored outfit myself.''

The fashion trend from whites to brights signified another trend taking place in the world of tennis, which had deeper implications for the future of the sport. By the early 1970s, things had changed in a sport that had remained the same for a long time. In the summer of 1972, *Life* magazine reported that 100 years earlier, ''There was just one tennis court in the United States. It was shaped like an hourglass, as were the ladies playing on it.'' By the time the article was published, there were an estimated 100,000 U.S. courts in all and 5,000 new ones being added each year.

Whatever the reasons, the trend continued, and by the mid-1970s, it looked as though there was no end in sight. Was it really more than a passing fad? A 1974 *Sports Illustrated* article claimed, ''Now Everybody Has the Bug,'' and warned:

> Once, like gout, it afflicted only the rich, but today tennis fever is epidemic. And it will sneak up on you, too, if you don't watch out.
>
> Twenty-one million Americans, drawn like fruit flies to a vast ripening vine, now play tennis at one level of incompetence or another. This national mania is not without value. Golf courses are no longer as crowded, for one thing, and there aren't as many drunks driving home after a match. Unlike golf, tennis has no par to alert man to his inferiority. He can reach new depths without the need of a 19th-hole elixir to ease the pain. A swig of Gatorade will usually do it.

Of course, all the enthusiasm generated by the sport brought the prospect of endless opportunity for inventors, businessmen, and consumers alike. A 1976 *Time* magazine article called ''Those Super Rackets'' told of the increasing popularity of rackets ''designed to bestow court greatness on weekend hackers.''

> The names—YFG-50, Boron XT, and the XRC—conjure up visions of supersonic test plans or supersonic racing cars. But the sobriquets belong to tennis rackets, crafted in strange shapes of exotic materials.

In search of a bigger "sweet spot," more power, and control, manufacturers have imbedded boron fibers in an epoxy matrix, reinforced nylon throat pieces with quartz, turned to builders of nuclear reactors for ultrasonic welding techniques, and altered the spacing of strings. The physics laboratories at Princeton where Albert Einstein once worked have been used to experiment with variants of torque and longitudinal flex.

There was a technological revolution occurring in the tennis world during the mid-1970s, reflecting the will of inventors who felt that if colored clothes and neighborhood courts were gaining acceptance, then tennis rackets would have to keep up with the times. Head was one of those inventors. Yet precisely as this period of technological innovation was reaching its peak, the popularity of the sport began to decline sharply. Prince came on the scene in the midst of the turmoil:

> The enormous, swelling U.S. tennis boom peaked in the late 1970s; total sales of rackets dropped precipitously from 8.3 million in 1977 to 4.9 million the next year and continued to drift downward to 3.2 million in 1981. (See **Exhibit 3**.)
>
> The manufacturers are anything but sure why this has happened, but they cite a couple of possibilities. The sport became such a social craze that many would-be players bought rackets before they found it wasn't as easy on the court as it seemed to be on TV. Beyond that, the manufacturers point to the cyclical nature of individual sports in general. Among recent fads, roller skating has hit the skids and racquetball has fizzled (ruining a secondary market for many racket manufacturers). Today, indoor exercise equipment is the rage.
>
> The simultaneous collapse of the market and the fact that the oversize Prince was just beginning its roll, left the giants of the industry searching for defensive strategies. The small, tightly strung world of tennis-racket makers is haunted by a paralyzing question: how to compete with that peculiar, triumphant slammer of the fuzzy yellow ball, the oversized Prince racket. Invented just six years ago by technological iconoclast Howard Head and at first considered nothing more than an amusing novelty, the Prince last year grabbed the commanding share of the high-priced market.
>
> Prince's share of the market for upper-bracket rackets—those selling for $50 and up— exploded from 8.5 percent in 1979 to 30.7 percent in 1981—AMF Head's share meanwhile slipped from 31.6 percent to 26.3 percent while Wilson's fell like a dropshot, from 19.2 percent to 10.7 percent.
>
> This left industry strongmen trying to persuade customers to trade up to more expensive "weapons," as manufacturers call rackets.[2]

Still, not everyone was convinced that Prince was the ultimate weapon. While many players swore by their new rackets, most experts during this peak period of experimentation agreed with Chicago tennis pro Calvin Head (clearly no relation to Howard Head), who claimed that the advantages of the new designs and materials were largely psychological.

"We're all trying to find that little secret, but it's all in the mind," he said. Another pro, disgusted by the stampede to new rackets, said, "People will do anything to improve their game except work on their strokes."

Head's oversized racket enjoyed its immediate success even though this professional skepticism had combined with a general decline in the tennis industry. Prince

---

[2]Ibid.

succeeded even though a majority of pros agreed with renowned California teacher Vic Braden who insisted:

> I don't care what kind of racket it is. I once saw Bobby Riggs beat a guy with a broom . . . the only difference the Prince rackets make is that now when you serve, you will hit both your legs rather than just one.

Design—Prince Rackets

Head arrived at the ultimate design of his oversized racket after a period of persistent trial and error. This was not, however, his first shot at racket design, as *Fortune* magazine noted:

> Head had fooled with tennis rackets before. While still with the Head Company, he had taken to shaving the wooden rims of cheap Korean imports and tacking on aluminum siding in an unsuccessful attempt to strengthen them. By 1974, he was frustrated enough with his own game to give the racket another try. It was either that or take up golf, and Head hated golf.

Just as he had looked for a ski that would keep him from tumbling down the mountain, he was searching for a racket that would save him from embarrassment on the court:

> The parallel story in Prince, to compare it with Head, was that I was simply looking for a racket that would be more stable to an off-center hit. I tried to fix it by putting weights on the rim of the frame. It didn't work.
>
> Then, I had a genuine breakthrough. I realized that I shouldn't add any weight, but should spread the weight out. I knew this would increase the inertia and therefore, the stability of the racket. That was my invention.

The only problem was that the result was a funny-looking contraception resembling a snowshoe, not a tennis racket. As one journalist observed:

> He knew it sounded silly (who would play with a paddle the size and shape of a snowshoe?), but he had to give it a try. The result was a racket two inches wider than conventional models, made of aluminum to bear the extra strain of the longer strings. Displeased with the too-round lines of his first designs, Head extended the strung area of the racket into the handle region to soften the curve.[3]

Although Howard Head's Prince racket was later expanded into various materials (his graphite racket was the first of its kind), it was the new shape as well as the dimensions of the racket that were its engineering breakthroughs. By making the racket only two inches wider with a three inch longer hitting surface in the throat, Head had increased the torsional stability of the racket and the size of its "sweet spot" by an extraordinary degree. The earlier 70-square-inch racket had a mean way of twisting in the hand to an off-center hit. As Head described it, "Suddenly, a sport, which had a somewhat limited following because of technical difficulty, became accessible to a

---

[3]Arthur Fisher, "Super Racket," *Popular Science,* Spring 1977.

much broader range of players. The market expanded, and the sport was just plain more fun. The parallels with the metal ski were obvious.'' But while the new racket worked very well, its appearance, as one tennis buff wrote, sparked a very important question:

> ''Is it legal?''
>
> That's what they asked me when I stepped onto a tennis court brandishing the new Prince racket. It's not a surprising reaction. For the last 75 years or so, tennis players had been used to seeing rackets of roughly the same size and shape. The first really radical change in that geometry is the Prince—an outlandish object resembling a deranged snowshoe. The surface area of the head is a full 50 percent larger than that of a conventional design. Reason? To let you hit more balls and hit them better.
>
> Is that legal? Absolutely. The rules of the game specify all sorts of things about the court, the net, and the ball, but state only that the player must strike the ball with an ''implement.'' You are entitled, if the fancy takes you, to whack a tennis ball with a pool cue, butterfly net, or the door off an old pickup.[4]

The Patent

It was legal, yes, but the patent office initially said that it wasn't a novel enough idea to merit the issuance of a coveted patent. It did no good simply to assert that this racket was better than the old fashioned kind. The question, ''How much better?'' had to be answered, and Howard Head was not to be denied. After working with Princeton consulting engineer Ken Wright, Head determined that the racket's ''coefficient of restitution'' could supply the quantifying data. (The coefficient of restitution at any spot on the racket head is the ratio of the velocity of the incoming ball as compared with the velocity of the ball leaving the strings.)

Using high-speed photography, he measured the size of where the coefficients were .3 and .4 and .5 on his new Prince racket as compared with these same zones on ordinary rackets. He found that in every case, these zones on the Prince were three to four times bigger than corresponding zones on conventional 70-square-inch rackets. He even found that there was one zone of .6 on his new racket that didn't exist on an ordinary racket. That was the crucial point. There was now measurable proof that at least by one criterion the Prince racket produced more than three times improved performance with only a 60 percent increase in area. (See **Exhibit 4**.)

Students of business might have thought it strange that Head seemed to have a great idea that he was taking out and showing to anyone he came in contact with, apparently unconcerned that his invention could be copied. But his experience in development led him to take the necessary precautions of meticulous documentation and also to go through the required legal groundwork. He had actually applied for patents as early as 1974, and the patent was finally issued as Patent No. 3,999,756 in May of 1976. It was good for 17 years, covered a wide range of racket shapes and sizes, and was, according to a 1977 *Popular Science* article, ''the broadest tennis racket patent ever granted.''

---

[4]Ibid.

Where the Prince was not able to achieve patent protection, for example in Germany and Japan, other companies began to produce rackets of Prince's size and shape. Prince's lawyers were, however, able to secure judgments that prevented those adaptations from being sold in the United States, causing one competitor to muse, "Howard's brilliance really shone at its brightest when he got that patent. It's like getting a patent on a size 9 shoe."[5]

Head explained that this discovery was more "a bit of black magic" than a work of brilliance. He had given the Prince its new shape with the intention of achieving a more aesthetically pleasing design, and it was this alteration that had made the racket's sweet spot 3.78 times bigger than that of a conventional racket. The enlarged sweet spot, combined with the racket's wider head, gave players four times the chance of hearing the clear sound of a center hit shot.

With good feedback from experimental rackets in the field, and with patent in sight, the decision was made to move Prince full speed ahead into the racket business. It was none too soon, as Howard Head explained:

> It was a dramatic moment in this little million-dollar company called Prince Ball Machine Company. We had noticed that our sales of ball machines had remained virtually constant for the last year but that profits had diminished from 15 to 7 percent. Luckily we faced up to the fact that the problem was simply an inherent limit to the size of the ball machine market. There just weren't that many players out there who were interested in that form of practice. The market wasn't there.

Sales of the Prince racket took off just in time, for it had become clear that the ball machine market was saturated. Head had discovered two things simultaneously: that he could not propel the ball machine onto an expanding sales trajectory, and that the potential for racket sales was enormous. The Prince racket had picked up precisely where the ball machine left off, but if Mr. Head was to realize the racket's potential, there were still many obstacles to overcome.

Marketing

Howard Head consistently emphasized the fact that at no time in his career did he stress a growth imperative:

> I will never try to make my company grow for growth's sake, but I have people who do—marketing people. My compulsion is simply to make the best sliding-down-the-hill implement for skiers and the best tennis ball hitting implement for tennis players, and in both sports a different piece of equipment fine tuned to each category of athlete.

At Prince, Head did encounter problems in achieving the latter aim—of providing a racket for players in all segments of the market:

> In 1976, we went into production. In that year, we sold 70,000 rackets, in 1977 we sold 160,000 rackets. I expected to be going up to 250,000 and then 400,000 in the years following, but suddenly there was a leveling off.

---

[5]McQuade, "Prince Triumphant."

Why this slowdown? For one thing, very few young people were buying the new rackets, including the oversized Prince. A Beverly Hills tennis shop salesman reported in November of 1976 that most Prince sales were made to men over 40 "searching for a tennis fountain of youth." A young tournament player summed it up by saying, "When somebody shows up with a fancy stick, some other kid will say, 'Oh you need a bionic racket, huh?' Nobody wants to look like a sissy."

Head was well aware of this problem:

Sitting afar I had the perspective and the vision to know that the problem with this racket was that it was being swallowed up by lady club players, elderly men, and beginners, but it was not being accepted by professionals, young college players, or class A players. It finally sank into me, and more quickly than in the case of the Head skis, that these guys had a valid complaint that the rackets were too spongy, strung too softly, and had a frame that was too flexible for the hard hitting young players.

Mal Bash explained further:

I can remember in early 1976 that we started to get complaints from our customers. They said that the racket didn't play well, that it vibrated badly, and that it made noises when the ball was hit.

Howard and I did some investigation on the problem and came to the conclusion that Prince rackets were not being strung tightly enough. The Prince needed to be strung 15 to 20 pounds tighter than a conventional racket.

So we wrote and rewrote extensive stringing instructions in an attempt to educate the consumer on how the racket should be strung.

Then people started complaining that the racket couldn't be strung on certain machines. Howard said that we had to solve this problem, and I said that I didn't know enough about all of the different kinds of machines. He told me to go out and buy them all, and I did just that. After stringing the rackets on every single machine on the market, we modified our stringing instructions accordingly.

This was not enough, however, to attract the segment of the market that was missing. Mr. Head described the aging group of players who still composed the majority of his most visible customers:

These guys were moderately gentle players anyhow—they were either seniors or getting along. They were not the kind of people who were going to lead the class A players, the younger touring pros, the college players, and the juniors to us. In any case, we increased the string tension, but it still did not attract many of the really good players to our racket. About 1977, I felt this slowdown taking place, and I decided that we must go on a search for a new racket, a stiffer racket with a stiffer frame and a frame that could be strung much tighter. I approached that in two ways. We wanted the tubular aluminum frame racket, which later became the Prince Pro, and we wanted the graphite fiber racket, which later became the Prince Graphite.

Just a couple of years later, Mr. Head's goals for reversing this slowdown in sales had more than been realized, and while he may never have stressed growth per se, he had a strong feeling that even more people should be using his racket. The slowdown was over, and he was now dreaming of even greater market penetration and hoping that every tennis player in the world would soon be using a Prince. The Pro and the Graphite were selling like hotcakes, adding to the Classic's steady share. Further growth seemed inevitable, prompting Head to envision an expanded line of new rackets in an assortment of different sizes, shapes, and colors designed to cater to players in every category. His main obstacle in achieving this goal would come from within his own company:

> In 1979, we were past our leveling-off period, with sales soaring from $9 million to $18 million and with a great increase in profits and margins. It was late in the fall of 1980 that my president, who was a superlative administrator, organizer, leader, and motivator said to me, "Howard you ought to look through the profit plan." I said all right, and I looked at it. I said, "Tell me what it means, give me the gist of it, and what is our sales increase projected for next year?" "Howard, we are projecting a 25 percent sales increase," he said, and I said, "Say that again!" He said, "You know, Howard, I am responsible for the company, and I am working for you, and I don't want to overpromise you. I am willing to project a 25 percent sales increase, and I'm sure we may do even better."
>
> I said, "I don't think I'm hearing you right. We grew 100 percent last year, didn't we?" He said, "Yes, but Howard, I don't want to promise you too much." Honest to God, my head started swimming. I told him that we were going to project a continuation of the 100 percent growth and that I would be responsible for it. That's how the thing went. Where would we have gotten the product to sell if I hadn't pressed the issue?

For Mr. Head, the word *marketing* conjured up images of a mind-set very different from his own. When asked about the marketing department of his company, he responded:

> It is not my favorite area just because of the kind of thinking they do. They are much more timid than I would be if I were in the marketing department. If I felt that we could make a better tennis ball hitting implement for a wider number of players, I would not be worried about the fact that the image of Prince is a 110-size racket. I would make the better implement first and worry about the marketing effect later. I don't like the word *marketing*, but I do like products.

Mr. Head's ongoing obsession with simplicity and with the efficient delivery of product to consumer was also evident in his attitude toward distributors and sales representatives:

> Past experience led us to conclude that marketing through distributors was an error and that we should standardize on shipment through the home office in Princeton.
>
> The country was divided quite early into about eight territories with a sales rep from each area in charge. Some of these were from big organizations and some were individual reps, but this is not an area in which I have been strongly interested. It has remained my conviction that the product either sells itself or it doesn't.

Manufacturing

It was in the area of manufacturing that Howard Head had learned perhaps the most valuable lesson of his years at the Head Ski Company. The time and energy wasted on problems related to manufacturing was said to be one of the main reasons that Mr. Head, so accustomed to being at the front of the pack, was kept from capitalizing on a major technological breakthrough in ski design. He said:

If we had not been doing our own manufacturing, we could have ordered this company and that company to do research and switch us over into fiberglass. The fact is that we were unable to do that fast enough. I think I knew that since I had this compulsion to direct everything and do everything myself that I would not succeed in that conversion.

The second time around, he realized the importance of doing what he did best and letting someone else do the rest. He explained:

At Prince, we do not waste our energies on the frustration of manufacturing. At Head, we ate ourselves up in the manufacturing process I had invented, and we remained total amateurs at it. In the case of Prince, our manufacturing is done exclusively by pros responsible for their own work.

At the beginning, these "pros" were the Maark Corporation, no strangers to Mr. Head. Late in the 1960s, during his final days at the Head Ski Company, Howard Head became interested in tennis and began selling conventional-sized aluminum rackets under the Head label. He had the rackets made to specification by Maark, an aluminum designer and fabricator near Princeton, New Jersey.

In 1974, when Prince manufacturing was ready to begin selling the oversized racket, Head again turned to his friends at Maark to manufacture the first model, known as the Prince Classic.

Head's previous relationship with Maark proved invaluable. As he once said, he would have been too tired to start the project from scratch had he not known someone who could make that first batch of rackets for him. After presenting the idea of the Prince racket to Prince's board of directors in the fall of 1974, the decision was made to get some test rackets produced by Maark the following year. When asked what kind of expenditure that involved, Head explained the nature of this "strategic alliance":

Maark was smart. They wouldn't charge me a cent for the first experimental racket, nor for the next 6, nor for the final 100 experimental rackets that we needed for confirmation. They were putting me under a moral obligation so that if this racket worked they were going to get the business.

They knew that I was trustworthy, and I think they thought from my history that, goofy as this thing looked, I must have had a good reason for pursuing it. My track record with Head skis was a good one.

Maark's initial pricing policy paid off well. They developed a great relationship with Prince, and they supplied the first production Prince racket, which was known as the Classic. They made it from aluminum extrusion of their own design. It was a good serviceable frame and reached wide acceptance with the beginner and the average player. However, this is the racket that turned out to be too flexible and was unable to be strung tightly enough to make it acceptable to the good player.

In 1978, aware of the flattening in sales and the need for a stiffer racket that would withstand tighter stringing, Mal Bash went to Maark and asked it to make a tubular racket as opposed to the extruded frame. Maark rejected this design. Bash became indignant at Maark's rejection of his plans for the new racket. As he explained it:

I walked out of the meeting at that point. I was really feeling like I was going down the wrong track. Here were two guys who had made and designed the first really successful aluminum racket (the Head Pro), and both of these guys had previously come from Alcoa. They had a lot of knowledge about aluminum, but they were just too old and tired to listen.

Head explained the ramifications:

> Maark was getting reasonably fat and they were enjoying our relationship with them. Then we came to them with a change which we knew was the future of the tennis racket world. This is like it was with Head back in 1965 when I knew in my gut that the wave of the future was going to be the fiberglass ski. But we were unable to make the leap to a totally new technology. This is what was happening with Maark.

The people at Prince knew they needed a tubular aluminum frame. But where would they get it? Mal Bash looked through the *Thomas Registry* and contacted 15 to 20 aluminum fabricators. They all said they were not interested because the new design would be too prone to stress corrosion, a propensity toward internal cracking. Bash then tried Alcoa itself but it wouldn't do it. So he reached out overseas and found the largest tennis racket manufacturer in the world in Taiwan, Kunnan Lo. Kunnan produced beautifully crafted rackets but only in cheap soft alloys. It knew nothing of the high-tempered alloy that Prince would need for its new tubular frame. Head explained how they finally got the product they were looking for:

> Almost at wit's end, Bash thought of an extremely imaginative solution. He decided that what we had to do was to buy high-strength aluminum tubing from Alcoa who would draw it for us, put it in an intermediate temper condition, and ship it over to Taiwan. We would then have Kunnan Lo take over to form the racket for us, put on the handle, anodize it, polish it, put on all the cosmetics, and ship it back to America where we would sell them. The best thing is that we made Kunnan Lo responsible for working its way successfully through the stress corrosion problem so we didn't have to worry about it. We didn't go to Taiwan because we could get rackets cheaper there; we went to Taiwan because the work ethic was so strong. I still remember watching them in that plant—they were dedicated to their work the way earlier American craftsmen were. Furthermore, they demonstrated an entrepreneurial capacity to work their way successfully through all problems.

Howard Head and Mal Bash breathed a gigantic sigh of relief when their relationship with Kunnan Lo was firmly established and they could get an unlimited supply of rackets from the company. Once established with Kunnan Lo, the Maark association continued out of an old loyalty, but it was no longer essential to the survival of Prince. Eventually, the relationship with Maark broke down altogether. This was at least in part due to a strange turn of events. A year after Maark had begun to manufacture the Prince Classic, it was acquired by AMF and so, incestuous though it seemed, Prince and Head rackets were popping out of the shipping door of the same factory.

With the supply problems of the tubular aluminum alloy for the Prince Pro out of the way, Prince turned its attention to the possibility of a graphite racket that, in some respects, would outperform even the Pro in stiffness and resilience. It got the first rackets produced by a large American company. The racket was immediately successful, which led to a small crisis for Prince. The supplier abruptly tried to hold Prince up with an arbitrary 50 percent price increase. Mal Bash solved the problem by withdrawing all the tooling from the company and trucking it down the road to another outfit called Grafalloy who, even though its experience had been solely in graphite golf club shafts, was willing to take on tennis racket design. The transition was successfully completed.

With the advent of the superior Pro and Graphite models, Howard Head had attracted the kind of young professional and college players for whom he had designed this new product.

Mr. Head's success in achieving this end was perhaps best demonstrated by the success of Pam Shriver who, with Prince Pro in hand, became the youngest player ever to get to the finals of the U.S. Open, beating Martina Navratilova along the way. The Prince Graphite was now enjoying a strong position on the market, boosting sales out of the previous slump. Head proudly told the story:

> In 1980, we had profits of $2 million on $18 million in sales. The very next year, with the new rackets, sales doubled again to $34 million with profits of $4.5 million, which is 15 percent after taxes.

Finance

In the area of finance, Prince was vastly different from the Head Ski Company. Head Ski was financed initially with $6,000 from Howard Head's personal funds.

During the winter, he had moved into a $20-a-month basement apartment, living in his father's old overcoat when his wore out. He borrowed money, and when that ran out, he could no longer pay the airplane mechanics who had been helping him. They worked for over a year without a cent of pay.

But through the next two years, when ski after ski failed, they labored with Head to build the ski he was determined to make. To help make ends meet, Howard Head got a part-time job designing special research equipment for Johns Hopkins University. This paid for the aluminum, glue, plywood, and some special new components and equipment.

After the company got off the ground, things were a little easier for Head and his employees. In 1953, Mr. Head sold 40 percent of the stock in the company for $60,000. This, together with retained earnings and normal bank debt, financed expansion until there was a public offering of common stock and convertible debentures. With the outside financing, Head's stock position was diluted to 18 percent.

Prince was financed very differently—solely out of earnings, even with the stupendous growth. Prince had no outside financing, and there were no outside investors. After Howard Head's initial purchase of stock, no additional capital was raised. Eventually, Howard Head bought out most of the original stockholders who cofounded the company and, at one point, he wound up with about 80 percent. This later diminished to 67 percent, due to stock bonuses that he gave to employees. "I totally owned the company in a sense," he said. "There were no outside stockholders, and no board of directors except in an advisory way."

Organization

Whereas Mr. Head's problems with finance and manufacturing had improved dramatically based upon lessons learned at the Head Ski Company, delegation and management continued to be a burden for him. Head believed that any improvement in these areas at Prince was mainly a result of his physical location:

> I recognized shortly after the sale that in the early days of Head I was hurting my own company by glowering over everyone's shoulders.

Head recognized the classic problems of the entrepreneur when he spoke of the Head Ski Company as it was in 1967:

> I think this is typical of the kind of business that is started solely from an entrepreneurial product basis, by someone with no interest or skills in management or business. Such an entrepreneur never stops to plan. The consuming interest is to build something new and to gain acceptance. The entrepreneur has to pick up the rudiments of finance and organizational practices as he goes along. This type of business is fantastically efficient as long as it remains at a certain level. One man can make all of the important decisions.
>
> At Head Ski Company, this approach worked quite successfully until about 1955 when we sold 10,000 pairs of skis and reached the $500,000 sales level. The next five years from 1955 to 1960 saw a number of disorganized attempts to acquire and use a more conventional pyramidal organizational system. To put it succinctly, what was efficient at the $500,000 level was increasingly inefficient as we reached $1 million, then $2 million in sales. One man just couldn't handle it. It was like trying to run an army with only a general and some sergeants. There were just no officers, to say nothing of an orderly chain of command.
>
> With Prince, fates have decreed that I live in Baltimore while the company is up in Princeton. If I lived in Princeton and went into that office every day, no matter what I learned at Head, it would not stop me from impeding the effectiveness of the company by nitpicking and impeding my own effectiveness by wasting all my energy on details that somebody else could handle better.

Looking toward the future, Head had reached the point where he did have to address himself to the difficult task of reviewing the people he had chosen to be his "officers." He often found himself at odds with them, first at Head Ski Company and now at Prince Manufacturing Inc.

He had learned a valuable lesson at Head Ski about the necessity of compatibility of objectives among the owner and the top officers within an organization. In January of 1967, Howard Head appointed Hal Seigle to be chief executive officer of Head Ski Company, and though Head himself called Seigle a man with "proven professional management skills," he also felt that Seigle did not place a strong enough emphasis on product. "Under Seigle," Head explained, "I got increasingly frustrated because we were so diametrically different. He was a manager who focused on broad aspects of company organization and expansion by acquisition. From my standpoint he did not pay enough attention to detail and he was not product oriented."

Head had hoped that his problems with the top officer of his first company would not repeat themselves with those at his second, but this was not to be.

Jack Murray became the president of Prince in early 1979, and Howard Head credited him with "shepherding the company through its spectacular growth, partly on his own ability and partly because there is a great marriage between his motivational character and my vision and creativity." Head claimed that Murray's leadership was "absolutely essential" and that the results in the company during his time as president "speak for themselves about how effective he is." Furthermore, Head pointed out one of Murray's strongest assets—and one that Head claimed he himself would like to possess—Murray "knows the names of everybody in the company."

But it was Murray who was reluctant to project the 100 percent increase in sales, which Mr. Head felt was sure to occur in 1981. Head also disagreed with Murray on the issue of an inflationary price increase of 10 percent. Murray felt that the profit margin at the time was sufficient and that a price increase was unwarranted. Head maintained that the company enjoyed the position of having an exclusive product and that he merely wanted to keep up with inflation.

Jim Baugh was the marketing director under Jack Murray, and as Head claimed, a "strong ally" of Murray's. Head explained:

> He is a very conservative thinker, even more conservative than Jack, in terms of projection. He is very, very afraid that Prince will kill itself by expanding its image to include a midsize racket line. The midsized racket has already hit the market, and for Prince to admit that this racket might have something is frightening to a marketing man.

Mal Bash, who came to play a vital role in the development of Prince, was called by Head the "single most important man at Prince. He had been hired back in the ball machine days as head of quality control. Within a couple of years, he got the title of factory manager, and then quite soon he became vice president of engineering and manufacturing." Head praised Bash profusely:

> Actually he is less of a manager than a doer. What *vice president* doesn't reflect is the initiative and the drive and the toughness with which he personally went to see Grafalloy and forced them to make a good graphite racket for us. He would take nothing but excellence. He dug them out and grappled with them, and he wouldn't take anything but good results from them. He also went to Taiwan, and instead of doing what a normal Taiwanese customer does, which is to get wined and dined and womened all over the place, he shocked them by insisting that he personally go in and out of the shop day after day. He was watching what these guys were doing and how they bent the aluminum and how they heat-treated it. I give Mal a very high ranking as a major force in the company. . . .

Even after his experience in hiring the various officers within his organization, Head still maintained this idealistic vision:

> I always had the dream that right out there would be a different chief executive officer who would have all my imagination and all my vision and all my critical judgment and all my creativity and all my positives, and who at the same time was a superlative manager, remembered faces, knew all the boys, loved people, people loved him back. . . . It's only as I look back on it in a philosophical way that I see how crazy it is to expect all these qualities in one person. It would be like expecting Leonardo DaVinci to play a great game of soccer. . . .

Head also said that if there was one thing he would emphasize, it would be that his first requirement in hiring someone to be a part of his vision of growth would be

> their attachment to me, either because they were like me or because they respected me or were fascinated by the project. I would avoid people whose views were diametrically different from mine, as in the case of Seigle and some of the earlier marketing people at Prince. . . .

Toward the Future

Mr. Head had done well financially from a personal standpoint. He earned a handsome sum in royalties on top of retained earnings, and as he explained the financial structure of this income:

> The royalties were indeed earnings to me, quite independent of my share in the earnings of the company. There is an interesting point regarding the royalties—they were received by me as capital gains (i.e., 22 percent), but they were expense to the company (50 percent). Originally I assumed that when the patent was issued I would give ownership of it to Prince. But my patent attorney was adamant that I keep title to the patent in my own name in order to take advantage of the tax law that provides for the above anomaly.

Howard Head didn't like the word *marketing,* he "never had a sales quota," and he believed that "word of mouth was always the primary salesman."

The Prince racket, like the Head ski, was a better product, and Head's only interest was in exclusive products that worked better for the consumer, even if they looked a little funny:

> The skis broke, they were shiny, and the bottom froze, but people found something magic about them. The parallel in Prince is that it looked ludicrous, as evidenced by a big article in the *New York Times* called "Tennis Racket or Barn Door?" which appeared after the company was in production.
>
> I think word of mouth has clearly been the key to boosting sales at Prince, because we've always been faced with a faint snobbism of using that "unfair racket" or that "big racket" or that "oversized racket."

In 1981, Head saw the company through the $35 million mark. He predicted gross sales of $60 million for the following year, and while he was excited about the prospects such enormous growth would bring, he was justifiably concerned about his ability to continue to manage an operation of this size. (See **Exhibit 5** for consolidated balance sheets and 1982 business plan.)

The issue wasn't financial. The question was, how much was possible? In his own mind, Head questioned if the company was prepared to grow, or if there were further measures he would have to take in order to reach the next plateau. Did he have the right people working within an effective organizational framework? Was the distribution process running smoothly enough to handle the enormous volume such rapid growth would bring? And perhaps most importantly, what would his own role be if he were to stay on at the helm? How should this role adapt to the inevitable changes soon to occur? Was it within his capacity to broaden the organization or was it time to sell and exit gracefully while luck was with him? It had come time to answer these difficult questions, and he had no one with whom he could share these concerns.

Exhibit 1   **Prince Financial Summary**

Year Ended	Rackets	Gross Sales	Net Earned	Percent
July 1971		$ 32,200	$ 830	2.6%
July 1972		100,000	15,000	15.0
July 1973		580,000	106,000	18.3
July 1974		1,151,000	150,000	13.0
July 1975		1,165,000	74,000	6.4
July 1976	70,000	2,946,000	227,000	7.7
July 1977	160,000	5,051,700	329,000	6.5
July 1978	180,000	7,142,900	200,500	2.8
December 1979	190,000	9,411,800	340,900	3.6
December 1980	300,000	17,785,900	1,668,000	9.4
December 1981	600,000	34,937,800	4,397,600	12.6
(December 1982 projected)	1,000,000	58,675,000	6,560,000	12.2

Exhibit 2   Chronology

1969	Howard Head sells Head Ski Company to AMF for $16 million.
1970	Retires. Renovates new home. With new tennis court.
July 1971	Orders Prince ball machine upon advice of tennis pro; began dialog to ''debug'' machine.
October 1971	Buys 27 percent of Prince for $27,000; becomes chairman of the board and de facto chief engineer.

	Gross Sales	Net Earned	Percent
1972	$ 100,000	$ 15,000	15%
1973	600,000	100,000	17
1974	1,100,000	150,000	14
1975	1,200,000	75,000	6

1974	Begins racket experimentation, first using weights, then conceived spreading weight out (thus increasing area).
1974–75	Controlled testing of experimental model begins.
May 1975	HH decides to go into production: 35,000 rackets necessary minimum order from Maark. (Sold 70,000)
1976	Patent #3,999,756 granted: Import of patent in scope and ownership.

	Rackets	Gross Sales	Net Earned	Percent
1976	70,000	$3,500,000	$250,000	8%
1977	160,000	5,000,000	330,000	7
1978	180,000	7,000,000	200,000	3
1979	190,000	9,500,000	350,000	4

1978	Noted need for Pro and Graphite. Also, exclusive license with Wilson.
1979	Manufacturing problem is solved (Kunnan Lo and Grafalloy).

	Rackets	Gross Sales	Net Earned	Percent
1980	300,000	$18,000,000	$1,700,000	9%
1981	600,000	35,000,000	4,400,000	13
(Projection)				
1982	1,100,000	$58,000,000	$7,000,000	12

EXHIBIT 2   *(concluded)*

Balance Sheet, July 31, 1971
(unaudited)

Assets

Current assets

Cash.	$ 902.95	
Accounts receivable	4,764.74	
Inventory, at cost	7,442.87	
Total current assets		$13,110.56
Other assets		
Patents	502.56	
Organization expense	132.50	
Security deposits.	450.00	
Total other assets		1,085.06
		$14,195.62

Liabilities and Stockholders' Equity

Current liabilities

Accounts payable	$5,402.43	
Loans payable—stockholders.	6,100.00	
Accrued federal and state income taxes	307.41	
Other accrued liabilities	355.88	
Total current liabilities		$12,165.72
Stockholders' equity		
Capital stock.	1,200.00	
Retained earnings—net income for year	829.90	
Total stockholders' equity		2,029.90
		$14,195.62

EXHIBIT 3   **Industry Overview**

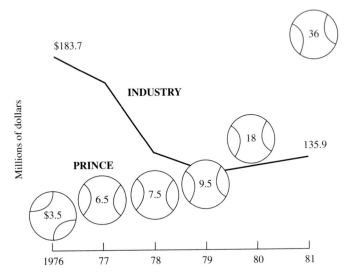

Tennis stumbled in 1977 and racket sales fell severely. But Prince Manufacturing, represented by the bouncing tennis balls, came on like a summer storm, starting behind the mountain in 1976 and drenching the competition. Industry sales are reported at retail. Prince's are its wholesale receipts, the only figures available; a common retail markup is around 40%.

SOURCE: National Sporting Goods Association, Prince Manufacturing Co.

EXHIBIT 4   **Prince vs. Conventional Racket**

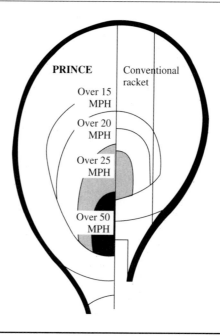

Exhibit 5   Financials

Consolidated Balance Sheets as of December 31, 1977–1981

	1981	1980	1979
Assets			
Current assets			
Cash	$ 924,815	$ 410,212	305,964
Receivables	5,324,384	3,299,985	1,618,597
Inventories	4,478,500	2,178,769	858,842
Prepaid expenses	156,163	100,486	57,867
Total current assets	$10,883,862	$5,989,452	$2,841,270
Plant and equipment, at cost	1,181,022	$ 693,779	$ 576,192
Less accumulated depreciation and amortization	287,225	171,104	104,210
Net plant and equipment	$ 893,797	522,675	471,982
Other assets	40,097	80,409	134,334
Total assets	$11,817,756	$6,592,536	3,447,586
Liabilities and stockholders' equity			
Current liabilities			
Notes payable	—	—	$ 450,000
Current installments of long-term debt	$ 42,723	$ 42,723	97,208
Accounts payable	1,212,955	813,237	670,548
Accrued expenses	1,268,375	733,998	367,645
Taxes currently payable	1,343,651	1,485,131	266,878
Deferred income taxes	283,499	206,499	87,499
Total current liabilities	$ 4,151,203	$3,281,588	$1,939,778
Long-term debt, excluding current installments	$ 42,041	84,084	127,607
Deferred income taxes	9,000	9,000	4,000
Stockholders' equity:			
Common stock without par value	249,643	249,643	75,965
Retained earnings	7,373,869	2,976,221	1,308,236
	$ 7,623,512	3,225,864	$1,384,201
Less cost of shares in treasury	8,000	8,000	8,000
Total stockholders' equity	$ 7,615,512	3,217,864	1,376,201
Total liabilities and stockholders' equity	$11,817,756	$6,592,536	$3,447,586

EXHIBIT 5   *(continued)*

Consolidated Statement of Earnings and Retained Earnings
1981, 1980, and 1979
Years Ended December 31,

	1981	1980	1979
Net sales	$34,937,800	$17,785,896	$9,411,759
Cost of sales	16,905,951	8,818,221	5,443,393
Gross profit	18,031,849	8,967,675	3,968,366
Selling expenses	5,816,675	3,019,782	1,738,475
Administrative expenses	3,477,287	2,142,262	1,337,883
	9,293,962	5,162,044	3,076,358
Operating profit	$ 8,737,887	$ 3,805,631	$ 892,008
Other income (expenses)			
Royalty income	437,597	253,341	108,252
Royalty expense	(1,119,945)	(574,580)	(274,492)
Interest expense	(22,969)	(71,943)	(76,818)
Miscellaneous	115,078	4,536	1,965
Net other income (expenses)	(590,239)	(388,646)	(241,093)
Earnings before income taxes	8,147,648	3,416,985	650,915
Income taxes			
Current	3,673,000	1,626,000	249,584
Deferred	77,000	123,000	60,416
	3,750,000	1,749,000	310,000
Net earnings	4,397,648	1,667,985	340,915
Retained earnings beginning of year	2,976,221	1,308,236	967,321
Retained earnings end of year	$ 7,373,869	$ 2,976,221	$1,308,236

EXHIBIT 5   *(concluded)*

1982 Business Plan
Statement of Earnings
Foreign and Domestic

	Total	*Domestic*	*Foreign*
Total			
Racquets	$58,359	$39,601	$18,758
Racquet accessories	2,999	2,549	450
Machines	1,450	1,234	216
Total	$62,808	$43,384	$19,424
Cost of sales	31,540	19,626	11,914
Gross profit	31,268	23,758	7,510
Percent of net sales	50%	55%	39%
Operating expenses			
Sales and marketing	11,220	8,522	2,698
Warehouse and shipping	697	481	216
Administrative and general	3,937	2,949	988
Research and engineering	791	546	245
Total	$16,645	$12,498	$ 4,147
Operating profit	14,623	11,260	3,363
Percent of net sales	23%	26%	17%
Royalty and interest			
Royalty income	$ 450	$ 310	$ 140
Royalty expense	(1,975)	(1,412)	(563)
Interest income	200	138	62
Total	$(1,325)	$ (964)	$ (361)
Income			
Pretax income	$13,298	$10,296	$ 3,002
Percent of net sales	21%	24%	15%